INSPIRE / PLAN / DISCOVER / EXPERIENCE

GREAT BRITAIN

Burnsall village in the Yorkshire Dales

GREAT BRITAIN

CONTENTS

Telephone box on a rainy day

DISCOVER 6

EXPERIENCE 52

NEED TO KNOW 570

DISCOVER

View over Oxford's spires and rooftops

WELCOME TO
GREAT BRITAIN

Sumptuous stately homes and glorious gardens. Epic mountains and cosmopolitan cities. Inspirational museums and world-famous festivals. Dazzling in its diversity, with a rich cultural tapestry part woven by the interlocking histories of its three constituent nations – England, Scotland and Wales – Great Britain offers enough thrilling experiences to fill a lifetime of exploring. Whatever your dream trip entails, this DK Eyewitness Travel Guide is the perfect companion.

① Sunbathing on Brighton Beach.

② Medieval cottages on the front quad of Worcester College, Oxford.

③ Piccadilly Circus and Regent Street, London.

④ Snowdon Mountain Railway, North Wales.

Separated from mainland Europe by the merest sliver of sea, Great Britain has some of the continent's most spectacular scenery. From the jagged peaks of the Scottish Highlands and the towering sea cliffs of Pembrokeshire to the desolate moors of the Peak District and the sweeping sands of Norfolk and Northumberland, there are miles of spectacular terrain to hike, bike and explore. Many centuries of civilization are etched across this timeless landscape, from mysterious menhirs to noble mansions. Gripping reminders of a tumultuous past – evident in ruined abbeys and countless brooding castles – add to the intrigue.

As well as being rich in history, you'll find Great Britain's dynamic cities surging forward with restless energy. Beyond the pomp and politics, London remains an unparalleled entrepot of global cultures, its innovative museums and galleries and diverse music, theatre and culinary scenes competing with the world's best. Edinburgh and Cardiff showcase Scottish and Welsh culture with exuberance and elan, while regional cities – from Liverpool to Newcastle, Bristol to Glasgow – are thriving, enhanced by eye-catching architecture and exciting regeneration projects.

We've broken Great Britain down into easily navigable chapters, with detailed itineraries, expert local knowledge and colourful, comprehensive maps to help you plan the perfect trip. Whether you're here for a flying visit or a grand tour, this Eyewitness guide will ensure that you see the very best Great Britain has to offer.

REASONS TO LOVE
GREAT BRITAIN

Spectacular landscapes, world-beating museums, postcard-pretty villages, glorious pubs and one of the greatest capital cities on the planet - there are so many reasons why visitors fall in love with Great Britain. Here are some of our favourites.

1 SUMPTUOUS STATELY HOMES

Marvel at the opulent country piles of Britain's old money - the real stars of many a costume drama. Classics include Hatfield House *(p242)*, Longleat *(p271)* and Hardwick Hall *(p340)*.

A PINT IN THE PUB 2

Whether for a swift pint or a leisurely Sunday lunch, the pub is the beating heart of British social life. From aged taverns to modern gastropubs, they're an essential part of any visit.

3 GREAT CITIES

Britain's cities are vibrant places, encompassing medieval treasure troves and rejuvenated Victorian metropolises. And how many other countries can boast three dynamic capitals?

MUSIC SCENE *4*

From the Arctic Monkeys to Led Zeppelin, Britain is a leader in the global music industry. Whether you're after folk, funk or classical you'll find somewhere to indulge your passion.

HIKING IN THE LAKE DISTRICT *5*

The sublime landscape of rugged fells, serene lakes and lush green valleys in the Lake District offers some of the most rewarding hiking in Britain (*p356*).

QUIRKY FESTIVALS *6*

Watching a crowd chase a wheel of cheese down a steep hill? Chances are you've stumbled upon one of Britain's many weird and wonderful local festivals.

PICTURESQUE VILLAGES 7

For many the essence of British life is found in its villages – often little more than a church, a pub and a handful of picturesque cottages with lovingly tended gardens. Head out into the sticks to appreciate the slow pace of life.

POMP AND CEREMONY 8

From the Changing of the Guard at Buckingham Palace *(p74)* to the flag-waving party of the Last Night of the Proms *(p45)*, Britain knows how to put on a good show.

9 GLORIOUS GARDENS

Whether you're after classical landscapes or exotic greenhouses, Britain offers an incredible array of gorgeous gardens, not to mention the many flower shows.

10 COASTAL ADVENTURES

Fish and chips on the beach; windswept walks along clifftop paths; the icy tingle of a dip in the North Sea: some of Britain's best experiences can be had by the ocean.

LONDON'S WORLD-CLASS MUSEUMS 11

Spend a day with the Old Masters at the National Gallery (p68) or meet a roaring dinosaur at the Natural History Museum (p94) – all without spending a penny.

GREAT BRITISH GRUB 12

Nothing beats Britain's comfort food staples such as steak and kidney pie; bangers and mash; Cornish pasties; or haggis, neeps and tatties, all prepared with love and attention.

EXPLORE
GREAT
BRITAIN

This guide divides Great Britain
into four main sections: London
(p54); England *(p144)*; Wales *(p424)*
and Scotland *(p478)*. These have
been split into 17 colour-coded
sightseeing areas, as shown on
the map below.

**THE HIGHLANDS
AND ISLANDS**
p542

Stornoway

Ullapool

Western Hebrides

Hebrides

Inner

Fort William

Oban

Ayr

*Atlantic
Ocean*

Londonderry

Larne   Stranraer

**NORTHERN
IRELAND**

Belfast

Sligo   Enniskillen

*Isle of
Man*

Newry

Douglas

*Irish
Sea*

Longford

**REPUBLIC OF
IRELAND**

Galway   Dublin   Holyhead

Portlaoise

Wicklow

Limerick

Tralee   Waterford   Rosslare

Fishguard

Cork   Pembroke

*Celtic
Sea*

0 kilometres	100
0 miles	100

N
↑

Truro

1 London's world-famous Tower Bridge at sunset.

2 The National Gallery, London.

3 Punting on the River Cam, a quintessential Cambridge experience.

4 Looking north down Danby Dale from Blakey Rigg in the wild North York Moors National Park.

With so much to see and do in Great Britain it can be difficult to know where to start. This itinerary, taking you through dynamic cities and spectacular landscapes, will help you make the most of your visit.

2 WEEKS

A Grand Tour of Great Britain

Day 1

Starting in London, immerse yourself in royal history at the Tower of London *(p118)*. Then head to the South Bank for a lunch of street food at Borough Market *(p128)*. Walk past Shakespeare's Globe to Tate Modern *(p120)* to see its cutting-edge art. Continue walking west along the river to the London Eye *(p85)*. After enjoying sweeping views from one of its pods, cross the Hungerford Bridge to Covent Garden and settle into dinner accompanied by live music at Sarastro *(126 Drury Lane)*.

Day 2

Visit the National Gallery *(p68)* to see one of the world's greatest art collections. After lunch in the gallery café walk south along Whitehall, passing 10 Downing Street to reach Big Ben and the Houses of Parliament *(p70)*. Cross the street to visit Westminster Abbey *(p72)*. Jump on the tube to Leicester Square for dinner in Chinatown at Shu Xiangge *(p79)*.

Day 3

Take the train from London Euston to Birmingham *(p324)*, Britain's third-largest city. Explore the centre with its outstanding Victorian buildings and visit the Birmingham Museum & Art Gallery for the world's best collection of pre-Raphaelite paintings. Lunch in the museum's Edwardian Tea Rooms. Then catch the train to Stratford-upon-Avon *(p310)*, the birthplace of the Bard, and pop into Shakespeare's Birthplace museum. After arranging car hire for the following morning, dine at the historic Lambs Restaurant *(12 Sheep St)* and stay at the Woodstock Guest House *(30 Grove Rd)*.

Day 4

Begin by driving to the world-famous university city of Cambridge *(p196)*. First, visit the magnificent King's College Chapel *(p198)* before wandering around several other colleges. Lunch at The Chophouse on King's Parade before spending the afternoon punting on the river. If time allows, visit the excellent Fitzwilliam Museum. After dinner at The Eagle *(p198)* hunker down at the stylish University Arms hotel *(Regent St)*.

Day 5

Drive north to Ely to visit its gorgeous cathedral *(p202)*. Afterwards, continue to pretty Stamford *(p338)* for lunch at The George *(71 St Martin's)*, one of England's greatest coaching inns, before driving to York *(p374)*. Visit York Minster and wander around the Shambles, a narrow cobbled street with Elizabethan buildings. Dine at Skosh *(p375)*, then turn in for the night at the swanky The Grand *(Station Rise)*.

Day 6

Start the day by heading north to the medieval remains of Rievaulx Abbey *(p394)*, which stand tall in a handsome valley. Then continue to Hutton-le-Hole *(p395)* for a traditional pub lunch at The Crown. Continuing north, cross the wild scenery of the North York Moors National Park *(p392)* to reach Durham *(p410)*. Take an hour to explore Durham's beautiful Norman cathedral before heading to Alnwick, which has an enchanting castle *(p419)*. Dine at the magical Alnwick Garden Treehouse *(Denwick Lane)*. Then stay overnight at the Tate House guesthouse *(11 Bondgate Without)*.

→

1

2

3

Day 7

Today you'll start with soaring Bamburgh Castle (p418) before continuing on to Holy Island (p416), reached via a tidal causeway. After visiting Lindisfarne Castle, stop for lunch at The Ship Inn. Drive into Scotland to the Rosslyn Chapel (p507) and admire its exquisite stonework. It's just another half hour to Edinburgh (p492) – arrive in time for a dinner of fresh seafood at Ondine (p495). Stay overnight at the 94DR boutique guest house (94 Dalkeith Rd).

Day 8

Feel the lively pulse of Edinburgh by strolling the Royal Mile with its numerous attractions. Choose from the Palace of Holyroodhouse, the Scottish National Gallery and the National Museum of Scotland, but be sure to visit the castle (p496). In the afternoon, visit the superb Scottish National Gallery of Modern Art in the well-heeled West End. Round off the day by exploring Leith (p501), a trendy district where the old docks have been creatively redeveloped. Dine at the waterside Shore Restaurant (3 The Shore).

Day 9

Heading south from Edinburgh, cross the gentle, green landscapes of the Borders to reach Melrose, an enchanting town adorned by its abbey ruins (p505). Close by is Abbotsford (p506), the fascinating former lair of Sir Walter Scott. In the afternoon drive to Windermere (p360), set amid the wondrous scenery of England's Lake District. After a cruise on the lake have dinner and stay overnight at the nearby Drunken Duck (p361).

Day 10

Begin at Grasmere (p358), where you can visit Dove Cottage, once the home of celebrated poet William Wordsworth. Carry on to the pretty market town of Keswick (p356) for lunch at Fellpack (p361) before undertaking the 40-minute hike to see the enigmatic Druid Castlerigg Stone Circle. After returning to Keswick enjoy a three-hour scenic drive to Cockermouth, followed by Wasdale Head, and then along the Hardknott Pass to finish up at Ambleside (p360). Round off the day with dinner at Lucy's On A Plate (Church St).

1 Bamburgh Castle on the
Northumberland coast.

2 Walkers in the Eildon Hills
overlooking Melrose, Scottish Borders.

3 Windermere in the Lake
District National Park.

4 Admiring art in the Scottish
National Gallery, Edinburgh.

5 Chester town centre at dusk.

6 The café bar at the Harbourmaster
hotel in Aberaeron, West Wales.

Day 11

Set off early to vibrant Manchester (p346). After visiting the fascinating People's History Museum head along King and Bridge streets for lunch at Mr Thomas's Chop House (p349). Spend the afternoon exploring Albert Square, home to a splendid town hall, and urbane Deansgate, one of the main thoroughfares. Head south to explore the Whitworth Art Gallery's superb collections. Back in the city centre, enjoy drinks and dinner at the rooftop 20 Stories (p349). Bed down at the grand Midland Hotel (16 Peter St).

Day 12

Head to the ancient Roman town of Chester (p354) and spend the morning wandering around The Rows, old galleried shopping arcades, and the city walls. Fuel up at Chez Jules before a 76-km (47-mile) drive to the Welsh seaside resort of Llandudno (p448), with its splendid beach. Take the sea air before continuing to Caernarfon (p448) to explore its fairytale castle tucked up against the Menai Straits. Wander the narrow streets of the

town centre before eating and sleeping in the plush Plas Dinas Country House (p449).

Day 13

Tour the impressive medieval fortress at Harlech (p444), then continue along the coast to the pretty town of Aberaeron (p471). Enjoy a tasty lunch here at Naturally Scrumptious (18 Market St) and check in early at the Harbourmaster Hotel (1 Quay Parade) before driving into the Pembrokeshire Coast National Park (p456) whose dramatic Coast Path follows the spectacular seashore. Hike along a section of the path before returning to Aberaeron.

Day 14

Head south from Aberaeron to Swansea (p472). Start by exploring the National Waterfront Museum and the Glynn Vivian Art Gallery with its beautiful local pottery. After lunch, head to the Mumbles on the Gower Peninsula and enjoy the beautiful coastal scenery (p472). Back in Swansea, round off your trip with dinner at Gallini's on Fishmarket Quay by the old docks.

Bookshop Browsing

There's nothing quite like scouring the shelves of a good bookshop. Stalwart Waterstones appears in most towns, while the flagship Blackwells store, founded in 1879 on Broad Street in Oxford, is a bookaholic's dream. It's the independent shops that particularly reward a visit, however. In Bath, have an expert prescribe books catered to your tastes at Mr B's Emporium *(www.mrbsemporium.com)* or head to Barter Books in Alnwick *(p419)*, where a model railway runs around the groaning bookcases. In London, don't miss a visit to Daunt Books *(www.dauntbooks.co.uk)*, with its superb travel section. You can explore the capital's 100-plus independents with the London Bookshop Map app.

$\rightarrow$

Daunt Books, with its Edwardian galleries, in London

GREAT BRITAIN FOR
BOOKWORMS

Home to some of the world's best-loved fictional characters and celebrated authors, Great Britain beckons bibliophiles from far and wide. There are opportunities aplenty to browse in bookshops, attend a literary festival and tread the streets that inspired readers' favourite tomes.

Children's Favourites

Unleash your inner wizard by boarding the train at Platform 9¾ at London's Kings Cross station or master the art of broomstick flying at Alnwick Castle *(p419)*. Many other kids' favourites are celebrated up and down the country. Look out for Peter Rabbit and friends at Beatrix Potter's home in the Lake District *(p360)*, head out on the trail of Roald Dahl in Cardiff *(p466)* or take your daemon on a tour of Philip Pullman's *His Dark Materials* in Oxford *(p232)*.

$\leftarrow$

Starting a magical school journey at Platform 9¾ in London's King's Cross

1476

The first printing press in England was established by William Caxton at Westminster.

TOP 3 BEAUTIFUL LIBRARIES

Bodleian Library
Take a tour of the refined Oxford University library *(p235)*.

John Rylands Library
Manchester's Neo-Gothic masterpiece has a collection of rare books *(www.library.manchester.ac.uk)*.

Liverpool Central Library
This book haven has a spiral staircase and a splendid glass-domed roof *(www.liverpool.co.uk/libraries)*.

Celebrate the Written Word

See authors in action, discover your next favourite writer and browse for new books at Britain's literary festivals. Cheltenham, Edinburgh, Oxford and Bath each host popular annual events, but the cream of the crop is arguably Hay Festival. Held in Hay-on-Wye *(p462)*, this spring bookfest attracts high-profile literati from across the globe.

←

Festival-goer at Hay Festival in Hay-on-Wye, a "book town" in Wales's Brecon Beacons

Literary Giants

Get under the skin of literary titans by exploring the places they lived and worked in. Visit the Bard's birthplace in Stratford-upon-Avon *(p310)*; walk the Brontë Way to see key landmarks in the three sisters' lives; visit Chawton in Hampshire *(p184)*, where Jane Austen wrote her most famous works; or feel the power of nature that inspired the Romantics in the Lake District *(p356)*.

↑ Crossing Haworth Moor on the Brontë Way in West Yorkshire

Modern Giants

Britain's cities have provided an open stage for architecture's leading players since World War II, with buildings ranging from the Brutalist concrete slabs of the 1960s to 21st-century steel-and-glass skyscrapers. Standouts include Birmingham's chainmail-like Selfridges store in the Bull Ring shopping centre, the sensuously curved Sage Gateshead concert venue and London's Shard *(p129)*, the tallest building in Western Europe.

←

Curving structure of the Sage Gateshead, in northeast England

GREAT BRITAIN FOR
ARCHITECTURE

Sumptuous stately homes, imposing castles, lofty Gothic cathedrals – over the centuries, Britain's builders have created a staggering showcase of architectural treasures. As dynamic cities continue to morph and develop, there's always something new to grab architecture lovers' attention.

Stately Pleasure Domes

From Tudor beginnings the grand country house reached its zenith in the 18th and 19th centuries. Everyone has their favourite, whether it be the Elizabethan extravagance of Burghley House *(p338)*, Chatsworth House's Palladian perfection *(p333)* or Vanbrugh's Baroque masterpieces – Blenheim Palace *(p238)* and Castle Howard *(p382)*.

THE NATIONAL TRUST

The National Trust was formed as a charity in 1895 to preserve the nation's valuable historic landscapes and finest buildings. It protects many of Britain's castles and stately homes, parks and gardens, as well as vast tracts of countryside and coastline. National Trust properties are denoted by an NT symbol throughout this book.

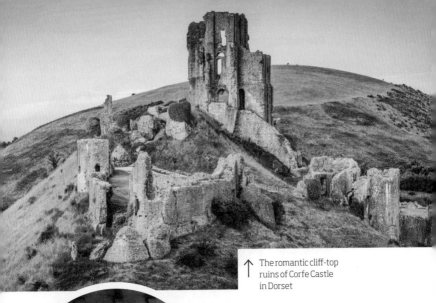

↑ The romantic cliff-top ruins of Corfe Castle in Dorset

Forbidding Fortresses

For almost a millennium, castles have stood sentinel along the faultlines of British history, an enduring visual link with a tumultuous and bloody past. From the mighty fortresses that garland the Anglo-Scottish border to Edward I's formidable structures, Britain's castles always provide a great day out, especially over summer weekends when you'll find pageantry aplenty.

←

The magnificent Great Hall, the largest room in Warwick Castle

Prayers in Stone

Encompassing the hulking, walled creations of the early Normans and the modern masterpieces of Liverpool *(p353)* and Coventry *(p325)*, Britain's cathedrals represent its architectural apotheosis. The statistics alone are staggering: Winchester has the longest medieval nave in Europe *(p170)*; Salisbury's spire is the tallest in Britain *(p266)*; while the dome of Wren's St Paul's still dwarfs almost all others *(p116)*. Be prepared to be moved by these awe-inspiring, magisterial spaces.

↑ Burghley House near Stamford, a grand 16th-century mansion

→

The dome of St Paul's Cathedral seen from the Millennium Bridge, London

Pioneering Gardens

Green-fingered Brits take a keen interest in garden design – the most pioneering gardens attract visitors in their thousands. Join the throng at the splendid Eden Project *(p280)*, whose vast glassy biomes hold an extraordinary range of plant life drawn from every corner of the globe. Of comparable size is the National Botanic Garden of Wales *(p472)*, whose single-span glasshouse, designed by Norman Foster, is the largest in the world. Crowning them all is the magnificent Royal Botanic Gardens, Kew *(p143)* where you can get up-close to the trees on the unique Treetop Walkway.

→

The Temperate House in Kew Gardens, home to 1,500 species

GREAT BRITAIN FOR
GREEN FINGERS

Wander through the grand gardens that surround many a stately home, explore a platoon of art gardens that combine magnificent scenery with modern sculpture, or enjoy scores of leafy city parks. Those with green fingers are spoilt for choice in each and every part of Great Britain.

CAPABILITY BROWN

Lancelot "Capability" Brown (1716–1783) was the supreme landscape gardener of Georgian England. He favoured the move away from formal gardens to man-made pastoral settings. You can admire his handiwork at a string of stately homes, such as Chatsworth *(p333)*, Stowe *(p243)* and Blenheim Palace *(p238)*. Mimicking nature, immaculate green lawns run down to artificial curving lakes, which occupy the middle distance and are given perspective by a clump or island of trees. These are, indeed, the best views in England.

Victorian Gardens

Taking full advantage of Britain's trading prowess, the Victorians imported plants, trees and shrubs from all over the world to create wooded arboretums such as those that are the hallmark of the Plantation Garden in Norwich *(p201)* and Cragside estate in Northumberland *(p421)*. To see intensely colourful flower beds wander around Bodnant Garden near Conwy *(p438)*.

Sculpture Gardens

A range of glorious natural settings host striking works of art all over Britain, from the wild uplands of Yorkshire Sculpture Park (p405) to the tranquil grounds of an Edinburgh estate, site of the Jupiter Art and Sculpture Park (www.jupiterartland.org), to the Cumbrian hills of Grizedale Forest (p361), whose footpaths offer a delightful medley of modern sculpture. The garden of the former home of Barbara Hepworth in St Ives has beautiful displays of her works (p283). For a more unusual experience, seek out the hidden sculptures in eerie Tout Quarry on the Isle of Portland (p273).

← *Zodiac Heads* by Ai Weiwei in Yorkshire Sculpture Park

TOP 3 FLOWER SHOWS

Chelsea Flower Show
🌐 rhs.org.uk
The most famous flower and landscape gardens show in the UK takes place over five days in May in the grounds of the Royal Hospital Chelsea in London.

Hampton Court Flower Show
🌐 rhs.org.uk
Held in early July at Hampton Court Palace near London (p138), this is the largest flower show in the world.

Chatsworth Flower Show
🌐 chatsworth.org
The gardens of Chatsworth House in Derbyshire (p333) host this flower show in June.

↑ Formal Tudor hedges in the knot garden at Hampton Court Palace

↑ Bodnant Garden near Conwy, Wales, founded by a Victorian industrialist

Tudor Gardens

In Tudor times, throughout the 16th century, British garden design was influenced by Renaissance Italy. Regularity and formality were all the rage. The "knot garden", with its geometric flower beds and closely manicured shrub hedges, became very popular – Hampton Court Palace (p138), on the edge of London, has a fine example. Water features and fountains are key at Aberglasney, one of Wales's finest gardens, while loggias and pavilions, such as those at Hever Castle (p177), offer leisurely views of its award-winning garden.

Festive Flavours

See top chefs in full flow and support independent food producers at a food festival. To tap into the latest trends, bag a ticket for Taste of London, an alfresco jamboree in June in Regent's Park, or graze to your heart's content at Abergavenny Food Festival. Other foodie events showcase local specialities: from oysters in Whitstable to cheese in Cardiff to sausages in Lincoln.

→

Stalls at Abergavenny Food Festival in Wales, held every September

GREAT BRITAIN FOR
FOODIES

Once written off by the food cognoscenti, Britain has undergone little short of a culinary revolution in the last few decades. Creative chefs pick up Michelin stars and farmers' markets and street food vendors bring artisan know-how and innovative new trends to local food scenes.

Open to the World

Ever since medieval merchants first brought exotic spices to British shores, Britons have absorbed culinary influences from across the globe, and nowadays are as likely to tuck into a Mexican burrito or a Vietnamese banh mi as bangers and mash. Chicken tikka masala eclipsed fish and chips as the nation's favourite dish some years ago; head to Bradford, London's Brick Lane and Birmingham to sample the best.

Chinatown in London, with great dim sum restaurants ↑

Catch of the Day

Firm, flaky cod, freshly caught and crisply battered; fat, juicy scallops, tossed in butter with a hint of garlic; delicate oysters, slurped fresh from the shell. With ocean on all sides, it's little wonder that seafood in Britain is a treat, especially in coastal villages and towns. Fish and chips, of course, is a national favourite – you'll find a chippy in every town, often with an excruciatingly punning name – and Scottish smoked salmon is legendary. There are plenty of local favourites to try, too, from kippers in Craster in Northumberland to Norfolk crabs in Cromer.

← Battered fish and chips, satisfying and ubiquitous

TOP 5 **BRITISH CHEESES**

Caerphilly
This fresh, mild and crumbly Welsh cheese is a top choice.

Cheddar
Often imitated but never bettered, and nothing else is as good on toast. Somerset produces the best.

Cornish Yarg
Creamy, semi-hard and fresh-tasting cow's milk cheese with a mouldy nettle rind.

Stilton
Strong, with a creamy texture, this blue-veined king of cheeses is especially popular at Christmas.

Wensleydale
From Hawes in North Yorkshire, this cheese has a crumbly texture and mild but tangy taste.

A Taste of Britain

From steak and kidney pie to treacle sponge, hearty native dishes are a delight. You'll find distinctive local flavours on your travels, too. In Scotland, the definitive dish is spicy, nutty haggis, while warming Lancashire hotpot is a favourite in northwest England. There's even more variety among Britain's sweet treats, from crumbly Welsh cakes to flaky Aberdeen butteries – salty, sweet and wholly delicious.

↑ Haggis, served with neeps (swede) and tatties (potatoes), a Scottish classic

Geology Rocks

Craggy peaks, jagged coastline, disused quarries: Britain's rock-climbing scene is wonderfully varied. Tackle the iconic rocky ridges of the Roaches in the Peak District or Yorkshire's wonderfully named Gordale Scar gorge. At sea, scramble along the cliffs of Pembrokeshire; back on dry land, scale the heights of Snowdonia for a view to end all views.

A climber at the Roaches overlooking Tittisworth Valley, Peak District

GREAT BRITAIN FOR
NATURE LOVERS

From the wild moors of Devon to the lofty fells of the Lake District, the landscapes of Britain are staggeringly beautiful and a veritable nature playground. Come rain or shine, a trip into the countryside is a joy. Lace up your boots and head out on an adventure worth writing home about.

TOP 3 WILD SWIMMING SPOTS

River Waveney, Outney Common, Suffolk
Home river to the god-father of British wild swimming, writer and environmentalist Roger Deakin, with a blissful, bucolic setting.

Fairy Pools of Skye, Glenbrittle
Crystal-clear pools at the foot of the Cuillin Mountains.

Blue Lagoon, Abereiddi, Pembrokeshire
Former slate quarry with wonderful, brilliant-blue waters.

Hiking Heaven

With miles upon miles of footpaths, Britain is a walker's paradise. Long-distance trails include the West Highland Way (westhighlandway.org) and Pembrokeshire Coast Path. For hill hikes with stunning views, choose from the Cairngorms, Brecon Beacons or the Lake District.

Take to the Water

Being an island nation, it's no surprise that Britain offers a rich array of water-based activities. Take to the lakes in a canoe (Loch Lomond or the Lake District can't be beaten), surf the waves at Cornwall's Fistral Beach or Porthleven, dive World War II wrecks off the Orkney Islands, or jump into cool waters for a wild swim.

$\longrightarrow$

Riding a wave off Porthleven in Cornwall, a great spot for surfing,

Starry, Starry Skies

Home to some of the darkest skies in Europe, Britain offers a good chance of spotting the Milky Way and major constellations. The Brecon Beacons, Dartmoor National Park, Bodmin Moor and Kielder Water & Forest Park are four of Britain's best stargazing spots.

$\longleftarrow$

The Milky Way at Great Staple Tor in Dartmoor National Park

BRITAIN'S NATIONAL PARKS

Created in 1949, the National Parks and Access to the Countryside Act of Parliament led to vast swathes of the Great British outdoors being designated National Parks. Independently managed, Britain's 15 parks (which include many of the places mentioned on these two pages) make up some of Britain's most breathtaking landscapes; the natural beauty, wildlife and heritage of each are protected by National Parks Partnerships. Find out more at www.nationalparks.uk.

↑ Rannoth Moor on the West Highland Way in Scotland

A Gin Renaissance

Traditionally, British gin divides into two main types: juniper-led, slightly citrussy London Dry, which covers many of the best-known brands, and the earthier Plymouth gin. To learn more, join a tour at gin-making stalwarts Plymouth Gin in Devon, at London Sipsmith, or at one of the micro-distilleries in Liverpool, Manchester or Norwich.

←

Plymouth Gin, made by the oldest British distillery

GREAT BRITAIN
BY THE GLASS

Celebration, commiseration or just a good old chinwag: the British accompany practically every occasion with a drop of their favourite tipple. Pint of ale, refreshing gin and tonic, a warming dram of Scottish whisky or a reassuring cup of tea – what's it to be?

Mine's a Pint

Draught bitter, drunk at cellar temperature, is the most traditional British beer. Brewed from malted barley, hops, yeast and water, and usually matured in a wooden cask, it comes in a variety of flavours and hues, from straw-coloured, pale and golden ales to malty stouts and porters. Pop into your nearest pub and ask to taste a few varieties before you buy.

↑ Celebrating with beer, one of Britain's most popular drinks

Sparkling Success

British wine production - helped in no small measure by ever-warmer summers - is growing and many wines have gained plaudits from all over the world. Sparkling wines dominate the scene, produced on the sunny, south-facing chalk slopes of southern England. Sample some of the best on a vineyard tour in Kent or Sussex, or book a weekend break in Gloucestershire's Three Choirs Vineyard *(www.three-choirs-vineyards.co.uk)*.

←

Grapes in a vineyard in East Sussex, part of Britain's maturing wine industry

PUT THE KETTLE ON

In Britain there's nothing that a good cup of tea won't solve, and so it's little wonder that Britons consume some 60 billion cups a year. Popularized in Britain in the 1660s, tea today is drunk with an essential splash of milk - anathema to the rest of the world, but to Brits, tea without milk is quite simply not a proper cuppa.

A Wee Dram

North of the border, no special occasion is complete without a drop of *uisce beathe* - the water of life. More than half of Scotland's malt whiskies come from Speyside, said to have a perfect balance of climate, terrain and pure spring water. Check out some of the distilleries on two wheels, with a fortifying swig at each, on Speyside's Malt Whisky Trail *(www. maltwhiskytrail.com)*, or try out the peatier, punchier island malts of Islay – an acquired taste for some, liquid heaven for others *(islay.com/about-islay/islay-distilleries)*. *Sláinte!*

↑ Pushing a barrel of whisky at Edinburgh Castle, and *(inset)* a Scotsman with a whisky

Walking Wonderland

In 2012, Wales became the first country in the world to have a dedicated footpath the full length of its coastline (walescoastpath.gov.uk). Work is well underway for England to go one step further: knitting together new stretches with long-established trails such as the glorious South West Coast Path (p287), the England Coast Path will, once complete, become the longest continuous coastal trail in the world. For news on progress and the latest sections to be unveiled, see www.nationaltrail.co.uk.

$\rightarrow$

Footpath leading past Durdle Door on the Jurassic Coast in Dorset

GREAT BRITAIN
ON THE COAST

Nobody in Britain lives more than 128 km (80 miles) from the sea. With over 18,000 km (11,000 miles) of coastline – and that's before you've counted the islands – it's little wonder that, whether for a muddy walk or a weekend retreat, the seaside is a favourite for locals and visitors.

Explorers of the High Seas

From the Tudor Age of Exploration to Olympic mastery of water-based sports, Britons have long pushed the boundaries of the possible on the ocean. Learn the stories of these seafarers, and see some of the most famous ships in history in the maritime museums and dockyards that protect Britain's naval heritage. Follow in the footsteps of Francis Drake in Plymouth (p300); head to Portsmouth to board Nelson's HMS *Victory* (p182), to Bristol to explore Brunel's masterpiece, the SS *Great Britain* (p254), and to Dundee to relive Scott's polar voyage aboard the RRS *Discovery* (p537). To celebrate the feats of modern sailing legends such as Robin Knox-Johnston and Ellen MacArthur visit the National Maritime Museum Cornwall in Falmouth (p291).

$\leftarrow$

RRS *Discovery*, Dundee, the ship on which Captain Scott undertook his first expedition to the Antarctic in 1901–4

TOP 4 HIDDEN BEACHES

Par Beach, St Martin's, Isles of Scilly
Crystal-clear waters and powdery white sands.

Bamburgh, Northumberland
Serene sands against a castle backdrop (p418).

Man O War, Dorset
Reachable only on foot, this Jurassic Coast gem is by Durdle Door (p274).

Scarista, Harris
Stunning dune-backed beach in the wilds of the Outer Hebrides (p553).

Coastal Wildlife

With its soaring cliffs and hidden creeks, Britain's shores provide a haven for coastal wildlife. Take a boat to Skomer (p457) to spot puffins, or venture to the lagoons of East Anglia to see waders. In summer, sightings of basking sharks are common off Cornwall, while dolphins frolick in Moray Firth (p560) and Ceredigion Bay (p469).

Puffins on Skomer Island, off the Pembrokeshire coast

Beside the Seaside

Salty-fresh sea breezes, the tangy aroma of vinegar-drenched chips and herring gulls screeching overhead – Britain's seaside resorts are an assault on the senses. In the south, Brighton (p164) is the star, while up north, there's nowhere more fun than brash Blackpool (p369). Riding a wave of regeneration, many coastal towns, such as Margate (p174) and Newquay (p294), offer a great escape.

→

Sunbathing on pebbled Brighton Beach by the pier

A Musical Pilgrimage

Home to the Cavern Club, The Beatles and British Music Experience *(www. british musicexperience.com)*, Liverpool is an essential first stop for a musical Magical Mystery Tour *(p350)*. Over in Manchester, you can re-create the iconic Smiths album cover at Salford Lads' Club. Meanwhile, the streets of London are littered with rock'n'roll memorials: pay tribute to Amy Winehouse in Camden Market *(p142)*, and explore the haunts that inspired the Thin White Duke on a tour of Bowie's Brixton in South London.

$\rightarrow$

Bronze statue of
The Beatles on
Liverpool's Waterfront

GREAT BRITAIN FOR
MUSIC FANS

From bhangra to Britpop, prog to punk and metal to grime, British artists have created a diverse music scene – to say nothing of the British contribution to classical, jazz and other genres. Plug into the latest sounds at a legendary music venue, or pack your tent and wellies and head for a fun summer festival.

Festival Fun

The great British summer brings with it a cornucopia of music festivals. Glastonbury *(p269)* remains the grand-daddy of them all, an exhilarating celebration of the arts that lures some of the world's biggest stars, but there are also hundreds of smaller, more intimate get-togethers. Over in the classical world, headline gatherings include Glyndebourne's festival of opera *(p181)* and the eight-week Prom season at the Royal Albert Hall *(p95; www.bbc.co.uk/proms)*.

Live Music Venues

A cultural melting pot for homegrown talent, British cities provide a wealth of live music venues. London teems with atmospheric locations, from the tiny sweatbox of the 100 Club *(www.the100club. co.uk)* to the ethereal Union Chapel *(www.unionchapel. org.uk)*. Jazz fans should make for the iconic Ronnie Scott's *(www.ronniescotts.co.uk)*, while for classical concerts, Wigmore Hall *(www.wigmore-hall.org.uk)* is the cream of the crop. Tap into the Welsh music scene at Cardiff's Clwb Ifor Bach *(www.clwb.net)* and get raucous at Glasgow's King Tut's *(www. kingtuts.co.uk)*.

 ←

Ronnie Scott's Jazz Club on Frith Street, Soho, London

TOP 4 **RECORD STORES**

Rough Trade East, London
🆆 roughtrade.com
With launches and gigs, plus its own label, this indie stalwart is much more than just a store.

Monorail, Glasgow
🆆 monorailmusic.com
A strong community ethos has kept this shop an essential dot on the Glasgow music map.

Vinyl Exchange, Manchester
🆆 vinylexchange.co.uk
Legend of the Northern Quarter – with fair pricing, too.

Spillers, Cardiff
🆆 spillersrecords.com
Opened in 1894, this is the world's oldest record store.

↑ The Malvern Hills, which inspired several leading British composers

Pastoral Symphonies

If urban grit forged Britain's world-beating pop scene, its classical composers have found inspiration in the more bucolic surroundings of the countryside. Head to the rolling Malvern Hills to experience the landscapes that awakened Edward Elgar's creative spirit *(p321)*, and where lifelong friends Gustav Holst and Ralph Vaughan Williams took country rambles together. Benjamin Britten's opera *Peter Grimes*, meanwhile, was inspired by the desolate beauty of his native Suffolk coast; celebrate his legacy at the annual Aldeburgh Festival *(p208)*.

↑ Festival-goers at the world-famous Glastonbury, Somerset

35

Birth of the Modern

Scottish inventor James Watt patented the first steam engine in 1776, kick-starting the Industrial Revolution. The dark satanic mills of the 19th century have given way to a cleaner, greener landscape, but many attractions bring Britain's industrial heritage alive. Plumb the depths of a mineshaft at Blaenavon's Big Pit *(p473)*, pull a locomotive by hand at Ironbridge's Enginuity *(p309)* or experience the deafening sounds of an 1860s cotton mill at Manchester's Museum of Science and Industry *(p347)*.

Looking at an early computer, Museum of Science and Industry ↑

ROMAN SITES — TOP 4

Hadrian's Wall
Watch archaeologists dig up Roman history beside the 2nd-century ramparts *(p414)*.

Roman Baths, Bath
Meet the Romans at this sacred spa *(p258)*.

Caerleon
This well-preserved amphitheatre once hosted gladiatorial contests *(p474)*.

Fishbourne Roman Palace
See splendidly preserved mosaics and the earliest surviving gardens in Britain *(p183)*.

GREAT BRITAIN FOR
HISTORY BUFFS

With three nations, long periods of internecine fighting, an often fractious relationship with its neighbours and a controversial global legacy, Britain has a rich and complex history. A vast array of museums and historic attractions makes unravelling the past as fun as it is edifying.

Living History

Ever fancied sporting a doublet and hose or embracing your inner Viking? Up and down Great Britain, festivals of living history allow Brits to indulge two of their favourite passions: expounding on history while dressing up in extravagant outfits. The festivals can range from boisterous affairs to elaborate attempts to re-create famous moments from the past. Annual events include re-enactments of the battles of Hastings (Oct; *p179*) and Tewkesbury (Jul; *p245*), while the Up Helly Aa Viking festival in Shetland *(p546)*, a madcap 24-hour marathon of flaming torches, winged helmets, sheepskin and shouting, brightens the January gloom.

→

Re-enactment of the Battle of Hastings on the site of the original battle at Battle Abbey

On the Tudor Trail

Genius or madman? Shrewd leader or tyrannical despot? Few historical figures keep as firm a grip on the public imagination as Henry VIII. Wander the poignant skeletal remains of Fountains Abbey *(p390)* and Tintern Abbey *(p474)*, or piece together the story of Anne Boleyn at Hever Castle *(p177)* and the Tower of London *(p118)* – all of these suffered at the destructive hands of this formidable monarch. On a more cheerful note, in Hampton Court *(p177)* Henry created one of the most exquisite palaces in England. Follow in his footsteps and you'll be enthralled.

$\rightarrow$

Atmospheric stone ruins of Tintern Abbey in Monmouthshire, Wales

Britain at War

As cataclysmic World War II passes out of living memory, Britain's wartime monuments, memorials and museums deserve a visit. Tap into the story of the Enigma codebreakers at Bletchley Park *(p243)*; explore the nerve centre of the wartime government at the Churchill War Rooms *(p82)*; see Spitfires take to the sky at IWM Duxford *(p215)*; and visit the Holocaust Exhibition at the Imperial War Museum London *(p84)*.

$\leftarrow$

Statue of mathematician Alan Turing, a chief codebreaker at Bletchley Park, by Stephen Kettle

Public Art

The urban and rural landscapes of Britain are dotted with public art. Among contemporary works, Antony Gormley's cast-iron figures in *Another Place* on Crosby Beach near Liverpool and Andy Scott's *The Kelpies*, dramatic horse-head sculptures near Falkirk *(p524)*, lead the charge. The beautiful *Scallop* by Maggi Hambling on Aldeburgh Beach is dedicated to Benjamin Britten, while Shrewsbury's modernist *Quantum Leap* by architects Pearce & Lal celebrates Charles Darwin. The Fourth Plinth in Trafalgar Square, hosting rotating artworks, is always a subject of hot debate.

→

Cast-iron figure by Antony Gormley looking out to sea on Crosby Beach

GREAT BRITAIN FOR
ART LOVERS

Every city in Great Britain has a major gallery, featuring a dazzling array of artists. These public galleries are supplemented by the collections in a multitude of stately homes, plus the many modern and contemporary spots housing cutting-edge art.

Glorious Galleries

British artists are well represented in galleries, not just in London but beyond. See the world's best collection of Pre-Raphaelites at the Birmingham Museum & Art Gallery *(p324)* and 20th-century British greats at Leeds Art Gallery *(p400)* and Liverpool's Walker Art Gallery *(p353)*. The Kelvingrove Museum and Art Gallery in Glasgow displays the stars of the Glasgow Style and Scottish Colourist Movement *(p353)*, while in Manchester The Lowry Centre *(p348)* specializes in the distinctive Northern landscapes by the eponymous artist.

→

Marble statues, figures and busts in Liverpool's, Walker Art Gallery

Art in Country Houses

Great Britain abounds with stately homes full of art purchased by their aristocratic owners on extended shopping tours of continental Europe. Audley End in Essex (p214) and Temple Newsam House near Leeds (p400) have splendid collections of 18th-century art, while Petworth House in West Sussex (p183) displays works by J M W Turner and Van Dyck and murals by Louis Laguerre. Kenwood House in North London (p141) is a treasure trove of art, with works by Rembrandt, Vermeer, Reynolds and Gainsborough.

Mural above the Grand Staircase, Petworth House

EVENTS AND EXPERIENCES

Take your sketchpad to a gallery and be inspired. You can either draw whatever takes your fancy or attend an artist-led drawing session, such as those often held at London's National Portrait Gallery (p80) during its Friday Lates and at the National Gallery (p68) on Friday lunchtimes. Many galleries and museums throughout Britain hold children's art activities, as well as frequent workshops, courses, talks and tours – check individual websites for details.

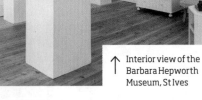

↑ Interior view of the Barbara Hepworth Museum, St Ives

Artists' Homes

The former homes of some of Britain's best-loved artists are now fascinating gallery-museums where you can explore in their footsteps. The Tudor Kelmscott Manor (p228), deep in the Cotswolds, holds exquisite furniture, fabrics and wallpapers by William Morris. In Sudbury, the house where Thomas Gainsborough was born displays a collection of paintings by England's finest portrait painter (p215); nearby, Flatford Mill (p219) was owned by John Constable's father and was the site where Constable painted many of his works. In Cornwall, the Barbara Hepworth Museum and Sculpture Garden (p283) includes the studio where she worked for almost 30 years.

A Night at the Museum

There's no better way for kids to experience London's Science Museum *(p94)* than at their regularly held Astronights sleep-overs, which offer science shows and breakfast. London's Natural History Museum *(p94)* has joined in with "Dino Snores" sleep-overs – there are even nights for adults too, but don't tell the kids!

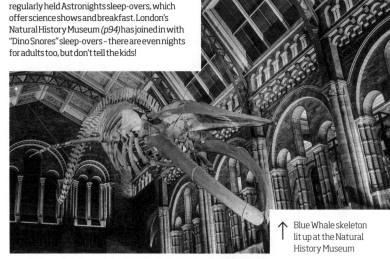

↑ Blue Whale skeleton lit up at the Natural History Museum

GREAT BRITAIN FOR
FAMILIES

Come rain or shine, there are numerous exciting activities for kids and adults alike the length of Great Britain. From theme parks to beautiful sandy beaches, storytelling centres to interactive exhibits, there is plenty of fun to be had by the whole family.

↑ The twists and turns of Alton Towers' Nemesis ride

Adventure Thrills

Great Britain has an enviable collection of adventure parks with something for everyone. At Norfolk's Bewilderwood *(www.bewilderwood.co.uk)*, little kids can enjoy a boat ride or clamber up and down climbing frames, while at Diggerland *(www.diggerland. com)*, which has locations in Kent, Devon, Yorkshire and Durham, kids can steer a go-kart or career around in a mini Land Rover. The big-deal theme park, however, is Alton Towers *(www.altontowers. com)* in Staffordshire, with its many hurtling rides. Nemesis and Galactica in particular promise to get your adrenaline pumping.

Hands-On Exhibits

Great Britain's museums will spark young minds with a range of activities. Everything interactive is the hallmark of Magna *(p404)* in Rotherham, from an inflatable zone where kids bounce around at alarming speeds, to galleries themed on air, earth, fire and water. Edinburgh's Dynamic Earth *(p499)* lets youngsters play with various materials to learn about the planet, while Enginuity *(p309)* at Ironbridge gets kids engaged with technology.

↑ The interactive and inspiring Dynamic Earth exhibition

Telling Tales

Budding young writers will love the Roald Dahl Museum *(p240)* at Great Missenden, with the chance to write their own tales to rival those of one of the world's greatest storytellers. For a literary adventure, kids can follow the whimsical carryings-on of Julia Donaldson's *The Gruffalo* along Gruffalo Trails *(www.forestryengland.uk/gruffalo)* dotted across Great Britain.

← Kids experimenting with arts and crafts at the Roald Dahl Museum

Swimming in the large salt water Tinside Lido in Plymouth ↓

Make a Splash

Scores of sandy beaches make for perfect day trips across Great Britain. Enjoy a dip in the sea at St Ives *(p282)* in Cornwall or tuck into an ice cream at Southwold *(p208)* in Suffolk. If you'd rather avoid sand between your toes, head to a lido. The Jubilee Pool in Penzance *(www.jubileepool.co.uk)* is open all year with geothermal heating, while Tinside Lido *(p300)* in Plymouth has beautiful sea views to enjoy in summer while the kids swim.

FUN PLACES TO STAY

One of the easiest ways to have a one-of-a-kind trip is by staying in quintessentially British accommodation. Break away from the normal and sleep in a treehouse at Clowance Treehouse *(www. luxurylodges.com/ clowance)* in the heart of the Cornish countryside, or at the lush Tinkers Treehouse *(www.canopyandstars. co.uk)* in Sussex. For something with a more historical flavour, stay in a mock medieval wooden cottage at Knight's Village at Warwick Castle *(p314)*.

Eccentric Events

If you're looking for a taste of local life, you'll find it at the cheese-rolling race down Cooper's Hill in Gloucestershire in May or the Bog-snorkelling Championship in Llanwrtyd Wells in Wales, which takes place in August. In the winter, head to Ottery St Mary in Devon to see lighted tar barrels carried through the streets.

Participating in the odd cheese-rolling race down Cooper's Hill

GREAT BRITAIN'S
QUIRKINESS

With a well-deserved reputation for eccentricity, Great Britain is an island where the bizarre can somehow seem steadfastly normal. Whether it be strange museums – pencils and lawnmowers spring to mind – or quirky festivals and events, some highly unusual experiences await.

GET GURNING

Gurning, a rural English tradition, can be traced back to the 13th century. The whole point is to twist and manipulate your face into a horrible pose, usually by projecting the lower jaw and covering the upper lip with the lower lip; this particularly favours those without any teeth. If gurning takes your fancy, or you're simply curious, head to the annual World Gurning Championships *(www. egremoncrabfair.com)*, which are held in Lancashire at the Egremont Crab Fair in late September. Be warned: it's not a pretty sight!

Wacky Lodgings

Dodge the mundane by staying at one of Britain's unconventional hotels. Kitted out in the style of a prison cell, the Penny Rope Bed Chamber *(www.quirkykent.co.uk)* in Margate occupies the basement of a Georgian house. In Lancashire, you can bed down in a converted Lynx helicopter *(www.glampsites.com)*.

Venture into a Village

Nowhere is a more curious and whimsical place to visit than Portmeirion (p440) in Wales, where the eccentric architect Clough William-Ellis built his own private village in a colourful and bizarre Italianate style in the 20th century. Another rich man, Stuart Ogilvie, was also prompted to build his own village – Thorpeness – in Suffolk, which features a Peter Pan boating lake and the House in the Clouds, a converted water tower.

→

Exploring the unusual and vibrant Portmeirion village in Wales

Extraordinary Homes

It's easy to depart from the average stately home. In Nottinghamshire you'll find old newspapers used as bedding at Mr Straw's House (www.nationaltrust.org.uk/mr-straws-house), while Cragside (p421) in Northumberland is packed with Lord Armstrong's assorted gadgets. The idiosyncratic Sir John Soane's Museum (p123) in London even includes an Egyptian sarcophagus.

←

The mass of ceramics that fill London's Sir John Soane's Museum

Kooky Museums

Dive into Great Britain's subversive side at one of its niche museums. Go on a journey of graphite and pencil discovery at the Derwent Pencil Museum (p356) in the Lake District, or explore the world of lawnmowers at the British Lawnmower Museum (www.lawnmowerworld.co.uk) in Southport. At the Laurel and Hardy Museum (p366), located in Ulverston, you can explore the iconic duo's life and times.

→

↑ Margate's underground, prison-themed Penny Rope Bed Chamber

A range of memorabilia on display at the Laurel and Hardy Museum

A YEAR IN
GREAT BRITAIN

JANUARY

Burns Night (25 Jan). Scots everywhere celebrate poet Robert Burns' birth with drinks and feasts.

Up Helly Aa (late Jan). A Viking longboat is carried through Lerwick, Shetland, in this Viking festival.

△ **Chinese New Year** (late Jan or early Feb). London's Chinatown celebrates the New Year with a parade, performances and plenty of food.

FEBRUARY

△ **Six Nations Rugby** (early Feb–late Mar). A keenly fought rugby contest involving the four Home Nations plus France and Italy, with matches at Twickenham, Cardiff and Edinburgh.

Shrovetide Football (Shrove Tuesday and Ash Wednesday). Madcap 8-hour match-cum-brawl through the streets of Ashbourne, Derbyshire.

MAY

May Day (early May). Folk and pagan-related festivals include Hastings' Jack in the Green, and, in Cornwall, Padstow's 'Obby 'Oss.

Glyndebourne Festival Opera Season (May–Sep). World-class productions are staged in the grounds of a Sussex country house.

△ **Chelsea Flower Show** (late May). A five-day horticultural show at London's Royal Hospital.

JUNE

Trooping the Colour (early Jun). Military pageantry in London for the Queen's Birthday Parade.

Royal Academy Summer Exhibitions (mid-Jun–mid-Aug). Large and varied London show of new work by many artists.

△ **Glastonbury Festival** (late Jun). Iconic five-day festival of contemporary music held in Somerset.

SEPTEMBER

Braemar Gathering (1st Sat). Kilted clansmen from all over the country toss cabers, shot put, dance and play the bagpipes.

△ **Great North Run** (Sep or Oct). Tyne and Wear hosts the largest half-marathon in the world.

St Ives Festival (mid–late Sep). Two-week celebration of art, music, poetry and theatre in the picturesque Cornish seaside town.

OCTOBER

Canterbury Festival (mid-Oct–early Nov). Music, drama and the arts in one of the biggest festivals in the southeast.

Battle of Hastings Re-enactment (mid-Oct). This re-enactment of the 1066 battle draws participants from all over the world to East Sussex.

△ **London Film Festival** (second half of Oct). Some 300 British and international films are screened at cinemas large and small around the city.

MARCH

△ **St David's Day** *(1 Mar)*. Wales's national day is celebrated with parades and concerts.

Cheltenham Gold Cup *(mid-Mar)*. One of the two most prestigious National Hunt events (with April's Grand National at Aintree, Liverpool).

The Boat Race *(late Mar or early Apr)*. Oxbridge rowing crews take to the river between Putney Bridge and Chiswick Bridge in London.

APRIL

△ **St George's Day** *(23 Apr)*. Celebrations are held in honour of England's patron saint and William Shakespeare's birthday, with special events at Stratford-upon-Avon.

London Marathon *(late Apr)*. Thousands pound the city's streets, from the world's best runners to fancy-dressed fundraisers.

Beltane Fire Festival *(30 Apr and 1 May)*. This spring festival features bonfires in Edinburgh.

JULY

Wimbledon Tennis Championships *(early–mid-July)*. One of the world's most prestigious tennis tournaments takes place over two weeks in Wimbledon, London.

△ **Pride in London** *(early July)*. Thousands parade through the streets of London to celebrate the LGBT+ community.

The Proms *(mid-July–mid-Sep)*. Eight-week festival of classical and orchestral music, concluding with the over-the-top, uproarious Last Night of the Proms.

AUGUST

Edinburgh International Festival and Edinburgh Festival Fringe *(early–late Aug)*. Great Britain's greatest celebration of arts and culture takes place over three weeks.

National Eisteddfod *(early Aug)*. Traditional arts competitions in Welsh; venue changes every year.

Cowes Week *(mid-Aug)*. The UK's premier sailing regatta takes places on the Isle of Wight.

△ **Notting Hill Carnival** *(last Mon)*. Europe's largest street festival is a riotous celebration of Afro-Caribbean music and culture in West London.

NOVEMBER

Guy Fawkes Night *(5 Nov)*. Fireworks and bonfires all over the country, with the biggest and wildest celebrations in Lewes, East Sussex.

△ **Lord Mayor's Show** *(2nd Sat)*. A procession of floats accompany the Lord Mayor in his gold state coach as it makes its way across London.

Remembrance Day *(2nd Sun)*. Services and parades at the Cenotaph in Whitehall, London.

DECEMBER

Christmas markets *(from late Nov)*. Copious amounts of mulled wine are consumed as Christmas markets are set up countrywide, with the biggest in Birmingham, Leeds, Manchester and London.

△ **New Year's Eve** *(31 Dec)*. Celebrated everywhere, but particularly boisterously at Hogmanay in Edinburgh and across Scotland, with midnight pyrotechnics and street parties.

A BRIEF
HISTORY

With a long and turbulent history, Great Britain's three countries – Wales, Scotland and England – have been welded together as a nation both by military conquest and dynastic accident. Though they share (for the most part) a common tongue, they cling fiercely to their own distinct identities.

Ancient Britain

Great Britain has been inhabited for roughly half a million years. The earliest archaeological remains include bones and flint tools. The Bronze Age, which began around 2,500 BC, witnessed the evolution of farming and livestock-rearing and the construction of stone and timber circles – most famously at Stonehenge (p264). With the advent of the Iron Age around 800 BC scores of hillforts were erected – such as those on the South Downs (p190)– and archaeological finds from this time have included splendid jewellery.

1 17th-century map of Great Britain and Ireland.

2 A 19th-century engraving of druids at Stonehenge.

3 Ancient Roman mosaic in Berkshire.

4 King Alfred's galleys in battle with the Vikings.

Timeline of events

c 500,000 BC
First evidence of human habitation in Great Britain.

c 2500 BC
Beginning of the Bronze Age.

c 800 BC
Iron Age begins, with construction of hillforts.

43 AD
The Roman Emperor Claudius invades Britain.

The Romans

Julius Caesar (100–44 BC) and his Roman legionnaires first landed in Kent in 55 BC, but it wasn't until 43 AD that the Romans invaded Great Britain, conquering southeast England, and then pushed north, building roads and establishing military outposts. By around 80 AD, England and much of Wales were firmly in their grasp. Emperor Hadrian (76–138) marked the northern frontier with the construction of Hadrian's Wall. Roman Britain lasted for 400 years. Trade flourished and peace prevailed – but Roman power ultimately waned.

The Saxons and Vikings

In the 4th century AD, Saxons and Angles from northern Germany regularly raided Roman Britain. By 700 AD, England had been invaded and parcelled up into a series of Anglo-Saxon kingdoms, with Wessex in the south predominating under Alfred the Great (848–899). However, the power of Wessex was subject to another threat. Sailing across the ocean in their mighty longships, the Vikings of Scandinavia were bent on settlement, resulting in endemic warfare into the 11th century.

↑ Bust of Emperor Hadrian, who began building a defensive wall in 122

793 AD
An early Viking raid destroys the monastery at Lindisfarne.

843 AD
Kenneth MacAlpine unites Scotland.

871 AD
Alfred the Great becomes King of Wessex.

973 AD
King Edgar of Wessex crowned the first king of England.

The Middle Ages

In 1066, William the Conqueror (1028–1087) sailed across the Channel from France and defeated the Saxons at the Battle of Hastings. He was then crowned king and both he and his successors ruled a feudal kingdom with local barons exercising regional control. The tension between royal and regional authority plagued England and led to both the curtailing of royal power in the signing of the Magna Carta in 1215 and, much later, to a prolonged period of civil war – the Wars of the Roses. Only in 1485, with the defeat of Richard III (1452–1485) and the accession of the first Tudor king, Henry VII (1457–1509), was order restored.

Tudor Renaissance

Under the Tudors (1485–1603), England blossomed into a major European power. Henry VIII (1491–1547) broke ties with Papal Rome to establish an independent Church of England and his daughter, Elizabeth I (1533–1603), defended England by defeating the Spanish Armada. Elizabeth steered a diplomatic course between her Catholic and Protestant subjects and kept

1 *The Battle of Hastings in 1066* painted by François-Hypolite Debon. ↑

2 An old naval print of the Defeat of the Spanish Armada in 1588.

3 Portrait of Charles II by Peter Lely.

Did You Know?

The Union rose, the floral emblem of England today, was created by Henry VII.

Timeline of events

1066
Battle of Hastings; William the Conqueror becomes king of England.

1215
Signing of the Magna Carta at Runnymede.

1220s
Edward I (1239-1307) of England sets about conquering Wales.

1349
The Black Death - (bubonic plague) breaks out in Great Britain.

1485
Richard III dies at the Battle of Bosworth Field; accession of Henry VII.

3

a firm grip on Wales via the Anglo-Welsh gentry; independent Scotland proved more problematic to Elizabeth as it was allied to France, England's bitter enemy, and the Scottish royals failed to control their own kingdom. One such royal, Mary Queen of Scots (1542–1587), was usurped and fled to exile in England, where her scheming against Elizabeth led to her execution.

The Stuarts

Elizabeth I died childless and her throne passed to James Stuart (1566–1625), the king of Scotland, thereby uniting the two kingdoms. James was an imprudent man, a trait he shared with his son, Charles I (1600–1649), who proceeded to antagonize his Protestant Parliament. The result was a Civil War (1639–1651), whose key engagements were fought in England, where Oliver Cromwell's (1599–1658) Parliamentarians crushed the Royalists. Charles I was executed and Cromwell became the Lord Protector of a republican Commonwealth, which did not last. The Stuarts returned to the throne (a period known as the Restoration) under Charles II (1630–1685) and the dynasty staggered on until the death of Queen Anne (1665–1714), who was succeeded by George I.

DEFEAT OF THE SPANISH ARMADA

Spain was England's main rival for supremacy on the seas. In 1588 Philip II sent 100 powerfully armed galleons towards England, bent on invasion. The English fleet - under Lord Howard, Francis Drake, John Hawkins and Martin Frobisher - sailed from Plymouth and destroyed the Spanish navy in a famous victory.

1538

The Pope excommunicates Henry VIII for his break with Rome.

1603

James VI of Scotland becomes James I of England, uniting the two kingdoms.

1639

Outbreak of the Civil War, also known as the Wars of the Three Kingdoms.

1714

Death of Queen Anne, the last of the Stuarts.

Georgian Britain

The reigns of George I (1660–1727) and George II (1683–1760) were lacklustre, with royal power leaching into the hands of a series of prime ministers. Two serious Jacobite rebellions (*p487*) – led by the deposed Stuarts – were defeated and Britain began to accumulate its Empire, though it did lose the United States during the reign of George III (1738–1820). The Industrial Revolution picked up pace in the late 18th century, with the digging of canals, the sinking of coal mines and the construction of the world's first iron bridge in 1781, whilst British pre-eminence in Europe was secured by the defeat of Napoleon's France at the Battle of Waterloo in 1815.

The Victorians

During the long reign of Queen Victoria (1819–1901), Great Britain became the most powerful country in the world, its economy buoyed both by the success of its manufacturing industry and the exploitation of its ever-expanding empire. The great figures of Victorian Britain – such as Charles Darwin and Charles Dickens – cut an international profile, while a

↑ The leading Victorian novelist and social critic Charles Dickens c 1860

Timeline of events

1783

Britain defeated by its American colonists in the Revolutionary War.

1805

Nelson wins the Battle of Trafalgar; British maritime supremacy secured.

1859

Charles Darwin publishes his seminal *Origin of Species*.

1914–18

World War I; Britain declares war on Germany and her allies.

Methodist-led religious revival resulted in the ban on slavery across the Empire in 1833. Crowning the Victoria era was the Great Exhibition of 1851, an unequalled display of industrial might and engineering virtuosity, although factory conditions were dire and urban poverty a major blight.

The Modern Era

In the 1900s, Britain's supremacy faded. After staggering through the Great Depression of the 1930s it took an economic and military pounding during World War II. After the war, a reforming Labour government established the much-admired National Health Service and Britain began to recover, enjoying an economic and cultural boom in the 1960s. The 1970s was a more troubled decade, which ended with the Conservative Margaret Thatcher coming to power, resulting in increasing social antagonisms and a widening of the gap between rich and poor. In the 21st century there have been two contentious referendums – one on Scottish independence in 2014, which failed, the other on the UK leaving the European Union in 2016, with the vote to leave (Brexit) winning by a narrow majority.

1 Portrait of George III by Allan Ramsay. ↑

2 The Great Exhibition of 1851 in Crystal Palace.

3 Men receiving free coffee during the Great Depression in 1933.

4 A pro-EU march.

Did You Know?

Sir Robert Walpole was Britain's longest serving prime minister from 1721 to 1742.

1939–45

World War II; for a second time, Britain declares war against Germany and her allies.

1967

Abortion (April) and homosexuality (July) legalized in Britain.

2012

Queen's Diamond Jubilee celebrations, marking the 60th year of her reign.

2016–19

Referendum vote to leave the EU, followed by protracted negotiations and bitter debates in parliament.

EXPERIENCE

Brighton Beach and West Pier

LONDON

The City of London skyline

EXPLORE
LONDON

This section divides London into four colour-coded sightseeing areas, as shown below, and an area beyond the centre. Find out more about each area on the following pages.

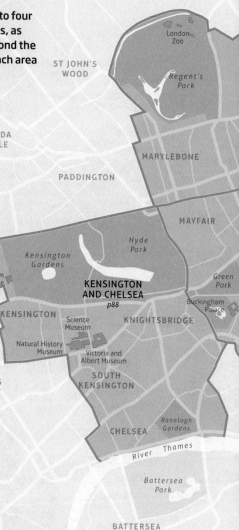

CAMDEN

London Zoo

Regent's Park

ST JOHN'S WOOD

MAIDA VALE

MARYLEBONE

PADDINGTON

NOTTING HILL

MAYFAIR

Hyde Park

Kensington Gardens

HOLLAND PARK

Kensington Palace

Green Park

KENSINGTON AND CHELSEA
p88

Buckingham Palace

Holland Park

KENSINGTON

KNIGHTSBRIDGE

Science Museum

Natural History Museum

Victoria and Albert Museum

HAMMERSMITH

EARL'S COURT

SOUTH KENSINGTON

Ranelagh Gardens

CHELSEA

River Thames

FULHAM

Battersea Park

BATTERSEA

PARSON'S GREEN

PUTNEY

WANDSWORTH

CLAPHAM

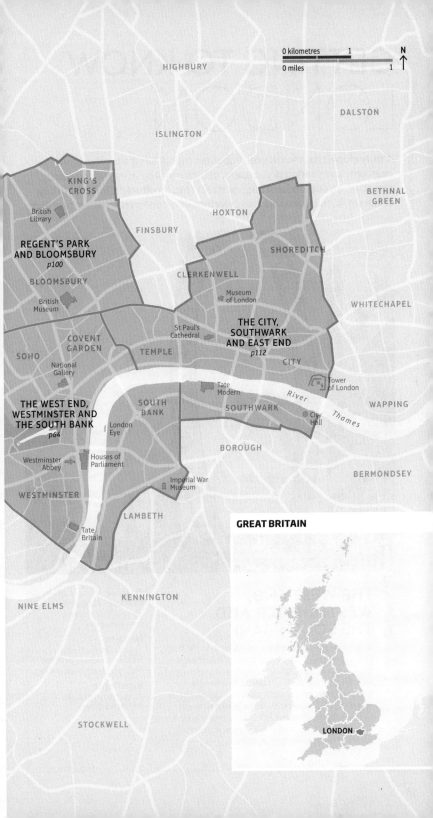

0 kilometres 1
0 miles 1

N

HIGHBURY

DALSTON

ISLINGTON

KING'S
CROSS

BETHNAL
GREEN

British
Library

HOXTON

FINSBURY

**REGENT'S PARK
AND BLOOMSBURY**
p100

SHOREDITCH

BLOOMSBURY

CLERKENWELL

British
Museum

Museum
of London

WHITECHAPEL

COVENT
GARDEN

St Paul's
Cathedral

**THE CITY,
SOUTHWARK
AND EAST END**
p112

SOHO

TEMPLE

CITY

National
Gallery

Tower
of London

Tate
Modern

River

WAPPING

**THE WEST END,
WESTMINSTER AND
THE SOUTH BANK**
p64

SOUTH
BANK

SOUTHWARK

Thames

London
Eye

City
Hall

Westminster
Abbey

Houses of
Parliament

BOROUGH

BERMONDSEY

WESTMINSTER

Imperial War
Museum

LAMBETH

GREAT BRITAIN

Tate
Britain

KENNINGTON

NINE ELMS

BERMSEY

STOCKWELL

LONDON

GETTING TO KNOW
LONDON

A truly global city, the UK's cosmopolitan capital has it all: mind-blowing museums and soaring skyscrapers; opulent royal palaces and cosy pubs; street art, street food and bags of street chic. If culture fatigue or big city ennui set in, there are countless swathes of green space in which to reboot.

PAGE 64

THE WEST END, WESTMINSTER AND THE SOUTH BANK

With its theatres, restaurants, pubs and clubs, the West End is London's 24-hour entertainment hub, a magnet for visitors and a well-placed launching pad for much of what the city has to offer. To the south is Westminster, seat of government for a millennium and synonymous with some of London's most iconic buildings. Across the river, the lively South Bank forms one of London's most welcoming open-air public spaces, focused on its line-up of first-class cultural institutions.

Best for
Iconic London landmarks, eating out and a buzzing, lively atmosphere

Home to
National Gallery, Houses of Parliament, Westminster Abbey, Buckingham Palace, Tate Britain

Experience
A tour of the art treasures in the National Gallery

PAGE 88

KENSINGTON AND CHELSEA

With its mansion blocks and garden squares, the Royal Borough of Kensington and Chelsea is one of London's most well-to-do areas, with upmarket shops and restaurants to match. The principal focus for visitors is the cluster of magnificent museums along South Kensington's Exhibition Road. From here, it's a short hop to the leafy expanse of Hyde Park, a tranquil place for a picnic, or for renting out a rowing boat on the inky waters of The Serpentine.

Best for
World-class free museums, upmarket shopping and beautiful neighbourhoods

Home to
Victoria and Albert Museum

Experience
The weird and wonderful collections of the Natural History Museum

$\rightarrow$

PAGE 100

REGENT'S PARK AND BLOOMSBURY

Regent's Park, fringed by Georgian terraces, is the busiest of the royal parks, its canalside location providing universal appeal. To the south, beyond traffic-choked Marylebone Road, is Marylebone, a genteel area with one of London's more high-brow high streets. Bohemian, laidback Bloomsbury is the student quarter, home to university campuses, independent bookshops and large garden squares. To its north, after a major regeneration, King's Cross is now a culinary, commercial and artsy hotspot.

Best for
Canal walks, Georgian architecture and a strong literary heritage

Home to
British Museum

Experience
Some of the world's greatest treasures at the British Museum

PAGE 112

THE CITY, SOUTHWARK AND EAST END

Bustling during the week but eerily deserted at the weekend, the City is both financial centre and historic heart, where towering skyscrapers sit cheek-by-jowl with reminders of London's ancient past. Beyond the City, the once-deprived East End is now a well-established hipster hub, with an alluring energy. South of the Thames, Southwark's Bankside is always thronged with visitors to its top-drawer attractions and has a fine concentration of waterside pubs and street-food markets.

Best for
Skyscraper views, street food and getting up close to London's staggering history

Home to
St Paul's Cathedral, Tower of London, Tate Modern

Experience
Striking modern and cutting-edge contemporary art at Tate Modern

PAGE 134

BEYOND THE CENTRE

Big-name draws beyond the city's central core include the legendary markets of Camden and Portobello, exquisite Kew Gardens, the maritime treasures of Greenwich and – in Hampton Court – London's finest royal palace. But the biggest attraction of venturing beyond the centre is to escape the crowds and explore the vibrant local neighbourhoods of this thrillingly multicultural, endlessly surprising city.

Best for
Royal palaces, green spaces and local life

Home to
Greenwich, Hampton Court

Experience
A dip in chilly Hampstead Heath Ponds

7 DAYS
in London

Day 1

Start by taking the lift to the to top of the Shard *(p129)* – there's no better vantage point from which to survey London. Down at street level, stroll along the cobbled alleys of Southwark and stop for lunch at London's last galleried pub, the 17th-century George *(p129)*. In the afternoon head west along the Thames, popping into the cavernous Tate Modern *(p120)* to see what's new in the world of contemporary art. Finish up the afternoon by taking a spin on the London Eye *(p85)*, followed by a dinner of Peruvian tapas at Casita Andina *(31 Great Windmill Street)*. It's just a short stroll from here to Ronne Scott's, London's most famous jazz club *(p78)*.

Day 2

Visit St Paul's Cathedral *(p116)*, Christopher Wren's Baroque masterpiece. Continue west to the Inns of Court *(p122)* for a picnic and stroll around the leafy gardens and passageways of this lawyers' hidey-hole, which have seen some of the most major events of English history. From here it's a 15-minute walk to the idiosyncratic

Sir John Soane's Museum *(p123)*. For the evening, head to super-cool Shoreditch where there are plenty of trendy places to eat, drink and relax in, not least Brick Lane *(p130)*, the curry capital of London.

Day 3

Head to the City and explore the Museum of London *(p124)*, which provides an excellent history of the capital. Have lunch at the historic Leadenhall Market *(p125)*. After, take the train to Greenwich *(p136)* to discover centuries of maritime history at the Old Royal Naval College and the National Maritime Museum. Then pop up to the Royal Observatory with its planetarium. In the evening, walk to Greenwich park to enjoy sunset views and then wander down to the north end towards the village until you find a restaurant that takes your fancy.

Day 4

Spend the morning exploring the specimens and skeletons at the Natural History Museum *(p94)*, housed in a

1 The Milliennium footbridge leading towards St. Paul's Cathedral. ↑

2 Skeletons in the National History Museum.

3 Street food at Southbank Centre Food Market.

4 The Victorian Leadenhall Market in the City.

5 The Palm House, Kew Gardens.

stunning Victorian building. For lunch have a picnic in nearby Hyde Park (p96). In the afternoon spend a few hours exploring the Victoria & Albert Museum (p92) with its world-beating collections of fine and applied art and design. Dine on excellent Polish cuisine at Daquise (p95) and, if you've pre-booked tickets, enjoy a performance at the Royal Albert Hall (p95).

Day 5

In the morning, visit Camden Town to enjoy the alternative vibe of Camden Market (p142). Browse the stalls and grab a casual lunch here. Then jump on the Northern Line to the villages of Hampstead and Highgate (p140). Take a scenic leisurely walk between the two via Hampstead Heath and the atmospheric Victorian Highgate Cemetery. Finish the day with a relaxed dinner at one of Highgate's excellent pubs, such as The Southampton Arms.

Day 6

Take a walk in Regent's Park (p108), one of London's most splendid royal parks. Then

visit the Sherlock Holmes Museum on Baker Street (p109) to explore the re-created house of the famous sleuth. Head over to the British Museum (p104), and after lunch in the café, spend the afternoon exploring its stunning collections. After-wards, amble through neighbouring Bloomsbury, once the haunt of the rich and influential, to Granary Square (p110) behind King's Cross station, and dine at one of the many buzzing restaurants.

Day 7

Escape the throngs of central London by catching the train (30 mins) from Waterloo to Kew Bridge, footsteps from the glorious greenery of the Royal Botanic Gardens, Kew (p143), Europe's prime botanical gardens. Give yourself at least two hours to enjoy Kew – and have lunch here too. In the afternoon, meander over to Kew Pier and take the river boat (1 hr 30 mins) to Hampton Court, one of England's finest Tudor houses (p138). Afterwards, return to Waterloo by train (50 mins) and finish the day by eating at the nearby Southbank Centre Food Market.

THE WEST END, WESTMINSTER AND THE SOUTH BANK

Westminster has been at the centre of political and religious power in England for 1,000 years. In the 11th century King Canute was the first monarch to found a palace here, beside the church that, some 50 years later, Edward the Confessor would enlarge into England's greatest abbey, giving the area its name (a minster is an abbey church). Over the following centuries the offices of state were established nearby, many of them in Whitehall. This grand street was named after the former Palace of Whitehall, established by Henry VIII in the 16th century as home to the royal court. Royal hunting grounds were laid out in what is today St James's Park and spread beyond to modern-day Soho and other parts of the West End.

In the 18th century the stretch of marshy land across the river from Westminster was drained and developed, becoming known as the South Bank. By the end of World War II the land lay bomb-damaged and derelict. It was redeveloped for the 1951 Festival of Britain with the construction of the Royal Festival Hall, and later the Southbank Centre. The new millennium was marked on the South Bank with the raising of the London Eye, Europe's tallest cantilevered observation wheel.

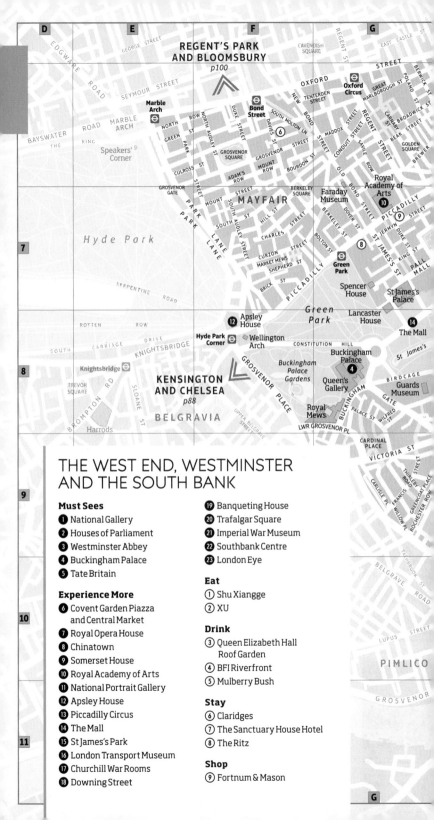

THE WEST END, WESTMINSTER AND THE SOUTH BANK

Must Sees

1. National Gallery
2. Houses of Parliament
3. Westminster Abbey
4. Buckingham Palace
5. Tate Britain

Experience More

6. Covent Garden Piazza and Central Market
7. Royal Opera House
8. Chinatown
9. Somerset House
10. Royal Academy of Arts
11. National Portrait Gallery
12. Apsley House
13. Piccadilly Circus
14. The Mall
15. St James's Park
16. London Transport Museum
17. Churchill War Rooms
18. Downing Street
19. Banqueting House
20. Trafalgar Square
21. Imperial War Museum
22. Southbank Centre
23. London Eye

Eat

1. Shu Xiangge
2. XU

Drink

3. Queen Elizabeth Hall Roof Garden
4. BFI Riverfront
5. Mulberry Bush

Stay

6. Claridges
7. The Sanctuary House Hotel
8. The Ritz

Shop

9. Fortnum & Mason

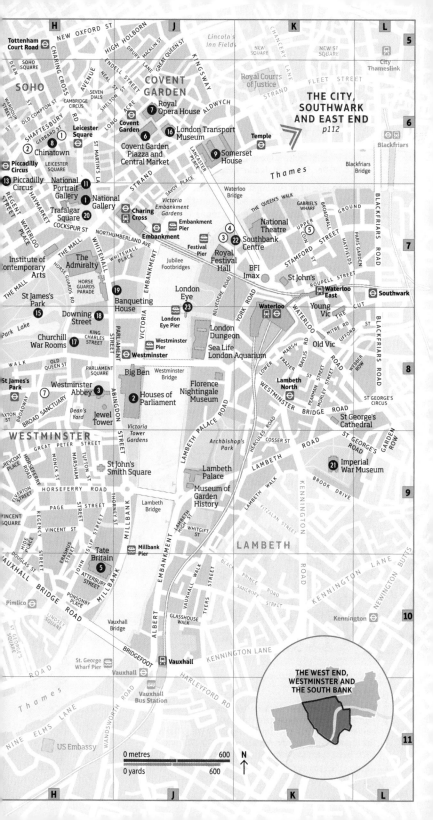

❶ 🍷 🍴 ☕ 🛍️

NATIONAL GALLERY

📍H7 🚇Trafalgar Square WC2 🚉Charing Cross, Leicester Sq,
Piccadilly Circus 🚆Charing Cross 🕐10am-6pm daily (to 9pm Fri)
📅1 Jan, 24-26 Dec 🌐nationalgallery.org.uk

Erected in the heart of the West End in order to be accessible by all,
the National Gallery houses some of the most famous paintings in the
world, by masters such as Rubens, Velázquez, Monet and Van Gogh.

The National Gallery has flourished
since its inception. In 1824 the House
of Commons was persuaded to buy
38 major paintings, including works
by Raphael and Rubens, and these
became the start of a national
collection. Today the gallery has
more than 2,300 paintings produced
in the Western European painting
tradition. The main gallery building,
designed in Greek Revival style by
William Wilkins, was built between
1833 and 1838. It was subsequently
enlarged and the dome added in 1876.
To its left lies the Sainsbury Wing,
financed by the grocery family and
completed in 1991.

The Collection

The National Gallery's paintings are
mostly kept on permanent display.
The collection spans late-medieval
times to the early 20th century,
covering Renaissance Italy and the
French Impressionists. There are
works by artists such as Botticelli,
Leonardo, Monet and Goya, and
highlights include Van Eyck's *Arnolfini
Portrait*, Velázquez's *Rokeby Venus*,
Raphael's *The Madonna of the Pinks*
and Van Gogh's *Sunflowers*.

→
The National Gallery,
overlooking Trafalgar Square

←
Groups of visitors
studying works by
the masters in the
airy galleries

GALLERY GUIDE

Most of the collection is housed on one floor divided into
four wings. The paintings hang chronologically, with the
earliest works (1200-1500) in the Sainsbury Wing. The West,
North and East Wings cover 1500-1600, 1600-1700 and 1700-
1930. Lesser paintings from all periods are on the lower floor.

Did You Know?

Close examination of the *Madonna of the Veil* showed it was a 19th-century fake, and not by Botticelli.

↑ Pausing for thought in front of some of the gallery's masterpieces

2 🖉 Ⓜ️ 🖥️ 🛍️

HOUSES OF PARLIAMENT

📍J8 🏠London SW1 🚇Westminster 🚆Victoria ⛴Westminster Pier
🕐For details on visiting and to buy tickets, check website ❌Recesses: mid-Feb, Easter, Whitsun, summer (late Jul–early Sep), conference (mid-Sep–mid-Oct), mid-Nov, Christmas 🌐parliament.uk/visit

At the heart of political power in England is the Palace of Westminster. Built in Neo-Gothic style, it lies beside the Thames near Westminster Bridge and makes an impressive sight, especially with the distinctive Elizabeth Tower.

For over 500 years the Palace of Westminster has been the seat of the two Houses of Parliament, called the Lords and the Commons. The Commons is made up of elected Members of Parliament (MPs) of different political parties; the party – or coalition of parties – with the most MPs forms the Government, and its leader becomes Prime Minister. MPs from other parties make up the Opposition. Commons debates are impartially chaired by an MP designated as Speaker. The Government formulates legislation which must be agreed to in both Houses before it becomes law.

↑ The Houses of Parliament, designed by Sir Charles Barry

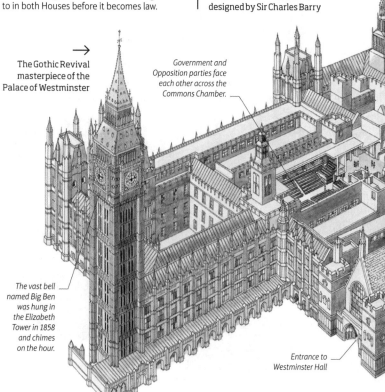

→ The Gothic Revival masterpiece of the Palace of Westminster

Government and Opposition parties face each other across the Commons Chamber.

The vast bell named Big Ben was hung in the Elizabeth Tower in 1858 and chimes on the hour.

Entrance to Westminster Hall

Timeline

1605
▽ Guy Fawkes and others try to blow up the king and Houses of Parliament.

1941
▽ Chamber of House of Commons destroyed by World War II bomb.

1042
△ Work starts on first palace for Edward the Confessor.

1834
△ Palace destroyed by fire; only Westminster Hall and the Jewel Tower survive.

People who come to meet their MP wait under a ceiling of rich mosaics in the Central Lobby.

The Lords Chamber is upholstered in red.

Sovereign's entrance

Westminster Hall is one of the surviving parts of the original Palace of Westminster, dating from 1097.

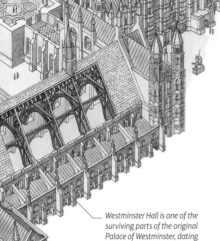

↑ The green leather benches of the Commons Chamber, where the government sits

③ ⚔️ Ⓜ️ 🖥️ 🛍️

WESTMINSTER ABBEY

📍 H8 🏛️ Broad Sanctuary SW1 🚇 St James's Park, Westminster 🚆 Victoria, Waterloo 🕐 Check website for specific parts of the church 🌐 westminster-abbey.org

The final resting place of 17 of Britain's monarchs and numerous political and cultural icons, the glorious Gothic Westminster Abbey is the stunning setting for coronations, royal marriages and Christian worship.

Within the abbey walls are some of the best examples of medieval architecture in London and one of the most impressive collections of tombs and monuments in the world. The first abbey church was established in the 10th century by St Dunstan and a group of Benedictine monks. The present structure dates largely from the 13th century; the new French-influenced design was begun in 1245 at the behest of Henry III. The abbey has been the fittingly sumptuous setting for all royal coronations since 1066.

The interior presents a diverse array of architectural and sculptural styles, from the austere French Gothic of the nave, through Henry VII's stunning Tudor chapel, to the riotous 18th-century monuments. The latest addition is the 2018 Weston Tower, which provides access to the triforium and its Queen's Diamond Jubilee Galleries, packed wth historical treasures.

The West Front towers were designed by Nicholas Hawksmoor.

← The Westminster Abbey choir singing from their stalls in the quire

Timeline

1050
▲ New Benedictine abbey church begun by Edward the Confessor.

1245
New church begun to the designs of Henry of Reyns.

1269
▲ Body of Edward the Confessor is moved to a new shrine in the abbey.

1540
▲ Monastery dissolved on the orders of King Henry VIII.

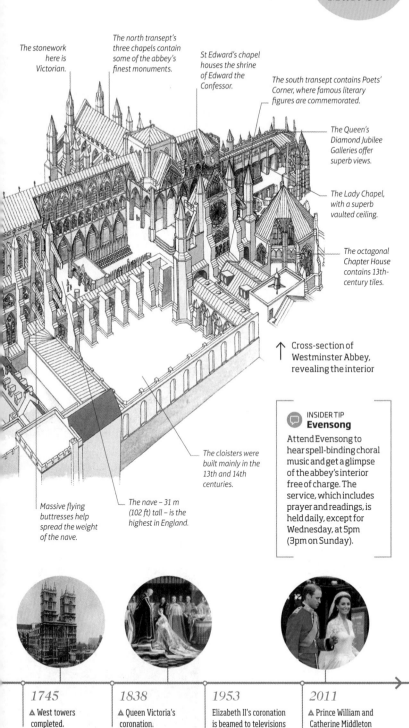

The stonework here is Victorian.

The north transept's three chapels contain some of the abbey's finest monuments.

St Edward's chapel houses the shrine of Edward the Confessor.

The south transept contains Poets' Corner, where famous literary figures are commemorated.

The Queen's Diamond Jubilee Galleries offer superb views.

The Lady Chapel, with a superb vaulted ceiling.

The octagonal Chapter House contains 13th-century tiles.

↑ Cross-section of Westminster Abbey, revealing the interior

The cloisters were built mainly in the 13th and 14th centuries.

Massive flying buttresses help spread the weight of the nave.

The nave – 31 m (102 ft) tall – is the highest in England.

> **INSIDER TIP**
> **Evensong**
>
> Attend Evensong to hear spell-binding choral music and get a glimpse of the abbey's interior free of charge. The service, which includes prayer and readings, is held daily, except for Wednesday, at 5pm (3pm on Sunday).

1745
△ West towers completed.

1838
△ Queen Victoria's coronation.

1953
Elizabeth II's coronation is beamed to televisions across the nation.

2011
△ Prince William and Catherine Middleton marry in the abbey.

State guests are presented and royal christenings take place in the Music Room.

The Victorian Ballroom, used for state banquets and ceremonies.

② (160 m/ 525 ft)

①

→

Buckingham Palace, official home of the British monarch

④

BUCKINGHAM PALACE

♀ G8 ⌂ SW1 ⊖ St James's Park, Victoria, Green Park 🚇 Victoria ⊙ State Rooms and Garden: mid-Jul–Sep 9:30am–7pm (to 6pm in Sep); selected dates Dec–May, check website 🖥 rct.uk

The Queen's official London residence is one of the capital's best recognized landmarks. Visit its opulent state rooms for a glimpse of how the royals live.

Both administrative office and family home, Buckingham Palace is the official London residence of the British monarch. The palace is used for ceremonial occasions for visiting heads of state as well as the weekly meeting between the Queen and the Prime Minister. John Nash converted the original Buckingham House into a palace for George IV (reigned 1820–30). Both he and his brother, William IV (reigned 1830–37), died before work was completed, and Queen Victoria was the first monarch to live at the palace. She added a fourth wing to incorporate more bedrooms and guest rooms.

THE CHANGING OF THE GUARD

Palace guards, dressed in traditional red tunics and tall furry hats, march from Wellington Barracks to Buckingham Palace, parading for 45 minutes while the palace keys are handed over by the old guard to the new at this colourful and musical military ceremony. Crowds gather to watch this striking show of pageantry (www.changing-guard.com).

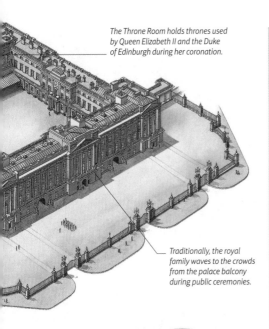

The Throne Room holds thrones used by Queen Elizabeth II and the Duke of Edinburgh during her coronation.

Traditionally, the royal family waves to the crowds from the palace balcony during public ceremonies.

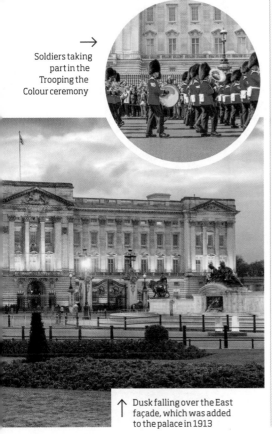

→ Soldiers taking part in the Trooping the Colour ceremony

↑ Dusk falling over the East façade, which was added to the palace in 1913

①

The Queen's Gallery

⌂ Buckingham Palace Rd SW1 🕐 10am–5:30pm daily (late-Jul–Sep: 9:30am–5:30pm; last adm: 4:15pm) 🚫 Between exhibitions, check website

Britain's royal family possesses one of the finest and most valuable art collections in the world, rich in the work of Old Masters, such as Johannes Vermeer and Leonardo da Vinci. The Queen's Gallery hosts a rolling programme of the Royal Collection's most impressive masterpieces, with temporary exhibitions featuring fine art, porcelain, jewels, furniture and manuscripts.

②

Royal Mews

⌂ Buckingham Palace Rd SW1 🕐 Apr–Oct: 10am–5pm daily; Nov, Feb–Mar: 10am–4pm Mon–Sat 🚫 Subject to closure at short notice, check website; Dec–Jan

Head to the Royal Mews to discover plenty of royal pomp. Stables and coach houses, designed by Nash in 1825, accommodate the horses and coaches used by the royal family on state occasions. The Mews' extensive collection of coaches, motorcars and carriages includes the Irish State Coach, bought by Queen Victoria for the State Opening of Parliament; the open-topped 1902 Royal Landau, used to give the crowds the best view of newlywed royal couples; and the Glass Coach, also used for royal weddings. The newest coach is the Diamond Jubilee State Coach, built in 2012. The star exhibit is the Gold State Coach: built for George III in 1761, with panels by Giovanni Cipriani, it has been used at every coronation since 1821.

TATE BRITAIN

THE NATIONAL
COLLECTION OF
BRITISH ART

The stately façade ↑
of Tate Britain, home
of British art

⑤ 🅜 🍴 🖵 🛍

TATE BRITAIN

📍H10 🏛Millbank SW1 🚇Pimlico 🚆Victoria, Vauxhall 🚢Millbank Pier
🕐10am–6pm daily (till 9:30pm first Fri of every month, except Jan)
📅24–26 Dec 🌐tate.org.uk

The nation's largest collection of British art, spanning the 16th to the 21st centuries, is held in a fabulous Neo-Classical building facing the river. The works include sculpture and modern installation pieces and a separate wing is given over to the moody paintings of British artist J M W Turner.

The gallery exhibits a broad range of British art, from Tudor portraits and 18th-century landscapes to a large sculpture collection and modern art. Displays change frequently and the gallery's broad definition of British art stretches to work by non-British artists who spent time in the country, such as Canaletto and James Whistler. The gallery opened in 1897, founded on the private collection of the sugar merchant Henry Tate and works from the older National Gallery. The Tate includes seven rooms added to display the paintings of J M W Turner, one of Britain's most revered artists. The Turner Bequest, as it is known, was left to the nation by Turner on his death in 1851. It is displayed in its own wing, called the Clore Gallery, and consists of some 300 oil paintings, 300 sketchbooks and about 20,000 watercolours and drawings. Major temporary exhibitions here always draw huge crowds.

↑ Turner's *Peace – Burial at Sea* (1842), a tribute to his friend and rival David Wilkie

↑ Inside the gallery, where art graces every corner

TURNER PRIZE

Every other year, Tate Britain exhibits the shortlisted works for the prestigious and often controversial Turner Prize, which was established in 1984. Representing all visual arts, four contemporary artists are shortlisted annually on the basis of their work during the preceding year, before a panel of judges picks the winner. Among the most sensational of the boundary-testing winners have been Damien Hirst's Mother and Child, Divided (1995) and the ceramics of Grayson Perry (*right*) in 2003.

 ←
Window-shopping
and snacking in the
Apple Market,
Covent Garden

EXPERIENCE MORE

   6

Covent Garden Piazza and Central Market

📍 J6 🚇 Covent Garden WC2 🚉 Covent Garden, Leicester Sq 🚆 Charing Cross 🌐 coventgarden.london

One of London's most distinct and animated squares, Covent Garden comprises a bustling piazza filled with street performers and a market alive with shops, cafés and the occasional opera singer.

The central, covered Apple Market, designed in 1833 for fruit and vegetable whole-salers, today houses an array of stalls and small shops selling designer clothes, books, arts and crafts, decorative items and antiques. The 17th-century architect Inigo Jones planned this area as an elegant residential square, but the Victorian buildings on and around the piazza now, including the Royal Opera House, are almost entirely commercial. The market stalls continue south into the neighbouring Jubilee Hall, which was built in 1903. The colonnaded Bedford Chambers on the north side give a hint of Inigo Jones's plan, although these buildings are not original either, having been rebuilt and partially modified in 1879. Despite the renovations, the tradition of street entertainers in the piazza has endured since at least the 17th century.

   7

Royal Opera House

📍 J6 🚇 Bow St WC2 🚇 Covent Garden 🌐 roh.org.uk

Built in 1732, the first theatre on this site served as more of a playhouse, although many of Handel's operas and oratorios were premiered here. Like its neighbour, the Theatre Royal Drury Lane, the building proved prone to fire and burned down in 1808 and again in 1856. The present opera house was designed in 1858 by E M Barry. John Flaxman's portico frieze, depicting tragedy and comedy, survived from the previous building of 1809.

The Opera House has had both high and low points during its history. In 1892, the first British performance of Wagner's *Ring* cycle was conducted here by Gustav Mahler. Later, during World War I, the building was used as a storehouse by the government. Today, it is home to the Royal Opera and Royal Ballet companies – the best tickets can cost over £200 (though restricted-view tickets up in the "slips" can be had for as little as £12; in addition, free musical performances take place in the foyer at lunchtime on Fridays and Sundays). Back-stage tours are available.

   8

Chinatown

📍 H6 🚇 Gerrard St and around W1 🚇 Leicester Sq, Piccadilly Circus 🌐 chinatown.co.uk

Though much smaller than its equivalents in New York

THE HEART OF SOHO

Beating a path through Soho is Old Compton Street, a busy thoroughfare of restaurants, bars, clubs and shops. Home for centuries to poets, writers and musicians, it is now an LGBT+ hub, the Admiral Duncan pub leading a pack of popular bars and clubs. Turn off on Frith Street to see iconic jazz club Ronnie Scott's and Bar Italia; above the latter, John Logie Baird first demonstrated TV in 1926.

City and San Francisco, London's Chinatown packs a punch. There are restaurants aplenty and a constant buzz that attracts countless locals and visitors.

Chinatown occupies the small network of pedestrianized streets north of Leicester Square and revolves around the main drag, Gerrard Street. Historically, London's Chinese community, which totals more than 120,000, came predominantly from Hong Kong and was concentrated initially in Limehouse, in the East End. The current base in Soho was established in the 1960s, though the Chinese population is now widely dispersed across the city.

Today, Chinatown is an intense little precinct marked by ornamental archways and, more often than not, strewn with paper lanterns. The area is packed over-whelmingly with authentic Oriental restaurants and Chinese supermarkets, with bakeries and bubble tea shops, plus herbal medicine, acupuncture and massage centres, filling the gaps.

Somerset House

J6 **Strand WC2**
Temple, Charing Cross
Charing Cross
Embankment Pier
8am–11pm daily
somersethouse.org.uk

This grand Georgian building, with four Neo-Classical wings around a huge stone courtyard, is an innovative arts and cultural centre. It is also a popular venue for outdoor summer cinema, art fairs and installations, and an ice rink in the winter months.

Somerset House is best known as the home of the **Courtauld Gallery**, the city's premier collection of Impressionist paintings.

Built in the 1770s, its first resident was the Royal Academy of Arts. Later tenants included the Navy Board at the end of the 1780s. The building retains some striking architectural features, including the classical grandeur of the Seamen's Waiting Hall and the five-storey rotunda staircase called Nelson's Stair, both in the South Wing. Strolling through the wing from the courtyard leads to a riverside terrace featuring an open-air summer café and a

restaurant. Below are the modern Embankment Galleries with exhibitions ranging from photography to design and fashion.

Courtauld Gallery
Until early 2021
courtauld.ac.uk

EAT

Shu Xiangge
Specialists in traditional Sichuan hotpots, with 80 different ingredients to add to their fragrant, communal broths.

H6 **10 Gerrard St**

£ £ £

***

XU
This restaurant re-creates the look of a 1930s Taipei social club, with wood panelling and murals. The food fuses Taiwanese and Cantonese cuisine.

H6 **30 Rupert St**
xulondon.com

£ £ £

↑ Taking a break in the large courtyard of Somerset House

Did You Know?

The Royal Academy was Britain's first independent fine arts school.

🔟 Royal Academy of Arts

📍 **G7** 🏠 **Burlington House & 6 Burlington Gardens, Piccadilly W1** 🚇 **Piccadilly Circus, Green Park** 🕐 **10am-6pm daily (to 10pm Fri)** 🌐 **royalacademy.org.uk**

Founded in 1768, the Royal Academy is one of Britain's oldest art institutions. Though it holds one of the nation's great art collections it is perhaps best known for its annual Summer Exhibition, which comprises a mix of around 1,200 new works by established and unknown painters, sculptors and architects. Celebrating its 250th anniversary in 2018, the Royal Academy expanded its exhibition spaces and linked two majestic Italianate buildings – Burlington House and Burlington Gardens – via a bridge. The addition of several galleries, including the Vaults and the Collection Gallery, allows more space to display highlights from the exceptional permanent collection, which includes works by Michelangelo and Constable, as well as the work of contemporary artists.

🔢 National Portrait Gallery

📍 **G7** 🏠 **2 St Martin's Place WC2** 🚇 **Charing Cross, Leicester Sq** 🕐 **10am-6pm Sat-Thu, 10am-9pm Fri** 🌐 **npg.org.uk**

With over 210,000 separate works spanning six centuries, the National Portrait Gallery (NPG) holds the world's greatest collection of portraits. The gallery tells the story of Britain from the 16th century to the present day through the portraits, photographs and sculptures of a wide cast of the nation's main figures. Subjects include the royal family, artists, musicians, thinkers, politicians and writers. There are also regular temporary exhibitions. The top-floor Portrait Restaurant has fabulous views over Trafalgar Square.

> 💬 **INSIDER TIP**
> **Lunchtime Learning**
>
> The NPG's Lunchtime Lectures (£4) are a great way to dig a bit deeper into aspects of the collection. They take place on Thursdays, are delivered by staff or by visiting speakers and last approximately one hour. Buy tickets online or in person.

Key figures in British history lining the walls at the National Portrait Gallery ↑

Apsley House

F8 **Hyde Park Corner W1** **Hyde Park Corner**
Apr-Oct: 11am-5pm Wed-Sun; Nov-Mar: 10am-4pm Sat & Sun
english-heritage.org.uk

This townhouse at Hyde Park Corner was completed by Robert Adam for Baron Apsley in 1778. Fifty years later it was enlarged and altered to provide a grand home for the Duke of Wellington. His dual career as both soldier and politician brought him victory against his archenemy Napoleon at Waterloo (1815) and two terms as prime minister (1828–30 and 1834). Against sumptuous silk hangings and gilt decoration is the duke's art collection: works by Goya, Velázquez, Titian and Rubens hang alongside displays of porcelain, silver and furniture. Ironically, the duke's memorabilia is dominated by Canova's colossal statue of Napoleon.

→
Looking down the flag-decorated Mall towards Buckingham Palace

Piccadilly Circus

H6 **W1** **Piccadilly Circus**

Dominated by neon billboards, Piccadilly Circus is a hectic traffic junction surrounded by shops and restaurants. It began as an early 19th-century crossroads between Piccadilly and John Nash's Regent Street and was briefly an elegant space, edged by stucco façades, but by 1910 the first electric advertisements had been installed. For years people have congregated at its centre, beneath the iconic 1892 winged statue of the Shaftesbury Memorial Fountain, which has been renamed in the public imagination after Eros, the Greek god of love.

The Mall

G8-H7 **SW1** **Charing Cross, Green Park**

This broad triumphal approach from Trafalgar Square to Buckingham Palace was created by Aston Webb when he redesigned the front of the palace and the Victoria Monument in 1911. The spacious tree-lined avenue follows the course of an old path at the edge of St James's Park. The path was laid out in the reign of Charles II, when it became London's most fashionable promenade. The Mall is used for royal processions on special occasions. Flagpoles down both sides fly the national flags of foreign heads of state during official visits. The Mall is closed to traffic on Sundays.

SHOP

Fortnum & Mason
The finest foods in beautifully designed packaging are the hallmarks of Fortnum & Mason. Established in 1707, this is one of the city's most renowned and extravagant stores.

G7 **181 Piccadilly**
fortnumand mason.com

15

St James's Park

H8 **SW1** **St James's Park** **5am–midnight daily** **royalparks.org.uk**

In summer, office workers sunbathe in between the flowerbeds of the capital's most ornamental park. In winter, the sunbathers are replaced with overcoated civil servants discussing affairs of state as they stroll by the lake, eyed by its resident ducks, geese and pelicans (which are fed at 2:30pm daily).

Originally a marsh, the park was drained by Henry VIII and incorporated into his hunting grounds. On his return from exile in France, Charles II had it remodelled in the more continental style as pedestrian pleasure gardens, with an aviary along its southern edge (hence Birdcage Walk, the name of the street that runs alongside the park, where the aviary once was).

It is a hugely popular place to escape the city's hustle and bustle, with an appealing view of Buckingham Palace, a café, which is open daily, and an attractive lake.

16

London Transport Museum

J6 **Covent Garden Piazza WC2** **Covent Garden** **10am–6pm daily** **ltmuseum.co.uk**

This collection of buses, trams and underground trains ranges from the earliest horse-drawn omnibuses to a present-day Hoppa bus. Housed in the Victorian Flower Market of Covent Garden built in 1872, the museum is particularly good for children, who can sit in the driver's seat of a bus or an underground train, operate signals and chat to an actor playing a 19th-century Tube-tunnel miner.

London's bus and train companies have long been prolific patrons of artists, and the museum holds a fine collection of 19th-, 20th- and 21st-century commercial art. Copies of some of the best works by distinguished artists, such as Paul Nash and Graham Sutherland, are on sale in the shop. Original works can be seen at the museum's depot in Acton.

17

Churchill War Rooms

H8 **Clive Steps, King Charles St SW1** **Westminster** **Jul & Aug: 9:30am–7pm daily (last adm: 5:45pm); Sep–Jun 9:30am–6pm daily (last adm: 5pm)** **iwm.org.uk**

This intriguing slice of 20th-century history is a warren of cellars below the government office buildings north of Parliament Square. It was here that the War Cabinet – first under Neville Chamberlain, then Winston Churchill from 1940 – met during World War II when German bombs were falling on London. The rooms include living quarters for ministers and military leaders

Did You Know?

In the Churchill War Rooms, Churchill's hotline to Roosevelt was disguised as a toilet.

and a Cabinet Room, where strategic decisions were taken. They are laid out as they were when the war ended, complete with Churchill's desk, communications equipment, and maps for plotting battles and strategies. The Churchill Museum records and illustrates the wartime prime minister's life and career.

18

Downing Street

H8 **SW1** **Westminster** **To the public**

Number 10 Downing Street has been the official residence of the British Prime Minister since 1732. It contains a Cabinet Room in which government policy is decided, an impressive State Dining Room and a private apartment; outside is a well-protected garden.

Next door at No. 11 is the official residence of the

← Making World War II come alive in the Map Room, part of the Churchill War Rooms

Chancellor of the Exchequer, who is in charge of the nation's financial affairs. In 1989, iron gates were erected at the Whitehall end of Downing Street for security purposes.

⑲

Banqueting House

⑨J7 **🏠Whitehall SW1** **🚇Charing Cross, Westminster** **🕐10am–5pm daily** **🚫Public hols & for functions; check website** **🌐hrp.org.uk**

Completed by Inigo Jones in 1622, this was the first building in central London to embody the Palladian style of Renaissance Italy. In 1629 Charles I commissioned Rubens to paint the ceiling with scenes exalting the reign of his father, James I. They symbolize the divine right of kings, disputed by the Parliamentarians, who executed Charles I outside the building in 1649 *(p49)*.

⑳

Trafalgar Square

⑨H7 **🏠WC2** **🚇🚉Charing Cross**

London's main venue for rallies and outdoor public meetings was conceived by John Nash and was mostly constructed during the 1830s. The 52-m (169-ft) column commemorates Admiral Lord Nelson, Britain's most famous sea lord, who died heroically at the Battle of Trafalgar in 1805. It dates from 1842; 14 stonemasons held a dinner on its flat top before the statue of Nelson was finally installed. Edwin Landseer's four lions guard its base. The north side of the square is now taken up by the National Gallery *(p68)*, with Canada House on the west side and South Africa House on the east. Three plinths support statues of the great and the good; funds ran out before the fourth plinth, on the northwest corner, could be filled. It now hosts one of London's most idiosyncratic art displays, as artworks are commissioned specially for it, and change every year or so.

↑ Trafalgar Square and its fountains, with South Africa House on the right

DRINK

Queen Elizabeth Hall Roof Garden

There are great views of the River Thames from the lawn of this rooftop bar.

Q K7 **🏠** Southbank Centre **🕐** Apr-Oct **🌐** southbankcentre. co.uk

BFI Riverfront

A buzzing balcony bar facing the river under the curve of Waterloo Bridge. There are DJ sets on Saturdays.

Q K7 **🏠** BFI Southbank **🕐** Wed-Sat **🌐** benugo.com

Mulberry Bush

This comfy, charming pub serves good food, ales and craft beers.

Q K7 **🏠** 89 Upper Ground **🌐** mulberrybushpub. co.uk

21 🏠🍴🖥🛍

Imperial War Museum

Q K9 **🏠** Lambeth Rd SE1 **🚇** Waterloo, Lambeth North, Elephant & Castle **🚆** Waterloo, Elephant & Castle **🕐** 10am-6pm daily **🌐** iwm.org.uk

With great creativity and sensitivity, the immersive exhibitions at the terrific Imperial War Museum provide a fascinating insight into the history of war and themes of conflict.

Inevitably the two World Wars feature heavily at the Imperial War Museum; however, they are covered in innovative ways. In the First World War Galleries, for example, there are original exhibits such as a re-created trench, while some of the most fascinating World War II exhibits relate more to the impact on the lives of people at home than to the business of fighting. One display focuses on the experiences of a London family, including the effects of food rationing and regular air raids. The Holocaust Exhibition (last admission 5:30pm) is a particularly poignant experience, while other highly original permanent displays include Curiosities of War, which is full of unexpected items such as a wooden horse used to train new recruits in World War I and a makeshift sofa built by troops stationed in Afghanistan. More conventionally, there are tanks, artillery and aircraft, including a Mark 1 Spitfire and a Harrier jet, on show in the main atrium.

Spitfire planes in the Imperial War Museum and the 19th-century building housing the collection *(inset)* ↓

Southbank Centre

K7 **Belvedere Rd, South Bank SE1** **Waterloo, Embankment** **Waterloo, Waterloo East, Charing Cross** **Festival Pier, London Eye Pier, Mon-Fri** **southbankcentre.co.uk**

With an art gallery and three world-class auditoriums for music, dance and other events lined up along the river, the Southbank Centre is one of London's pre-eminent cultural and performance venues.

London's high-profile and much-respected arts centre takes centre stage among the other great institutions on the South Bank: the National Theatre and the British Film Institute. The Southbank Centre itself comprises four main venues: the Royal Festival Hall, the Hayward Gallery, the Queen Elizabeth Hall and the Purcell Room. The centre's always buzzing, with bars and restaurants slotted into and between the terraces, platforms, walkways and rooftops of this concrete complex.

Performances at the Southbank Centre focus on classical music, but there is also opera, folk, world music and all kinds of leftfield genres, plus comedy and dance. Regular festivals staged here include the London Jazz Festival, Women of the World (WOW) Festival, the London Literature Festival and Meltdown.

↑ The London Eye observation wheel, on the River Thames

London Eye

J7 **Jubilee Gardens, South Bank SE1** **Waterloo, Westminster** **Apr-Aug: 10am-8:30pm daily; Sep-Mar: 11am-6pm daily (times can vary, check website)** **Mid-Jan (for maintenance)** **london eye.com**

The London Eye is a 135-m (443-ft) observation wheel that was installed on the South Bank to mark the Millennium. Its 32 enclosed passenger capsules offer a gentle, 30-minute ride as the wheel makes a full turn, with breathtaking views over London and for up to 42 km (26 miles) around on a clear day. Towering over one of the world's most familiar riverscapes, it has understandably captured the hearts of Londoners and visitors alike, and is one of the city's most popular attractions.

Trips on the wheel are on the hour and half-hour. You can pick up your tickets at County Hall (adjacent to the Eye) at least 30 minutes before boarding time. Booking is highly recommended in the summer, when tickets sell out days in advance.

> **Performances at the Southbank Centre focus on classical music, but there is also opera, folk, world music and all kinds of leftfield genres, plus comedy and dance.**

A SHORT WALK
COVENT GARDEN

Distance 1.5 km (1 mile) **Time** 25 minutes
Nearest Tube Leicester Square

Although no longer alive with the calls of fruit and vegetable market traders going about their business, visitors, residents and street entertainers throng Covent Garden Piazza, much as they would have done centuries ago. Pause to people-watch as you stroll through this buzzing area, popping into vibrant boutiques and historic pubs along the way.

*Bright and colourful **Neal Street** and **Neal's Yard** are home to lots of charming shops and cafés.*

*A replica of a 17th-century monument marks the junction at **Seven Dials**.*

*The airy **Thomas Neal's Centre** houses designer shops and the Donmar Warehouse Theatre.*

***Ching Court** is a Post-Modernist courtyard by architect Terry Farrell.*

***St Martin's Theatre** is home to the world's longest-running play: The Mousetrap.*

***Stanfords**, established in 1852, is the largest map and guide retailer in the world.*

*Parts of the **Lamb & Flag,** one of London's oldest pubs, date from 1623.*

*The exclusive **Garrick Club** is one of the oldest in the world.*

New Row is lined with little shops and cafés.

***Goodwin's Court** is a charming, albeit small, alley lined with former Georgian-era shops.*

Did You Know?

Eliza Doolittle, of George Bernard Shaw's *Pygmalion* (1913), was a flower seller in Covent Garden.

Locator Map
For more detail see p66

↑ Plants in a wooden market
barrow in Covent Garden

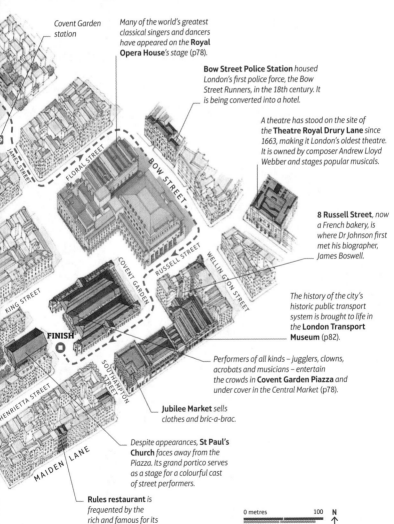

Covent Garden station

Many of the world's greatest classical singers and dancers have appeared on the **Royal Opera House**'s stage (p78).

Bow Street Police Station *housed London's first police force, the Bow Street Runners, in the 18th century. It is being converted into a hotel.*

A theatre has stood on the site of the **Theatre Royal Drury Lane** *since 1663, making it London's oldest theatre. It is owned by composer Andrew Lloyd Webber and stages popular musicals.*

8 Russell Street, *now a French bakery, is where Dr Johnson first met his biographer, James Boswell.*

The history of the city's historic public transport system is brought to life in the **London Transport Museum** (p82).

Performers of all kinds – jugglers, clowns, acrobats and musicians – entertain the crowds in **Covent Garden Piazza** *and under cover in the Central Market (p78).*

Jubilee Market *sells clothes and bric-a-brac.*

Despite appearances, **St Paul's Church** *faces away from the Piazza. Its grand portico serves as a stage for a colourful cast of street performers.*

FINISH

Rules restaurant *is frequented by the rich and famous for its typically English food.*

| 0 metres | 100 | N |
| 0 yards | 100 | ↑ |

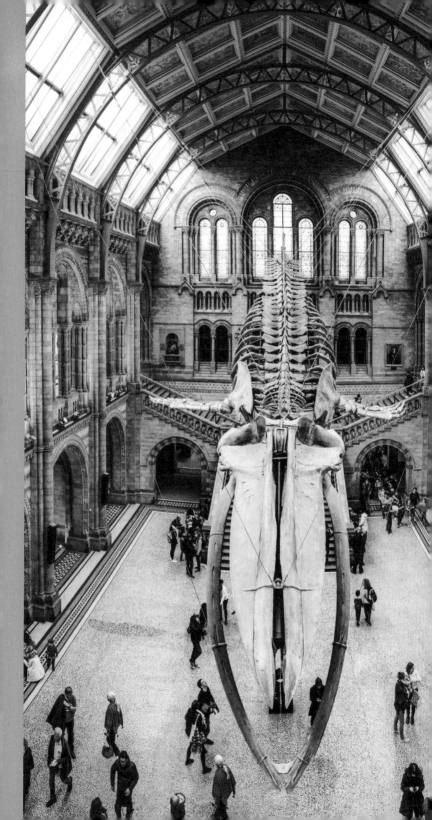

KENSINGTON AND CHELSEA

The tone was set for Kensington from the late 17th century when William III and Mary II bought Kensington Palace. With the arrival of the royal court, it soon became a highly desirable residential area, as it still is today, attracting the wealthy as well as those who sought to sell them goods. It remained largely rural until the late 18th century when a period of urban expansion slowly began, with Knightsbridge among the first spots to be developed. It was in the 1850s that the pace of transformation really exploded, the fuse lit by the Great Exhibition of 1851. Held in Hyde Park, the exhibition was the brainchild of Queen Victoria's husband, Prince Albert, who sought to demonstrate and promote British industry and invention. It was a huge success and the profits were ploughed into the creation of a permanent showcase for the arts and sciences in South Kensington. The great museums and the Royal Albert Hall are all part of that legacy.

Formerly a riverside village, Chelsea first became fashionable in Tudor times when Henry VIII had a small palace (long vanished) built here. In the 18th and 19th centuries artists, such as Turner, Whistler and Rossetti, were attracted by the river views. With its trendsetting boutiques, the King's Road was at the centre of 1960s Swinging London and became the hangout of popular cultural icons, such as the Rolling Stones.

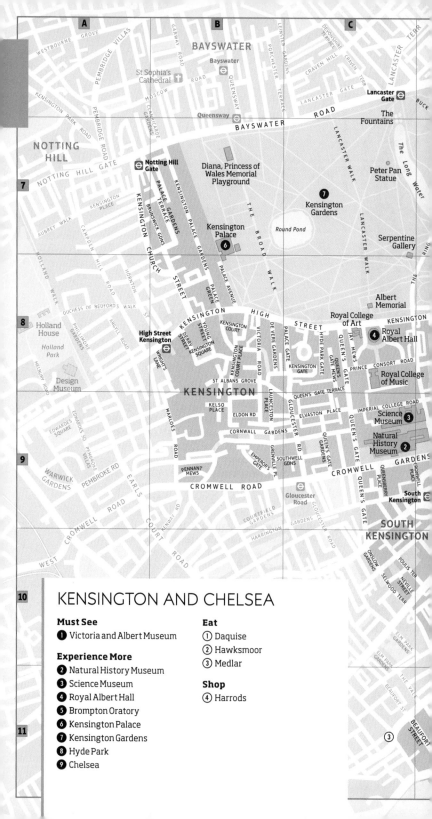

KENSINGTON AND CHELSEA

Must See
1. Victoria and Albert Museum

Experience More
2. Natural History Museum
3. Science Museum
4. Royal Albert Hall
5. Brompton Oratory
6. Kensington Palace
7. Kensington Gardens
8. Hyde Park
9. Chelsea

Eat
1. Daquise
2. Hawksmoor
3. Medlar

Shop
4. Harrods

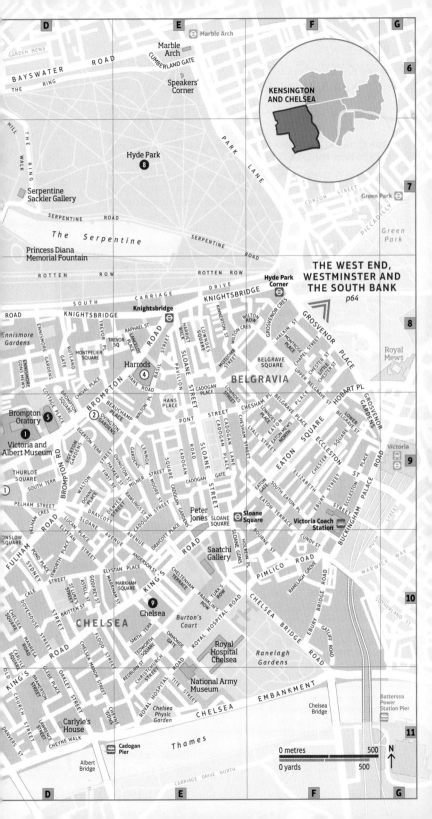

❶ Ⓜ 🍴 🖥 🛍

VICTORIA AND ALBERT MUSEUM

📍 D9 🏠 Cromwell Road SW7 🚇 South Kensington 🕐 10am–5:45pm daily (to 10pm Fri) 🚫 24–26 Dec 🌐 vam.ac.uk

Housed in Victorian splendour, as well as modern, state-of-the-art galleries, the V&A is the world's leading museum of art and design, with its collection spanning 5,000 years of furniture, glass, textiles, fashion, ceramics and jewellery.

The Victoria and Albert Museum (V&A) contains one of the world's broadest collections of art and design, with exhibits ranging from early Christian devotional objects to cutting-edge furniture. Originally founded in 1852 to inspire design students as the Museum of Manufactures, it was renamed by Queen Victoria in 1899 in memory of Prince Albert. The museum has undergone extensive renovation since the early 2000s, including the opening in 2017 of a new quarter on Exhibition Road, encompassing the Sackler Courtyard and the underground Sainsbury Gallery, and an expanded Photography Centre in 2018.

↑ The grand Cromwell Road entrance to the V&A

←
The welcoming neon information desk at the museum

GALLERY GUIDE

The V&A has six levels. Level 1 houses the China, Japan and South Asia galleries, the Fashion Gallery and the Cast Courts. The British Galleries are on Levels 2 and 4. Level 3 contains the 20th Century galleries and silver, ironwork, paintings and photography. The glass display is on Level 4. The Ceramics Galleries and Furniture are on Level 6. The fantastic European galleries from 300 to 1815 are on Level 1.

↑ The reading room of the National Art Library in the V&A

Did You Know?

The V&A was the first museum to have its own restaurant. The original refreshment rooms are still in use today.

↑ Large-scale works that were once part of buildings in the Medieval & Renaissance Gallery

Interior of the Science Museum, housing a huge number of scientific objects

Science Museum

C9 **Exhibition Rd SW7**
South Kensington
10am-6pm daily (last adm: 5:15pm) **science museum.org.uk**

Centuries of continuing scientific and technological development lie at the heart of the Science Museum's massive collections. The hardware displayed is magnificent: from steam engines to aeroengines; spacecraft to the very first mechanical computers. Equally important is the social context of science – what discoveries and inventions mean for day-to-day life – and the process of discovery itself.

EXPERIENCE MORE

Natural History Museum

C9 **Cromwell Rd SW7**
South Kensington
10am-5:50pm daily (to 10:30pm last Fri of month) **nhm.ac.uk**

The richly sculpted stonework of the cathedral-like Natural History Museum (NHM) conceals an iron and steel frame, a revolutionary construction technique when the museum opened in 1881. The imaginative displays tackle fundamental issues such as the planet's ecology and evolution, the origin of species and the development of human beings – all explained through the latest technology, interactive techniques and traditional displays.

The central Hintze Hall showcases the museum's collections and explores humanity's relationship with the planet. It is dominated by the huge suspended skeleton of a blue whale.

The museum is divided into four sections: the Blue Zone, Green Zone, Red Zone and the Orange Zone. In the Blue Zone, the Ecology exhibition explores the complex web of the natural world through a replica of a moonlit rainforest buzzing with the sounds of insects. One of the most popular exhibits is the Dinosaur Gallery, which includes animatronic models of dinosaurs. The Vault, in the Green Zone, holds a dazzling collection of gems, crystals, metals and meteorites from around the world. The Darwin Centre is the largest curved structure in Europe. The eight-storey-high cocoon houses a vast collection of insects and plants.

TOP 5 **UNMISSIBLE EXHIBITS IN THE NHM**

Triceratops Skull
The gigantic skull of a plant-eating three-horned dinosaur.

Latrobe Gold Nugget
A rare crystallized gold nugget from Australia weighing 717 g (25 oz).

Butterflies
A tropical butterfly house (open Mar-Sep).

Archaeopteryx
This valuable fossil of a feathered dinosaur provided the link between birds and dinosaurs.

Earthquake Simulator
Experience the effects of an earthquake in this simulation.

The museum is spread over five floors and includes the high-tech Wellcome Wing at its western end. The basement features excellent hands-on galleries for children, including The Garden. The Energy Hall dominates the ground floor and is dedicated to steam power, with the still-operational Harle Syke Mill Engine of 1903. Here too are Exploring Space and Making the Modern World, a highlight of which is the display of the scarred Apollo 10 spacecraft, which carried three astronauts to the moon and back in May 1969.

In Challenge of Materials, on the first floor, our expectations of materials are confounded by exhibits such as a bridge made of glass and a steel wedding dress, while the renovated Medicine Galleries chart some of the most extra-ordinary achievements in the world of medicine over the last 400 years. The Flight gallery on the third floor is packed with early flying contraptions, fighter planes, aeroplanes and the Launchpad.

The Wellcome Wing offers four floors of interactive technology, including "Who Am I?" (first floor), a fascinating exhibition exploring the science of you. With an IMAX 3D Cinema and the SimEx simulator ride, it is a breathtaking addition to the museum.

Royal Albert Hall

📍 C8 🏛 Kensington Gore SW7 🚇 South Kensington ⏰ For performances daily; box office: 9am–9pm daily 🌐 royalalberthall.com

The vast oval hall named after Queen Victoria's beloved consort, Prince Albert, was opened in 1871 and has mainly functioned as a concert venue, but it has also hosted a wide variety of other events over the years. Today, it is probably most famous for the summer Proms (p45).

A short walk north of Albert Hall, in Kensington Gardens, is the grandiose **Albert Memorial**. Designed by leading Victorian architect George Gilbert Scott and unveiled in 1876, it is made up of a vast decorative Gothic canopy within which sits a gilded statue of Prince Albert sculpted by John Foley.

Eight large allegorical sculptures stand at the corner of the memorial and at the base of the steps leading up to it: four representing industry; the other four the Empire.

Albert Memorial

🕖 South Carriage Dr, Kensington Gardens W2 ⏰ 6am–dusk 🌐 royalparks.org.uk

← The Prince Consort statue in front of the Royal Albert Hall

EAT

Daquise
Enjoy contemporary Polish fine dining in this artsy stalwart of the South Kensington restaurant scene.

📍 D9 🏛 20 Thurloe St 🌐 daquise.co.uk

£££

Hawksmoor
This is a smart branch of one of the city's renowned steak specialists.

📍 D9 🏛 3 Yeomans Row 🌐 thehawksmoor.com

£££

Medlar
Widely lauded Medlar serves high-quality European cuisine with a French bent in understated elegance.

📍 C11 🏛 438 Kings Rd 🌐 medlarrestaurant.co.uk

£££

5

Brompton Oratory

📍 D9 🏛 Brompton Rd SW7
🚇 South Kensington
🕐 6:30am-8pm Mon-Sat,
7:30am-8pm Sun
🌐 bromptonoratory.co.uk

The Italianate Oratory is
a lavish monument to the
19th-century English Catholic
revival. It was established
as a base for a community
of priests by John Henry
Newman (later Cardinal
Newman), who introduced
the Oratorian movement to
England in 1848. The church
was opened in 1884, and the
dome and façade added in
the 1890s.

The interior holds many
fine monuments. The 12
huge 17th-century statues
of the apostles are from
Siena Cathedral, the Baroque
Lady Altar (1693) is from the
Dominican church at Brescia,
Italy, and the 18th-century
altar in St Wilfred's Chapel is
from Rochefort in Belgium.

6

Kensington Palace

📍 B7 🏛 Kensington Gdns
W8 🚇 High St Kensington,
Queensway 🕐 Mar-Oct:
10am-6pm daily; Nov-
Feb: 10am-4pm daily
🌐 hrp.org.uk

Kensington Palace was the
main residence of the royal
family from the 1690s until the
1830s, when the court moved
to Buckingham Palace. It has
seen a number of important
royal events. In June 1837,
Princess Victoria of Kent was
woken to be told that her
uncle William IV had died and
she was now queen – the start
of her 64-year reign. After the
death of Princess Diana in
1997, mourners turned the
gates into a field of bouquets.
Half the palace still holds royal
apartments, but the rest is
open to the public. Highlights
include the 18th-century state
rooms with ceilings and
murals by William Kent, along
with the King's Staircase.

> 💬 INSIDER TIP
> **On the Water**
>
> Rent a pedalo or
> rowing boat from the
> Boathouse (Apr-Oct)
> and enjoy a tranquil
> tour of Hyde Park's
> Serpentine lake. The
> brave can dive in for a
> swim at the lido during
> the summer months
> (Jun-early Sep).

7

Kensington Gardens

📍 C7 🏛 W2 🚇 Queensway,
Lancaster Gate 🕐 6am-
dusk daily 🌐 royalparks.
org.uk

The former grounds of
Kensington Palace became a
public park in 1841. They
contain three great attractions
for children: the innovative
Diana, Princess of Wales
Memorial Playground, the
bronze statue of J M Barrie's
fictional Peter Pan (1912) by
George Frampton, and the
Round Pond, where people
sail model boats. Also worth
seeing is the Orangery (1704),
once used by Queen Anne as a
"summer supper house", and
now an elegant café.

8

Hyde Park

📍 D7-E7 🏛 W2 🚇 Hyde
Park Corner, Knightsbridge,
Lancaster Gate, Marble
Arch 🕐 5am-midnight
daily 🌐 royalparks.org.uk

The ancient manor of Hyde
was part of the lands of
Westminster Abbey seized by
Henry VIII at the Dissolution of
the Monasteries in 1536 (p391).
James I opened Hyde Park to
the public in the early 17th

←

The ornate interior of
the Brompton Oratory,
completed in the 1880s

century, and it was soon one of the city's most fashionable public spaces. When it also became popular with duellists and highwaymen, William III had 300 oil lamps hung along Rotten Row, the first street in England to be lit artificially at night. Rotten Row is now used for horse riding. In the middle of the park, the Serpentine, a man-made lake, is used for boating and swimming. South of the Serpentine is the Princess Diana Memorial Fountain. The park is also a

A couple rowing ↑ on Hyde Park's Serpentine, and the large bronze Isis statue on the shore of the lake *(inset)*

rallying point for political demonstrations, while at Speaker's Corner, in the northeast, anyone has had the legal right to address the public since 1872. Sundays are particularly lively, with many budding orators.

9
Chelsea

📍 D10-F10 🚇 SW3
🚉 Sloane Square

Riverside Chelsea has been fashionable since Tudor times when Sir Thomas More, Henry VIII's Lord Chancellor, lived here. The river views attracted artists, and the arrival of the historian Thomas Carlyle and essayist Leigh Hunt in the 1830s began a literary connection. Blue plaques on the houses of Cheyne Walk celebrate former residents such as J M W Turner

(p76) and writers George Eliot, Henry James and T S Eliot.

Chelsea's artistic tradition is maintained by its galleries and antiques shops, many of them scattered on King's Road, which is also famous for its trendy fashion boutiques.

Founded by advertising mogul Charles Saatchi, the **Saatchi Gallery** hosts wide-ranging, innovative contemporary art exhibitions.

Wren's Royal Hospital, on Royal Hospital Road, was built in 1692 as a retirement home for soldiers and still houses 400 Chelsea Pensioners, who can be spotted in their uniform of scarlet coat and tricorn hat.

Saatchi Gallery
 🏛 Duke of York's HQ, King's Rd SW3 🚉 Sloane Square 🕐 10am–6pm daily 🌐 saatchigallery.com

---

SHOP

Harrods
The department store that could supply anything, from pins to an elephant – not quite true today, but Harrods remains as grand as ever.

📍 E8 🏛 87-135 Brompton Rd, Knightsbridge
🌐 harrods.com

A SHORT WALK
SOUTH KENSINGTON

Distance 2 km (1.5 miles) **Time** 30 minutes
Nearest Tube South Kensington

This area is characterized by its world-renowned museums, which are housed in grandiose buildings celebrating Victorian self-confidence. Take a stroll from the Albert Memorial in Hyde Park, past the Royal Albert Hall, to the Victoria and Albert Museum and admire the monuments to the royal couple that made London a world capital of industry and knowledge.

Did You Know?

The Royal Albert Hall was partly funded by selling seats on a 999-year lease.

David Hockney and Peter Blake are among the great artists who trained at the **Royal College of Art**.

The former **Royal College of Organists** *was decorated by F W Moody in 1876.*

Opened in 1870, the **Royal Albert Hall** *has a beautiful curved exterior (p95).*

Historic musical instruments are exhibited at the **Royal College of Music**.

The **Natural History Museum** *houses every-thing from dinosaurs to butterflies (p94).*

Visitors can experiment with interactive displays at the **Science Museum** (p94).

PRINCE CONSORT ROAD

IMPERIAL COLLEGE ROAD

EXHIBITION ROAD

CROMWELL ROAD

CROMWELL

0 metres 100
0 yards 100

N

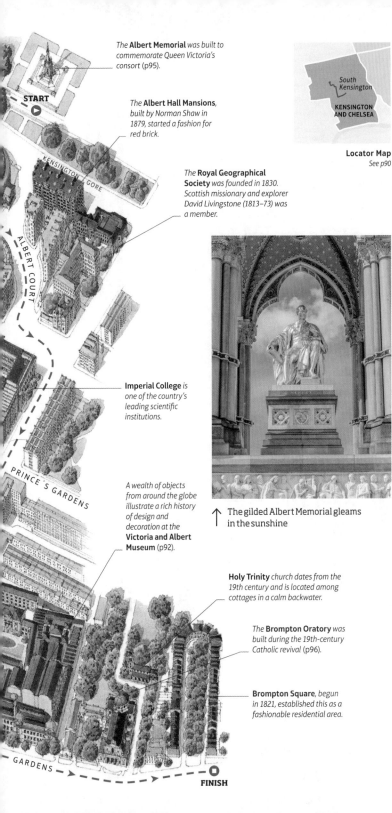

The **Albert Memorial** was built to commemorate Queen Victoria's consort (p95).

The **Albert Hall Mansions**, built by Norman Shaw in 1879, started a fashion for red brick.

The **Royal Geographical Society** was founded in 1830. Scottish missionary and explorer David Livingstone (1813–73) was a member.

START

KENSINGTON GORE

ALBERT COURT

Imperial College is one of the country's leading scientific institutions.

PRINCE'S GARDENS

A wealth of objects from around the globe illustrate a rich history of design and decoration at the **Victoria and Albert Museum** (p92).

Locator Map
See p90

South Kensington

KENSINGTON AND CHELSEA

↑ The gilded Albert Memorial gleams in the sunshine

Holy Trinity church dates from the 19th century and is located among cottages in a calm backwater.

The **Brompton Oratory** was built during the 19th-century Catholic revival (p96).

Brompton Square, begun in 1821, established this as a fashionable residential area.

GARDENS

FINISH

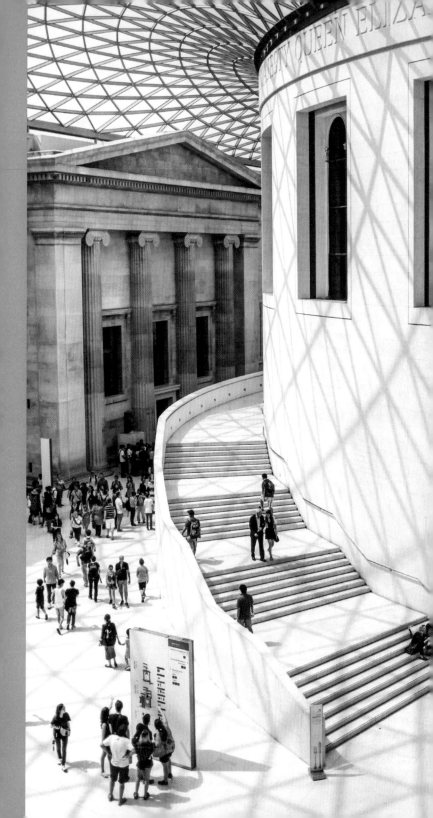

REGENT'S PARK AND BLOOMSBURY

Regent's Park was formally laid out in 1812, on land Henry VIII had used as hunting grounds, by John Nash, the architect responsible for the design of much of Regency London. Along the northern perimeter of the park runs the Regent's Canal, also designed by Nash in the early 19th century. The canal runs down to King's Cross and, along with the railways, helped drive the industrialization of the King's Cross area. Decades of decline after World War II were reversed in the first years of this century when St Pancras Station became the terminus for international trains to the rest of Europe. The area has been transformed into one of the capital's most cutting-edge shopping, business and leisure districts.

The handsome garden squares of nearby Bloomsbury date mainly from the Regency era, during which time Bloomsbury cemented itself as a place of learning and culture, already home to the British Museum, founded in 1753, followed by the University of London, founded in 1826. It was an apt location, therefore, for the homes and haunts of the avant-garde set known as the Bloomsbury Group, a network of learned and artistic friends and associates.

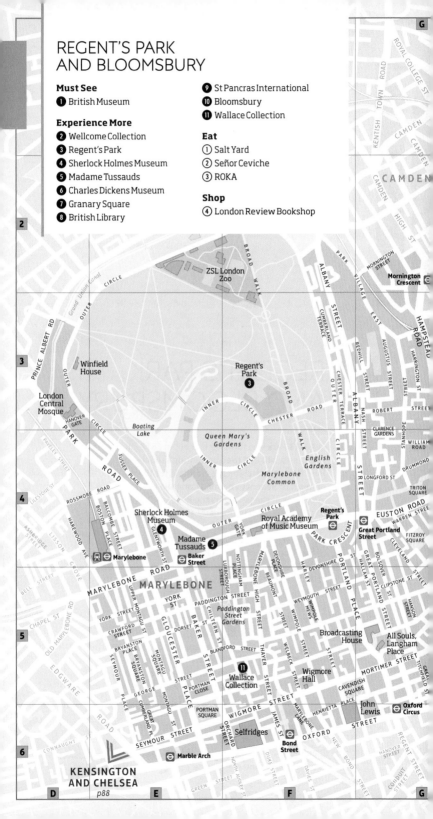

REGENT'S PARK
AND BLOOMSBURY

Must See
1 British Museum

Experience More
2 Wellcome Collection
3 Regent's Park
4 Sherlock Holmes Museum
5 Madame Tussauds
6 Charles Dickens Museum
7 Granary Square
8 British Library

9 St Pancras International
10 Bloomsbury
11 Wallace Collection

Eat
1 Salt Yard
2 Señor Ceviche
3 ROKA

Shop
4 London Review Bookshop

1

BRITISH MUSEUM

H5 ⬛ Great Russell St WC1 ⬤ Tottenham Court Road, Holborn, Russell Square
🚉 Euston ⏰ 10am–5:30pm daily (to 8:30pm Fri) 🌐 britishmuseum.org

The British Museum holds one of the world's greatest collections of historical and cultural artifacts. This immense hoard of treasure comprises over eight million objects spanning the history of mankind, from prehistoric times to today.

 INSIDER TIP
Eye Openers

The museum offers an excellent set of free tours. There are over a dozen daily "eye-opener tours" of individual rooms; and on Friday evenings the "spotlight tours" focus on specific exhibits such as the Rosetta Stone. There's no need to book, simply check the website for where and when to meet.

One of the oldest public museums in the world, the British Museum was established in 1753 to house the books, antiquities, and plant and animal specimens of the physician Sir Hans Sloane (1660–1753). The collection expanded rapidly and during the 19th century the museum acquired a mass of Classical and Middle Eastern antiquities, some of which still make up the top attractions here, such as the Rosetta Stone and the Parthenon sculptures. You can now see items drawn from a dizzying number of cultures and civilizations, from Stone Age Europe and Ancient Egypt to modern Japan and contemporary North America. There are sculptures and statues, mummies and murals, coins and medals, ceramics, gold and silver, prints, drawings and innumerable other man-made objects from every corner of the globe and every period of history.

In addition to the vast permanent collection, one of the largest in the world, the British Museum hosts regular special exhibitions, talks and events.

① The Rosetta Stone was the key to interpreting Egyptian hieroglyphs.

② The museum holds the largest collection of Egyptian mummies outside of Egypt.

③ Beautiful statues from the Parthenon in Ancient Greece.

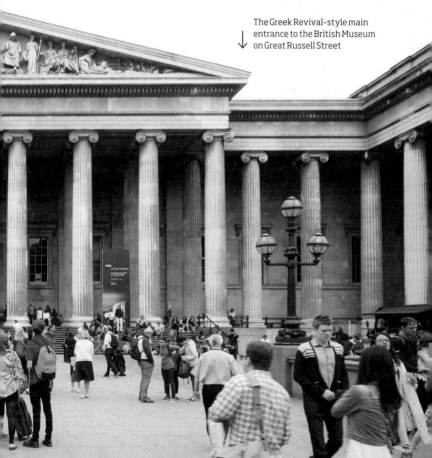

The Greek Revival-style main entrance to the British Museum ↓ on Great Russell Street

A World of Treasures

There are 95 galleries covering 4 km (2.5 miles) over three floors and eight levels of the museum, though the majority of exhibits are on the ground and upper floors. Ancient Egyptian artifacts are on the upper floor in Rooms 61 to 66 and in Room 4, beside the Great Court. The Greece, Rome and Middle East collections are also spread across the two main floors, though major items such as the Parthenon sculptures are in the large rooms of the ground floor to the west of the Great Court. The Africa collection is on the lower floor, while Asia exhibits are on the ground and upper floors on the north side. The Americas collection is located in the north-east corner of the main floor. The Sainsbury Gallery hosts major temporary exhibitions.

←

The world-famous Reading Room, designed by Norman Foster, at the centre of the museum's Great Court

Did You Know?

The Portland Vase, made before the birth of Christ, was reassembled after it was smashed by a visitor in 1845.

Inside the Enlightenment gallery, formerly the library of King George III ↑

Top Collections

GREAT COURT AND READING ROOM

The architectural highlight of the building is the Great Court, a breathtaking conversion of the original 19th-century inner courtyard. Opened in 2000, the court is now covered by a tessellated glass roof, creating Europe's largest indoor public square. At the centre of the Great Court is the glorious dome-roofed Reading Room of the former British Library, completed in 1857, where figures such as Mahatma Gandhi and Karl Marx studied.

Prehistoric and Roman Britain

▶ Highlights among the relics of ancient Britain on display include the gold "Mold Cape", a ceremonial Bronze Age cape found in Wales; an antlered headdress worn by hunter-gatherers 9,000 years ago; and "Lindow Man", a 1st-century AD victim of sacrifice who was preserved in a bog until 1984.

Europe

Sutton Hoo's treasure, the burial hoard of a 7th-century Anglo-Saxon king, is in Room 41. The artifacts include a helmet and shield, Celtic bowls, and gold and garnet jewellery. Exquisite timepieces include a 400-year-old clock from Germany, designed as a model galleon; in its day it pitched, played music and even fired a cannon. Nearby are the famous 12th-century Lewis chessmen. Baron Ferdinand Rothschild's (1839–98) Renaissance treasures are in Room 2a.

Middle East

Galleries devoted to the Middle East collections cover 7,000 years of history, with famous items such as 7th-century BC Assyrian reliefs from King Ashurbanipal's palace at Nineveh, two large human-headed bulls from 7th-century BC Khorsabad and the Black Obelisk of Shalmaneser III, an Assyrian king. The upper floors contain pieces from ancient Sumeria, part of the Oxus Treasure (which lay buried for over 2,000 years) and the diverse new Islamic World galleries.

Egypt

Egyptian sculptures in Room 4 include a fine red granite head of a king, thought to be Amenhotep III, and a huge statue of King Rameses II. Here too is the Rosetta Stone, used as a key for deciphering Egyptian hieroglyphs. An array of mummies, jewellery and Coptic art is upstairs.

Greece and Rome

◀ The Greek and Roman collections include the controversial Parthenon sculptures. These 5th-century BC reliefs decorated the temple to Athena on the Acropolis, Athens. Much of the temple was ruined, and what survived was removed by the British diplomat Lord Elgin. There is also the Nereid Monument and sculptures from the Mausoleum at Halicarnassus.

Asia

Fine porcelain, Shang bronzes (c 1500–1050 BC) and ceremonial bronze vessels are in the Chinese Collection. In the Sir Percival David gallery the Chinese ceramics date from the 10th to early 20th centuries. There is a fine collection of sculpture from the Indian subcontinent, including sculpted reliefs that once covered the walls of the Buddhist temple at Amaravati. A Korean section contains works of Buddhist art, and there is a traditional Japanese teahouse in Room 92.

Africa

African sculptures, textiles and graphic art are in Room 25. Famous bronzes from the Kingdom of Benin, set in due course to return to Nigeria, stand alongside modern African prints, paintings, drawings and colourful fabrics.

EXPERIENCE MORE

EAT

Salt Yard

Excellent tapas combining Spanish and Italian cuisines.

📍 G5 🏠 54 Goode St
🌐 saltyardgroup.co.uk

£££

Señor Ceviche

Delicious Peruvian street food.

📍 G5 🏠 18 Charlotte St
🌐 senor-ceviche.com

£££

ROKA

A contemporary Japanese *robatayaki* (barbecue) specialist.

📍 G5 🏠 37 Charlotte St
🌐 rokarestaurant.com

£££

---

②

Wellcome Collection

📍 H4 🏠 183 Euston Rd NW1
🚇 Euston, King's Cross, Warren St ⏰ 10am–6pm Tue–Sat (to 10pm Thu), 11am–6pm Sun, noon–6pm public hols
🌐 wellcomecollection.org

Sir Henry Wellcome (1853–1936) was a pharmacist and entrepreneur. His interest in medicine and its history, as well as archaeology and ethnography, led him to collect more than one million objects from around the world, now housed in this building.

The museum's permanent exhibition, Medicine Man, includes more than 900 diverse objects, ranging from Napoleon's toothbrush to Florence Nightingale's moccasins. Changing displays cover a range of engaging topics exploring medicine, art and the human condition.

The Wellcome Library is the world's largest collection of books devoted to the history of medicine.

---

③

Regent's Park

📍 D3–F4 🏠 NW1
🚇 Regent's Park, Baker St, Great Portland St ⏰ 5am–dusk daily 🌐 royalparks.org.uk

This land became enclosed as a park in 1812. Designer John Nash originally envisaged a kind of garden suburb, with 56 villas and a pleasure palace for the Prince Regent. In the event only eight villas were built (three survive round the edge of the Inner Circle).

The boating lake has many varieties of water birds and is marvellously romantic. Queen Mary's Gardens are a mass of

Did You Know?

AA Milne's Winnie-the-Pooh was inspired by a bear that lived in London Zoo 1914–34.

↑ Blossoming magnolia tree on a beautiful spring day in Regent's Park

The entrance and gift shop at the Sherlock Holmes Museum, on Baker Street

6

Charles Dickens Museum

📍J4 🏠48 Doughty St WC1 🚇Chancery Lane, Russell Sq 🕐10am–5pm Tue-Sun (last adm: 4pm) 🚪Occasionally Sat & Sun for events 🌐dickens museum.com

The novelist Charles Dickens lived in this early 19th-century terraced house for three of his most productive years (1837 to 1839). *Oliver Twist* and *Nicholas Nickleby* were written here, and this is where *The Pickwick Papers* was completed. Although Dickens had a number of London homes throughout his lifetime, this is the only one to have survived.

It is now a museum with some rooms laid out exactly as they were in Dickens's time. Others have been adapted to display a varied collection of articles associated with him.

The museum houses over 100,000 exhibits – from manuscripts, paintings and personal items, to pieces of furniture from Dickens's other homes, and first editions of many of his best-known works. As well as its permanent collection, the museum puts on special exhibitions and events, and runs a monthly "Housemaid's Tour".

wonderful sights and smells in summer, when visitors can also enjoy performances at the Open Air Theatre nearby.

The park is also the site for amateur sports leagues and competitions, and the home of **ZSL London Zoo**, a major research and conservation centre. Opened in 1828, the zoo houses more than 600 species, including Sumatran tigers and Asiatic lions.

ZSL London Zoo

 🕐10am–6pm daily (Mar, Sep & Oct: to 5pm; Nov-Feb: to 4pm; last adm: 1 hr before closing) 🌐zsl.org

4

Sherlock Holmes Museum

📍E4 🏠221b Baker St NW1 🚇Baker St 🕐9:30am–6pm daily 🌐sherlock-holmes.co.uk

Sir Arthur Conan Doyle's fictional detective was supposed to live at 221b Baker Street, which did not exist. The museum, labelled 221b, actually stands between Nos. 237 and 239, and is the only surviving Victorian lodging house in the street. It has been converted to resemble Holmes's flat, and is

furnished exactly as described in the books. Visitors can buy plaques, Holmes hats, Toby jugs and meerschaum pipes.

5

Madame Tussauds

📍E4 🏠Marylebone Rd NW1 🚇Baker St 🕐Times vary, check website 🌐madametussauds.com

This famous waxworks museum is divided into several areas, including the Party area where you can find celebrities, film stars, royals and figures from the world of pop music, and a *Star Wars* exhibit where iconic scenes from the movie series have been re-created.

The Marvel Super Heroes 4D Experience, an exclusive short film complete with water, wind and vibration effects, puts you right in the heart of the action. In the Spirit of London finale, visitors travel in stylized taxi-cabs through the city's history to "witness" events from the Great Fire of 1666 to the Swinging 1960s.

→

Bust of the author Charles Dickens, who lived in London for most of his life

7

Granary Square

H2 **King's Cross St Pancras** **kingscross.co.uk**

Urban regeneration has transformed this area behind King's Cross station into a cultural and social hub. The focus of the area is attractive Granary Square, which leads down to Regent's Canal. It is dominated by fountains that dance to an ever-changing pattern of lights, a magnet for small children on hot days. There are also good restaurants and bars, and a popular food market.

Occupying the former King's Cross Goods Yards offices, built in 1850, is the **House of Illustration**. These three small rooms form the UK's only gallery dedicated to illustration. Founded by Sir Quentin Blake, best known for his illustrations of Roald Dahl's children's books, the gallery stages an eclectic programme of exhibitions, past examples featuring work from Soviet Russia, Japan, Thailand and North Korea. Displays cover a broad range of techniques and mediums, including graphic design, animation, scientific drawings, picture books and political cartoons.

House of Illustration

 2 Granary Sq N1 **10am-6pm Tue-Sun** **houseofillustration.org.uk**

8

British Library

H3 **96 Euston Rd NW1** **King's Cross St Pancras** **9:30am-8pm Mon-Thu, 9:30am-6pm Fri, 9:30am-5pm Sat, 11am-5pm Sun** **bl.uk**

Designed in red brick by Sir Colin St John Wilson, this late 20th-century building houses the national collection of books, manuscripts and maps, as well as the British Library Sound Archive. A copy of nearly every printed book in the UK is held here – about 25 million – and can be consulted by those with a Reader Pass (you can pre-register for one online). Open to all are the temporary exhibitions in the Entrance Hall and PACCAR Galleries and, housing some of the library's most precious items, the Treasures Gallery, where, among other highlights, are the Lindisfarne Gospels, a Gutenberg Bible and Shakespeare's First Folio.

There are also regular talks, discussions and workshops. Pre-booking is advised for the tours, and there may be a fee for special exhibitions.

9

St Pancras International

H3 **Euston Rd NW1** **King's Cross St Pancras** **stpancras.com**

The London terminal for Eurostar rail services to continental Europe, St Pancras

is the most spectacular of the three rail termini along Euston Road, thanks to the frontage, in red-brick gingerbread Gothic, of the former Midland Grand Hotel, opened in 1874 as one of the most sumptuous hotels of its time. By 1935, now too expensive to run, it became office space. It was threatened with demolition in the 1960s but saved by a campaign led by the poet John Betjeman (there is a statue of him on the upper level of the station concourse). The hotel has since been restored.

10

Bloomsbury

📍 H4 📮 WC1 🚇 Russell Sq, Holborn, Tottenham Court Rd

Home to numerous writers and artists, Bloomsbury is dominated by the British Museum and the University of London and characterized by several fine Georgian squares. These include Russell Square, where the poet T S Eliot (1888–1965) worked for a publisher for 40 years; Queen Square, with a statue of Queen Charlotte, wife of George III; and Bloomsbury Square, laid out in 1661 by the 4th Earl of Southampton. A plaque here commemorates members of the Bloomsbury Group.

11

Wallace Collection

📍 F5 📮 Hertford House, Manchester Sq W1
🚇 Bond St, Baker St
🕐 10am–5pm daily
🌐 wallacecollection.org

The product of collecting by four generations of the Seymour-Conway family, who were Marquesses of Hertford, this fine private collection of European art was bequeathed to the state in 1897 on the condition that it would go on

Lounging on the artificial-grassed steps of Granary Square, by Regent's Canal

permanent public display with nothing added or taken away. Hertford House still retains the atmosphere of a grand 19th-century mansion.

The 3rd Marquess (1777–1842) used his Italian wife's fortune to buy works by Titian and Canaletto, along with numerous 17th-century Dutch paintings, including works by Van Dyck. The collection's particular strength is 18th-century French painting, sculpture and decorative arts, acquired by the 4th Marquess (1800–70) and his natural son, Sir Richard Wallace (1818–90). The Marquess had a taste for lush romanticism and among his acquisitions are Watteau's *Les Champs Elisées* (c.1720–21) and Boucher's twin paintings *The Setting of the Sun* (1752) and *The Rising of the Sun* (1753).

Other highlights of the Wallace Collection include Rembrandt's *Titus, The Artist's Son* (c.1657), Titian's *Perseus and Andromeda* (1554–6) and Hals's famous *Laughing Cavalier* (1624). There are also superb examples of Sèvres porcelain and Italian majolica.

SHOP

London Review Bookshop

A bookshop for people who are serious about books. The carefully chosen stock is testament to the highly respected literary credentials of its owners, the *London Review of Books* journal. There are knowledgeable staff members to help and chat, and a great little coffee shop too.

📍 J5 📮 14-16 Bury Pl
🌐 londonreview bookshop.co.uk

THE CITY, SOUTHWARK AND EAST END

The capital's financial district, the City, built on the site of the original Roman settlement, was, for many centuries, London in its entirety. Though royal government moved from here to the City of Westminster in the 11th century, the City's importance as a centre of trade remained and grew. Many of its original buildings were obliterated by the Great Fire of 1666, though its jumbled street plan stands as testament to a medieval past. After the fire, the architect Christopher Wren rebuilt dozens of the City's churches, with his magnificent dome for St Paul's Cathedral rising above them all.

Also in the 17th century traders began operating outside the City's gates at Spitalfields, where the now-famous market first emerged. As the market expanded people began to settle in its vicinity, notably Huguenots fleeing religious persecution in France, who also made homes in nearby Shoreditch. Waves of Irish, Jewish and Bangladeshi immigrants followed.

Southwark and its stretch of riverbank, known as Bankside, became the entertainment hub of London in the Middle Ages, a refuge for pleasure-seekers, prostitutes and gamblers. There were also several bear-baiting arenas in which plays were staged until the building of theatres such as The Globe in 1598. Shakespeare's Globe was rebuilt in 1997 close to its original site.

THE CITY, SOUTHWARK AND EAST END

Must Sees

1. St Paul's Cathedral
2. Tower of London
3. Tate Modern

Experience More

4. Inns of Court
5. St Bartholomew-the-Great
6. Barbican Centre
7. The Royal Exchange
8. Sir John Soane's Museum
9. Museum of London
10. Sky Garden
11. St Stephen Walbrook
12. Tower Bridge
13. City Hall
14. Monument
15. Guildhall
16. Borough Market
17. Southwark Cathedral
18. Shakespeare's Globe
19. HMS Belfast
20. The Shard
21. Old Spitalfields Market
22. Brick Lane
23. Hoxton
24. Dennis Severs' House
25. Geffrye Museum

Eat

1. José Pizarro
2. The Jugged Hare
3. Fenchurch
4. Nusa Kitchen
5. Dinerama
6. The Brick Lane Food Hall
7. Sunday Upmarket

Drink

8. Ye Olde Cheshire Cheese
9. Lamb Tavern
10. The Black Friar
11. Fox & Anchor
12. The Market Porter
13. Merchant House
14. The George

L

CITY

GRAHAM ST

LEVER

GOSWELL ROAD

SEWARD ST

ST JOHN ST

CLERKENWELL ROAD

Charterhouse

11 Barbican ⊖

CHARTERHOUSE STREET

LONG LANE

Smithfield Market

5 St Bartholomew-the-Great

GILTSPUR STREET

HOLBORN VIADUCT

FARRINGDON ST

NEWGATE ST

HIGH HOLBORN

BLOOMSBURY WAY

Holborn ⊖

HIGH HOLBORN

KINGSWAY

SHAFTESBURY AVE

HOLBORN

Chancery Lane ⊖

CHANCERY LANE

CURSITOR STREET

Sir John Soane's Museum 8

Lincoln's Inn Fields

LINCOLN'S INN FIELDS

NEW SQUARE

NEW FETTER LANE

Dr Johnson's House

City Thameslink

NEWGATE ST

St Paul's ⊖

LUDGATE HILL

St Paul's Cathedral 1

ℹ

QUEEN VICTORIA

THE WEST END, WESTMINSTER AND THE SOUTH BANK
p64

Hunterian Museum

Royal Courts of Justice

STRAND

FLEET STREET

St Bride's

NEW BRIDGE ST

ST MARTIN'S LA

Covent Garden ⊖

Central Market

STRAND

ALDWYCH

Somerset House

ESSEX ST

Temple ⊖

Inns of Court 4

MIDDLE TEMPLE LN

Inner Temple Gardens

TEMPLE AVENUE

10 The Black Friar

Blackfriars ⊖

Blackfriars Pier

Blackfriars Bridge

Millennium Bridge

VICTORIA EMBANKMENT

Thames

Waterloo Bridge

Waterloo Bridge

National Theatre

WATERLOO ROAD

STAMFORD STREET

Bankside Gallery

BLACKFRIARS

3 Tate Modern

SOUTHWARK STREET

THE CITY, SOUTHWARK AND EAST END

BLACKFRIARS ROAD

Southwark ⊖

UNION STREET

0 metres 500

0 yards 500

N ↑

J   K   L

① ⟨icons⟩

ST PAUL'S CATHEDRAL

♀L6 ⬢Ludgate Hill EC4 ⊖St Paul's, Mansion House
⬛City Thameslink, Blackfriars ⊙Cathedral:
8:30am-4:30pm Mon-Sat (last adm: 4pm); Galleries:
9:30am-4:15pm Mon-Sat ⬛stpauls.co.uk

Built between 1675 and 1710, Sir Christopher Wren's Baroque masterpiece has one of the largest cathedral domes in the world, standing 111m (365 ft) high and weighing 65,000 tonnes. The splendid cathedral has formed the lavish setting for many state ceremonies.

Following the Great Fire of London in 1666, the medieval cathedral of St Paul's was left in ruins. The authorities turned to Christopher Wren to rebuild it, but his ideas met with strong resistance from the conservative Dean and Chapter. Wren's 1672 Great Model plan was rejected and a watered-down plan was finally agreed in 1675. Despite the compromises, Wren created a magnificent Baroque cathedral. It has a strong choral tradition and is famed for its music, with regular concerts and organ recitals.

The balustrade was added against Wren's wishes.

Carvings on the pediment depict the Conversion of St Paul.

↑ Illustration of the exterior of St Paul's Cathedral

↑ The mighty dome of St Paul's, viewed from the Millennium Bridge

CHRISTOPHER WREN

Sir Christopher Wren (1632-1723) was a leading figure in the rebuilding of London after the Great Fire of 1666. He built 52 churches, 31 of which have survived. Nearly as splendid as St Paul's is St Stephen Walbrook, his domed church of 1672-7. Other landmarks are St Bride's, off Fleet Street, said to have inspired the trad-itional shape of wedding cakes, and St Mary-le-Bow in Cheapside.

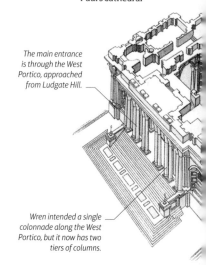

The main entrance is through the West Portico, approached from Ludgate Hill.

Wren intended a single colonnade along the West Portico, but it now has two tiers of columns.

The lantern weighs a massive 700 tonnes.

The Golden Gallery is at the highest point of the dome.

Windows at the top of the cone are visible through the oculus.

The brick cone located inside the outer dome supports the heavy lantern.

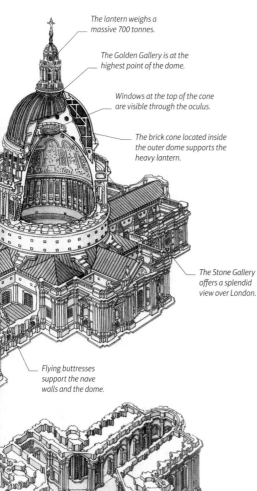

The Stone Gallery offers a splendid view over London.

Flying buttresses support the nave walls and the dome.

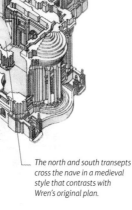

The north and south transepts cross the nave in a medieval style that contrasts with Wren's original plan.

↑ Cross-section of the interior of St Paul's Cathedral

Timeline

Must See

604

▽ Bishop Mellitus builds the first wooden St Paul's church; it burns down in 675 and is rebuilt shortly thereafter.

1087

▽ Bishop Maurice begins Old St Paul's: a Norman cathedral built of stone.

1708

▽ Wren's son Christopher, together with the son of a master stone mason, lays the last stone on the lantern.

2011

▽ Extensive restorations are completed using state-of-the-art conservation techniques.

2

TOWER OF LONDON

📍P7 🚇Tower Hill EC3 🚉Tower Hill, DLR Tower Gateway
🚂Fenchurch Street ⏰9am-5:30pm Tue-Sat, 10am-5:30pm Sun & Mon (Nov-Feb: to 4:30pm) 🌐hrp.org.uk

Founded in 1066 by William the Conqueror, the Tower of London has served as a fortress, palace and prison. Visitors flock here to see the Crown Jewels and hear tales of its dark and intriguing history.

The Tower has been a tourist attraction since the reign of Charles II (1660–85), when both the Crown Jewels and the Line of Kings collection of armour were first shown to the public. The area within the mighty walls houses the remaining parts of the Medieval Palace built by Henry III, as well as several towers that held prisoners, including Anne Boleyn, Thomas Cromwell and Catherine Howard. For much of its 900-year history, the Tower was somewhere to be feared. Those who had committed treason or threatened the throne were held within its dank walls – many did not get out alive, and some were tortured before meeting violent deaths on nearby Tower Hill. High-ranking prisoners could live in some comfort with servants, but the rest suffered hardship, torture and, ultimately, death.

The Crown Jewels

Comprising crowns, sceptres and orbs at coronations and other state occasions, the priceless Crown Jewels in the Jewel House have enormous historical significance. They mostly date from 1661 when Charles II ordered replacements for regalia destroyed by Parliament after the execution of Charles I.

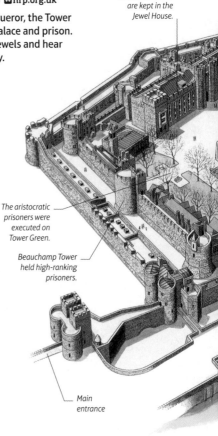

The Crown Jewels are kept in the Jewel House.

The aristocratic prisoners were executed on Tower Green.

Beauchamp Tower held high-ranking prisoners.

Main entrance

> 💬 INSIDER TIP
> **Tour with a Beefeater**
>
> Join a Yeoman Warder, or Beefeater, on a tour of the Tower. A lively retelling of tales of executions, plots and famous prisoners, it's an entertaining way to explore the Tower's history. Tours are included in the entry fee and set off every 30 minutes from near the main entrance, lasting for an hour.

Timeline

1066
△ William I erects a temporary castle.

1534–5
△ Thomas More is imprisoned and executed.

The White Tower displays armour worn by Tudor and Stuart kings.

The imposing Norman Tower of London, ↑ the setting for key historical events

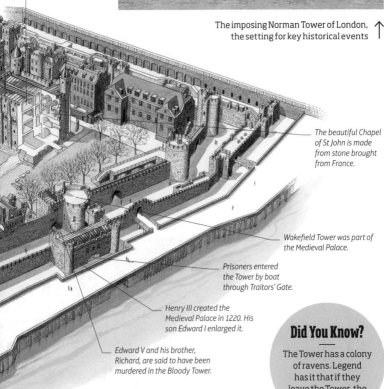

The beautiful Chapel of St John is made from stone brought from France.

Wakefield Tower was part of the Medieval Palace.

Prisoners entered the Tower by boat through Traitors' Gate.

Henry III created the Medieval Palace in 1220. His son Edward I enlarged it.

Edward V and his brother, Richard, are said to have been murdered in the Bloody Tower.

↑ Illustration showing the layout of the Tower of London

Did You Know?

The Tower has a colony of ravens. Legend has it that if they leave the Tower, the kingdom will fall.

1553–4
△ Lady Jane Grey is held and executed.

1603–16
△ Walter Raleigh is imprisoned in Tower.

1671
△ "Colonel Blood" tries to steal Crown Jewels.

1941
△ Prominent Nazi Rudolf Hess is held in the Queen's House.

(3) ⓜ ⓨ ⓓ ⓐ

TATE MODERN

📍L7 🏠Bankside SE1 🚇Pimlico 🚂Blackfriars, Southwark 🚉Blackfriars
🕙10am-6pm Sun-Thu, 10am-10pm Fri & Sat 📅24-26 Dec 🌐tate.org.uk

Looming over the southern bank of the Thames, Tate Modern, housed in the converted Bankside power station, holds one of the world's premier collections of modern and contemporary art. With an ever-changing roster of exhibitions, it is London's most visited gallery.

Opened to coincide with the new millennium, this Goliath of a gallery boasts a collection of over 70,000 works of modern art, featuring paintings and sculptures by some of the most significant artists of the 20th and 21st centuries, Pablo Picasso, Salvador Dalí, Mark Rothko and Francis Bacon among them. Lesser known artists and less mainstream media also abound, with pieces composed of bottle tops or, most famously, a porcelain urinal, in the guise of Marcel Duchamp's notorious *Fountain*. The focal point of the building is the awesome Turbine Hall, which is often filled by a specially commissioned work. Other exhibition spaces, including the galleries of the towering Blavatnik Building, feature collections on a single theme or hugely popular temporary shows.

INTERACTIVE ART

Tate Modern has created a series of interactive activities and experiences under its Bloomberg Connects umbrella. These products, including the Tate app, the digital Drawing Bar, which lets you create your own work of digital art, and the digital gallery, in which you can immerse yourself in the studios and cities of artists, enable members of the public to actively connect with art, artists and other visitors. The award-winning handheld multimedia guides present audio commentary alongside images, film clips and games.

One Two Three Swing! by SUPERFLEX, an installation in the Turbine Hall ↓

4.2 million
—
The number of bricks used to build the original Bankside power station.

1 The striking 99-m- (325-ft-) high chimney of Tate Modern reveals the building's former role as a power station.

2 Andy Warhol's silkscreen *Marilyn Diptych* (1962) is just one of Tate Modern's many notable works of modern art.

3 The Blavatnik Building extension has added a large number of galleries . It was built in 2016 to a design by Herzog & de Meuron, the original architects who converted the power station.

GREAT VIEW
Top of the Tower

On Level 10, the top floor of the fantastic Blavatnik Building extension, the 360-degree viewing terrace gives spectacular views of London. You can also enjoy more or less the same views, taking in St Paul's Cathedral, the rest of the City and beyond, from the restaurant on Level 9.

The well-tended gardens in front of Middle Temple ↑

EXPERIENCE MORE

4

Inns of Court

📍 K6 🚇 Temple

A cluster of atmospheric squares and gardens form the **Inner Temple** and Middle Temple, two of London's four Inns of Court, where law students are trained. The name Temple derives from the medieval Knights Templar, a religious order

> 💬 **INSIDER TIP**
> ### Summer Spot
> The best time to visit the Inns of Court is when the gardens are open: between noon and 3pm on weekdays. Middle Temple Gardens are only open in summer.

which protected pilgrims to the Holy Land and was based here until 1312. **Middle Temple** has a fine Elizabethan interior. Marble effigies of knights lie on the floor of the circular **Temple Church**, part of which dates from the 12th century. There are free organ recitals here at 1:15pm on Wednesdays.

Inner Temple

🏠 King's Bench Walk EC4
🕐 6am–8pm Mon–Fri; Sat & Sun: grounds only
🌐 innertemple.org.uk

Middle Temple

🏠 Middle Temple Ln EC4
🕐 For lunch (book ahead)
🌐 middletemplevenue.org.uk

Temple Church

 📞 020 7353 3470
🕐 10am–4pm Mon–Fri

5

St Bartholomew-the-Great

📍 L5 🏠 West Smithfield EC1
🚇 Barbican, St Paul's
🕐 8:30am–5pm Mon–Fri (mid-Nov–mid-Feb: to 4pm), 10:30am–4pm Sat, 8:30am–8pm Sun
🌐 greatstbarts.com

Hidden behind Smithfield meat market, this is one of London's oldest churches. The 13th-century arch, now topped by a Tudor gatehouse, used to be the entrance to the church until the old nave was pulled down during the Dissolution of the Monasteries (p391). The painter William Hogarth was baptized here in 1697. The church featured in the films *Four Weddings and a Funeral* and *Shakespeare in Love*.

institutions, with two cinemas, a concert hall, two theatres and gallery spaces. The centre is also home to a library, restaurants, cafés and bars, and a tropical conservatory. A dynamic programme of events typically includes seasons of plays by the Royal Shakespeare Company, concerts by the resident London Symphony Orchestra, and plenty of independent cinema. The centre has always made room for experimental, genre-defying performers and artists, so expect anything from multimedia art exhibitions to street dance operas. Jazz and world music also feature frequently.

7 🍴 🖥 🏛
The Royal Exchange

📍M6 🏠EC3 🚇Bank
🌐theroyalexchange.co.uk

Sir Thomas Gresham, an Elizabethan merchant and courtier, founded the Royal Exchange in 1565 as a centre for commerce of all kinds. The original building was centred on a vast courtyard. Queen Elizabeth I gave it its royal title and it is still one of the sites from which a new monarch is announced. Dating from 1844, this is the third splendid building on the site since Gresham's. The building is now a luxurious shopping centre with designer stores and a branch of the luxurious Fortnum & Mason *(p81)*.

8 🏛
Sir John Soane's Museum

📍J5 🏠13 Lincoln's Inn Fields WC2 🚇Holborn
🕐10am-5pm Wed-Sun, most bank hols
🌐soane.org

One of the most eccentric museums in London, this house was left to the nation by Sir John Soane in 1837, with a stipulation that nothing should be changed. The son of a bricklayer, Soane became one of Britain's leading late Georgian architects, developing a restrained Neo-Classical style of his own. After marrying the niece of a wealthy builder, he bought and reconstructed No. 12 Lincoln's Inn Fields. In 1813 he and his wife moved into No. 13 and in 1824 he rebuilt No. 14, adding a picture gallery and the mock medieval Monk's Parlour.

The collections are an eclectic gathering of beautiful, instructional and often simply peculiar artifacts in a warren of rooms. There are casts, bronzes, vases, antique fragments, paintings and a selection of bizarre trivia ranging from a giant fungus from Sumatra to a scold-bridle, a device designed to silence nagging wives. Highlights include the sarcophagus of Seti I, Soanes's own designs, including those for the Bank of England, models by leading Neo-Classical sculptors and the *Rake's Progress* series of satirical paintings (1734) by William Hogarth.

The building itself is full of architectural surprises and illusions. In the main ground floor room, cunningly placed mirrors play tricks with light and space, while an atrium stretching from the basement to the glass-domed roof allows light into every floor.

↑ A room filled with ancient statuary at the Sir John Soane's Museum

Did You Know?

The Inns have starred as locations in such films as *The Da Vinci Code* and *Pirates of the Caribbean*.

6 🍴 🖥 🏛
Barbican Centre

📍M5 🏠Barbican Estate EC2 🚇Barbican, Moorgate
🚉Moorgate, Liverpool Street 🕐9am-11pm Mon-Sat, 11am-11pm Sun; Art gallery: 10am-6pm daily (to 9pm Thu & Fri); Conservatory: noon-5pm Sun (check website for other days) 🌐barbican.org.uk

A Brutalist masterpiece, this residential, commercial and cultural complex is a fabulous anomaly in the City: an oasis of culture and community in London's financial district.

The soul at the concrete heart of the Barbican Estate, the Barbican Centre is one of London's largest arts

DRINK

Ye Olde Cheshire Cheese

This famous 17th-century pub features a warren of wood-panelled rooms and traditional booths.

📍K6 🏠145 Fleet St
📞020 7353 6170
🚫Sun

Lamb Tavern

Open since 1780, this glorious, traditional boozer in historic Leadenhall Market is often packed with City workers across its three floors. The Lamb Tavern is famous for selling its own beer.

📍N6 🏠10-12 Leadenhall Market
🚫Sat & Sun
🌐lambtavern leadenhall.com

The Black Friar

An unusual and sumptuous Art Nouveau public house built on the site of a Dominican priory, The Black Friar is decorated with friezes of monks breaking their vows.

📍L6 🏠174 Queen Victoria St
📞020 7236 5474

Fox & Anchor

Serving a wide range of beers, the splendid Victorian Fox & Anchor pub has etched glass, mahogany doors and private snugs at the back.

📍L5 🏠115 Charterhouse Street
🕐Daily (from 7am Mon-Fri)
🌐foxandanchor.com

↑ Visitors examining the displays at the fascinating Museum of London

Museum of London

📍M5 🏠150 London Wall EC2 🚇Barbican, St Paul's, Moorgate
🕐10am-6pm daily
🌐museumoflondon.org.uk

On the edge of the Barbican Estate, this museum provides a lively account of London life from prehistoric times to the present day through an eclectic set of displays.

Prehistory exhibits, such as flint hand axes found in the gravels under the modern city, begin on the entrance level, and visitors can walk through Roman and medieval London galleries to the War, Plague and Fire exhibit, which includes a display on the Great Fire of 1666.

On the lowest level, the history of London after the disastrous fire up to the present day is explored. The Lord Mayor of London's State Coach is on show here. Finely carved and painted, this gilded coach from c 1757 is paraded once a year during the Lord Mayor's Show. The Victorian Walk uses several original shopfronts to re-create the atmosphere of late 19th-century London. There are also the bronze and cast-iron Brandt Edgar lifts from Selfridges department store on Oxford Street and a 1964 Beatles dress printed with the faces of the Fab Four.

One of the newest galleries is the London 2012 Cauldron, the centrepiece of the opening and closing ceremonies at the London Olympics. Videos,

→
The Sky Garden, offering far-reaching, panoramic views of London

photographs, diagrams and the copper petal elements which rose together to form the Olympic Flame combine to describe the spectacle and the ingenuity of the design.

Sky Garden

📍N6 🏠 20 Fenchurch St EC3 🚇Bank, Monument ⏰10am-6pm Mon-Fri, 11am-9pm Sat & Sun (last adm: 1 hr earlier); advance booking essential 🌐skygarden.london

Completed in 2014, the Rafael Viñoly-designed skyscraper at 20 Fenchurch Street is commonly known as the "Walkie-Talkie", thanks to its unusual shape. It has been the most controversial of London's modern towers, partly because its shape and position make it particularly obtrusive on the London skyline. However, it is one of the few skyscrapers with free public access, provided that you book ahead for the Sky Garden, a large three-level viewing deck at the top of the building. Tickets are issued three weeks ahead and go

quickly for popular times. There are also several bars and restaurants. The Sky Garden is a perfect place from which to view London's other mega-structures: to the south, the Shard *(p129)*; and the north, Tower 42, the distinctive "Gherkin", and the Leadenhall Building, aka the "Cheesegrater".

St Stephen Walbrook

📍M6 🏠 39 Walbrook EC4 🚇Bank, Cannon St ⏰10am-4pm Mon, Tue & Thu, 11am-3pm Wed, 10am-3:30pm Fri 🌐ststephenwalbrook.net

The Lord Mayor's parish church was built by Sir Christopher Wren in the 1670s. The airy interior is flooded with light by a huge dome that appears to float above the eight columns and arches that support it. Original fittings, such as the decorative font cover and pulpit canopy, contrast with the stark simplicity of Henry Moore's massive white stone altar (1987). Free organ recitals take place at 12:30pm on Fridays and chamber music recitals at 1pm on Tuesdays (except Aug).

> 🔍 HIDDEN GEM
> ### Leadenhall Market
>
> This ornate Victorian shopping arcade was designed by Sir Horace Jones in 1881. It is home to boutique wine shops, cheesemongers and fine food shops, plus several traditional pubs and wine bars.

Tower Bridge

**⊙ P7 ⊘ SE1 ⊙ Tower Hill
⊙ Exhibition: 9:30am–
5:30pm daily (last adm:
5pm) ⊡ towerbridge.
org.uk**

This flamboyant piece of Victorian engineering, designed by Sir Horace Jones, was completed in 1894 and soon became a symbol of London. Its two Gothic towers contain the mechanism for raising the roadway to permit large ships to pass through, or for special occasions. When raised, the bridge is 40 m (135 ft) high and 60 m (200 ft) wide. Check the website for bridge lift times. The towers are made of a steel framework clad in stone, linked by two high-level walkways.

The bridge houses The Tower Bridge Exhibition, with interactive displays bringing the bridge's history to life. There are fine river views from the walkways, including through the glass floor, and a look at the magnificent Victorian steam engine room that powered the lifting machinery until 1976, when the system was electrified.

Did You Know?

Nicknames for City Hall include the Snail and the Onion.

City Hall

**⊙ N7 ⊘ The Queen's Walk
SE1 ⊙ London Bridge
⊙ 8:30am–6pm Mon–Thu,
8:30am–5:30pm Fri
⊡ london.gov.uk/about-us**

The Norman Foster-designed domed glass building near Tower Bridge is the head-quarters for London's Mayor and the Greater London Authority. Anyone can visit the building and look in on the assembly chamber, or sit in on Mayor's Question Time when assembly members interrogate the mayor on London issues (check the website for dates). On the lower ground floor are tempo-rary exhibitions and a café. Outside, the stone amphi-theatre, known as the Scoop, hosts free summer events.

Monument

**⊙ N6 ⊘ Monument St
EC3 ⊙ Monument
⊙ Apr–Sep: 9:30am–6pm;
Oct–Mar: 9:30am–5:30pm
(last adm: 5pm)
⊡ themonument.info**

This Doric column, designed by Sir Christopher Wren to commemorate the Great Fire of London that devastated the original walled city in September 1666, is the tallest and finest isolated stone column in the world. Constructed in Portland stone and topped with a bronze flame, the Monument took six years to build and is 62 m (205 ft) high: this is the exact distance west to Pudding Lane, where the fire is believed to have started. Reliefs around the base show Charles II restoring the city after the tragedy.

The column has 311 tightly spiralled steps that lead to a tiny viewing platform. The steep climb is well worth the

Tower Bridge, an enduring symbol of London

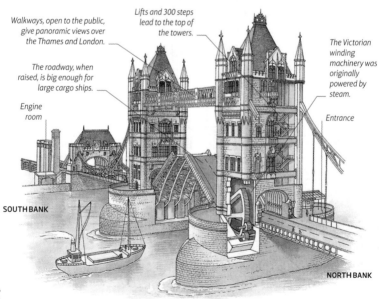

Walkways, open to the public, give panoramic views over the Thames and London.

Lifts and 300 steps lead to the top of the towers.

The roadway, when raised, is big enough for large cargo ships.

The Victorian winding machinery was originally powered by steam.

Engine room

Entrance

SOUTH BANK

NORTH BANK

Visitors admiring Pre-Raphaelite paintings in the Guildhall Art Gallery

EAT

José Pizarro
Sample a range of classic Spanish tapas and inventive dishes at this laid-back tapas restaurant and bar.

🗺 N5 🏠 36 Broadgate Circle 🌐 josepizarro. com

💷💷💷

The Jugged Hare
This gastropub serves excellent game dishes (including the one after which it is named), plus Sunday roasts.

🗺 M5 🏠 49 Chiswell St 🌐 thejuggedhare.com

💷💷💷

Fenchurch
Modern British cuisine is on the menu at this elegant rooftop restaurant in the Walkie Talkie tower.

🗺 N6 🏠 1 Sky Garden Walk 🌐 skygarden. london/fenchurch-restaurant

💷💷💷

Nusa Kitchen
Offering excellent value, this lunchtime pit stop serves fabulous, hearty Southeast Asian soups and dishes. It's one of several branches in the City.

🗺 M5 🏠 Masons Ave 🌐 nusakitchen.co.uk

💷💷💷

---

effort as the views from the top are spectacular and include a good vista of the dome of St Paul's.

15
Guildhall

🗺 M5 🏠 Guildhall Yard EC2 🚇 St Paul's ⏱ Great Hall: 10am–4:30pm Mon-Sat (May–Sep: daily) 🚫 Occasionally for events 🌐 guildhall.cityoflondon. gov.uk

Guildhall has been the administrative centre of the City for at least 800 years. For centuries its Great Hall was used for trials, and many people were condemned to death here, including, in 1606, the Jesuit priest Henry Garnet, one of the Gunpowder Plot conspirators.

Overlooking the Great Hall at one end are the figures of legendary giants Gog and Magog, the guardians of the City, while statues of notable figures such as Sir Winston Churchill and Lord Horatio Nelson line its 46-m- (150-ft-) long sides. Each year, a few days after the Lord Mayor's parade, the prime minister addresses a banquet here.

On the south side of Guildhall Yard is a Wren-designed church, St Lawrence Jewry, while on the east side is the **Guildhall Art Gallery**. It houses the studio collection of 20th-century artist Sir Matthew Smith, portraits from the 16th century to the present day, 18th-century works including John Singleton Copley's *Defeat of the Floating Batteries at Gibraltar*, and numerous Victorian works.

In 1988, the foundations of a **Roman amphitheatre** were discovered beneath the gallery. Built in AD 70 and with a capacity of about 6,000 spectators, the arena would have hosted animal hunts, executions and gladiatorial combat. Public access to the atmospheric ruins is through the art gallery.

Guildhall Art Gallery and Roman Amphitheatre
⏱ 10am–5pm Mon-Fri, noon–4pm Sun
🌐 cityoflondon.gov.uk

Anyone can visit City Hall and look in on the Assembly chamber, or sit in on Mayor's Question Time when assembly members interrogate the mayor on London issues.

16 Borough Market

♀ M7 🚏 8 Southwark St SE1 🚇 London Bridge ⏰ 10am-5pm Wed-Thu, 10am-6pm Fri, 8am-5pm Sat (some stalls also 10am-5pm Mon & Tue) 🌐 borough market. org.uk

Borough Market has existed in some form or another for over a thousand years. It moved to its current location in 1756. Today, it is an extremely popular fine food market, known for gourmet goods as well as quality fruit and vegetables and organic meat, fish and dairy produce.

17 Southwark Cathedral

♀ M7 🚏 Montague Close SE1 🚇 London Bridge ⏰ 9am-5pm Mon-Fri, 9:30am-3:45pm & 5-6pm Sat, 12:30-3pm & 4-6pm Sun 🌐 cathedral. southwark.anglican.org

Although this church, formerly known as St Mary Overie and then St Saviour's, did not

Borough Market, housed in 1850s buildings; flame-grilled burgers at one of the hot food stalls *(inset)*

become a cathedral until 1905, some parts of it date back to the 12th century, when the building was attached to a priory, and many of its medieval features remain. The memorials are quite fascinating and include a late 13th-century wooden effigy of an unknown knight. The medieval poet John Gower is buried in the cathedral in a colourful painted tomb. John Harvard, the first benefactor of Harvard University, was born in Southwark and baptized here in 1607. A chapel is named after him.

In 2000, the cathedral was restored in a multi-million-pound programme which included the addition of new buildings housing a shop and a refectory. The exterior has also been landscaped to create a herb garden, with the attractive Millennium Courtyard leading to the riverside.

18 Shakespeare's Globe

♀ L7 🚏 21 New Globe Walk SE1 🚇 Southwark, London Bridge ⏰ Exhibition: 9:30am-5pm daily; performances: late Apr-mid-Oct 🌐 shakespeares globe.com

Opened in 1997, this circular building is a faithful repro-duction of an Elizabethan theatre, close to the site of the original Globe where many of Shakespeare's plays were first performed. It was built using handmade bricks and oak laths, fastened with wooden pegs rather than metal screws, and its thatched roof is the first to have been allowed in London since the Great Fire

> **The Sam Wanamaker Playhouse is an atmospheric reproduction of a Jacobean indoor candlelit theatre, with performances all year round.**

of 1666. Open to the elements (although the seating area is covered), the main theatre offers one of London's most stimulating theatrical experiences but operates only in the summer. A second theatre, the Sam Wanamaker Playhouse, is an atmospheric reproduction of a Jacobean indoor candlelit theatre, with performances all year round.

Beneath the theatre, Shakespeare's Globe Exhibition covers many aspects of Shakespeare's work and times.

 19

HMS Belfast

📍N7 ⏷The Queen's Walk SE1 ⬚London Bridge, Tower Hill ⏰10am–6pm daily (Nov–Feb: to 5pm; last adm: 1 hr before closing) ⬚iwm.org.uk/visits/hms-belfast

Originally launched in 1938 to serve in World War II, the famous warship HMS *Belfast* was instrumental in the destruction of the German battle cruiser *Scharnhorst* in the battle of North Cape, and also played a key role in the Normandy Landings. After the war, it was sent to work for the United Nations in Korea. The ship remained in service with the Royal Navy until 1965.

Since 1971, *Belfast* has been a floating museum. Some of the ship has been re-created to show how it was in 1943, when it participated in sinking the German battle cruiser. Other displays portray life on board during World War II.

On selected weekends children can participate in activities and events on board.

 20

The Shard

📍N7 ⏷London Bridge St SE1 ⬚London Bridge ⏰The View from the Shard: 10am–10pm daily, with seasonal variations; check website (last adm: 1 hr before closing) ⬚theviewfromtheshard.com

Designed by Italian architect Renzo Piano, the Shard is one of the tallest buildings in Western Europe. At 310 m (1,016 ft) high, it dominates the London skyline, its appearance changing with the weather due to the crystalline façade that reflects the sky. The building's 95 floors are home to offices, apartments, the five-star Shangri-La hotel, half a dozen bars and restaurants and Britain's highest observation gallery, The View from the Shard, which allows visitors 360-degree panoramas of up to 64 km (40 miles).

DRINK

The Market Porter
A marvellous selection of traditional English ales is offered at this bustling pub next to Borough Market.

📍M7 ⏷9 Stoney St ⬚themarketporter.co.uk

Merchant House
Hidden away down an alley, this basement bar and lounge with a mercantile theme serves exceptional cocktails, whisky, gin and rum.

📍M6 ⏷13 Well Court, off Bow Lane ⬚merchanthouse.bar

The George
Owned by the National Trust, The George is the only remaining galleried coaching inn in London. In summer there is outside seating in the yard.

📍M7 ⏷75-77 Borough High St ⬚greeneking-pubs.co.uk

→
The Shard, one of London's most iconic modern buildings

EAT

Dinerama

The best spot for street food after dark, this old truck depot also offers craft beers and cocktails.

N4 19 Great Eastern St Wed-Sat

£££

The Brick Lane Food Hall

Choose from treats from Poland, Ethiopia, Japan, Korea and more inside a red-brick warehouse.

P4 Old Truman Brewery, Brick Lane Sat & Sun

£££

Sunday Upmarket

Artsy stalls serve delicious international street food.

P4 Old Truman Brewery, Brick Lane Sun

£££

Alfresco tables at a bar in the Old Truman Brewery, Brick Lane

---

 21

Old Spitalfields Market

P5 16 Horner Sq E1 Liverpool St, Aldgate Market stalls: 10am-6pm Fri-Wed (to 5pm Sun), 7am-6pm Thu oldspitalfieldsmarket.com

Produce has been traded at Spitalfields Market since 1682, though the original covered market buildings date to 1887. The vegetable market moved out in 1991, after which today's version of the market – known for antiques, fashion, bric-a-brac and crafts stalls – started to take shape. Today the market space is a mix of

restaurants, shops and traditional market stalls. It is open every day; Thursdays are good for antiques and collectibles, and every other Friday for vinyl records, but it is on Sundays that the crowds really arrive, in search of vintage clothing and unique items. This is also a major foodie destination, with superb street food from top names, both global and local – from Pacific poké and Burmese tea leaf salad to East Anglian oysters and the unrivalled Reuben sandwich from the iconic Monty's Deli.

22

Brick Lane

P4 E1 Liverpool St, Aldgate East Shoreditch High St Market: 10am-5pm Sun visitbricklane.org

Once a lane running through brickfields, Brick Lane has long been synonymous with the area's British-Bangladeshi community.

Today curry houses sit next to hip galleries and quirky boutiques. Shops and houses, some dating from the 18th century, have seen immigrants of many nationalities, and ethnic foods, spices, silks and saris are all on sale here. In the 19th century this was mainly a Jewish quarter, and some Jewish shops remain, most famously a 24-hour bagel shop at No. 159. On Sundays, a large market is held here and in the surrounding streets. Towards the northern end of Brick Lane is the Old Truman Brewery, home to a mix of bars, shops and stalls: separate markets at weekends sell food, vintage clothes and new fashion.

23

Hoxton

N3 N1, E2 Old St

Hoxton, at the heart of hipster London, is a loosely defined district that revolves around its two main streets: Old Street and Kingsland Road. This once-gritty landscape of Victorian warehouses is now home to trendy places to eat, pricey clothes stores and a significant percentage of the city's newer street art. Clubs and bars radiate out from the Shoreditch High Street and Old Street junction, some of them on neatly proportioned Hoxton Square, just behind Old Street.

24

Dennis Severs' House

📍N4 🏠18 Folgate St E1 🚇Liverpool St 🕐Noon–2pm & 5–9pm Mon, 5–9pm Wed & Fri, noon–4pm Sun 🌐dennissevershouse.co.uk

The late designer and performer Dennis Severs re-created this historical interior that takes you on a journey from the 17th to the 19th centuries. The rooms are like a series of *tableaux vivants*, as if the occupants had simply left for a moment. This theatrical experience is highly removed from the usual museum re-creations and is truly unique.

The Geffrye Museum takes you on a trip through various room settings, each providing an insight into domestic interiors from 1600 to the present day.

25

Geffrye Museum

📍N3 🏠136 Kingsland Rd E2 🚇🚇 Old St, Liverpool St 🚉Hoxton 🕐Times vary, check website 🌐geffrye-museum.org.uk

This delightful museum is housed in a set of restored almshouses built in 1715 on land bequeathed by Sir Robert Geffrye, a 17th-century Lord Mayor of London. The museum takes you on a trip through various typical middle-class room settings, each providing an insight into domestic interiors from 1600 to the present day. Each room

contains superb examples of British furniture of the period. Outside, a series of period garden "rooms" show designs and planting schemes popular in urban gardens between the 16th and 20th centuries.

After a major two-year redevelopment programme, the main museum building is reopening with expanded spaces, which will allow many more collections to be displayed, in spring 2020. Talks and other events take place regularly in the front gardens.

The front gardens of the Geffrye Museum; one of the museum's period interiors *(inset)* ↓

A SHORT WALK
SOUTHWARK

Distance 2 km (1.25 miles) **Time** 20 minutes
Nearest Tube Southwark

Out of the jurisdiction of the City authorities, Southwark was the place for illicit pleasures from medieval times until the 18th century. The 18th and 19th centuries brought new business, and docks, warehouses and factories were built to meet the demand. Today, a riverside walk here provides spectacular views of St Paul's and takes in Tate Modern, a regenerated Borough Market, the recreation of Shakespeare's Globe Theatre and the Shard.

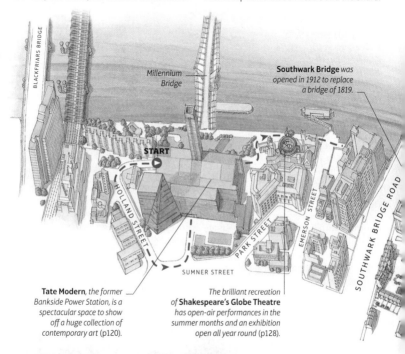

Millennium Bridge

Southwark Bridge *was opened in 1912 to replace a bridge of 1819.*

START

BLACKFRIARS BRIDGE

HOLLAND STREET

PARK STREET

EMERSON STREET

SOUTHWARK BRIDGE ROAD

SUMNER STREET

Tate Modern, *the former Bankside Power Station, is a spectacular space to show off a huge collection of contemporary art (p120).*

The brilliant recreation of **Shakespeare's Globe Theatre** *has open-air performances in the summer months and an exhibition open all year round (p128).*

0 metres 100
0 yards 100
N ↑

The spacious Turbine Hall, part of the grand entrance to Tate Modern

↑ The historic Anchor pub, a popular drinking establishment since the time of Shakespeare

Locator Map
For more detail see p114

THE CITY, SOUTHWARK AND EAST END

Southwark

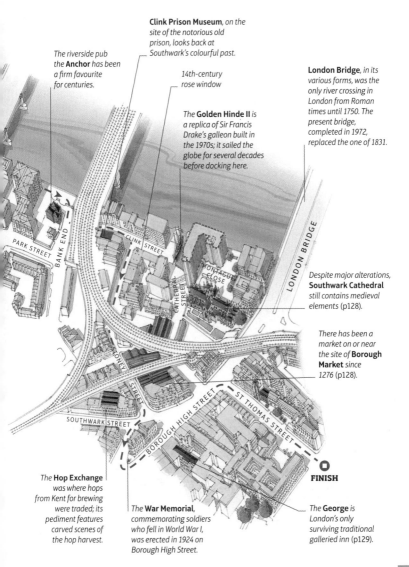

Clink Prison Museum, *on the site of the notorious old prison, looks back at Southwark's colourful past.*

The riverside pub the **Anchor** *has been a firm favourite for centuries.*

14th-century rose window

The **Golden Hinde II** *is a replica of Sir Francis Drake's galleon built in the 1970s; it sailed the globe for several decades before docking here.*

London Bridge, *in its various forms, was the only river crossing in London from Roman times until 1750. The present bridge, completed in 1972, replaced the one of 1831.*

PARK STREET

BANK END

CLINK STREET

MONTAGUE CLOSE

CATHEDRAL STREET

LONDON BRIDGE

Despite major alterations, **Southwark Cathedral** *still contains medieval elements (p128).*

There has been a market on or near the site of **Borough Market** *since 1276 (p128).*

STONEY STREET

SOUTHWARK STREET

BOROUGH HIGH STREET

ST THOMAS STREET

FINISH

The **Hop Exchange** *was where hops from Kent for brewing were traded; its pediment features carved scenes of the hop harvest.*

The **War Memorial**, *commemorating soldiers who fell in World War I, was erected in 1924 on Borough High Street.*

The **George** *is London's only surviving traditional galleried inn (p129).*

BEYOND THE CENTRE

Over the centuries London has steadily expanded, swallowing up the scores of settlements that surrounded it, though many of these areas have maintained their old village atmosphere and character. London's royals, aristocrats and, later, its wealthy industrialists, sought refuge from the city in the manor houses they built a short distance to the north and west of the centre. To the east, in Greenwich, is the Old Royal Naval College. The maritime heritage in Greenwich is shared by Canary Wharf across the river, the site of the historic 19th-century docklands.

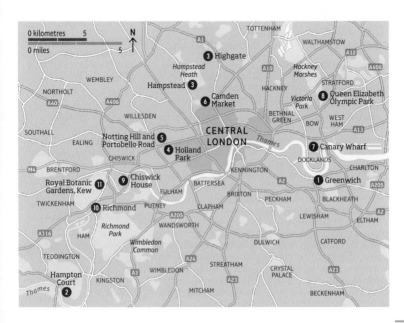

↑ The structure holding the copper hull of the impressive Cutty Sark

❶

GREENWICH

⬛SE10 ⊜Cutty Sark DLR ⬛Greenwich, Maze Hill
⬛Greenwich Pier 🔲62 Huguenot St; 021 876 2861

With illustrious royal and naval connections, Maritime Greenwich is a UNESCO World Heritage Site. In Tudor times it was the site of a palace enjoyed by Henry VIII, now occupied by the Old Royal Naval College; the royal hunting grounds are today Greenwich Park.

①

Cutty Sark

⬛King William Walk SE10
🕐10am–5pm daily (last adm: 4:15pm) 🌐rmg.co.uk

Launched in 1869 as a tea carrier, this vessel is a survivor of the clippers that crossed the Atlantic and Pacific oceans in the 19th century. It was something of a speed machine in its day, returning in 1884 from Australia in just 83 days – 25 days faster than any other ship. It made its final voyage in 1938. In a glass enclosure, it is open to visitors, who can explore the cargo decks and sleeping quarters below and be entertained by the costumed "crew". There are interactive displays on navigation and life on board.

②

National Maritime Museum

⬛Romney Rd SE10
🕐10am–5pm daily
🌐rmg.co.uk

This substantial museum celebrates Britain's seafaring heritage, from early British trade through its emergence as a leading maritime nation to the expeditions of Captain Cook, and from the Napoleonic Wars through to the modern day. In the Tudor and Stuart Seafarers gallery, a digital recreation of the Deptford royal dockyard in 1690 is brought alive, while the Polar Worlds section draws together artifacts from the quests of Shackleton and Scott in the Arctic and Antarctic. In the

Nelson, Navy, Nation gallery, the star exhibit is the uniform that Lord Horatio Nelson was wearing when he was shot at the Battle of Trafalgar in 1805.

Throughout the museum there are numerous activities for children, such as navigating a ship around the world on al huge floor map.

③

Old Royal Naval College

⬛King William Walk SE10 🕐10am–5pm daily; grounds: 8am–11pm daily
🚫Some Sat 🌐ornc.org

A landmark of Greenwich, these ambitious buildings by Sir Christopher Wren were built to house naval pensioners on the site of the old 15th-century royal palace, where Henry VIII, Mary I and

Did You Know?

The ceiling mural in the Old Royal Naval College is the largest figurative painting in Great Britain.

Elizabeth I were born. The Painted Hall, which was intended as a dining room for the retired seamen, was opulently decorated in Baroque *trompe l'oeil* style by Sir James Thornhill in the early 18th century.

---

④

The Queen's House

🏠 Romney Rd SE10
🕐 10am–5pm daily
🌐 rmg.co.uk

The Palladian Queen's House, designed by Inigo Jones for James I's first wife, was completed in 1637 for Henrietta Maria, Charles I's queen consort. From 1821 to 1933 the Royal Hosptial School was housed here.

Highlights include the perfectly cubic Great Hall and the spiral "tulip staircase". The palace is filled with superb works of art, including paintings by Gainsborough, Stubbs and Hogarth.

⑤

Royal Observatory

🏠 Greenwich Park SE10
🕐 10am–5pm daily (to 6pm Easter & Jun–Sep) 🌐 rmg.co.uk

The courtyard of the Royal Observatory in the middle of Greenwich Park is where the meridian (0° longitude) that divides Earth's eastern and western hemispheres passes through. Visitors flock to be photographed standing with a foot on either side of it. In 1884, Greenwich Mean Time became the basis of time measurement for most of the world. At the Astronomy Centre you can explore how scientists first began to map the stars and see world-changing inventions, including the UK's largest refracting telescope. The original build-ing, Flamsteed House, was designed by Sir Christopher Wren and contains old instru-ments belonging to the Astronomer Royals, including

EAT & SHOP

Greenwich Market

This historic covered market is particularly strong on arts and crafts and vintage and antique items, but kooky clothes and accessories and food stalls feature too.

📍 N9 🏠 Greenwich Church St SE10
🌐 greenwich market.london

Edmond Halley, as well as the sea clocks of John Harrison, including the H4 – arguably the most important timepiece ever made. There is also a state-of the art planetarium, the only one in London.

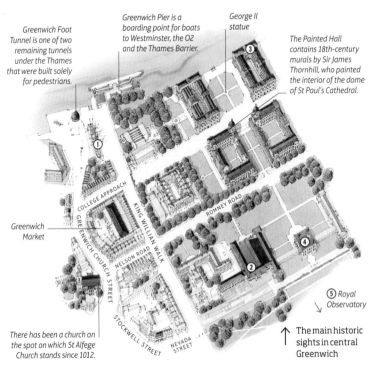

Greenwich Foot Tunnel is one of two remaining tunnels under the Thames that were built solely for pedestrians.

Greenwich Pier is a boarding point for boats to Westminster, the O2 and the Thames Barrier.

George II statue

The Painted Hall contains 18th-century murals by Sir James Thornhill, who painted the interior of the dome of St Paul's Cathedral.

Greenwich Market

There has been a church on the spot on which St Alfege Church stands since 1012.

⑤ *Royal Observatory*

↑ The main historic sights in central Greenwich

The formal Privy Garden on the south side of Hampton Court Palace ↑

2 🥾 🍴 💻 🛍

HAMPTON COURT

🏠 East Molesey, Surrey KT8 9AU 🚇 Hampton Court ⛴ Hampton Court pier (summer only) 🕙 10am-6pm daily (Oct-Mar: to 4:30pm) 🌐 hrp.org.uk

With its impressively preserved palace, beautifully manicured gardens and location on the River Thames, the former stomping ground of Tudor king Henry VIII makes for an irresistible attraction.

Glorious Hampton Court began life in 1514 as the riverside country house of Cardinal Wolsey, Henry VIII's Archbishop of York. Later, in 1528, in the hope of retaining royal favour, Wolsey offered it to the king. Hampton Court was twice rebuilt and extended, first by Henry himself and then, in the 1690s, by King William and Queen Mary, who employed Christopher Wren as architect. There is a striking contrast between Wren's Classical royal apartments and the Tudor turrets, gables and chimneys elsewhere. The inspiration for the gardens comes largely from the time of William and Mary, who created a vast, formal Baroque landscape with avenues and exotic plants. Inside the palace, highlights include the Great Hall, built by Henry VIII, as well as the state apartments of the Tudor court.

> **FLOWER SHOW**
>
> The world's biggest flower show takes place every July at Hampton Court. Displays feature show gardens, floral marquees, talks and demonstrations, with a focus on environmental issues. Book tickets at www.rhs.org.uk.

1528

▽ Cardinal Wolsey gives the Tudor palace to Henry VIII to try to keep favour with the king.

1647

▽ Charles I is imprisoned at Hampton Court Palace by Oliver Cromwell.

1702

▽ Antonio Verrio paints the ceiling above the Grand Staircase leading to the William III State Apartments.

1992

▽ The State apartments, which were damaged by a fire in 1986, are reopened.

1 The King's Staircase is decorated with murals by William Kent.

2 A visitor browses plant displays at RHS Hampton Court Flower Show.

3 The Great Hall was used as a banqueting room and for entertainments.

EXPERIENCE MORE

DRINK

The Spaniards Inn
Dickensian pub with a beer garden and an open fire in winter.

⌂ Spaniards Rd
ⓦ thespaniards
hampstead.co.uk

─────────────

The Southampton Arms
Serving a great range of independent ales.

⌂ 139 Highgate Rd
ⓦ thesouthampton
arms.co.uk

─────────────

The Holly Bush
A cosy old pub with low ceilings and great grub.

⌂ 22 Holly Mount
ⓦ hollybush
hampstead.co.uk

❸

Hampstead and Highgate

⌂ NW3, N6 ⊖ Hampstead, Highgate, Archway
🚉 Hampstead Heath

A hilltop Georgian village with many perfectly maintained houses, Hampstead has long been home to a community of artists and writers.

Keats House (1816) is an evocative tribute to the poet John Keats (1795–1821), who lived here for two years before his death from consumption at the age of 25. Mementoes of Keats and of Fanny Brawne, the neighbour to whom he was engaged, are on show.

The **Freud Museum** is dedicated to Sigmund Freud (1856–1939), the founder of psychoanalysis. At the age of 82, Freud fled from Nazi persecution in Vienna to this Hampstead house where he lived and worked for the last year of his life.

The open spaces of

Did You Know?

The Freud Museum has a collection of contemporary art open for public viewing.

Hampstead Heath offer woods, meadows, lakes and ponds for bathing and fishing, and fine views of the city from Parliament Hill. High on the edge of the Heath, **Kenwood House** is a splendid 18th-century mansion filled with Old Master paintings, including works by Van Dyck, Vermeer, Turner (p76), Reynolds and Rembrandt.

A fashionable retreat in the 16th century, Highgate still has an exclusive feel. Its main draw is **Highgate Cemetery**, whose famous residents include the Victorian novelist George Eliot (1819–80) and Karl Marx (1818–83).

↑ The London skyline from the green environs of Hampstead Heath

↑ Islamic tile decoration in Leighton House's Arab Hall

The highlight is the Arab Hall, which displays Leighton's collection of 13th- to 17th-century Islamic tiles.

Design Museum
◎ ⓘ ⌂ 224-238 Kensington High St W8 ⊖ High St Ken, Earls Crt ⏲ 10am-6pm daily ⓦ designmuseum.org

18 Stafford Terrace
⊛ ⊛ ⓘ ⌂ W8 ⊖ High St Ken ⏲ 2-5:30pm Wed, Sat & Sun ⓦ rbkc.gov.uk

Leighton House
⊛ ⊛ ⓘ ⌂ 12 Holland Park Rd W14 ⊖ High St Ken ⏲ 10am-5:30pm Wed-Mon ⓦ rbkc.gov.uk

---

❺ Notting Hill and Portobello Road

⌂ W11 ⊖ Notting Hill Gate, Ladbroke Grove

In the 1950s and 60s, Notting Hill became a centre for the Caribbean community and today it is a vibrant part of London. It is also home to a famous street carnival, which began in 1965 and takes over the entire area on the August bank holiday weekend.

Nearby, bustling Portobello Road market has hundreds of stalls and shops selling a range of collectables.

Keats House
⊛ ⊛ ⓘ ⌂ Keats Grove NW3 ⏲ Mar-Oct: 11am-5pm Wed-Sun; Nov-Feb: 11am-5pm Fri-Sun ⓦ cityoflondon.gov.uk

Freud Museum
ⓘ ⌂ 20 Maresfield Gdns NW3 ⊖ Finchley Rd ⏲ Noon-5pm Wed-Sun (Aug & Sep: also Mon) ⓦ freud.org.uk

Kenwood House
⊛ ◎ ⓘ ⊛ ⌂ Hampstead Lane NW3 ⏲ 10am-5pm daily (Nov-Mar: to 4pm) ⓦ english-heritage.org.uk

Highgate Cemetery
⊛ ⊛ ⌂ Swains Lane N6 ⏲ Eastern Cemetery: 10am-5pm daily (Nov-Feb: to 4pm); Western Cemetery: daily by guided tour only ⓦ highgatecemetery.org

---

❹ Holland Park

⌂ W8, W14 ⊖ Holland Park

This park is more intimate than the large royal parks such as Hyde Park (p96). On the south side is the **Design Museum**, showcasing contemporary design, from architecture and household goods to fashion and graphics.

Late Victorian houses around the park include **18 Stafford Terrace**, formerly known as Linley Sambourne House. Built in about 1870, it features china ornaments and heavy velvet curtains. Sambourne was a political cartoonist for the satirical magazine *Punch*, and many of his drawings adorn the walls.

Leighton House, built for the Neo-Classical painter Lord Leighton in 1866, is stuffed with *objets d'art* and paintings, some by Leighton himself.

NOTTING HILL CARNIVAL

Celebrating Caribbean culture, Europe's largest street carnival takes place in the area around Notting Hill, Ladbroke Grove and Westbourne Park. Its centrepiece is a parade of flamboyant floats accompanied by steel bands, costumed dancers and mobile sound systems. Along the route are static sound systems, stages and food stalls.

Victorian former
warehouses at Camden
Market

present. A highlight is the
re-creation of the dark and
dangerous "Sailortown" of
Wapping in the 1850s.

**Museum of London
Docklands**
No.1 Warehouse,
West India Quay E14
Canary Wharf 10am-
6pm daily museum
oflondonorg.uk/museum0-
london-docklands

6
Camden Market

NW1 Camden Town,
Chalk Farm 10am-6pm
daily; some cafés
and bars open later
camdenmarket.com

Packed at weekends, Camden
Market is a series of interconnected markets running
along Chalk Farm Road and
Camden High Street. The
market has been at the
forefront of alternative fashion
since the days of punk, and
the current jumble of vintage
clothes and jewellery, arts
and crafts, records and music
memorabilia maintains the
market's place among the
most original shopping
destinations in the city. This
is also street food heaven,
with scores of stalls, cafés and
informal restaurants dishing
out authentic nosh from all
over the world. Some of the
more interesting stalls are in
the Stables Market towards
Chalk Farm, where you will also
find a statue of the late singer-
songwriter Amy Winehouse, a
Camden habituée.

7
Canary Wharf

E14 Canary Wharf,
West India Quay DLR

London's most ambitious
commercial development
opened in 1991, when the
first tenants moved into the
50-storey One Canada Square.
At 235 m (700 ft), it continues
to dominate the city's eastern
skyline with its pyramid-
shaped top. The tower stands
on what was the West India
Dock, closed, like all the
London docks, between the
1960s and the 1980s, when
trade moved to Tilbury. Today,
Canary Wharf is thriving, with
a major shopping complex,
cafés and restaurants.

A few minutes' walk
north of Canary Wharf is
the **Museum of London
Docklands**, occupying a late
Georgian warehouse. This
museum tells the story of
London's docks and their links
from Roman times to the

8
Queen Elizabeth
Olympic Park

1 Hackney Wick,
Stratford, Pudding Mill
Lane E20 Stratford
International 24 hrs
daily; info point 10am-3pm
daily queenelizabeth
olympicpark.co.uk

Home of the 2012 London
Olympic Games, this east
London site was transformed
from an area of industrial

Did You Know?

The oldest potted plant
(since 1775) in the
world, *Encephalartos
altensteineii,* is in
the Palm House.

wasteland into a world-class sporting hub, with striking venues such as the aquatics centre and the velodrome dotted amid meandering waterways and surrounded by wildflower gardens.

Renamed the Queen Elizabeth Olympic Park to commemorate the Queen's Diamond Jubilee in 2012, the site is now a permanent leisure attraction.

Chiswick House

🏠 Burlington Lane W4 🚇 Chiswick ⏰ Apr–Oct: 10am–5pm Wed–Mon & bank hols; gardens: 7am–dusk daily 🌐 chiswick houseandgardens.org.uk

Completed in 1729 to the design of its owner, the third Earl of Burlington, this is a fine example of a Palladian villa. Built around a central octagonal room, the house is packed with references to ancient Rome and Renaissance Italy.

Chiswick was Burlington's country residence and this house was built as an annexe to a larger, older house (since demolished). It was designed for recreation and entertaining. Some of the ceiling paintings are by William Kent. The layout of the garden, now a public park, is much as Burlington designed it.

Free tours of the house are included with admission on Sundays at 2:30pm.

🔟

Richmond

🚇🚆 Richmond

The supremely picturesque village of Richmond took its name from a palace built by Henry VII in 1500; the remains can be seen off the green. Nearby is vast Richmond Park, formerly Charles II's royal hunting ground. Today the park is a national nature reserve and deer still graze among the chestnuts, birches and oaks. In spring, the highlight is the Isabella Plantation with its spectacular azlaeas. The rest of the park is covered with heath, bracken and trees. Richmond Gate, in the northwest corner, was designed by Capability Brown (*p24*) in 1798.

↑ The iconic Palm House at the Royal Botanic Gardens, Kew

TOP 3 **SPLENDID HOUSES NEAR RICHMOND**

Syon House
🌐 syonpark.co.uk
This mansion is known for its spectacular conservatory and lavish Neo-Classical interiors created by Robert Adam in the 1760s.

Ham House
🌐 nationaltrust.org.uk Built in 1610, this house has beautiful parks and formal gardens.

Marble Hill House
🌐 english-heritage.org.uk
A grand Palladian villa, Marble Hill House was built in 1724–9 for the mistress of George II.

⓫

Royal Botanic Gardens, Kew

🏠 Kew, Richmond TW9 🚇 Kew Gardens 🚆 Kew Bridge ⏰ From 10am (closing times vary, check website) 🌐 kew.org

On the riverbank to the south of Richmond village, the Royal Botanic Gardens, Kew is a UNESCO World Heritage Site, home to the world's most diverse collection of living plants – about 30,000 in total. Kew's reputation was first established by the British naturalist and plant hunter Sir Joseph Banks, who worked here in the late 18th century. The former royal gardens were created by Princess Augusta, the mother of George III, on the 3.6-ha (9-acre) site in 1759. The ornate Palm House was designed by Decimus Burton in the 1840s and this famous jewel of Victorian engineering houses palms and other exotic plants in tropical and subtropical conditions.

ENGLAND

Durdle Door natural limestone arch near Lulworth in Dorset

EXPLORE
ENGLAND

This guide divides England into
11 colour-coded sightseeing areas, as
shown on the map below. Find out more
about each area on the following pages.

Edinburgh

Glasgow

Ayr

SCOTLAND

Stranraer

Whitehaven

NORTHERN
IRELAND

Sligo

Isle of Man

Douglas

Irish Sea

Longford

REPUBLIC OF
IRELAND

Dublin

Holyhead

Galway

Bangor

Portlaoise

Wicklow

Limerick

Aberystwyth

Waterford

Rosslare

WALES

Fishguard

Cork

Pembroke

Swansea

Cardiff

Celtic Sea

Barnstaple

Taunton

DEVON AND
CORNWALL
p276

Exete

Plymouth

Truro

| 0 kilometres | 60 |
| 0 miles | 60 |

N
↑

Scilly Isles

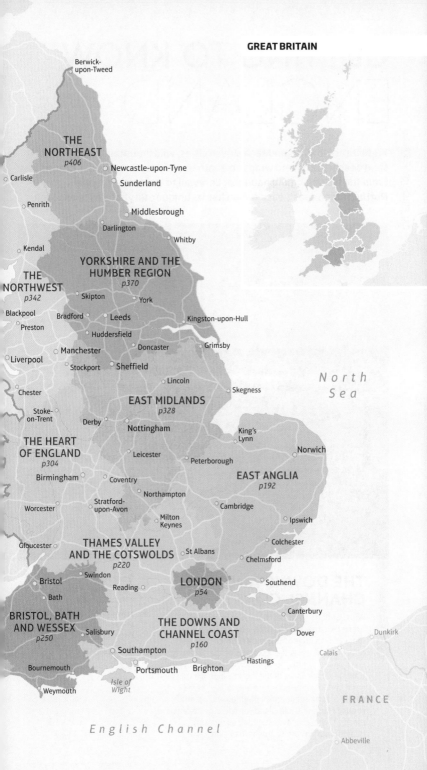

Berwick-
upon-Tweed

THE
NORTHEAST
p406

Carlisle

Newcastle-upon-Tyne

Sunderland

Penrith

Middlesbrough

Darlington

Kendal

Whitby

YORKSHIRE AND THE
HUMBER REGION
p370

THE
NORTHWEST
p342

Skipton

York

Blackpool

Bradford

Leeds

Kingston-upon-Hull

Preston

Huddersfield

Manchester

Doncaster

Grimsby

Liverpool

Stockport

Sheffield

Chester

Lincoln

Skegness

Stoke-
on-Trent

EAST MIDLANDS
p328

*North
Sea*

Derby

Nottingham

THE HEART
OF ENGLAND
p304

Leicester

King's
Lynn

Norwich

Birmingham

Coventry

Peterborough

Worcester

Stratford-
upon-Avon

Northampton

EAST ANGLIA
p192

Milton
Keynes

Cambridge

Ipswich

Gloucester

THAMES VALLEY
AND THE COTSWOLDS
p220

St Albans

Colchester

Chelmsford

Swindon

Bristol

Reading

LONDON
p54

Southend

Bath

Canterbury

BRISTOL, BATH
AND WESSEX
p250

Salisbury

THE DOWNS AND
CHANNEL COAST
p160

Dover

Dunkirk

Southampton

Calais

Bournemouth

Portsmouth

Brighton

Hastings

Weymouth

*Isle of
Wight*

FRANCE

English Channel

Abbeville

GETTING TO KNOW
ENGLAND

Prehistoric wonders and tech-driven cities, wild mountain peaks and soft-sand beaches: England wraps an enormous variety into modest proportions. From the old smuggling haunts of Cornwall to the castle-studded Northumbrian coast, each region has its unique storybook of tales to tell.

PAGE 160

THE DOWNS AND CHANNEL COAST

With London's sprawl confined by a far-sighted Green Belt, the populous and – by and large – moneyed counties of England's southeast remain remarkably unspoiled, encompassing the sweeping chalk uplands of the North and South Downs and the tranquil sunken lanes of the Weald. Along the coast – most famed for its towering white cliffs – there's plenty of buzz at bohemian Brighton and up-and-coming Margate, while inland you'll find handsome market towns, mighty castles and an array of beautifully manicured gardens to explore.

Best for
Buzzy seaside towns and gorgeous gardens

Home to
Brighton, Winchester, Canterbury

Experience
Shopping in the Lanes, Brighton

EAST ANGLIA

PAGE 192

Basking under endless skies, flat but far from featureless East Anglia sits aside from Britain's main north–south axis, preserving an independent-minded air of detachment. The ancient university town of Cambridge, and Norwich, with its magnificent cathedral, are the main city draws but this unhurried rural corner of the country offers much more, from the cultured seaside resorts of Southwold and Aldeburgh to the blissfully peaceful Broads, a haven for wildlife best explored by boat.

Best for
Pretty pastel villages and painterly skies

Home to
Cambridge, Norwich, Ely Cathedral

Experience
Watery adventures: punting on the Cam and boating on the Broads

THAMES VALLEY AND THE COTSWOLDS

PAGE 220

The lush green Thames Valley and the chalky uplands of the Chilterns offer serene pockets of pastoral beauty and play host to some unmissable sights. The region's stately homes, from Jacobean Hatfield House to Baroque Blenheim Palace, are among England's finest, while Oxford's dreaming spires offer one of Britain's most harmonious architectural set-pieces. West of Oxford are the Cotswolds, a picture-perfect landscape of rolling hills and warm, honey-stone villages that feel like they've barely changed in centuries.

Best for
Magnificent stately homes and quintessential English villages

Home to
Windsor Castle, the Cotswolds, Oxford, Blenheim Palace

Experience
Puzzling over the curios of the Pitt Rivers Museum, Oxford

$\rightarrow$

PAGE 250

BRISTOL, BATH AND WESSEX

From the plunging ravine of Cheddar Gorge to the drama and majesty of the Dorset coast, this varied region makes for a thrilling introduction to the West Country. Explore the street art and cutting-edge cultural and culinary scenes of Bristol, one of Britain's most dynamic cities; nearby Bath, meanwhile, retains the elegance of its Georgian heyday. Further afield, don't miss the evocative ruins of Glastonbury Abbey; prehistoric Stonehenge; and the exquisite sandy bays of the Isle of Purbeck.

Best for
Iconic ancient monuments and a fossil-studded coastline

Home to
Bristol, Bath, Stourhead, Stonehenge, Salisbury Cathedral

Experience
Wandering the honey-coloured streets of Georgian Bath

PAGE 276

DEVON AND CORNWALL

Sea-battered cliffs and windswept moors; hidden coves and verdant valleys: opportunities for the romance of the wild draw writers, artists and lovers of the great outdoors to England's myth-steeped southwestern corner. Beyond the pasties and pirates, Cornwall lives up to its reputation for picturesque fishing villages, exquisite seafood, golden sands and pounding surf. Home to the sparkling English Riviera and the lonely expanse of Dartmoor, Devon is more than its match.

Best for
Secluded beaches, lush gardens and sinfully rich cream teas

Home to
Eden Project, St Ives, Dartmoor National Park, Exmoor National Park

Experience
Savouring a seafood feast in Padstow

THE HEART OF ENGLAND

The green shires of England's heart are sprinkled with chocolate-box villages and peaceful market towns lined with streets of crooked, half-timbered buildings. The region's proud past as the cradle of the Industrial Revolution is brought brilliantly to life at Ironbridge Gorge. Meanwhile, buoyed by prestigious architectural projects and cultural initiatives, the cosmopolitan cities of Birmingham and Coventry – UK City of Culture in 2021 – have eyes firmly set on the future.

Best for
Industrial heritage and picturesque villages

Home to
Ironbridge Gorge, Stratford-upon-Avon, Warwick Castle

Experience
Goggling at the medieval Mappa Mundi in Hereford Cathedral

EAST MIDLANDS

Spanning the pancake-flat agricultural heartlands of Lincolnshire – home to the alluringly well-preserved historic centres of Lincoln and Stamford – and the craggy heights of the Peak District, with its heather-covered moors, wooded dales and deep limestone caverns, the East Midlands packs in surprising variety. In between, search out superb country mansions and the spruced-up towns of Nottingham, Leicester and Derby, each shirking off post-industrial gloom with a slew of attractions old and new.

Best for
Fine historic mansions and wild moors

Home to
Peak District National Park, Burghley House

Experience
Tucking into a Bakewell pudding after a hike in the Peaks

→

PAGE 342

THE NORTHWEST

World-class art, music and football, a strong sense of civic pride and a rollicking nightlife give the two great cities of the northwest – Manchester and Liverpool – an irrepressible swagger and energy. Heading north, rural Lancashire is one of England's best-kept secrets, the empty landscapes of the Ribble Valley and the Forest of Bowland a tranquil counterpoint to the shamelessly brash, irresistibly fun seaside resort of Blackpool. But for most visitors, it's the majestic Lake District – indisputably the nation's most dramatic and alluring landscape – that makes this one of Britain's best-loved corners.

Best for
Dynamic cities, seaside thrills and England's most spectacular countryside

Home to
Manchester, Liverpool, Chester, Lake District National Park

Experience
A night out in Manchester's Northern Quarter

PAGE 370

YORKSHIRE AND THE HUMBER REGION

Yorkshire conjures up images of emerald green dales patchworked with drystone walls, ghostly abbey ruins, flower-bedecked market towns and cosy pubs. Wander the cobbled alleys of medieval York, hike the mighty cliffs of Flamborough Head and follow the Brontë trail in Haworth, and you'll soon agree with all trueborn Yorkshire folk that "God's Own Country" is a place apart.

Best for
Proud heritage and rugged landscapes

Home to
York, Castle Howard, Yorkshire Dales National Park, Fountains Abbey, North York Moors National Park

Experience
Indulging your Dracula fantasies in Gothic Whitby

PAGE 406

THE NORTHEAST

Craggy islands home to nesting puffins, colourful fishing villages, dune-backed golden sands and a string of massive medieval strongholds define the rugged north-eastern coast. There's abundant natural beauty inland, too, in the wide open spaces of the North Pennines and Northumberland National Park, the latter cut through by Hadrian's Wall, a dramatic reminder of the Romans' tenure in Britain. The wall snakes east to the fringes of Newcastle upon Tyne, known for its eye-catching architecture and raucous nightlife; south lies Durham, dominated by its ravishing cathedral and castle.

Best for
Romantic coastal castles and unspoilt wilderness

Home to
Durham, Newcastle upon Tyne, Hadrian's Wall

Experience
Browsing the bursting shelves at Barter Books, Alnwick

7 DAYS
in Southeast England

Day 1

Start in the ancient town of Canterbury (p172). Wander its narrow lanes and visit the magnificent Cathedral. After lunch at Tiny Tim's Tearoom (34 St Margaret's St), with its outstanding range of sandwiches, teas and cakes, head to the adjacent Canterbury Tales, where costumed guides fill you in on Geoffrey Chaucer's original stories. Afterwards catch the train (35 mins) to the seaside resort of Margate (p174), home of the Turner Contemporary art gallery. Stroll the beach before returning to Canterbury, where you could catch a show at the Marlowe Theatre (www. marlowetheatre.com). For dinner and a hotel, head for ABode (30–33 High St).

Day 2

Hire a car and drive southeast to Dover (p175) to explore its splendid castle. After taking a peek at Dover's famous white cliffs, drive to Rye (p178) and wander around its medieval cobbled streets. Carry on inland, traversing some of Kent's finest scenery to reach enchanting Leeds Castle (p174), surrounded by its reedy moat. After

visiting the castle, return to the coast to Hastings (p179), and grab a dinner of fish and chips on the beach at Maggie's (www maggiesfishand chips.co.uk). Stay the night at boutique B&B The Laindons (23 High St).

Day 3

It's a short drive from Hastings to Battle Abbey (p179). Here you can walk around the site of the Battle of Hastings. Then continue to Eastbourne (p180) – walk along the pier and relax on the beach. Have lunch at the Lamb Inn (36 High Street) and then continue to Brighton (p164). Explore the exuberant Pavillion and then browse the independent shops in the Lanes. In the evening enjoy some live music at the Brighton Music Hall (www. brightonmusic hall.co.uk). Stay overnight at the classy MyHotel (17 Jubilee St).

Day 4

Spend the morning in Brighton, soaking up the atmosphere and strolling out along the Victorian pier. Take lunch at Food for Friends (p156), Brighton's

1 Medieval cobbled street in Rye.

2 Royal Pavilion in Brighton.

3 Nave of Winchester Cathedral.

4 Lavender field at Snowshill in the Cotswolds.

5 Punting on the River Cherwell in Oxford.

foremost vegetarian restaurant, and then drive to the imposing ramparts and immaculate gardens of Arundel Castle (p182). Afterwards, it's a scenic short drive to the delightful town of Chichester (p183), famous for its cathedral and the remarkable Fishbourne Roman Palace. Eat at the Field & Fork (4 Guildhall St), where the trout is particularly delicious, and bed down at Musgrove House (63 Oving Rd).

Day 5

Drive to Winchester (p168), where you can visit the splendid cathedral (p170), wander the city centre and pop into 8 College Street, where Jane Austen spent the last few weeks of her life in 1817. Take lunch at the River Cottage Canteen (Abbey Mill Gardens, The Broadway), which occupies a splendidly renovated old mill, and then carry on to Windsor and its mighty castle (p224). It will take you a couple of hours at least to explore the castle, after which you can push on to well-heeled Henley-on-Thames (p246) to eat at The Angel on the Bridge, right by the river, and stay at the Hotel du Vin (New St).

Day 6

In the morning, set off to the university town of Oxford (p232), whose compact centre is graced by handsome, historic colleges – Christ Church, Merton and Magdalen are just three of the most beautiful to visit. After a late lunch in the Covered Market go punting on the river. Afterwards, either visit the top-ranking Ashmolean Museum or head 18 km (11 miles) to Blenheim Palace, one of the country's grandest stately homes. Finish off the day with an Italian dinner at Branca (p233) and turn in at the Bath Place (4–5 Hollywell St).

Day 7

Spend the day touring the bucolic land-scapes of the Cotswolds (p226). Begin by visiting Burford, with its enchanting church, followed by Kelmscott Manor, the former home of William Morris, Bibury, with its iconic Arlington Row cotttages and Chipping Campden, which still has the appearance of a medieval wool town. From here it's not far to the lavender fields at Snowshill, a glorious sight in summer.

→

1. Lyme Regis harbour, Dorset.

2. The rainforest biome in the Eden Project.

3. The Great Bath in the Roman Baths complex, Bath.

4. Salisbury Cathedral cloister.

5 DAYS
in Southwest England

Day 1

Start your tour in Salisbury *(p268)*. Explore the Market Square and visit the beautiful cathedral, admiring its spire, the highest in England. Lunch at Fisherton Mill *(108 Fisherton St)*, a combined art gallery and café. In the afternoon, explore the world-famous prehistoric standing stones at Stonehenge *(p264)* and the stone circle and ancient earthworks at Avebury *(p270)*. In the evening head to the charming town of Bath *(p256)*. Dine at Sotto Sotto *(p257)* before turning in for the night at the cosy Harrington's City Hotel *(8–10 Queen St)*.

Day 2

Start your exploration of Bath by visiting the Roman Baths and the Royal Crescent before having lunch at the hipster Wild Café *(10a Queen St)*. In the afternoon, drive south to Lyme Regis *(p273)* and take a stroll around the centre of this picture-perfect resort with a well-protected harbour. Continue to Torquay *(p296)*, a classic English seaside resort where you can dine on excellent seafood at the appealing Number 7 Fish Bistro *(7 Beacon Hill)* and bed down at the imaginatively decorated The 25 Boutique B&B *(25 Avenue Rd)*.

Day 3

In the morning, stroll the streets of the enchanting fishing village of Fowey *(p292)* before visiting the Eden Project *(p280)*, a garden lover's paradise. Eat here, and then drive to St Michael's Mount *(p289)*, a granite islet that rises steeply from the

ocean. Tour the Mount before journeying on to beguiling St Ives *(p282)*. In the evening, enjoy a tasty dinner at the town's informal Cornish Deli *(3 Chapel St)* and settle down for the night at the Primrose House B&B *(Primrose Valley)*.

Day 4

Begin by visiting St Ives's splendid art galleries – Tate St Ives and the Barbara Hepworth Museum and Sculpture Garden. Then journey onto Padstow *(p293)*, a bustling fishing port with a string of outstanding seafood restaurants – try lunch at the smart Prawn on the Lawn *(p292)*. Suitably refreshed, carry on to Tintagel *(p294)* to visit its splendid ruined castle. In the early evening head to scenic Boscastle for a pub dinner at the Napoleon Inn on the High Street and book a bed at The Old Rectory B&B in nearby St Juliot.

Day 5

In the morning, cut inland from Boscastle to travel across the windswept landscapes of Dartmoor National Park *(p284)*. Pause to stretch your legs in minuscule Princetown at the heart of Dartmoor, and grab lunch at the Fox Tor Café *(2 Two Bridges Rd)*. In the afternoon, continue to Glastonbury *(p269)*, home to one of the world's most famous contemporary music festivals. Visit Glastonbury Abbey and take the 30-minute hike up to the summit of Glastonbury Tor to enjoy the views. Eat at the Hundred Monkeys Café *(52 High St)* and spend the night at the family-run Magdalene House on Magdalene Street.

7 DAYS
in Northern England

Day 1

Start in Liverpool (*p350*) with a stroll around Albert Dock, where you can visit either the Tate Liverpool art gallery or the Mersey Maritime Museum. Lunch at Leaf (*p352*) and spend the early afternoon at The Beatles Story, which gives the low-down on the Fab Four. Afterwards, walk up to the Pier Head and take a ferry ride on the River Mersey – a Liverpool highlight. In the evening, sample the Modern British menu at The Art School (*p352*), and then go bar-hopping along Seel Street. Stay the night at the historic Titanic Hotel (*Stanley Dock, Regent Rd*) and arrange car hire for the the rest of the tour.

Day 2

Discover the beautiful landscapes of the Lake District (*p356*) beginning at low-key Windermere (*p360*), where a cruise on the lake is a must. Journey on to the picturesque village of Ambleside for lunch at the Tower Bank Arms (*p361*). In the afternoon, visit Hill Top, Beatrix Potter's old cottage, and then, if the sun is out, continue onto Hawkshead, a

starting point for the delightful Tarns How Walk (*p361*). For dinner and a bed for the night, head to the delightful Drunken Duck in Barnsgate, Ambleside (*p361*).

Day 3

In the morning, arrive in Grasmere (*p358*) to wander around the village and visit Dove Cottage, world-famous as the one-time home of William Wordsworth. Fans of the poet will also be keen to visit nearby Rydal Mount, where Wordsworh lived for a large part of his life. Take lunch at the Rydal Mount tearoom and then drive to the pretty village of Elterwater (*p361*). Spend the afternoon undertaking the Great Langdale walk and end your day at the Old Dungeon Ghyll (*Great Langdale, Ambleside*), a charming old restaurant and hotel in an idyllic location just several miles from Elterwater.

Day 4

Spend the morning driving across the Pennines, the dramatic mountain range bisecting northern England. Continue

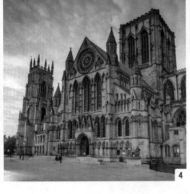

1. The Tyne Bridge and the Sage Gateshead in Newcastle.

2. The idyllic landscape of the western fells of the Lake District National Park.

3. The Beatles statues by Andrew Edwards on the Liverpool waterfront.

4. York Minster in the city of York.

5. The North Yorkshire town of Whitby.

onto the handsome town of Hexham (p415), where you can visit the abbey and enjoy lunch at the Bouchon Bistrot (www. bouchonbistrot.co.uk). From here, visit Hadrian's Wall (p414), built to mark the northern perimeter of the Roman Empire. The three-hour hike here between the major Roman forts – Chesters, Vindolanda and Housesteads – is truly memorable. Stay the night in Hexham at the luxurious Carraw B&B (www.carraw.co.uk).

Day 5

Explore the lively city of Newcastle (p412), strolling the banks of the River Tyne before continuing onto Northumberland's most cutting-edge art gallery, the Baltic Centre for Contemporary Art. Lunch at the Baltic before pressing on to Durham (p410), where visiting the splendid Norman cathedral and castle will take up the afternoon. For dinner in Durham, sample the Modern British cuisine of Finnbarr's Restaurant (Aykley Heads House). If it's outside of university term, stay the night in Durham Castle, which lets rooms out to visitors when the students are away.

Day 6

Arrive in charming Whitby (p392) and explore its quaint centre before wandering over to the abbey with its fine sea views. Lunch at the cosy Magpie Café (14 Pier Rd) and then enjoy more stunning coastal scenery on the way to Robin Hood's Bay. In the late afternoon, double back to Whitby to eat and drink at the Duke of York pub (124 Church St), staying the night at the idiosyncratic La Rosa Hotel (p393).

Day 7

Begin the day by heading south to Castle Howard (p382) and spend the rest of the morning touring this grand stately home set in magnificent grounds. Eat at the Courtyard Café before driving to the nearby beautiful historic city of York (p374). Spend the afternoon wandering York's delightful centre and be sure to visit both York Minster and the Jorvik Viking Centre. Round off the day with dinner at Café No.8 (8 Gillygate) and bed down at The Bar Convent (17 Blossom St), set in an 18th -century working convent.

THE DOWNS AND CHANNEL COAST

England's southeast coast has been the first point of call for newcomers throughout history. The Romans built fortifications along the Channel Coast in the 1st century, later incorporated into Dover Castle and Portchester Castle, and built towns and villas inland. Fishbourne Palace near Chichester is a fine example. In the 6th century, St Augustine came to Kent from Rome to convert the Anglo-Saxons and made Canterbury the centre of the church in England, which it remains today.

As London consolidated its status as the focus and capital of the country, the counties between the city and the coast became favoured places for the monarchs and the nobility to show their wealth and prestige, and a number of lavish mansions arose. Leeds Castle in Kent, a stronghold built by the Normans, was a royal residence for several centuries; designed to impress, Knole acquired the vast number of 365 rooms; and like many other grand houses of the time, Petworth in West Sussex employed Capability Brown to design its deer park and grounds. The Royal Pavilion at Brighton, built for George IV in 1822, is embellishment taken to excess.

THE DOWNS AND CHANNEL COAST

Must Sees

1. Brighton
2. Winchester
3. Canterbury

Experience More

4. Margate
5. Leeds Castle
6. Rochester
7. Whitstable
8. Dover
9. Royal Tunbridge Wells
10. Knole
11. Hever Castle
12. Romney Marsh
13. Rye
14. Bodiam Castle
15. Winchelsea
16. Hastings
17. Eastbourne
18. Lewes
19. Steyning
20. Portsmouth
21. Arundel Castle
22. Chichester
23. Petworth House
24. Beaulieu
25. Chawton
26. Guildford
27. New Forest
28. Isle of Wight

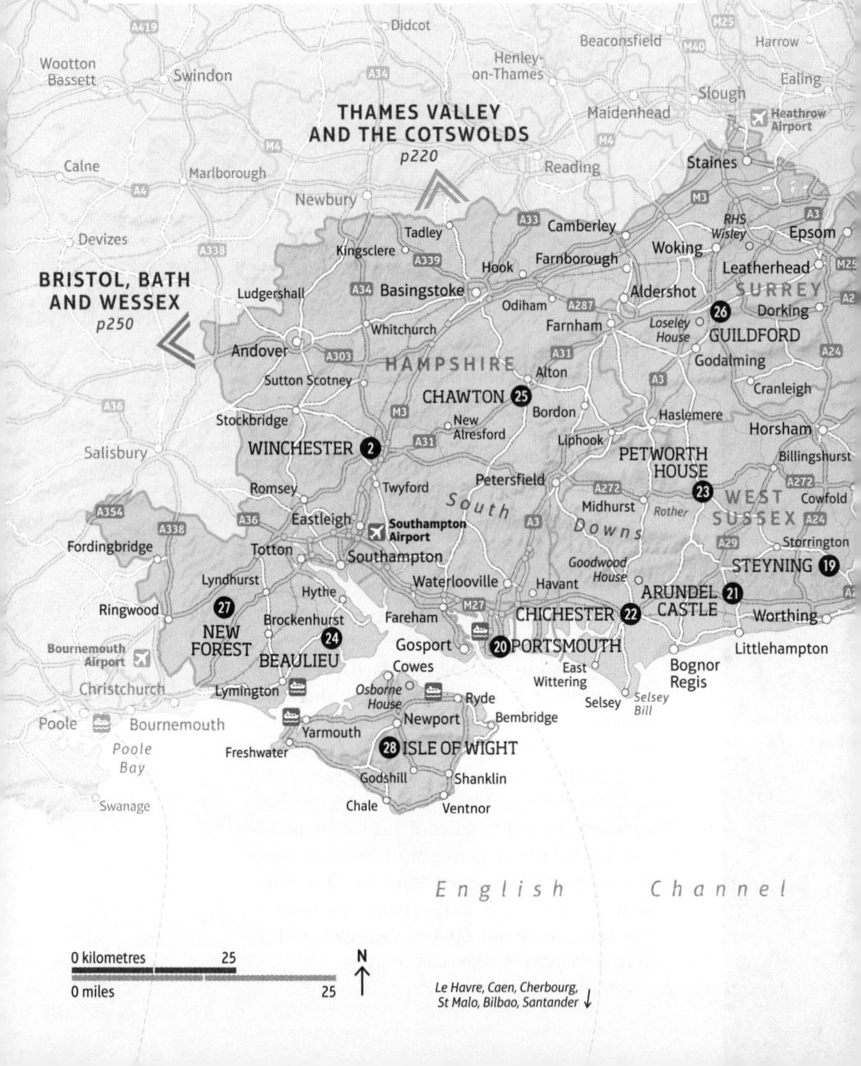

THAMES VALLEY AND THE COTSWOLDS
p220

BRISTOL, BATH AND WESSEX
p250

0 kilometres   25
0 miles   25

N
↑

Le Havre, Caen, Cherbourg, St Malo, Bilbao, Santander ↓

English Channel

❶

BRIGHTON

📍 East Sussex 🚉 Brighton 🚌 Pool Valley ℹ️ Brighton Centre, King's Rd; www.visitbrighton.com

London's nearest South Coast resort, Brighton has always attracted a sophisticated crowd. The spirit of the Prince Regent lives on, not only in his splendid Pavilion, but in the city's buzzing nightlife, independent shops, thriving LGBT+ scene and progressive politics.

Brighton Palace Pier

📍 Madeira Drive
🌐 brightonpier.co.uk

Opened in 1899, the large Brighton Palace Pier (also known simply as Brighton Pier) retains a Victorian ambience while catering for modern visitors with game arcades, bars, fish and chip restaurants and funfair rides, such as a roller-coaster, dodgems and carousels.

②

West Pier

🌐 westpier.co.uk

A distinctive landmark west of Brighton Pier, the now-derelict West Pier was built in 1866 and had a popular concert hall in its heyday. Its popularity declined from the 1950s and it eventually closed in 1975.

Brighton Museum & Art Gallery

📍 Royal Pavilion Gardens
🕙 10am–5pm Tue–Sun
🌐 brightonmuseums.org.uk

This lovely museum and art gallery, part of the Royal Pavillion Estate, has wonderfully varied exhibits ranging from art and design, fine art and fashion to natural sciences and archaeology, all enhanced by state-of-the-art interactive displays.

→
Displays in the Brighton Museum & Art Gallery

↑ Brighton's Victorian pleasure pier, also known as the Palace Pier

④
Volk's Electric Railway

⌂ Aquarium Station to Black Rock Station
⊙ Spring and summer

Opened in 1883, Volk's is the world's oldest operating public elecric railway. It provides a fun ride along the Brighton seafront from the pier to the marina in season, taking about 12 minutes, and can carry up to 80 passengers.

The son of a German clock-maker, Magnus Volk, who designed the railway, was an inventor and pioneering electrical engineer born in Brighton in 1851.

Did You Know?

Brighton is the only town in Britain with a Grade I- listed pier.

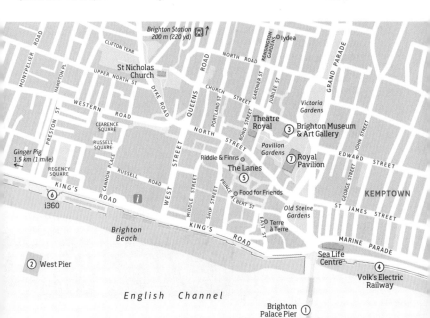

EAT

Food for Friends
Knockout vegetarian and vegan delights in a light-filled interior.

17-18 Prince Albert St
foodforfriends.com

£££

Ginger Pig
A traditional but classy pub just off the seafront offering delicious British food sourced from local suppliers.

3 Hove St, Hove
thegingerpigpub.com

£££

Terre à Terre
An acclaimed restaurant in The Lanes serving world-inspired vegetarian dishes.

71 East St
terreaterre.co.uk

£££

Iydea
This award-winning vegetarian café serves delicious, freshly prepared dishes.

17 Kensington Gardens From 5:30pm
iydea.co.uk

£££

Riddle & Finns
The flagship of this champagne and oyster bar chain in The Lanes serves superb fresh seafood and fish in a casual setting.

12B Meeting House Lane riddleand finns.co.uk

£££

(5) (🏛)

The Lanes

The original streets of the fishing village of Brighthelstone, this is the oldest part of Brighton. The maze of narrow alleys, completed around the middle of the 18th century, is full of independent shops and boutiques and forms the city's most popular shopping district. It is packed with all sorts of shops, from antiques stores and jewellers to gift shops and clothes boutiques. Head north of the Lanes for North Laine, another lively shopping district full of independent shops lining wider thoroughfares.

---

(6)

i360

Lower King's Rd
10am–7:30pm daily (to 9:30pm Fri & Sat)
britishairwaysi360.com

This breathtaking "vertical cable car" is a sleek glass pod that rises 137 m (450 ft) up a

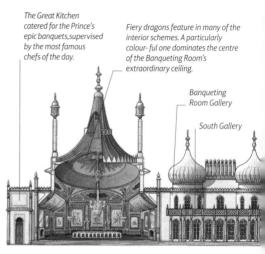

The Great Kitchen catered for the Prince's epic banquets, supervised by the most famous chefs of the day.

Fiery dragons feature in many of the interior schemes. A particularly colour-ful one dominates the centre of the Banqueting Room's extraordinary ceiling.

Banqueting Room Gallery

South Gallery

↑ Colourful bunting adorning the Lanes shopping area

giant silver needle to provide superb 360° vistas. At the foot of the needle is a fine beachside restaurant. Inside the pod is the "Skybar", open at night for a unique view of the stars over the sea.

> **For the Royal Pavilion Nash drew heavily from Islamic buildings such as the Taj Mahal, but called this design his "Hindu style".**

⑦ 🎨 🎭 🖥 🏛
Royal Pavilion

🏛 Old Steine, Brighton
🕐 Apr–Sep: 9:30am–5:45pm daily; Oct–Mar: 10am–5:15pm daily (last adm: 45 mins before closing)
🗓 25 & 26 Dec 🌐 brighton museums.org.uk

The Prince of Wales's opulent seaside retreat, designed to echo the palaces of Mughal India, epitomises the extravagant pleasures of Brighton in its 19th-century heyday and its quirky charm today. As sea bathing became increasingly popular in the mid-18th century, Brighton was transformed into England's most fashionable seaside resort. Its gaiety soon appealed to the rakish Prince of Wales, who became George IV in 1820. When, in 1785, at the age of 23 he

secretly married Mrs Fitzherbert, a 29-year-old Catholic widow, it was here that they conducted their liaison. He acquired a farmhouse near the shore, and in 1815, once he had become Regent – just one small step to the throne – he employed Henry Holland and later John Nash to transform it into a lavish Oriental palace.

Completed in 1823, the exotic exterior of this seaside retreat has remained largely unaltered. Queen Victoria sold the Pavilion to the town of Brighton in 1850. The delightful Regency Pavilion gardens have been restored following Nash's original 1820s plans.

The splendid Royal Pavilion, constructed with Bath stone, with an exuberant interior

↓

The central Dome is an imposing onion dome decorated with delicate tracery. Nash drew heavily from Islamic buildings such as the Taj Mahal, but called this design his "Hindu style".

A 70-piece orchestra played for the Prince's guests in the exquisitely decorated Music Room with crimson and gold murals.

Muezzin-like turrets

Cast iron dome

Music Room Gallery

Yellow Bow Rooms

WINCHESTER

 Hampshire 🚉🚌 ℹ Guildhall, High St;
www.visitwinchester.co.uk

Capital of the ancient kingdom of Wessex, the city of
Winchester was also the headquarters of the Anglo-
Saxon kings until the Norman Conquest (p48). William
the Conqueror built one of his first English castles
here. The only surviving part of the castle is the Great
Hall, erected in 1235 to replace the original. It is now
home to the legendary Round Table.

💬 INSIDER TIP
**Winchester
River Walk**

Starting at the
cathedral, this lovely
circular walk along the
riverside path leads to
St Catherine's Hill, at
the top of which there
are sweeping views of
the South Downs and
the city. You then reach
the Hospital of St Cross,
followed by Winchester
College, before arriving
back at the cathedral.

Westgate Museum

🏛 High St 📞 01962 869864
🕐 Mid-Feb-Oct: Sat & Sun
(Jul & Aug daily)

Housed above one of the
two surviving 12th-century
gatehouses in the city wall,
this room (once a prison) has
walls covered in prisoners'
graffiti and a 16th-century
painted ceiling, moved here
from Winchester College,
England's oldest fee-paying,
or "public" school. There are
great views from the roof.

Great Hall and
Round Table

🏛 Castle Ave 🕐 10am-5pm
daily 🌐 hants.gov.uk/
greathall

The 13th-century Great
Hall is the only part of the
former Winchester Castle that
was spared destruction by
Oliver Cromwell in the 17th
century and is one of the
finest surviving medieval
aisled halls in England. On the
wall is the iconic Round Table,
designed in legend by King
Arthur (p294), who had it

The historic city of Winchester on the edge of the South Downs

shaped so none of his knights could claim precedence. It was said to have been built by the wizard Merlin but was actually made in the 13th century. Outside the Great Hall is Queen Eleanor's Garden, a tranquil, re-created medieval garden.

③

Wolvesey Castle

🏠 College St 🕐 Apr-Oct: 10am-5pm daily 🌐 english-heritage.org

Winchester has been an ecclesiastical centre for many centuries. Wolvesey Castle (built around 1110) was the home of the cathedral's bishops in the Middle Ages. The extensive ruins evoke the former grandeur of the castle. In 1554 Queen Mary and Prince Philip II of Spain celebrated their wedding with a banquet here.

The Round Table in Winchester's Great Hall, steeped in history and myth

④

Winchester College

🏠 College St 🕐 For guided tours only 🌐 winchestercollege.org

Established by William Wykeham, Bishop of Winchester, in 1393, this distinguished private school offers daily guided tours of the beautiful Gothic chapel, the dining hall, cloisters and a 17th-century open classroom where exams still take place.

⑤

Hospital of St Cross

🏠 St Cross Rd 🕐 Apr-Oct: 9:30am-5pm Mon-Sat, 1-5pm Sun; Nov-Mar: 10:30am-3:30pm Mon-Sat 🌐 hospitalofstcross.co.uk

The Hospital of St Cross is an almshouse founded in the 12th century by Henry of Blois, a grandson of William the Conqueror, and is said to be the oldest charitable institution in England. A secular establishment, it is run by the 25 Brothers of St Cross, who are appointed by the Hospital Trust. In the Middle Ages it sheltered and provided food and drink for those in need. Today weary strangers may still claim the "Wayfarer's Dole" from the Brothers – a horn (cup) of ale and a crust of bread, given out since medieval times.

EAT

Wykeham Arms

Dating to 1755, when it was a coaching inn, this wonderful historic pub is full of bric-a-brac and serves a wide range of drinks to accompany a varied menu. Lord Nelson is said to have stayed here.

🏠 75 Kingsgate St 🌐 wykehamarmswinchester.co.uk

££££

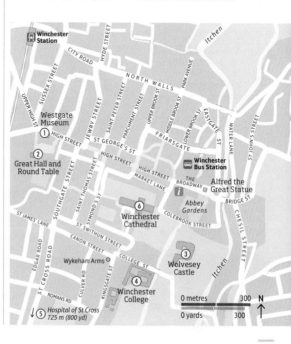

⑥ 🤿 Ⓜ 🖥

WINCHESTER CATHEDRAL

🏠 **The Close** 🕐 9:30am–5pm Mon–Sat, 12:30–3pm Sun
🌐 winchester-cathedral.org.uk

This magnificent building is one of the largest Gothic cathedrals in Europe. The first church was built here in 648, but the present building was begun in 1079 and was originally a Benedictine monastery. Much of the Norman architecture remains, although some of the domestic buildings used by the monks, including the refectory and cloister, were destroyed during the Dissolution of the Monasteries (p391).

Among the highlights of the cathedral are the exquisitely beautiful 12th-century illuminated Winchester Bible, intricately carved medieval choir stalls and wall paintings. It is also the resting place of Saxon royalty, bishops and the writer Jane Austen, who died in Winchester in 1817 and is buried near the entrance in the north aisle of the nave. Informative guided tours of the crypt and the cathedral are included in the admission price. For an additional fee, the tower tour takes you up onto the nave roof, from where there are superb views across Winchester.

WILLIAM WALKER

The water table is very near the surface here, so when, in the early 20th century, the cathedral's east end was in dire need of work to underpin its foundations, it had to be done underwater. From 1906 to 1911, William Walker, a deep-sea diver, worked 6 hours a day laying sacks of cement beneath the unsteady walls until the building was safe.

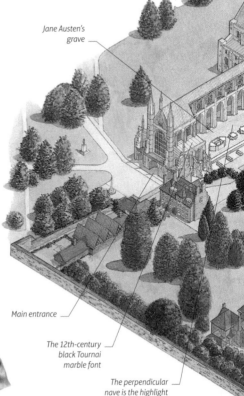

Jane Austen's grave

Main entrance

The 12th-century black Tournai marble font

The perpendicular nave is the highlight of the building.

Winchester Cathedral's façade and its vaulted nave *(inset)*, the longest of any Gothic cathedral in Europe

The magnificent choirstalls (c 1308) are England's oldest.

The Lady Chapel was rebuilt by Elizabeth of York (c 1500) after her son was baptized here.

Author Izaac Walton (1593–1683) is depicted in the 1914 stained-glass Anglers' Window.

← The Cathedral, sitting amid green space and historic buildings

The Library has over 4,000 books, including the 12th-century Winchester Bible..

Prior's Hall

The Close still retains some lovely timber-framed buildings dating to the time when this was the Priory of St Swithun.

The Norman Chapterhouse ceased to be used in 1580. Only the Norman arches survive.

❸

CANTERBURY

⌂ Kent 🚃🚌 ℹ The Beaney, 18 High St; www.canterbury.co.uk

The beautiful city of Canterbury has been a major Christian pilgrimage site for the last 900 years, since the building of its glorious cathedral in 1070 and the martyrdom of Thomas Becket a century later.

Its position on the London to Dover route meant Canterbury was an important Roman town even before the arrival of St Augustine in 597 to convert the Anglo-Saxons to Christianity. The town soon became the centre of the Christian Church in England.

The first Norman archbishop, Lanfranc, ordered a new **cathedral** to be built on the ruins of the Anglo-Saxon cathedral in 1070. It was enlarged and rebuilt many times and as a result embraces examples of all styles of medieval architecture. The most poignant moment in its history came in 1170 when Thomas Becket was murdered here. Four years after his death a fire devastated the cathedral and the Trinity Chapel was built to house Becket's remains. The shrine quickly became an important religious site.

For a glimpse into the city's ancient past, visit the **Canterbury Roman Museum** and the ancient city walls, which include the Westgate Towers, England's oldest surviving medieval gateway. Experience medieval Canterbury at **The Canterbury Tales**, which brings Geoffrey Chaucer's famous pilgrimage stories to life. Slightly beyond the city centre, adjacent to the ruins of St Augustine's Abbey, is St Martin's Church, the oldest in England, where St Augustine first worshipped.

Canterbury Cathedral

♿⊘ ⌂ 11 The Precincts, Canterbury ⌚ 9am–5:30pm Mon–Sat (to 5pm winter), 12:30–2:30pm Sun 🆆 canterbury-cathedral.org

Canterbury Roman Museum

♿ ⌂ Longmarket, Butchery Lane ⌚ 10am–5pm daily 🆆 canterburymuseums.co.uk

The Canterbury Tales

♿⊘ ⌂ St Margaret's St ⌚ Apr–Oct: 10am–5pm daily (Sep & Oct: to 4pm); Nov–Mar: 10am–4pm Wed–Sun 🆆 canterburytales.org.uk

↑ Traditional old houses lining the River Stour in Canterbury

GEOFFREY CHAUCER

Considered to be the first great English poet, Geoffrey Chaucer (c 1345–1400) wrote what is thought by many to be one of the greatest and most entertaining works of early English literature, the *Canterbury Tales* – a rumbustious account of a group of pilgrims travelling from London to Becket's shrine in 1387. The pilgrims represent a cross-section of 14th-century English society.

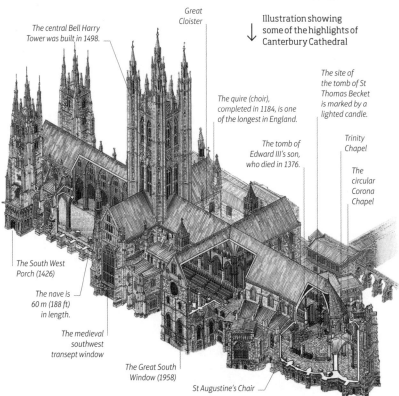

→ Illustration showing some of the highlights of Canterbury Cathedral

The central Bell Harry Tower was built in 1498.

Great Cloister

The quire (choir), completed in 1184, is one of the longest in England.

The site of the tomb of St Thomas Becket is marked by a lighted candle.

The tomb of Edward III's son, who died in 1376.

Trinity Chapel

The circular Corona Chapel

The South West Porch (1426)

The nave is 60 m (188 ft) in length.

The medieval southwest transept window

The Great South Window (1958)

St Augustine's Chair

EXPERIENCE MORE

4

Margate

 Kent   The Droit House, Stone Pier; www.visitthanet.co.uk

A classic seaside resort with fine sand beaches, Margate is a draw not only for its amusement park, Dreamland, but also for the **Turner Contemporary** art gallery. This spectacular modern building celebrates the town's connections with J M W Turner and hosts eclectic exhibitions.

Just south is a 19th-century estate, **Quex Park**. The adjoining **Powell-Cotton Museum** has a fine collection of predominantly African art and artifacts, as well as wildlife dioramas.

To the west is a Saxon church, built within the remains of the bleak Roman coastal fort of Reculver. Access to Reculver is any time during daylight hours.

Turner Contemporary

⊚ ⊕ ⊓ Rendezvous
⊙ 10am–6pm Tue–Sun
⊎ turnercontemporary.org

Quex Park & Powell-Cotton Museum

⊘ ⊚ ⊕ ⊓ Birchington
⊙ 10am–5pm Tue–Sun
(House: Apr–Oct: 1–4pm daily) ⊎ quexpark.co.uk

5

Leeds Castle

⊓ Maidstone, Kent
⊟ Bearsted, then bus
⊙ 10:30am–5:30pm daily (Oct–Mar: to 4pm)
⊟ 1st w/e Nov
⊎ leeds-castle.com

Surrounded by a lake that reflects the warm buff stone of its crenellated turrets, Leeds is among the most beautiful castles in England. Celebrating its 900th anniversary in 2019, it has been continuously inhabited and its present appearance is the result of centuries of rebuilding and extensions, most recently in the 1930s.

Leeds has many royal connections going back to 1278, when it was given to Edward I by a courtier seeking favour. Henry VIII loved the castle and visited it often to escape the plague in London. It contains a life-sized bust of Henry VII from the late 16th century. Leeds passed out of royal ownership when Edward VI gave it to Sir Anthony St Leger in 1552 as a reward for helping to pacify the Irish.

↓ The striking architecture of the Turner Contemporary art gallery in Margate

6

Rochester

 Kent ⊞ ⊟ ⊓ 95 High St; 01634 338141

Clustered at the mouth of the River Medway are the towns of Rochester and Chatham, both rich in naval history.

England's tallest Norman keep is at **Rochester Castle**, worth climbing for the views over the Medway. The town's medieval history is still visible, with the original city walls on view in the High Street, along with wall paintings in the cathedral, built in 1088.

In Chatham, the **Historic Dockyard** is now a museum of shipbuilding and the Age of Sail. **Fort Amherst** nearby was built in 1756 to protect the dockyard from attack and has 1,800 m (5,570 ft) of tunnels to explore that were hewn by Napoleonic prisoners of war.

EXPERIENCE The Downs and Channel Coast

Sea view from the top of the iconic white cliffs of Dover ↑

Rochester Castle

 ⬜ Castle Hill
☎ 01634 335882
⏰ 10am–4pm daily (Apr–Sep: to 6pm; last adm: 45 mins before closing)

Historic Dockyard

⬜ Dock Rd, Chatham ⏰ Feb–Nov: 10am–6pm daily (Feb: to 3pm; Mar & Nov: to 4pm) 🌐 thedockyard.co.uk

Fort Amherst

⬜ Dock Rd, Chatham ⏰ 8am–4pm daily 🌐 fortamherst.com

7

Whitstable

⬜ Kent 🚆 🚌 ℹ 34 Harbour St; 01227 770060

Celebrated for its oysters since Roman times, Whitstable is the prettiest of the old fishing towns on the North Kent coast, with brightly painted buildings, atmospheric alleyways, a busy little harbour and a long shingle beach lined with colourful huts. Plenty of lively restaurants specialize in local seafood. The bustling Whitstable Oyster Festival takes place each July, a tradition dating from Norman times. There are also many art and craft shops. On the beach, the walk westwards is especially lovely.

8

Dover

⬜ Kent 🚆 🚌 ℹ Dover Museum, Market Sq; www.whitecliffscountry.org.uk

Its proximity to the European mainland makes Dover the leading port for cross-Channel travel. Its famous white cliffs exert a strong pull on returning travellers.

Due to its strategic position and large natural harbour, Dover has played a key role in the nation's defences. Built on the site of a Saxon fort, **Dover Castle** helped defend the town from 1198, when Henry II first built the keep, right up to World War II, when it was used as the command post for the Dunkirk evacuation.

Some 3 km (2 miles) inland, one of the most significant sites in England's early history is the ruin of **Richborough Roman Fort**. Now a grassy site, this was where, in AD 43, Claudius's Roman invaders made their first landing.

Dover Castle

⬜ Castle Hill
⏰ Times vary, see website
🌐 english-heritage.org.uk

Richborough Roman Fort

⬜ Richborough
⏰ Apr–Sep: 10am–6pm daily; Oct: 10am–5pm Wed–Sun; Nov–Mar: 10am–4pm Sat & Sun 🌐 english-heritage.org.uk

EAT

Whitstable Oyster Company
Kentish oysters headline the menu at this seafood specialist.

⬜ Horsebridge, Whitstable
🌐 whitstableoyster company.com

££££

Hantverk & Found
An unconventional seafood café-restaurant with a daily changing, locally sourced menu.

⬜ 16–18 King St, Margate
⏰ Mon–Wed & Sun pm
🌐 hantverk-found.co.uk

££££

The Allotment
Unpretentious yet stylish, this restaurant serves local meat dishes and afternoon teas.

⬜ 9 High St, Dover
⏰ Sun & Mon
🌐 theallotment restaurant.com

££££

Al fresco eating at the elegant Pantiles, Royal Tunbridge Wells

DRINK

The Mount Edgcumbe

You can sup local ales and craft beers in a number of intimate spaces, including a sandstone cave, at this pub with a terrace overlooking Tunbridge Wells Common.

◫ The Common, Royal Tunbridge Wells
ⓦ themount edgcumbe.com

The Duke of York

At the heart of the Pantiles, this 18th-century pub with a wooden ceiling offers a cosy spot for a pint in the winter and outside tables in the summer.

◫ 17 The Pantiles, Royal Tunbridge Wells
ⓦ dukeofyork tunbridgewells.co.uk

The Bucks Head

A classic English country pub with oak beams, a log fire and wood panelling.

◫ Park Lane, Godden Green, near Knole Park
ⓦ buckshead sevenoaks.co.uk

❾ Royal Tunbridge Wells

◫ Kent ▣▣ ⓘ The Corn Exchange, The Pantiles; www.visittunbridge wells.com

Helped by royal patronage, the town became a popular spa after mineral springs were discovered in 1606. The Pantiles – the colonnaded and paved promenade – was laid out in the 1700s.

Nearby manor house **Penshurst Place**, built in the 1340s, has an 18-m-(60-ft-) high Great Hall.

Penshurst Place

⊗ ⓣ ⊜ ⓐ ◫ Tonbridge, Kent ◷ Apr–Oct: Daily (House & Toy Museum: noon–4pm; Gardens: 10:30am–6pm) ⓦ penshurstplace.com

❿

Knole

◫ Sevenoaks, Kent
▣ Sevenoaks then taxi
◷ Mar–Oct: 11am–5pm Tue–Sun, public hols pm; Park: dawn–dusk daily
ⓦ nationaltrust.org.uk

This huge Tudor mansion was built in the late 15th century

and was seized by Henry VIII from the Archbishop of Canterbury at the Dissolution (p391). In 1566 Queen Elizabeth I gave it to her cousin Thomas Sackville. His descendants have lived here ever since, including the writer Vita Sackville-West (1892–1962). The house is well known for its 17th-century furniture, such as the elaborate bed made for James II. The 405-ha (1,000-acre) park has deer and lovely walks.

East of Knowle, **Ightham Mote** is the most complete medieval manor house in England, with parts dating back to the 1320s. Its stone-and-timber building has over 70 rooms and a grand courtyard. Rooms are decorated in a range of styles from across the centuries, including a 15th-century chapel with an ornate 16th-century painted oak ceiling and a drawing room with hand-painted 18th-century Chinese wallpaper. The house is surrounded by a placid moat, crossed by three bridges, and is set in beautifully manicured gardens.

About 40 km (25 miles) southeast, **Sissinghurst Castle Garden** has gardens created by Vita Sackville-West and her husband Harold Nicolson in the 1930s.

The moat around Hever Castle, where Anne Boleyn lived as a young woman

Ightham Mote

 Ivy Hatch, Sevenoaks ◷Mar-Oct: 11am-5pm daily; Dec: 11am-3pm daily; Gardens: 10am-5pm daily (Nov & Dec: to 4pm) ⓦnationaltrust.org.uk

Sissinghurst Castle Garden

Cranbrook ◷Mar-Oct: 11am-5:30pm daily ⓦnationaltrust.org.uk

Hever Castle

Edenbridge, Kent
Edenbridge Town
◷Jan-Mar & Nov: noon-4:30pm Wed-Sun; Apr-Oct & Dec: noon-6pm daily
ⓦhevercastle.co.uk

This small, moated castle was the 16th-century home of Anne Boleyn, the doomed wife of Henry VIII, executed for adultery. She lived here as a young woman, and the king often visited her while staying at Leeds Castle. In 1903 Hever was bought by William Waldorf Astor, who began a restoration programme, building a Neo-Tudor village alongside it for guests and servants. The moat and gatehouse date from around 1270.

Inside the house, visitors can see Anne Boleyn's bedroom and other apartments, while the gardens are filled with sculptures, grottoes and imaginative topiary.

To the northwest of Hever is **Chartwell**, the family home of one of Britain's greatest politicians, Sir Winston Churchill. Before he became prime minister in 1940, he expended a lot of his energy on improving Chartwell, and with Lady Churchill he created magnificent gardens, with lakes, black swans, a rose garden and gorgeous views over the Kent Weald. His greatest hobby was painting, and his studio is lined with beautiful landscapes and portraits he painted at Chartwell and on his international travels.

After he died, Lady Churchill left the house almost immediately, and the main rooms are still preserved very much as she left them. Enormously atmospheric, they are full of books, photos, cigar stubs, letters, memorabilia and gifts from various world figures, giving a rich sense of Sir Winston's life and personality.

Chartwell

Mapleton Rd, Westerham, Kent ◷Times vary, check website ⓦnationaltrust.org.uk

---

KENT: THE GARDEN OF ENGLAND

With its fertile soil, mild climate and regular rainfall, the Kentish countryside has flourished as a fruit-growing region ever since its first orchards were planted by the Romans. The orchards are dazzling during the blossoming season, and in the autumn the branches sag under the weight of ripening fruit - a familiar sight that inspired the journalist, politician and farmer William Cobbett (1763-1835) to describe the area as "the very finest as to fertility and diminutive beauty in the whole world."

Romney Marsh

🏛 Kent 🚉 Ashford
🚌 Ashford, Hythe
ℹ Dymchurch Rd, New
Romney; www.kent
wildlifetrust.org.uk

Once upon a time, Romney Marsh and its neighbour Walland Marsh were entirely covered by the sea at high tide. The Romans drained the Romney section, and Walland Marsh was reclaimed during the Middle Ages. Together they formed a large area of fertile land, particularly suitable for the Romney Marsh sheep bred for the quality of their wool.

Fourteen medieval churches are scattered over the Marsh. Dungeness, a desolate spot at the southeastern tip of the area, is dominated by a lighthouse and a nuclear power station. It is also the southern terminus of the Romney, Hythe and Dymchurch Light Railway. From April to October, this takes passengers 23 km (14 miles) up the coast to Hythe on trains one third the conventional size. Visit www. rhdr.org.uk for more details.

The Kent Wildlife Trust Visitor Centre explores the Marsh's history and wildlife.

Rye

🏛 East Sussex 🚉 🚌
ℹ Strand Quay; www.visit
1066country.com/rye

In 1287, a huge storm diverted the River Rother so that it met the sea at Rye, and for more than 300 years thereafter, this charming fortified town was one of the main Channel ports. The brick-and-timber warehouses on Strand Quay survive from the prosperous days when Rye was a thriving port. In the 16th century the harbour began to silt up, and the town is now 3 km (2 miles) inland.

Cobbled Mermaid Street, lined with houses jutting out at unlikely angles, has hardly altered since the 14th century. On this street, the Mermaid Inn, rebuilt around 1420, is Rye's largest medieval edifice. On nearby West Street, Lamb House was the residence of Henry James from 1897 to 1914. Built in 1722, this fine Georgian house is now a writer's museum. Ypres Tower on Pump Street, built under Henry II in 1250 as a defence against the French, contains a museum with exhibits of medieval artifacts.

About 6 km (4 miles) southeast of Rye, Camber Sands is a popular beach for swimming and kite- and windsurfing. West of the beach, near Brede Lock, are the ruins of Camber Castle, one of the coastal forts built by Henry VIII.

↑ Novices chamber, part of the Battle Abbey ruins on the site of the Battle of Hastings

⑭ Bodiam Castle

🏠 Nr Robertsbridge, E Sussex 📞 01580 830196
🚉 Robertsbridge then taxi
🕐 11am–5pm daily (Mar–Oct: to 4pm)

Surrounded by a wide moat, this late 14th-century castle, with its wooden portcullis and spiral staircases, is one of the most romantic in England.

Previously believed to have been built as a defence against French invasion, it is now thought to have been intended as a home for a Sussex knight. During the Civil War in 1642–51 *(p49)*, Parliamentary soldiers removed the roof to restrict the castle's use as a base for Charles I's troops. It has been uninhabited since. With the exception of the roof, it was restored in 1919 by Lord Curzon, who gave it to the nation.

To the east is **Great Dixter**, a 15th-century manor house restored by Sir Edwin Lutyens in 1910. The late Christopher Lloyd created a magnificent garden with a blend of terraces and borders, and a great nursery, too.

← Charming half-timbered houses lining cobbled Mermaid Street, Rye

Great Dixter

🏠 Northiam, Rye
🕐 Apr–Oct: 11am–5pm Tue–Sun & public hols
🌐 greatdixter.co.uk

---

⑮ Winchelsea

🏠 East Sussex 🚉🚌
🌐 winchelsea.com

Just 3 km (2 miles) south of Rye is the small town of Winchelsea. At the behest of Edward I, it was moved to its present position on higher ground in 1288, when most of the old town on lower and to the southeast was submerged by the same storm that diverted the River Rother in 1287. Winchelsea is probably Britain's first coherently planned medieval town. Although not all of it was built as originally planned, its rectangular grid survives today, as does the Church of St Thomas Becket (begun c 1300) at its centre. The church has several well-preserved, superbly carved medieval tombs in the chantry. The three windows (1928–33) in the Lady Chapel were designed by Douglas Strachan as a memorial to those who died in World War I.

The beach below the town is one of the finest on the southeast coast.

⑯ Hastings

🏠 East Sussex 🚉🚌
ℹ Muriel Matters House, Breeds Place; www.visit 1066country.com

This seaside town was one of the first Cinque Ports (a confederation of five port towns founded for military and trade purposes) and is still a thriving fishing port. In the 19th century, the area to the west of the Old Town was built up as a seaside resort, which left the narrow, characterful streets of the old fishermen's quarter intact.

Eleven km (7 miles) from Hastings is the small town of Battle, whose central square is dominated by the gatehouse of **Battle Abbey**. William the Conqueror built this on the site of his great victory, reputedly placing the high altar where Harold fell, but the abbey was destroyed in the Dissolution *(p391)*. Visitors can take an evocative walk around the actual battlefield.

Battle Abbey

🏠 High St, Battle
📞 01424 775705 🕐 Apr–Oct: 10am–6pm daily; Nov–Mar: 10am–4pm Sat & Sun

---

> **BATTLE OF HASTINGS**
>
> In 1066, William the Conqueror's army from Normandy, France, landed on the south coast of England, aiming to take Winchester and London. Hearing that King Harold and his army were camped just inland from Hastings, William confronted them. He won the battle after Harold was mortally wounded by an arrow to the eye. Audio guides, along with displays and a film at the visitor's centre bring the battle to life.

⓱

Eastbourne

🏛 East Sussex 🚆🚌
ℹ Cornfield Rd; www.
visiteastbourne.com

With its pier and beachside promenade, Eastbourne is a classic Victorian seaside resort. It is also the starting point of the South Downs Way (p190) and an excellent base for touring the South Downs. The path begins at Beachy Head, the spectacular 163-m (536-ft) chalk cliff just on the outskirts of the town. From here it is a bracing walk to the clifftop at Birling Gap, with views to the Seven Sisters. To the west of Eastbourne is **Seven Sisters Country Park** (p191).

Just north is the village of Alfriston, with an ancient market cross and a 15th-century inn, The Star. Nearby is the 14th-century **Clergy House**, which became the first National Trust property in 1896.

Bexhill-on-Sea, 19 km (12 miles) east of Alfriston, features the 1935 Art Deco **De La Warr Pavilion**, which hosts art exhibitions and has a café with fabulous sea views.

Seven Sisters Country Park

🍴🛒🏛 Exceat, Seaford
🕐 Apr–Sep: 10:30am–4:30pm daily; Mar & Nov: 11am–4pm Sat & Sun; Oct: 11am–4pm daily 🌐 sevensisters.org.uk

Clergy House

🍴🏛🚾 🏛 Alfriston
🕐 Mar–Oct: 10:30am–5pm Sat–Wed (Jul & Aug: also Fri)
🌐 nationaltrust.org.uk

De La Warr Pavilion

🍴🛒🏛 🏛 Marina, Bexhill-on-Sea 🕐 10am–6pm daily
🌐 dlwp.com

⓲

Lewes

🏛 East Sussex 🚆
ℹ 187 High St; www.
staylewes.org

The ancient county town of Sussex was a strategic site for the Saxons because of its high vantage point over the coastline. William the Conqueror built a wooden castle here in 1067; this was replaced by a large stone structure whose remains can be visited today. In 1264 it was the site of a

HIDDEN GEM
Farleys House

Tucked in the countryside 16 km (10 miles) east of Lewes is the former home of photographer Lee Miller and Surrealist artist Roland Penrose, where they lived for 35 years from 1949. It displays their works and those by their friends, who included Picasso and Man Ray (www.farleyshouse.co.uk).

critical battle in which Simon de Montfort and his barons defeated Henry III, enabling them to establish the first English Parliament, though this victory was shortlived.

The Tudor **Anne of Cleves House** is a museum of local history, although Anne of Cleves, Henry VIII's fourth wife, never actually lived here.

On Guy Fawkes Night (p45) lighted tar barrels are rolled to the river and various effigies, including of the Pope and Guy Fawkes, are burned. This commemorates the town's 17 Protestant martyrs burnt at the stake by Mary I.

Nearby are the 16th-century **Glynde Place**, a fine courtyard house, and the art-filled **Charleston**, the former country home of Vanessa Bell and Duncan Grant, members the Bloomsbury Group *(p111)*. Also nearby is **Glyndebourne** opera house that plays host to the namesake festival (May–Aug).

Anne of Cleves House

⊘ ⊕ 🏠 Lewes ⊙ Times vary, check website 🆆 sussexpast.co.uk

Glynde Place

⊘ ⊘ ⊟ ⊕ 🏠 Lewes ⊙ May-Jun: 2-5pm daily 🆆 glynde.co.uk

Charleston

⊘ ⊘ ⊟ ⊕ 🏠 Lewes ⊙ Mar-Oct: 11:30am-5pm Wed, noon-5pm Sun & bank hols 🆆 charleston.org.uk

Glyndebourne

⊘ ⊘ ⊟ ⊕ 🏠 Lewes 🆆 glyndebourne.com

19

Steyning

🏠 West Sussex 🚌
🛈 9 Causeway, Horsham; www.steyning southdowns.co.uk

This charming little town below the Downs is full of well-preserved timber-framed houses from the Tudor era and earlier. In Saxon times, Steyning was an important port on the River Adur, and a splendid 12th-century church is evidence of its medieval prosperity. In the 14th century the river silted up, but the town later became a coaching stop. Just to the southeast of the centre of Steyning are the gaunt ruins of a Norman motte-and-bailey defensive fort, Bramber Castle. Also in Bramber, once a separate village, is **St Mary's House**, a timber-framed manor built around 1470, with fine panelled rooms and beautiful gardens with topiary figures.

St Mary's House

⊘ ⊘ ⊟ 🏠 Bramber ⊙ May-Sep: 2-6pm Thu, Sun & public hols (also Wed in Aug) 🆆 stmarysbramber.co.uk

EAT

Limetree Kitchen

The eclectic menu here features Asian flavours in both mains and sharing plates. There's a stripped-back, shabby-chic interior and a simple terrace.

🏠 14 Station St, Lewes 🕐 Sun pm, Mon & Tue 🆆 limetreekitchen.co.uk

Ⓕ ⓕ ⓕ

Tiger Inn

This country pub has a log fire for cold days and outdoor tables in the summer. The menu offers hearty dishes, such as ploughmans lunches and bangers and mash.

🏠 East Dean, Eastbourne 🆆 beachyhead.org.uk

Ⓕ ⓕ ⓕ

↑ Walking along the beach by the huge Seven Sisters chalk cliffs near Eastbourne

Portsmouth

🅰 Hampshire 🚇🚌 ⓘ The Hard Interchange; www.visitportsmouth.co.uk

Once a vital port, this vibrant city has a fascinating naval history. **Portsmouth Historic Dockyard** is the hub of the city's main sights. Among these is the hull of the *Mary Rose*, the favourite of Henry VIII (*p48*), which capsized on its maiden voyage in 1545. Recovered from the sea bed in 1982, it has been reunited, in the **Mary Rose Museum**, with many of the 19,000 16th-century objects that have been raised from the wreck. Nearby is the dockyard's most famous exhibit, HMS *Victory*, the English flagship on which Admiral Nelson was killed at Trafalgar. **The D-Day Story** is a museum that tells the story of the 1944 Allied landing in Normandy, France.

Portchester Castle, on the north edge of the harbour, was fortified in the 3rd century and is a great example of Roman sea defences. The Normans later used the Roman walls to enclose a castle – only the keep survives – and a church.

Less warlike attractions include the **Charles Dickens Birthplace Museum**, the house where the author was born in 1812 (*p174*), and the

striking **Spinnaker Tower**, rising to 170 m (558 ft) above Portsmouth; the views from the top are quite magnificent.

Portsmouth Historic Dockyard

⊘⊜⛾🍴🛍 🅰 Victory Gate, HM Naval Base 🕙 10am-5:30pm daily (Nov-Mar: to 5pm) 🌐 historicdockyard.co.uk

Mary Rose Museum

⊘⛾🍴 🅰 Portsmouth Historic Dockyard 🕙 10am-5:30pm daily (Nov-Mar: to 5pm) 🌐 maryrose.org

The D-Day Story

⊘⊜⛾🛍 🅰 Museum Rd 🕙 10am-5:30pm daily (Nov-Mar: to 5pm) 🌐 theddaystory.com

Portchester Castle

⊘⛾🅱🛍🅗 🅰 Church Rd, Portchester 🕙 Apr-Oct: 10am-6pm daily (Oct: to 5pm); Nov-Mar: 10am-4pm Sat & Sun 🌐 english-heritage.org.uk

Charles Dickens Birthplace Museum

⊘⛾ 🅰 393 Old Commercial Rd 🕙 Apr-Sep & 7 Feb: 10am-5:30pm Fri-Sun 🌐 charlesdickensbirthplace.co.uk

Spinnaker Tower

⊘⊜🛍 🅰 Gunwharf Quays 📞 023 9285 7520 🕙 10am-5:30pm daily

㉑

Arundel Castle

🅰 Arundel, West Sussex 🚉 Arundel 🕙 Apr-Oct: 10am-5pm Tue-Sun & public hols (Aug: daily; last adm: 4pm) 🌐 arundelcastle.org

Dominating the small river-side town, this vast, grey hilltop castle, surrounded by

←

HMS *Victory*, one of the highlights of Portsmouth Historic Dockyard

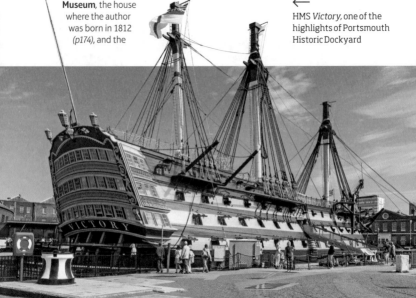

castellated walls, was originally built by the Normans. In the 16th century it was acquired by the powerful Dukes of Norfolk, the country's senior Roman Catholic family, whose descendants still live here. They rebuilt it after the original was virtually destroyed by Parliamentarians in 1643, and then once more in Gothic Revival style in the 19th century.

Chichester

🏠 West Sussex 🚉🚌
ℹ The Novium, Tower St; www.visitchichester.org

A well-preserved market town, Chichester is dominated by its **cathedral**, consecrated in 1108. The spire is said to be the only English cathedral spire visible from the sea. Also of interest is the cathedral's unique detached bell tower, dating from 1436.

There are two carved stone panels in the choir, dating from 1140. Modern works include paintings by Graham Sutherland (1903–80) and a stained-glass window by Marc Chagall (1887–1985).

The refurbished **Fishbourne Roman Palace**, between Chichester and Bosham, is the largest Roman villa in Britain. Constructed from AD 75, the palace featured advanced technology such as underfloor heating and indoor plumbing for baths. It was destroyed by fire in 285. The north wing has some of the finest mosaics in Britain, including one of Cupid.

To the north is the 18th-century **Goodwood House**. Its magnificent art collection features a number of works by Canaletto (1697–1768) and Stubbs (1724–1806).

↑ The interior of Chichester Cathedral, seen from the choir

Chichester Cathedral
🅿️🚗🏛 🏠 West St ⏰ 7:15am–6:30pm daily (to 5pm Sun)
🌐 chichestercathedral.org.uk

Fishbourne Roman Palace
♿🅿️🚗🏛 🏠 Roman Way
⏰ 10am–5pm daily; mid-Dec–Feb & Nov: 10am–4pm Sat & Sun 🌐 sussexpast.co.uk

Goodwood House
♿🅿️🚗🏛 🏠 Goodwood
⏰ Mar–Oct: 1–4:30pm Sun & Mon (Aug: Sun–Thu)
🔒 For special events; check website 🌐 goodwood.com

Petworth House

🏠 Petworth, West Sussex
🚉 Pulborough then bus
⏰ House: 11am–5pm daily (Nov–Feb: to 4pm); Park: 10am–5pm daily (Nov–Feb: to 4pm) 🌐 national trust.org.uk

This late 17th-century house was immortalized in a series of famous views by the painter J M W Turner. Some

> **ENGLISH WINE**
>
> There are more than 500 vineyards in Great Britain, most of them in the English southern counties of Kent and Sussex, where the drier, warmer climate provides better growing conditions. Sparkling varieties make up the bulk of production, such as Denbies (Surrey), Chapel Down (Kent) and Breaky Bottom (Sussex). Still whites are now appearing in increasing numbers too.

of his best paintings are on display here and are part of Petworth's outstanding art collection, which also includes works by Titian, Van Dyck and Gainsborough. Also well represented is ancient Roman and Greek sculpture, notably the 4th-century BC *Leconfield Aphrodite*, widely thought to be by Praxiteles.

The Carved Room is decorated with intricately carved wood panels of birds, flowers and musical instruments, by Grinling Gibbons (1648–1721).

The large deer park includes some of the earliest work of Capability Brown (*p24*).

> **A well-preserved market town, Chichester is dominated by its cathedral, consecrated in 1108. The spire is said to be the only English cathedral spire visible from the sea.**

←
Visitors admiring a vintage car in front of the National Motor Museum, Beaulieu

EAT

Boathouse
A beautiful spot on the waterfront to enjoy freshly caught fish, lobster and crab.
Steephill Cove, Isle of Wight PO38 Wed & Oct-Apr steephill-cove.co.uk
£££

The Elderflower
Imaginative seasonal dishes as well as crowd-pleasers like fish and chips are offered at this New Forest eatery.
4-5 Quay St, Lymington SO41 Sun pm, Mon & Tue elderflower restaurant.co.uk
£££

The Terrace
Local game and seafood are on the menu, along with produce from the organic kitchen garden.
The Montagu Arms, Beaulieu SO42 Mon & Tue montagu armshotel.co.uk
£££

24

Beaulieu

Brockenhurst, Hampshire Brockenhurst then taxi 10am-5pm daily (Jun-Sep: to 6pm) beaulieu.co.uk

Palace House, once the gatehouse of Beaulieu Abbey, contains the finest collection of vintage cars in the country at the National Motor Museum, along with boats used in the James Bond films.

There is also an exhibition of monastic life in the ruined abbey, founded in 1204 by King John for Cistercian monks.

Just south, the maritime museum at **Buckler's Hard** tells the story of shipbuilding in the 18th century. The yard employed 4,000 men at its peak but declined when steel began to be used.

Buckler's Hard
Beaulieu 10am-4:30pm daily (Apr-Sep: to 5pm) bucklershard.co.uk

25

Chawton

Hampshire Alton, then bus or taxi The Library, The Square, Petersfield; www.visit-hampshire.co.uk

This tranquil village, with its woods, ponds and cottages, is the site of **Jane Austen's House**, where the author lived with her mother and sister for the last eight years of her life. Chawton is where she wrote all her major novels, including *Sense and Sensibility* and *Pride and Prejudice*. Now a museum, the house displays her letters and furniture.

Just outside the village is **Chawton House**, a 1580s manor house that once belonged to Austen's brother Edward, who added a pretty walled rose garden. The house is now a centre for the study of women's writing between 1600 and 1830.

Jane Austen's House
Chawton Village Green Feb-May & Sep-Dec: 10:30am-4:30pm daily; Jun-Aug: 10am-5pm daily Jan jane-austens-house museum.org.uk.

Chawton House
Chawton House: late Mar-Oct: noon-4:30pm Mon-Fri, 11am-5pm Sun & public hols; Library: by appt all year Nov-late Mar chawtonhouse.org

26

Guildford

Surrey 155 High St; www.guildford.gov.uk

The county town of Surrey incorporates the remains of a small refurbished Norman castle. The high street is lined with Tudor buildings, such as the impressive Guildhall, and the huge red-brick cathedral, completed in 1954, dominates the town's skyline.

Guildford stands at the end of the North Downs, a range of chalk hills that are popular for walking. The area also has two famous beauty spots: Leith Hill and Box Hill. The view from the latter is well worth the short, steep climb from West Humble.

To the north of Guildford is **RHS Wisley** with 97 ha (240 acres) of beautiful gardens. To the southwest is **Loseley House**, a lavishly decorated mansion set in extensive gardens and unchanged since 1562.

RHS Wisley

⊛ ⊕ ☺ ⌂ ☐ Off A3
☐ 10am–6pm Mon–Fri, 9am–6pm Sat, Sun & bank hols
ⓦ rhs.org.uk

Loseley House

⊛ ⊛ ☺ ⌂ ☐ Surrey
☐ House: May–Jul: noon–4pm Mon–Thu, 1–5pm Sun; Gardens: May–Aug: 11am–5pm Sun–Thu (Aug: Mon–Wed only) ⓦ loseleypark.co.uk

---

COWES WEEK

Cowes Week is one of the largest regattas in the world. Every August, as many as 1,000 boats compete across dozens of racing classes, animating the waters of the Solent. The first race was held in 1826, when just seven yachts took part.

New Forest

☐ Hampshire
🚊 Brockenhurst
🚌 Lymington then bus
ℹ New Forest Heritage Centre, High St, Lyndhurst; www.thenewforest.co.uk

Despite its name, this vast expanse of heath and woodland is one of the few primeval oak woods in England. It was a popular hunting ground of Norman kings.

Today its many visitors share it with the New Forest ponies, unique to the area, and over 1,500 fallow deer.

Isle of Wight

☐ Isle of Wight 🚢 From Lymington, Southampton, Portsmouth ℹ The Guildhall, High St, Newport; www.visitisleofwight.co.uk

A visit to **Osborne House**, the favoured seaside retreat of Queen Victoria and Prince Albert, is alone worth the ferry ride from the mainland. Furnished much as they left it, the house provides a great insight into royal life. The Swiss Cottage, built for the royal children to play in, is now a museum attached to Osborne House. Next to it you can see the bathing machine used by the queen to preserve her modesty while taking her to the edge of the sea.

The other main sight on the island is the 11th-century **Carisbrooke Castle**. A walk on its outer wall and the climb to the top of its keep offer spectacular views.

The island is a base for ocean sailing, especially during Cowes Week. Aside from its many sandy, family-friendly beaches, the scenic highlight is the Needles, three towers of rock jutting out of the sea at the western end. This is only a short walk from Alum Bay, with its multi-coloured cliffs and sand.

Osborne House

⊛ ⊕ ☺ ⌂ ⌂ 🅮 ☐ East Cowes
☐ Apr–Sep: 10am–6pm daily; Oct–Mar: Times vary, check website ⓦ english-heritage.org.uk

Carisbrooke Castle

⊛ ⊛ ☺ ⌂ ⌂ 🅮 ☐ Newport
☐ Apr–Sep: 10am–6pm daily; Oct–Mar: Times vary, check website ⓦ english-heritage.org.uk

↑ A grey pony and her foal on the expansive heathland of the New Forest

A SHORT WALK
RYE

Distance 2 km (1.5 miles) **Time** 20 minutes
Nearest bus station Station Approach

This ancient and charming fortified town was part of the Cinque Ports federation, a group of seaports on the Kent coast that provided military services to the Crown in the 12th–13th century. Its compact medieval centre makes for a lovely walk along a maze of picturesque cobbled streets lined with well-preserved half-timbered houses full of art galleries, antiques shops, tea rooms and arts and crafts stores. Climb to the top of St Mary's Church tower for great views of the River Rother flowing through the marshes.

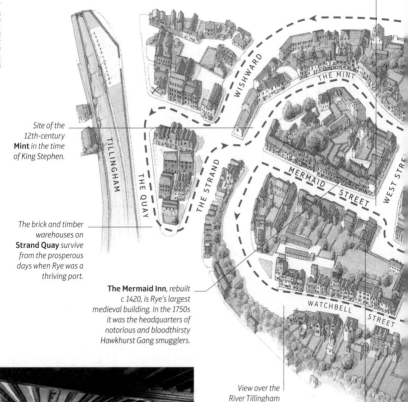

*The delightful cobbled **Mermaid Street**, lined with historic timbered houses, is one of Britain's prettiest streets.*

*Site of the 12th-century **Mint** in the time of King Stephen.*

*The brick and timber warehouses on **Strand Quay** survive from the prosperous days when Rye was a thriving port.*

The Mermaid Inn, rebuilt c 1420, is Rye's largest medieval building. In the 1750s it was the headquarters of notorious and bloodthirsty Hawkhurst Gang smugglers.

WISHWARD

THE MINT

TILLINGHAM

THE QUAY

THE STRAND

MERMAID STREET

WEST STREET

WATCHBELL STREET

View over the River Tillingham

*The fine Georgian **Lamb House** was built in 1722. George I stayed here and writer Henry James (1843–1916) lived here.*

← The Mermaid Inn, rich in history

↑ Ypres Tower, built in the Middle Ages as part of the town's defences

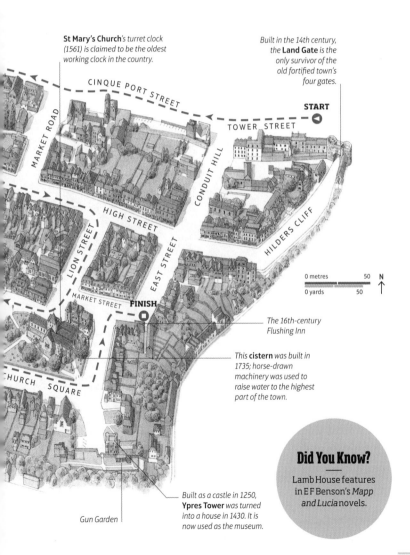

St Mary's Church's turret clock (1561) is claimed to be the oldest working clock in the country.

Built in the 14th century, the **Land Gate** is the only survivor of the old fortified town's four gates.

START

TOWER STREET

CINQUE PORT STREET

MARKET ROAD

CONDUIT HILL

HIGH STREET

HILDERS CLIFF

LION STREET

EAST STREET

MARKET STREET

FINISH

CHURCH SQUARE

0 metres 50

0 yards 50

N

The 16th-century Flushing Inn

This **cistern** was built in 1735; horse-drawn machinery was used to raise water to the highest part of the town.

Gun Garden

Built as a castle in 1250, **Ypres Tower** was turned into a house in 1430. It is now used as the museum.

Did You Know?

Lamb House features in E F Benson's *Mapp and Lucia* novels.

A DRIVING TOUR
NEW FOREST

THE DOWNS AND
CHANNEL COAST
New Forest

Length 77 km (48 miles) **Stopping-off points** Each town has cafés and pubs serving food. In Fordingbridge, the George is located beside the River Avon.

The New Forest got its name when it was made a new royal hunting preserve by William the Conqueror shortly after he seized England in 1066. Now a national park, it retains some ancient laws – especially the right for local inhabitants to graze animals across the entire forest. These include the famous New Forest ponies, which roam freely through the villages. Look out for England's largest deer herds as you drive through the gorgeous mix of heath and woodland scenery.

Locator Map
For more detail see p162

Rufus Stone *marks the spot where cruel King William II – known as Rufus because of his red face – is said to have been killed.*

Minstead, *a little village of old thatched cottages, was a favourite of Sir Arthur Conan Doyle, creator of Sherlock Holmes.*

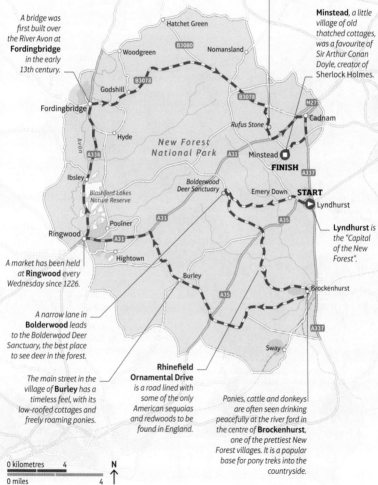

A bridge was first built over the River Avon at **Fordingbridge** *in the early 13th century.*

A market has been held at **Ringwood** *every Wednesday since 1226.*

A narrow lane in **Bolderwood** *leads to the Bolderwood Deer Sanctuary, the best place to see deer in the forest.*

The main street in the village of **Burley** *has a timeless feel, with its low-roofed cottages and freely roaming ponies.*

Lyndhurst *is the "Capital of the New Forest".*

Rhinefield Ornamental Drive *is a road lined with some of the only American sequoias and redwoods to be found in England.*

Ponies, cattle and donkeys are often seen drinking peacefully at the river ford in the centre of **Brockenhurst**, *one of the prettiest New Forest villages. It is a popular base for pony treks into the countryside.*

0 kilometres 4

0 miles 4

N

6,500
—
The number of animals who roam the New Forest freely.

Gorgeous scenery and vibrant flowers at a common in the New Forest at sunrise ↑

A LONG WALK
SOUTH DOWNS WAY

Distance 160 km (100 miles) **Walking time** 8-9 days **Terrain** The path leads mostly along farm tracks. Except for some steep slopes, walking conditions are reasonably easy.

The South Downs are a range of steep chalk ridges extending across Sussex into Hampshire. The South Downs Way trail runs along the tops of the downs for 160 km (100 miles) from Eastbourne to Winchester, providing views over the Weald countryside to the north, and southwards down to the sea. There are lovely walks around beauty spots along the path. Iron Age hillforts are also dotted across the downs, built to take advantage of the high ground.

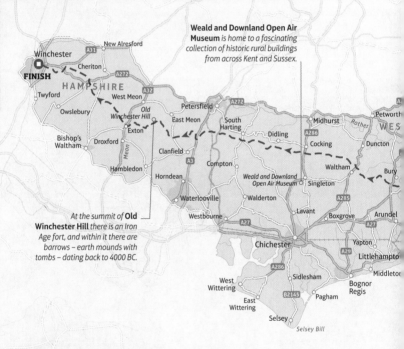

Weald and Downland Open Air Museum *is home to a fascinating collection of historic rural buildings from across Kent and Sussex.*

At the summit of **Old Winchester Hill** *there is an Iron Age fort, and within it there are barrows – earth mounds with tombs – dating back to 4000 BC.*

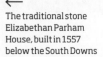

← The traditional stone Elizabethan Parham House, built in 1557 below the South Downs

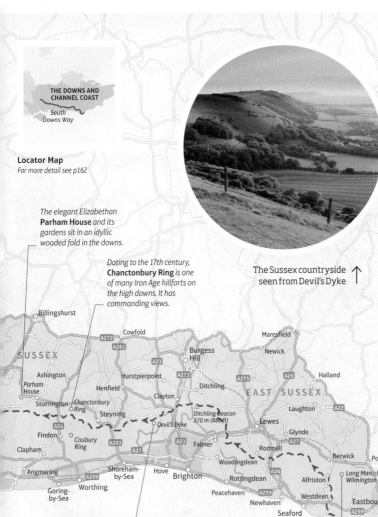

Locator Map
For more detail see p162

THE DOWNS AND CHANNEL COAST

South Downs Way

The elegant Elizabethan **Parham House** and its gardens sit in an idyllic wooded fold in the downs.

Dating to the 17th century, **Chanctonbury Ring** is one of many Iron Age hillforts on the high downs. It has commanding views.

The Sussex countryside seen from Devil's Dyke ↑

Billingshurst

Cowfold

A272

A281

Maresfield

Newick

SUSSEX

Ashington

Burgess Hill

A23

A273

A275

A26

Halland

Hurstpierpoint

Parham House

Henfield

Ditchling

EAST SUSSEX

Storrington

Chanctonbury Ring

Clayton

Laughton

A22

Steyning

Ditchling Beacon
270 m (880ft)

Lewes

Findon

Devil's Dyke

Glynde

Clapham

Cissbury Ring

A283

A27

Falmer

Rodmell

Berwick

Polegate

Angmering

Shoreham-by-Sea

Woodingdean

A259

Hove

Brighton

Rottingdean

A26

Alfriston

Long Man of Wilmington

START

Goring-by-Sea

Worthing

Peacehaven

Westdean

Eastbourne

Newhaven

A259

Seaford

Seven Sisters Country Park

Beachy Head

Devil's Dyke is a long, deep cleft in the downs. According to legend it was dug by the Devil in an attempt to let in the sea and flood the Christian villages to the north.

The series of majestic chalk cliffs in the **Seven Sisters Country Park** peak and dip along the coast between Eastbourne and Seaford.

The Long Man of Wilmington is a strange figure cut into the hillside. No one knows when the figure appeared, but theories range from the Stone Age to the 17th century.

Did You Know?

The entire coastline of the South Downs is a marine conservation zone.

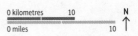

| 0 kilometres | 10 |
| 0 miles | 10 |

N ↑

EAST ANGLIA

East Anglia's name derives from the Angles, the people from northern Germany who settled here during the 5th and 6th centuries. For a brief time in the 7th century East Anglia was the most powerful of the Anglo-Saxon kingdoms of England. The ship burial and treasures found at Sutton Hoo are testament to the great wealth of the Anglo-Saxon kings.

Colchester is the oldest recorded town in England and was the site of the first permanent Roman colony after the Roman invasion of Britain.

Much of the region remained as swampy marshes (Fens) until the 17th century, when it was drained. The peaty oil proved ideal for arable farming and today East Anglia grows about a third of Britain's vegetables. During the Middle Ages the region also became very rich from a booming wool and textiles industry, with Norwich as its major weaving town. Cambridge University was also founded during this time of prosperity. However, these industries declined in East Anglia in the 18th century after they moved north during the Industrial Revolution.

Due to its flat, open landscape, the region became a base for the Royal Air Force in the fight against Nazi Germany during World War II.

EAST ANGLIA

Must Sees

1 Cambridge
2 Norwich
3 Ely Cathedral

Experience More

4 The Broads
5 The Fens
6 King's Lynn
7 Sandringham
8 Blickling Hall
9 Lowestoft
10 Framlingham Castle
11 Great Yarmouth
12 Aldeburgh
13 Southwold
14 Dunwich
15 Colchester
16 Maldon
17 Kentwell Hall
18 Ipswich
19 Bury St Edmunds
20 Coggeshall
21 Huntingdon
22 Anglesey Abbey
23 Audley End
24 Saffron Walden
25 Talliston House
26 Lavenham
27 Newmarket
28 Imperial War Museum Duxford

North Sea

Hunstanton

Heacham

Dersingham

Brancaster
Wells-next-the-Sea
Cley-next-the-Sea
Sheringham
Cromer
Mundesley

Burnham Market
Docking
Little Walsingham
Holt
Roughton
North Walsham

Syderstone
Saxthorpe

7 SANDRINGHAM

Harpley

Fakenham
Aylsham

8 BLICKLING HALL

Smallburgh
Stalham
Winterton-on-Sea

6 KING'S LYNN

Guist
Reepham
Coltishall

THE BROADS

Bawdeswell
Wroxham

Middleton
Litcham
East Dereham
Drayton
Norwich Airport
Ranworth
Acle

Caister-on-Sea

Bure

4

2 NORWICH

11 GREAT YARMOUTH

Swaffham
Shipdham
Cringleford

NORFOLK

Downham Market
Wymondham

Yore

Gorleston-on-Sea

Northwold
Watton
Attleborough
Newton Flotman

Loddon

Somerleyton Hall

Southery
Feltwell

Mundford

Wissey

Bungay
Beccles

9 LOWESTOFT

Littleport
Brandon
Lakenheath
Thetford
Garboldisham
Diss
Harleston

Wrentham

13 SOUTHWOLD

Mildenhall
Soham

Stanton
Botesdale
Eye
Laxfield
Halesworth
Blythburgh

Walberswick

14 DUNWICH

Wicken Fen Nature Reserve
Kentford

Culford
Ixworth

Peasenhall
Yoxford

Minsmere Reserve

27 NEWMARKET

19 BURY ST EDMUNDS

FRAMLINGHAM CASTLE **10**

Saxmundham

National Stud

Ickworth House

Haughley

12 ALDEBURGH

Wickhambrook

Stowmarket
Needham Market
Wickham Market

Orford Ness

KENTWELL HALL **17**

SUFFOLK

26 LAVENHAM

Woodbridge

Sutton Hoo

Orford

Linton

Long Melford
Bramford

18 IPSWICH

Haverhill
Clare
Hadleigh

Debden

Great Yeldham
Sudbury
East Bergholt

Felixstowe

Finchingfield
Halstead
Dedham
Manningtree

Harwich

haxted

London Stansted Airport

Braintree

15 COLCHESTER

Beth Chatto Gardens

Walton-on-the-Naze

25

20 COGGESHALL

Frinton-on-Sea

TALLISTON HOUSE

Tiptree
Brightlingsea

Leaden Roding
Great Waltham
Witham

Clacton-on-Sea

Chelmsford

Great Baddow

ESSEX

West Mersea

Hook of Holland

Chipping Ongar

16 MALDON

Blackwater

Bradwell-on-Sea

Ingatestone
South Woodham Ferrers
Burnham-on-Crouch

Billericay
Rayleigh

Crouch

Foulness Island

Brentwood

London Southend Airport

Basildon
Benfleet

Grays

Canvey Island
Southend-on-Sea

Tilbury

Thames

Sheerness

THE DOWNS AND CHANNEL COAST
p160

Isle of Sheppey

Herne Bay

EAST ANGLIA

CAMBRIDGE

⌂ Cambridgeshire ✈ Stansted ▯ Cambridge
🚌 Drummer St ❢ The Guildhall, Peas Hill;
www.visitcambridge.org

Cambridge has been an important trading centre since Roman times. Its famous university dates to the 13th century, when a group of religious scholars broke away from Oxford. While student life dominates its streets, the city is also a regional hub and lies at the heart of "Silicon Fen", one of the most important clusters of high-tech businesses in Europe, with a focus on biosciences.

Fitzwilliam Museum

⌂ Trumpington St ◷ Tue-Sun, public hols ▯ 1 Jan, Good Friday, 24-26 & 31 Jan
ⓦ fitzmuseum.cam.ac.uk

Part of the University of Cambridge, this massive Neo-Classical building contains some exceptional works of art, particularly paintings and ceramics. The core of the collection was bequeathed in 1816 by the 7th Viscount Fitzwilliam. Other gifts have since greatly enhanced the range of exhibits.

Works by Titian (1488–1576) and the 17th-century Dutch masters, including Hals and Cuyp, stand out among the paintings. French Impressionist gems include Monet's *Le Printemps* (1866) and Renoir's *La Place Clichy* (1880), while Stanley Spencer's *Self-Portrait with Patricia Preece* (1937) is a key British painting.

A collection of miniatures includes the earliest surviving depiction of Henry VIII. In the same gallery are some dazzling illuminated manuscripts, notably the 15th-century *Metz Pontifical*, a French liturgical work.

The impressive Glaisher collection of European ceramics includes a unique display of English delftware from the 16th and 17th centuries. Handel's bookcase contains folios of his work, and nearby is Keats' original manuscript for *Ode to a Nightingale* (1819).

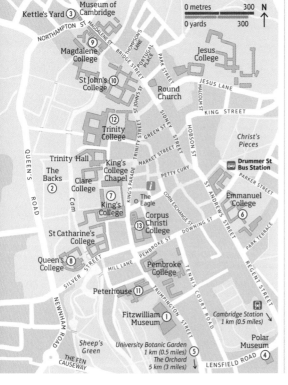

Museum of Cambridge

Kettle's Yard ③
Magdalene College ⑨
St John's College ⑩
Jesus College
Round Church
Trinity College ⑫
Trinity Hall
The Backs ②
Clare College
King's College Chapel
King's College ⑦
St Catharine's College
Queen's College ⑧
The Eagle ❢
Corpus Christi College ⑬
Emmanuel College ⑥
Christ's Pieces
Drummer St Bus Station
Pembroke College
Peterhouse ⑪
Fitzwilliam Museum ①
Sheep's Green
University Botanic Garden 1 km (0.5 miles) ⑤
The Orchard 5 km (3 miles)
Cambridge Station 1 km (0.5 miles)
Polar Museum ④

NORTHAMPTON ST · MAGDALENE ST · THOMPSON'S LANE · BRIDGE STREET · PORTUGAL PLACE · ST JOHN'S ST · PARK STREET · JESUS LANE · MALCOLM ST · KING STREET · SIDNEY STREET · GREEN ST · TRINITY STREET · MARKET STREET · HOBSON ST · ST ANDREWS STREET · PARKER STREET · KING'S PARADE · PETTY CURY · CORN EXCHANGE ST · DOWNING ST · REGENT STREET · PARK TERRACE · QUEEN'S ROAD · Cam · SILVER STREET · PEMBROKE ST · MILL LANE · TENNIS COURT ROAD · TRUMPINGTON STREET · TRUMPINGTON ST · LENSFIELD ROAD · NEWNHAM ROAD · THE FEN CAUSEWAY

0 metres 300
0 yards 300
N ↑

②

The Backs

The river Cam runs through the rear grounds of several adjoining colleges (St John's, Trinity, Trinity Hall, Clare, King's and Queen's), creating a picturesque strip of lawns, gardens and grazing land known as the Backs – as in, the backs of the colleges. The view across the Backs to

↑ A punt gliding down the Cam past the Backs of the colleges

King's College Chapel (p198) is one of the finest and best-known in England.

Kettle's Yard

🏠 Castle St 🕐 11am-5pm Tue-Sun 🌐 kettlesyard. co.uk

This beautiful house contains the University's modern and contemporary art gallery. The permanent collection consists of paintings, sculptures and objects, particularly by the British avant-garde of the early 20th century, collected by the former owners of the house, Jim Ede and his wife. There are also changing modern and contemporary art exhibitions.

PUNTING ON THE CAM

Punting captures the essence of carefree college days: a student leaning on a long pole, lazily guiding the flat-bottomed river craft along, while passengers stretch out, relax and enjoy the scenery. Punting is popular with both students and visitors, who can hire punts from boatyards along the river - with a chauffeur if required. Punts do sometimes capsize, and novice polers should prepare to get soaked.

Polar Museum

🏠 Lensfield Rd 🕐 10am-4pm Tue-Sat

This fascinating museum within the Scott Polar Institute charts the history of polar exploration with displays of clothing, maps, paintings, photographs, journals and other artifacts used during explorations of the Arctic and Antarctic. There is a section devoted to Inuit peoples.

University Botanic Garden

🏠 1 Brookside 🕐 Apr-Sep: 10am-6pm daily; Feb, Mar, Oct: 10am-5pm daily; Nov-Jan: 10am-4pm daily

A delightful oasis just off Trumpington Street, as well as an important academic resource, the garden has been on this site since 1846. It has a superb collection of trees and a sensational water garden. The winter garden is one of the finest in the country.

← Cambridge's beautiful historic centre, with colleges, cafés and shops

EAT

The Eagle

The city's most famous pub is a must. See where Crick and Watson "discovered" DNA and view the poignant WWII graffiti in the RAF Bar.

🏠 Benet St 🌐 greene-king-pubs.co.uk

£££

The Orchard

Grantchester's famous orchard tea garden has served its superb cream teas to the likes of Rupert Brooke and Virginia Woolf.

🏠 47 Mill Way, Grantchester 🌐 the orchardteagarden.co.uk

£££

---

⑥

Emmanuel College

🏠 St Andrews St 🌐 emma.cam.ac.uk

Built in 1677, Sir Christopher Wren's (p116) chapel is the highlight of this college, which has a Puritan tradition. Some of the intricate interior details, particularly the plaster ceiling and Amigoni's altar rails (1734), are superb.

---

⑦

King's College

🏠 King's Parade 🌐 kings.cam.ac.uk

One of the grandest of the University's 31 colleges, King's was founded by Henry VI in 1441. Henry decided that its chapel – a superb example of late medieval architecture – should dominate the city and himself specified its dimensions: 88 m (289 ft) long,

12 m (40 ft) wide and 29 m (94 ft) high. The chapel's famous choir is best-known for its lovely Festival of Nine Lessons and Carols, broadcast worldwide on Christmas Eve.

---

⑧

Queens' College

🏠 Queen's Lane 🌐 queens.cam.ac.uk

Built in 1446, Queens' has a marvellous collection of Tudor buildings, notably the half-timbered President's Gallery in the charming Cloister Court. The Principal Court is 15th century, as is Erasmus's Tower, named after the Dutch scholar. The college has buildings on both sides of the Cam, linked by the Mathematical Bridge, built in 1749. Though the bridge appears to be an arch, it is built entirely of straight timbers using a complicated engineering design.

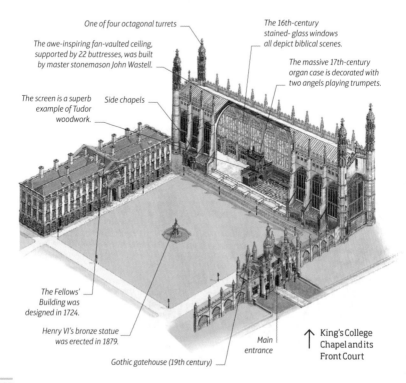

One of four octagonal turrets

The awe-inspiring fan-vaulted ceiling, supported by 22 buttresses, was built by master stonemason John Wastell.

The 16th-century stained-glass windows all depict biblical scenes.

The massive 17th-century organ case is decorated with two angels playing trumpets.

The screen is a superb example of Tudor woodwork.

Side chapels

The Fellows' Building was designed in 1724.

Henry VI's bronze statue was erected in 1879.

Main entrance

Gothic gatehouse (19th century)

↑ King's College Chapel and its Front Court

↑ The Fountain in Trinity's Great Court, at one time the college's main water supply

 (9)

Magdalene College

Magdelene St ⓦmagd.cam.ac.uk

Pronounced "maudlin", this college was established in 1482. The diarist Samuel Pepys (1633–1703) was a student here and left his large library to the college on his death. The 12 red-oak bookcases hold over 3,000 books. Magdalene was the last all-male Cambridge college: it started admitting women students only in 1988.

(10)

St John's College

ⒶSt John's St ⓦjoh.cam.ac.uk

An imposing turreted brick and stone gatehouse of 1514 provides a fitting entrance to John's, the second largest Cambridge college, and its rich store of 16th- and 17th-century buildings. Its hall, most of it Elizabethan, has portraits of famous alumni, including the poet William Wordsworth (p358). St John's

spans the Cam; its Bridge of Sighs (1831) was based on its Venetian namesake.

 (11)

Peterhouse

ⒶTrumpington St ⓦpet.cam.ac.uk

The oldest Cambridge college is also one of the smallest. The hall still has original features from 1284 but its best details are later – a Tudor fireplace backed with 19th-century tiles by William Morris (p228).

 (12)

Trinity College

ⒶTrinity St ⓦtrin.cam.ac.uk

The largest college was founded by Henry VIII in 1546 and has a massive court and hall. The entrance gate, with statues of Henry and James I (added later), was built in 1529 for King's Hall, an earlier college incorporated into Trinity. As a result of a student prank, Henry holds not his original sword, but a wooden

chair leg. The chapel, built in 1567, has statues of college members, notably Roubiliac's statue of Isaac Newton (1755).

 (13)

Corpus Christi College

ⒶKing's Parade ⓦcorpus.cam.ac.uk

Across the road just down from King's, this college was founded in 1352 by the local trade guilds, anxious to ensure that education was not the sole prerogative of church and nobility. Its Old Court is remarkably well preserved and looks today much as it would have done when built in the 14th century.

 INSIDER TIP
Visiting the Colleges

Cambridge colleges can usually be visited outside exam times, but opening hours vary; check the noticeboards at the entrance of each college. Some colleges charge admission.

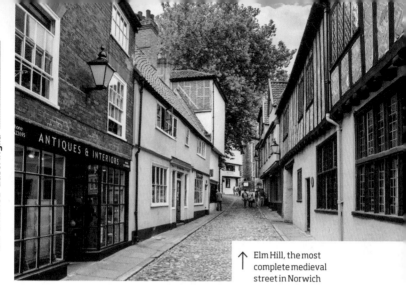

↑ Elm Hill, the most complete medieval street in Norwich

2

NORWICH

🄰 Norfolk ✈ 🚇 Norwich 🚌 Surrey St 🛈 The Forum, Millennium Plain; www.visitnorwich.co.uk

In the heart of the fertile East Anglian countryside, Norwich, one of the best-preserved medieval cities in Britain, today has a welcoming atmosphere, with laid-back boutiques and bars tucked away in its maze of narrow streets, and a vibrant live-music scene.

①

Norwich Cathedral

🄰 The Close ⏰ 7:30am–6pm daily 🌐 cathedral.org.uk

This magnificent building was founded in 1096 by Bishop Losinga and built with both English and French stone. The precinct originally included a monastery, and the surviving cloister is the most extensive in England. The spire, added in the 15th century, is at 96 m (315 ft) the second tallest in England after Salisbury (p266). In the majestic nave, soaring Norman pillars and arches support a 15th-century vaulted roof whose stone bosses have been beautifully restored.

Easier to appreciate at close hand is the elaborate wood carving in the choir, both over and under the stalls; one scene shows a small boy being smacked. Not to be missed is the 14th-century Despenser Reredos in St Luke's Chapel, hidden for years to prevent its destruction by Puritans.

Beneath the east outer wall is the grave of Edith Cavell, the Norwich-born nurse who was arrested and executed in 1915 by the Germans for helping Allied soldiers escape from occupied Belgium.

Tombland, the old Saxon marketplace by the cathedral, is a lovely space lined with medieval buildings. From here it is a short walk down Wensum Street to Elm Hill (on your left), one of the finest medieval streets in England. This cobbled lane lined with Tudor buildings is Norwich's prettiest street.

②

Norwich Castle

🄰 Castle Meadow ⏰ 10am–4:30pm Mon–Sat, 1–4:30pm Sun 🌐 museums.norfolk.gov.uk

The brooding keep of this 12th-century castle, a prison for 650 years, became a museum in 1894. It houses significant archaeology and natural history collections, as well as the world's largest collection of British ceramic teapots. The art gallery is

---

DRINK

Cinema City

There is an atmospheric bar, with a good selection of wines and bottled beers, in the equally ambient dining rooms at this arthouse cinema, which is housed in a splendid, Grade 1-listed 14th-century merchant's house.

🄰 St Andrew's St 🌐 norwichdiningrooms.co.uk

HIDDEN GEM
Plantation Garden

About 550 m (600 yds) from the city centre on Earlham Road, this delightful secret garden has woodland paths, flower beds, fountains, an Italianate terrace and a greenhouse.

dominated by works from the Norwich School, a group of early 19th-century landscape artists that included John Crome (1768–1821), often compared with Constable, and John Sell Cotman (1782–1842), known for his watercolours.

Museum of Norwich

🏠 Bridewell Alley 🕐 10am-4:30pm Tue-Sat 🌐 museums.norfolk.gov.uk

One of the oldest houses in Norwich, this 14th-century flint-faced building was once a jail for women and beggars. It now houses an exhibition of local industries, including the textile, shoe, chocolate and mustard trades.

Strangers' Hall

🏠 Charing Cross 🕐 10am-4pm Wed, 1-4:30pm Sun 🕐 23 Dec-mid-Feb 🌐 museums.norfolk.gov.uk

This 14th-century merchant's house is a museum of local history. The first "strangers" to inhabit it were immigrant Dutch and Flemish weavers in the 16th century. It has a fine 15th-century Great Hall and a maze of rooms showing domestic life from Tudor to Victorian times.

The Sainsbury Centre for Visual Arts

🏠 University of East Anglia (on B1108) 🕐 10am-6pm Tue-Fri, 10am-5pm Sat & Sun 🕐 23 Dec-2 Jan 🌐 scva.ac.uk

This important art gallery was built in 1978 to house the collection of Robert and Lisa Sainsbury, given to the University of East Anglia in 1973. The collection's strength is in its modern European art, including works by Modigliani, Picasso, Bacon, Giacometti and Moore. There is also ethnographic art from Africa, the Pacific and the Americas. The striking building was designed by Norman Foster, one of Britain's most innovative architects.

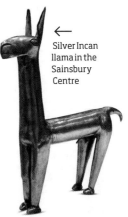

← Silver Incan llama in the Sainsbury Centre

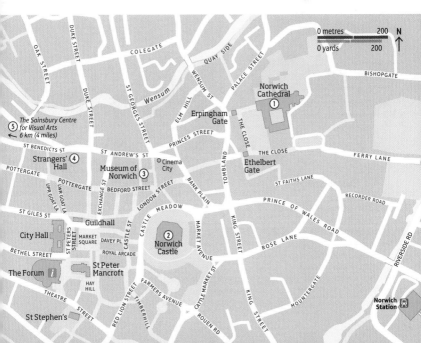

3 ⟐ ⟐ ▣ ◱

ELY CATHEDRAL

⌂ Ely, Cambridgeshire ⏰ 7am–6:30pm daily (winter: to 5:30pm Sun) 🌐 elycathedral.org

One of the marvels of the medieval world, magnificent Ely Cathedral is more than 900 years old and is highly regarded for its size and beauty. Visible for miles around, the cathedral is often referred to as "The Ship of the Fens".

The cathedral is located in the centre of the small, historic city of Ely, which was built on a chalk hill. The hill was the last stronghold of Anglo-Saxon resistance under Hereward the Wake, who hid in the cathedral until the Normans crossed the Fens in 1071. Begun in 1083, the cathedral took 268 years to complete. It survived the Dissolution (*p391*) but was closed for 17 years by Cromwell, who lived in Ely for a time. Particular highlights include the nave with its spectacular roof of painted panels, the Octagon Tower, regarded as a masterpiece of engineering and the vast, beautiful Lady Chapel. Visitors can also explore the medieval monastic buildings, parkland and meadows surrounding the cathedral.

The lantern's glass windows admit light into the dome.

↑ The lantern in the exceptionally beautiful Octagon Tower

💬 INSIDER TIP
Choral Evensong

Harking back to medieval tradition, the cathedral still retains a resident choir of choristers. Atmospheric Choral Evensong, sung by the world-famous choir, takes place at 5:30pm on most days.

Stained glass museum

↑ Illustration showing a section of the interior of Ely Cathedral

The Octagon Tower was built in 1322 when the Norman tower collapsed. Its roof, the lantern, took an extra 24 years to build and weighs 200 tonnes.

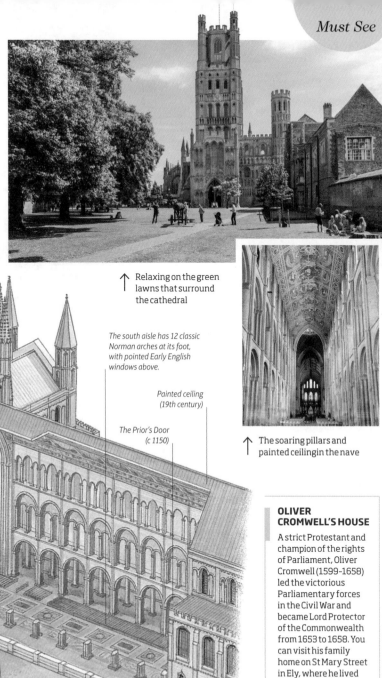

↑ Relaxing on the green lawns that surround the cathedral

The south aisle has 12 classic Norman arches at its foot, with pointed Early English windows above.

Painted ceiling (19th century)

The Prior's Door (c 1150)

↑ The soaring pillars and painted ceiling in the nave

This tomb is that of Alan de Walsingham, designer of the unique Octagon.

OLIVER CROMWELL'S HOUSE

A strict Protestant and champion of the rights of Parliament, Oliver Cromwell (1599–1658) led the victorious Parliamentary forces in the Civil War and became Lord Protector of the Commonwealth from 1653 to 1658. You can visit his family home on St Mary Street in Ely, where he lived when he was the local tithe collector. There is an interesting exhibition on the Civil War with interactive displays (www.oliver cromwellshouse.co.uk).

EXPERIENCE MORE

❹
The Broads

🏠 Norfolk 🚉 Hoveton &
Wroxham or Norwich, then
bus 🚏 Station Rd, Hoveton
(Apr–Oct) or Whitlingham
Country Park, Trowse
(year-round); www.broads-
authority.gov.uk

These tranquil lakes and
waterways south and northeast of Norwich, joined by six
rivers, were formed by
medieval peat diggings that
flooded when the water level
rose in the 13th century.

In summer the 200 km
(125 miles) of beautiful open
waterways, uninterrupted by
locks, teem with boating
enthusiasts. You can either
hire a boat yourself or take
one of the many trips on offer
to view the plants and wildlife
of the area. Wroxham, the
unofficial capital of the
Broads, is the starting point
for many of these excursions.

Run by the Norfolk Wildlife
Trust, the **Broads Wildlife
Visitor Centre** is a large
thatched floating information
centre with displays on all
aspects of the area, and a
bird-watching gallery.

In the centre of Ranworth
is St Helen's Church, which has
a magnificent medieval
screen, a 15th-century
illuminated manuscript and
spectacular views over the
entire area from its tower.

**Broads Wildlife
Visitor Centre**

🕐 🏠 Ranworth Broad
📞 01603 270479 🕐 Apr–Oct:
10am–5pm daily

❺
The Fens

🏠 Cambridgeshire/Norfolk
🚉 Ely, Downham Market,
March 🚏 7 York Row,
Wisbech; www.visit
cambridgeshirefens.org

Up until the 17th century,
this eerily flat, fertile
expanse was a swamp and
settlement was possible
only on "islands", such as Ely
(*p202*). Through the 17th
century, speculators,
recognizing the value of the
peaty soil for farmland,
brought in Dutch experts to
drain the Fens. However, as
the peat dried, it contracted,
and the Fens have slowly
been getting lower.
Powerful electric pumps
now keep them drained.

Fourteen kilometres
(9 miles) from Ely, **Wicken Fen
Nature Reserve**'s large
expanse of undrained Fen
provides a habitat for a wide
range of water life, wildfowl
and wild flowers. It is one of
Europe's most important
wetlands, home to many
species of birds, plants and
dragonflies The boardwalk
allows easy access.

**Wicken Fen Nature
Reserve**

🕐 🕐 🏠 Lode Lane, Wicken,
Ely 📞 01353 720274
🕐 Nature reserve: dawn–
dusk; Visitor centre: 10am–
5pm daily

❻
King's Lynn

🏠 Norfolk 🚉 🚌
🚏 Custom House,
Purfleet Quay; www.
visitwestnorfolk.com

Formerly Bishop's Lynn, this
town's name was changed at
the Reformation to reflect
political reality. In the Middle

WINDMILLS ON THE
FENS AND BROADS

The stiff breezes from the North Sea made
windmills an obvious power source for
East Anglia well into the 20th century,
and today they are an evocative and
recurring feature of the landscape. On the
Broads and Fens, some were used for
drainage, while others, such as that at
Saxtead Green, ground corn. On the
Broads, many of them have been restored
to working order.

↑ Sandringham House, a peaceful country retreat for the royal family

Ages it was one of England's most prosperous ports, shipping local grain and wool to Europe. There are still a few surviving warehouses and merchants' houses by the River Ouse from this period. At the north end of the town, **True's Yard Fisherfolk Museum** contains a fisherfolk yard, with two cottages and a smokehouse, the last remnants of the fishing community. Other historic buildings include the 15th-century Trinity Guildhall and St Margaret's Church dating to 1101; inside there is a fine Elizabethan screen..The **Custom House**, overlooking the river, was built in the 17th century as a merchant exchange. It houses an exhibition dedicated to the town's colourful maritime history.

True's Yard Fisherfolk Museum

⊛ ⊜ 🏠 🏠 North St ⏰ 10am-4pm Tue-Sat 🚫 24 Dec-mid-Jan 🌐 truesyard.co.uk

Custom House

🏠 Purfleet Quay 📞 01553 763044 ⏰ Times vary, call to check

Did You Know?

The Queen spends every Christmas at Sandringham.

Sandringham

🏠 Norfolk 🚌 From King's Lynn ⏰ Easter-Oct: 11am-5pm daily 🚫 1 week Jul 🌐 sandringhamestate.co.uk

This Norfolk estate has been in royal hands since 1862, when it was bought by the Prince of Wales, who later became Edward VII. The 18th-century house was elaborately refurbished by the prince and retains an Edwardian atmosphere. The large former stables house a museum whose exhibits range from a 1939 fire engine to estate cars used by the royal family over the years. There are extensive gardens and a park.

EAT

Market Bistro

This family-run spot serves a seasonal, local menu in a renovated 17th-century house with a fireplace and wooden beamed ceiling.

🏠 11 Saturday Market Place, King's Lynn 🚫 Sun & Mon, Tue lunch 🌐 marketbistro.co.uk

£££€

Bure River Cottage

A great seafood restaurant on the Broads with a menu of locally sourced fish and shellfish, including char-grilled lobster and squid.

🏠 27 Lower St, Horning 🚫 Sun & Mon 🌐 burerivercottage restaurant.co.uk

£££€

8   NT

Blickling Hall

⌂ Aylsham, Norfolk
🚂 Norwich, then bus
🕐 House: noon-5pm daily
(Nov-Mar: 11am-3:30pm);
Garden: 10am-5:30pm daily
(Nov-Mar: 10:30am-4pm)
🌐 nationaltrust.org.uk

Approached from the east, its symmetrical Jacobean front framed by trees and flanked by two yew hedges, Blickling Hall offers one of the most impressive vistas of any country house in the area.

Anne Boleyn, Henry VIII's doomed second queen, spent her childhood here. However, very little of the original house remains. Most of the present structure dates from 1628, when it was home to James I's Chief Justice, Sir Henry Hobart. Later, in 1767, John Hobart, the 2nd Earl of Buckinghamshire, celebrated the Boleyn connection with reliefs in the Great Hall depicting Anne and her daughter, Elizabeth I. The spectacular Long Gallery, dating to the 1620s, has a ceiling depicting symbolic representations of learning.

The Peter the Great Room marks the 2nd Earl's service as ambassador to Russia and was built to display a huge, stunning tapestry (1764) of the tsar on horseback, a gift from Catherine the Great. It also has portraits (1760) of the ambassador and his wife by Gainsborough.

9

Lowestoft

⌂ Suffolk 🚂 🚌
🌐 lovelowestoft.co.uk

The most easterly town in Britain was long a rival to Great Yarmouth, both as a holiday resort and a fishing port. The coming of the railway in the 1840s gave the town an advantage over other resorts, and the solid Victorian and Edwardian boarding houses are evidence of its popularity. The town's fishing industry has declined, and there are now only a few small fishing boats operating.

Lowestoft Museum, in a 17th-century house, has a good display of the fine porcelain made here in the

Did You Know?

Black Shuck is a mythical black dog that is said to roam the East Anglian countryside.

18th century, as well as exhibits on local archaeology and domestic life.

Ten kilometres (6 miles) northwest of Lowestoft is **Somerleyton Hall**, built in Jacobean style on the foundations of a smaller mansion. Its gardens are a real delight, and there is a genuinely baffling yew hedge maze.

Lowestoft Museum
⏸🅿 ⌂ Oulton Broad
🕐 Apr-Oct: 1-4pm Fri-Wed,
10:30am-4pm Thu
🌐 lowestoftmuseum.org

Somerleyton Hall
⏸🅿 ⌂ On B1074
🕐 Easter Sun-Sep: 10am-5pm
Tue, Thu, Sun & public hols
(Wed: garden only)
🌐 somerleyton.co.uk

Yachts moored at the Oulton Broad marina, Lowestoft ↑

↑ Great Yarmouth's colourful Britannia Pier, with shows and amusement arcades

10

Framlingham Castle

🏠 Framlingham, Suffolk
📞 01728 724189
🚉 Wickham Market then taxi ⏰ 10am-6pm daily (Nov-Mar: 10am-4pm Sat & Sun only)

Perched on a hill, the small village of Framlingham has long been an important strategic site, even before the present castle was built in 1190 by the Earl of Norfolk. Little of the castle from that period survives except the powerful curtain wall and its towers; walk round the top of it for fine views of the town.

Mary Tudor, daughter of Henry VIII, was staying here in 1553 when she heard she was to become queen.

To the southeast, on the coast, is the 16-sided keep of **Orford Castle**, built for Henry II as a coastal defence at around the same time as Framlingham. A short climb to the top of the castle gives fantastic views.

Orford Castle

🏠 Orford ⏰ 10am-6pm daily (Nov-Mar: 10am-4pm Sat & Sun only)
🌐 english-heritage.org.uk

11

Great Yarmouth

🏠 Norfolk 🚉 🚌 ℹ Marine Parade; www.great-yarmouth.co.uk

For centuries, herring fishing was the major industry of this port. Over-fishing led to a depletion of stocks and, for the port to survive, it started to earn its living from servicing container ships and North Sea oil rigs.

It is also the most popular seaside resort on the Norfolk coast and has been since the 19th century, when Dickens *(p174)* gave it useful publicity by setting part of his novel *David Copperfield* here. The **Elizabethan House Museum** has a large, eclectic display which illustrates the social history of the area.

In the old part of the town, around South Quay, are a number of charming traditional **Row Houses**, including the 17th-century Old Merchant's House. The latter retains its superb plaster ceiling, oak panelling and a collection of wall anchors. The house across the court has been furnished as it was in 1942.

Elizabethan House Museum

🏠 4 South Quay
⏰ Apr-mid-Jul: 10am-4pm Sun-Fri; mid-Jul-Sep: 10am-4pm daily
🌐 nationaltrust.org.uk

Row Houses

🏠 South Quay
⏰ Apr-Sep: 11am-4pm Mon-Fri 🌐 english-heritage.org.uk

EAT

The Courtyard
Hidden away in one of the Row Houses, this Italian restaurant serves generous platefuls of tasty pasta and seafood dishes.

🏠 75 Howard St South, Great Yarmouth
📞 01493 330622

£ £ £

Bucks Arms
In a 17th-century coaching inn, this pub serves meat and fish dishes. There's plenty of outdoor seating.

🏠 Blickling
🌐 bucksarms.co.uk

£ £ £

Dusk falling on illuminated Southwold Pier, stretching into the calm sea

12

Aldeburgh

🏠 Suffolk 🚌 ℹ️ Aldeburgh Cinema, 51 High St; www.eastsuffolk.gov.uk/visitors

Best known today for the music festivals at Snape Maltings, Aldeburgh has been a port since Roman times (the Roman area is underwater). Erosion has resulted in the fine Tudor Moot Hall, once far inland, today being close to the beach. Its ground floor is now **Aldeburgh Museum**. The large timbered court room above can only be reached by the original outside staircase.

The church, also Tudor, had a large stained-glass window installed in 1979 as a memorial to composer Benjamin Britten. **The Red House** was Britten's home from 1957 to 1976.

Aldeburgh Museum

🏠 Moot Hall, Market Cross Pl ⏰ Times vary, check website 🌐 aldeburgh museum.org.uk

The Red House

🏠 Golf Lane 📞 01728 451700 ⏰ Mar-Oct: 1-5pm Tue-Sun 🌐 brittenpears.org

---

13

Southwold

🏠 Suffolk 🚌 ℹ️ The Library, North Green; www.east suffolk.gov.uk/visitors

This unspoiled, picture-postcard seaside resort has a long pier and charming whitewashed villas clustered around small greens. The railway line which connected it with London was closed in 1929, isolating this Georgian town from an influx of day-trippers.

> The tiny village of Dunwich is all that remains of a "lost city" that was consigned to the sea by erosion.

This was also once a large port, as evidenced by the size of the 15th-century St Edmund King and Martyr Church, worth a visit for the 16th-century painted screens. **Southwold Museum** tells the story of the Battle of Sole Bay, which was fought offshore between the English and Dutch navies in 1672. On the seafront, the **Sailors' Reading Room**, built in 1864 to encourage seamen to stay away from drinking and embrace reading instead, now displays maritime artifacts.

Inland, at Blythburgh, the 15th-century Holy Trinity Church dominates the surrounding landscape.

Southwold Museum

🏠 9-11 Victoria St ⏰ Apr-Oct: 2-4pm daily 🌐 southwoldmuseum.org

Sailors' Reading Room

🏠 East Cliff ⏰ 9am-5pm daily 🌐 southwoldsailors readingroom.co.uk

---

ALDEBURGH MUSIC FESTIVAL

Composer Benjamin Britten (1913-76), who was born in Lowestoft, Suffolk, moved to Snape in 1937. In 1945 his opera *Peter Grimes* - inspired by the poet George Crabbe (1754-1832), once a curate at Aldeburgh - was performed in Snape. Since then the area has become a hub of musical activity. In 1948, Britten began the Aldeburgh Music Festival, held every June. He acquired the Maltings at Snape and converted it into a music venue, opened by the Queen in 1967. It has since become the focus of an annual series of musical events held in churches and halls throughout the entire region.

14

Dunwich

🅐 Suffolk

The tiny village of Dunwich is all that remains of a "lost city" that was consigned to the sea by erosion. In the 7th century it was the seat of the powerful East Anglian kings. In the 13th century it was still the biggest port in Suffolk and some 12 churches were built. But the land was being eroded at the alarming rate of about a metre (3 ft) a year, and the last original church collapsed into the sea in 1919. **Dunwich Museum** tells the fascinating story of this city lost to the sea.

Dunwich Heath, to the south, runs down to a sandy beach and is a notable nature reserve. Further south, **Minsmere Reserve** has observation hides for bird-watching.

Dunwich Museum

🅐 St James's Street
🕒 Mar: 2–4pm Sat & Sun only; Apr–Oct: 11:30am–4pm daily
🌐 dunwichmuseum.org.uk

Dunwich Heath

🅐 Nr Dunwich
🕒 Dawn–dusk daily
🌐 nationaltrust.org.uk

Minsmere Reserve

🅐 Minsmere, Westleton 🕒 Dawn–dusk daily 🌐 rspb.org.uk

EAT

The Butley Orford Oysterage

Oysters, grown at the local Butley Creek, are a must here, but don't miss the fish pie either.

🅐 Market Hill, Orford
🌐 pinneysoforford. co.uk

The Lighthouse

Enjoy mouthwatering steaks, fresh fish, duck and vegan options in an upbeat two-floor dining room. There is also a courtyard for the summer months.

🅐 77 High St, Aldeburgh
🌐 lighthouse restaurant.co.uk

Aldeburgh Fish & Chip Shop

The owners have the local fish and chips market sewn up – and deservedly so, given the crispy chips and the freshly caught cod, haddock and plaice.

🅐 226 High St, Aldeburgh
🕒 Mon; Tue, Wed & Sun pm 🌐 aldeburgh fishandchips.co.uk

Sutherland House

The menu is weighted towards seafood but also features flavourful meat dishes, served in a medieval building.

🅐 56 High St, Southwold
🕒 Mon 🌐 sutherland house.co.uk

↑ Red deer, one of many animal species in the nature reserve at Dunwich Heath

⑮

Colchester

🅰 Essex 🚍🚌 ℹ Hollytrees Museum, Castle Park; www.visitcolchester.com

The oldest recorded town in Britain, Colchester was the effective capital of southeast England when the Romans invaded in AD 43, and it was here that the first permanent Roman colony was established.

After Queen Boudica burnt the town in AD 60, a 2-mile (3-km) wall was erected, 3 m (10 ft) thick and 9 m (30 ft) high, to deter future attackers. You can still see these walls and the surviving Roman town gate, which is the largest in Britain.

During the Middle Ages Colchester developed into an important weaving centre. In the 16th century, a number of immigrant Flemish weavers settled in an area west of the castle, known as the Dutch Quarter, which still retains its original tall houses and steep, narrow streets.

Colchester Castle has the oldest and largest Norman keep still standing in England. Twice the size of the White Tower at the Tower of London *(p118)*, it was constructed in 1076 on the platform of a Roman temple dedicated to Claudius, using stones and tiles from other Roman buildings. The castle houses a museum with displays on the story of the town from prehistoric times to the Civil War, when Colchester was besieged for 11 weeks in 1648 before being captured by Cromwell's troops. There is also a medieval prison here.

Close to the castle, an elegant Georgian town house built in 1719 contains the charming **Hollytrees Museum**

→ A sailing barge returning to its riverside port at sunset, Maldon

Did You Know?

"Twinkle, Twinkle, Little Star" was written in 1806 by Jane Taylor in Colchester.

of social history, which records the day-to-day lives of people in Colchester and changing technology over 300 years. Clock-making was once an important craft in the town, as celebrated in displays here. Young visitors especially will enjoy exploring the miniature world of the doll's house, and learning about the origin of the famous nursery rhyme "Twinkle, Twinkle, Little Star".

Just to the south of Hollytrees Museum is **Firstsite**, a visual arts centre housed in a striking modern building. It hosts changing art displays, film screenings and talks. The only permanent exhibit is the ancient Roman Berryfield Mosaic, which was discovered on the site .

Ten kilometres (6 miles) east of Colchester, in Elmstead Market village, the **Beth Chatto Gardens** started in the 1960s as an experiment by the eminent gardening writer. She wanted to test her belief that it is possible to create a garden in the most adverse

conditions. The dry and windy slopes, boggy patches, gravel beds and wooded areas support plants best suited to each particular environment.

Colchester Castle

♿🅿🕐 🅰 Castle Park 🕐 10am–5pm Mon–Sat, 11am–5pm Sun 🌐 colchester. cimuseums.org.uk

Hollytrees Museum

🕐 🅰 Castle Park 🕐 10am–5pm Mon–Sat 🌐 colchester. cimuseums.org.uk

Firstsite

😊 🅰 Lewis Gardens, High St 🕐 10am–5pm daily 🌐 firstsite.co.uk

Beth Chatto Gardens

♿🅿🕐 🅰 Elmstead Market 🕐 10am–5pm daily (Nov–Feb: to 4pm) 🚫 22 Dec–5 Jan 🌐 bethchatto.co.uk

⑯

Maldon

🅰 Essex 🚆 Chelmsford then bus ℹ Wenlock Way; www. visitmaldondistrict.co.uk

This delightful old town on the River Blackwater, its High Street lined with shops and inns from the 14th century on, was once an important harbour. It is perhaps best known for its production of Maldon sea salt, which is panned

Colourful market stalls at Ipswich's Corn Exchange, in front of the town hall

in the traditional way. A fierce battle here in 991, when Viking invaders defeated the Saxon defenders, is told in *The Battle of Maldon*, one of the earliest known Saxon poems. The battle is also celebrated in the *Maldon Embroidery* on display in the **Maeldune Heritage Centre**. This magnificent 13-m- (42-ft-) long embroidery, designed by a local artist, depicts the history of Maldon from 991 to 1991 and took 86 women three years to complete.

East of Maldon, at Bradwell-on-Sea, is the sturdy church of St Peter's-on-the-Wall, a simple stone building that stands isolated on the shore. It was built in 654, from the stones of a former Roman fort, by St Cedd, an Anglo-Saxon monk who used it as his cathedral. The church was restored in the 1920s.

Maeldune Heritage Centre

Ⓜ 🏠 Market Hill Ⓞ Mid-Feb–Dec: 11am–4pm daily Ⓦ maelduneheritage centre.co.uk

🔟7 Kentwell Hall

🏠 Long Melford 🚉 Sudbury, then taxi Ⓞ Noon–4pm daily in summer (gardens: from 11am) Ⓦ kentwell. co.uk

In the picturesque village of Long Melford, Kentwell Hall is a beautiful Tudor mansion surrounded by a moat and splendid gardens. It also has a rare-breeds farm and hosts Tudor re-enactment events.

🔟8 Ipswich

🏠 Suffolk 🚉🚌
ℹ️ St Stephen's Lane; www. allaboutipswich.com

Suffolk's county town has a largely modern centre but several buildings remain from earlier times. It rose to prominence after the 13th century as a port for the rich Suffolk wool trade *(p212)*.

The town's museum and art gallery, **Christchurch Mansion**, is a Tudor house from 1548, in which Elizabeth I stayed in 1561. It also has the best collection of Constable's

paintings outside London, including four marvellous Suffolk landscapes, as well as paintings by Gainsborough.

In the town centre is St Margaret's, a 15th-century church built in flint and stone with a double hammerbeam roof and 17th-century painted ceiling panels.

Christchurch Mansion

Ⓜ😊🏠 Soane St
Ⓞ 10am–5pm Tue–Sun (Nov–Feb: to 4pm) Ⓦ ipswich. cimuseums.org.uk

---

SUTTON HOO

East of Ipswich, Sutton Hoo (www.national trust.org.uk/sutton-hoo) is a 7th-century royal burial site with a hoard of Anglo-Saxon treasures. A museum houses a reconstructed burial mound, plus the original treasures from the Horseman's Mound, where a young man was buried with his horse, and replicas of the treasure found in the King's Mound (the originals are in the British Museum, p104).

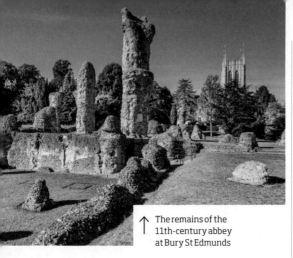

↑ The remains of the 11th-century abbey at Bury St Edmunds

Dating from 1140, **Coggeshall Grange Barn** is the oldest surviving timber-framed barn in Europe. Inside is a display of historic farm wagons and woodworking tools. The half-timbered merchant's house, **Paycocke's**, was built around 1500 and has a beautifully panelled interior and fine display of Coggeshall lace.

Coggeshall Grange Barn

 ⊕ ⊗ ⚐ Grange Hill ☎ 01376 562226 🕙 Apr–Oct: from 11am daily

Paycocke's

⊕ ⊗ ⚐ West St ☎ 01376 561305 🕙 Apr–Oct: 11am–5pm daily

㉑
Huntingdon

⚐ Cambridgeshire 🚆🚌 🌐 visitcambridge.org

More than 300 years after his death, Oliver Cromwell still dominates the small town where he was born in 1599. **Cromwell Museum**, his former school, traces his life with pictures and mementos, including his death mask.

Cromwell remains one of the most controversial figures in British history. An MP before he was 30, he became embroiled in the disputes between Charles I and Parliament over taxes and religion. In the Civil War (p49) he proved an inspired

---

⑲
Bury St Edmunds

 ⚐ Suffolk 🚆🚌 ℹ The Apex, Charter Square; www.visit-burystedmunds.co.uk

The last Saxon king of East Anglia, St Edmund was decapitated by Danish raiders in 870. Legend has it that a wolf picked up the severed head – an image that appears in a number of medieval carvings. Edmund was canonized in 900 and buried in Bury, where in 1014 King Canute built an abbey in his honour, the wealthiest in England until its destruction in the Dissolution of the Monasteries (p391). The abbey ruins lie in the town centre.

Nearby are two large 15th-century churches, built when the wool trade made the town wealthy. St James's was designated a cathedral in 1914. A stone slab in the northeast corner of St Mary's marks the tomb of Mary Tudor.

Just below the market cross in Cornhill stands the large 12th-century **Moyse's Hall**, a merchant's house that is now the local history museum. A little south is The Nutshell, which claims to be Britain's smallest pub, open since 1867.

Five kilometres (3 miles) southwest of Bury is the late 18th-century **Ickworth House**, an eccentric Neo-Classical mansion. Its art collection includes works by Reynolds and Titian. There are also fine displays of silver, porcelain and sculpture.

Moyse's Hall

 ⊕ ⊘ ⚐ Cornhill 🕙 10am–5pm Mon–Sat, noon–4pm Sun 🚫 Public hols 🌐 moyseshall.org

Ickworth House

⊕ ⊛ ⊘ ⊗ ⚐ Horringer 🕙 Times vary, check website 🌐 nationaltrust.org.uk

---

⑳
Coggeshall

⚐ Essex 🌐 visitessex.com

This town has two of the most important medieval and Tudor buildings in the country.

THE RISE AND FALL OF THE WOOL TRADE

Wool was a major English export from the 13th century and by 1310 some ten million fleeces were exported every year. Around 1350 Edward III decided it was time to establish a home-based cloth industry and encouraged Flemish weavers to come to Britain. Many settled in East Anglia, particularly Suffolk, and their skills helped establish a flourishing trade. This time of prosperity saw the construction of the sumptuous churches, such as the one at Stoke-by-Nayland, that we see today - East Anglia has more than 2,000 churches. The cloth trade began to decline in the late 16th century with the development of water-powered looms. These were not suited to the area, which never regained its former wealth.

general and, after refusing the title of king, was made Lord Protector in 1653, four years after King Charles I was beheaded. Just two years after Cromwell's death, the monarchy was restored by popular demand, and his body was removed from Westminster Abbey (p72) to hang on gallows.

The museum was also the former school of diarist Samuel Pepys, who lived at nearby Bampton.

Cromwell Museum
⊙ 🏠 Grammar School Walk
🕙 11am–4pm Tue-Sun & public hols (Nov-Mar: to 3pm)
🌐 cromwellmuseum.org

Anglesey Abbey

🏠 Lode, Cambridgeshire
📞 01223 810080
🚉 Cambridge or Newmarket, then bus
🕙 House: 11am-5pm daily (to 4pm in winter); Garden: 9:30am-5:30pm daily (to 4:30pm in winter)

The original abbey was built in 1135 for an Augustinian order, but only the crypt, with its vaulted ceiling on marble and stone pillars, survived the Dissolution (p391). This was later incorporated into a manor house whose treasures include furniture from many periods and a rare seascape by Gainsborough. The superb garden was created in the 1930s by Lord Fairhaven.

Walking along an avenue lined with beech trees at Anglesey Abbey; the façade of the stately home (inset)
↓

EAT

Pea Porridge
The Mediterranean-influenced fine cuisine here consists of unfussy but delectable seasonal offerings.

🏠 28-29 Cannon St, Bury St Edmunds 🔒 Sun & Mon 🌐 peaporridge.co.uk

£ £ £

Maison Bleue
This stylish restaurant in a 17th-century building serves modern French dishes with an emphasis on fish.

🏠 30-31 Churchgate St, Bury St Edmunds 🔒 Sun & Mon 🌐 maisonbleue.co.uk

£ £ £

Audley End

▣ Saffron Walden, Essex
▣ Audley End then taxi
▣ Times vary, check website ▣ 24 Dec–Jan & certain days in Jan, Feb & Mar ▣ english-heritage.org.uk

This was the largest house in England when built in 1603–14 for Thomas Howard, Lord Treasurer and 1st Earl of Suffolk. James I joked that Audley End was too big for a king but not for a Lord Treasurer. Charles II, his grandson, disagreed and bought it in 1667. He seldom went there, however, and in 1701 it was given back to the Howards, who demolished two thirds of it.

What remains is a Jacobean mansion, retaining its original hall and many fine plaster ceilings. The Scottish Neo-Classical architect Robert Adam remodelled some of the interior in the 1760s, and these rooms have been restored to his original designs. At the same time,

"Capability" Brown (p24) landscaped the magnificent 18th-century park.

24
Saffron Walden

▣ Essex ▣ Audley End then bus ▣ 1 Market Place; www.visitsaffronwalden.gov.uk

This medieval market town acquired its name in the 16th century, when the saffron crocus was grown and traded here. A long-running market is still going strong, animating the central square twice a week. The surrounding streets and narrow lanes shelter shops, cafés, tea rooms and pubs. Also in the heart of town is St Mary's, the largest parish church in Essex, and, just beyond, seven interlinked gardens collectively known as Bridge End Garden.

> Each room of Talliston House is a separate world, a re-creation of a distinct time and place, from a guestroom in the Alhambra Palace to a bohemian Victorian watchtower.

25

Talliston House

▣ Great Dunmow, Essex
▣ Braintree ▣ For tours (see website) ▣ talliston.com

This extraordinary fairytale-like house, 25 years in the making, was a semi-detached ex-council residential property prior to 1990. That year, the owner John Trevillian began to deconstruct the original three-bedroom layout to create what is today an extra-ordinary 13-room labyrinth. Each room is a separate world, a re-creation of a distinct time and place, from a guestroom in the Alhambra Palace in Granada and a mid-20th-century Cambodian treehouse to a bohemian Victorian watchtower. The fun extends to the outside, where a teepee and a 1930s Gothic courtyard complete the jamboree.

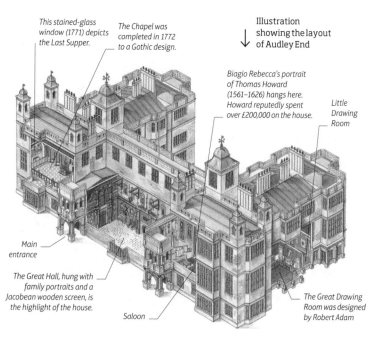

This stained-glass window (1771) depicts the Last Supper.

The Chapel was completed in 1772 to a Gothic design.

Illustration showing the layout of Audley End ↓

Biagio Rebecca's portrait of Thomas Howard (1561–1626) hangs here. Howard reputedly spent over £200,000 on the house.

Little Drawing Room

Main entrance

The Great Hall, hung with family portraits and a Jacobean wooden screen, is the highlight of the house.

Saloon

The Great Drawing Room was designed by Robert Adam

Lavenham

26

🏠 Suffolk 🛈 Lady St; www.
heartofsuffolk.co.uk

Lavenham is a treasure trove
of beautiful timber-framed
houses ranged along streets
whose pattern is virtually
unchanged from medieval
times. For 150 years, between
the 14th and 16th centuries, it
was the prosperous centre of
the Suffolk wool trade. No
fewer than 350 of the town's
well-preserved buildings are
Grade II listed, including the
fine **Little Hall**.

   Gainsborough's House, the
birthplace of the artist, has a
fine collection of his paintings,
drawings and prints.

Little Hall

🏠 Market Place 🕙 10am-
1pm Mon, 1-4pm Tue-Sun
🖥 littlehall.org.uk

Gainsborough's House

🏠 Sudbury 🕙 10am-
5pm Mon-Sat, 11am-5pm Sun
🗓 24 Dec-2 Jan, Good Fri
🖥 gainsborough.org

Newmarket

27

🏠 Suffolk 🚌 🛈 Palace
House, Palace St; www.
discovernewmarket.co.uk

Newmarket has been the
headquarters of British horse
racing since James I decided
that its open heaths were
ideal for testing the mettle
of his fastest steeds against
those of his friends. The first
ever recorded horse race was
held here in 1622. Charles II
shared his grandfather's
enthusiasm and after the
Restoration *(p49)* moved the
whole court to Newmarket
for the sport.

   There are now over 2,500
horses in training in and
around the town and two
racecourses staging regular
race meetings from around
April to October. You can view

 Assorted aircraft inside a huge hangar at
the Imperial War Museum Duxford

the horses being exercised
on the heath in the early
morning, and visit the
National Stud. The National
Horseracing Museum, in the
restored palace and stables
built by Charles II in 1651,
comprises the **National
Heritage Centre for
Horseracing and Sporting
Art** and a racing yard where
ex-racehorses are retrained.

National Stud

🏠 Newmarket
🕙 Mid-Feb-Oct: tours only
🖥 nationalstud.co.uk

National Heritage Centre
for Horseracing and
Sporting Art

🏠 Palace House,
Palace St 🕙 10am-5pm daily
🖥 palacehousenewmarket.
co.uk

28

Imperial War Museum
Duxford

🏠 Duxford, Cambridgeshire
🚉 Whittlesford Parkway
then bus 🕙 10am-6pm
daily 🖥 iwm.org.uk

Located in an aerodrome
built during World War I, this
impressive branch of the
Imperial War Museums was
a Royal Air Force station until
1961. It is now Britain's largest
aviation museum and

showcases the military aircraft
that once regularly took off
from its airfield, including
World War II iconic Spitfires
and Lancaster Bombers.
Hundreds of other aircraft
spanning the history of
military aviation are also
on display in the vast hangars
that house the permanent
exhibition, including classics
of civil aviation, most notably
a Concorde. There are also
regular captivating air shows.

EAT

Eight Bells

Locally sourced game
and meat are spiced
with imaginative sides
like Suffolk bacon jam.

🏠 18 Bridge St,
Saffron Walden
🖥 8bells-pub.co.uk

££££

Tea Amo

This cosy tea room
serves home-made
cakes and cream teas.

🏠 5 Cross St, Saffron
Walden 🗓 Sun
🖥 teaamo.co.uk

££££

A DRIVING TOUR
NORTH NORFOLK COASTAL TOUR

Length 45 km (28 miles) **Stopping-off points** Holkham Hall makes a pleasant stop for a picnic lunch. There are some good pubs in Wells-next-the-Sea

This tour takes you through some of the most beautiful areas of East Anglia; nearly all of the north Norfolk coast has been designated an Area of Outstanding Natural Beauty. The sea has dictated the character of the area. With continuing deposits of silt, once busy ports are now far inland and the shingle and sand banks that have been built up are home to a huge variety of wildlife. Do bear in mind when planning your journey that this popular route can get congested during summer.

Did You Know?

The Hunstanton Cliffs were under the sea between 135 and 70 million years ago, and are full of fossils.

The magnificent **Hunstanton Cliffs** *tower 18 m (60 ft) above the beach. Their three bands of colour are made from limestone and red and white chalk.*

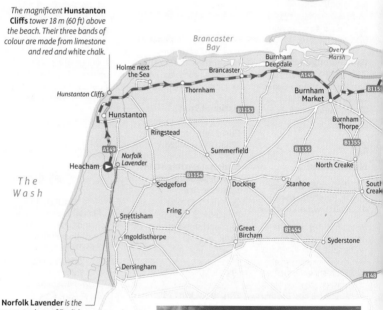

Norfolk Lavender *is the largest producer of English Lavender. This whole area is at its best in July and August when the fields are a blaze of purple.*

→ Vibrant lavender fields at Norfolk Lavender on a summer day

North Norfolk
Coastal Tour

EAST
ANGLIA

Locator Map
For more detail see p194

↑ A coastal footpath by the red
chalk Hunstanton Cliffs

Holkham Hall, *a Palladian home, is magnificent. Set in a beautiful landscaped park, it houses an impressive collection of art and Classical sculptures.*

Due to silting, the port of **Wells-next-the-Sea** *is now 1.5 km (1 mile) from the sea. Its popular sandy beach is lined with colourful beach huts on stilts.*

In the 13th century, **Blakeney Marshes** *was a substantial trading port. Today, the marsh is inhabited by England's largest colony of grey seals and hundreds of sea birds.*

Cley Windmill *overlooks Cley Marshes which became, in 1926, the first nature and bird reserve in Britain.*

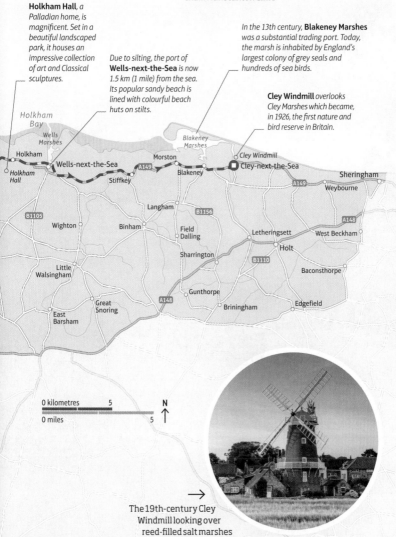

Holkham Bay

Wells Marshes

Holkham

Holkham Hall

Wells-next-the-Sea

Stiffkey

Morston

Blakeney

Blakeney Marshes

Cley Windmill
Cley-next-the-Sea

A149

Sheringham

Weybourne

B1105

Wighton

Langham

Binham

B1156

Field Dalling

Sharrington

B1110

Letheringsett

Holt

West Beckham

A148

Little Walsingham

Gunthorpe

Briningham

Baconsthorpe

A148

East Barsham

Great Snoring

Edgefield

0 kilometres 5
0 miles 5

N
↑

→
The 19th-century Cley
Windmill looking over
reed-filled salt marshes

Boating on the River Stour near Dedham through the landscape immortalized by Constable ↑

A LONG WALK
CONSTABLE WALK

EAST ANGLIA

Constable Walk

Distance 5 km (3 miles) **Walking time** 1 hour
Terrain This trail is along flat grass, gravel paths a and a
river-side footpath with kissing gates.

This walk in Constable country follows one of the most
picturesque sections of the River Stour. The route taken would
have been familiar to the landscape painter John Constable
(1776–1837). Constable's father, a wealthy merchant, owned
Flatford Mill, which was depicted in many of the artist's
paintings. Constable claimed to know and love "every stile
and stump, and every lane" around East Bergholt.

Locator Map
For more detail see p194

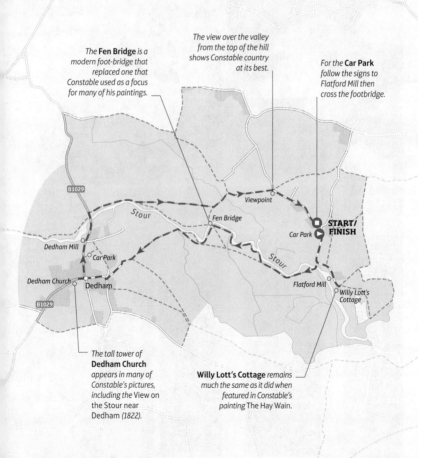

The **Fen Bridge** is a
modern foot-bridge that
replaced one that
Constable used as a focus
for many of his paintings.

The view over the valley
from the top of the hill
shows Constable country
at its best.

For the **Car Park**
follow the signs to
Flatford Mill then
cross the footbridge.

Viewpoint

B1029

Stour

Fen Bridge

**START/
FINISH**

Car Park

Stour

Dedham Mill

Car Park

Dedham Church

Dedham

B1029

Flatford Mill

*Willy Lott's
Cottage*

The tall tower of
Dedham Church
appears in many of
Constable's pictures,
including the View on
the Stour near
Dedham (1822).

Willy Lott's Cottage remains
much the same as it did when
featured in Constable's
painting The Hay Wain.

0 metres   500   **N**
0 yards   500   ↑

THAMES VALLEY AND THE COTSWOLDS

This area has been inhabited for thousands of years, shown by the large number of prehistoric remains, including a remarkable chalk hillside figure, the White Horse of Uffington. Nearer to London is St Albans, a town steeped in Roman history. The pleasant countryside of the Chiltern Hills and of the Thames Valley itself appealed to aristocrats who built stately homes close to London, and many of these are among the grandest in the country. The area also abounds with royal connections. Windsor Castle has been a residence of kings and queens since William the Conqueror chose this strategic site above the Thames and began building in 1070. It played a critical role in 1215, when King John set out from here to sign the Magna Carta at Runnymede on the Thames. Further north, Queen Anne had Blenheim Palace built for her military commander, the 1st Duke of Marlborough. Elizabeth I spent part of her childhood at Hatfield House, and some of the Tudor palace still stands. Around these great houses grew picturesque villages, with half-timbered buildings and, as you move towards the Cotswolds, houses built in attractive buff-coloured stone.

THAMES VALLEY AND THE COTSWOLDS

Must Sees

1. Windsor Castle
2. The Cotswolds
3. Oxford
4. Blenheim Palace

Experience More

5. Roald Dahl Museum
6. ZSL Whipsnade Zoo
7. St Albans
8. Waddesdon
9. Vale of the White Horse
10. Warner Bros. Studio Tour – The Making of Harry Potter
11. Hatfield House
12. Woburn Abbey
13. Stowe
14. Bletchley Park
15. Cheltenham
16. Gloucester
17. Tewkesbury

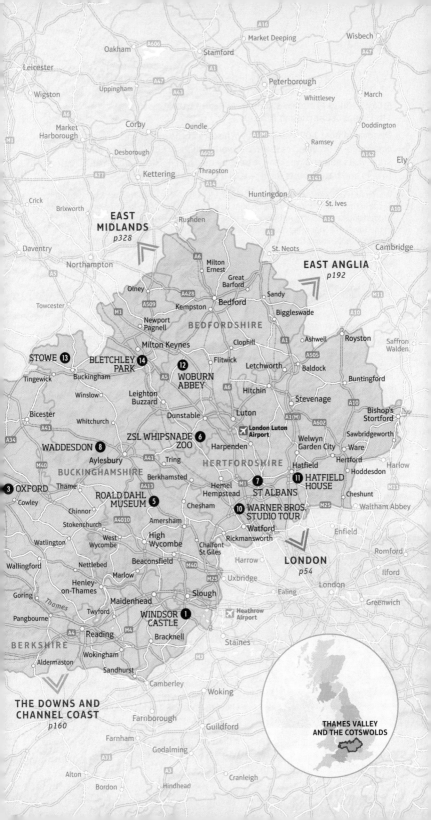

WINDSOR CASTLE

⌂ Castle Hill ⊞ ⊙ 9:30am–5:30pm (Nov–Feb: to 4:15pm; last adm
1 hr 15 mins before closing) ⓦ rct.uk

Discover almost 1,000 years of royal history at the oldest and largest
continuously occupied castle in the world. Windsor Castle is used for
state visits and as a weekend retreat by the Queen. The impressive
towers and battlements form part of a fully working castle.

William the Conqueror chose the site for the
castle in the 11th century as it was on high
ground and just a day's journey from his base
in the Tower of London. Successive monarchs
have made alterations that render it a remarkable monument to royalty's changing tastes.
Henry II and Edward III were responsible for the
bulk of the work until the castle was remodelled
by George IV in 1823. George V's affection for it
was shown when he chose Windsor for his
family surname in 1917.

Pick up an audio guide – the commentary
takes you through the highlights of the State
Apartments and St George's Chapel.

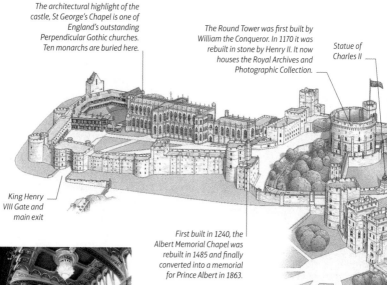

The architectural highlight of the castle, St George's Chapel is one of England's outstanding Perpendicular Gothic churches. Ten monarchs are buried here.

The Round Tower was first built by William the Conqueror. In 1170 it was rebuilt in stone by Henry II. It now houses the Royal Archives and Photographic Collection.

Statue of Charles II

King Henry VIII Gate and main exit

First built in 1240, the Albert Memorial Chapel was rebuilt in 1485 and finally converted into a memorial for Prince Albert in 1863.

↑ The banqueting hall in the Waterloo Chamber, adorned in red and gold

WINDSOR

Dwarfed by the enormous castle on the hill above –
in fact its original purpose was to serve the castle's
needs – the town of Windsor is full of quaint Georgian
shops, houses and inns. The most prominent building
is the Guildhall, where Prince Charles and Camilla
Parker-Bowles were married in 2005. Eton College,
one of the most prestigious schools in Britain, lies just
a short walk away. Windsor Great Park stretches from
the castle 5 km (3 miles) to Snow Hill. To the southeast
is the meadow of Runnymede, where King John was
forced to sign the Magna Carta.

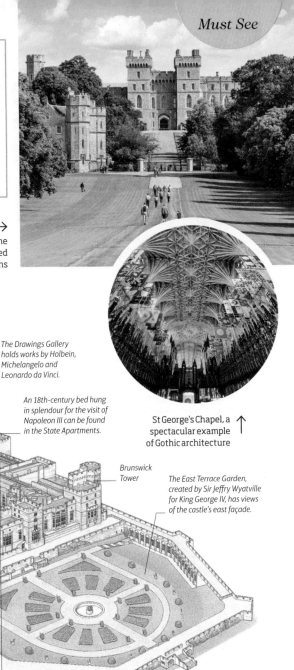

INSIDER TIP
Changing the Guard

Time your visit with the Changing the Guard spectacle. Led by a regimental band, the guards march from the barracks through the town to the Guard Room. Check the website for timings.

→

The long approach to the castle entrance, framed by manicured lawns

The Audience Chamber is where the Queen greets her guests.

The Drawings Gallery holds works by Holbein, Michelangelo and Leonardo da Vinci.

The Queen's Ballroom

An 18th-century bed hung in splendour for the visit of Napoleon III can be found in the State Apartments.

St George's Chapel, a ↑ spectacular example of Gothic architecture

Brunswick Tower

The East Terrace Garden, created by Sir Jeffry Wyatville for King George IV, has views of the castle's east façade.

Queen's Tower

Clarence Tower

Waterloo Chamber banqueting hall was created in 1823.

↑ Illustration of Windsor Castle's expansive grounds

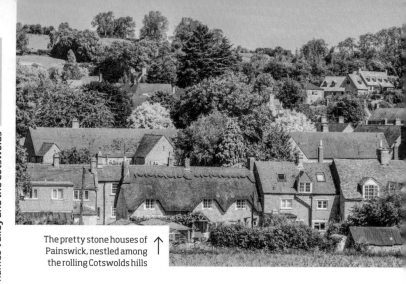

The pretty stone houses of Painswick, nestled among the rolling Cotswolds hills ↑

2

THE
COTSWOLDS

 Gloucestershire, Oxfordshire, Warwickshire, Wiltshire, Worcestershire cotswolds.com

Running through five counties, including Oxfordshire and Gloucestershire, this Area of Outstanding Natural Beauty is full of idyllic small towns and villages characterized by pretty sandstone cottages notable for their steep, gabled roofs. It offers some of the most scenic landscapes and walks in England.

①
Painswick

 Gloucestershire
 Stroud, then 66 bus
 St Mary's Church, New St;
www.painswicktourist
info.co.uk

Known as the "Queen of the Cotswolds", this beautifully preserved hilltop town on the Cotswold Way is certainly among the prettiest in the area. It built its wealth on the wool trade from the 15th to the 19th centuries, but today the only tangible industry is art; the winding, narrow streets are home to a large number of artists' studios and galleries.

②
The Slaughters

 Gloucestershire
 Victoria St, Bourton on the Water

The chocolate-box-pretty villages of Upper and Lower Slaughter, separated by about a mile of the River Eye, are so called for the boggy land on which they were built, known in Old English as "slohtre". There is no sign of any bog now but these hamlets retain their medieval charm. The best way to take them in is to walk between them along the river, which narrows to a stream in places.

EAT

Made by Bob
Open for breakfast and lunch, this buzzing bistro and deli offers British and Mediterranean dishes.

 26 Market Pl, The Corn Hall, Cirencester
 foodmadebybob.com

£££

―――――――――

Lamb Inn
Classic British dishes and afternoon teas in a 15th-century inn.

 Sheep St, Burford
 cotswold-inns-hotels. co.uk

£££

―――――――――

5 North St
A family-run restaurant dedicated to top drawer, modern British food

 5 North St, Winchcombe
 5northstreet restaurant.co.uk

£££

③
Chipping Campden

 Gloucestershire High St; www.chippingcampden online.org

This perfect Cotswold town presents a unified picture of golden-coloured and lichen-patched stone. Inside the 15th-century St James's Church, one of the finest in the Cotswolds, are many elaborate tombs and a magnificent brass dedicated to wool merchant William Grevel, who built Grevel House (c.1380) on the High Street, the oldest in a fine row of buildings, distinguished by a double-storey bay window.

Viscount Campden donated the Market Hall in 1627. His contemporary, Robert Dover, founded the "Cotswold Olimpicks". This 1612 version included such painful events as the shin-kicking contest. The games still take place on the first Friday after each Spring Bank Holiday. The setting for the games is a spectacular natural hollow on Dover's Hill, worth climbing on a clear day for the marvellous views over the Vale of Evesham.

④
Cirencester

 Gloucestershire Park St; www. cirencester.com

The town of Cirencester is known as the capital of the Cotswolds. At its heart is a marketplace where a popular market is held every Monday and Friday. Overlooking the market is St John the Baptist Church, whose "wineglass" pulpit (1515) is one of the few pre-Reformation pulpits to survive in England. To the west is Cirencester Park, a country house laid out by the 1st Earl of Bathurst from 1714, surrounded by a massive yew hedge. The modern **Corinium Museum** displays a fabulous hoard of Roman finds, including mosaics, as well as Anglo-Saxon and medieval exhibits.

Corinium Museum
 Park St 10am-5pm Mon-Sat, 2-5pm Sun (Mar-Oct: to 4pm)
 coriniummuseum.org

> HIDDEN GEM
> **Superb Mosaics**
>
> Cirencester was an important centre of mosaic production during Roman times. Chedworth Roman Villa, 13 kilometres (8 miles) north, has a particularly glorious example, which celebrates the Four Seasons.

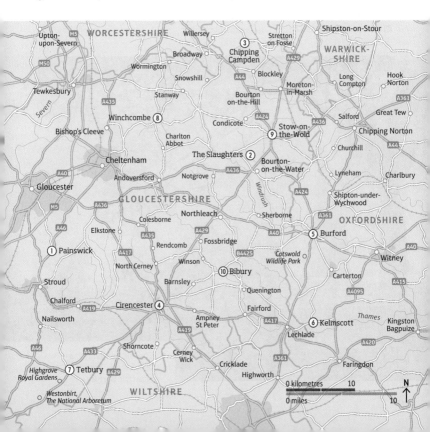

Burford

🏠 Oxfordshire 🛈 33a High St; www.oxfordshire cotswolds.org

A charming small town, Burford has hardly changed since Georgian times, when it was an important coach stop between Oxford and the West Country. Cotswold stone houses, inns and shops, many built in the 16th century, line its main street. The large church at the end of the High Street was begun in 1125 and has a 15th-century spire and several ornate tombs, most notably that of Sir Lawrence and Lady Tanfield (1625).

A few miles south of Burford is the popular **Cotswold Wildlife Park**, home to over 260 different species of mammals, reptiles and birds.

Cotswold Wildlife Park

♿ 🅿 🍴 🏠 Burford ⏰ 10am–6pm daily (Nov–Mar: to 5pm) 🌐 cotswoldwildlifepark.co.uk

 Kelmscott

🏠 Oxfordshire 🌐 kelmscott.org.uk

The designer, writer and publisher William Morris lived in this pretty Thameside village from 1871 until his death in 1896. He shared his house, the classic Elizabethan **Kelmscott Manor**, with painter Dante Gabriel Rossetti (1828–82), who later left after an affair with Morris's wife Jane. Morris and his followers in the Arts and Crafts movement were attracted by the medieval feel of the village and several cottages were later built in Morris's memory. Today the manor has works of art by members of the movement and Morris's textile patterns and furniture. Morris is buried in the village churchyard

Kelmscott Manor

♿ 🍴 🏠 Kelmscott ⏰ Apr–Oct: 11am–5pm Wed & Sat (house & garden) 🌐 sal.org.uk/kelmscott-manor

Did You Know?

William Morris's wife Jane was the model for many Pre-Raphaelite paintings.

⑦ **Tetbury**

🏠 Gloucestershire 🚉 Kemble 🚌 From Cirencester 🛈 33 Church St; www.visittetbury.co.uk

With a twice-weekly market, a clutch of antiques shops and a history stretching back 1,300 years, Tetbury is one of the larger, busier towns in the Cotswolds, though still small by national standards. Most of its buildings, including the handsome pillared Market House, the wool merchants' houses and weavers' cottages, date from the 16th and 17th centuries, when the town

↑ The tall, slender tower of St John the Baptist Church in Burford

prospered from the wool trade. A mile to the southwest of the town are the glorious, innovative **Highgrove Royal Gardens** at the private residence of The Prince of Wales and the Duchess of Cornwall.

A couple of miles southwest of Tetbury is **Westonbirt, The National Arboretum**, where treetop walkways and trails allow visitors to explore parkland and gardens heaving with 2,500 species of trees from around the globe.

Highgrove Royal Gardens

 ⬜ Doughton
🕙 Apr–Oct: by pre-booked guided tour on selected dates only, check website
🌐 highgrovegardens.com

Westonbirt, The National Arboretum

 ⬜ Westonbirt
🕙 Mar–Nov: 9am–4:30pm daily (Dec–Feb: to 4pm)
🌐 forestryengland.uk

---

⑧

Winchcombe

🏛 Gloucestershire
🚉 Winchcombe (summer only) 🚌 From Cirencester
🛈 High St; www.winchcombe.co.uk

Nestling photogenically in a valley on a number of official walking routes, Winchcombe makes a great stop for hungry, tired walkers, with its restaurants, pubs, tea rooms and places to stay.

This was a major centre of the Anglo-Saxon kingdom of Mercia, mentioned in the Domesday Book of 1086, and a commercially successful town in the Middle Ages.

The splendid **Sudeley Castle** was the home and the final resting place of Catherine Parr, the last and surviving wife of Henry VIII.

Sudeley Castle

 ⬜ Winchcombe
🕙 Mid-Mar–Oct: 10am–5pm daily 🌐 sudeleycastle.co.uk

↑ The highly picturesque cottages on Arlington Row, a Cotswolds landmark, in Bibury

---

⑨

Stow-on-the-Wold

🏛 Gloucestershire 🚌 From Cirencester 🛈 St Edwards Hall; www.stowinfo.co.uk

Perched 244 m (800 ft) atop Stow Hill, this is the loftiest town in the Cotswolds. The large square at its centre, surrounded by smart stone town houses now occupied by tea rooms, antiques shops and pubs, is testament to the once-renowned annual trade fairs that were held here from the 14th century. Today it is famous for the Stowe Horse Fair, held twice a year.

---

⑩

Bibury

🏛 Gloucestershire 🚌 From Cirencester 🌐 bibury.com

William Morris described this quintessential Cotswolds village, which straddles the River Coln, as the "most beautiful village in England". The stone buildings, many of them 17th-century weavers' cottages, line the river and the twisted nest of streets. One such row of cottages – Arlington Row – is one of England's most iconic streets.

STAY

The Painswick Hotel

This Grade II listed building overlooking the Painswick Valley has stylish rooms.

🏛 Kemps Ln, Painswick
🌐 thepainswick.co.uk

£££

Number 4 at Stow

Set within its own grounds, this compact boutique hotel offers 18 stylish rooms.

🏛 Fosseway, Stow-on-the-Wold
🌐 hotelnumber4.co.uk

£££

The Close Hotel

A 16th-century manor house with spacious rooms and a fabulous walled garden.

🏛 Long St, Tetbury
🌐 cotswolds-inns-hotels.co.uk

£££

BUILDING WITH COTSWOLD STONE

The Cotswolds are a range of limestone hills running over 80 km (50 miles) in a north-easterly direction from Bath *(p256)*. The thin soils here are difficult to plough but ideal for grazing sheep, and the wealth engendered by the medieval wool trade was poured into building majestic churches and opulent town houses. Stone quarried from these hills was used to build London's St Paul's Cathedral *(p116)*, as well as the villages, barns and manor houses that make the local landscape so picturesque.

COTSWOLD STONE TOWNS AND VILLAGES

Many of the villages in the Cotswolds are built almost entirely from stone. Huge deposits of limestone in the region resulted in a wealth of stone buildings. Masons worked from distinctive local designs that were handed down from generation to generation.

STONE GARGOYLES

Gargoyles appear on the outside of churches in the Cotswolds, often in the form of animal heads with gaping mouths or human heads with their tongues sticking out. Typical 15th-century gargoyles reflect a combination of pagan and Christian beliefs. Fertility figures, always important in rural areas, were incorporated into Christian festivals. Human faces often caricatured local church dignitaries. Animal gods represented qualities such as strength in pagan times.

↑ Picturesque cottages on the famous Arlington Row in Bibury

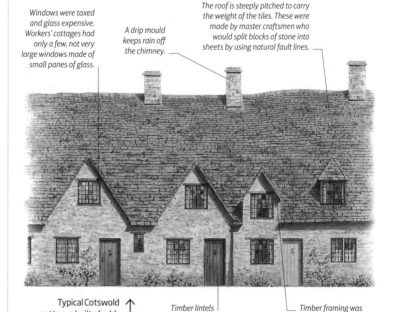

Windows were taxed and glass expensive. Workers' cottages had only a few, not very large windows made of small panes of glass.

A drip mould keeps rain off the chimney.

The roof is steeply pitched to carry the weight of the tiles. These were made by master craftsmen who would split blocks of stone into sheets by using natural fault lines.

Typical Cotswold cottages built of odd-shaped stones ↑

Timber lintels and doors

Timber framing was cheaper than stone, and was used for the upper rooms in the roof.

VARIATIONS IN STONE

The golden brown to cream stone that is typically seen in Cotswold villages is a Jurassic oolitic limestone. Cotswold stone is warmer-toned in the north due to being stained with iron, pearly in central areas and light grey in the south. The stone seems to glow with absorbed sunlight. It is a limestone that is easily carved and can be used for many purposes, from buildings to bridges, headstones and gargoyles.

① Lower Slaughter

Lower Slaughter *(p226)* is built of honey-coloured stone and gets its name from the Anglo-Saxon word slough, or muddy place. It has a low stone bridge over the River Eye.

② Stow-on-the-Wold

Market cross, a late medieval stone cross in Stow-on-the-Wold *(p229)*, is one of many found in the Cotswolds.

③ Dry-Stone Walling

Dry-stone walling is an ancient technique used in the Cotswolds and such walls can be seen throughout the region. The stones are held in place without mortar.

④ Stone Tombs

Fine, richly carved 17th- and 18th-century limestone tombs can be found in the churchyard in Painswick *(p226)*.

Wool merchants' houses were built of fine ashlar (dressed stone) with ornamental cornerstones, doorframes and windows.

The eaves here have a dentil frieze, so-called because it resembles a row of teeth.

The door frame has a rounded pediment on simple pilasters.

→ An early Georgian merchant's house in Painswick

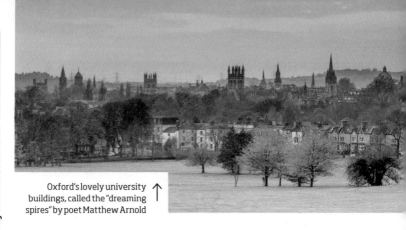

↑ Oxford's lovely university buildings, called the "dreaming spires" by poet Matthew Arnold

 3

OXFORD

🏠 Oxfordshire 🚉 Oxford 🚌 Gloucester Green
🛈 15-16 Broad St; www.experienceoxfordshire.org

Oxford is more than just a university city, but with 38 colleges, inevitably the city centre is dominated by institutions related to its huge academic community, such as Blackwell's bookshop, which stocks over 20,000 titles. The two rivers, the Cherwell and the Isis (the upper reaches of the Thames), provide lovely riverside walks, or you can hire a punt and spend a few hours on the water.

 ①

Ashmolean Museum

🏠 Beaumont St ⏰ 10am-5pm daily (to 8pm last Fri of the month) 🌐 ashmolean.org

One of the best British museums outside London, the Ashmolean is based on a collection put together in the 17th century by two John Tradescants, father and son. On their death, their cabinet of curiosities was acquired by the antiquarian Elias Ashmole, who donated it to the university. It is housed in a Neo-Classical building of 1845.

Spacious galleries, added in 2009, lead off a striking atrium and staircase. The collections comprise Greek, Roman and Indian artifacts, ancient Egyptian mummies, Anglo-Saxon treasures and modern Chinese painting, all of world-class standard. Highlights of the Western art galleries include the world's greatest collection of drawings by Raphael (1483–1520), Bellini's *St Jerome Reading in a Landscape* (late 15th century), Turner's *Venice: The Grand Canal* (1840) and Picasso's *Blue Roofs* (1901).

The second-largest coin collection in Britain is housed here. One of the most notable pieces is a rare Oxford crown,

Did You Know?

The Ashmolean, founded in 1683, was the first museum in the world to be opened to the public.

minted in Oxford during the Civil War in 1644. Perhaps the most famous item is the smal gold and enamel ornament known as the Alfred Jewel, which dates from the 9th century. Another key exhibit is the lantern that belonged to Guy Fawkes.

 ②

Pitt Rivers Museum

🏠 Parks Rd ⏰ Noon-4pm Mon, 10am-4:30pm Tue-Sun
🌐 prm.ox.ac.uk

Entrance to this fascinating museum is through the adjacent Museum of Natural History, which houses dinosaur relics and a stuffed dodo. The Pitt Rivers has an extensive ethnographic collection – masks and totems from Africa and the Far East – and archaeological displays, including exhibits collected by the explorer Captain Cook, are shown in densely packed cases, giving the museum a magical atmosphere.

 ③

Oxford Botanic Garden

🏠 Rose Lane ⏰ Times vary, check website
🌐 botanic-garden.ox.ac.uk

Britain's oldest botanic garden was founded in 1621 – one ancient yew tree survives

from that period. The entrance gates were designed by Nicholas Stone in 1633. The delightful garden has an original walled garden, a rock garden and an insectivorous plant house.

④ Carfax Tower

Carfax Sq **01865 792653** **Daily**

The tower is all that remains of the 14th-century Church of St Martin, demolished in 1896 so that the adjoining road could be widened. You can climb to the top for panoramic views. Carfax was the crossing point of the original north–south and east–west routes through Oxford: its name derives from the Latin *quadrifurcus* (four-forked).

⑤ University Church of St Mary the Virgin

High St **9:30am–5pm Mon–Sat, noon–5pm Sun** **university-church.ox. ac.uk**

This, the official university church, is said to be the most visited parish church in England. The oldest parts date from the early 13th century and include the tower, from which there are fine views. Its Convocation House served as the university's first library until the Bodleian *(p235)* was founded in 1488. The church is where the three Oxford Martyrs *(p236)* were pronounced heretics in 1555.

EAT

Vaults & Garden
Busy café in the vaulted Congregation House of the University Church, serving snacks, cooked breakfasts and a varied lunch menu, including vegetarian options.

University Church of St Mary the Virgin, Radcliffe Sq **thevaults andgarden.com**

£££

Branca
This large, vibrant brasserie specializes in Italian dishes. The bar is a great place for cocktails. There is also a large garden terrace for alfresco dining in warm weather.

111 Walton St, Jericho **branca.co.uk**

£££

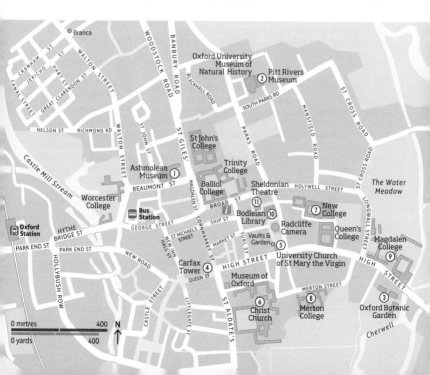

↑ Christ Church, Oxford's largest college with some 600 students on its roll

⑥ Christ Church

🏛 St Aldate's
🌐 chch.ox.ac.uk

The best way to view the largest of the Oxford colleges is to approach it through the meadows from St Aldate's. Christ Church dates from 1525, when Cardinal Wolsey founded it as an ecclesiastical college to train cardinals. Like most of the colleges, it is designed around a series of quadrangles or "quads": interconnected rectangular courtyards. The upper part of the tower in Tom Quad was built by Sir Christopher Wren (p116) in 1682 and is the largest in the city. When its bell, Great Tom, was hung in 1648, the college had 101 students, which is why the bell is rung 101 times at 9:05pm, to mark the curfew that was once the rule for students. The odd timing is because Oxford is technically 5 minutes behind Greenwich Mean Time. Christ Church has produced 13 British prime ministers in the last 200 years. The Renaissance magnificence of Christ Church's Hall inspired the film-makers of the Harry Potter series. Beside the main quad is the 12th-century Christ Church Cathedral, one of the smallest in England.

The impressive Christ Church Picture Gallery holds masterpieces dating from 1300 to 1750, focusing on the Italian Renaissance, with works by da Vinci and Michelangelo.

WALKING TOURS

Oxford Official Walking Tours (www.experienceoxfordshire.org) runs a number of excellent guided walks taking in the colleges as well as special-interest tours on themes such as Harry Potter, Alice in Wonderland and Inspector Morse.

⑦ New College

🏛 Hollywell St
🌐 new.ox.ac.uk

One of the grandest colleges, New College was founded by William of Wykeham in 1379 to educate clergy to replace those killed by the Black Death of 1348 (p48). Highlights of its magnificent chapel on New College Lane, restored in the 19th century, are the 14th-century misericords and El Greco's (1541–1614) painting of St James. Its gardens are enclosed by the 13th-century city walls.

⑧ Merton College

🏛 Merton St
🌐 merton.ox.ac.uk

This is the oldest college (1264) in Oxford. Much of its hall is original, including a sturdy decorated door. The chapel choir contains allegorical reliefs representing music, arithmetic, rhetoric and grammar. Merton's Mob Quad served as a model for the later colleges. It vies with the Old Court in Cambridge's Corpus Christi (p199) for the title of oldest college quadrangle.

→ The 18th-century New Building, Magdalen College, where C S Lewis had a room

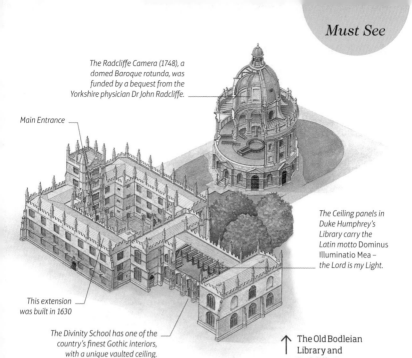

The Radcliffe Camera (1748), a domed Baroque rotunda, was funded by a bequest from the Yorkshire physician Dr John Radcliffe.

Main Entrance

The Ceiling panels in Duke Humphrey's Library carry the Latin motto Dominus Illuminatio Mea – the Lord is my Light.

This extension was built in 1630

The Divinity School has one of the country's finest Gothic interiors, with a unique vaulted ceiling.

↑ The Old Bodleian Library and Radcliffe Camera

⑨

Magdalen College

🏛 High St 🌐 magd.ox.ac.uk

Magdalen is perhaps the most iconic and beautiful Oxford college, with its 15th-century quads in contrasting styles backing onto the Cherwell. Every May Day at 6am, the college choir sings from the top of Magdalen's bell tower (1508) – a 16th-century custom to mark the start of summer.

⑩

Bodleian Library

🏛 Broad St ⏰ 9am-5pm Mon-Sat, 11am-5pm Sun 🌐 bodleian.ox.ac.uk

The first university library was founded at the site of the University Church in 1320. A new library was built at its current location in 1488 by Humphrey, Duke of Gloucester (1391–1447) and brother of Henry V. It was refounded in 1602 by Thomas Bodley, a wealthy scholar, and has seen additions and expansions over the centuries. The library is one of the six copyright deposit libraries in the UK – it is entitled to receive a copy of every book published in Britain.

⑪

Sheldonian Theatre

🏛 Broad St ⏰ Times vary, check website 🌐 admin. ox.ac.uk/sheldonian

Completed in 1669, this was designed by Christopher Wren (p116), and paid for by Gilbert Sheldon, Archbishop of Canterbury, as a location for university degree ceremonies. The design of the D-shaped building is based on the Theatre of Marcellus in Rome. The octagonal cupola built in 1838 offers a famous view from its huge lantern. The theatre's painted ceiling shows the triumph of religion, art and science over envy, hatred and malice.

A SHORT WALK
OXFORD

Distance 2.5 km (1.5 miles) **Time** 30 minutes
Nearest bus station Gloucester Green

The development of England's first university created Oxford's spectacular skyline of tall towers and "dreaming spires". A great place to explore on foot, Oxford is full of history and interesting buildings. A walk around the city centre will take you past eminent colleges and other university buildings, as well as Radcliffe Square, perhaps one of the most beautiful squares in Europe.

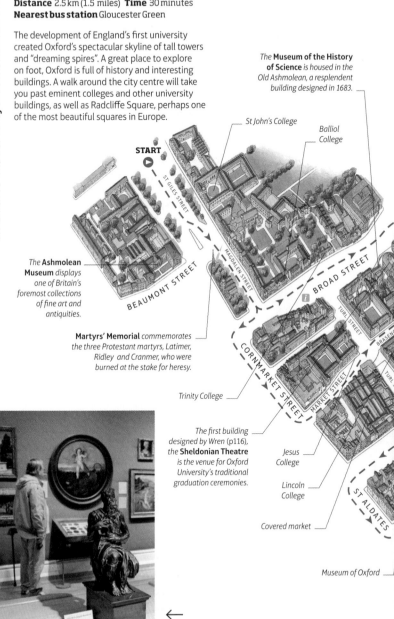

The **Museum of the History of Science** is housed in the Old Ashmolean, a resplendent building designed in 1683.

St John's College

Balliol College

START

ST GILES STREET

The **Ashmolean Museum** displays one of Britain's foremost collections of fine art and antiquities.

MAGDALEN STREET

BEAUMONT STREET

BROAD STREET

TURL STREET

BRASENOSE

TURL ST

Martyrs' Memorial commemorates the three Protestant martyrs, Latimer, Ridley and Cranmer, who were burned at the stake for heresy.

CORNMARKET STREET

MARKET STREET

Trinity College

The first building designed by Wren (p116), the **Sheldonian Theatre** is the venue for Oxford University's traditional graduation ceremonies.

Jesus College

Lincoln College

Covered market

ST ALDATES

Museum of Oxford

←
Western Art galleries in the Ashmolean Museum

0 metres   100
0 yards   100

N ↑

↑ Radcliffe Camera and All Souls College on Radcliffe Square, at the heart of the university

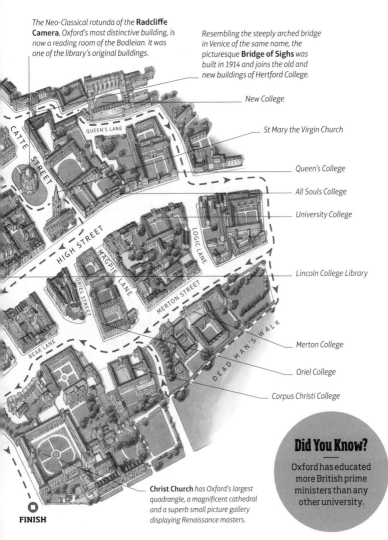

The Neo-Classical rotunda of the **Radcliffe Camera**, *Oxford's most distinctive building, is now a reading room of the Bodleian. It was one of the library's original buildings.*

Resembling the steeply arched bridge in Venice of the same name, the picturesque **Bridge of Sighs** *was built in 1914 and joins the old and new buildings of Hertford College.*

New College

St Mary the Virgin Church

Queen's College

All Souls College

University College

Lincoln College Library

Merton College

Oriel College

Corpus Christi College

CATTE STREET

QUEEN'S LANE

HIGH STREET

MAGPIE LANE

ORIEL STREET

LOGIC LANE

MERTON STREET

BEAR LANE

DEADMAN'S WALK

O
FINISH

Christ Church *has Oxford's largest quadrangle, a magnificent cathedral and a superb small picture gallery displaying Renaissance masters.*

Did You Know?

Oxford has educated more British prime ministers than any other university.

④ 🚲 🎭 🍴 💬 🛍️

BLENHEIM PALACE

📍 **Woodstock, Oxfordshire** 🚊 **Oxford** 🚌 **53 from Oxford train station**
🕐 **Palace and gardens: 10am–5:30pm daily; Park: 9am–6pm daily**
🌐 **blenheimpalace.com**

Designed by Nicholas Hawksmoor and Sir John Vanbrugh in the early 1700s, Blenheim Palace is a Baroque masterpiece and is the only British historic house to be named a UNESCO World Heritage Site. The vast, splendid gardens and parkland make for glorious walks.

After John Churchill, the 1st Duke of Marlborough, defeated the French at the Battle of Blenheim in 1704, Queen Anne gave him the Manor of Woodstock and had this palatial house built for him. It was also the birthplace of Winston Churchill in 1874, who was a descendant of the Dukes of Marlborough, and houses an exhibition with displays on the life, work, paintings and writings of the former British prime minister. Today Blenheim is home to the 12th duke. Visitors can wander through 300 years of history in splendid rooms full of tapestries, paintings, china and statues. Capability Brown (p24) designed parts of the beautiful landscaped gardens and park, which include a yew maze, lakes, a rose garden, arboretum and the Grand Bridge designed by Vanbrugh.

The Grand Bridge, begun in 1708, has a 31-m (101-ft) main span and contains rooms within its structure.

The Chapel features a marble monument to the 1st Duke of Marlborough and his family.

→
The layout of the magnificent Blenheim Palace

The magnificent water terraces were laid out in the 1920s by French architect Achille Duchêne in 17th-century style.

WOODSTOCK

Located about 13 km (18 miles) northwest of Oxford, the small, quiet town of Woodstock grew up as a coach stop around the Royal Hunting Lodge, which later became Blenheim Palace. With its pretty stone houses, antiques shops, traditional pubs and tea rooms, it is a relaxing place to take afternoon tea after a visit to the palace. The Oxfordshire Museum on Park Street has displays on local history, art and wildlife.

Blenheim Palace with its water terraces and a fountain; the lavish Red Drawing Room *(inset)*

Blenheim Palace: The Untold Story exhibition.

Grinling Gibbons lions (1709)

Clock tower

The Great Hall has a splendid ceiling by Thornhill (1716).

East gate

The Italian Garden contains the Mermaid Fountain (early 1900s) by US sculptor Waldo Story.

The Green Drawing Room has a full-length portrait of the 4th Duke by George Romney (1734–1802).

Third State Room

Great Court

Second State Room

First State Room

Red Drawing Room

Green Writing Room

The Saloon's walls and ceiling have detailed paintings by French artist Louis Laguerre (1663–1721).

The Long Library was designed by Vanbrugh as a picture gallery. The portraits include one of Queen Anne by Sir Godfrey Kneller (1646–1723).

Did You Know?

Blenheim is the only building in England other than royal buildings to have "Palace" in its title.

EXPERIENCE MORE

⑤

Roald Dahl Museum

📍 81-83 High St, Great Missenden, Buckinghamshire 🚉 Great Missenden ⏰ 10am-5pm Tue-Fri, 11am-5pm Sat & Sun 🌐 roalddahl.com/museum

The magical world of Roald Dahl's stories comes to life in this museum, where interactive exhibits allow children to record dreams in a "dream bottle" or try their hand at creative writing.

⑥

ZSL Whipsnade Zoo

📍 Nr Dunstable, Bedfordshire 🚉 Hemel Hempsted or Luton then bus ⏰ 10am-6pm daily (Sep-Oct: to 5pm; Nov-Feb: to 4pm) 🌐 zsl.org

The rural branch of London Zoo, this was one of the first

↑ Coming up with inspiration at the Ideas Table in the Roald Dahl Museum

zoos to minimize the use of cages, confining animals safely but without constriction.

At 240 ha (600 acres), it is one of Europe's largest conservation parks, with more than 2,500 species. You can drive through some areas or hop aboard a steam train. Popular attractions are the Cheetah Rock exhibit and the Butterfly House.

⑦

St Albans

📍 Hertfordshire 🚉 St Albans City, St Albans Abbey ℹ️ Alban Arena Civic Centre; www.enjoy stalbans.com

This thriving market town is best known for its **Cathedral**, an outstanding example of medieval architecture. It was begun in 793, when King Offa of Mercia founded the abbey in honour of St Alban, Britain's first Christian martyr, put to death by the Romans in the 3rd century. The oldest parts, which still stand, were first built in 1077 and are easily recognizable as Norman by the round-headed arches and windows. They form part of the 84-m (276-ft) nave – the longest in England. It was at the cathedral that

the English barons drafted the Magna Carta document (p267), which King John was then forced to sign.

On the site of one of the first British cities that the Romans established in Britain, the **Verulamium Museum** displays well-preserved Roman artifacts, notably some breathtaking mosaic floors, including one depicting the head of a sea god and another of a scallop shell. On the basis of excavated plaster fragments, a Roman room has been re-created, its walls painted in geometric patterns.

→ Waddesdon's gardens; an ornate room in the 19th-century manor house (inset)

Between here and St Albans Cathedral are a hypocaust with a mosaic, remnants of the ancient city wall and one of the original gates.

St Albans Cathedral
⌖ ♿ ☐ Sumpter Yard
🕐 8:30am-5:30pm daily
Ⓦ stalbanscathedral.org

Verulamium Museum
⌖ ♿ ☐ St Michael's St
🕐 10am-5pm Mon-Sat,
2-5pm Sun Ⓦ stalbans
museums.org.uk

Waddesdon
☐ Nr Aylesbury, Buckinghamshire
🚉 Aylesbury 🕐 House: late Mar-Oct: noon-4pm Wed-Fri, 11am-4pm Sat & Sun; Grounds: late Mar-Oct: 10am-5pm Wed-Sun; see website for winter hours
Ⓦ waddesdon.org.uk

Waddesdon Manor was built in 1874–85 by Baron Ferdinand de Rothschild and designed by French architect Gabriel-Hippolyte Destailleur in the style of a French 16th-century chateau. The manor houses a fine collection of French 18th-century decorative art,

as well as Savonnerie carpets and Sèvres porcelain. The garden, originally laid out by French landscape gardener Elie Lainé, is renowned for its seasonal displays.

Ⓨ Vale of the White Horse
☐ Oxfordshire 🚉 Didcot
ℹ Roysse Court, The Guildhall, Abingdon, 01235 522711; 19 Church St, Wantage, 01235 760176

This lovely valley gets its name from the huge chalk horse, measuring 100 m (350 ft) from nose to tail, carved into the hillside above Uffington. It is believed to be Britain's oldest hillside carving and has sparked many legends: some say it was cut by the Saxon leader Hengist (whose name means "stallion" in German), while others believe it is to do with Alfred the Great, thought to have been born nearby. It is, however, a great deal older than either of these stories suggest, having been dated at around 1000 BC.

The best view of the horse is to be had from Uffington village, which is also worth

visiting for the **Tom Brown's School Museum**. This 17th-century school house contains exhibits devoted to the author Thomas Hughes (1822–96). Hughes set the early chapters of his Victorian novel *Tom Brown's Schooldays* here. The museum also contains material about excavations on White Horse Hill.

Tom Brown's School Museum
⌖ ☐ Broad St, Uffington
🕐 Easter-Oct: 2-5pm Sat, Sun & public hols Ⓦ museum. uffington.net

↑ Visiting the Diagon Alley set from the Harry Potter movies at the Warner Bros. Studio Tour

EAT

Paris House

The menu at this restaurant in a mock-Tudor house combines Asian and British flavours. It is best experienced by ordering one of the signature six- to ten-course tasting menus.

 Woburn Park ⏰ Mon–Wed 🅦 parishouse.co.uk

£££

The Muddy Duck

Southwest of Stowe, this contemporary pub is well worth a visit for the mix of classic, top-quality pub grub and innovative British tapas.

 Main St, Hethe ⏰ Sun dinner 🅦 themuddy duckpub.co.uk

£££

10

Warner Bros. Studio Tour – The Making of Harry Potter

📍 Leavesden, Hertfordshire 🚉 Watford Junction then shuttle bus ⏰ Times vary, check website 🅦 wbstudio tour.co.uk

Visitors to the Warner Bros. Studio can see original scenery, costumes and props from the Harry Potter movies. Among the sets are the iconic Great Hall and Diagon Alley. The self-guided tour offers glimpses into the off-camera world of the film-makers, including how green-screen effects brought to life the monsters and marvels of Harry's world. Tickets must be booked in advance.

11

Hatfield House

📍 Hatfield, Hertfordshire 🚉 Hatfield ⏰ Easter–Sep: 11am–5pm Wed–Sun & public hols 🅦 hatfield-house.co.uk

One of England's finest Jacobean houses, Hatfield House was built between 1607 and 1611 for the powerful statesman Robert Cecil.

Its chief historical interest, though, lies in the surviving wing of the original Tudor Hatfield Palace, where Queen Elizabeth I spent much of her childhood. She held her first Council of State here when she was crowned in 1558. The palace was partly demolished in 1607 to make way for the new house, which now contains mementos of her life, including the famous *Rainbow* portrait painted around 1600 by Isaac Oliver.

12

Woburn Abbey

📍 Woburn, Bedfordshire 🚉 Flitwick then taxi ⏰ Easter–Aug: 11am–5pm daily; Garden & Deer Park: 10am–6pm daily (Fri–Sun in winter) 🅦 woburnabbey.co.uk

The abbey was built in the mid-18th century on the foundations of a large 12th-century Cistercian monastery. Its mix of styles include those of Henry Flitcroft and Henry Holland. The grounds are also

> In the space of nearly 100 years Stowe was transformed by the addition of monuments, Greek and Gothic temples, grottoes, statues, artificial lakes and "natural tree plantings.

popular for their extensive safari park and attractive deer park, home to nine species, including the Manchurian Sika deer from China.

Woburn's magnificent state apartments house an impressive private art collection which includes Gower's *Armada Portrait* of Queen Elizabeth I (1588) and works by Reynolds (1723–92) and Canaletto (1697–1768).

13

Stowe

A Buckingham, Buckinghamshire **B** Milton Keynes then bus **C** 10am-5pm daily (Nov-Mar: to 4pm) **W** nationaltrust. org.uk

One of the most ambitious landscaped gardens in Britain, Stowe is also a fine example of the 18th-century passion for improving on nature to make it conform to fashionable notions of taste. In the space of nearly 100 years the original garden, first laid out around 1680, was enlarged and transformed by the addition of monuments, Greek and Gothic temples, grottoes, statues, ornamental bridges, artificial lakes and "natural" tree plantings.

Most of the leading designers and architects of the period contributed to the design, including Sir John Vanbrugh and Capability Brown (p24).

From 1593 to 1921 the property was owned by the Temple and Grenville families – later the Dukes of Buckingham – until the large Palladian house, **Stowe House**, at its centre was converted into an elite boys' school.

Stowe House

 C During school term for guided tours only; for other days, check website **W** stowe.co.uk/house

14

Bletchley Park

A Sherwood Drive, Bletchley MK3 **B** Bletchley **C** 9:30am-5pm daily (Nov-Feb: to 4pm) **W** bletchley park.org.uk

During World War II, this mansion on a leafy estate near Milton Keynes housed the British Government Code and Cypher School. This is where Alan Turing and his colleagues broke the German Enigma code. Examples of the code-breaking machines and a series of restored rooms across the site, where many of the code breakers worked their eight-hour shifts, leave a vivid impression of what happened here and what was at stake.

HIDDEN GEM
MK Gallery

Just 3 km (5 miles) north of Bletchley Park, in Milton Keynes, this superb gallery offers changing exhibitions of cutting-edge international art, design and architecture (www.mkgallery.org).

↑ An elegant Palladio-inspired bridge reflected in the lake at Stowe

↑ Cheltenham's shaded Promenade, lined with elegant stores

 15

Cheltenham

🏛 Gloucestershire 🚉🚌
ℹ Clarence St; www.
visitcheltenham.com

Cheltenham's reputation for elegance was first gained in the late 18th century, when high society flocked to the spa town following the example set by George III. Many gracious terraced houses were built in Neo-Classical style, along broad avenues. These survive around the Queen's Hotel, near Montpellier, a lovely Regency arcade lined with crafts and antiques shops, and in the Promenade, with its smart department stores and couturiers. In the more modern Regency Arcade, the star attraction is the 1985 clock by Kit Williams: visit on the hour to see fish blowing bubbles over the onlookers' heads.

The **Wilson Art Gallery & Museum** houses a collection of furniture and other items made by members of the influential Arts and Crafts movement, whose strict principles of utilitarian design were laid down by William Morris (*p228*).

The **Pittville Pump Room** (1825–30), modelled on the Greek Temple of Ilissos in Athens, is frequently used for performances during the town's renowned annual festivals of music (Jul) and literature (Oct).

The event that really attracts the crowds is the Cheltenham Festival, the country's premier National Hunt race meeting held every March.

The Wilson Art Gallery & Museum

😊🏛 🏛 Clarence St
🕐 9:30am–5:15pm Tue–Sat (to 7:45pm Thu), 11am–4pm Sun 🌐 cheltenhammuseum.
org.uk

Pittville Pump Room

🏛 Pittville Park 🕐 10am–4pm Wed–Sat 🔒 For functions 🌐 cheltenhamtownhall.
org.uk

 16

Gloucester

🏛 Gloucestershire 🚉🚌
ℹ 28 Southgate St; www.
visitgloucester.co.uk

Gloucester has played a prominent role in the history of England. It was here that William the Conqueror ordered a vast survey of all the land in his kingdom for tax purposes, which was to be recorded in the Domesday Book of 1086.

Gloucester was popular with the Norman monarchs, and in 1216 Henry III was crowned in its magnificent cathedral. The solid, dignified nave was begun in 1089. Edward II is buried near the high altar. Many pilgrims came to honour his tomb, leaving behind generous donations. In 1331, these were used to fund

> **Gloucester was popular with the Norman monarchs, and in 1216 Henry III was crowned in its magnificent cathedral. The solid, dignified nave was begun in 1089.**

the wonderful east window and the cloisters, where the fan vault was developed and then copied in other churches all over the country.

The impressive buildings around the cathedral include College Court, with its **House of the Tailor of Gloucester** museum, in the house that the children's author Beatrix Potter *(p360)* used as the setting for her illustrations of that story. A museum complex has been created in the Gloucester Docks, part of which is still a port, linked to the Bristol Channel by the Gloucester and Sharpness Canal (opened in 1827). In the old port, and housed in a Victorian warehouse, the **National Waterways Museum Gloucester** relates the history of Britain's canals via a series of interactive galleries. There are boat trips, too.

House of the Tailor of Gloucester

ⓒ ⛫ College Court ⏰ 10am–4pm Mon-Sat ⓦ tailor-of-gloucester.org.uk

↑ Charming half-timbered cottages along the River Avon, Tewkesbury

National Waterways Museum Gloucester

⊛ ☺ ⓒ ⛫ Llanthony Warehouse, Gloucester Docks ⏰ Apr-Oct: 10am–5pm daily (Nov-Mar: Tue–Sun) ⓦ canalrivertrust.org.uk

Tewkesbury

⛫ Gloucestershire ℹ 100 Church St; www. visittewkesbury.info

This lovely town sits on the confluence of the rivers Severn and Avon. It has one of England's finest Norman abbey churches, St Mary the Virgin, which locals saved during the Dissolution of the Monasteries *(p391)* by paying Henry VIII £453. Around the church, with its bulky tower and Norman façade, timbered buildings are crammed within the bend of the river. Warehouses are a reminder of past wealth, while the pretty, but redundant, Borough Mill on Quay Street also harks back to a more prosperous age.

The Medieval Festival (Jul) sees re-enactments of the Battle of Tewksbury of 1471, accompanied by period-style entertainers such as minstrels.

← Fan vaulting and stained-glass windows in Gloucester Cathedral's cloisters

A DRIVING TOUR
TOURING
THE THAMES

Length 75 km (50 miles) **Stopping-off points**
The picturesque town of Henley has a large
number of riverside pubs for lunch.

The Thames between Pangbourne and Eton is
leafy and romantic and best seen by boat. If
time is short travel by car: the road keeps close
to the riverbank for much of the way. Swans glide
gracefully below ancient bridges and elegant
herons stand impassive at the river's edge. Huge
beech trees overhang the banks, which are lined
with fine houses, their gardens sloping to the
water. This tranquil scene has inspired painters
and writers through the ages.

1440
The year Eton College
was founded by
King Henry VI.

The white weather-boarded
Hambleden Mill *was operational
until 1955 and is one of the
largest on the Thames as well as
one of the oldest in origin.*

The 140-ha (350-acre)
Beale Park *was created
to preserve this beautiful
stretch of river intact and
breed endangered birds.*

The lovely old river town of
Henley *has houses and
churches dating from the
15th and 16th centuries.*

Pishill
Stonor
Nettlebed
Fawley
Skirmett
Frieth

Highmoor
Chechendon
Woodcote
OXFORDSHIRE
Henley-on-Thames
Harpsden

Goring-on-Thames
Sonning Common
Binfield Heath
Wargrave

Lower Basildon
Beale Park
START
Pangbourne
Whitchurch Mill
Sonning Bridge
Sonning
Twyford

Caversham
Hurst
Woodley

*Kenneth Grahame (1859–1932),
author of* The Wind in the
Willows, *lived in* **Pangbourne**.
*The village was used as the setting
by artists Ernest Shepard in 1908
and Arthur Rackham in 1951 to
illustrate the book.*

Reading
Whitley
Earley
Winnersh

Whitchurch Mill, *a charming village,
linked to Pangbourne by a Victorian
toll bridge, has a picturesque church
and one of the many disused
watermills that once harnessed
the power of this stretch of river. .*

The 18th-century
Sonning Bridge
*is made up of 11
brick arches of
varying width.*

← Approaching Sonning Bridge while boating on the Thames on a beautiful clear day

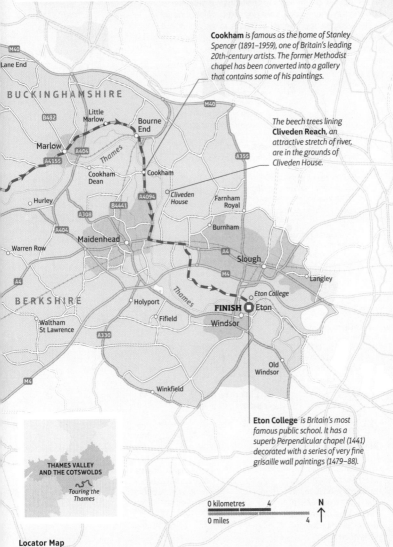

Cookham *is famous as the home of Stanley Spencer (1891–1959), one of Britain's leading 20th-century artists. The former Methodist chapel has been converted into a gallery that contains some of his paintings.*

The beech trees lining **Cliveden Reach**, *an attractive stretch of river, are in the grounds of Cliveden House.*

FINISH Eton

Eton College *is Britain's most famous public school. It has a superb Perpendicular chapel (1441) decorated with a series of very fine grisaille wall paintings (1479–88).*

THAMES VALLEY AND THE COTSWOLDS

Touring the Thames

Locator Map
For more detail see p222

0 kilometres   4

0 miles   4

N
↑

A DRIVING TOUR
COTSWOLDS GARDEN TOUR

Length 40 km (25 miles) **Stopping-off points** Hidcote Manor has excellent lunches and teas. Kiftsgate Court and Sudeley Castle also have restaurants offering lunches and snacks.

The charming Cotswold stone buildings perfectly complement the lush gardens for which the region is famous. This picturesque route from Stow-on-the-Wold to Cheltenham is designed to show every type of garden, from tiny cottage plots, brimming with bell-shaped flowers and hollyhocks, to the grand landscaped gardens of manor houses The route follows the escarpment of the Cotswold Hills, taking in spectacular scenery and some of the prettiest villages on the way.

In **Broadway** village, wisteria and cordoned fruit trees cover 17th-century cottages with their immaculate gardens.

The Cotswold stone **Snowshill Manor** contains an extraordinary collection of objets d'art, from bicycles to Japanese armour. There are walled gardens and terraces .The colour blue is a recurrent theme.

The Jacobean **Stanway House** has many lovely trees in its grounds and a pyramid above a cascade of water.

Cheltenham Imperial Gardens on the Promenade were laid out in 1817–18 to encourage people to walk from the town to the spa (p244).

South Littleton

Honeybourne

Badsey

B4035

Weston-sub-Edge

A46

A44

WORCESTER-SHIRE

Sedgeberrow

Broadway

Wormington

Little Beckford

B4077

Snowshill Manor

Stanway House

B4077

Gotherington

Winchcombe

Bishop's Cleeve

Sudeley Castle

B4632

Windrush

Southam

GLOUCESTERSHIRE

Cheltenham
FINISH

Brockhampton

A436

Andoversford

💬 INSIDER TIP
Broadway

Broadway has a choice of good eateries, from traditional pubs and teashops to the deluxe historic Lygon Arms on the High Street, which serves local dishes and drinks and delicious afternoon tea.

Restored **Sudeley Castle** is complemented by box hedges, topiary and an Elizabethan knot garden. Catherine Parr, Henry VIII's widow, died here in 1548 (p229).

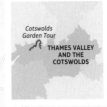

Cotswolds
Garden Tour

**THAMES VALLEY
AND THE
COTSWOLDS**

Locator Map
For more detail see p222

The charmingly naturalistic
Kiftsgate Court Garden *lies
opposite Hidcote Manor. It has
many rare and unusual plants
on a series of hillside terraces,
including the enormous "Kiftsgate"
Rose, nearly 30 m (100 ft) high.*

Started in the early years of the 20th
century, the beautiful **Hidcote Manor
Gardens** *pioneered the idea of a
garden as a series of outdoor "rooms",
enclosed by high yew hedges and
planted according to theme.*

One of the most picturesque gardens
in the Cotswolds is set on a hill around
the stone **Mill Dene** *water mill.*

Batsford Arboretum *holds a huge
collection of trees and shrubs from
around the world, with a focus on the
Far East, especially Japanese maples,
magnolias and pines.*

Bourton House Garden *surrounds an
18th-century manor house. It includes a
knot garden, water features and magnificent
wide herbaceous borders.*

Meon
Vale

Kiftsgate Court
Garden

Mickleton

Ilmington

Hidcote Manor
Gardens

B4632

Shipston-on-Stour

B4035

A429

Chipping
Campden

Stretton
on Fosse

B4081

A3400

B4479

Todenham

Blockley

Mill Dene

Batsford
Arboretum

Great
Wolford

A44

Bourton-on-the-Hill

Bourton
House

Moreton
in-Marsh

A44

Sezincote

A429

Longborough

Condicote

Evenlode

B4077

A424

A436

Stow-on-
the-Wold

START

Sezincote, *a 200-year
old house built in the
style of an Indian Mughal
palace, has formal
landscaped grounds
with spring-fed pools,
waterfalls and a grotto.*

0 kilometres   5

0 miles   5

N
↑

A greenhouse at Hidcote Manor ↑
Gardens in Gloucestershire

249

The dramatic stones of Stonehenge at dawn

BRISTOL, BATH AND WESSEX

This region of mellow countryside and prosperous cities has a rich history. Three thousand years ago, the downs of the Salisbury Plain were home to the settlers who created the mysterious stone circles at Stonehenge and Avebury and other prehistoric sites. Later, the Celts founded fortresses such as Dorchester's vast Maiden Castle, followed by the Romans who built England's first spa resort at Bath. In the 6th century the area became a stronghold of Celtic resistance against the Saxons. However, the Anglo-Saxon King Alfred was the first to unite the region as the kingdom of Wessex, which is roughly the modern counties of Hampshire, Dorset and Somerset.

In the early 1700s, Bristol, the area's largest city, became a transatlantic port, and its grand buildings bear witness to the wealth acquired from the subsequent slave, tobacco and wine trades. At the same time, the building of the Georgian terraces and circuses of Bath made the town supremely fashionable. George III 's regular visits to Weymouth set it on the map as a seaside resort, and with the introduction of the railway line in the 19th century, Bournemouth and its fine sandy beaches became popular.

BRISTOL, BATH AND WESSEX

Must Sees

1. Bristol
2. Bath
3. Stourhead
4. Stonehenge
5. Salisbury Cathedral

Experience More

6. Salisbury
7. Cheddar Gorge
8. Wells
9. Glastonbury
10. Bradford-on-Avon
11. Corsham
12. Avebury
13. Longleat House
14. Lacock
15. Abbotsbury
16. Shaftesbury
17. Dorchester
18. Weymouth
19. Sherborne
20. Lyme Regis
21. Isle of Purbeck
22. Corfe Castle
23. Wimborne Minster
24. Poole
25. Bournemouth

SOUTH AND
MID-WALES
p452

Kingstone

Pontrilas

Monmouth

Raglan

Usk

Portishead

Clevedon

Bristol Airport

Congresbury

Weston-super-Mare

Cardiff

Cowbridge

Wenvoe

Penarth

Llantwit Major

Barry

Bristol Channel

CHEDDAR GORGE 7

Cheddar

Burnham-on-Sea

Highbridge

Puriton

Street

SOMERSET

Brue

Axe

Lynmouth

Ilfracombe

Porlock

Minehead

Watchet

Dunster

Washford

Exmoor

Exford

Braunton

Barnstaple

Exton

Brendon Hills

Quantock Hills

Bridgwater

Somerton

Langport

DEVON AND
CORNWALL
p276

Taunton

Wellington

Corfe

Hatch Beauchamp

Great Torrington

South Molton

Witheridge

Tiverton

Ilminster

Chard

Crewkerne

Winsham

Beaminster

Merton

Hatherleigh

Copplestone

Honiton

Charmouth

Bridport

Okehampton

Exeter Airport

Exeter

Ottery St. Mary

20

LYME REGIS

Sidmouth

Lyme Bay

BRISTOL, BATH
AND WESSEX

Exmouth

Dawlish

Teignmouth

Torquay

Paignton

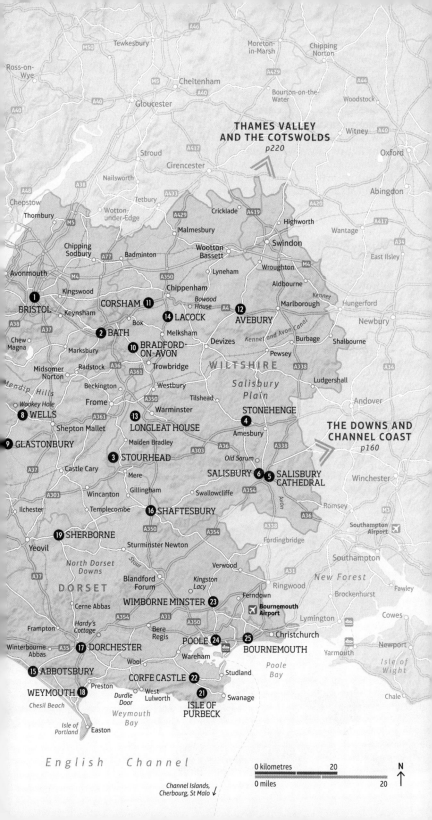

❶

BRISTOL

 Bristol Bristol Temple Meads visitbristol.co.uk

A major port at the mouth of the River Avon, Bristol grew rich on the maritime trade in wine, tobacco and, in the 17th century, slaves. The oldest part of the city lies around Broad, King and Corn streets, known as the Old Quarter. In the lively old dock area, bars, cafés, restaurants and art galleries line the waterside.

①

Clifton Suspension Bridge

 Leigh Woods; www.cliftonbridge.org.uk

The defining symbol of Bristol, the Clifton Suspension Bridge was designed by Isambard Kingdom Brunel, who won the commission at the age of 23. Completed in 1864, the bridge spans the dramatic Avon Gorge from Clifton to Leigh Woods. The brilliant visitor centre provides an interesting and entertaining background to its history. From Easter to October, there are excellent free tours of the bridge, starting from the centre at 3pm on Saturdays, Sundays and bank holidays.

②

Brunel's SS Great Britain

 Gas Ferry Rd 10am–6pm (Mar–Nov: to 4:30pm) daily ssgreatbritain.org

It was from Bristol that, in 1497, John Cabot sailed on his historic voyage to North America. In the 19th century, the city pioneered the era of the ocean-going steam liner with the construction of the SS Great Britain. Designed by Isambard Kingdom Brunel, this was the world's first large iron passenger ship. Launched in 1843, she travelled 32 times round the world before being abandoned in the Falkland Islands in 1886. The ship has been restored and contains an exhibition, Being Brunel.

③

St Mary Redcliffe

 Redcliffe Way Daily stmaryredcliffe.co.uk

This magnificent 14th-century church was claimed by Queen Elizabeth I to be "the fairest in England". The church owes much to the generosity of William Canynge the Elder and Younger, both famous mayors of Bristol. Inscriptions on the tombs of merchants and sailors tell of lives devoted to trade. Look out for the maze roof boss in the north aisle. Regular musical events are held here.

BANKSY

As mysterious as he is prolific, Bristol-born Banksy is the world's best-known, yet secretive, graffiti artist. There are excellent tours taking in his works around the city (which include Mild Mild West and Masked Gorilla), together with other excellent street art, or you can devise your own itinerary at www.bristol-street-art.co.uk.

↑ The Bristol skyline with the University buildings in the foreground

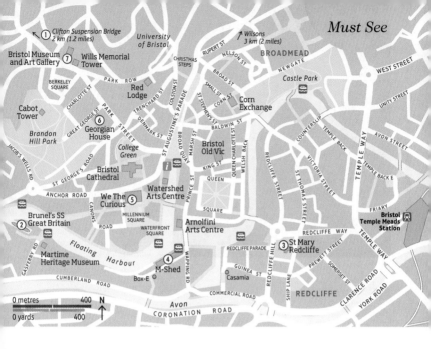

Map labels

Clifton Suspension Bridge
2 km (1.2 miles)

University of Bristol

Wilsons
3 km (2 miles)

BROADMEAD

Bristol Museum and Art Gallery ⑦

Wills Memorial Tower

RUPERT ST
NELSON ST
NEWGATE
WEST STREET

CHRISTMAS STEPS
BROAD ST
SMALL ST

BERKELEY SQUARE
PARK ROW

Red Lodge

Castle Park

UNITY STREET

Cabot Tower

CHARLOTTE ST
GREAT GEORGE ST
PARK STREET

ST AUGUSTINE'S PARADE
COLSTON ST
ST STEPHEN'S ST
CORN ST

Corn Exchange

COUNTERSLIP
TEMPLE BACK
AVON STREET

Brandon Hill Park

⑥ Georgian House

TRENCHARD ST
DENMARK ST

BALDWIN ST

Bristol Old Vic

TEMPLE BACK E

JACOB'S WELLS RD

College Green

BOYD QUAY
MARSH ST

QUEEN CHARLOTTE ST
WELSH BACK

VICTORIA STREET

ST GEORGE'S ROAD

Bristol Cathedral

We The Curious ⑤

Watershed Arts Centre

KING ST
QUEEN

ST THOMAS STREET

FRIARY

Bristol Temple Meads Station

ANCHOR ROAD

MILLENNIUM SQUARE

SQUARE

REDCLIFFE WAY

Brunel's SS Great Britain ②

CANONS ROAD

Arnolfini Arts Centre

TEMPLE WAY

Maritime Heritage Museum

Floating Harbour

WATERFRONT SQUARE

WAPPING RD

③ St Mary Redcliffe

REDCLIFFE PARADE
REDCLIFFE HILL

PREWETT STREET
SOMERSET ST

CASTERBY RD

④ M-Shed

Box-E

GUINEA ST
Casamia

SHIP LANE

CLARENCE ROAD
YORK ROAD

CUMBERLAND ROAD

COMMERCIAL ROAD

REDCLIFFE

Avon
CORONATION ROAD

0 metres 400
0 yards 400
N

Must See

---

④

M-Shed

🏠 Princes Wharf ⏰ 10am–5pm Tue–Sun 🌐 bristol museums.org.uk

The city's history is told in this museum in a 1950s harbourside transit shed, through film, photographs and objects. There are also several historic vessels moored in the Wharf.

---

⑤

We The Curious

🏠 Anchor Rd ⏰ 10am–5pm daily (to 6pm Sat & Sun) 🌐 wethecurious.org

On the harbourside, this exciting science centre has

---

several hundred interactive, hands-on exhibits to enable you to explore the inner workings of the world around us, and a 3-D planetarium with full surround-sound.

---

⑥

Georgian House

🏠 7 Great George St ⏰ Apr–Dec: 11am–4pm Sat–Tue 🌐 bristolmuseums.org.uk

Daily life in a wealthy 1790s Bristol merchant's house is reimagined here in rooms including the drawing room and the servants' area.

---

⑦

Bristol Museum and Art Gallery

🏠 Queen's Rd ⏰ 10am–5pm Tue–Sun 🌐 bristol museums.org.uk

The varied collections include Egyptology, fossils, Roman finds, Chinese glass and fine paintings. Bristol artists include Sir Thomas Lawrence, Francis Danby and Banksy.

Did You Know?

Author J K Rowling was born in Chipping Sodbury, just a few miles from Bristol.

EAT

Box-E

Fantastic little outfit in an old shipping container with a small but ambitious menu.

🏠 Unit 10, 1 Cargo Wharf 🌐 boxebristol.com

££££

Casamia

Spanish-run, Michelin-starred restaurant for a special occasion.

🏠 The General, Lower Guinea St 🌐 casa miarestaurant.co.uk

£££

Wilsons

Food of great distinction, combined in exciting dishes.

🏠 Chandos St 🌐 wilsons restaurant.co.uk

££££

↑ Bath Abbey, built, like much of the city, from the local warm-toned Bath stone

2

BATH

🔼 Somerset 🚉 Bath Spa 🛈 Bridgwater House, 2 Terrace Walk; www.visitbathco.uk

The beautiful and compact city of Bath is set among the rolling green hills of the Avon valley. Its lively, traffic-free heart is full of museums, cafés and enticing shops, while its characteristic honey-coloured Georgian houses form an elegant backdrop.

① 🏛

Bath Abbey

🔼 Abbey Churchyard
🕒 Times vary, check website 🌐 bathabbey.org

This splendid abbey was supposedly designed by divine agency. According to legend, Bishop Oliver King dreamed of angels going up and down to heaven, which then inspired the ladders carved on the west front façade. The bishop began work in 1499, rebuilding a church that had been founded in the 8th century. Memorials cover the walls and the varied Georgian inscriptions make fascinating reading. The spacious interior is remarkable for the fan vaulting of the nave, an addition made by Sir George Gilbert Scott in 1874.

② 🎨 🏛

No. 1 Royal Crescent

🔼 Royal Crescent 🕒 10am–5pm daily 🚫 1 Jan, 25 & 26 Dec 🌐 no1royalcrescent.org.uk

Bath rose to prominence in the 18th century as one of England's's most fashionable spa towns, and as a result the city now has some of the finest Georgian architecture in the country. Highlights are the Circus, a daring circular "square" of distinguished townhouses designed by John Wood the Elder (1704–1754), and above all the magnificent Royal Crescent, created by his son, John Wood the Younger in the 1770s

No. 1 Royal Crescent is now a handsome museum that gives visitors a taste of what life was like for 18th-century aristocrats, such as the Duke of York, who stayed here. You can also see the servants' quarters, the spit powered by a dog made to run in a wheel, and Georgian mousetraps.

JANE AUSTEN

The one name most synonymous with Bath is Jane Austen, whose six years here informed some of her greatest novels, notably *Persuasion*. Devotees will certainly want to pay a visit to the Jane Austen Centre on 40 Gay Street, whose exhibits include the only known waxwork of the author. A plaque outside the door at no. 4 Sydney Place marks her first dwelling in Bath.

> **According to legend, Bishop Oliver King dreamed of angels going up and down to heaven, which inspired the ladders carved on the Abbey's west front façade.**

(3) 🎨 🖥 🛍

Holburne Museum of Art

🏛 Great Pulteney St
🕐 10am–5pm daily (from 11am Sun & public hols)
🚫 1 Jan, 24–26 Dec
🌐 holburne.org

This historic building is named after William Holburne of Menstrie (1793–1874), whose collections form the nucleus of the display of fine and decorative arts, including superb silver and paintings by Gainsborough and Stubbs.

 (4) 🎨 🖥 🛍

Assembly Rooms and Fashion Museum

🏛 Bennett St 🕐 10:30am–5pm daily 🚫 25 & 26 Dec
🌐 fashionmuseum.co.uk

The Assembly Rooms were built in 1769 as a meeting place for the elite and as a backdrop for glittering balls. Jane Austen's *Northanger Abbey* (1818) describes the gossip and flirtation that went on here. In the basement is a collection of costumes from the 1500s to the present day.

↑ The Holburne Museum, a tranquil delight housing a splendid collection of fine and decorative arts

EAT

Menu Gordon Jones

Seven-course tasting menus are cooked with imagination and flair; fantastic organic wines.

🏛 2 Wells Way 🌐 menu gordonjones.co.uk

£££

Noya's Kitchen

Homely but high-class Vietnamese: exquisite morsels form the five-course set menu.

🏛 7 St James's Parade
🌐 noyaskitchen.co.uk

£££

Sotto Sotto

Consummate Italian restaurant located in an atmospheric brick-vaulted cellar.

🏛 10 North Parade
🌐 sottosotto.co.uk

£££

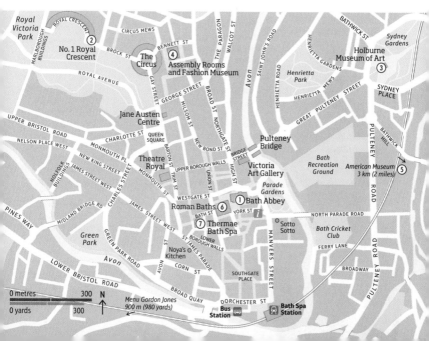

Royal Victoria Park
Royal Crescent
Marlborough Buildings
Circus Mews
(2) No. 1 Royal Crescent
Brock St
Royal Avenue
Bennett St
The Circus
(4) Assembly Rooms and Fashion Museum
Walcot St
The Paragon
Bathwick St
Sydney Gardens
Henrietta Gardens
Holburne Museum of Art (3)
Henrietta Park
Henrietta Mews
Henrietta Road
Saint John's Road
Avon
Gay Street
George Street
Broad St
Northgate St
Great Pulteney Street
Sydney Place
Bathwick Hill
Upper Bristol Road
Jane Austen Centre
Charlotte St
Queen Square
Milsom St
New Bond St
Pulteney Bridge
Bridge St
Nelson Place West
Monmouth Pl
New King Street
Barton St
Trim St
Union St
Upper Borough Walls
High St
Victoria Art Gallery
Bath Recreation Ground
American Museum 3 km (2 miles) (5)
Pulteney Road
Theatre Royal
Monmouth St
Westgate St
Parade Gardens
Molox Buildings
James Street West
Charles Street
James Street West
Green Park Road
Bath St
York St
Roman Baths (6) (1) Bath Abbey
North Parade Road
Pines Way
Midland Bridge Rd
(7) Thermae Bath Spa
Lower Borough Walls
Sotto Sotto
Manvers Street
Bath Cricket Club
Ferry Lane
Green Park
Avon
St James Parade
Noya's Kitchen
Corn St
Southgate Place
Broadway
Lower Bristol Road
Broad Quay
Dorchester St
Bus Station
Bath Spa Station

0 metres 300
0 yards 300
N
Menu Gordon Jones 900 m (980 yards)

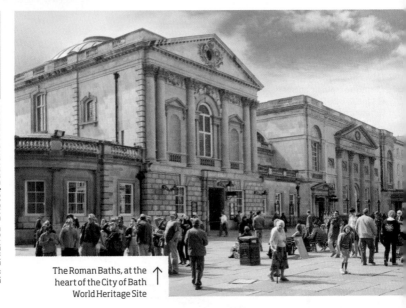

The Roman Baths, at the heart of the City of Bath World Heritage Site

American Museum

🏛 Claverton Manor, Claverton Down 🕐 Mid-Mar-Oct: 10am-5pm Tue-Sun 🌐 american museum.org

Founded in 1961, this was the first American museum to be established in Britain. The rooms in the 1820 manor house are decorated in many styles, from the rudimentary dwellings of the first settlers to the opulent style of 19th-century homes. The museum has special sections on Shaker furniture, quilts and American Indian art, and a replica of George Washington's Mount Vernon garden of 1785.

Roman Baths

🏛 Entrance in Abbey Churchyard 🕐 Daily; times vary, check website 🚫 25 & 26 Dec 🌐 romanbaths.co.uk

According to legend, Bath owes its origin to the Celtic king Bladud, who discovered the curative properties of its natural hot springs in 860 BC. In the 1st century, the Romans built baths around the spring, as well as a temple dedicated to the goddess Sulis Minerva, who combined the atrributes of the Celt water goddess Sulis and the Roman goddess Minerva. The medieval monks

← Impressive folk art on display at the American Museum

of Bath Abbey also exploited the springs' properties, but it was when Queen Anne visited in 1702–3 that Bath reached its zenith as a fashionable watering place. Beau Nash, Bath's Master of Ceremonies, commissioned the building of the adjoining Grand Pump Room, where Bath's high society gathered to meet, exchange gossip and "take the waters". Gradually the whole complex was rebuilt in noble Neo-Classical style to echo the bath's Roman origins.

The Great Bath, at the heart of the Roman complex, was

only rediscovered in the 1870s. Leading off this magnificent pool were various bathing chambers which became increasingly sophisticated; extensive excavations have revealed the remarkable skill of Roman engineering. Artifacts from the digs and fragments of the original structure are displayed on the lower levels. The Pump Room remains an elegant tearoom.

Did You Know?

Bath is the only entire city in the UK to be labelled a UNESCO World Heritage Site.

Thermae Bath Spa

🏠 Hot Bath St 🕐 9am–9:30pm daily (last adm: 7pm); not open to under-16s 🚫 1 Jan, 25 & 26 Dec 🌐 thermaebathspa.com

While bathing is not allowed in the Roman Baths, the opening of the Thermae Bath Spa in 2006 once again made Bath a popular day-spa destination. There are three pools fed by natural thermal waters: the New Royal Bath has two baths including an open-air rooftop pool with superb views over the city; across the road, the oval Cross Bath is a more intimate open-air bath, ideal for shorter sessions. Also on offer are spa treatments and massage.

↑ A rooftop dip at Thermae Bath Spa overlooking the city

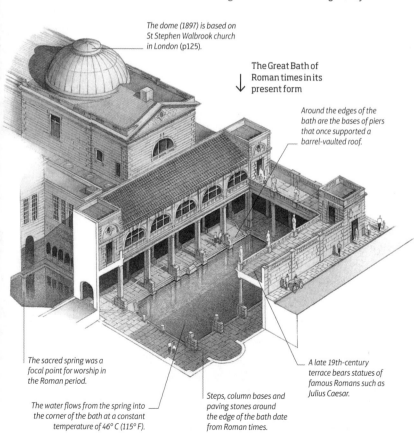

The dome (1897) is based on St Stephen Walbrook church in London (p125).

↓ The Great Bath of Roman times in its present form

Around the edges of the bath are the bases of piers that once supported a barrel-vaulted roof.

A late 19th-century terrace bears statues of famous Romans such as Julius Caesar.

The sacred spring was a focal point for worship in the Roman period.

The water flows from the spring into the corner of the bath at a constant temperature of 46° C (115° F).

Steps, column bases and paving stones around the edge of the bath date from Roman times.

A SHORT WALK

BATH

Distance 1.5 km (1 mile) **Time** 15 minutes
Nearest bus station Dorchester St

Bath owes its magnificent Georgian townscape to the bubbling pool of water at the heart of the Roman Baths. The Romans transformed Bath into England's first spa resort and it regained fame as a spa town in the 18th century. At this time the two John Woods (Elder and Younger), both architects, designed the city's Palladian-style buildings. Many houses bear plaques recording the numerous famous people who have resided here.

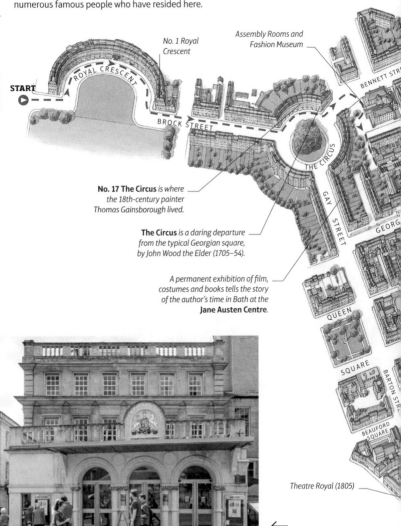

No. 1 Royal Crescent

Assembly Rooms and Fashion Museum

START

ROYAL CRESCENT

BROCK STREET

BENNETT STREET

THE CIRCUS

GAY STREET

GEORG

No. 17 The Circus *is where the 18th-century painter Thomas Gainsborough lived.*

The Circus *is a daring departure from the typical Georgian square, by John Wood the Elder (1705–54).*

A permanent exhibition of film, costumes and books tells the story of the author's time in Bath at the **Jane Austen Centre.**

QUEEN

SQUARE

BARTON STREET

BEAUFORD SQUARE

Theatre Royal (1805)

←
The elegant façade of the Theatre Royal, a fine example of Georgian architecture

↑ The historic, shop-lined Pulteney Bridge spanning the River Avon in Bath's centre

The **Museum of Bath at Work** celebrates 2,000 years of Bath's working heritage.

Milsom Street and New Bond Street contain some of Bath's most elegant shops.

Built in the 1st century, the **Roman Baths** complex is one of Britain's greatest memorials to the Roman era.

Did You Know?

Bath has its own currency, the Oliver, which can be used as a discount voucher in shops.

0 metres   100
0 yards   100

N ↑

The charming **Pulteney Bridge** (1769–74), designed by Robert Adam, is lined with shops and links the town centre with the magnificent Great Pulteney Street.

FINISH

The splendid **Bath Abbey** stands at the heart of the old city in the Abbey Church Yard, a paved courtyard enlivened by buskers. Its unique façade features stone angels climbing Jacob's Ladder to heaven.

Courting couples came to the pretty riverside **Parade Gardens** park for secret liaisons in the 18th century.

The tearooms in the **Pump Rooms** once formed the social hub of the 18th-century spa community.

Sally Lunn's House (1482) is one of Bath's oldest houses.

LANSDOWN ROAD
PARAGON
STREET
BROAD STREET
WALCOT STREET
SOM STREET
NEW BOND STREET
UPPER BOROUGH WALLS
UNION STREET
HIGH STREET
GRAND PARADE
ORANGE GROVE
PIERREPOINT STREET
CHEAP STREET
WESTGATE STREET
YORK STREET

3 🏛 🚲 🍴 ☕ 🛍 🏠 NT

STOURHEAD

📍 Stourton, Wiltshire 🚉 Gillingham (Dorset) then taxi
🕐 9am–6pm daily (winter: to 5pm) 🌐 nationaltrust.org.uk

Located at the source of the River Stour, Stourhead is a large estate with stunning landscape gardens and a Palladian villa set among ancient woods and farmland.

Among the finest examples of 18th-century landscape gardening in Britain, the garden was begun in the 1740s by Henry Hoare (1705–85), who inherited the estate and transformed it into a breathtaking work of art. He created the lake as the centerpiece of the garden, surrounding it with rare trees and plants, and Neo-Classical Italianate temples, mystical grottoes, ornate follies and bridges. The Palladian-style house, built by Colen Campbell (1676–1729), dates from 1724.

Did You Know?

C Hoare & Co., founded in 1672 by Richard Hoare, is the oldest privately owned bank in the UK.

The Grotto is an artificial cave with a pool and a life-size statue of the guardian of the River Stour, sculpted by John Cheere in 1748.

Modelled on the Pantheon in Rome, this elegant temple was designed by architect Henry Flitcroft. It was built as a visual centrepoint for the garden.

Gothic Cottage (1806)

Iron Bridge

A walk of 3 km (2 miles) around the lake provides artistically contrived vistas.

Stourhead's famous lake was created by damming the River Stour in the 1750s. The path around it evokes the journeys of Aeneas in Virgil's Aeneid.

Inspired by Italian originals and dedicated to the sun god Apollo, this circular temple was also created by architect Henry Flitcroft.

📷 PICTURE PERFECT
Floral Photos

Stourhead is beautiful all year round, but in spring, the rhododendrons, and in autumn, the vibrant colours of the trees, make for exceptional photos. The view from the Temple of Apollo is particularly attractive.

Fragrant rhododendrons bloom in the spring, and azaleas explode into colour later in the summer. There are also many fine cypresses, Japanese pines and other exotic trees.

Turf Bridge

The Temple of Flora (1744) is dedicated to the Roman goddess of flowers.

The parish church of St Peter contains monuments to the Hoare family. The medieval Bristol Cross, nearby, was brought from Bristol in 1765.

Stourhead estate, with its picturesque lake and sweeping gardens ↑

← The expansive landscaped gardens, with Iron Bridge and the Pantheon in view

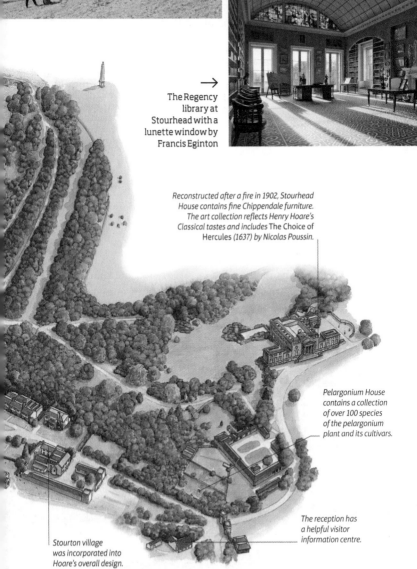

→ The Regency library at Stourhead with a lunette window by Francis Eginton

Reconstructed after a fire in 1902, Stourhead House contains fine Chippendale furniture. The art collection reflects Henry Hoare's Classical tastes and includes The Choice of Hercules (1637) by Nicolas Poussin.

Pelargonium House contains a collection of over 100 species of the pelargonium plant and its cultivars.

The reception has a helpful visitor information centre.

Stourton village was incorporated into Hoare's overall design.

④ (icons) EH

STONEHENGE

📍 Off A303, Wilts 🕐 Apr, May & Sep-mid-Oct: 9:30am-7pm; Jun-Aug: 9am-8pm; mid-Oct-Mar: 9:30am-5pm (Stone Circle Access visit available outside these hours); book ahead 🌐 english-heritage.org.uk

Built in several stages from about 3000 BC, Stonehenge is Europe's most famous prehistoric monument, a masterpiece of Neolithic engineering and building. No trip to Great Britain is complete without visiting the vast, awe-inspiring stone circle.

We can only guess at the rituals that took place at Stonehenge, but the alignment of the stones leaves little doubt that the circle is connected with the sun and the passing of the seasons, and that its builders possessed an understanding of both arithmetic and astronomy. Despite popular belief, the circle was not built by the Druids, an Iron Age priestly cult in Britain from around 250 BC – Stonehenge was abandoned more than 1,000 years before this time. Its monumental scale is all the more impressive given that the only tools available were made of stone, wood and bone. Its builders must have been able to command immense resources and vast numbers of people to transport and erect the stones.

Ringing the horizon around Stonehenge are scores of prehistoric circular barrows, or burial mounds, where members of the ruling class were honoured with burial close to the temple site. Ceremonial bronze weapons and other finds excavated around Stonehenge and other local prehistoric sites can be seen in the visitor centre at Stonehenge and Salisbury Museum (p268).

> **The alignment of the stones leaves little doubt that the circle is connected with the sun and the passing of the seasons.**

WILTSHIRE'S OTHER PREHISTORIC SITES

The open countryside of the Salisbury Plain made this area a major centre of prehistoric settlement, and today it is covered in many ancient remains.

Built out of chalk blocks around 2750 BC, Silbury Hill is Europe's largest prehistoric earthwork, but its purpose remains a mystery. Nearby, West Kennet Long Barrow is the biggest chambered tomb in England. Built as a communal burial site around 3250 BC, it was in use for several centuries.

Old Sarum, a 400 BC Iron Age hill fort, is located just north of Salisbury. The Romans, Normans and Saxons all left their mark here. Visitors can walk along the Iron Age ramparts, which give great views, and see the remains of the 11th-century castle and cathedral.

The Heel Stone casts a long shadow straight to the heart of the circle on Midsummer's Day.

The Slaughter Stone, named by 17th-century historians who believed Stonehenge to be a place of human sacrifice, is one of a pair marking the entrance to the interior.

Horseshoe of Bluestones

The Bluestone Circle was built around 2500 BC out of some 80 slabs quarried in the Preseli Hills in south Wales.

The Avenue forms a ceremonial approach to the site.

The Sarsen Circle was erected around 2500 BC and is capped by lintel stones held in place by mortise and tenon joints.

Horseshoe of Sarsen Trilithons

The Outer Bank, dug around 3000 BC, is the oldest known phase of Stonehenge.

Illustration of Stonehenge showing what it probably looked like 4,000 years ago ↑

> 💬 **INSIDER TIP**
> **Visiting**
>
> Entry is by timed tickets. Visitors can get up close to the stone circle itself only on a pre-booked self-guided tour – for this you have to request a Stone Circle Access visit online at least two months in advance.

↑ The mysterious Stonehenge circle of standing stones

⑤ Ⓜ 🍴 🛍 🎁

SALISBURY CATHEDRAL

🏠 The Close, Salisbury 🅿 🕐 9am–5pm Mon–Sat; noon–4pm Sun
🌐 salisburycathedral.org.uk

An outstanding example of Early English Gothic architecture, Salisbury Cathedral was built in the 13th century over the short space of 38 years. Its landmark spire – the tallest surviving in England – was an inspired afterthought added in 1280–1310.

The cathedral was built between 1220 and 1258 from locally sourced Purbeck marble and Chilmark stone. The Gothic design is typified by tall, sharply pointed lancet windows. The stunning West Front façade is decorated by rows of symbolic figures and saints in niches. The Chapter House contains the best preserved of only four surviving original Magna Carta issued in 1215. In the north aisle is the world's oldest working mechanical clock, dating to 1386. The highlight of the cathedral, however, is its octagonal spire, which was a tremendous technical feat for its medieval builders.

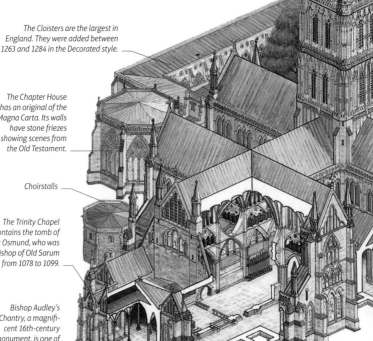

The graceful spire soars to a height of 123 m (404 ft).

A tour of the tower takes visitors up to a gallery at the base of the spire with views of the city and Old Sarum (p264).

The Cloisters are the largest in England. They were added between 1263 and 1284 in the Decorated style.

The Chapter House has an original of the Magna Carta. Its walls have stone friezes showing scenes from the Old Testament.

Choirstalls

The Trinity Chapel contains the tomb of St Osmund, who was bishop of Old Sarum from 1078 to 1099.

Bishop Audley's Chantry, a magnificent 16th-century monument, is one of several chapels around the altar.

INSIDER TIP
Tower Tour

Take a 100-minute tour of the tower and climb 332 steps to the base of the spire where there are panoramic views of the city and the surrounding countryside. Advance booking online is recommended.

① The West Front façade is decorated with elaborate statues and columns.

② The expansive Cloister Garden is a peaceful place for visitors to relax.

③ Designed by William Pye, the font was added in 2008. Its water reflects the cathedral's elegant ceiling.

Numerous stained-glass windows depict stories from the Bible.

The clock, dating from 1386, is believed to be the oldest working mechanical clock in the world.

The nave is divided into ten bays by columns of polished Purbeck marble.

North transept

↑ Salisbury Cathedral, with its elegant Gothic architecture and spire

MAGNA CARTA

To protect themselves and the Church from arbitrary taxation, the powerful English barons compelled King John to sign a "great charter" in 1215. This laid down the foundations for an independent legal system and granted certain rights. It contains over 60 clauses, including the right to a fair trial. It was written in Latin by a scribe on parchment. To this day it remains a symbol of justice, fairness and the importance of human rights.

EXPERIENCE MORE

⑥
Salisbury

🏠 Wiltshire 🚆🚌
ℹ️ Fish Row; www.
visitwiltshire.co.uk

Founded in 1220, Salisbury sits where the rivers Avon, Nadder and Bourne meet. The **Salisbury Museum** explores the history of the area, with displays on early man, Stonehenge and the original hilltop settlement of Old Sarum (*p264*).

Built by a wealthy family in 1701, **Mompesson House** gives an indication of aristocratic life in the 18th century. Nearby, **Wilton House** has been home to the Earls of Pembroke for over 400 years. The house, converted from a nunnery and largely rebuilt by Inigo Jones in the 17th century, includes one of the original Tudor towers, a fine collection of art and a landscaped park.

Salisbury Museum

⊛ ⊜ 🏠 The Close
⏰ 10am–5pm Mon–Sat (Jun–Sep: also noon–5pm Sun)
🌐 salisburymuseum.org.uk

Mompesson House

⊛ ⊜ (NT) 🏠 The Close ⏰ Mid-Mar–Oct: 11am–5pm daily
🌐 nationaltrust.org.uk

Wilton House

⊛ ⊛ ⊜ 🏠 Wilton ⏰ Easter & May–Aug: 11:30am–5pm Sun–Thu & bank hol Sat
🌐 wiltonhouse.co.uk

⑦
Cheddar Gorge

🏠 The Cliffs, Cheddar, Somerset 🚌 From Weston super-Mare ⏰ 10am–5pm daily 🌐 cheddargorge.co.uk

This is a spectacular ravine cut through the Mendip plateau by fast-flowing streams during the interglacial phases of the last Ice Age. Cheddar has given its name to a rich cheese that originates from here and is now produced worldwide. The caves in the gorge provide the perfect environment of constant temperature and high humidity for storing and maturing the cheese. "Cheddar Man", a 9,000-year-old skeleton, is displayed at the Museum of Prehistory.

Hiking amid the majestic landscape of Cheddar Gorge, in the Mendip plateau ↑

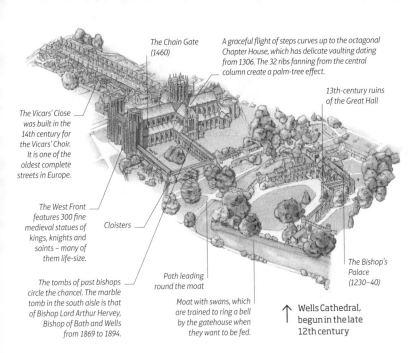

The Chain Gate (1460)

A graceful flight of steps curves up to the octagonal Chapter House, which has delicate vaulting dating from 1306. The 32 ribs fanning from the central column create a palm-tree effect.

13th-century ruins of the Great Hall

The Vicars' Close was built in the 14th century for the Vicars' Choir. It is one of the oldest complete streets in Europe.

The West Front features 300 fine medieval statues of kings, knights and saints – many of them life-size.

Cloisters

The tombs of past bishops circle the chancel. The marble tomb in the south aisle is that of Bishop Lord Arthur Hervey, Bishop of Bath and Wells from 1869 to 1894.

Path leading round the moat

Moat with swans, which are trained to ring a bell by the gatehouse when they want to be fed.

The Bishop's Palace (1230–40)

↑ Wells Cathedral, begun in the late 12th century

---

⑧

Wells

🏠 Somerset 🚌
ℹ️ Cathedral Green; www.wellssomerset.com

Named after St Andrew's Well, the sacred spring that bubbles up near the 13th-century Bishop's Palace, the tranquil city of Wells is famous for its imposing cathedral, which was begun in the late 1100s and is considered one of the most beautiful in England. Penniless Porch, where beggars once received alms, leads from the bustling marketplace to the calm of the cathedral close.

To the northeast of Wells lies the impressive cave complex of **Wookey Hole**, which has a wide range of popular attractions, including a live circus show, a maze and pirate adventure golf.

Wookey Hole

🏠 Off A371
🕙 10am–5pm daily (winter: to 4pm) 🚫 Dec & Jan: Mon-Fri 🌐 wookey.co.uk

⑨

Glastonbury

🏠 Somerset 🚌
ℹ️ St Dunstan's House, Magdalene St; www.glastonbury.uk

Shrouded in Arthurian myth and rich in mystical association, Glastonbury was once one of the most important destinations for pilgrims in England. Now thousands flock here for the annual festival and the summer solstice on 21 June. Over time, history and legend have united, and the monks who founded Glastonbury Abbey, around AD 700, found it profitable to encourage the association between Glastonbury and the mythical "Blessed Isle" known as Avalon – said to be the last resting place of King Arthur and the Holy Grail (p294). The abbey was left in ruins after the Dissolution of the Monasteries. Visible for miles around, Glastonbury Tor is a hill crowned by St Michael's Tower, which is all that remains of a 14th-century church.

GLASTONBURY FESTIVAL

Conceived by local farmer Michael Eavis, Glastonbury Festival has grown from a small hippy affair in 1970 into one of the world's largest festivals. The vast set-up, on Eavis's own Worthy Farm site, hosts everything from comedy to art and meditation, but ultimately it's all about the music.

10
Bradford-on-Avon

⬚ Wiltshire ⬚
ℹ 50 St Margaret St; www.
bradfordonavon.co.uk

This lovely Cotswold-stone town is full of flamboyant houses built by wealthy wool and cloth merchants in the 17th and 18th centuries. One fine Georgian example is Abbey House, on Church Street. Further along, St Laurence Church is a remarkably complete Saxon building founded in the 8th century. Converted to a school and cottage in the 1100s, it was rediscovered in the 19th century when a vicar recognized the characteristic cross-shaped roof.

At one end of the medieval Town Bridge is a small stone cell, built as a chapel in the 13th century but later used as a lock-up for vagrants. A short walk away is the spectacular 14th-century **Tithe Barn** (used for storing rents and tithes). Canoe trips down the canal are popular.

Tithe Barn
ⓑⓗ ⬚ Pound Lane
🕐 10:30am–4pm daily
🌐 english-heritage.org.uk

11
Corsham

⬚ Wiltshire ℹ 31 High St;
www.corsham.gov.uk

The streets of Corsham are lined with stately Georgian

↑ A summer's day at a riverside pub near the Town Bridge in Bradford-on-Avon

houses in Cotswold stone. St Bartholomew's Church has an elegant spire and the carved alabaster tomb (1960) of Lady Methuen, whose family founded Methuen publishers. The family acquired **Corsham Court** in 1745 with its collection of Flemish, Italian and English paintings, including works by Van Dyck, Lippi and Reynolds.

Corsham Court
⬚ Off A4 ⬚ Apr–Sep: 2–5:30pm Tue–Thu, Sat & Sun; Oct–Mar: 2pm–4:30pm Sat & Sun ⬚ Dec 🌐 corsham-court.co.uk

12
Avebury

⬚ Wiltshire ⬚ Swindon then bus ℹ Green St; www.nationaltrust.org.uk

Built around 2500 BC, the Avebury Stone Circle surrounds the village of Avebury and was probably once some form of religious centre. Although the stones are smaller than those at Stonehenge, the circle itself is larger. In the 18th century,

superstitious villagers smashed many of the stones, believing the circle to have been a place of pagan sacrifice.

The original form of the circle is best appreciated by a visit to the **Alexander Keiller Museum** to the west of the site, which illustrates in detail the construction of the circle.

Another attraction of note in Avebury is St James's Church, which has a rare 15th-century choir screen.

Alexander Keiller Museum
⬚ Off High St
🕐 Times vary, check website 🌐 nationaltrust.org.uk

→
The imposing Gothic Revival architecture of Lacock Abbey

> **INSIDER TIP**
> **Wadworth Brewery Tour**
>
> In Devizes, southeast of Corsham, Wadworth Brewery (www. wadworth.co.uk) runs tours that illustrate the company's history and brewing techniques. Tastings are included.

⓲
Longleat House

🏠 Warminster, Wiltshire
🚂 Frome then taxi 🕐 Mid-Feb-mid-Mar: 10am-5pm Fri-Mon; mid-Mar-Oct & late Nov-early Jan: 10am-7pm daily 🌐 longleat.co.uk

The architectural historian John Summerson coined the term "prodigy house" to describe the exuberance of Elizabethan architecture that is so well represented at Longleat. The house was started in 1540, when John Thynne bought the ruins of a priory on the site. Over the centuries subsequent owners have added their own touches. The present owner, the 7th Marquess of Bath, is renowned for his erotic murals. Less controversial are the Breakfast Room and Lower Dining Room (dating from the 1870s), modelled on Venice's Ducal Palace. Today, the Great Hall is the only remaining room which belongs to Thynne's time.

Parts of the grounds, landscaped by "Capability" Brown (p24), were turned into an expansive safari park in 1966, where wolves, rhinos and other animals roam freely; there are myriad other attractions too, such as a large hedge maze, adventure castle and mini-train.

⓮
Lacock

🏠 Wiltshire

The picturesque village of Lacock has provided the backdrop to many costume dramas, including *Downton Abbey*. The meandering River Avon forms the boundary to the north side of the church-yard, while humorous stone figures look down from St Cyriac Church. Inside the 15th-century church is the splendid Renaissance-style tomb of Sir William Sharington (1495–1553). He acquired **Lacock Abbey** after the Dissolution, but it was a later owner, John Ivory Talbot, who had the buildings remodelled in the Gothic Revival style. The abbey is famous for the window (in the south gallery) from which his descendant William Henry Fox Talbot, an early pioneer of photography, took his first picture in 1835. A 16th-century barn has been converted to the **Fox Talbot Museum**, which has displays on his experiments.

Designed by Robert Adam in 1769, **Bowood House** includes the laboratory where Joseph Priestley discovered oxygen in 1774, and a fine collection of sculpture, costumes, jewellery and paintings. Italianate gardens surround the house while the lake-filled grounds, landscaped by "Capability" Brown, contain a Doric temple and grotto.

Lacock Abbey
 🏠 Lacock
🕐 11am-5pm daily (Nov-Feb: 11:30am-3pm Sat & Sun)
🌐 nationaltrust.org.uk

Fox Talbot Museum
🏠 Lacock
🕐 10:30am-5:30pm daily (Nov-Feb: 11am-4pm)
🌐 nationaltrust.org.uk

Bowood House
🏠 Derry Hill, nr Calne 🕐 Apr-Oct: 11am-5:30pm daily 🌐 bowood.org

15
Abbotsbury

🏠 Dorset 🚹 West Yard Barn, West St; www.abbotsbury-tourism.co.uk

The name Abbotsbury recalls the town's 11th-century Benedictine abbey, of which little but the huge tithe barn, built around 1400, remains.

The earliest records of the **Swannery** date to 1393. Mute swans come to nest here in the breeding season, attracted by the reed beds along the Fleet, a brackish lagoon protected from the sea by Chesil Beach.

Swannery

⊗⊖⊕ 🏠 New Barn Rd 📞 01305 871858 ⏰ Mid-Mar–Oct: 10am–5pm daily

16
Shaftesbury

🏠 Dorset 🚌 🚹 8 Bell St; www.shaftesburytourism.co.uk

Hilltop Shaftesbury, with its cobbled streets and 18th-century cottages, is often used as a setting for period films. Picture-perfect Gold Hill is lined on one side by a wall of the demolished abbey, founded by King Alfred in 888. Only the excavated remains of the abbey church survive.

17
Dorchester

🏠 Dorset 🚌 🚹 The Library, Charles St; www.visit-dorset.com

The county town of Dorset is still recognizably the town in which Thomas Hardy based his novel *The Mayor of Casterbridge* (1886). The original manuscript of the novel is displayed at the **Dorset County Museum**. Dorchester has the only example of a Roman town house in Britain. The remains reveal architectural details including a fine mosaic.

To the north lies Cerne Abbas village. The giant chalk fertility figure on the hillside here is thought to represent either the Roman god Hercules or an Iron Age warrior.

East of Dorchester is Bere Regis, the Kingsbere of *Tess of the D'Urbervilles*, where the tombs of the family whose name inspired the novel may be seen in the Saxon church. **Hardy's Cottage** is where the writer was born and **Max Gate** is where he lived from 1885 until his death.

Dorset County Museum

⊗⊜⊕ 🏠 High West St 🔄 For renovation till Nov 2020 🌐 dorsetcountymuseum.org

Hardy's Cottage

⊗⊕⊕ NT 🏠 Higher Bockhampton ⏰ 11am–5pm daily (Nov–Feb: 11am–4pm Thu–Sun) 🌐 nationaltrust.org.uk

Max Gate

⊗⊕⊕ NT 🏠 Alington Ave, Dorchester ⏰ 11am–5pm daily (Nov–Feb: 11am–4pm Thu–Sun) 🌐 nationaltrust.org.uk

Did You Know?

Maiden Castle, a little south of Dorchester, is the largest Iron Age hill fort in Britain.

Colourful fishing cottages along the harbour in Weymouth ↑

18

Weymouth

 Dorset 🚉🚌🚆
🌐 visit-dorset.com

Weymouth's popularity as a seaside resort began in 1789, when George III paid the first of many summer visits here. His statue is a prominent feature on the seafront. Here gracious Georgian terraces look across to the beautiful expanse of Weymouth Bay. Different in character is the old town around Custom House Quay with its boats and old seamen's inns. In 1944 the town played host to over 500,000 troops in advance of the D-Day Landings; **Nothe Fort** has displays of World War II memorabilia.

A little south of Weymouth on the Isle of Portland is Tout Quarry (open 24 hours), a delightful stone sculpture park and nature reserve in an abandoned stone quarry. From here there are stunning views of Chesil Beach.

Nothe Fort

⊗⊜⊙ 🅰 Barrack Rd
📞 01305 766626 🕒 Apr-Oct: 10:30am–4:30pm daily; Mar & Nov: 10:30am–4:30pm Sun

←

Charming cottages lining the cobbled street on Gold Hill, Shaftesbury

19

Sherborne

 Dorset 🚉🚌 🛈 Digby Rd; www.visit-dorset.com

Few British towns have such a wealth of unspoilt medieval buildings. In 1550, Edward VI founded Sherborne School, thereby saving the Abbey Church and other monastic buildings that might otherwise have been demolished in the Dissolution (*p391*).

Sherborne Castle, built by Sir Walter Raleigh in 1594, is a wonderfully varied building that anticipates the flamboyant Jacobean style. Raleigh also lived briefly in the 12th-century **Old Castle**, which now stands in ruins.

Sherborne Castle

⊗⊜⊙ 🅰 Off A30 🕒 Apr-Oct: 11am–5pm Tue–Thu, Sat, Sun & public hols
🌐 sherbornecastle.com

Old Castle

⊗⊜⊛ 🅰 Off A30 🕒 Easter-Oct: 11am–5pm daily
🌐 english-heritage.org.uk

20

Lyme Regis

 Dorset 🛈 Church St; www.lymeregis.org

Lyme Regis is the most picturesque resort on the Jurassic Coast, which holds UNESCO World Heritage status. The Victorian pioneer fossil-hunter Mary Anning unearthed the first complete Ichthyosaurus and Plesiosaurus extinct marine reptiles here, and you can see her story in the **Lyme Regis Museum**. Encircling the harbour is the famous Cobb breakwater, which gives great views along the coast and to the Georgian houses along the seafront.

Lyme Regis Museum

⊗⊛ 🅰 Bridge St
🕒 Apr-Oct: 10am–5pm daily (to 4pm Sun); Nov-Mar: 10am–4pm Wed–Sun
🌐 lymeregismuseum.co.uk

> ### JURASSIC COAST
>
> Stretching some 153 km (95 miles) between East Devon and Dorset, the Jurassic Coast (www.jurassic coast.org) is a diverse landscape that records 185 million years of the Earth's history. Iconic landmarks include the Durdle Door natural rock arch near Lulworth and the spectacular rust-red sandstone sea stacks in Ladram Bay, East Devon. This is one of Britain's premier fossil-hunting regions, with Lyme Regis the fossil capital.

㉑
Isle of Purbeck

⬛ Dorset 🚉 Wareham
🚤 Shell Bay, Studland
ℹ Shore Rd, Swanage;
www.swanage.gov.uk

The Isle of Purbeck, which is in fact a peninsula, is the source of the grey shelly limestone, known as Purbeck marble, from which the castle and nearby houses were built. The geology changes to the south-west at Kimmeridge, where the muddy shale is rich in fossils and oil reserves.

The Isle, a World Heritage site, is fringed with unspoilt beaches like Studland Bay, with white sand and a nature reserve rich in birdlife. Sheltered Lulworth Cove is almost encircled by white cliffs, and there is a fine clifftop walk to Durdle Door (p273), a natural chalk arch.

The main resort in the area is Swanage, the port where Purbeck stone was transported by ship to London. Unwanted masonry from demolished buildings was shipped back, and this is how Swanage got its ornate town hall façade, designed by Wren around 1668.

㉒
Corfe Castle

⬛ Dorset 🚉 Wareham then bus ⏰ 10am–6pm daily (Oct: to 5pm; Nov–Feb: to 4pm)
🌐 nationaltrust.org.uk

The ruins of the 11th-century Corfe Castle crown a rocky pinnacle above the charming village that shares its name. In 1635 the castle was purchased by Sir John Bankes, whose wife and her retainers held out against Parliamentary troops in a six-week siege during the Civil War (p49). The castle was eventually taken, and in 1646 Parliament had it blown up to prevent it being used again. From the ruins there are far-reaching coastal views.

㉓
Wimborne Minster

⬛ Dorset 🚌 ℹ 29 High St;
www.wimborne.info

The fine collegiate church of Wimborne Minster, founded in 705 by Cuthburga, sister of King Ina of Wessex, fell prey to Danish raiders in the 10th century. Today's imposing grey church dates from the refounding by Edward the Confessor in 1043. Stonemasons made use of the local Purbeck marble, carving beasts, biblical scenes, and a mass of zig-zag decoration.

The 16th-century **Priest's House Museum** has rooms furnished in the style of different periods and an enchanting hidden garden.

Kingston Lacy is a sumptuous mansion designed for the Bankes family after the destruction of Corfe Castle. It has outstanding paintings.

Priest's House Museum
🎨 🛍 ⏰ ⬛ High St ⏰ Check website 🚫 24 Dec–2 Jan
🌐 priest-house.co.uk

Kingston Lacy
🎨 🍴 🛍 🚻 NT ⬛ On B3082
⏰ House: 11am–5pm daily (Nov–Feb: to 4pm); Gardens: 10am–6pm daily (Nov–Feb: to 4pm) 🌐 nationaltrust.org.uk

→ Dramatic landscape of vertiginous cliffs on the Isle of Purbeck

People enjoying a drink in the sunshine at a pub on the quay, Poole

Poole

⌂ Dorset 🚗🚌🚉 ⓘ 4 High St; www.pooletourism.com

Situated on one of the largest natural harbours in the world, Poole is an ancient, still thriving seaport. The quay is lined with old warehouses, modern apartments and a marina. The **Poole Museum**, partly housed in 15th-century cellars alongside the quay, has four floors of galleries.

Nearby **Brownsea Island** is given over to a woodland nature reserve with egrets, herons and red squirrels.

Poole Museum

🅿 ⌂ 4 High St 📞 01202 262600 🕐 10am-5pm daily (Nov-Mar: to 4pm)

Brownsea Island

🅿🅿😊🐦🚻 🕐 Mid-Mar-Oct: daily (boat trips leave every 30 mins) 🌐 national trust.org.uk

Bournemouth

⌂ Dorset ✈🚗🚉 ⓘ Pier Approach; www. bournemouth.co.uk

Bournemouth has an almost unbroken sweep of sandy beach, extending from the mouth of Poole Harbour to Hengistbury Head. To the west there are clifftop parks and gardens, interrupted by wooded river ravines known as "chines". The varied and colourful garden of **Compton Acres** was conceived as a museum of garden styles.

The **Russell-Cotes Art Gallery and Museum**, housed in a late Victorian villa, has an extensive collection, with many fine Oriental and Victorian artifacts.

East of Bournemouth, Christchurch Priory is 95 m (310 ft) in length – one of the longest churches in England.

The original nave, dating from around 1093, is an impressive example of Norman architecture, but the highlight is the intricate stone reredos, which features a Tree of Jesse tracing the lineage of Christ.

Hengistbury Head is well worth climbing for grassland flowers and sea views, while Stanpit Marsh, to the west of Bournemouth, is an excellent spot for viewing wading birds.

Compton Acres

🌸🍴🚻 ⌂ Canford Cliffs Rd 🕐 10am-6pm daily (Nov-Good Friday: to 4pm) 🌐 comptonacres.co.uk

Russell-Cotes Art Gallery and Museum

🍴🚻 ⌂ Eastcliff 🕐 10am-5pm Tue-Sun 🌐 russell cotes.com

EAT

Guildhall Tavern
This venerable seafood restaurant with smart maritime decor serves crab, lobster, oysters, scallops and loads more.

⌂ 15 Market St, Poole 🕐 Sun & Mon 🌐 guild halltavern.co.uk

£££

Lola's
A scrumptious menu starring classic tapas dishes might just make you think you are on the Spanish coast.

⌂ 95 Commercial Rd, Bournemouth 🌐 lolasrestaurant.co.uk

£££

DEVON AND CORNWALL

Parts of Devon and Cornwall – in particular the moorland areas – were settled by hunter-gatherers in the middle Stone Age. During the Iron Age, Cornwall became a refuge for Celtic tribes and an independent British polity was established here. Its people were even regarded as a separate ethnic group, with their own language, Brythonic, shared with the Welsh and the Bretons – although this language and identity had largely faded by the 18th century.

The heyday of this isolated corner of England was the buccaneering age of sea voyages by Francis Drake and Walter Raleigh during the 16th century. Meanwhile, inland, the wild moorland of Bodmin and Dartmoor provided inspiration for countless romantic tales, many of which were associated with King Arthur who, according to legend, was born at Tintagel on Cornwall's north coast.

At the beginning of the 19th century, the tin and copper mines of Devon and Cornwall were among the largest enterprises anywhere in Europe, at the forefront of the Industrial Revolution. These industries may have left their mark, quite literally, on the landscape, but these days it's tourism that largely sustains the local economy, thanks to the area's array of exotic gardens, pretty coves and first-class beaches.

DEVON AND CORNWALL

Barnstaple o
Bideford Bay

Hartland
Point

CLOVELLY 19

Hartland

A39

Morewenstow

Kilkhampton

BUDE 17

Bude Bay

Marham-
church

Poundstock

Boscastle

TINTAGEL 15

A39

Hallworthy

Delabole

Port Isaac

Camelford

Altarnun

Polzeath

Bodmin Moor

PADSTOW 14

Wadebridge

A30

Colliford
Reservoir

Constantine Bay

St Issey

CORNWALL

A39

Watergate Bay

BODMIN 13

Liskeard

Cornwall Airport Newquay

St Columb
Major

Lanhydrock

A38

NEWQUAY 16

Bugle

Lostwithiel

Ligger Bay

Newlyn
East

EDEN PROJECT 1

St Blazey

Perranporth

ST AUSTELL 11

12

Looe

St Agnes

A30

A39

FOWEY

Polperro

Portreath

TRURO 9

Lost Gardens
of Heligan

Mevagissey

ST IVES

Redruth

Treliske

Portloe

Zennor

2

Hayle

Camborne

Penryn

St Just-in-Roseland

Chysauster

Poldark
Mine

St Mawes

Pendeen

Marazion

ST MICHAEL'S
MOUNT

10

PENZANCE 6

7

FALMOUTH

Sennen

Trewidden

Newlyn

Glendurgan

Lands
End

Mousehole

8

HELSTON

Porthcurno

Mullion

St Keverne

LIZARD PENINSULA 8

Coverack

Ruan Minor

Lizard
Point

Lizard

*Atlantic
Ocean*

Tamar

Scilly Isles

*Roscoff,
Santander*

❶ ⊗ ♨ ☐ ⬚

EDEN PROJECT

📍 Bodelva, St Austell, Cornwall 🚉 St Austell 🚌 Dedicated bus service from St Austell 🕐 9:30am–6pm daily (Jul & Aug: to 6:30pm) 🌐 edenproject.com

A global garden for the 21st century, the spectacular Eden Project is nestled in a huge crater, providing a dramatic setting in which to tell the fascinating story of plants, people and places.

Hundreds of octagonal and pentagonal plastic cells supported by steel frames form the biomes, which mimic the environments of warmer climes. The hot and humid Rainforest Biome houses the largest enclosed rainforest in the world while the Mediterranean Biome re-creates the warm temperate climate and landscapes of the Mediterranean, South Africa, California and Western Australia. The relationship between humans and nature is interpreted in sculptures by artists throughout the site. The Core education centre hosts exhibitions and workshops. For an aerial view, you can ride over the biomes on a 660-m (2,165-ft) zip wire, the longest in England.

Building Eden

Cornwall's declining china clay industry left behind many disused pits which the Eden Project made ingenious use of. After partly infilling a pit, the biomes were constructed using a record 370 km (230 miles) of scaffolding.

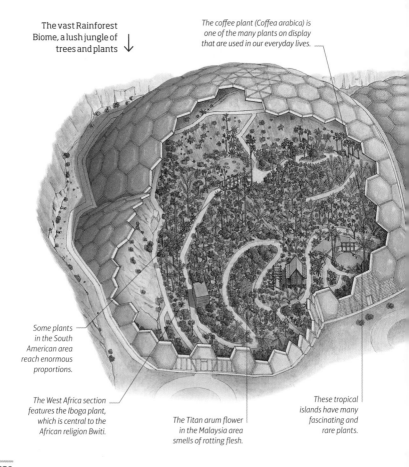

The vast Rainforest Biome, a lush jungle of trees and plants ↓

The coffee plant (Coffea arabica) is one of the many plants on display that are used in our everyday lives.

Some plants in the South American area reach enormous proportions.

The West Africa section features the Iboga plant, which is central to the African religion Bwiti.

The Titan arum flower in the Malaysia area smells of rotting flesh.

These tropical islands have many fascinating and rare plants.

The Eden Project's iconic geodesic domes, and the interior of the Mediterranean biome *(inset)*

Did You Know?

The Eden Project hosts music concerts called the Eden Sessions towards the end of June every year.

Transparent hexagons made of ultra-light high-tech plastic

The entrance to both the Rainforest and Mediterranean biomes is via the Link, where the Eden Bakery is located.

STAY

YHA

The Eden Project's unique on-site youth hostel is housed in recycled shipping containers, blending in with its eco-friendly surroundings. Bedrooms have good en-suite bathrooms. You can even bring your own tent (or hire one) to pitch in the garden in the summer months.

🏠 Eden Project, Bodelva
🌐 yha.org.uk

£ £ £

❷

ST IVES

🏠 Cornwall 🚌🚉 🛈 St Ives Library, Gabriel St; www.stives-cornwall.co.uk

With its whitewashed cottages, flower-filled gardens and beautiful sandy beaches, this historic fishing town combines coastal charm with a prestigious artistic heritage. The town is famous for the colony of artists that settled here in the 1920s, and today hosts Tate St Ives along with scores of small galleries and studios.

①

Tate St Ives

🏠 Porthmeor Beach
🕐 10am–5:20pm daily
🌐 tate.org

Perched above Porthmeor Beach with sweeping views of the ocean, this major art gallery showcases works by 20th-century modern British artists linked to St Ives and nearby Newlyn and hosts changing special exhibitions. Housed in a striking white modernist building, on the site of an old gasworks, it opened in 1993 and was the first regional outpost of London's Tate gallery (p76), founded by sugar baron and champion of British art Henry Tate. Within its light-filled galleries is an impressive range of work by St Ives

School artists, including iconic pieces by leading figures such as Barbara Hepworth, Ben Nicholson, Alfred Wallis, Peter Lanyon and Naum Gabo, as well as abstract pieces by associated international artists such as Brancusi, Mark Rothko and Piet Mondrian.

②

Beaches

With one of the mildest climates in Great Britain, St Ives is a beach-lover's paradise. A string of golden beaches stretches along St Ives Bay as far as Godrevy Lighthouse. The smallest beach, Porthgwidden, has soft golden sand and is very sheltered, making it great for children and family trips. Just a stone's throw from the centre of St Ives, Porthmeor is popular with both surfers and swimmers. The star beach, however, is sweeping Porthminster with its crescent of golden sand in a glittering bay of clear water. It also has an 18-hole golf course and a beach café serving great local dishes.

ST IVES ARTISTS

In the 1920s, St Ives, already known among painters for the clarity of its light, became a magnet for aspiring artists. Ben Nicholson and his then wife, Barbara Hepworth, formed the nucleus of a group of artists that made a major contribution to the development of abstract art in Europe. Other prolific artists associated with what became known as the St Ives School include the potter Bernard Leach and the painter Patrick Heron, whose *Coloured Glass Window* dominates the Tate St Ives entrance. Much of the art on display at Tate St Ives is abstract and illustrates new responses to the rugged Cornish landscape, the human figure and the ever-changing patterns of sunlight on sea.

↑ St Ives's sheltered beach basking beneath supremely beautiful skies

Must See

EAT

Cellar Bistro
Dine among upcycled and vintage bric-a-brac; the menu is largely gluten-free.

⌂ 29-31 Fore St
ⓦ cellar-bistro.co.uk

ⓔⓔⓔ

Porthmeor Beach Café
While away an hour or two on the breezy terrace, tucking into shared small plates.

⌂ Porthmear Beach
ⓦ porthmeor-beach.co.uk

ⓔⓔⓔ

---

③

St Ives Museum

⌂ Wheal Dream
🕒 Apr-Oct: 10:30am-4:30pm Mon-Fri, 10:30am-3:30pm Sat ⓦ museumsin cornwall.org.uk

Run entirely by volunteers, this quirky independent museum contains a treasure-trove of artifacts related to local history and life, from the earliest times until the town's modern transformation into a tourist destination. The fascinating collections include mining, boat building, fishing, farming, Victorian clothes, photographs and wartime memorabilia. There is also a studio where films of local interest are shown.

---

④

Barbara Hepworth Museum and Sculpture Garden

⌂ Barnoon Hill 🕒 10am-5:20pm daily ⓦ tate.org

Run by the Tate, this museum presents the works of one of Britain's most important 20th-century artists in the house and garden (formerly named Trewyn Studio) where she lived and worked from 1949 until 1975. Sculptures in bronze, stone and wood are displayed outdoors and in the house, where there are also paintings and drawings. The garden was designed by Barbara Hepworth in collaboration with a friend, the composer Priaulx Rainier.

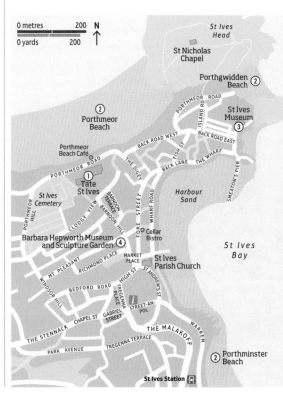

③

DARTMOOR NATIONAL PARK

⌂ Devon 🚂 Exeter, Plymouth, Totnes then bus ℹ Tavistock Rd, Princetown; www.dartmoor.gov.uk

A mix of sheltered wooded valleys and barren moorland peppered with granite rock formations and Bronze Age remains, Dartmoor was one of the first areas in England to be designated a National Park, in 1951.

The dramatic landscape of central Dartmoor is one of contrasts, providing an impressive variety of striking vistas. The high, open moorlands served as the eerie backdrop for the Sherlock Holmes tale *The Hound of the Baskervilles* (1902), while one of Britain's most famous prisons, Dartmoor Prison, is surrounded by weathered outcrops of stone

←

Hay tor Rocks, one of the most remarkable of Dartmoor's many tors

Walk across the splendid moorlands of Dartmoor and Exmoor along the Two Moors Way (also known as The Coast to Coast Path). Some 188 km (117 miles) in length, it starts at Wembury Bay in south Devon and finishes at Lynmouth on the north Devon coast, slicing through a small section of Somerset along the way. Suitable for both day and longer-distance walkers, the routes are explained on www.twomoorsway.org.

tors (rock formations) in Princetown village. Also dotting the landscape are scores of ancient remains of standing stones and mysterious hut circles that have survived thanks to the durability of granite. Creating pockets of tranquility, streams tumble through wooded and boulder-strewn ravines forming waterfalls, and thatched cottages nestle in the sheltered valleys and villages around the margins of the moor. Dartmoor ponies, here for centuries, can be seen grazing on the moors.

↑ Walker looking out over the beautiful Dartmoor landscape at sunrise

Highlights

St Michael de Rupe

▷ Legend has it that the Devil tried to prevent the construction of this church, perched atop Brent Tor, by moving the stones. Whatever the truth, there has been a church here since the 12th century. Reached by a footpath, there are stunning views over Dartmoor from here.

Postbridge

▽ In the centre of the moor and set on the River Dart, the village of Postbridge is a good starting point for walks on the moor. There is a medieval "clapper" bridge here, which was built to enable pack horses to carry mined tin across the river.

Lydford Gorge

There is a circular 5-km (3-mile) walk through this remote ravine.

Castle Drogo

This magnificent early 20th-century mock castle - said to be the last castle built in England - was designed by architect Edwin Lutyens for the grocery magnate Julius Drewe. From the house there are lovely walks through the gorge of the River Teign.

Hound Tor

▷ The remains of this village lie on the eastern edge of Dartmoor. The settlement consists of a cluster of 13th-century stone longhouses - in which the family lived at one end and the animals at the other - on land originally farmed in the Bronze Age.

Buckland-in-the-Moor

◁ One of the many pretty villages on the southeastern side of Dartmoor, Buckland-in-the-Moor has thatched stone cottages and a small granite church.

Did You Know?

The Exmoor pony is the oldest of the native British ponies.

4

EXMOOR NATIONAL PARK

⌂ Somerset / Devon 🚃 Tiverton Parkway, then bus 🛈 National Park Centres: Lee Rd, Lynton; 7-9 Fore St, Dulverton; The Steep, Dunster; www.exmoor-nationalpark.gov.uk

For walkers, Exmoor offers 1,000 km (620 miles) of wonderful public paths and varied, dramatic scenery of moorland, river valleys and cliffs, while the tamer perimeters of the national park offer less energetic attractions – everything from traditional seaside entertainments to picturesque villages and ancient churches.

The majestic cliffs plunging into the Bristol Channel along Exmoor's northern coast are interrupted by lush, wooded valleys carrying rivers from the high moorland down to sheltered fishing coves. Inland, wild rolling hills are grazed by sturdy Exmoor ponies, horned sheep and local wild red deer. Buzzards wheel over the bracken-clad terrain looking for prey.

←

Walker on Dunkery Beacon, Exmoor's highest point, at sunset

SOUTH WEST COAST PATH

Running across the northern edge of Exmoor National Park is the wonderful South West Coast Path, which begins in Minehead in Somerset and then snakes its way around the coast of Cornwall to Poole in Dorset. Some 1,014 km (630 miles) in length, it is the longest national trail in the UK and passes through diverse, stunning scenery, taking in geology, wildlife and heritage along the way *(www.southcoastpark.org.uk)*.

Exmoor ponies grazing on heather-covered moorland on Porlock Common, and Dunster Castle *(inset)*

Situated at the point where the East and West Lyn rivers meet the sea, Lynmouth is a picturesque fishing village. Above Lynmouth stands hilltop Lynton. The two villages are connected by a water-powered funicular railway which since the 19th century has shuttled 263 m (862 ft) up a steep bank. The short ride offers impressive views of the spectacular Jurassic Coast.

Lynmouth is an excellent starting point for walks on Exmoor. There is a gorgeous 3-km (2-mile) trail that leads southeast to tranquil Watersmeet House, a former fishing lodge that is now a fabulous tearoom with a splendid garden. Set in a wooded valley, this is the spot where the East Lyn and Hoar Oak Water join together in a tumbling cascade.

East of here are charming Porlock village, with winding streets, thatched houses and a lovely old church, and Minehead, a major resort built around a pretty quay. Dunster is one of Exmoor's oldest villages, with an ancient castle, parts of which date to the 13th century, and an unusual octagonal Yarn Market (c 1609), where local cloth was once sold.

On the western edge of Exmoor, the village of Combe Martin lies in a sheltered valley. On the main street, lined with Victorian villas, is the 17th-century Pack o' Cards inn, built by a gambler to resemble a pack of cards, with 52 windows, one for each card in the pack.

> **Inland, wild rolling hills are grazed by Exmoor ponies, horned sheep and local wild red deer. Buzzards wheel over the bracken-clad terrain looking for prey.**

EXPERIENCE MORE

5

Exeter

Devon | Dix's Field; www.visitexeter.com

Devon's capital, Exeter is built high on a plateau above the River Exe. The city is encircled by substantial sections of Roman and medieval wall.

The **Cathedral Church of St Peter** is one of the most gloriously ornamented cathedrals in Britain. Except for the two Norman towers, it dates mainly to the 14th century and is built in the style known as Decorated due to the swirling geometric patterns of the stonework. The West Front, the largest single collection (66) of medieval figure sculptures in England, includes kings, apostles and prophets. Among the tombs around the choir is that of Edward II's treasurer, Walter de Stapledon (1261–1326), who was murdered by a mob in London. A tour of the cathedral's roof affords spectacular citywide views and allows visitors to see the elaborate clock mechanism.

The family-friendly **Royal Albert Memorial Museum and Art Gallery** has a wonderfully varied collection, including Roman remains, a zoo of stuffed animals, West Country art and a particularly good ethnographic display, including a Samurai warrior. You can discover the city's past in the fun, interactive Making History gallery, and the Finders Keepers display explores the morality of collecting and the story behind the artifacts.

HIDDEN GEM
Bill Douglas Cinema Museum

Optical media before the invention of cinema and film-makers' production archives are among the displays at this museum in Exeter focusing on moving images in Britain *(www.bdcmuseum.org.uk)*.

Cathedral Church of St Peter

Cathedral Close
Times vary, check website
exeter-cathedral.org.uk

Royal Albert Memorial Museum and Art Gallery

Queen St
10am–5pm Tue–Sun
rammuseum.org.uk

6

Penzance

Cornwall | Station Approach; www.lovepenzance.co.uk

Penzance is a bustling resort with a climate so mild that palm trees and subtropical plants grow happily in the lush Morrab Gardens. The town commands fine views of St Michael's Mount and a great sweep of clean sandy beach.

The main road through the town is Market Jew Street, at the top of which stands the magnificent domed Market House (1837). Chapel Street

The majestic interior of the Cathedral Church of St Peter, in Exeter

is lined with curious buildings, like the flamboyant Egyptian House (1835), with its richly painted façade and lotus bud decoration, and Admiral Benbow Inn (1696), which has a pirate perched on the roof.

The **Penlee House Gallery and Museum** has pictures by the Newlyn School of artists, who painted outdoors, aiming to capture the fleeting impressions of wind, sun and sea. Newlyn *(p282)*, Cornwall's largest fishing port, is a short distance south of Penzance, while to the north is **Chysauster**, a fine example of a Romano-British village.

From Penzance, regular boat services depart for the Isles of Scilly, an enchanting, unspoilt archipelago with white-sand beaches forming part of the same granite mass as Land's End, Bodmin Moor and Dartmoor. Along with

tourism, flower-growing is the main source of income – fields of scented narcissi and pinks only add to the exceptional wild beauty of the islands.

Penlee House Gallery and Museum

 🅐 Morrab Rd
🕐 10am-5pm Mon-Sat (Nov-Mar: to 4:30pm)
🆆 penleehouse.org.uk

Chysauster

 🅐 Off B3311 🕐 Apr-Oct: 10am-6pm daily (Sep: to 5pm 🆆 english-heritage. org.uk

---

7 🅐 🍴 🥤 🛍 NT

St Michael's Mount

🅐 Marazion, Cornwall
🚢 From Marazion (Mar-Oct) or on foot at low tide 🕐 Mid-Mar-Oct: 10:30am-5pm Sun-Fri 🆆 nationaltrust. org.uk

According to many Roman historians, the mount was the island of Ictis, an important

centre for the Cornish tin trade during the Iron Age. It is dedicated to the archangel St Michael, who is said to have appeared here in AD 495.

When the Normans conquered England in 1066 *(p48)*, they were struck by the island's resemblance to their own Mont-St-Michel, whose Benedictine monks were then invited to build an abbey here. The abbey was absorbed into a fortress during the Dissolution *(p391)*, when Henry VIII set up coastal defences to counter an attack from France. In 1659, the mount was bought by Colonel John St Aubyn, whose descendants turned the fortress into a magnificent house.

Did You Know?

It was from St Michael's Mount that the Spanish Armada was first spotted in 1588.

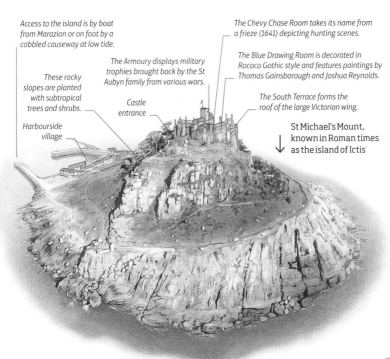

Access to the island is by boat from Marazion or on foot by a cobbled causeway at low tide.

The Chevy Chase Room takes its name from a frieze (1641) depicting hunting scenes.

The Blue Drawing Room is decorated in Rococo Gothic style and features paintings by Thomas Gainsborough and Joshua Reynolds.

The Armoury displays military trophies brought back by the St Aubyn family from various wars.

These rocky slopes are planted with subtropical trees and shrubs.

Castle entrance

The South Terrace forms the roof of the large Victorian wing.

Harbourside village

St Michael's Mount, known in Roman times as the island of Ictis

↑ Sunbathing on a sheltered beach on the Lizard Peninsula

8

Helston and the Lizard Peninsula

🏠 Cornwall
🚌 From Penzance
🌐 visithelston.com

The attractive town of Helston makes a good base for exploring the windswept coastline of the Lizard Peninsula. The town is famous for its Furry Dance, which welcomes spring with dancing through the streets (p44); the **Museum of Cornish Life, Helston** explains the history of this ancient custom. The Georgian houses and inns of Coinagehall Street are a reminder that Helston was once a thriving stannary town where tin ingots were brought for weighing and stamping before being sold. Locally mined tin was brought downriver to a harbour at the bottom of this street until access to the sea was blocked in the 13th century by a shingle bar that formed across the estuary. The bar created the freshwater lake, Loe Pool, now skirted by an attractive walk. In 1880, Helston's trade was taken over by a new harbour created to the east on the River Helford, at Gweek. Today, Gweek is the home of the **Cornish Seal Sanctuary**, where sick seals are nursed before being returned to the sea.

Cornwall's tin mining industry, from Roman to recent times, is covered at **Poldark Mine**, where underground tours show the working conditions of 18th-century miners.

Further south is Britain's most southerly tourist attraction, the **Lizard Lighthouse Heritage Centre**. Built in 1619, the tower was automated in 1998. Interactive displays describe the workings of a lighthouse.

Local shops sell souvenirs carved from serpentine, a soft greenish stone which forms the unusual-shaped rocks that rise from the sandy beach at Kynance Cove.

Museum of Cornish Life, Helston

🕐 🏠 Market Place, Helston
🕐 10am–4pm Mon–Sat
🌐 museumofcornishlife.co.uk

Cornish Seal Sanctuary

♿ 🅿 🕐 🏠 Gweek
🕐 10am–5pm daily
🌐 sealsanctuary.co.uk

Poldark Mine

♿ 🅿 🕐 🏠 Wendron 🕐 Mid-April–Nov: dates vary, check website 🌐 poldarkmine.org.uk

Lizard Lighthouse Heritage Centre

♿ 🕐 🏠 3 Lighthouse Rd, Lizard, Helston 🕐 Times vary, check website
🌐 trinityhouse.co.uk

CORNISH SMUGGLERS

In the days before income tax, the main form of government income came from tax on imported luxury goods, such as brandy and perfume. Huge profits were to be made by evading these taxes. With its coves and rivers penetrating deep into the mainland, Cornwall was prime smuggling territory; estimates put the number of people involved, including women and children, at 100,000. Some people resorted to deliberate wrecking, setting up deceptive lights to lure vessels onto the sharp rocks, in the hope of plundering the wreckage.

DRINK

Beerwolf Books
What could be better than books and beer? Combining a freehouse and a bookshop in a novel and quite brilliant concept, this place also hosts frequent live music and other events.

⌂ 3 Bells Court, Falmouth
ⓦ beerwolfbooks.com

⑨ Truro

⌂ Cornwall 🚃🚂
🛈 30 Boscawen St; www.visittruro.org.uk

The administrative capital of Cornwall's many gracious Georgian buildings reflect its prosperity during the tin mining boom of the 1800s. In 1876 the 16th-century parish church was rebuilt to create the first new cathedral to be built in England since Wren built St Paul's in the 17th century. With its central tower, lancet windows and spires, the cathedral is an exuberant building that looks more French than English.

The **Royal Cornwall Museum** explores the history of the county with displays on tin mining, Methodism and smuggling.

Royal Cornwall Museum
◎◎ ⌂ River St ◔ Apr–Oct: 10am–4pm Mon–Sat; Nov–Mar: 10am–4pm Tue–Sat ⓦ royalcornwallmuseum.org.uk

---

⑩ Falmouth

⌂ Cornwall 🚃🚌🚂
🛈 11 Market Strand; www.falmouth.co.uk

Falmouth stands at the point where seven rivers flow into a long stretch of water called the Carrick Roads. Numerous creeks are ideal for boating excursions to view the varied scenery and birdlife. The town has the third largest naturally deep harbour after Sydney and Rio de Janeiro. On the harbour waterfront stands the **National Maritime Museum Cornwall**, part of a large waterside complex that includes cafés, shops and restaurants. The museum is dedicated to Cornwall's great maritime tradition and contains Britain's finest public collection of historical and contemporary small craft.

Pendennis Castle and St Mawes Castle, opposite, were built by King Henry VIII. Towards the town centre is the **Falmouth Art Gallery**, with an important art collection.

National Maritime Museum Cornwall
◎◎◎ ⌂ Discovery Quay, Falmouth ◔ 10am–5pm daily ⓦ nmmc.co.uk

Pendennis Castle
◎◎◎◎◎◎ ⌂ The Headland ◔ Apr–Oct: 10am–6pm daily; Nov–Mar: 10am–4pm Sat, Sun ◔ 26 Dec–1 Jan ⓦ english-heritage.org.uk

Falmouth Art Gallery
⌂ The Moor ◔ 10am–5pm Mon–Sat ⓦ falmouth artgallery.com

← Cathedral Lane, a charming, shop-lined alley in the centre of Truro

↑ A sleeping giant in the atmospheric The Lost Gardens of Heligan, St Austell

⓫

St Austell

 Cornwall 🚌 ⬡
ℹ Texaco Service Station, Southbourne Rd; www.staustellbay.co.uk

The busy town of St Austell is the capital of the local china-clay industry, which rose to prominence in the 18th century.

At the **Wheal Martyn China Clay Museum**, displays evoke the history and human impact of clay quarrying, while nature trails weave through the abandoned clay works.

South of St Austell **The Lost Gardens of Heligan** aim to restore the extraordinary gardens created by the Tremayne family from the 16th century to World War I.

Wheal Martyn China Clay Museum

⬡⬡⬡⬡ Carthew ⬡10am-4pm daily ⬡24 Dec-mid-Jan
⬡ wheal-martyn.com

The Lost Gardens of Heligan

⬡⬡⬡⬡⬡ Pentewan
⬡10am-6pm daily (Oct-Mar: to 5pm) ⬡heligan.com

⓬

Fowey

⬡ Cornwall 🚢 ℹ5 South St; www.fowey.co.uk

The river, creeks and gentle waters of the Fowey (pronounced Foy) estuary were probably the inspiration for *The Wind in the Willows*, whose author Kenneth Grahame spent holidays here. The picturesque charm of the village is undeniable, with its tangle of tiny steep streets and its views across the estuary to Polruan.

The Church of St Fimbarrus marks the end of the ancient Saint's Way footpath from Padstow, a reminder of the Celtic missionaries who arrived here to convert people to Christianity. Inside, there are some fine 17th-century memorials to the Rashleigh family whose seat, Menabilly, became Daphne du Maurier's home and featured as Manderley in *Rebecca* (1938).

For a closer look at the town of Polruan and a tour

DAPHNE DU MAURIER

The period mystery romances of writer Daphne du Maurier (1907-89) are inextricably linked with the wild Cornish landscape where she grew up. *Jamaica Inn* established her reputation in 1936, and with the publication of *Rebecca* two years later she found herself one of the most popular authors of her day.

of the busy harbour, there are a number of river trips up the little creeks. At the estuary mouth are the twin towers from which chains were once hung to demast invading ships – an effective form of defence.

Up-river from Fowey is the tranquil town of Lostwithiel. Perched on a hill just to the north are the remains of the Norman **Restormel Castle**.

Restormel Castle

 ⟁ Lostwithiel
📞 01208 872687 🕐 Apr-Oct: 10am-5pm daily (Nov: to 4pm)

Bodmin

⟁ Cornwall 🚆 Bodmin Parkway 🚌 Bodmin
ℹ️ Mount Folly Sq, Bodmin; www.bodminlive.com

Bodmin, Cornwall's ancient county town, lies on the sheltered western edge of the great expanse of moorland that shares its name. The history and archaeology of the town and moor are covered by **Bodmin Town Museum**.

South of Bodmin, amid the **Lanhydrock** estate's wooded acres and formal gardens, stands a massive Victorian manor house, rebuilt after a fire in 1881 but retaining some Jacobean features.

The wilderness of Bodmin Moor is noted for its network of prehistoric field boundaries. The main attraction, however, is the 18th-century Jamaica Inn, made famous by Daphne du Maurier's tale of smuggling and romance. Today there is a museum telling the story of smuggling and a room devoted to the author.

Bodmin Town Museum

📷 ⟁ Mount Folly Sq, Bodmin
📞 01208 77067 🕐 Easter-Oct: 10:30am-4:30pm Mon-Fri, 10:30am-2:30pm Sat

Lanhydrock

⟁ Bodmin
🕐 House: Mar-Oct: 11am-5:30pm daily; Gardens: mid-Feb-Dec: 10am-5:30pm daily
🌐 nationaltrust.org.uk

Padstow

⟁ Cornwall 🚌
ℹ️ North Quay; www.padstowlive.com

A picturesque fishing port, chic Padstow is best known as a magnet for foodies. Celebrity chef Rick Stein opened his first seafood restaurant here in 1975. The cobbled streets

behind the quay are full of boutiques, art galleries and delicatessens. The Padstow Museum displays a range of artifacts including items from the annual Obby Orse (Hobby Horse) May Day ritual.

CORNISH GARDENS

Eden Project
An enormous array of plants in two biomes-one Mediterranean, the other Rainforest *(p280)*.

Lanhydrock
Immaculate parkland, formal gardens and woodland walks.

Lost Gardens of Heligan
Explore jungle, lakes, woods and stunning wildflower meadows.

Trelissick Feock
🌐 nationaltrust.org.uk
Renowned for its hydrangeas and Mediterranean species, plus great sea views.

Trewidden
🌐 trewiddengarden.co.uk
A maze of tree ferns, azaleas, camellias and magnolias.

↑ Small boats in the charming harbour of the village of Fowey

15

Tintagel

⌂ Cornwall 🚃 Bossiney Rd;
www.visitboscastle
andtintagel.com

The romantic and mysterious ruins of **Tintagel Castle**, built around 1240 by Earl Richard of Cornwall, sit high on a hilltop surrounded by slate cliffs. Access to the castle is via two steep staircases clinging to the cliffside where pink thrift and purple sea lavender abound. The earl was persuaded to build in this isolated, windswept spot by the popular belief that this was the birthplace of the legendary King Arthur.

A clifftop path leads from the castle to Tintagel's church, which has Norman and Saxon masonry. In Tintagel village the **Old Post Office** is a rare example of a 14th-century restored and furnished Cornish manor house.

A short distance to the east is pretty Boscastle village. The River Valency runs down the middle of the main street to the fishing harbour, which is sheltered from the sea by

high slate cliffs. Access from the harbour to the sea is via a channel cut through the rocks.

Tintagel Castle

⌘ 🏠 ♿ ⌂ Tintagel Head
🕐 10am-7pm daily 🌐 english-heritage.org.uk

Old Post Office

⌘ 🏠 NT ⌂ Fore St 🕐 Mar-Oct: 10:30am-5:30pm daily; book ahead 🌐 nationaltrust.org.uk

---

KING ARTHUR

The legendary figure of King Arthur may have some historical basis. He was probably a chieftain who led British resistance to the Saxon invasion of the 6th century. Geoffrey of Monmouth's *History of the Kings of Britain* (1139) related many Arthurian legends – how he became king by removing the sword Excalibur from a stone, his final battle with Mordred, and the story of the Knights of the Round Table.

16

Newquay

⌂ Cornwall 🚃 🚌
ℹ Macus Hill; www.visitnewquay.org

Starting life as an Elizabethan sailing port, Newquay quickly became one of Cornwall's biggest pilchard fisheries. The arrival of the railway in the 1870s made it the county's most popular beach resort.

→ The dramatic coastal landscape around the ruins of Tintagel Castle

Today, as the UK's surfing capital, Newquay attracts surfers from all over Europe.

Bude

🏠 Cornwall 🚻 Crescent Car Park; www.visitbude.info

The expanse of clean golden sand that draws visitors today once made Bude a bustling port. Shelly, lime-rich sand was transported along a canal to inland farms where it was used to neutralize the acidic soil. The canal was abandoned in 1880 but a short stretch survives, providing a haven for birds such as kingfishers and herons.

Bideford

🏠 Devon 🚌 🚻 Burton Art Gallery, Kingsley Rd; www.visitdevon.co.uk

Strung out along the estuary of the River Torridge, Bideford thrived on importing tobacco from the New World. Some 17th-century merchants' houses survive in Bridgeland Street, including the splendid bay-windowed house at No. 28 (1693). Beyond is Mill Street, leading to the parish church and the fine medieval bridge. The quay stretches from here to a park and a statue that commemorates Charles Kingsley, whose novels helped bring visitors to the area in the 19th century.

To the west of Bideford, the late 19th-century village Westward Ho!, named after Charles Kingsley's popular novel, is notable for its good surfing and the oldest golf club in England, the Royal North Devon. Also to the west is **Hartland Abbey**, built as a monastery in around 1157, now a family home. The BBC filmed parts of *Sense and Sensibility* here. Visitors can enjoy a museum and gardens.

In Torridge Valley, the 290-km (180-mile) Tarka Trail follows the route taken by the title character in Henry Williamson's *Tarka the Otter* (1927). Part of the trail runs along a disued railway line beside the Torridge and can be enjoyed by walkers and cyclists. The trail passes close to the magnificent **Rosemoor Garden**. Day trips run from either Bideford or Ilfracombe (depending on the tide) to Lundy Island, which is abundant in birds and wildlife.

Hartland Abbey

♿ 🎁 🏠 Near Bideford ⏰ Apr–Sep: 11am–5pm Sun–Thu (house: from 2pm) 🌐 hartlandabbey.com

Rosemoor Garden

♿ 🍴 🎁 🏠 Great Torrington ⏰ 10am–5pm daily (Apr–Sep: to 6pm) 🌐 rhs.org.uk/gardens/rosemoor

---

Clovelly

🏠 Devon 🌐 clovelly.co.uk

Clovelly has been renowned as a beauty spot since the novelist Charles Kingsley (1819–75) wrote about it in his stirring story of the Spanish Armada, *Westward Ho!* (1855). Privately owned, the village has steep, traffic-free cobbled streets rising up the cliff from the harbourside and gardens brimming with brightly coloured flowers. There are superb views from the lookout points and fine coastal paths from the tiny quay.

Hobby Drive is a scenic 5-km (3-mile) approach on foot to the village, running through woodland along the coast. The road was constructed in 1811–29 to give employment to local men who had been made redundant at the end of the Napoleonic Wars.

❷⓪ Torbay

🏠 Torbay 🚆🚌 Torquay, Paignton ℹ 5 Vaughan Parade, Torquay; www. englishriviera.co.uk

The seaside towns of Torquay, Paignton and Brixham form an almost continuous resort around the great sweep of sandy beach and blue waters of Torbay. Because of its mild climate, semi-tropical gardens and exuberant Victorian hotel architecture, this popular coastline has been dubbed the English Riviera.

Torre Abbey includes the remains of a monastery founded in 1196. The mansion dates back to the 17th century, and houses an art gallery and museum, though other rooms have been preserved as they were in the 1920s, when it was a private residence. **Torquay Museum** nearby covers natural history and archaeology, including finds from **Kents Cavern**, on the outskirts of the town. This is one of England's most important prehistoric sites, and the spectacular caves include displays on people and animals who lived here up to 350,000 years ago.

The charming miniature town of **Babbacombe Model Village** is north of Torquay, while 1.5 km (1 mile) inland is the lovely village of Cockington. It is possible to visit the preserved Tudor manor house, church and thatched cottages and watch craftsmen at work.

In Paignton, the celebrated **Paignton Zoo** teaches children about the planet's wildlife, and from here you can take the steam railway – an ideal way to visit Dartmouth.

Torre Abbey

♿🐕♻️🅿️🏠 🏠 King's Drive, Torquay 🕐 Mar–Dec: 10am–5pm Tue–Sun (Apr, May & Aug: also bank hols 🚫 25 Dec 🌐 torre-abbey.org.uk

Torquay Museum

♿🐕🅿️ 🏠 Babbacombe Rd, Torquay 🕐 10am–4pm daily 🚫 Christmas week 🌐 torquaymuseum.org

Kents Cavern

♿🐕🍽️🅿️ 🏠 Ilsham Rd, Torquay 🕐 10:30am–4pm daily 🌐 kents-cavern.co.uk

Babbacombe Model Village

♿🍽️ 🏠 Hampton Ave, Torquay 🕐 10am–4pm daily (to 9pm Thu) 🌐 model-village.co.uk

Paignton Zoo

♿🍴🍽️ 🏠 Totnes Rd, Paignton 🕐 10am–6pm daily (Sep–Mar: to 4:30pm) 🌐 paigntonzoo.org.uk

---

❷① Barnstaple

🏠 Devon 🚆🚌 ℹ The Square; www. staynorthdevon.co.uk

Barnstaple is an important distribution centre for the whole region. The massive glass-roofed Pannier Market (1855) has stalls of organic food, much of it produced locally. Nearby is St Peter's Church with its twisted broach spire, said to have been

↑ Sunset falling on the marina at Torquay, one of the towns making up the Torbay area

→

A street lined with colourful cottages in the village of Appledore

caused by a lightning strike warping the timbers in 1810. On the Strand is a wonderful arcade topped with a statue of Queen Anne, now the Heritage Centre. Nearby is the 15th-century bridge and the **Museum of Barnstaple and North Devon**, where displays cover local history and the 700-year-old pottery industry, as well as otters and other local wildlife. The Tarka Trail *(p295)* circuits around Barnstaple; 56 km (35 miles) of it can be cycled.

Just west of Barnstaple, Braunton "Great Field" covers over 120 ha (300 acres) and is a well-preserved relic of medieval open-field cultivation. Beyond lies Braunton Burrows, one of the most extensive wild-dune reserves in Britain. It is a must for plant enthusiasts, who are likely to spot sea kale, sea holly, sea lavender and horned poppies. The sandy beaches at nearby Croyde and Woolacombe are popular surfing spots. There are also calmer areas of warm shallow water and rock pools.

Arlington Court and National Trust Carriage Museum, north of Barnstaple, is packed with treasures. It has a collection of horse-drawn vehicles and model ships. The grounds feature magnificent perennial borders and a lake.

Museum of Barnstaple and North Devon
🕐 🏛 The Square 🕙 10am-4pm Mon-Sat ⏱ 24 Dec-1 Jan 🌐 barnstaplemuseum.org.uk

Arlington Court and National Trust Carriage Museum
🏛 Arlington 🕙 Mid-Feb-Oct: 11am-5pm daily; Nov & Dec: 11am-4pm Sat & Sun 🌐 nationaltrust. org.uk

㉒

Appledore

🏛 Devon 🛈 Bideford; www.appledore.org

Appledore's remote position at the tip of the Torridge Estuary has helped to preserve its charms intact. Busy boatyards line the long riverside quay, which is also the departure point for fishing trips and ferries to the sandy beaches of Braunton Burrows on the opposite shore. Time-worn Regency houses line the main street that runs parallel to the quay, and behind is a network of narrow cobbled lanes with 18th-century fishermen's cottages. Several shops retain their original bow windows and sell crafts, antiques and souvenirs.

Uphill from the quay is the **North Devon Maritime Museum**, with an exhibition on the experiences of Devon emigrants to Australia and displays explaining the work of local shipyards. The tiny Victorian Schoolroom, which is affiliated with the museum, shows videos on local trades like fishing and shipbuilding.

North Devon Maritime Museum
🏛 Odun Rd 🕙 Apr-Oct: 10:30am-5pm 🌐 northdevon maritimemuseum.co.uk

The seaside towns of Torquay, Paignton and Brixham form an almost continuous resort around the great sweep of sandy beach and blue waters of Torbay.

SHOP

Drift

An independent record store whose stock of vinyl is consistently rated one of England's best.

🏠103 High St, Totnes
🕐Sun 🌐drift records.com

Me and East

A little shop selling local arts and crafts, including jewellery, woodwork, ceramics, prints and textiles.

🏠24 Leechwell St, Totnes 🕐Sun & Mon 🌐meandeast.com

Tom Wood Antiques and Coins

A wonderful little curiosity shop whose owner is a font of knowledge on just about anything.

🏠7 St Lawrence Lane, Ashburton, nr Buckfastleigh 📞01364 653997 🕐Sun & Mon

Low tide at the beach at Bigbury-on-Sea, looking towards Burgh Island ↑

23 Totnes

🏠Devon 🚉🚌🚲
🌐englishriviera.co.uk

One of the most ecologically minded towns in the UK, vibrant Totnes is committed to sustainable food, energy and buildings. It is set at the highest navigable point on the River Dart, with a Norman **castle** perched high on the hill above. Linking the two is the steep High Street, lined with bow-windowed Elizabethan houses. Bridging the street is the Eastgate, part of the medieval town wall. Life in the town's heyday is explored in the **Totnes**

Elizabethan Museum, which also has a room devoted to the mathematician Charles Babbage (1791–1871), who is regarded as the pioneer of modern computers. There is a **Guildhall** and a church with a delicately carved and gilded rood screen. On Tuesdays in the summer, market stallholders dress in colourful Elizabethan costume.

A few miles north of Totnes, **Dartington Hall** has 10 ha (25 acres) of lovely gardens and hosts a music school every August, when concerts are held in the timbered 14th-century Great Hall.

Totnes Castle

♿ 🅱️ 🏠Castle St 🕐Apr–Oct: 10am–6pm daily; Nov–Mar: 10am–4pm Sat & Sun 🌐english-heritage.org.uk

Totnes Elizabethan Museum

🏠Fore St 🕐Apr–Sep: 10am–4pm Mon–Fri 🌐totnes museum.org

Guildhall

🏠Ramparts Walk 📞01803 862147 🕐Apr–Oct: 11am–3pm Mon–Fri 🕐Public hols

Dartington Hall

🏠Gardens: dawn–dusk daily 🌐dartington.org

24 Burgh Island

🏠Devon 🚉Plymouth then taxi ℹ️The Quay, Kingsbridge; www.burghisland.com

The short walk across the sands at low tide from Bigbury-on-Sea to Burgh Island takes you back to the era of the 1920s and 1930s. It was here that the millionaire Archibald Nettlefold built the luxury Burgh Island hotel in 1929. Created in Art Deco style with a natural rock

CELEBRITY ISLAND

Burgh Island and its eponymous hotel have long been celebrity haunts – the Beatles were among its guests, and prior to D-Day Churchill and Eisenhower met here. The island also provided the inspiration for Agatha Christie's novels *And Then There Were None* and *Evil Under the Sun*. At low tide, you can walk to the island; at other times, it is accessed by a 1969 restored sea tractor.

sea-bathing pool, this was the exclusive retreat of figures such as the Duke of Windsor and Noël Coward. The restored hotel is worth a visit to see the photographs of its heyday and the Art Deco fittings.

㉕

Buckfastleigh

 Devon 🚉 ℹ 80 Fore St; 01364 644522

This market town, situated on the edge of Dartmoor (*p284*), is dominated by **Buckfast Abbey**. The original abbey, founded in Norman times, fell into ruin after the Dissolution of the Monasteries and it was not until 1882 that a small group of French Benedictine monks set up a new abbey here. The fine abbey was completed in 1938 and lies at the heart of a thriving community. The fine mosaics and modern stained-glass window are also the work of the monks. Buckfast Tonic Wine ("Buckie"), wine fortified with caffeine, was created in the 1880s by the French Benedictine monks and is still made today at the abbey. Nearby is the **Buckfast Butterfly Farm and Dartmoor Otter Sanctuary**,

and the South Devon Steam Railway terminus where steam trains leave for Totnes.

Buckfast Abbey

ⓣ ⓐ Ⓗ Buckfastleigh
🕐 10am-3pm daily
ⓦ buckfast.org.uk

Buckfast Butterfly Farm and Dartmoor Otter Sanctuary

⊗ ⓐ Ⓗ Buckfastleigh
🕐 10am-5pm daily
ⓦ ottersandbutterflies.co.uk

㉖

Dartmouth

 Devon 🚢 ℹ Mayors Ave; www.discoverdartmouth.com

Historically an important port, it was from Dartmouth that English fleets set sail to join the Second and Third Crusades. Some 18th-century houses adorn the cobbled quay of Bayards Cove, while carved timber buildings line the 17th-century Butterwalk,

home to the **Dartmouth Museum** with its impressive collection of maritime artifacts. To the south is **Dartmouth Castle** (1388).

About 13 km (8 miles) north is **Greenway House**, the 1950s former holiday home of Agatha Christie and her family.

Dartmouth Museum

⊗ ⓐ Ⓗ Butterwalk
ⓒ Easter-Oct: 10am-4pm Mon -Fri & Sat, 1-4pm Sun & Mon; Nov-Easter: 1-4pm daily
ⓦ dartmouthmuseum.org

Dartmouth Castle

⊗ ⊜ ⓐ ᴱᴴ Ⓗ Castle Rd
ⓒ 10am-6pm daily (Nov-Easter: 10am-4pm Sat & Sun)
ⓦ english-heritage.org.uk

Greenway House

⊗ ⊜ ⓐ ᴺᵀ Ⓗ Greenway Rd, Galmpton ⓒ 10:30am-5pm daily (Nov-Easter: 11am-4pm Sat & Sun) ⓦ nationaltrust.org.guk

→
A ship in a bottle, part of the collection on display at the Dartmouth Museum

27

Buckland Abbey

📍 Yelverton, Devon 🚌 From Yelverton ⏰ 11am–5pm daily (Jan–mid-Feb: 10am–4pm Sat & Sun) 🌐 national trust.org.uk

Founded by Cistercian monks in 1278, Buckland Abbey was converted to a house after the Dissolution of the Monasteries and became the home of Sir Francis Drake from 1581. Many of the original monastic buildings survive in a garden setting, notably the 14th-century tithe barn *(p284)*. Drake's life is recalled through paintings and memorabilia in the house.

28

Plymouth

📍 Plymouth 🚗🚌🚆 ℹ️ The Mayflower, The Barbican; www.visitplymouth.co.uk

The tiny port from which Drake, Raleigh, the Pilgrim Fathers, Cook and Darwin all set sail on pioneering voyages has grown into a substantial city. Old Plymouth clusters around the Hoe, the famous patch of turf on which Sir Francis Drake is said to have calmly finished his game of bowls as the Spanish Armada approached the port in 1588. Today the Hoe is a park and parade ground surrounded by memorials to

↑ The coast seen from Mount Edgcumbe Park, Plymouth

naval men, including Drake himself. Just south is Tinside Lido, a lovely 1935 Art Deco swimming pool. Nearby is Charles II's **Royal Citadel**, built to guard the harbour in the 1660s (book your visit in advance). On the harbour is the **National Marine Aquarium**. Just west is the Mayflower Stone and Steps, the spot where the Pilgrim Fathers set sail for the New World in 1620. The popular **Plymouth Mayflower Exhibition** explores the story

of the *Mayflower* and the creation of the harbour. A boat tour of the harbour is the best way to see the dockyards. There are also splendid views of various fine gardens, such as **Mount Edgcumbe Park**, scattered around the coastline. East of the city, the 18th-century **Saltram House** has two rooms by Robert Adam and portraits by Reynolds, who was born in nearby Plympton.

Royal Citadel
📍 The Hoe ⏰ For tours only, check website 🌐 english-heritage.org.uk

National Marine Aquarium
📍 Rope Walk, Coxside ⏰ 10am–5pm daily 🌐 national-aquarium.co.uk

Plymouth Mayflower Exhibition
📍 3–5 The Barbican ☎ 01752 306330 ⏰ 9am–5pm daily (Nov–Mar: 10am–4pm Sat)

SIR FRANCIS DRAKE

Sir Francis Drake (c1540–1596) was the first Englishman to circumnavigate the globe and was knighted by Elizabeth I in 1580. To many, however, Drake was just an opportunistic rogue, renowned for his exploits as a "privateer", the polite name for a pirate. Drake further endeared himself to queen and people by his part in the victory over Philip II's Spanish Armada *(p48)*, defeated by bad weather and the buccaneering spirit of the English.

Mount Edgcumbe Park

 ☐ Cremyll, Torpoint 🚌 From Torpoint car park ⏰ House: Apr-Sep: 11am-4:30pm Sun-Thu 🌐 mountedgcumbe.gov.uk

Saltram House

☐ Plympton ⏰ Noon-4:30pm daily 🌐 nationaltrust.org.uk

---

29 🚲 Ⓜ 📷 🏛

Morwellham Quay

☐ Near Tavistock, Devon 🚉 Gunnislake ⏰ 10am-5pm (winter: to 4pm) daily 🌐 morwellham-quay.co.uk

Morwellham Quay was a neglected industrial site until 1970, when members of a local trust began restoring the abandoned cottages, schoolhouse, farmyards, quay and copper mines to their original condition.

Today, Morwellham Quay is a thriving industrial museum, where you can easily spend a whole day partaking in the typical activities of a Victorian village, from preparing the shire horses for a day's work, to riding a tramway deep into a copper mine in the hillside behind the village. The museum is brought to life by characters in costumes, some of whom give demonstrations throughout the day. You can watch, or lend a hand to the cooper while he builds a barrel, attend a lesson in the schoolroom, take part in Victorian playground games or dress up in 19th-century hooped skirts, bonnets, top hats or jackets. The staff, who convincingly play the part of villagers, lead visitors through Victorian life and impart a huge amount of information about the history of this small copper-mining community.

---

30 🚲 🍴 📷 🏛 ⓃⓉ

Cotehele

☐ St Dominick, Cornwall 🚉 Calstock ☎ 01579 351346 ⏰ House: mid-Mar-Oct: 11am-4pm daily; Nov-Dec: 10:30am-4pm daily; Grounds: dawn-dusk daily

Magnificent woodland and lush river scenery make Cotehele (pronounced Coteal) one of the most delightful spots on the River Tamar and a rewarding day can be spent exploring the estate. Far from civilization, tucked into its wooded fold in the Cornish countryside, Cotehele has slumbered for 500 years. The main attraction is the house and valley garden at its centre. Built mainly between 1489 and 1520, it is a rare example of a medieval house, set around three courtyards with a magnificent open hall, kitchen, chapel and a warren of private parlours and chambers. The romance of the house is enhanced by colourful terraced gardens to the east, leading via a tunnel into a richly planted valley garden. The path through this garden passes a large domed medieval dovecote and descends to a quay, to which lime and coal were once shipped, and now features a restored sailing barge and a small maritime museum. There are fine views up and down the winding reed-fringed Tamar from Prospect Tower, and a gallery on the quayside specializes in local arts and crafts.

→

The medieval mansion at Cotehele, an estate on the River Tamar

---

EAT

Gallery Restaurant

A memorable fine-dining experience is guaranteed at this lavish hotel restaurant, courtesy of exciting dishes (such as citrus cured halibut with mint and cobnuts) and impeccable service.

☐ Boringdon Hall Hotel, Plympton, Plymouth 🚫 Mon & Tue 🌐 boringdonhall.co.uk

£££

St Elizabeth's

This top-notch hotel restaurant uses local ingredients and although the emphasis is very much on seafood, the menu offers much more besides, including delicious Sunday roasts.

☐ St Elizabeth's House Hotel, Plympton, Plymouth 🌐 stelizabeths.co.uk

£££

A DRIVING TOUR
PENWITH

Length 50 km (30 miles) **Stopping-off points** There are pubs and cafés in most villages. Sennen Cove makes a pleasant midway stop.

This driving tour passes through a spectacular, remote Cornish landscape, dotted with relics of the tin mining industry, picturesque fishing villages and many prehistoric remains. The magnificent coastline varies between gentle rolling moorland in the north and the rugged, windswept cliffs that characterize the dramatic south coast. The beauty of the area, combined with the clarity of light, has attracted artists since the late 19th century. Their work can be seen in Newlyn, St Ives and Penzance.

Did You Know?

Cornwall has its own language. It is not widely spoken but is taught in some schools.

*Derelict engine-houses clinging to the cliffside at **Botallack Mine** are a vivid reminder of the region's former industry of tin mining.*

↑ Engine-houses perched on the edge of cliffs at Botallack

Land's End *is England's most westerly point and noted for its dramatic and wild landscape. A local exhibition reveals its history, geology and wildlife.*

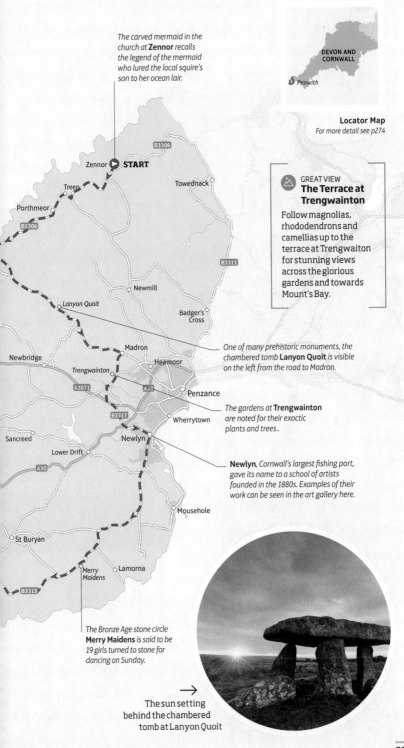

The carved mermaid in the church at **Zennor** recalls the legend of the mermaid who lured the local squire's son to her ocean lair.

DEVON AND CORNWALL

Penwith

Locator Map
For more detail see p274

Zennor ▷ **START**

GREAT VIEW
The Terrace at Trengwainton

Follow magnolias, rhododendrons and camellias up to the terrace at Trengwaiton for stunning views across the glorious gardens and towards Mount's Bay.

One of many prehistoric monuments, the chambered tomb **Lanyon Quoit** is visible on the left from the road to Madron.

The gardens at **Trengwainton** are noted for their exoctic plants and trees..

Newlyn, Cornwall's largest fishing port, gave its name to a school of artists founded in the 1880s. Examples of their work can be seen in the art gallery here.

The Bronze Age stone circle **Merry Maidens** is said to be 19 girls turned to stone for dancing on Sunday.

→ The sun setting behind the chambered tomb at Lanyon Quoit

303

THE HEART OF ENGLAND

Early settlement of this region of remote and heavily wooded countryside was sparse until Saxon colonists penetrated the river valleys around the 6th century. In the area on the border with Wales, known as the Marches, 11th-century castles at Shrewsbury and Ludlow recall the time when the Welsh were locked in fierce conflict with Norman barons and the Marcher Lords.

It was for very good reason that the Heart of England was once known as the workshop of the world. An industrial powerhouse of a region comprising Coventry, Birmingham, the Potteries (present-day Stoke-on-Trent) and their hinterlands were synonymous with the manufacture of iron, textiles and ceramics in the 18th and 19th centuries.

During World War II, the Midlands suffered significant air-raid damage – the ruins of the old Coventry Cathedral are perhaps the most visible modern-day reminder of the Blitz. As heavy industry began to decline in the 1970s and 1980s, museums developed to commemorate the towns' industrial heyday and explain the manufacturing processes that were once taken for granted in the fascinating Ironbridge Gorge industrial site.

THE HEART OF ENGLAND

Must Sees

1. Ironbridge Gorge
2. Stratford-upon-Avon
3. Warwick Castle

Experience More

4. Stoke-on-Trent
5. Warwick
6. Shrewsbury
7. Ludlow
8. Ledbury
9. Leominster
10. Ross-on-Wye
11. Great Malvern and the Malverns
12. Worcester
13. Hereford
14. Birmingham
15. Coventry

THE HEART OF ENGLAND

❶

IRONBRIDGE GORGE

📍 Shropshire 🚌 Telford then bus 🌐 ironbridge.org.uk

A World Heritage Sight, Ironbridge Gorge was one of the most important centres of the Industrial Revolution. It was here, in 1709, that Abraham Darby I (1678–1717) pioneered the use of inexpensive coke, rather than charcoal, to smelt iron ore. The use of iron in bridges, ships and buildings transformed Ironbridge Gorge into one of the world's great iron-making centres. Industrial decline in the 20th century led to the Gorge's decay, but today it has been restored as an exciting complex of industrial history, with several museums strung along the scenic wooded banks of the River Severn.

❶ 🔸🖥️🛍️

Coalport China Museum

📍 High St, Telford 🕐 Times vary, check website

In the mid-19th century the Coalport Works was one of the largest porcelain manu-facturers in Britain. Today the china workshops have been converted into a museum, where visitors can watch demonstrations of the various stages of making porcelain.

❷ 🔸🛍️

Coalbrookdale Museum of Iron

📍 Coach Rd, Coalbrookdale, Telford 🕐 Times vary, check website

Abraham Darby I's original blast furnace forms the cen-trepiece of this museum which traces the history of iron and the men who made it.

The museum also explores the history of the Darby dynasty, a Quaker family who had a great impact on the Coalbrookdale community. Cast-iron statues, many of them commissioned for the 1851 Great Exhibition, are among the Coalbrookdale Company products on display. One of the Darby family's homes in Coalbrookdale, Rosehill House, is open during the summer.

---

❸ 🔸🛍️

Museum of the Gorge

📍 Coach Rd, Coalbrookdale, Telford 🕐 Times vary, check website

This Victorian building is home to the Museum of the Gorge and has displays illustrating the history of the Severn and the development of the water industry. The highlight of the

THE IRON BRIDGE

Abraham Darby III (grandson of the first man to smelt iron with coke) cast the world's first iron bridge in 1779, thereby revolutionizing building methods in the process. Spanning the Severn, the bridge is a monument to the ironmaster's skills. The tollhouse on the south bank charts the bridge's construction.

Did You Know?

The Iron Bridge was the first large bridge to be made of cast iron in the world.

museum is a wonderful 12-m (40-ft) model of the Gorge as it would have appeared in 1796, complete with foundries, cargo boats and lovely growing villages.

④

Jackfield Tile Museum

🏠 Salthouse Rd, Telford
🕐 Times vary, check website

There have been potteries in this area since the 17th century, but it was the Victorian passion for decorative tiles that made Jackfield famous. This museum has a collection of the decorative floor and wall tiles that were produced here. You can watch small-scale demonstrations of

traditional methods of tile-making, including the kilns and the decoration workshops.

⑤

Enginuity

🏠 10 Wellingon Rd, Coalbrookdale, Telford
🕐 Times vary, check website

Kids will love this hands-on interactive science centre where they can learn to generate electricity using water and dams or move a steam locomotive with their hands.

⑥

Blists Hill Victorian Town

🏠 Legges Way, Madeley, Telford 🕐 Times vary, check website

This enormous open-air museum re-creates Victorian life in an east Shropshire coalfield town. Here, people in period costume perform tasks such as iron forging. The site has period housing,

↑ Re-creation of iron forging at Blists Hill Victorian Town

a church and a Victorian school. The highlight of Blists Hill is a complete foundry that still produces wrought iron. Other attractions include steam engines, a chemist, a candle-makers and a sweetshop.

↓ Strolling across the elegantly arching Iron Bridge

②

STRATFORD–UPON-AVON

🏠 Warwickshire 🛫 Birmingham, 32 km (20 miles) NW of Stratford-upon-Avon 🚌 Alcester Rd 🚆 Bridge St
ℹ️ Bridge Foot; www.visitstratforduponavon.co.uk

This small Tudor market town, with mellow half-timbered buildings and tranquil walks beside the tree-fringed River Avon, is the most visited tourist attraction outside London, with eager hordes flocking to see sights connected to William Shakespeare, Britain's greatest dramatist, born here in 1564.

Shakespeare's Birthplace

🏠 Henley St ⏰ Jan-Mar & Nov-Dec: 10am-4pm daily; Apr-Oct: 10am-5pm daily
🌐 shakespeare.org.uk

Bought for the nation in 1847, Shakespeare's Birthplace was restored from its state of disrepair to its original Elizabethan style. Objects associated with Shakespeare's father, John, a glovemaker and wool merchant, are on display. There is a birth room, in which

Shakespeare was supposedly born, and another room has a window etched with visitors' autographs, including that of Sir Walter Scott (p507).

② 🎭 🏠

Shakespeare's New Place

🏠 22 Chapel St ⏰ Jan-Mar & Nov-Dec: 10am-4pm daily; Apr-Oct: 10am-5pm daily
🌐 shakespeare.org.uk

This was the site of the house where Shakespeare lived from

1597 until his death in 1616. The house was demolished in 1759 and has been replaced with a garden with displays and artworks commemorating his family life and evoking some of the major works he wrote while he lived here. The Knot Garden with a deep pool has been beautifully restored.

Nearby, on the façade of the Town Hall, is a statue of the Bard, the gift of legendary Shakespearean actor David Garrick (1717–79).

③

Shakespeare's School Room and Guildhall

🏠 Church St ⏰ 11am-5pm daily 🌐 shakespeares schoolroom.org

Here you can learn about Shakespeare's formative

Did You Know?

The RSC is the only theatre company with its own on-site armoury.

↑ Visitors thronging the pretty streets of Stratford, home to the Bard of Avon

THE ROYAL SHAKESPEARE COMPANY (RSC)

The RSC, founded in 1960, is renowned for its interpretations of Shakespeare's work. It has featured the brightest and best theatrical talent, from Laurence Olivier and Vivien Leigh to Helen Mirren and Kenneth Branagh. The RSC also tours, with regular seasons in London, Newcastle and even New York.

Stratford has two main stages run by the RSC – the Royal Shakespeare Theatre and the Swan Theatre, both on Waterside. Tours of the Royal Shakespeare Theatre take place regularly at 10:30am or 2:45pm – see www.rsc.org.uk for details and to book.

childhood years at the King Edward VI School, located within the Guildhall, and about the inspiration that led him to become a great playwright. Visit the classroom where he received a grammar-school education between 1571 and 1578 and experience the space where he first watched performances by the country's greatest actors of the day. This fun interactive visitor experience includes films, soundscapes, interpretive panels and knowledgeable guides. The medieval Guildhall itself is home to some rare wall paintings from this period.

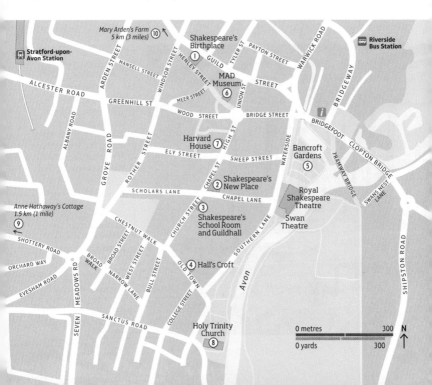

Mary Arden's Farm 5 km (3 miles) ⑩

Stratford-upon-Avon Station

Riverside Bus Station

Shakespeare's Birthplace ①

MAD Museum ⑥

Harvard House ⑦

Bancroft Gardens ⑤

Shakespeare's New Place ②

Royal Shakespeare Theatre

Swan Theatre

Shakespeare's School Room and Guildhall ③

Anne Hathaway's Cottage 1.5 km (1 mile) ⑨

Hall's Croft ④

Holy Trinity Church ⑧

ALCESTER ROAD
ARDEN STREET
MANSELL STREET
WINDSOR STREET
HENLEY STREET
GUILD
TYLER ST
PAYTON STREET
WARWICK ROAD
GREENHILL ST
MEER STREET
UNION STREET
STREET
WOOD STREET
BRIDGE STREET
BRIDGEWAY
BRIDGEFOOT
CLOPTON BRIDGE
ALBANY ROAD
GROVE ROAD
ROTHER STREET
ELY STREET
HIGH ST
CHAPEL ST
SHEEP STREET
WATERSIDE
SCHOLARS LANE
CHAPEL LANE
TRAMWAY BRIDGE
SWANS NEST LANE
CHESTNUT WALK
CHURCH STREET
SOUTHERN LANE
SHOTTERY ROAD
ORCHARD WAY
BROAD STREET
WEST STREET
BULL STREET
OLD TOWN
Avon
SHIPSTON ROAD
EVESHAM ROAD
MEADOWS RD
BROAD WALK
NARROW LANE
COLLEGE STREET
SANCTUS ROAD
SEVEN

0 metres   300
0 yards   300

N ↑

> The beautifully furnished Jacobean Hall's Croft, built in 1613, displays fascinating exhibits on medicine in the 16th and 17th centuries.

(4)

Hall's Croft

🏠 Old Town ⏰ Apr-Oct: 9am-5pm daily; Nov-Mar: 10am-4pm daily
🌐 shakespeare.org.uk

Home of Shakespeare's daughter Susanna and her husband, the renowned physician John Hall, this beautifully furnished Jacobean town house, built in 1613, displays fascinating exhibits on medicine in the 16th and 17th centuries. The tranquil walled garden contains aromatic medicinal herbs.

(5)

Bancroft Gardens

Located on the River Avon next to the Royal Shakespeare Theatre, Bancroft Gardens is a beautiful green space of lawns and gardens next to a boat-lined canal. There are statues of Shakespeare and of famous characters from some of his plays, including Hamlet, Lady Macbeth, Falstaff and Prince Hal, symbolizing philosophy, tragedy, comedy and history.

(6)

MAD Museum

🏠 4-5 Henley St ⏰ 10am-5pm Mon-Fri (Oct-Mar: to 4:30pm), 10am-5:50pm Sat, Sun & public hols
🌐 themadmuseum.co.uk

The only museum of its kind in the UK, MAD showcases mechanical art, kinetic art and automata by pioneering artists from around the world. Visitors can interact with moving machines, high-tech robots and innovative contraptions. This is a great family-friendly attraction.

(7)

Harvard House

🏠 High St ⏰ To the public

Built in 1596, this ornate house was the home of Katherine Rogers, whose son, John Harvard, emigrated to

> 💬 INSIDER TIP
> **Shakespeare's Family Homes**
>
> Five of the most significant buildings associated with the Bard contain museums run by the Shakespeare Birthplace Trust. The Full Story ticket offers admission to all five properties at a 60 per cent discount for £22.50 (children aged 3-17 £14.50). Buy tickets online at www.shakespeare.org.uk.

←

Hall's Croft, home to the elder of Shakespeare's two daughters

Holy Trinity Church
on the banks of
the Avon, and a
colourful stained-
glass window inside
the church *(inset)*

America in 1637. On his death he left money and a small library to the New College in Cambridge, Massachusetts. In gratitude, they renamed the college in his honour.

Holy Trinity Church

 Old Town

This church, founded in 1210, is where Shakespeare was baptised, where he worshipped and where he was buried. Shakespeare's grave and copies of the parish register entries recording his birth and death can be seen. There are also some fine 16th- and 17th-century tombs.

Did You Know?

The first real theatre in Stratford was a wooden affair built in 1769 by the actor David Garrick.

Anne Hathaway's Cottage

 22 Cottage Lane, Shottery ⏰ Apr–Oct: 9am–5pm daily; Nov–Mar: 10am–4pm daily 🌐 shakespeare.org.uk

At Shottery, once a separate village 1.5 km (1 mile) west of the centre of Stratford, is the home of Shakespeare's wife before their marriage. This beautiful thatched cottage, built in 1463, contains lovely period furniture. Anne Hathaway was born here in 1556; the site was then a farm, and the Hathaways were prominent sheep farmers. You can wander around the beautiful garden (which was previously the farm yard), the orchard and the arboretum.

Mary Arden's Farm

🏠 Station Rd, Wilmcote ⏰ Apr–Oct: 9am–5pm daily; Nov–Mar: 10am–4pm daily 🌐 shakespeare.org.uk

Some 5 km (3 miles) west of Stratford is the home of Shakespeare's grandparents and the childhood home of his mother, born Mary Arden, and her seven sisters. Shakespeare's father, John Shakespeare, was a tenant farmer on their land. This great family-friendly attraction lets you experience the sights, sounds and smells of a working Tudor farm and includes demonstrations of falconry and Tudor music and dance.

3 ⚔️ 🎨 🍴 ☕ 🏛️

WARWICK CASTLE

🏠 Castle Lane, Warwick 🚉🚌 ⏰ From 10am daily; closing times vary, check website 🌐 warwick-castle.com

Warwick's magnificent castle was founded in 1068 by William the Conqueror. The well-preserved medieval fortress is filled with family-friendly attractions that bring the castle's history to life.

EXPERIENCE **The Heart of England**

The original Norman castle was rebuilt in the 13th and 14th centuries, when outer walls and towers were added, mainly to display the power of the great feudal magnates the Beauchamps and, in the 1400s, the Nevilles, the Earls of Warwick. The castle passed in 1604 to the Greville family who transformed it into a great country house. In 1978 the owners of Madame Tussauds (p109) bought the castle and set up tableaux of waxworks to illustrate its history.

The Mound has remains of the motte-and-bailey castle.

Merlin: The Dragon Tower houses characters from the BBC TV series Merlin.

Princess Tower

The Great Hall and State Rooms display a collection of family treasures from around the world.

Dramatic displays re-create medieval life as "Warwick the Kingmaker", Richard Neville, prepared for battle in the Wars of the Roses.

The Mill and Engine House

↑ Armoury on display in the Great Hall

Timeline

1068
▽ Norman motte-and-bailey castle built.

1264
Simon de Montfort, champion of Parliament against Henry III, attacks Warwick Castle.

1268–1445
Much of the present castle built by the Beauchamp family, Earls of Warwick.

1449–1471
▷ Richard Neville, Earl of Warwick, plays leading role in Wars of the Roses.

1478
Castle reverts to Crown after murder of Richard Neville's son-in-law.

↑ Canoeing along the River Avon, which flows past the castle

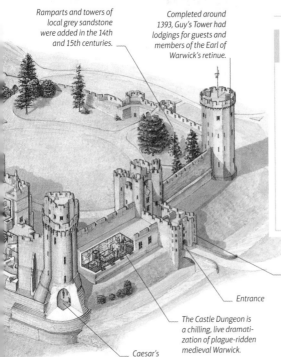

Ramparts and towers of local grey sandstone were added in the 14th and 15th centuries.

Completed around 1393, Guy's Tower had lodgings for guests and members of the Earl of Warwick's retinue.

EVENTS AT WARWICK CASTLE

From jousting tournaments and trebuchet firings to themed evenings, medieval banquets with live entertainment and bowman shows, events and activities take place every day at the castle. Entrance to the dungeon includes live actors and special effects. Check the website to see what's on before you visit.

The Gatehouse is defended by portcullises and "murder holes", through which boiling pitch was dropped onto attackers beneath.

— Entrance

The Castle Dungeon is a chilling, live dramatization of plague-ridden medieval Warwick.

Caesar's Tower

↑ The fortress complex, with its formidable ramparts and towers

1604
▷ James I gives castle to Sir Fulke Greville.

1642
Castle is besieged by Royalist troops.

1600–1800
Interiors remodelled and gardens landscaped.

1871
▷ Fire damages the Great Hall.

1890s–1910
Visits from future Edward VII.

EXPERIENCE MORE

❹
Stoke-on-Trent

◻ Stoke-on-Trent 🚗🚌
🛈 Potteries Museum and
Art Gallery, Bethesda St;
www.visitstoke.
co.uk

From the mid-18th
century, Staffordshire
became a hub for mass-
produced ceramics, from
fine bone china to utilitarian
products. In 1910 the towns of
Longton, Fenton, Hanley,
Burslem, Tunstall and Stoke
merged to form the
conurbation of Stoke-on-Trent,
also known as the Potteries.
The **Gladstone Pottery
Museum**, a Victorian complex
of kilns and galleries holds
demonstrations of traditional
pottery techniques. At the
World of Wedgwood visitors
can see the famous blue
jasperware and watch
demonstrations. Founded in
1985, the **Emma Bridgewater
Factory** creates lovely
earthenware pottery.
Guided tours are available.
About 16 km (10 miles)
north of Stoke-on-Trent is
Little Moreton Hall *(p318)*,
a fine Tudor manor house.

Gladstone Pottery Museum
🅿️ 🚻 ♿ ◻ Uttoxeter Rd,
Longton ◷ 10am-5pm Tue-
Sat (Oct-Mar: to 4pm)
🆆 stokemuseums.org.uk/
visit/gpm

STAFFORDSHIRE POTTERY

An abundance of water, marl, clay and easily mined
coal to fire the kilns enabled Staffordshire to develop
as a ceramics centre; and local supplies of iron, copper
and lead were used for glazing. In the
18th century, pottery
became widely accessible
and affordable. Josiah
Wedgwood (1730-95)
introduced simple,
durable crockery - though
his best-known design is
the blue jasperware decorated
with white Classical themes.

World of Wedgwood
🅿️ 🚻 ♿ 🍽️ ◻ Wedgwood
Drive, Barlaston ◷ 10am-
5pm daily 🆆 worldof
wedgwood.com

Emma Bridgewater Factory
🅿️ 🚻 ♿ ◻ Litchfield St
◷ 9:30am-5:30pm Mon-Sat,
10am-4pm Sun 🆆 emma
bridgewaterco.uk

Little Moreton Hall
🅿️ 🚻 ♿ 🍽️ ◻ Congleton
◷ Times vary, check website
🆆 nationaltrust.org.co.uk

❺
Warwick

◻ Warwickshire 🚗🚌
🛈 The Courthouse, Jury St;
www.visitwarwick.co.uk

Despite a major fire in 1694,
Warwick retains some
medieval architecture. At the
west end of the High Street, a

row of medieval guild buildings was transformed in 1571
by the Earl of Leicester to
create the **Lord Leycester
Hospital**, a refuge for retired
soldiers. In Church Street is
Beauchamp Chapel (1443-64),
containing the tombs of the
Earls of Warwick.

Lord Leycester Hospital
🅿️ 🍽️ ◻ 60 High St ◷ 10am-
4pm Tue-Sun (Apr-Oct: to
5pm) 🆆 lordleycester.com

❻
Shrewsbury

◻ Shropshire 🚗🚌
🛈 The Music Hall, The
Square; www.original
shrewsbury.co.uk

Shrewsbury is almost an
island, enclosed by a loop
of the River Severn. A red
sandstone **castle**, originally
from 1066-74 but rebuilt over
the centuries, guards the
entrance to the town and
now houses the Shropshire
Regimental Museum. In AD 60
the Romans built the garrison
town of Viroconium, modern
Wroxeter, 8 km (5 miles)

←

The tomb of Ambrose Dudley,
Earl of Warwick, in the
Beauchamp Chapel, Warwick

↑ Ludlow Castle and the River Teme surrounded by vibrant autumnal foliage

east of Shrewsbury. Finds from the excavations are displayed at **Shrewsbury Museum and Art Gallery**. The town's medieval wealth as a centre of the wool trade is evident in the many fine timber-framed buildings along the High Street, Butcher Row, and Wyle Cop.

Shrewsbury Castle

⊛ 🏛 🅰 Castle St ⏱ Times vary, check website 🚫 Late Dec–mid-Feb 🌐 shropshire regimentalmuseum.co.uk

Shrewsbury Museum and Art Gallery

⊛ 🏛 🅰 The Music Hall, Market Sq ⏱ 10am–5pm Mon–Sat, 11am–4pm Sun 🌐 shrewsburymuseum. org.uk

---

🔍 HIDDEN GEM
Bishop's Castle

About 71 km (44 miles) from Shrewsbury, this small market town with pastel-painted Georgian and red-brick Victorian buildings is bursting with independent shops, restaurants and pubs. It even has its own walking festival (May).

7
Ludlow

🅰 Shropshire 🚇 ℹ️ Ludlow Assembly Rooms, 1 Mill St; www.ludlow.org.uk

Ludlow attracts visitors with its splendid castle, small shops and lovely Georgian and half-timbered Tudor buildings, but perhaps the biggest draw to the town is the quality food on offer. Ludlow is also an important area of geological research and the **museum** has fossils of the oldest known animals and plants.

The ruined **castle**, on cliffs high above the River Teme, was built in 1086, damaged in the Civil War (*p49*) and abandoned in 1689. Prince Arthur (1486–1502), brother of Henry VIII, died in the castle. His heart is buried in St Laurence Church at the other end of Castle Square.

Ludlow Museum

⊛ 🅰 Buttercross 📞 01584 871970 ⏱ 10am–4pm Fri–Sun 🚫 24 Dec–1 Jan

Ludlow Castle

⊛ 🏛 🅰 Castle Square ⏱ 10am–5pm daily (Nov–Feb: to 4pm) 🌐 ludlowcastle.com

---

EAT

The Fish House
A popular spot for sumptuous platters of glorious seafood.

🅰 51 Bullring, Ludlow 🚫 Sun–Tue 🌐 thefish houseludlow.co.uk

£££

Mortimers
The accent here is firmly on modern British/French cuisine. Try the scallops with truffle.

🅰 17 Crove St, Ludlow 🚫 Sun & Mon 🌐 mortimers ludlow.co.uk

£££

The Walrus
This modern restaurant offers a seasonal menu and local produce.

🅰 5 Rousehill, Shrewsbury 🚫 Sun–Tue 🌐 the-walrus.co.uk

£££

TUDOR MANOR HOUSES

Many striking manor houses were built in central England during the Tudor Age, a time of relative peace and prosperity. The abolition of the monasteries meant that vast estates were broken up and sold to secular landowners, who built houses to reflect their new status. In the Midlands, wood was the main building material, and the gentry flaunted their wealth by using timber panelling, often decorated with ancient motifs such as vines and trefoils, for flamboyant effect.

LITTLE MORETON HALL

The impressive Moreton family home *(p316)* was built between 1504 and 1610 from a number of box-shapes fitted together. Wood panelling, glass windows and jetties displayed the family's wealth.

Did You Know?

Long galleries, often located on the upper floor, were a typical feature of a Tudor family home.

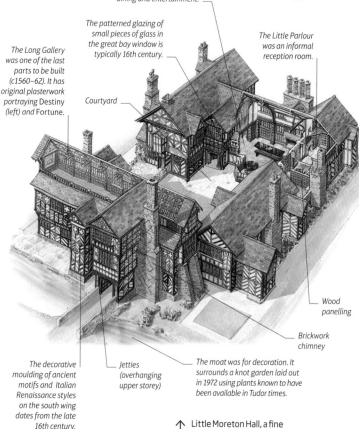

The Great Hall (c1504–08) is the oldest part of the house and in Tudor times was the most important. The open-plan hall was the main communal area for dining and entertainment.

The patterned glazing of small pieces of glass in the great bay window is typically 16th century.

The Little Parlour was an informal reception room.

The Long Gallery was one of the last parts to be built (c1560–62). It has original plasterwork portraying Destiny (left) and Fortune.

Courtyard

The decorative moulding of ancient motifs and Italian Renaissance styles on the south wing dates from the late 16th century.

Jetties (overhanging upper storey)

The moat was for decoration. It surrounds a knot garden laid out in 1972 using plants known to have been available in Tudor times.

Wood panelling

Brickwork chimney

↑ Little Moreton Hall, a fine example of a 16th-century Tudor manor house

TUDOR MANSIONS AND TUDOR REVIVAL

There are many sumptuously decorated Tudor mansions in the Midlands. In the 19th century Tudor Revival architecture became a very popular "Old English" style, intended to evoke family pride and values rooted in the past.

1 Hardwick Hall

Hardwick Hall in Derbyshire *(p340)*, created by Bess of Hardwick and designed by the architect Robert Smythson in the 1500s, is one of the finest Tudor mansions in Great Britain. Such buildings are known as "prodigy" houses due to their gigantic size. The house contains a large number of 16th- and 17th-century fine embroideries, tapestries and furniture.

2 Charlecote Park

A brick mansion built by Sir Thomas Lucy in 1551–59 on the edge of Stratford-upon-Avon in Warwickshire, Charlecote Park was heavily restored in Tudor style in the 19th century but has a fine original gatehouse. According to legend, the young William Shakespeare *(p310)* was caught poaching deer in the park.

3 Moseley Old Hall

The red-brick exterior of Moseley Old Hall in Staffordshire conceals its early 17th-century timber frame. The King's Room is where Charles II hid in 1651 after the Battle of Worcester, the final battle of the English Civil War *(p49)*. The mansion has fine gardens planted with period plants, including a knot garden.

4 Packwood House

A timber-framed mid-Tudor house with extensive 17th-century additions, Packwood House in Warwickshire has a lovely garden of herbacious borders and clipped yew trees dating from the 17th century, which is supposed to represent the Sermon on the Mount. The house contains a splendid collection of 16th-century furniture and beautiful textiles.

5 Wightwick Manor

Built in 1887–93 in Wolverhampton, Wightwick Manor is a fine example of Tudor Revival architecture and is one of the few remaining houses in Britain furnished under the influence of the Arts and Crafts movement. It has superb late 19th-century furniture and a collection of Pre-Raphaelite paintings by Rossetti, Burne-Jones and their contemporaries.

Ledbury's Church Lane, a cobbled street lined with half-timbered buildings

8 Ledbury

 Herefordshire 🔲🔲 **ℹ** **Ice Bytes, 38 The Homend; www.visitledbury.info**

Ledbury's main street is lined with timbered houses like the Market Hall, which dates from 1655. Church Lane, a cobbled lane running up from the High Street, has lovely 16th-century buildings: the **Heritage Centre** and **Butcher Row House** are

both now museums. St Michael and All Angels Church has a detached bell tower, ornate Early English decoration and interesting monuments.

Heritage Centre
🏠 Church Lane ⏰ Easter–Oct: 10:30am–4:30pm daily

Butcher Row House
🏠 Church Lane ☎ 01531 635069 ⏰ Easter–Oct: 11am–5pm daily (Oct: to 3pm)

9 Leominster

 Herefordshire 🔲 **ℹ** **11 Corn Sq; www. leominstertourism.co.uk**

Leominster (pronounced "Lemster") has been a wool-manufacturing centre for 700 years. In the town centre, the magnificent Grade II-listed Grange Court was carved with bold and bizarre figures in 1633. Nearby, the priory has an imposing Norman portal decorated with mythical birds and beasts.

South of the town, the gardens and parkland at **Hampton Court Castle** include island pavilions and a maze. To the west of town, along the River Arrow, are the villages of Eadisland and Pembridge, with their well-kept gardens and timber-framed houses. **Berrington Hall**, 5 km (3 miles) north of Leominster, designed by Henry Holland (1745–1806),

is a Neo-Classical house set in grounds by "Capability" Brown. Inside are beautifully preserved ceiling decorations and period furniture.

Northeast of Leominster is Tenbury Wells, which enjoyed brief popularity as a spa in the 19th century. The River Teme flows through it, full of minnows, trout and other fish, and was loved by the composer Sir Edward Elgar, who came to seek inspiration on its banks. A few miles south of Tenbury Wells lies **Witley Court and Gardens**. The landscaped gardens contain a splendid Perseus and Andromeda fountain that fires up regularly during the day.

Hampton Court Castle
⊘⊘🅿️🏠 **Nr Hope Under Dinmore** ⏰ Apr–Oct: 10:30am–5pm daily 🔲 hamptoncourtcastle.co.uk

Sunset at Ross-on-Wye, with St Mary's Church in the background

STAY

The Feathers
Beyond the black and white frontage of this Tudor building you'll find rooms with original wooden beams.

🏠 25 High St, Ledbury 🔲 feathersledbury.co.uk

💲💲💲

Bridge House Hotel
Regency-style guesthouse nestled on the banks of the Wye with six elegant rooms and manicured gardens.

🏠 Wilton Rd, Ross-on-Wye 🔲 bridgehouse rossonwye.co.uk

💲💲💲

Berrington Hall

 Berrington
🕙 11am–5pm daily (Nov–mid-Feb: 11am–4pm Sat & Sun)
ⓦ nationaltrust.org.uk

Witley Court and Gardens

Worcester Rd, Great Witley 🕙 10am–6pm daily (Nov–Feb: 10am–4pm Sat & Sun) ⓦ english-heritage.org.uk

---

⑩ Ross-on-Wye

Ⓐ Herefordshire 🚌
ⓦ visitrosswye.com

The town of Ross sits on a cliff of red sandstone above the water meadows of the River Wye. There are opportunities for canoeing and views over the river from the clifftop gardens, given to the town by a local benefactor, John Kyrle (1637–1724). Kyrle was lauded by the poet Alexander Pope (1688–1744) in his *Moral Essays on the Uses of Riches* (1732) for using his wealth in a practical way, and he came to be known as "The Man of Ross". There is a memorial to Kyrle in St Mary's Church.

Goodrich Castle, 8 km (5 miles) south of Ross, is a 12th-century red sandstone fort on a rock above the river.

Goodrich Castle

 Goodrich
🕙 10am–6pm daily (Nov–Mar: 10am–4pm Sat & Sun)
ⓦ english-heritage.org.uk

---

⑪ Great Malvern and the Malverns

Ⓐ Worcestershire 🚃🚌
🛈 21 Church St; www.visitthemalverns.org

The ancient granite rock of the Malvern Hills rises from the plain of the River Severn, its 15 km (9 miles) of glorious scenery visible from afar.

Malvern was originally a spa village. The water gushing from the hillside at St Ann's Well is still bottled and sold throughout Britain. The town is also home to the famous Morgan cars (book online for a factory tour: www.morgan-motor.co.uk).

Malvern's architecture is mostly Victorian, but older buildings include the Priory Church, which was founded in 1085 and has 15th-century stained-glass windows and medieval misericords.

DRINK

Bottles Wine Bar

The wines stocked here from all over the world are best enjoyed with a plate or two of tapas.

⌂ 22-24 New St, Worcester ⓦ bottles wine.co.uk

The Cardinal's Hat Inn

Worcester's oldest pub has lots of small spaces to cosy up in and sup on the terrific local ales.

⌂ 31 Friar St, Worcester ⓦ the-cardinals-hat.co.uk

Tonic

This cool craft beer bar serves a rotating selection of draught ales and a vast range of gins, plus cocktails.

⌂ 36 Foregate St, Worcester ⓒ Sun ⓦ tonic-worcester.co.uk

⓬

Worcester

⌂ Worcestershire
🚇 🚌 ⓘ High St; www.visitworcestershire.org

Worcester's architectural highlight is the cathedral, off College Yard, which suffered a collapsed tower in 1175 and a disastrous fire in 1203, before the present structure was started in the 13th century. The nave and central tower were completed in the 1370s after building was severely interrupted by the Black Death. The most recent and ornate addition was made in 1874, when Sir George Gilbert Scott designed the High Gothic choir, incorporating 14th-century carved misericords.

The tomb of King John, a masterpiece of medieval carving, sits in front of the altar. Prince Arthur, Henry VIII's brother, is buried in the chantry chapel south of the altar. Below is the huge Norman crypt from the first cathedral (1084).

From the cathedral cloister, a gate leads to College Green and out into Edgar Street with its Georgian houses. Here the **Museum of Royal Worcester**

> Some of Worcester's finest timber buildings are in Friar Street: most notable is The Greyfriars, built around 1480, full of atmospheric wood-panelled rooms.

displays Royal Worcester porcelain dating to 1751. On the High Street, north of the cathedral, the 1721 Guildhall is adorned with statues of Stuart monarchs, reflecting the city's Royalist allegiances.

Some of Worcester's finest timber buildings are in Friar Street: most notable is **The Greyfriars**, built around 1480, full of atmospheric wood-panelled rooms. The **Commandery**, originally an 11th-century hospital, was rebuilt in the 15th century and used by Charles I as a base during the Civil War. Now a museum, it has a fine hammerbeam roof.

Elgar's Birthplace was the home of composer Sir Edward Elgar (p321) and contains a wealth of memorabilia.

Museum of Royal Worcester

♿ Ⓢ Ⓣ Ⓟ 🍴 ⌂ Severn St
🕐 10am–5pm Mon–Sat, 10am–4pm Sun
ⓦ museumofroyal worcester.org

↑ Hereford's half-timbered Black and White House, dating from the 17th century

The Greyfriars
⊗😊(NT) ⬛Friar St ◐Mid-Feb–mid-Dec: 11am–5pm Tue–Sat (Nov–Feb: to 4pm) Ⓦnationaltrust.org.uk

Commandery
⊗😊🕐 ⬛Sidbury ☎01905 361821 ◐Feb–Dec: 10am–5pm Tue–Sat, 1:30–5pm Sun

Elgar's Birthplace
⊗😊🕐(NT) ⬛Lower Broadheath ☎01905 333224 ◐10am–5pm daily (Nov–Feb: to 4pm)

Hereford
⬛Herefordshire 🚌🚆 Ⓦvisitherefordshire.co.uk

Once the capital of the Saxon kingdom of West Mercia, Hereford is today a pretty town serving a primarily rural community. A cattle market is held here on Wednesdays, and local produce is sold at the covered market in the town centre. The Jacobean timber-framed **Black and White House** of 1621 is now

Looking towards the altar in Worcester Cathedral, started in the 1200s

a museum of local history. In the cathedral, only a short stroll away, interesting features include the Lady Chapel, in richly ornamented Early English style, the *Mappa Mundi* and the Chained Library, whose 1,500 books are tethered by iron chains to bookcases as a precaution against theft. The story of these national treasures is told through models, original artifacts and interactive displays. The best place for an overall view of the cathedral is Bishop's Meadow, south of the centre, which leads down to the banks of the Wye.

Hereford's many rewarding museums include the **Hereford Museum and Art Gallery**, noted for its Roman mosaic and for watercolours

by local artists, and the **Cider Museum**, where visitors can discover the history of traditional cider making by exploring the champagne cellars and learning how the barrels are made. There are still around 30 traditional cider-makers operating in Herefordshire.

During the 12th century, Oliver de Merlemond made a pilgrimage from Hereford to Spain. Impressed by several churches he saw on the way, he brought French masons over to England and introduced their techniques to this area. One result was Kilpeck Church, 10 km (6 miles) southwest, which is full of splendid carvings including tail-biting dragons and snakes. At Abbey Dore, 6 km (4 miles) west, the Cistercian abbey church is complemented by the lovely, serene riverside gardens and tranquil arboretum of Abbey Dore Court.

Black and White House
⊗🕐 ⬛High St ◐10am–4pm Tue–Sat, 11:30am–2:30pm Sun Ⓦherefordshire.gov.uk

Hereford Museum and Art Gallery
🕐 ⬛Broad St ◐10am–4pm Tue–Fri, 10am–12:30pm Sat Ⓦherefordshire.gov.uk

Cider Museum
⊗⊗😊🕐 ⬛Ryelands St ◐10:30am–4:30pm Mon–Sat Ⓦcidermuseum.co.uk

THE MAPPA MUNDI
Hereford Cathedral's most celebrated treasure is the *Mappa Mundi*, the Map of the World drawn in 1290 by a clergyman, Richard of Haldingham. The world is depicted here on biblical principles: Jerusalem is at the centre, the Garden of Eden figures prominently, and monsters inhabit the margins of the world.

14

Birmingham

🏛 Birmingham 🚇🚌🚍
ℹ Library of Birmingham, Centenary Sq; www. visitbirmingham.com

Brum, as it is affectionately known to its inhabitants, grew up as a major centre of the Industrial Revolution in the 19th century. The vast range of manufacturing trades led to the rapid development of grim factories and cramped housing. Since the clearance of these areas after World War II, the city has raised its cultural, architectural and civic profile.

Set away from the massive Bullring shopping centre, Birmingham's 19th-century Neo-Classical **Birmingham Museum and Art Gallery** houses outstanding works by Pre-Raphaelite artists such as Edward Burne-Jones (1833–98), who was born in the city.

The **Library of Birmingham,** opened in 2013, is a stunning piece of architecture and includes art gallery and performance spaces.

Thinktank, Birmingham Science Museum celebrates the city's contribution to the world of railway engines and aircraft, and to the motor trade.

Birmingham's extensive canal system is now used mainly for leisure boating (p326), and several warehouses have been converted into galleries. One such converted Gothic warehouse contains the **Ikon Gallery** of cutting-edge contemporary art.

A little south of the city centre, the **Barber Institute of Fine Arts** has an outstanding art collection, from Renaissance works to British 19th-century masterpieces to modern art. A little north of the centre, set in a public park , the lavish, red-brick **Aston Hall** was built in Jacobean style between 1618 and 1635 and is full of great paintings and textiles.

BACK TO BACKS

Back-to-back terraced houses were built to house the rapidly increasing working population in Britain's industrial towns. The Back to Backs on Birmingham's Hurst and Inge streets are the last surviving examples in England. Guided tours lead you through several houses restored by the National Trust and show how ordinary people lived between the 1840s and 1970s. Pre-booking is essential (tel: 0121 666 7671).

Did You Know?

Birmingham has more canals than Venice, with 56 km (35 miles) of waterways.

Birmingham Museum and Art Gallery

🖼🏛 🏛Chamberlain Sq
🕐10am–5pm daily (from 10:30am Fri) 🌐birmingham museums.org.uk

Library of Birmingham

🖼 🏛Centenary Sq
🕐11am–7pm Mon & Tue, 11am–5pm Wed–Sat
🌐libraryofbirmingham.com

Thinktank, Birmingham Science Museum

🖼🖼🏛Millennium Point
🕐10am–5pm daily 🌐birming hammuseums.org.uk

↑ Victorian paintings at the Birmingham Museum and Art Gallery

Ikon Gallery

◎ ⓐ ⓓ 1 Oozells Sq ◷ 11am–5pm Tue–Sun ⓦ ikon-gallery.org

Barber Institute of Fine Arts

◎ ⓐ ⓓ University of Birmingham, Edgbaston ◷ 10am–5pm Mon–Fri, 11am–5pm Sat & Sun ⓦ barber.org.uk

Aston Hall

◈ ◎ ⓐ ⓓ Trinity Rd, Aston ◷ 11am–4pm Tue–Sun ⓦ birminghammuseums.org.uk

---

⓰ Coventry

ⓐ Coventry ⓡ ⓔ ⓘ Herbert Gallery, Jordan Well; www.visitcoventryand warwickshire.co.uk

As an armaments centre, Coventry was a prime target for German bombing raids in World War II, and in 1940 the cathedral was almost destroyed. After the war Sir Basil Spence (1907–76) built a modernist-style cathedral alongside the ruins. It includes sculptures by Sir Jacob Epstein.

The **Herbert Gallery and Museum** has displays on the 11th-century legend of Lady Godiva, who rode naked through the streets of Coventry to gain a pardon for the high taxes imposed by her husband upon his tenants. The **Coventry Transport Museum** has the largest collection of Britain's road transport in the world.

Herbert Gallery and Museum

◎ ⓐ ⓓ Jordan Well ◷ 10am–4pm Mon–Sat, noon–4pm Sun ⓦ theherbert.org

Coventry Transport Museum

◎ ⓐ ⓓ Hales St ◷ 10am–5pm daily ⓦ transport-museum.com

EAT

Pushkar
Fine Punjabi and North Indian cuisine is served in this stylish restaurant, which also offers great cocktails.

ⓓ 245 Broad St, Birmingham ◷ Sat & Sun lunch ⓦ pushkardining.com

ⓔⓔⓔ

Maribel
Dine on gougère, smoked eel, and sea bass with fennel and caviar at this outstanding spot.

ⓓ 6 Brindleyplace, Birmingham ◷ Sun & Mon ⓦ maribel restaurant.co.uk

ⓔⓔⓔ

Purnell's
Michelin-starred chef Glyn Purnell crafts exquisite modern British food with a French and Asian slant.

ⓓ 55 Cornwall St, Birmingham ◷ Sun & Mon ⓦ purnells restaurant.com

ⓔⓔⓔ

← The entrance to Coventry Cathedral, next to the ruins of the original building

CANALS OF THE MIDLANDS

One of England's first canals opened in 1761, built in the northwest by the 3rd Duke of Bridgewater to link the coal mine on his Worsley estate with Manchester's textile factories. This heralded the start of a canal-building boom and, by 1805, a 4,800-km (3,000-mile) network of waterways had been dug across the country, linking into the natural river system. Canals provided the cheapest, fastest way of transporting goods until competition arrived from the railways in the 1840s. Cargo transport ended in 1963, but today nearly 3,200 km (2,000 miles) of canals are still navigable for those who wish to take a leisurely cruise on a narrowboat.

Did You Know?

The Midlands has the biggest concentration of navigable waterways in England.

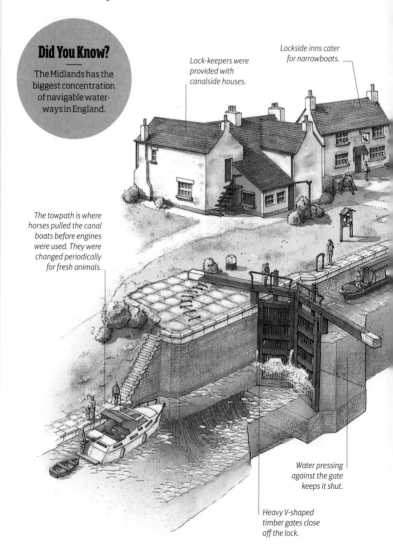

Lock-keepers were provided with canalside houses.

Lockside inns cater for narrowboats.

The towpath is where horses pulled the canal boats before engines were used. They were changed periodically for fresh animals.

Water pressing against the gate keeps it shut.

Heavy V-shaped timber gates close off the lock.

CANAL ART

In the late 19th century the decoration of a traditional English narrow-boat often included paintings of roses and castles, with local variations in style. This has seen a revival in modern times with the emergence of leisure boating, and roses and castles-themed decoration on narrowboats is a relatively common sight on English canals today. Modern narrowboats are used for holidays or even as permanent residences.

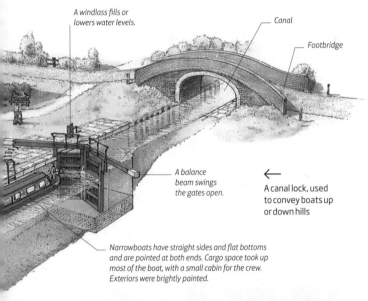

A windlass fills or lowers water levels.

Canal

Footbridge

A balance beam swings the gates open.

← A canal lock, used to convey boats up or down hills

Narrowboats have straight sides and flat bottoms and are pointed at both ends. Cargo space took up most of the boat, with a small cabin for the crew. Exteriors were brightly painted.

↑ Boats on one of Birmingham's many canals created during the Industrial age

EAST MIDLANDS

Evidence suggests that the East Midlands has been settled since prehistoric times. The remains of Iron Age hillforts are scattered across the region, especially within the Peak District. The Romans made Leicester the capital of the East Midlands while mining for lead and salt and building an extensive network of roads and fortresses. Their influence was also manifest in spa towns such as Buxton, where remains of Roman baths have been found. In the early 10th century, the region was divided between land controlled by the Vikings in the north and an area in the south under Saxon rule.

During the Middle Ages, profits from the wool trade enabled towns such as Lincoln to prosper, before the onset of mass industrialization in the late 18th century began to shape much of the landscape elsewhere. The flatlands of south Derbyshire (Britain's first factory was in Derby), Leicestershire and Nottinghamshire became replete with coalmines and factories, though by the late 19th century most of these had fallen by the wayside. These days, the East Midlands owes its character to a conjunction of the pastoral with the urban: spa resorts, historic villages and stately homes happily coexist within a landscape forever wedded to its industrialized past.

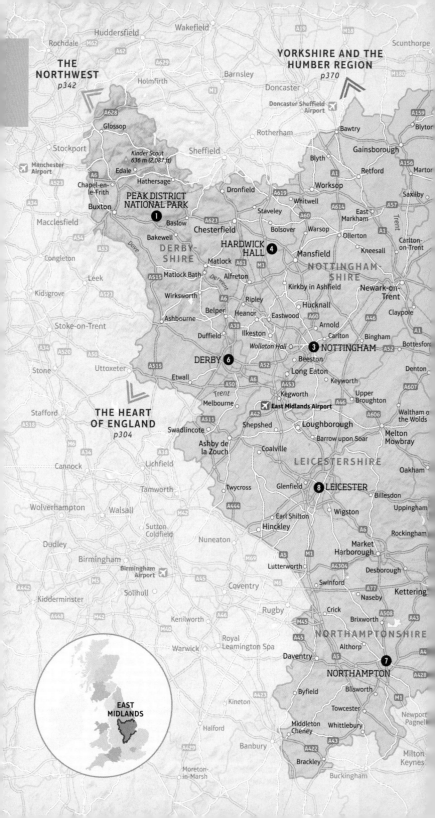

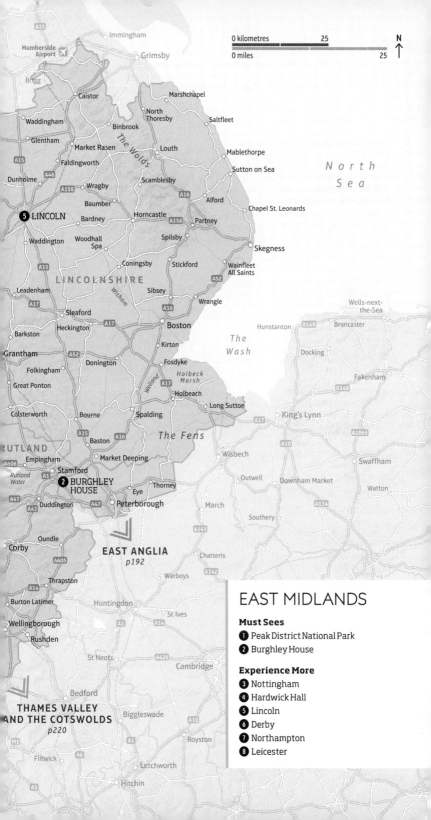

North Sea

Immingham
Grimsby
Humberside Airport
Brigg
Marshchapel
Caistor
Waddingham
North Thoresby
Saltfleet
Binbrook
Glentham
Market Rasen
Louth
Mablethorpe
Faldingworth
The Wolds
Sutton on Sea
Dunholme
Wragby
Scamblesby
Alford
Baumber
Chapel St. Leonards
LINCOLN
Bardney
Horncastle
Partney
Waddington
Woodhall Spa
Spilsby
Skegness
Coningsby
Stickford
Wainfleet All Saints
LINCOLNSHIRE
Sibsey
Wrangle
Leadenham
Withan
Sleaford
Barkston
Heckington
Boston
Grantham
Kirton
The Wash
Folkingham
Donington
Fosdyke
Hunstanton
Wells-next-the-Sea
Brancaster
Great Ponton
Welland
Holbeck Marsh
Docking
Fakenham
Colsterworth
Bourne
Spalding
Holbeach
Long Sutton
King's Lynn
RUTLAND
Baston
The Fens
Wisbech
Empingham
Market Deeping
Swaffham
Rutland Water
Stamford
Outwell
Downham Market
Watton
BURGHLEY HOUSE
Eye
Thorney
Duddington
Peterborough
March
Southery
Oundle
EAST ANGLIA
p192
Chatteris
Corby
Warboys
Thrapston
Huntingdon
Burton Latimer
St Ives
Wellingborough
St Neots
Rushden
Cambridge
Bedford
Biggleswade
THAMES VALLEY AND THE COTSWOLDS
p220
Royston
Flitwick
Letchworth
Hitchin

0 kilometres   25
0 miles   25
N

EAST MIDLANDS

Must Sees
1 Peak District National Park
2 Burghley House

Experience More
3 Nottingham
4 Hardwick Hall
5 Lincoln
6 Derby
7 Northampton
8 Leicester

❶

PEAK DISTRICT NATIONAL PARK

⌂Derbyshire ⊕peakdistrict.gov.uk

Spreading across the Pennines' southern tip are the beautiful hills and dales of the Peak District National Park, dotted with small stone villages, characterful towns and grand stately homes. England's first national park is today one of its most popular, with wild and beautiful heather-covered moors to its north, west and east, the wooded dales of the River Dove to its south, and the stone-walled meadows which descend through sheltered valleys on the eastern edge.

① Buxton

⌂Derbyshire 🚃🚌
🛈The Pump Room;
www.visitbuxton.co.uk

Buxton, source of the world-famous mineral water, was developed as a spa town by the 5th Duke of Devonshire during the late 1700s. It has many fine Neo-Classical build-ings, including the Devonshire

Royal Hospital (1790), originally stables, at the town's entrance. The Crescent (1780–90) was built to rival Bath's Royal Crescent (p256). It is currently being restored as part of a major programme of spa redevelopment.

The town's Natural Mineral Baths opened in 1854 at the southwest end of the Crescent, on the site of the ancient Roman baths, set over a spring where water surges from the ground at a rate of 7,000 litres (1,540 gallons) an hour, and at a temperature of 27° C (80° F). While bottled Buxton water is, naturally, for sale all over the town, you can fill your own bottles for free at the public fountain, St Ann's Well, opposite the Baths.

With the advent of the railway in 1863 the Baths soon became too crowded for the smart set, and the elegant, marbled Pump Room was built in 1884, opposite the Crescent. Steep gardens known as the Slopes lead down from here to the small **Buxton Museum and Art Gallery**, with geological and archaeological displays. At the bottom of the Crescent are the Pavilion Gardens, pleasure gardens laid out before a magnificent 19th-century iron and glass pavilion and the splendidly restored Opera House, where a music and arts festival is held in summer. The gardens are a lovely recreational area, with cafés

Map. Kinder Scout 636 m (2,087 ft). High Peak. Derwent Moor. SOUTH YORKSHIRE. Edale ⑤. A57. A6013. Whiteley Wood. Hope. Bamford. Castleton ⑥. Chapel-en-le-Frith. Bradwell. Old Moor. Hathersage. A6187. Peak Forest. Eyam Moor. Totley. Dove Holes. A623. Grindleford. A625. DERBYSHIRE. Eyam. Big Moor. A621. Tideswell. A623. Wardlow. Curbar Gap. Wormhill. Wye. Calver. Buxton ①. Blackwell. Little Longstone. Baslow. Harpurhill. A6. A619. Ashford. Edensor. ② Chatsworth House and Gardens. Earl Sterndale. A515. Bakewell ③. Haddon Hall. Monyash. A6. Rowsley. Longnor. Youlgreave. Dove. Derwent. Two Dales. STAFFORD-SHIRE. A515. Friden. Winter. Matlock. A6. Hulme End. Biggin. A5012. Matlock Bath ④. Aldwark. Cromford. A6. 0 kilometres 5. 0 miles 5. N.

Did You Know?

At the time of building, the dome of Buxton's Royal Hospital was the largest unsupported dome in the world.

↑ Purple heather in the Peak District landscape against a vibrant sunset

and an ice-cream parlour, a boating lake, bandstand and miniature railway.

Buxton Museum and Art Gallery

🏛 📍 Terrace Rd ⏰ 10am–5pm Tue–Sat; Easter–Sep: also noon–4pm Sun 🌐 derbyshire.gov.uk

---

②

Chatsworth House and Gardens

📍 Bakewell, Derbyshire ⏰ Times vary, check website 🌐 chatsworth.org

Chatsworth is one of Britain's most impressive stately homes. Originally a Tudor mansion built in 1552 by Bess of Hardwick, it was replaced in Baroque style by the 1st Duke of Devonshire between 1687 and 1707. Today it hosts a particularly fine collection of artwork, including a Sculpture Gallery. The house has a 42-ha (105-acre) garden, landscaped in the 1760s by Capability Brown (pXX) and developed in the mid-1800s by Joseph Paxton, best known

for designing London's Crystal Palace. Alongside some terrific walks and trails, there is a fabulous working farmyard and a woodland playground. The grounds are perhaps best-known, however, for their elaborate, gravity-fed system of water features. A masterpiece of hydraulic engineering, their highlights are the soaring Emperor Fountain and the spectacular 300-year-old Cascade, an infinite ribbon of water tumbling over a broad flight of 24 rock-cut steps.

---

③

Bakewell

📍 Derbyshire 🚌 ℹ️ Old Market Hall; 01629 816558

Flanking the banks of the River Wye, Bakewell is the ancient capital of the Peak District, a pretty market town that makes a great base for hikes along the nearby River Wye or for forays into the surrounding countryside. For all its lovely buildings, the town is synonymous with the local jam and almond paste

 GREAT VIEW
Curbar Gap

From the vast open moorland and gritstone formations of the Dark Peak to the limestone plateau and deep gorges of White Peak, the Peak District National Park affords many marvellous views, but few are better than the one from Curbar Gap, some 13 km (8 miles) northeast of Bakewell.

tart, Bakewell pudding, which was apparently invented by delicious mistake when a cook misinterpreted a recipe.

Nearby **Haddon Hall** is a grand Elizabethan manor house with superb terraced gardens. Although parts of it date back to the 12th century, it is considered one of the best-preserved and complete houses of the Tudor period.

Haddon Hall

 📍 5 km (3 miles) S of Bakewell ⏰ 10:30am–5pm daily (winter: to 4pm) 🚫 Nov 🌐 haddonhall.co.uk

STAY

East Lodge Country House Hotel

Ensconced within pretty gardens, this elegant hotel is the perfect base for forays into the Peak District.

⌂ Rowsley, Matlock
🌐 eastlodge.com

£££

Stonecroft Guesthouse

This detached Edwardian house has three rooms and offers an organic breakfast.

⌂ Edale, Hope Valley
🌐 stonecroftguest house.co.uk

£££

Grosvenor House

Superbly located in the heart of Buxton, Grosvenor offers eight attractive rooms.

⌂ 1 Broad Walk, Buxton 🌐 grosvenor buxton.co.uk

£££

---

④

Matlock Bath

⌂ Derbyshire 🚉 🚆 Matlock Station; www.matlock. org.uk

Matlock was developed as a spa from the 1780s. Interesting buildings include a former hydrotherapy centre (1853) on the hill above the town, now council offices. On the hill opposite is the mock-Gothic Riber Castle.

From Matlock, the A6 road winds through the beautiful Derwent Gorge to Matlock Bath. Here, cable cars run to the **Heights of Abraham** pleasure park, with caves, a nature trail and extensive views. Lead mining is the subject of the **Peak District Mining Museum**, with guided tours offered of the old Temple Mine across the road (best booked in advance). There is also a huge collection of mineral specimens here. Sir Richard Arkwright's **Cromford Mills** (1771), a World Heritage Site and the first ever water-powered cotton spinning mill, lies at the southern end of the gorge.

Heights of Abraham

🚡 🎟 🅿 ⌂ On A6 🕙 Feb-Oct: daily (Mar: Sat & Sun only) 🌐 heightsofabraham.com

Peak District Mining Museum

🚡 🎟 🅿 ⌂ The Pavilion, off A6 🕙 Apr-Oct: daily; Nov-Mar: Sat & Sun 🗙 25 Dec 🌐 peakdistrictleadmining museum.co.uk

Cromford Mills

🚡 🎟 🅿 ⌂ Mill Lane, Cromford 🕙 Daily 🗙 25 Dec 🌐 cromfordmills.org.uk

> **Visitors descend upon the delightful little valley village of Edale in their thousands to begin an assault on the 431-km (268-mile) Pennine Way trail.**

⑤
Edale

 Derbyshire 🚉
ℹ️ Fieldhead, 01433 670207

Visitors descend upon this delightful little valley village in their thousands to begin an assault on the 431-km (268-mile) Pennine Way trail. The village has a cluster of pretty gritstone houses, a 19th-century church and a pub or two, one of which, the Old Nags Head, was once the village blacksmiths. Edale is also known for its many quirky events, such as the Kinder Beer Barrel Challenge every autumn, and Spoonfest, a celebration of the carved wooden spoon every summer.

---

⑥ Castleton

ℹ️ Derbyshire ℹ️ Buxton Rd; 01629 816572

A popular staging post for walkers and cyclists, the picturesque village of

WALKING IN THE PEAK DISTRICT

The Peak District's most famous walking trail is the Pennine Way, Britain's first designated long-distance path. The 431-km (268-mile) route from Edale in Derbyshire to Kirk Yetholm on the Scottish border is a challenging upland hike, with long stretches of moorland. The Limestone Way runs through fine Peak District scenery from Castleton to Rocester in Staffordshire. The most popular stretch is the 44-km (26-mile) section between Castleton and Matlock. Another popular scenic route is the Tissington Trail, which follows the route of a disused railway line for 22 km (13 miles) from the market town of Ashbourne to Parsley Hay, passing through picturesque Tissington village and near to Dovedale, a dramatic limestone ravine in a stunning landscape.

Castleton – a designated conservation area – huddles under the ruins of Peveril Castle. Cavers descend here in big numbers, as the surrounding limestone hills are riddled with underground caverns. Several are open to visitors, including Peak Cavern and Speedwell Cavern, which offers a subterranean boat ride. A little further afield is Treak Cliff Cavern, where you can see The Pillar, the largest known piece of bluejohn. This semi-precious stone is unique to the Peak District, and you'll find jewellery crafted from it for sale in the village. Castleton's visitor centre is worth a peek, too, for its illuminating local history exhibition, complete with an interactive wall.

Walkers from Castleton traversing Rushup Edge, which faces Mam Tor, the "Shivering Mountain"

A DRIVING TOUR
PEAK DISTRICT

Length 60 km (40 miles) **Stopping-off points**
There are refreshments at Arkwright's Mill in
Cromford. Buxton has many pubs and cafés

The Peak District's natural beauty and sheep-grazed
crags contrast with the industrial buildings of nearby
valley towns. As you drive through the area, you'll
notice its two distinct types of landscape. In the
south are the gently rolling hills of the limestone
White Peak. To the north, west and east are the
wild, heather-clad moorlands of the Dark Peak
peat bogs, superimposed on millstone grit.

1951

The year the
Peak District was
designated Britain's
first National Park.

*The opera house in the lovely
spa town of **Buxton** (see
p332) is known as the
"theatre in the hills" because
of its magnificent setting.*

*The high plateau
above scenic **Edale**
(see p335) marks the
starting point of the
267-mile (429-km)
Pennine Way footpath.*

Alshop

Kinder Scout
636 m (2,087 ft)

Edale Moor

A624

Edale

Castleton

Chapel
Milton

Whaley
Bridge

A6

Winnats
Pass

B6061

Chapel-en-
le-Frith

Sparrowpit

Old Moor

Fernilee

A623

Peak Forest

Combs

Dove Holes

DERBYSHIRE

A5004

*Combs
Moss*

A6

Tideswell

Buxton

Fairfield

Miller's
Dale

A515

A6

Harpurhill

Taddington

A53

Monyash

Dove

A515

Longnor

Arbor
Low

Arbor Low, *a stone circle
known as the "Stonehenge
of the North", dates from
around 2000 BC and
consists of 46 recumbent
stones enclosed by a ditch.*

Sheen

Hartington

Hulme
End

Biggin

**STAFFORD-
SHIRE**

Alstonefield

Grindon

Stanshope

Manifold

Dove

FINISH

Dovedale

Mapleton

A52

↑ Crossing over stepping
stones at the scenic
Dovedale river valley

*Popular **Dovedale** is one of the prettiest
of the Peak District's river valleys, with
its stepping stones, thickly wooded
slopes and wind-sculpted rocks.*

Locator Map
For more detail see p306

Millstones and beautiful views over the rolling landscape at Hathersage ↑

There are spectacular panoramic views over the moors above **Hathersage**, which is thought to be "Morton" in Charlotte Brontë's Jane Eyre.

The village of **Eyam** is famous for its self-imposed quarantine to contain the plague of 1665–6. There is a fine Saxon cross in the churchyard.

Cromford Arkwright's Mill *was the world's first water-powered cotton mill. It stands next to the Cromford Canal, part of which can be toured by horse-drawn narrowboats in the summer.*

Crich Tramway Village *is a unique museum in a disused quarry. You can take rides on old trams from all over the world, along reconstructed Victorian streets.*

START

💬 INSIDER TIP
Seek out Sculptures

Kids will love the Sculpture Trail that winds through the woodlands at Crich Tramway Village. Look out for the Green Man and Giant Wood Ant.

0 kilometres   5

0 miles   5

N ↑

② 🚴 🏇 🍴 🛍

BURGHLEY HOUSE

📍 Off A1, SE of Stamford, Lincs 🚉 Stamford 🕐 Mid-Mar–Oct: 11am–4:30pm Sat-Thu 🗓 Sep: 4 days (horse trials) 🌐 burghley.co.uk

The wonderfully dramatic Burghley House is one of the largest and grandest houses of the Elizabethan era, built between 1555 and 1587 by William Cecil, 1st Lord Burghley (1520–98), who was Queen Elizabeth I's adviser and confidant for 40 years.

The roof line bristles with stone pyramids, chimneys disguised as Classical columns and towers shaped like pepper pots, all culminating in a symmetrical pattern when viewed from the west. The surrounding deer park is dotted with lime trees, many of which were planted by "Capability" Brown when the park was landscaped in 1760. The interior walls are lavishly decorated with Italian paintings of Greek gods and the Elizabethan "garden of surprises" features a moss house, swivelling bust of Julius Caesar and water jets. Historical learning activities are available all year in the education centre.

Did You Know?

The Burghley Horse Trials, a world-leading three-day event, is held at Burghley House every September.

STAMFORD

Located 1.5 km (1 mile) from Burghley House, Stamford is a show-piece town, famous for its churches and Georgian town houses. The town retains its medieval layout, with a warren of winding streets and cobbled alleys. The spires of the medieval churches (five survive of the original 11) give Stamford the air of a miniature Oxford. Barn Hill is the best place for a view of Stamford's Georgian architecture in all its variety. Below it is the Public Library, fronted by Tuscan columns. Inside is the Discover Stamford exhibition, which reveals the town's development through the ages (www.lincolnshire.gov.uk).

↓ Burghley House's elaborate interior and exterior design

Cupolas were very fashionable details, inspired by European Renaissance architecture.

Intricate examples of 19th-century wrought-iron work adorn the principal entrances.

A chimney has been disguised as a Classical column.

Mullioned windows were added in 1683 when glass became less expensive.

The Gatehouse, with its side turrets, is a typical feature of the "prodigy" houses of the Tudor era.

Featuring the Burghley crest, the West Front was finished in 1577 and formed the original main entrance.

→
An array of classical paintings, ornaments and sumptuous fabrics within the Third George Room

The Billiard Room has many fine portraits inset in oak panelling.

Gleaming copper pans hang from the walls of the fan-vaulted Old Kitchen, little altered since the Tudor period.

The Heaven Room features a wine cooler (1710) thought to be the largest in existence.

Obelisk and clock (1585)

The Great Hall has a double hammerbeam roof and was a banqueting hall in Elizabethan days.

In Hell Staircase, Verrio painted the ceiling to show Hell as the mouth of a cat crammed with tormented sinners.

Gods tumble from the sky and nymphs play on the walls and ceiling in Heaven Room by Antonio Verrio (1639–1707).

The Fourth George Room, one of a suite, is panelled in oak stained with ale.

→
A gold wrought-iron door marking the entrance at the west front

Paintings lining the walls at the Nottingham Castle Museum and Art Gallery ↑

EXPERIENCE MORE

Nottingham

◫ Nottinghamshire ▣▣
🛈 1-4 Smithy Row; www.
visit-nottinghamshire.
co.uk

Nottingham is still famed for the legend of Robin Hood. On the site of a Norman castle, the **Nottingham Castle Museum and Art Gallery** is an elegant 18th-century palace housing a fine collection of art. At the foot of the museum, Britain's oldest tavern, Ye Olde Trip to Jerusalem (1189), is still in business. Its name may refer to the 12th- and 13th-century crusades, but much of it is 17th century.

There are several museums nearby, including **Wollaton Hall and Deer Park**, an Elizabethan mansion housing a natural history museum.

Nottingham Castle Museum and Art Gallery

◉◈◉◉ ◫ Lenton Rd
◪ For renovation until late 2020; check website for latest details
🅦 nottinghamcastle.
org.uk

Wollaton Hall and Deer Park

◉◉◉ ◫ Wollaton
◷ 11am-4pm daily
🅦 wollatonhall.org.uk

Harwick Hall

◫ Doe Lea, Chesterfield, Derbyshire ◷ House: 11am-5pm daily (winter: to 3pm); Garden: 9am-6pm daily (winter: 10am-4pm)
🅦 nationaltrust.org.uk

A late 16th-century Elizabethan masterpiece, the sumptuous Hardwick Hall was the creation of Bess of Hardwick, Countess of Shrewsbury, who was second only to Queen Elizabeth I in terms of fortune at that time. Among the many highlights of this labyrinthine mansion are the Long Gallery, covered in wall-to-wall portraits and tapestries, and the High Great Chamber, complete with an exuberantly coloured plaster frieze – this room is where Bess received her most distinguished guests. The gardens, too, merit an extended

ROBIN HOOD OF SHERWOOD FOREST

England's most colourful folk hero was a legendary bowman whose adventures are depicted in numerous films and stories. He lived in Sherwood Forest, near Nottingham, with a band of "merry men", and robbed the rich to give to the poor. As part of an ancient oral tradition, Robin Hood figured mainly in ballads; the first written records of his exploits date from the 15th century. Today historians think that he was not one person but a composite of various outlaws who refused to conform to medieval feudal constraints.

marble and the splendid Angel Choir, home to the famous Lincoln Imp statue.

Lincoln Castle, built in the late 11th century by William the Conqueror, houses one of the four surviving copies of the Magna Carta.

Lincoln Cathedral

 🄰 4 Priorygate
🕒 7:15am–6pm daily
🅦 lincolncathedral.com

Lincoln Castle

 🄰 Castle Hill
🕒 10am–5pm daily (winter: to 4pm) 🅦 lincolncastle.com

---

❻
Derby

🄰 Derbyshire 🄸 Market Place; www.visitderby.co.uk

A major industrial player, Derby has enjoyed quite a resurgence in the 21st century. Many city-centre buildings have been spruced up, particularly around Market Place and the Cathedral Quarter. The most impressive of these is the cathedral itself, with its sturdy 16th-century tower. The **Derby Museum and Art Gallery**'s spectacular display of porcelain is trumped only by the gallery devoted to local artist Joseph Wright, whose paintings explore themes of science and technology.

Derby Museum and Art Gallery

🄰 The Strand 🕒 10am–5pm Tue–Sat, noon–4pm Sun 🅦 derbymuseums.org

---

❼
Northampton

🄰 Northamptonshire 🄸 Sessions House, George Row; www.visit northamptonshire.co.uk

This market town was once a centre for shoe-making, and the **Museum and Art Gallery** holds the world's largest

collection of footwear. Among many fine old buildings is the Victorian Gothic Guildhall.

Northampton Museum and Art Gallery

🄰 4–6 Guildhall Rd
📞 01604 838111
🕒 Times vary, call ahead

---

❽
Leicester

🄰 Leicestershire 🄸 51 Gallowtree Gate; www.visitleicester.info

In 2013, the remains of Richard III were discovered in a car park in the centre of Leicester. The life and times of this 15th-century monarch are recalled in the illuminating **King Richard III Visitor Centre**, next to the car park, on the site of the old Greyfriars church (his original burial site, though he was reinterred in Leicester Cathedral in 2015). The city's finest museum is the **New Walk Museum and Art Gallery**, which has a collection of Ancient Egyptian artifacts.

King Richard III Visitor Centre

 🄰 4A St Martins
📞 0300 300 0900 🕒 10am–4pm Mon–Fri & Sun, 10am–5pm Sat & bank hols

New Walk Museum and Art Gallery

🄰 53 New Walk
📞 0116 225 4900 🕒 11am–4:30pm Mon–Fri, 11am–5pm Sat & Sun

---

stroll, featuring parkland sculpture trails and stunning herbaceous borders.

---

❺
Lincoln

🄰 Lincolnshire 🄸 9 Castle Hill; www. visitlincoln.com

Lincoln is dominated by the magnificent Gothic **cathedral**, built in the 11th century and for many years the tallest building in the world. The soaring West Front crawls with outstanding statuary, while the vast interior features huge pillars of dark Purbeck

↑ A steep cobbled street in the historic centre of Lincoln

THE NORTHWEST

As well as the earliest evidence of human habitation in England (dating to around 11,000 BC), Northwest England also has the country's highest mountains, and for a long time remained a remote border-land. The Romans started documenting history with their arrival around 70 AD, when they usurped tribes such as the Brigantes and Carvetii and built a fortress in Chester to guard their northern border. Some 300 years later, after domination of England by the Anglo-Saxons and then the Normans, the northwest remained relatively lawless for centuries.

During the 18th century the northwest became increasingly orderly, but it was the 19th century that saw dramatic changes. Coal mining, textile manufacture and shipbuilding took off, and towns like Manchester and Liverpool grew into huge industrial cities and kingpins in the British Empire. The wealth spawned massive infrastructure and impressive buildings, but also urban deprivation and problems, which were exacerbated by the sharp decline of heavy industry from the 1950s onwards. Entertainment culture, including the Beatles and Manchester United; a growing interest in rural tourism in the Lake District; and various urban revitalization projects have since brought renewed dynamism to this beautiful region.

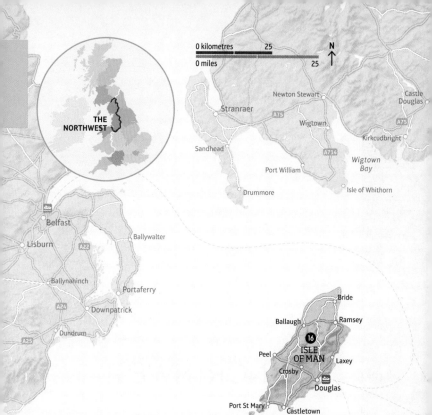

THE NORTHWEST

Must Sees

1 Manchester
2 Liverpool
3 Chester
4 The Lake District
National Park

Experience More

5 Penrith
6 Dalemain
7 Carlisle
8 Furness Peninsula
9 Cartmel
10 Kendal
11 Levens Hall
12 Carnforth
13 Lancaster
14 Ribble Valley
15 Blackpool
16 Isle of Man

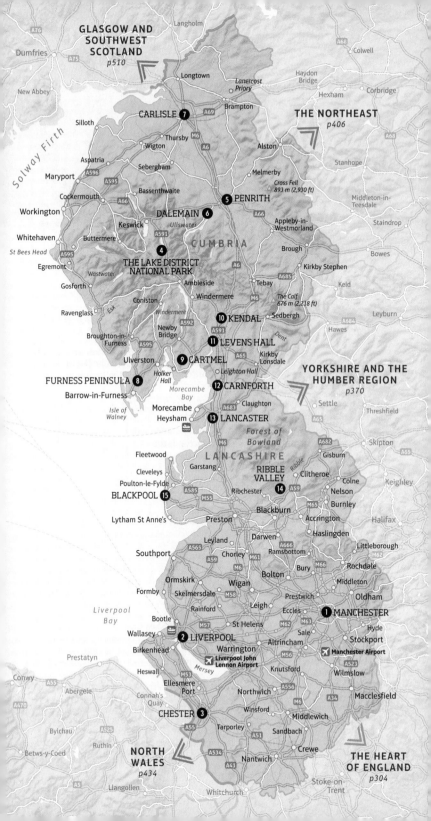

↑ The sun setting over Manchester and its various industrial buildings

❶

MANCHESTER

 Greater Manchester ✈18 km (11 miles) S of city 🚉 Piccadilly, Victoria, Oxford Rd 🚍 Coach: Chorlton St
🛈 1 Piccadilly Gardens; www.visitmanchester.com

From Roman origins (as Mamucium) to the 19th century, Manchester grew to become a massive industrial powerhouse, fuelled by the cotton trade. Today, famed for its Britpop legacy and footballing eminence, it is the north of England's premier shopping and media hub.

①

People's History Museum

📍 Bridge St 🕐 10am-5pm daily 🌐 phm.org.uk

Housed in a renovated Edwardian pumping station, this large, excellent national museum narrates the history of democracy in Britain and the story of people's lives at home, work and leisure from the early 19th century to the present day. The first gallery focuses on the theme of revolution, the birth of democratic ideas, trade unions and the main political parties and political movements up to 1945. The second gallery has displays on the struggle for equal rights from World War II onwards,

including gay rights, anti-raciscm initiatives, and major sociopolitical events such as the founding of the NHS, the Miners' Strike and the protests against the Poll Tax. The huge collection of political banners is the largest and most important of its kind in the world.

②

National Football Museum

📍 Cathedral Gdns 🕐 10am-5pm daily 🌐 national footballmuseum.com

The National Football Museum is housed in a striking, ski slope-shaped glass building. The visit begins with a glass elevator ride up the incline, then proceeds down through three staggered floors showcasing a huge collection of football memorabilia. A notable object on display is the ball from the 1966 World Cup Final.

Across the plaza is Manchester Cathedral; dating largely from the 19th century, it stands on a site that has been occupied by a church for more than a millennium.

THE PETERLOO MASSACRE

In 1819, the working conditions of Manchester's factory workers were so bad that social tensions reached breaking point. On 16 August, 50,000 people assembled in St Peter's Field to protest. Initially peaceful, the mood darkened and the poorly trained mounted troops panicked, charging the crowd. Eleven were killed and many wounded. The incident was called Peterloo (the Battle of Waterloo had taken place in 1815). Reforms such as the Factory Act came in later that year. In 2018 a statue of suffragette Emmeline Pankhurst was unveiled in St Peter's Square, site of the Peterloo Massacre.

③

Museum of Science and Industry

🏠 Liverpool Rd ⏰ 10am–5pm daily 🚫 1 Jan, 24–26 Dec 🌐 mosi.org.uk

The spirit of scientific enterprise and industrial might of Manchester's heyday is conveyed at the Museum of Science and Industry, one of the largest science museums in the world. Among the best sections are the Power Hall, a collection of working steam engines, the Electricity Gallery, tracing the history of domestic power, and an exhibition on the Liverpool and Manchester Railway.

---

④

Manchester Town Hall

🏠 Albert Square 🚫 For renovation until 2024 🌐 manchester.gov.uk

Manchester's majestic town hall was designed by Liverpool-born architect Alfred Waterhouse (1830–1905), who would later find fame with his Natural History Museum in London. The building was completed in 1877 in an English Gothic style. In the square in front of the town hall is Manchester's Albert Memorial, dedicated to the consort of Queen Victoria.

---

⑤

Manchester Art Gallery

🏠 Mosley St & Princess St ⏰ 11am–5pm Mon, 10am–5pm Tue–Sun 🚫 1 Jan, Good Fri, 24–26 & 31 Dec 🌐 manchesterartgallery.org

The original gallery building was designed in 1824 and contains a superb collection of British art, notably Pre-Raphaelites such as William Holman Hunt and Dante Gabriel Rossetti, early Italian, Flemish and French pieces and a vast array of decorative art objects, such as ceramics, glass, metalwork and furniture. Most special exhibitions are free, with accompanying events. The lively Clore Art Studio offers a combination of artworks and hands-on activities for children.

↑ Admiring one of the paintings on display at the fantastic Manchester Art Gallery

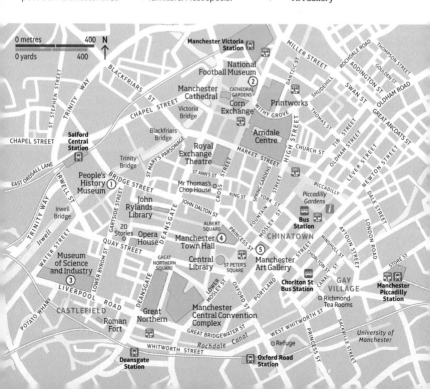

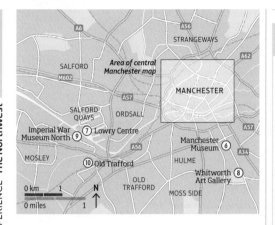

The Salford Quays area to the west of Manchester city centre (15 minutes by Metrolink tram) is home to MediaCityUK, which houses major national media outlets, such as the BBC and ITV. There are a host of restaurants, cafés and shops in this media hub. Guided 90-minute tours take you around the BBC's impressive site and the sets of some of British TV's most famous shows. You can book tours, or tickets to a recording, at www.bbc.co.uk/ showsandtours.

GREATER MANCHESTER

⑥ 🍴 🖥 🏛

Manchester Museum

🏠 Oxford Rd 🕐 10am–5pm daily 🚫 1 Jan, 24–26 Dec 🌐 museummanchester. ac.uk

Part of Manchester University, this museum opened in 1885 in a building designed by Alfred Waterhouse, the architect responsible for the city's magnificent town hall (p347). It houses around six million items from all ages and all over the world but specializes in Egyptology and zoology. The collection of ancient Egyptian artifacts is one of the largest in the UK and includes monumental stone sculpture and mummies displayed with their sarcophagi and funerary goods. Funerary masks, tomb models and mummified animals also appear in other sections. The zoological collections number over 600,000 objects, from stuffed animals to a cast of one of the most complete skeletons of a *Tyrannosaurus rex*.

⑦ 🍴 🖥 🏛

Lowry Centre

🏠 Pier 8, Salford Quays 🕐 10am–6pm daily 🌐 thelowry.com

On a prominent site beside the Manchester Ship Canal, the Lowry is an arts and entertainment complex that combines two theatres, a restaurant, terrace bars and cafés, art galleries and a shop. The centre is named after celebrated reclusive artist Laurence Stephen Lowry (1887–1976), who was born locally and lived all his life in

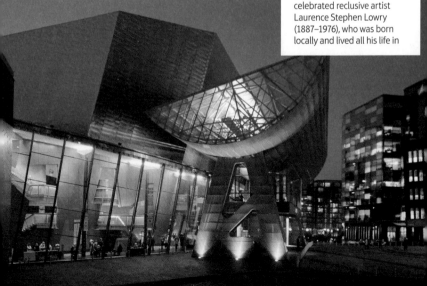

Imperial War Museum North, designed by Polish-born Daniel Liebeskind

the Manchester area. A rent collector by day, in his leisure hours he painted cityscapes dominated by the smoking chimneys of industry beneath heavy, soot-filled skies. The term "matchstick men" is frequently applied to the crowds of slight and ghostly figures peopling his canvases. Some of Lowry's work is displayed in one of the galleries here; another hosts changing temporary exhibitions. A 20-minute documentary, "Meet Mr Lowry", is screened throughout the day.

Whitworth Art Gallery

⌂ University of Manchester, Oxford Rd ⏰ 10am–5pm daily (to 9pm Thu) 🚫 Good Fri, 24 Dec–2 Jan ⓦ whitworth manchester.ac.uk

The Stockport-born machine tool manufacturer and engineer Sir Joseph Whitworth bequeathed money for this gallery, founded in 1889 and part of the University of Manchester since 1958. The red-brick building is from the Edwardian period, while the modern interior dates from the 1960s. The gallery houses a superb collection of drawings, sculpture, contemporary art, textiles and prints. Jacob Epstein's *Genesis* nude sits in the entrance, and there is an important collection of British watercolours. Look out, too, for the Japanese woodcuts and the collection of historical and modern wallpapers.

← The Lowry Centre, a shimmering, silvery cultural complex

Imperial War Museum North

⌂ Trafford Wharf Rd, Salford Quays ⏰ 10am–5pm daily 🚫 24–26 Dec ⓦ iwm.org.uk

This striking piece of modern architecture comes courtesy of Daniel Libeskind; the waterfront collision of three great aluminium shards represents a globe shattered by conflict. Inside, a vast space is used to display a small but well-presented collection of military hardware and ephemera, with nine "silos" devoted to exhibits on people's experiences of war. On the hour the lights are extinguished for an audiovisual display.

Old Trafford

⌂ Salford Quays ⏰ 9:30am–5pm Mon-Sat, 10am-4pm Sun (except match days) ⓦ manutd.com

A tour of Manchester United's football ground includes not only its museum but much interactive fun, such as a chance to test your own penalty-taking skills. The tour takes in the dressing rooms, the trophy room and the players' lounge and culminates in a walk down the tunnel, tracing the route taken by players at every home game.

EAT

Refuge
Globally inspired, eclectic sharing plates in a Victorian interior.

⌂ The Principal Hotel, Oxford St ⓦ refuge mcr.co.uk

£££

---

20 Stories
Immaculate modern British cuisine served in a rooftop setting.

⌂ 1 Hardman Sq ⓦ 20stories.co.uk

£££

Richmond Tea Rooms
Flamboyant Gay Village spot for grand cooked breakfast, lunch and tea.

⌂ Richmond St ⓦ rich mondtearooms.com

£££

Mr Thomas's Chop House
Gastropub with good-value traditional comfort food.

⌂ 52 Cross St ⓦ toms chophouse.com

£££

②

LIVERPOOL

🅰 Merseyside ✈ 11 km (7 miles) SE of city 🚉 Lime St
🚌 Norton St ⛴ Pier Head 🛈 Albert Dock; www.visit
liverpool.com

Liverpool owes much to its position on the western seaboard: as a major port it drew hordes of would-be emigrants to the New World from Europe. Many settled permanently in Liverpool, and a large, mixed community developed. Economic decline followed, but the 1960s saw Liverpool resurgent; in the 21st century urban regeneration has revitalized the city.

GREAT VIEW
City Vista

Take a 50-minute cruise on the Mersey Ferry for the best views of the Liverpool Waterfront. The commentary tells the city's fascinating history *(www.mersey ferries.co.uk)*.

① 🍴 ☕ 🛍
Albert Dock

🅰 3-4 The Colonnades
🌐 albertdock.com

The first docks opened in Liverpool in 1715 and at their peak stretched 11 km (7 miles) along the Mersey, but they suffered in the 20th century due to the decline in maritime trade. The Albert Dock, a handsome group of arcaded warehouses designed by Jesse Hartley in 1846, finally closed in 1972 but was triumphantly redeveloped and reopened a decade later. Now a vibrant visitor destination, it houses museums, including Tate Liverpool *(p352)*, galleries, shops, restaurants, cafés, bars and other lively attractions.

② 🎸 ☕ 🛍
The Beatles Story

🅰 Albert Dock 🕙 10am-6pm daily 🚫 25 & 26 Dec
🌐 beatlesstory.com

This walk-through exhibition relates the history of The Beatles' meteoric rise to fame, from their first record, *Love Me Do*, through Beatlemania to their last live appearance together in 1969. A highlight is the replica of the Cavern Club, birthplace of the group. The hits that mesmerized a generation are played throughout the museum. Limited-edition merchandise is on sale in the shop alongside T-shirts and posters.

BEATLES CITY TOURS

Locations associated with the Fab Four are revered as shrines in Liverpool. Bus and walking tours trace the hallowed ground of the Salvation Army home at Strawberry Fields and Penny Lane, as well as the boys' old homes. The most visited site is Mathew Street, where the Cavern Club first throbbed to the Mersey Beat. The original site is now a shopping arcade, but you can visit a replica.

← Liverpool past and present merging on the banks of the Mersey

and White Star liners. The exhibition on the Battle of the Atlantic in World War II includes models and charts. Another gallery deals with emigration to the New World.

International Slavery Museum

🏠 Albert Dock ⏰ 10am-5pm daily 🌐 liverpool museums.org.uk

Next door to the Maritime Museum is the International Slavery Museum, which explores the story of the transatlantic slave trade and its legacies through a range of highly moving and thought-provoking exhibitions. It also covers slavery today and issues of racism and discrimination through multimedia, artifacts and other displays.

Merseyside Maritime Museum

🏠 Albert Dock ⏰ 10am-5pm daily 📅 1 Jan, 24-26 Dec 🌐 liverpoolmuseums.org.uk

Devoted to the history of the Port of Liverpool, this large complex has good sections on shipbuilding and the Cunard

SHOP

The Bluecoat Display Centre
Beautifully designed, hand-made arts, crafts and jewellery by over 300 local artisans.

🏠 College Ln 🌐 bluecoat displaycentre.com

Probe Records
Cult vinyl store strong on punk, indie, funk, soul, reggae and hard-to-find discs.

🏠 School Ln 🌐 probe-records.co.uk

News from Nowhere
Left-wing bookshop and non-profit worker's co-op specializing in radical and intellectual books.

🏠 96 Bold St 🌐 news fromnowhere.org.uk

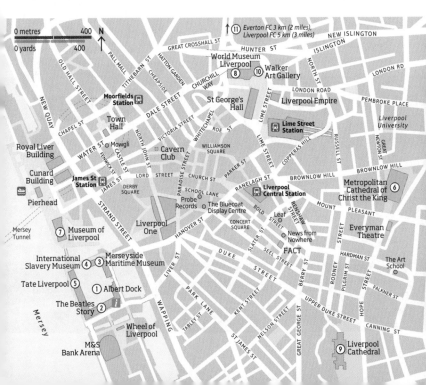

EAT

Mowgli

Sit-down Indian street food is served on steel plates and tiffin boxes in this colourful little spot. Booking recommended.

📍 3 Water St 🌐 mowgli streetfood.com

££££

The Art School

A good choice for contemporary takes on British classics; creative vegan options are also available.

📍 1 Sugnall St 🌐 theart schoolrestaurant.co.uk

££££

Leaf

There's always a lively buzz at this smart bistro with its modern decor. Regular live music.

📍 65-67 Bold St 🌐 thisisleaf.co.uk

££££

Tate Liverpool

📍 Albert Dock ⏰ 10am-6pm daily 🚫 Good Fri, 24-26 Dec 🌐 tate.org.uk/liverpool

Tate Liverpool has one of the best contemporary art collections outside London. Marked by bright blue and orange panels and arranged over three floors, the gallery was converted from an old warehouse by architect James Stirling. It opened in 1988 as the first outpost of Tate Britain (p76). Some special exhibitions charge a fee.

Metropolitan Cathedral of Christ the King

📍 Mount Pleasant ⏰ 7:30am- 6pm daily 🌐 liverpoolmetro cathedral.org.uk

Liverpool's Roman Catholic cathedral rejected traditional forms in favour of a striking modern design. Early plans, drawn up by Pugin and later by Edwin Lutyens in the 1930s, proved too expensive. The final version, brainchild of Sir Frederick Gibberd and built in 1962–7, is a circular building surmounted by a stylized crown of thorns 88 m (290 ft) high. Inside, the stained-glass lantern, designed by John Piper and Patrick Reyntiens, floods the circular nave with diffused blueish light. There is a fine bronze of Christ by Elisabeth Frink (1930–94).

Museum of Liverpool

📍 Pier Head, Albert Dock ⏰ 10am-5pm daily 🚫 1 Jan, 24-26 Dec 🌐 liverpool museums org.uk/mol

The Museum of Liverpool is housed in a stunning building on the waterfront. Inside,

This gallery houses one of the finest art collections in Britain, from the 14th to the 21st centuries.

visitors are told the story of this famous city, including its contributions to music, popular culture, sport and industry, as well as its role in the wider world. The café, located on the ground floor, has superb views of Albert Dock.

↑ The Pre-Raphaelite collection, one of the Walker Art Gallery's most popular attractions

World Museum Liverpool

🏛 William Brown St ⏰ 10am–5pm daily ✖ 25 & 26 Dec 🌐 liverpool museums.org.uk/wml

Six floors of exhibits in this excellent museum include collections of Egyptian, Greek and Roman pieces and displays on natural history, archaeology, space and time. Highlights include the hands-on Weston Discovery Centre, a planetarium, the Clore Natural History Centre, an aquarium and a Bug House.

Liverpool Cathedral

🏛 St James' Mount ⏰ 8am–6pm daily 🌐 liverpool cathedral.org.uk

Although Gothic in style, this building was completed only in 1978. The largest Anglican cathedral in the world, it is a fine red sandstone edifice designed by Sir Giles Gilbert Scott. The foundation stone was laid in 1904 by Edward VII

←

Admiring the interior *(inset)* of the unique Metropolitan Cathedral

but, dogged by two world wars, building work dragged on to modified designs. Today, the cathedral also houses works by important 20th- and 21st-century artists.

Walker Art Gallery

🏛 William Brown St ⏰ 10am–5pm daily 🌐 liverpoolmuseums.org. uk/wml

Founded in 1877 by local brewer and Liverpool mayor Sir Andrew Barclay Walker, this gallery houses one of the finest art collections in Britain, from the 14th to the 21st centuries. Paintings range from early Italian and Flemish works to Rubens, Rembrandt and the works of the French Impressionists, such as Degas' *Woman Ironing* (c 1892-5). Among the strong collection of British artists from the 18th century onwards are works by Millais, Turner and Gainsborough. Twentieth-century art includes iconic paintings by Sickert, Hockney and Lucian Freud, while the brilliant sculpture collection has pieces by John Gibson, Henry Moore and Rodin.

Liverpool & Everton Football Clubs

🏛 Anfield Rd; Goodison Park ⏰ To match ticket-holders and for guided tours only ✖ During fixtures 🌐 liverpoolfc.com; evertonfc.com

Some 5 km (3 miles) northeast of the centre lies Everton, Liverpool's football district, the home of its two major clubs: Liverpool FC and Everton FC, both with their own devoted following. They offer stadium tours. The much-decorated Liverpool FC also has a small museum to past successes.

 HIDDEN GEM
Model Village

10 km (6 miles) from the city centre in the Wirral is Port Sunlight, a Victorian garden village built by soap manufacturer William Hesketh Lever for his factory workers. The Lady Lever Art Gallery here houses his art collection, including Pre-Raphaelite paintings *(www.port sunlightvillage.com).*

❸

CHESTER

🏛 Cheshire 🚉 Chester 🚌 ℹ Town Hall, Northgate St;
www.visitchester.com

First settled by the Romans in AD 79 to defend fertile
land near the River Dee, Chester is one of the best-
preserved walled cities in Britain. The main streets are
lined with black-and-white timber buildings – a few are
medieval originals, but most are Victorian restorations.

GREAT VIEW
Tower Tour

Climb the spiral stairs
to the bell chamber on a
guided tour to the top of
the cathedral tower for
spectacular views over
the city. Guides narrate
fascinating tales from
over 900 years of
history as you climb.

①

City Walls

A good introduction to
Chester is to walk the 3-km
(2-mile) circuit along the old
city walls. Erected in Roman
times, the walls were rebuilt at
intervals. The most interesting
stretch is from the cathedral
to Eastgate, where there is a
wrought-iron clock built in
1899 for Queen Victoria's
Diamond Jubilee. The route to
Newgate leads to the remains
of a Roman amphitheatre
built in AD 100; the largest
in Britain, it seated 7,000
spectators. Just inside
Bridgegate is the Bear & Billet
pub, once a toll gate into the
city and Chester's oldest
timber-framed building,
dating to 1664.

②

The Rows

The Chester Rows, a series of
two-level arcades, with their
shops and continuous upper
gallery, anticipated today's
multistorey malls by several
centuries. Although their oriel
windows and decorative
timberwork date mostly from
the 19th century, the Rows
were first built in the 13th and
14th centuries, and some of
the original buildings are
still standing. The Rows
house a superb range of
independent shops.

③

Chester Cathedral

🌐 chestercathedral.com

Formerly the abbey church of
a Benedictine monastery, the
cathedral dates from the
11th to the early 16th century.
Even though it underwent
major restoration during the
19th century, the cathedral
retains much of its original
structure. The choir stalls
have splendid misericords
(carved ledges that are only
visible when the seats are
folded up), with scenes
including a quarrelling couple.
The lovely gardens are
worth a stroll and also
host a falconry centre.
The cathedral is often
used as a venue
for concerts.

Grosvenor Museum

Grosvenor St 10:30am-5pm Mon-Sat, 1-4pm Sun grosvenormuseum.westcheshiremuseums.co.uk

This museum presents the history of Chester from Roman times to the present day. Its galleries display paintings and sculpture, silverware and natural history exhibits, and there is an impressive collection of Roman tombstones. In its Period House, roomsets arranged in the styles of different eras show how life in a typical gentry townhouse evolved through the ages.

Dewa Roman Experience

Pierpoint Lane 9am-5pm Mon-Sat, 10am-5pm Sun (Dec-Jan: to 4pm) dewaromanexperience.co.uk

Immerse yourself in what life was like in Roman times at this hands-on exhibit at the heart of a Roman legionary

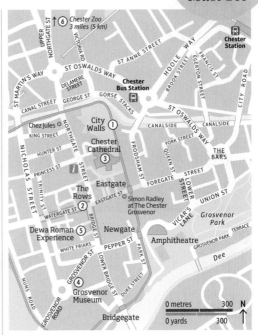

← Chester's medieval High Cross at the main junction of the distinctive Rows

fortress. Atmospheric reconstructions of a galley ship, a granary, a barracks, bathhouse and tavern help you experience this site as it was 2,000 years ago. The interactive experience includes trying on Roman armour, firing a catapult and building a mosaic. Excavations and ancient Roman artifacts from the site are on display.

Chester Zoo

Upton-by-Chester 10am-5pm daily chesterzoo.org

The UK's largest zoo holds some 500 animal species in 50 ha (125 acres) of beautiful gardens. Conservation is at the heart of this zoo, which is passionate about providing the highest standards of care for the animals and protecting native and international wildlife. There are a variety of tours and hands-on experiences, as well as daily talks.

EAT

Chez Jules
Despite the half-timbered exterior, this cheerful bistro is modern and airy inside. It specializes in classic French brasserie food.

71 Northgate St chezjules.com

£££

Simon Radley at The Chester Grosvenor
Holding a Michelin star since 1990, this is the go-to restaurant for formal dining. The focus is on tasting menus. Smart attire required.

58 Eastgate St chestergrosvenor.com

£££

↑ Ullswater, considered by many the most beautiful of all Cumbria's lakes

4

THE LAKE DISTRICT NATIONAL PARK

🏠 Cumbria 🚉 Penrith (from London or Glasgow); Windermere (from Manchester) ℹ️ Brockhole, off A591; www.lakedistrict.gov.uk

The painter John Constable (1776–1837) declared that the Lake District, now visited by 18 million people annually, had "the finest scenery that ever was". Swathes of rolling hills and mountains, glistening lakes, and ancient woodlands all contribute to this spectacular landscape.

① Ullswater

 ℹ️ Beckside car park, Glenridding; www. ullswater.com

The second largest lake in the Lake District after Windermere, Ullswater stretches from gentle farmland near Penrith to dramatic hills and crags at its southern end. In summer, two restored Victorian steamers ply regularly from Pooley Bridge to Glenridding. One of the best walks crosses the eastern shore from Glenridding to Hallin Fell and the moorland of Martindale. The spring bloom on the strip of land at Glencoyne Bay inspired Wordworth's "host of golden daffodils" in his poem "I wandered lonely as a cloud".

---

② Keswick

 ℹ️ Moot Hall, Market Sq; www.keswick.org

Popular with tourists since the end of the 18th century, Keswick has excellent visitor amenities, including a summer repertory theatre. The town prospered on wool and leather until, in Tudor times, deposits of graphite and copper were discovered and Keswick became an important centre for pencil manufacture. In World War II, hollow pencils were made to hide espionage maps on thin paper. The **Derwent Pencil Museum**, housed in a pencil factory, offers a fun insight into the world of pencils.

Among the many fine exhibits at the **Keswick Museum and Art Gallery** are original manuscripts of Lakeland writers, musical stones and other curiosities.

Derwent Pencil Museum

♿🚻☕ 🏠 Carding Mill Lane ⏰ 9:30am–5pm daily (last adm: 4pm) 🚫 1 Jan, 25 & 26 Dec 🌐 derwentart.com

Keswick Museum and Art Gallery

♿ 🏠 Fitz Park, Station Rd ⏰ 10am–4pm daily 🌐 keswickmuseum.org.uk

Did You Know?

Almost all of the major lakes in the Lake District are named "water" or "mere".

③

Cockermouth

🏧 🔢 88 Main St; www.
cockermouth.org.uk

Brightly coloured terraced
houses and restored workers'
cottages beside the river
count among the key
attractions in the busy market
town of Cockermouth, which
dates from the 12th century.
The elegant Georgian
Wordsworth House, where
the poet William Wordsworth
was born in 1770, is a must-see.
It displays some of the family's
possessions and is furnished
in late 18th century style.

The ruined Cockermouth
castle is occasionally open to
the public, most often during
the Cockermouth Festival,
which is held in July. Beer fans
can visit the Jennings Brewery
on Brewery Lane (www.
jenningsbrewery.co.uk) for
tours and tastings.

Wordsworth House

⊘ 🖰 NT 🏠 Main St 🕒 Mar-
Oct: 11am–5pm Sat–Thu
W nationaltrust.org.uk

---

④

Newlands Valley

🏧 Cockermouth 🔢 Moot
Hall, Market Sq, Keswick;
www.keswick.org

From the gently wooded
shores of Derwentwater, the
Newlands Valley runs through
a scattering of farms towards
rugged heights of 335 m
(1,100 ft) at the top of a pass,
where steps lead to a waterfall, Moss Force. Grisedale
Pike, Cat Bells and Robinson
all provide excellent fell walks.
Local mineral deposits were
mined here from Elizabethan
times. The hamlet of Little
Town was used as a setting by
Beatrix Potter *(p360)* in *The
Tale of Mrs Tiggywinkle*.

⑤

Buttermere

🏧 From Keswick 🔢 88 Main
St, Cockermouth; www.
visitcumbria.com

Interlinking with Crummock
Water and Loweswater,
Buttermere and its environs
represent some of the most
scenic countryside in the
region. Often known as the
"western lakes", the three are
remote enough not to
become too crowded. The
village of Buttermere, with its
handful of houses and inns, is
a popular starting point for
walks around all three lakes.

Buttermere is circled by
peaks: High Stile, Red Pike
and Haystacks. It was at the
latter that the ashes of A W
Wainwright, the celebrated
hill-walker and author of fell-
walking books, were scattered.

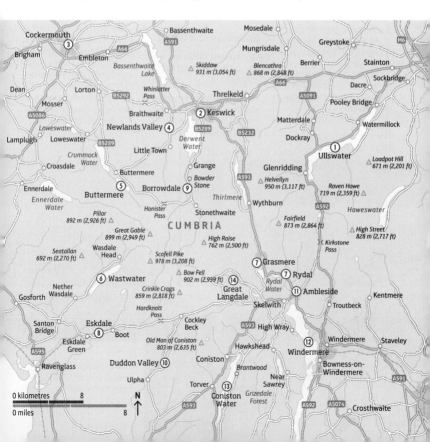

⑥
Wastwater

 Wasdale 🚹 Lowes Court Gallery, Egremont; 01946 820693

A silent reflection of truly awesome surroundings, brooding Wastwater is a mysterious, evocative lake. Along its eastern side loom walls of sheer scree over 600 m (2,000 ft) high. Beneath them the water looks inky black, whatever the weather, plunging an icy 80 m (260 ft) from the waterline to form England's deepest lake. You can walk along the scree, but it is an uncomfortable and very dangerous scramble.

Wasdale Head offers one of Britain's grandest views: the austere pyramid of Great Gable, centrepiece of a fine mountain range, alongside the huge forms of Scafell and Scafell Pike. This irresistible backdrop inspired the first serious British mountaineers, who flocked here during the 19th century, insouciantly clad in tweed jackets and carrying little more than a length of rope slung over their shoulders.

PICTURE PERFECT
Wastwater

You don't need to be a climber to get great shots of Wastwater. There are spectacular viewpoints on the road along the western edge and from paths to the shore at the top of the lake, especially when the water is dark-mirror still.

WILLIAM WORDSWORTH (1770-1850)

The best known of the Romantic poets, Wordsworth was born in the Lake District and spent most of his life there. After school in Hawkshead and a period at Cambridge he settled at Dove Cottage with his sister Dorothy and in 1802 married an old school friend, Mary Hutchinson. They lived simply, bringing up their children and enjoying walking and receiving visits from poets such as Coleridge and de Quincey. Wordsworth's prose works include one of the earliest guidebooks to the Lake District.

⑦
Grasmere and Rydal

🚉 Grasmere 🚹 Market Cross, Ambleside, 08442 250544

William Wordsworth lived in both these lakeshore villages. Fairfield, Nab Scar and Loughrigg Fell rise steeply above the lakes' reedy shores and offer good walking. The famous Grasmere Sports attract large crowds in August. The Wordsworth family is buried in St Oswald's Church, where crowds flock for the annual rushbearing ceremony. Most visitors head for **Dove Cottage**, where the poet spent his most creative years. The museum here includes such artifacts as the great man's socks. The Wordsworths also lived for many years at **Rydal Mount.** The grounds contain waterfalls and a summerhouse, and there are stunning views of Rydal Water and the surrounding fells. Dora's Field nearby is a blaze of daffodils in spring and the Fairfield Horseshoe offers a brisk walk.

← Looking out over Wasdale's scree slopes and Wastwater from Great Gable

→

Inn at Grange, one of the prettiest spots in Borrowdale

Dove Cottage

 Off A591 near Grasmere ◯ Mar–Dec: daily; check website for times
🔲 wordsworth org.uk

Rydal Mount

◯ Rydal ◯ Apr–Oct: 9:30am–5pm daily; Nov–Dec & Feb–Mar: 11am–4pm Wed–Sun 🔲 rydalmount.co.uk

---

⑧
Eskdale

🚩 Egremont; 01946 820693

The pastoral delights of Eskdale are the reward for driving the gruelling Hardknott Pass, whose steep gradients make it the most taxing journey in the Lake District. As you descend into Eskdale, rhododendrons and pines flourish in a landscape of small hamlets, narrow lanes and gentle farmland. The main settlements are the villages of Boot and Eskdale Green, and Ravenglass, the only coastal village in the Lake District National Park. A fun way to enjoy the area is to take the miniature Ravenglass & Eskdale railway (known as La'al Ratty), which runs for 11 km (7 miles) between Ravenglass and Dalegarth (for Boot), with seven request stops along the way (www.ravenglass-railway.co.uk).

---

⑨
Borrowdale

🚌 From Keswick 🚩 Moot Hall, Market Sq, Keswick

This romantic valley, subject of many a painter's creative endeavours, lies beside the densely wooded shores of Derwentwater under towering crags. It is a popular trip from Keswick, offering gentle valley walks. At the tiny hamlet of Grange, the valley narrows dramatically to form the "Jaws of Borrowdale". Other scenic stopping points include Rosthwaite, Stonethwaite and Watendlath, near the famous beauty spot of Ashness Bridge.

Grange is a good starting point for an 13-km (8-mile) walk around Derwentwater, or for a walk or drive south towards the more open farmland around Seatoller. If travelling down by road, look out for a sign to the Bowder Stone, a delicately poised boulder which may have fallen from the crags above or been deposited by a glacier millions of years ago.

---

⑩
Duddon Valley

🚩 The Old Town Hall, Broughton-in-Furness; www.duddon valley.co.uk

Also known as Dunnerdale, this picturesque tract of countryside inspired 35 of Wordsworth's sonnets. The prettiest stretch lies between Ulpha and Cockley Beck. In autumn the colours of heather-covered moors are particularly beautiful. Stepping stones and bridges span the river at intervals, the most charming being Birk's Bridge, near Seathwaite. At the southern end of the valley, where the River Duddon meets the sea at Duddon Sands, is the pretty village of Broughton-in-Furness. Note the stone slabs once used for fish in the market square.

TOP 5 TOP FIVE HIKES

Rydal Water
An easy lakeside walk in the footsteps of William Wordsworth.

Helm Crag
Climb up Grasmere's iconic lion-and-lamb-shaped fell for highly impressive views.

Langdale Pikes
See glorious, varied peaks rising above Stickle Tarn in the Langdale valley.

Helvellyn
A classic big mountain walk with stunning cliff-edge approaches.

Scafell Pike
The Lakes' highest peak requires determined clambering over big boulders to the summit.

Victorian architecture in Ambleside, at the head of Lake Windermere

boasts all of its original features. The **Stott Park Bobbin Mill** is the last working example of over 70 such mills in Cumbria that once served the textiles industry.

Beatrix Potter wrote many of her books at **Hill Top**, the 17th-century farmhouse at Near Sawrey, northwest of Windermere. The house is furnished with many of Potter's possessions and left as it was in her lifetime. The **Beatrix Potter Gallery** in Hawkshead holds annual exhibitions of her manuscripts and illustrations, while the **World of Beatrix Potter** in Crag Brow brings her popular characters to life in a fun exhibition that is guaranteed to excite the kids.

Blackwell Arts and Crafts House

⊛ ⊜ 🄰Bowness-on-Windermere 🕙10:30am–5pm daily 🅦blackwell.org.uk

Ambleside

🚌 𝒊Market Cross; www.ambleside online.co.uk

With good road connections to all parts of the Lakes, a range of restaurants and shops, a summer music festival and a cinema, Ambleside is an attractive base, especially for walkers. Sights include the remnants of the Roman fort of Galava, Stock Ghyll Force waterfall and the 17th-century Bridge House, now a National Trust information centre.

Windermere

🚂🚌 𝒊Victoria St, www.winderemereinfo.co.uk

At over 16 km (10 miles) long, this dramatic watery expanse is England's largest lake. Industrial magnates built mansions around its shores

long before the railway arrived. Stately Brockhole, now the national park's visitor centre, was one such grand estate. When the railway reached Windermere in 1847, it enabled crowds of workers to visit the area on day trips.

Today, a year-round car ferry service connects the lake's east and west shores (it runs between Ferry Nab and Ferry House), and summer steamers link Lakeside, Bowness and Ambleside on the north–south axis. Belle Isle, a wooded island on which stands a unique round house, is one of the lake's most attractive features, but landing is not permitted.

Bowness-on-Windermere, on the east shore, is a popular centre. Many of its buildings display Victorian details, and St Martin's Church dates back to the 15th century. The **Blackwell Arts and Crafts House** is one of Britain's most beautiful houses from the early 20th century. It still

---

BEATRIX POTTER AND THE LAKE DISTRICT

Although best known for her illustrated children's stories featuring characters such as Peter Rabbit and Jemima Puddleduck, Beatrix Potter (1866-1943) became a champion of conservation in the Lake District after moving there in 1906. She married William Heelis, devoted herself to farming, and was an expert on Herdwick sheep. To conserve her beloved countryside, she donated land to the National Trust.

Stott Park Bobbin Mill

 ⬢Finsthwaite
☎01539 531087 ⏰Apr-Oct:
10am-5pm Wed-Sun (daily in
Jul & Aug)

Hill Top

⬢Near Sawrey ⏰Feb-
Oct: daily 🌐nationaltrust.
org.uk

Beatrix Potter Gallery

⬢The Square,
Hawkshead ⏰Feb-Oct:
10am-4:30pm daily
🌐nationaltrust.org.uk

World of Beatrix Potter

⬢Crag Brow
⏰10am-5:30pm daily
🌐hop-skip-jump.com

---

⑬
Coniston Water

🅿 ℹConiston car park,
Ruskin Ave; www.coniston
tic.org

For the best view of this lovely
lake, you need to climb a little.
The 19th-century art critic,
writer and philosopher John
Ruskin had a fine view from
his house, **Brantwood**, where
his paintings can be seen
today. Contemporary art
exhibitions and events take
place throughout the year.

The green slate village of
Coniston, once a centre for
coppermining, now caters for
walkers. An enjoyable
excursion is the summer lake
trip from Coniston Pier on the
National Trust steam yacht,
Gondola, calling at Brantwood.
Alternatively, boats can be
hired at the Coniston Boating
Centre (www.conistonboating
centre.co.uk).

Dotted around Coniston
Water are Hawkshead, a quaint
village with timber-framed
houses, and Grizedale Forest,
scattered with woodland
sculptures and popular with
mountain bikers. Tarn Hows is
a landscaped tarn surrounded
by woods. Walkers can enjoy a
pleasant climb up the 803-m
(2,633-ft) Old Man of Coniston.

Brantwood

⬢Off B5285
⏰Mid-Mar-Nov: 10:30am-
5pm daily; Dec-mid-Mar:
10:30am-4pm Wed-Sun
🌐brantwood.org.uk

⑭
Great Langdale

🚌From Ambleside 🌐visit
cumbria.com

North of Coniston, the
stunning wild landscape of
Great Landale is one of the
Lake District's most popular
valleys for walkers and
climbers, who throng here to
take on fells such as Pavey
Ark, Pike o'Stickle, Crinkle
Crags and Bow Fell. The
gateway to the valley is the
supremely picturesque and
quaint village of Elterwater,
was once a site of a gun-
powder works.

EAT

Tower Bank Arms
This traditional 17th-
century inn serves
tasty dishes made
with locally sourced
ingredients.

⬢Near Sawrey,
Ambleside 🌐tower
bankarms.co.uk

€€€

Drunken Duck
High-class dishes are
served in a cosy interior
at this delightful
country gastropub.

⬢Barnesgate,
Ambleside 🌐drunken
duckinn.co.uk

€€€

Fellpack
Hearty recipes use
Cumbrian ingredients,
with dishes served
in "fellpots" - local
pottery bowls.

⬢19 Lake Rd, Keswick
🌐fellpack.co.uk

€€€

↑ Summer steamers and
boats on the shore of
Windermere at sunset

THE GEOLOGY OF THE LAKE DISTRICT

The Lake District, a UNESCO World Heritage site, contains some of England's most spectacular scenery. Concentrated in just 231 sq km (900 sq miles) are the highest peaks, deepest valleys and longest lakes in England. Today's landscape has changed little since the end of the Ice Age 10,000 years ago, the last major event in Britain's geological history. But the glaciated hills that were revealed by the retreating ice were once part of a vast mountain chain whose remains can also be found in North America. The mountains were first raised by the gradual fusion of two ancient landmasses which, for millions of years, formed a single continent. Eventually the continent broke into two, forming Europe and America, separated by the widening Atlantic Ocean.

GEOLOGICAL HISTORY

The diversity of the Lake District's scenery owes much to its geology. Some 450 million years ago, Earth's internal movements made two continents collide, and the ocean disappear, forming a mountain range. Magma altered the sediments and cooled into volcanic rock. In the Ice Age, glaciers excavated huge rock basins in the mountainsides. The glaciers retreated 10,000 years ago, their meltwaters forming lakes in valleys dammed by debris.

16

The number of different bodies of water that represent the Lake District.

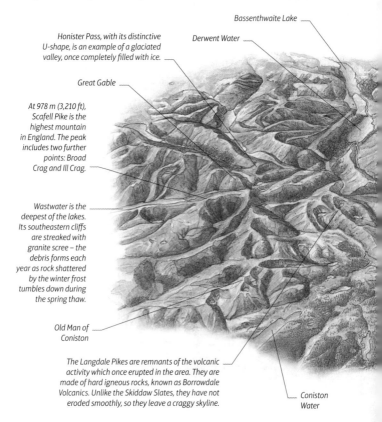

Honister Pass, with its distinctive U-shape, is an example of a glaciated valley, once completely filled with ice.

Great Gable

At 978 m (3,210 ft), Scafell Pike is the highest mountain in England. The peak includes two further points: Broad Crag and Ill Crag.

Wastwater is the deepest of the lakes. Its southeastern cliffs are streaked with granite scree – the debris forms each year as rock shattered by the winter frost tumbles down during the spring thaw.

Old Man of Coniston

The Langdale Pikes are remnants of the volcanic activity which once erupted in the area. They are made of hard igneous rocks, known as Borrowdale Volcanics. Unlike the Skiddaw Slates, they have not eroded smoothly, so they leave a craggy skyline.

Bassenthwaite Lake

Derwent Water

Coniston Water

SETTLEMENT OF THE LAKE DISTRICT

The sheltered valley floors with their benign climate and fertile soils are ideal for settlement. Farmhouses, dry-stone walls, pasture and sheep pens are an integral part of the landscape. Higher up, the absence of trees and bracken are the result of wind and a cooler climate. Old mine workings and tracks are the relics of once-flourishing industries.

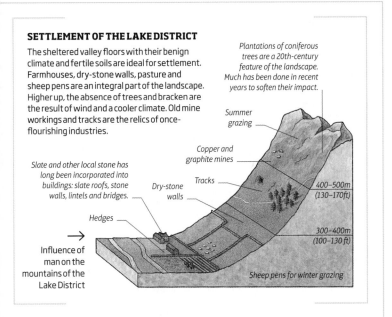

Plantations of coniferous trees are a 20th-century feature of the landscape. Much has been done in recent years to soften their impact.

Summer grazing

Copper and graphite mines

Tracks

Slate and other local stone has long been incorporated into buildings: slate roofs, stone walls, lintels and bridges.

Dry-stone walls

400–500m (130–170ft)

Hedges

300–400m (100–130 ft)

→

Influence of man on the mountains of the Lake District

Sheep pens for winter grazing

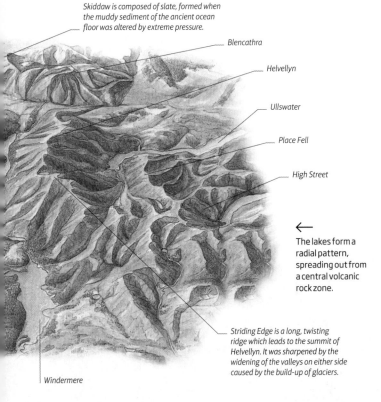

Skiddaw is composed of slate, formed when the muddy sediment of the ancient ocean floor was altered by extreme pressure.

Blencathra

Helvellyn

Ullswater

Place Fell

High Street

←

The lakes form a radial pattern, spreading out from a central volcanic rock zone.

Striding Edge is a long, twisting ridge which leads to the summit of Helvellyn. It was sharpened by the widening of the valleys on either side caused by the build-up of glaciers.

Windermere

EXPERIENCE MORE

5

Penrith

🏛 Cumbria
📍 Robinson's School, Middlegate; www. visiteden.co.uk

Timewarp shopfronts on the market square and a 14th-century **castle** of sandstone are Penrith's main attractions. There are some strange hogback stones in St Andrew's churchyard, allegedly a giant's grave, but more likely Anglo-Viking headstones.

Just northeast of Penrith, at Little Salkeld, is the intriguing Bronze Age circle (with 66 tall stones) known as Long Meg and her Daughters. Nine kilometers (6 miles) northwest of Penrith lies **Hutton-in-the-Forest**. The oldest part of this house is the 13th-century tower. Inside is a magnificent Italianate staircase, a panelled 17th-century Long Gallery, a delicately stuccoed Cupid Room dating from the 1740s, and several Victorian rooms. Outside, you can walk around the walled garden and topiary terraces, or explore the woods.

Penrith Castle

🏛 Ullswater Rd 🕖 7:30am–9pm (winter: to 4:30pm) daily
🌐 english-heritage.org.uk

Hutton-in-the-Forest

🏛 Off B5305 🕖 Apr–Sep: 11:30am–4pm Wed, Thu, Sun & public hols; Grounds: 10am–5pm Sun–Fri 🌐 hutton-in-the-forest.co.uk

6

Dalemain

🏛 Penrith, Cumbria
🚉 Penrith then taxi
🕖 Apr–Oct: 10:30am–3:30pm Sun–Thu 🌐 dalemain.com

A Georgian façade gives this fine house near Ullswater the impression of architectural unity, but it hides a much-altered medieval and Elizabethan structure with a maze of rambling passages.

TRADITIONAL CUMBRIAN SPORTS AND EVENTS

Cumberland wrestling is one of the most interesting sports to watch in the summer months. The combatants, often clad in longjohns and embroidered velvet pants, clasp one another in an armlock and attempt to topple each other over. Other traditional Lakeland sports include fell-racing, a gruelling test of speed and stamina up and down local peaks at ankle-breaking speed. Hound-trailing is also a popular sport, in which specially bred hounds follow an aniseed trail over the hills. The Egremont Crab Fair in September is famous for its face-pulling, or "gurning", competition.

→ Fragments of columns and sculptures at Carlisle's Tullie House Museum

Public rooms include a superb Chinese drawing room with hand-painted wallpaper and a panelled 18th-century drawing room. Several small museums occupy various outbuildings, and the gardens have a fine collection of fragrant shrub roses and a huge silver fir. Every March, the Marmalade Festival organizes a farmers' market plus tutor-led tastings, cookery demonstrations, competitions and other marmalade-related events.

7

Carlisle

🏛 Cumbria 🚉🚌
ℹ The Old Town Hall; www.discovercarlisle.co.uk

Due to its proximity to the Scottish border, this city has long been a defensive site.

↑ The sandstone ruins of Penrith Castle, built in the 1300s

Known as Luguvalium by the Romans, it was an outpost of Hadrian's Wall (*p414*). Carlisle was sacked and pillaged repeatedly by the Danes, the Normans and border raiders, and suffered damage as a Royalist stronghold under Cromwell (*p49*).

Today, Carlisle is the capital of Cumbria. In its centre are the timber-framed Guildhall and market cross, and fortifications still exist in the West Walls, drum-towered gates and its Norman **castle**. The castle tower has a small museum devoted to the King's Own Border Regiment. The cathedral dates from 1122 and features a decorative east window. Carlisle's **Tullie House Museum** re-creates the city's past with sections on Roman history and Cumbrian wildlife. Nearby lie the evocative ruins of **Lanercost Priory** (c.1166) and **Birdoswald Roman Fort**.

Carlisle Castle

🖐🎨🏛🅴🅷 🏛 Castle Way
🕐 10am-6pm daily (Nov-Mar: 10am-4pm Sat & Sun)
🌐 english-heritage.org.uk

Tullie House Museum

🖐🎫🏛🅴🅷 🏛 Castle St
🕐 10am-5pm Mon-Sat, 11am-5pm Sun 🌐 tulliehouse.co.uk

Lanercost Priory

🖐🏛🅴🅷 🏛 Nr Brampton
🕐 10am-6pm daily (Oct-Mar: to 5pm) 🌐 english-heritage.org.uk

Birdoswald Roman Fort

🖐🖥🏛🅴🅷 🏛 Gilsland, Brampton 🕐 10am-5pm daily (Nov-Mar: 10am-4pm Sat & Sun) 🌐 english-heritage.org.uk

---

EAT

Four and Twenty
An old bank has been turned into a hip setting for casual fine dining. The menu includes Cumbrian chorizo and superb Cumberland farmhouse cheddar cheese soufflé.

🏛 42 King St, Penrith
🕐 Sun & Mon
🌐 fourandtwenty penrith.co.uk

££££

David's
Fine dining in a plush Victorian townhouse. The traditional menu offers such dishes as lamb, guinea fowl and venison. There are vegetarian options too.

🏛 62 Warwick Rd, Carlisle 🕐 Sun & Mon 🌐 davidsrestaurant.co.uk

££££

↑ The priory church in Cartmel, with its soaring central nave and vibrant window

⑧

Furness Peninsula

🗺 Cumbria 🚌🚂 Barrow-in-Furness 🛈 Forum 28, Duke St, Barrow-in-Furness; www.barrowtourism.co.uk

Barrow-in-Furness is the peninsula's main town. Its **Dock Museum**, built over a Victorian dock, traces the history of Barrow using interactive displays.

Ruins of the red sandstone walls of **Furness Abbey** remain in the wooded Vale of Deadly Nightshade. It was founded by Savigniac monks in the mid-12th century and destroyed during the Reformation.

The historic town of Ulverston received its charter in 1280. Stan Laurel, of Laurel and Hardy fame, was born here in 1890. The **Laurel and Hardy Museum** has a cinema and memorabilia. In the nearby village of Gleaston is the **Gleaston Water Mill**, a 400-year-old, working corn mill.

Dock Museum

🖼 ♿ 🗺 North Rd, Barrow-in-Furness ⏰ 11am–4pm Wed–Sun & public hols 🌐 dockmuseum.org.uk

Furness Abbey

🖼 🅿 ♿ 🗺 Vale of Deadly Nightshade ⏰ Apr–Oct: 10am–6pm daily; Nov–Mar: 10am–4pm Sat & Sun 🌐 english-heritage.org.uk

Laurel and Hardy Museum

🖼 🗺 Upper Brook St, Ulverston ⏰ 10am–5pm daily 🌐 laurel-and-hardy.co.uk

Gleaston Water Mill

🗺 Gleaston ⏰ Apr–Sep: 11am–4:30pm Wed–Sun 🌐 watermill.co.uk

⑨

Cartmel

🗺 Cumbria 🛈 Main St, Grange-over-Sands; www.grangeoversands.net

A centre for gourmet dining and home of sticky toffee pudding, Cartmel has given its name to its surroundings, a hilly area of green farm-land

← A statue of Laurel and Hardy in Ulverston, on the Furness Peninsula

with mixed woodland and limestone scars. The highlight of this pretty village is the restored 12th-century priory church, with a stone-carved 14th-century tomb and beautiful misericords.

About 2 km (0.5 mile) southwest of Cartmel is **Holker Hall**, the former residence of the Dukes of Devonshire, with lavishly furnished rooms, stunning gardens and a deer park.

Holker Hall

🖼 🕙 🖼 🅿 🗺 Cark-in-Cartmel ⏰ Mid-Mar–Oct: 11am–4pm Wed–Sun & public hols 🌐 holker.co.uk

CROSSING THE SANDS

South of Cartmel, Morecambe Bay, a huge expanse of glistening tidal flats and sand, attracts thousands of wading birds and is one of the most important reserves in England. The sands are very dangerous due to ever-changing tides, but you can take a walk across the bay from Arnside to Kent's Bank village with an experienced, knowledgeable guide to enjoy the scenery.

EAT

L'Enclume
Fresh foraged produce is transformed with innovative methods into delicacies such as mousses or jellies at this acclaimed Michelin-starred restaurant in a former irongmonger's.

Cavendish St, Cartmel
lenclume.co.uk

£££

10

Kendal

Cumbria 25 Stramongate; www.golakes.co.uk

A busy market town, Kendal is the administrative centre of the region and the southern gateway to the Lake District. **Abbot Hall**, built in 1759, has an art gallery with paintings by Turner and Romney. The hall's stable block contains the **Museum of Lakeland Life & Industry**, with occasional workshops demonstrating local crafts and trades. There are dioramas of geology and wildlife in the **Kendal Museum**.

About 5 km (3 miles) south of the town is the 14th-century **Sizergh Castle**, with a fortified tower and a lovely garden.

Abbot Hall Art Gallery
10:30am-5pm Mon-Sat (winter: to 4pm), 11am-3pm Sun abbothall.org.uk

Museum of Lakeland Life & Industry
10:30am-5pm Mon-Sat (winter: to 4pm) lakelandmuseum.org.uk

Kendal Museum
Station Rd 10am-4pm Thu, Fri & Sat kendalmuseum.org.uk

Sizergh Castle
Off A591 & A590 Apr-Oct: noon-4pm daily nationaltrust.org.uk

11

Levens Hall

Near Kendal, Cumbria
From Kendal or Lancaster
Apr-early Oct: noon-4pm Sun-Thu (house); 10am-5pm (gardens)
levenshall.co.uk

The outstanding attraction of this Elizabethan mansion is its topiary, the world's oldest. However, the house itself also has much to offer. Built around a 13th-century tower, it contains fine Jacobean furniture and watercolours by landscape artist Peter de Wint (1784–1849). Also of note are the ornate ceilings, Charles II dining chairs, the earliest example of English patchwork and gilded hearts on the drainpipes.

The elegant grounds of Levens Hall, an Elizabethan mansion

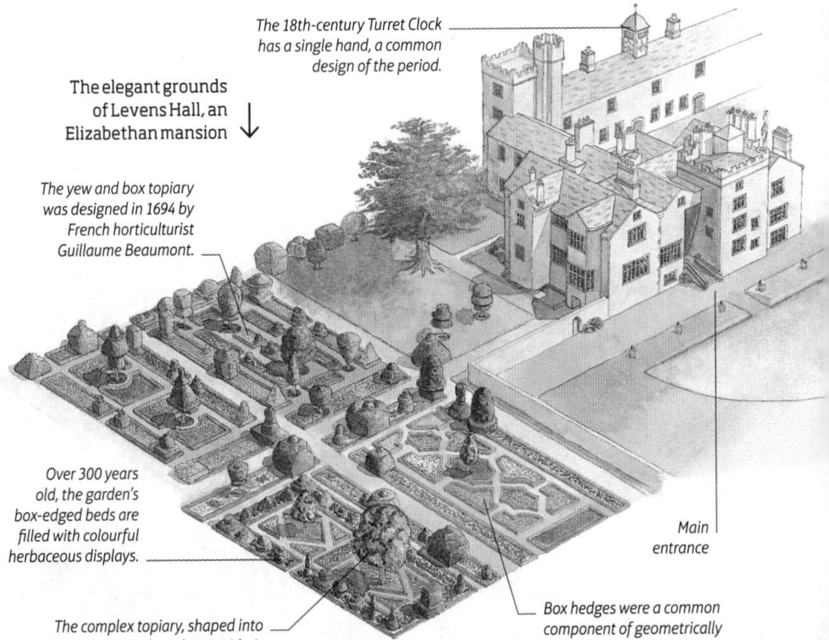

The 18th-century Turret Clock has a single hand, a common design of the period.
The yew and box topiary was designed in 1694 by French horticulturist Guillaume Beaumont.
Over 300 years old, the garden's box-edged beds are filled with colourful herbaceous displays.
The complex topiary, shaped into cones, spirals and pyramids, is kept in shape by gardeners. Some specimens are 6 m (20 ft) high.
Box hedges were a common component of geometrically designed gardens of this period.
Main entrance

⑫ Carnforth

📍Lancashire 🛈
Morecambe Old Station
Buildings; www.explore
morecambebay.org.uk

The small town of Carnforth, just inland of the estuary sands of Morecambe Bay, is best known for its beautifully preserved railway station, a key location for the 1945 film *Brief Encounter*. The **Carnforth Station Heritage Centre** celebrates the film.

Carnforth also provides a gateway to Arnside and Silverdale, two protected areas of rolling hills with attractive minor roads and paths, ideal for walkers and cyclists. **Leighton Hall**, a Georgian-style stately home with extensive gardens, lies adjacent to a bird reserve with otters and red deer.

Carnforth Station Heritage Centre

📍250 Warton Rd
🕘10am–4pm daily
🌐carnforthstation.co.uk

Leighton Hall

♿ 📍Silverdale 🕘May–Sep:
2–5pm Tue–Fri (Aug: also
Sun) 🌐leightonhall.co.uk

PENDLE WITCH TRIALS

The 1612 Pendle Witch Trials took place in Lancaster Castle and involved charging a dozen men and women with murder by witchcraft. At the time, the Pendle Hill area was seen as a lawless periphery where all sorts of religious non-conformism thrived and village healers performed magic for money. The trials led to ten of the accused being hanged, based on little more than local gossip and the testimony of a nine-year-old.

⑬ Lancaster

📍Lancashire 🚉🚌
🛈Meeting House Lane;
www.visitlancaster.org.uk

Named by the Romans after their camp on the other side of the River Lune, the county town of Lancaster grew into a prosperous port. **Lancaster Castle** dates back to the 11th century but was expanded over the years and was in use as a jail until 2011. It is still used as a Crown Court. The Shire Hall is decorated with 600 heraldic shields.

Also outstanding are the museum of furniture in the 17th-century **Judge's Lodgings**, and the **Maritime Museum**, with displays on the port's history.

Williamson Park is the site of the 1907 Ashton Memorial, a folly built by linoleum magnate and politician Lord Ashton. There are fine views from the top of this 67-m (220-ft) domed structure.

Lancaster Castle

♿♿♿ 📍Castle Parade
🕘9:30am–5pm daily
🌐lancastercastle.com

Judge's Lodgings

♿♿ 📍Church
St 📞01524
581241 🕘Apr–
Oct: 11am–
4pm daily

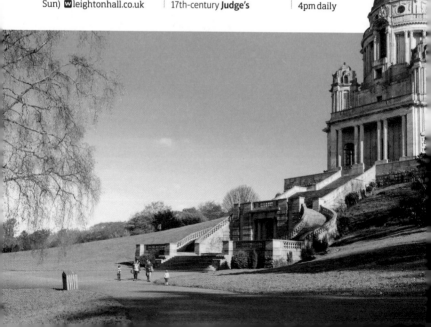

The Ferris wheel dominating Blackpool's Central Pier at sunset

Maritime Museum

◎◎◎ ⌂ Custom House, St George's Quay ◷ 10am–4pm daily (Nov–Mar: noon–4pm) ⊞ lancashire.gov.uk

---

14

Ribble Valley

⌂ Lancashire ▣ Clitheroe **ℹ** Station Rd, Clitheroe; www.visitribblevalley.co.uk

Clitheroe, a small market town with a hilltop castle, is a good centre for exploring the Ribble Valley's rivers, old villages such as Slaidburn, and acclaimed fine-dining scene. Ribchester has a **Roman Museum**, and there is a ruined Cistercian abbey at Whalley. To the east is 560-m (1,830-ft) Pendle Hill, with a Bronze Age burial mound at its peak.

Roman Museum

◎◎◎ ⌂ Ribchester ◷ 10am–5pm Mon–Fri, noon–4pm Sat & Sun ⊞ ribchesterromanmuseum.org

↑ The Ashton Memorial, a folly in Williamson Park, Lancaster

15

Blackpool

⌂ Lancashire ✈▣⊟ **ℹ** Festival House, Promenade; www.visitblackpool.com

Blackpool's resort life dates back to the 18th century, but it burst into prominence when the railway arrived in 1840. A wall of amusement arcades, bingo halls and fast-food stalls, plus the popular Pleasure Beach theme park and the famous Blackpool Tower, stretches behind the sands. The town attracts thousands of visitors in September and October when Illuminations line the roads for miles.

16

Isle of Man

ℹ Sea Terminal, Douglas; www.visitisleofman.com

With its cliff-fringed coasts, lush glens and barren hills, many dotted with ancient forts and Celtic crosses, the Isle of Man has UNESCO biosphere reserve status. Most visitors come for the annual TT (Tourist Trophy) motorbike race (May–Jun). Douglas, the main town, has a faded Victorian-era holiday resort feel.

EAT

Bay Horse Inn
This country pub offers modern takes on rustic fare like roast chicken and rack of lamb.

⌂ Bay Horse Bridge, Ellel, Lancaster ◷ Mon & Tue ⊞ bayhorseinn.com

€€€

Yorkshire Fisheries
A family-run, no-frills chippie that does fish 'n' chips to perfection.

⌂ 16 Topping St, Blackpool ◷ Sun ⊞ yorkshirefisheries.co.uk

€€€

Little Fish Café
The daily catch is turned into delicious creations at this quayside spot. Try the battered Manx queen scallops.

⌂ 31 North Quay, Douglas, Isle of Man ⊞ littlefishcafe.com

€€€

YORKSHIRE AND THE HUMBER REGION

Yorkshire is England's largest county and also one of its wildest. Dramatic scenery formed by Ice Age glaciers is still very much in evidence among the sheep farms and gentle hills of the Dales and the Moors national parks. The Romans were the first group of inhabitants to leave a major mark on the land by establishing what became the city of York. Most other layers of early Yorkshire history are also in evidence in York where Viking remnants co-exist with Anglo-Saxon fortifications and medieval structures. The 7th-century Angles introduced Christendom to Yorkshire and built its first abbeys. York and Yorkshire continued to be important as seats of national power. Three members of the House of York became kings of England, culminating in the 15th-century Wars of the Roses.

It wasn't until the arrival of 19th-century industrialization that York got some regional rivals. Then the mills of Leeds and Bradford, the shipyards and fisheries of Hull and the steelmakers of Sheffield ushered in an era of grand industrialist-built manor houses and viaducts that opened the countryside to railways, for which York remained the main hub. Periods of post-war industrial decline hit all the big cities hard, but time and diversification has seen them rebound and celebrate their past.

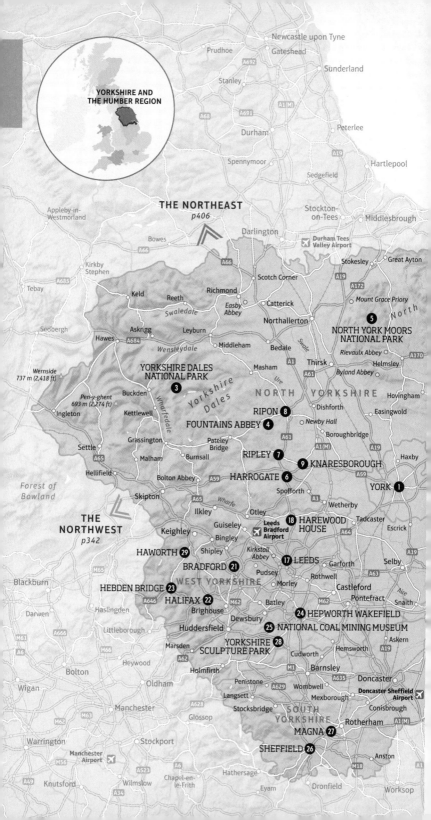

North
Sea

YORKSHIRE AND THE HUMBER REGION

Must Sees
1. York
2. Castle Howard
3. Yorkshire Dales National Park
4. Fountains Abbey
5. North York Moors National Park

Experience More
6. Harrogate
7. Ripley
8. Ripon
9. Knaresborough
10. Scarborough
11. Burton Agnes
12. Bempton Cliffs and Flamborough Head
13. Eden Camp
14. Beverley
15. Wharram Percy
16. Burton Constable
17. Leeds
18. Harewood House
19. Kingston upon Hull
20. Holderness and Spurn Head
21. Bradford
22. Halifax
23. Hebden Bridge
24. Hepworth Wakefield
25. National Coal Mining Museum
26. Sheffield
27. Magna
28. Yorkshire Sculpture Park
29. Haworth

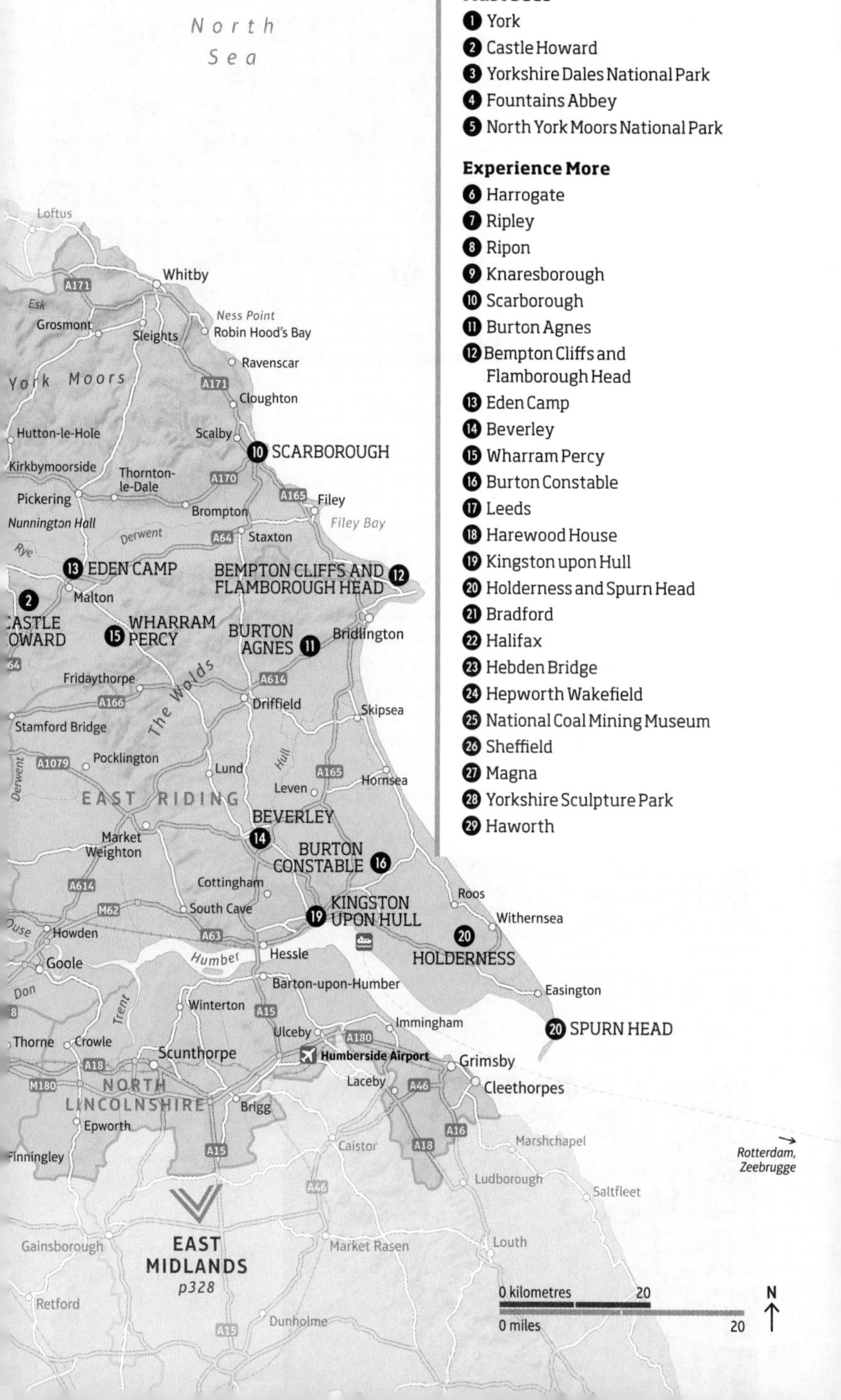

Loftus
Whitby
Esk
Grosmont
Ness Point
Sleights
Robin Hood's Bay
Ravenscar
York Moors
A171
Cloughton
Hutton-le-Hole
Scalby
10 SCARBOROUGH
Kirkbymoorside
Thornton-
le-Dale
A170
Filey
Pickering
Brompton
Filey Bay
Nunnington Hall
Derwent
Staxton
Rye
A64
13 EDEN CAMP
BEMPTON CLIFFS AND
FLAMBOROUGH HEAD 12
2
Malton
CASTLE
OWARD
15 WHARRAM
PERCY
BURTON
AGNES 11
Bridlington
Fridaythorpe
A614
A166
Driffield
Skipsea
Stamford Bridge
The Wolds
A1079
Pocklington
Lund
Hull
Derwent
Leven
A165
Hornsea
EAST RIDING
Market
Weighton
14 BEVERLEY
BURTON
CONSTABLE 16
A614
Cottingham
Roos
M62
South Cave
19 KINGSTON
UPON HULL
20
Withernsea
Ouse
Howden
A63
Hessle
HOLDERNESS
Goole
Humber
Easington
Don
Barton-upon-Humber
20 SPURN HEAD
3
Thorne
Crowle
Winterton
A15
Immingham
A18
Ulceby
A180
Grimsby
M180
NORTH
LINCOLNSHIRE
Scunthorpe
Humberside Airport
Laceby
A46
Cleethorpes
Epworth
Brigg
Finningley
A15
Caistor
A18
Marshchapel
A46
A16
Rotterdam,
Zeebrugge
Gainsborough
EAST
MIDLANDS
p328
Market Rasen
Ludborough
Saltfleet
Retford
A15
Dunholme
Louth

0 kilometres   20
0 miles   20

N

❶

YORK

⌂ York ✈ Leeds Bradford, 50 km (32 miles) NW ⊟ York
▭ Station Rd 🛈 1 Museum St; www.visityork.org

A multilayered history makes York's compact city centre a delight to explore, with evidence of its Roman, Saxon, Viking and medieval heritage at every turn of its narrow streets. Overlooking all is the magnificent York Minster *(p376)*, dating from the time when this Christian stronghold was England's second city.

①

York Castle Museum

⌂ The Eye of York
🕒 9:30am–5pm daily
🌐 yorkcastlemuseum.org.uk

Opened in 1938, this fine museum of social history is housed in two former 18th-century prisons. Period displays include a Jacobean dining room, a Victorian street, a moorland cottage and a 1950s front room. An exhibition explores the traditions of birth, marriages and death in Britain from 1700 to 2000. Another highlight is the Anglo-Saxon York Helmet, discovered in 1982.

②

Yorkshire Museum and St Mary's Abbey

⌂ Museum Gardens
🕒 10am–5pm daily
🌐 yorkshiremuseum.org.uk

Highlights of this museum include the 15th-century Middleham Jewel, 2nd-century Roman mosaics and an Anglo-Saxon silver gilt bowl. Part of the museum stands in the ruined Benedictine St Mary's Abbey *(p378)*.

③

Jorvik Viking Centre

⌂ Coppergate 🕒 10am–5pm daily (Nov–Mar: to 4pm) 🌐 jorvikvikingcentre.co.uk

Advance booking is advised for the popular Jorvik Viking Centre, built on the site of the original Viking settlement which archaeologists uncovered at Coppergate. Using new technology and

←

Victorian-era re-creation of the York street of Kirkgate in the York Castle Museum

York's bustling city centre and the colossal York Minster cathedral

remains and artifacts from the site, a dynamic vision of 10th-century York is re-created, bringing the Viking world to life. The centre's galleries contain many more fascinating artifacts, from earrings to frying pans, and visitors may handle a few. A short walk away, in the medieval church of St Saviour's, is the centre's sister attraction, DIG, where visitors can take part in an archaeological excavation.

Fairfax House

🏠 Castlegate ⏰ Feb-Dec: 10am-5pm Tue-Sun; Mon: tours only 🌐 fairfax house.co.uk

From 1755 to 1762 Viscount Fairfax built this fine Georgian townhouse for his daughter, Anne. Between 1920 and 1965 it was a cinema and dancehall. Today, visitors can see the bedroom of Anne Fairfax (1725–93), and a fine collection of 18th-century furniture, porcelain and clocks.

National Railway Museum

🏠 Leeman Rd ⏰ 10am-6pm daily (Nov-Mar: to 5pm) 🌐 nrm.org.uk

In what is the world's largest railway museum, nearly 200 years of history are explored using a variety of visual aids. Visitors can try wheel-tapping and shunting in the interactive gallery, or find out what made Stephenson's *Rocket* so successful. Exhibits include uniforms, rolling stock from 1797 onwards and Queen Victoria's Royal Train carriage, as well as the very latest rail innovations.

EAT

Il Paradiso del Cibo
This small Sardinian café-restaurant is well known locally for an authentic taste of Italy.

🏠 40 Walmgate
🌐 ilparadisodel ciboyork.com

£££

Skosh
Upbeat and open-plan, Skosh offers inventive British-international fusion food in tapas-sized portions, enabling you to sample several dishes.

🏠 98 Micklegate
🌐 skoshyork.co.uk

£££

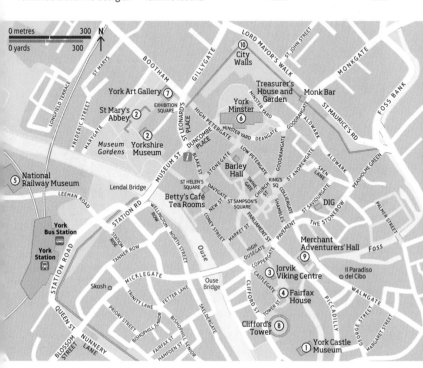

⑥ 🥢 🍴 🛍️

YORK MINSTER

🏛️ Deangate 🕐 9am–4:30pm Mon–Sat, 12:30–3pm Sun (major services may affect opening times) 🌐 yorkminster.org

The largest medieval Gothic cathedral north of the Alps, and seat of the Archbishop of York, York Minster is notable not only for its colossal size but also for its treasure trove of medieval stained glass.

York Minster is 158 m (519 ft) long and 76 m (249 ft) wide across the transepts; its Lantern Tower is the height of a 20-story building. The word "minster" refers to a missionary teaching church in Anglo-Saxon times. The first minster was a wooden chapel where King Edwin of Northumbria was baptized in 627. A Druid worshipper, he converted in order to marry the

daughter of the King of Kent (today, York is the only British cathedral to place mistletoe on the altar at Christmas, a Druid custom). There have been several cathedrals on or near the site, including an 11th-century Norman structure. The present minster was begun in 1220 and completed 250 years later. In 1984, fire damage led to a £2.25 million restoration programme.

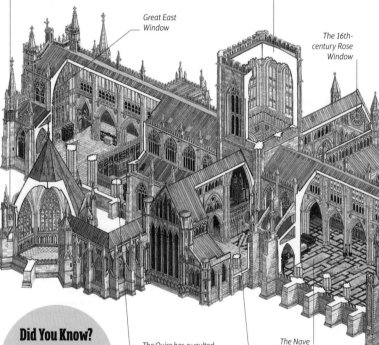

A Latin inscription near the entrance of the wooden, vaulted Chapter House (1260–85) reads: "As the rose is the flower of flowers, so this is the house of houses".

The central Lantern Tower was reconstructed in 1420–65 (after partial collapse in 1405) from a design by the master stonemason William Colchester.

Great East Window

The 16th-century Rose Window

Did You Know?

The minster has a staff of 15 masons and carvers, constantly working on the fabric of the building.

The Quire has a vaulted entrance with a 15th-century boss of the Assumption of the Virgin.

The Nave

Sited between the choir and the nave, the 15th-century stone Choir Screen depicts kings of England from William I to Henry VI, and has a canopy of angels.

↑ The nave, bisected by a stone screen behind which the choristers sit

The western towers with their 15th-century decorative panelling and elaborate pinnacles contrast with the simpler design of the north transept. The southwest tower is the minster belfry.

West Window

Great West Door

↑ York Minster, one of the finest medieval buildings in Europe

⑦ York Art Gallery

📍 Exhibition Sq ⏰ 10am–5pm daily 🌐 yorkartgallery.org.uk

This 1879 Italianate building holds a wide-ranging collection of paintings from western Europe dating from the early 1500s onwards. There is also a large, internationally significant collection of British and foreign studio ceramics, including work by Bernard Leach, William Staite Murray and Shoji Hamada. Expanded in 2015, the gallery hosts major international shows, and exhibits contemporary art in the Artists Garden.

⑧ Clifford's Tower

📍 Clifford's St ⏰ 10am–6pm Tue–Sun (Oct–Mar: to 4pm) 🌐 english-heritage org.uk

William the Conqueror's original wooden castle, sited here, was heavily damaged in 1069. The scene of anti-Jewish riots in 1190, the present tower dates to the 13th century and is a major landmark of York. The moated keep guarded a strategic gap in York's city walls, an area of swampy ground where the River Foss joins the River Ouse. Built by Henry III, the tower was named after the de Clifford family, who were constables of the castle. There are stunning panoramic views over the city from the top.

⑨ Merchant Adventurers' Hall

📍 Fossgate ⏰ 10am–4:30pm Sun–Fri, 10am–1:30pm Sat 🌐 theyorkcompany.co.uk

Built by a guild of Yorkshire merchants in 1357, this is one of the largest timber-framed medieval buildings in Britain. The Great Hall is probably the best example of its kind in Europe. Below the Great Hall is the hospital, which was used by the guild until 1900, and a private chapel. The homely café with its walled garden makes a good pit stop.

⑩ City Walls

🌐 yorkwalls.org.uk

For visitors, York's city walls are its finest free asset, offering a wonderful 2–3 hour walk. Walls were first built here as part of a Roman military camp but took much of their present shape in the 12th and 14th centuries. They are studded with imposing city gates called bars. The finest is Monk Bar, on Goodramgate, whose portcullis still works. In the Middle Ages, the rooms above it were rented out, and it was a prison in the 16th century. Decorative details include men holding stones ready to drop on intruders.

→ Clifford's Tower, which was formerly the keep of York Castle

NORTHERN ENGLAND ABBEYS

Northern England has some of the finest and best preserved religious houses in Europe. Centres of prayer, learning and power in the Middle Ages, the larger of these were designated abbeys and were governed by an abbot. Most were located in rural areas, considered appropriate for a spiritual and contemplative life. Viking raiders had destroyed many Anglo-Saxon religious houses in the 8th and 9th centuries, and it was not until William the Conqueror founded the Benedictine Selby Abbey in 1069 that monastic life revived in the north. New orders, Augustinians in particular, arrived from the Continent and by 1500 Yorkshire had 83 monasteries.

MONASTERIES AND LOCAL LIFE

As one of the wealthiest landowning sections of society, the monasteries played a vital role in the local economy. They provided employment, particularly in agriculture, and dominated the wool trade, England's largest export during the Middle Ages. By 1387 two-thirds of all wool exported from England passed through St Mary's Abbey *(p374)*, the largest wool trader in York.

ST MARY'S ABBEY

Founded in York in 1086, this Benedictine abbey was one of the wealthiest in Britain. It was granted royal and papal privileges and land, which led to a relaxing of standards by the early 12th century. The abbot was even allowed to dress in the same style as a bishop, and was raised by the pope to the status of a "mitred abbot". As a result, 13 monks left in 1132, to found Fountains Abbey *(p390)*.

HIDDEN GEM
Selby Abbey

A hidden gem of Yorkshire, the medieval Selby Abbey is located some 19 km (12 miles) south of York. It was the first monastery to be founded in the north after the Norman Conquest and is one of the most majestic abbey churches in England. It is still in use today as a parish church.

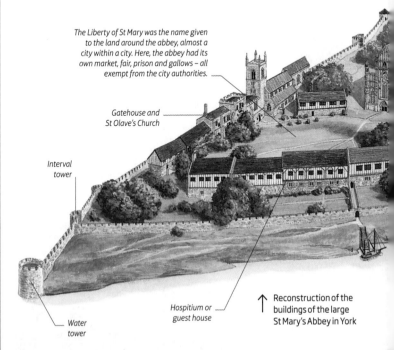

The Liberty of St Mary was the name given to the land around the abbey, almost a city within a city. Here, the abbey had its own market, fair, prison and gallows – all exempt from the city authorities.

Gatehouse and St Olave's Church

Interval tower

Hospitium or guest house

Water tower

↑ Reconstruction of the buildings of the large St Mary's Abbey in York

WHERE TO SEE ABBEYS TODAY

Fountains Abbey (p390) is the most famous of the numerous abbeys in the region. Other key Benedictine or Cistercian abbeys include Whitby (p392), Rievaulx (p394), Byland (p395) and Furness (p366). The northeast is famous for its early Anglo-Saxon monasteries at Hexham (p415) and Lindisfarne (p417).

1 Mount Grace Priory
Founded in 1398, Mount Grace Priory (p393) is the best-preserved Carthusian house in England. The former individual gardens and cells of each monk are all clearly visible.

2 Easby Abbey
This 1155 Premonstratensian house is located beside the River Swale, outside the pretty market town of Richmond. Among its remains are the 13th-century refectory and sleeping quarters and 14th-century gatehouse.

3 Kirkstall Abbey
Founded in 1152 by monks from Fountains Abbey, this Cistercian house is near Leeds. Its well-preserrved ruins include the church, the late Norman chapter house and the abbot's lodging.

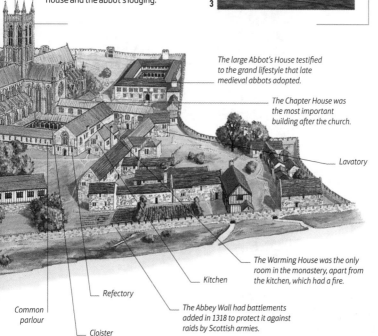

The large Abbot's House testified to the grand lifestyle that late medieval abbots adopted.

The Chapter House was the most important building after the church.

Lavatory

The Warming House was the only room in the monastery, apart from the kitchen, which had a fire.

Kitchen

The Abbey Wall had battlements added in 1318 to protect it against raids by Scottish armies.

Common parlour

Refectory

Cloister

A SHORT WALK
YORK

Distance 3 km (2 miles) **Time** 45 minutes
Nearest buses 29, 412, 5A, 840, 843

The city of York has retained so much of its medieval structure that walking into its centre is like entering a living museum. Many of the ancient timbered houses, perched on narrow, winding streets such as the Shambles, are protected by a conservation order and much of the centre is pedestrianized. The city's strategic position led to its development as a railway centre in the 19th century and the medieval core is close to the railway station, which is served by trains from all over the country.

York Minster, England's largest medieval church, was begun in 1220 (p376).

DEANGATE

START

HIGH PETERGATE   LOW PETERGATE

MINSTER YARD

One of the most attractive streets is **Stonegate**, *built over a Roman road.*

ST LEONARDS PLACE

DUNCOMBE PLACE

STONEGATE

York Art Gallery

St Mary's Abbey

BLAKE STREET

DAVYGATE

St Olave's Church *was founded in the 11th century in memory of St Olaf, King of Norway. To the left of the church is the small Chapel of St Mary on the Walls.*

MUSEUM STREET

LENDAL STREET

CONEY STREET

The **Yorkshire Museum** *is home to some of the most fascinating archaeological finds in the country (p374).*

Lendal Bridge

The 15th-century **Guildhall**, *situated beside the River Ouse, was rebuilt after bomb damage during World War II.*

OUSE

Ye Old Starre Inne *is one of the oldest pubs in York.*

← The Guildhall seen from the Gothic-style Lendal Bridge, opened in 1863

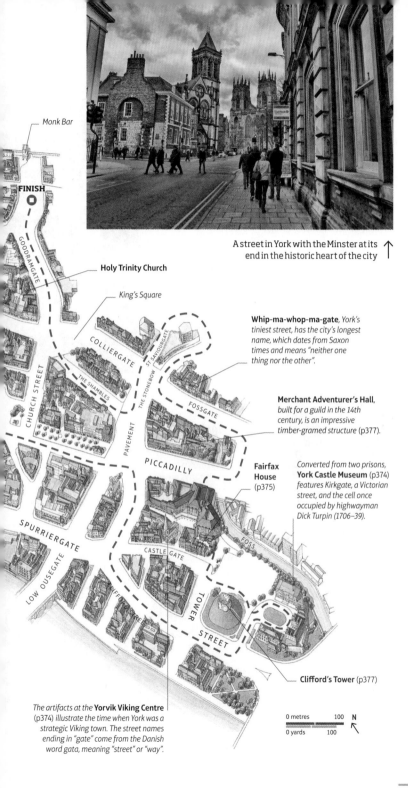

A street in York with the Minster at its end in the historic heart of the city ↑

Monk Bar

FINISH

GOODRAMGATE

Holy Trinity Church

King's Square

COLLIERGATE

THE SHAMBLES

CHURCH STREET

ST SAVIOURGATE

THE STONEBOW

FOSSGATE

PAVEMENT

PICCADILLY

SPURRIERGATE

LOW OUSEGATE

CASTLE GATE

FOSS

TOWER STREET

Whip-ma-whop-ma-gate, *York's tiniest street, has the city's longest name, which dates from Saxon times and means "neither one thing nor the other".*

Merchant Adventurer's Hall, *built for a guild in the 14th century, is an impressive timber-gramed structure (p377).*

Fairfax House (p375)

Converted from two prisons, **York Castle Museum** (p374) *features Kirkgate, a Victorian street, and the cell once occupied by highwayman Dick Turpin (1706–39).*

Clifford's Tower (p377)

The artifacts at the **Yorvik Viking Centre** *(p374) illustrate the time when York was a strategic Viking town. The street names ending in "gate" come from the Danish word gata, meaning "street" or "way".*

0 metres 100   N
0 yards 100

2 ✎ Ⓜ 🖥 🏛

CASTLE HOWARD

🚗 A64 from York 🚆 🕐 House: 10:30am–4pm daily; Grounds: 10am–6pm daily 🌐 castlehoward.co.uk

Built on the site of a former military castle, Castle Howard is a magnificent Baroque stately home that is surrounded by beautiful formal gardens and parkland. It is still owned and lived in by the Carlisle branch of the Howard family.

Castle Howard was the work of Charles, 3rd Earl of Carlisle. In 1699, he commissioned Sir John Vanbrugh, a man of dramatic ideas but with no previous architectural experience, to design a palace for him. Vanbrugh's grand designs of 1699 were put into practice by architect Nicholas Hawksmoor, and the main body of the house was completed by 1712. The West Wing was built in 1753–9, using a design by Thomas Robinson, son-in-law of the 3rd Earl. In the 1980s, Castle Howard was used as the spectacular location for the television adaptation of Evelyn Waugh's novel *Brideshead Revisited* (1945) and again in 2008 for a film version.

SIR JOHN VANBRUGH

Vanbrugh (1664–1726) trained as a soldier, but became better known as a playwright, architect and member of the Whig nobility. He collaborated with Hawksmoor over the design of Blenheim Palace, but his bold architectural vision, later greatly admired, was mocked by the establishment. Vanbrugh died while working on the garden buildings and grounds of Castle Howard.

Did You Know?

The towering dome was the first of its kind on a private house in Britain.

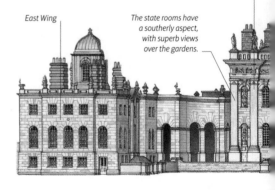

The front façade faces north, which was unusual for the 17th century.

East Wing

The state rooms have a southerly aspect, with superb views over the gardens.

The sweeping layout of Castle Howard, showing its main highlights ↑

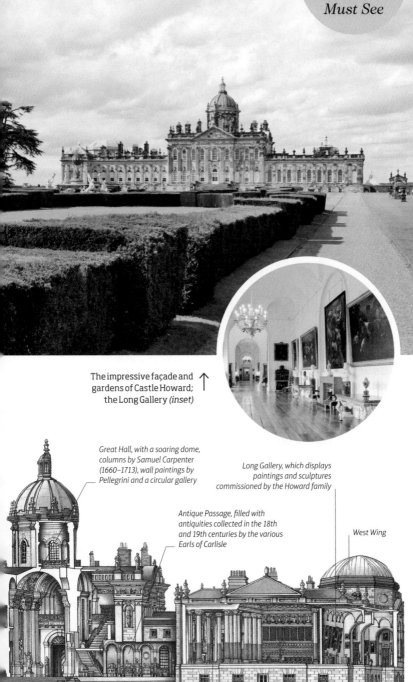

The impressive façade and gardens of Castle Howard; the Long Gallery *(inset)* ↑

Great Hall, with a soaring dome, columns by Samuel Carpenter (1660–1713), wall paintings by Pellegrini and a circular gallery

Long Gallery, which displays paintings and sculptures commissioned by the Howard family

Antique Passage, filled with antiquities collected in the 18th and 19th centuries by the various Earls of Carlisle

West Wing

North Front

Chapel, with stained-glass windows designed by Edward Burne-Jones and made by William Morris & Co.

Museum Room, which houses items such as a huge 17th-century Delft tulip vase

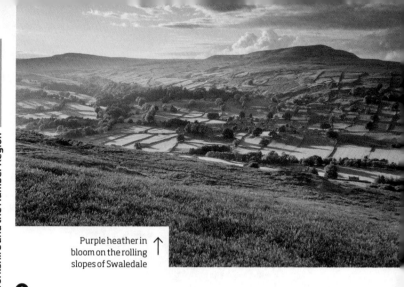

Purple heather in
bloom on the rolling
slopes of Swaledale ↑

❸

YORKSHIRE DALES NATIONAL PARK

🏠 North Yorkshire 🚉 Skipton ▦ 🌐 yorkshiredales.org.uk

This national park is formed from three principal dales – Swaledale,
Wharfedale and Wensleydale – and a number of smaller ones, such
as Deepdale. These steep-sided valleys, carved out in the Ice Age,
contrast with high moorland and grassy meadows to form a rich, scenic
landscape characterized by an age-old tradition of livestock farming.

SWALEDALE

Swaledale's prosperity was
founded largely on wool; it is
famous for the herds of hardy
sheep that graze on the wild,
high slopes even in the
harshest weather. The fast-
moving River Swale travels
from bleak moorland down
tumbling waterfalls to richly
wooded lower slopes, passing
through Reeth and Richmond.

This is fine cycling country:
the 2014 Tour de France took
the B6270 between Thwaite
and Hawes over Buttertubs
Pass, which takes its name
from a series of fluted limestone potholes known as the
Buttertubs. It is said that
farmers on their way to market
would lower their butter into
the holes to keep it cool.

①

Richmond

🌐 richmond.org

Swaledale's main point of entry
is this medieval town on the
Swale. Alan Rufus, 1st Earl of
Richmond, began building its
castle in 1071. An 11th-century
arch in the Norman keep leads
into a courtyard containing
Scolland's Hall (1080), one of
England's oldest buildings.
Richmond's market-place was
once the castle's outer bailey.
Its quaint, narrow streets gave
rise to the song *The Lass of
Richmond Hill* (1787), written
by Leonard McNallly. The
Georgian Theatre (1788) is the
only one of its age still extant.

Richmond Castle

♿ 🏠 Tower St 📞 0870
3331181 🕐 Apr–Oct: 10am–
6pm daily; Nov–Mar: 10am–
4pm Sat & Sun

②

Swaledale Folk Museum

🏠 Reeth 🕐 10am–5pm
daily 🌐 swaledale
museum.org

Reeth, once a lead-mining
centre, houses this museum
in a former Methodist
Sunday School. Displays
include wool-making and
mining artifacts and brass
band memorabilia.

WENSLEYDALE

The largest of the dales, Wensleydale is famous for its cheese and for the television series *All Creatures Great and Small*, based on the books by country vet James Herriot, which was filmed here. It is easy walking country for anyone seeking an alternative to major moorland hikes.

___

③

Dales Countryside Museum

🅐 Station Yard, Hawes
🕐 10am–5pm daily 🆆 dales countrysidemuseum.org.uk

In a former railway goods warehouse in Hawes, capital of Upper Wensleydale, is this fascinating museum, filled with items from local life and industry in the 18th and 19th century. These include cheese-making equipment; Wensleydale cheese was created by monks at nearby Jervaulx Abbey. There is also a ropemaking works a short walk away. Hawes, one of the highest-altitude market towns in England, is a thriving centre where thousands of cattle and sheep are auctioned each summer. For a Wensleydale cheese experience, just outside the town centre is the Wensleydale Creamery, with tours and demonstrations, a farm shop and a restaurant.

④

Hardraw Force

🅐 Hardraw, near Hawes

At the tiny village of Hardraw is England's tallest single-drop waterfall, with no outcrops to interrupt its 29-m (96-ft) fall. It became famous in Victorian times when the daredevil Blondin walked across it on a tightrope. Today, you can walk right under it and look through the water without getting wet. Buy your ticket and start the walk to the falls at the Green Dragon Inn.

> **Wensleydale is famous for its cheese and for the television series *All Creatures Great and Small*, based on the books by country vet James Herriot.**

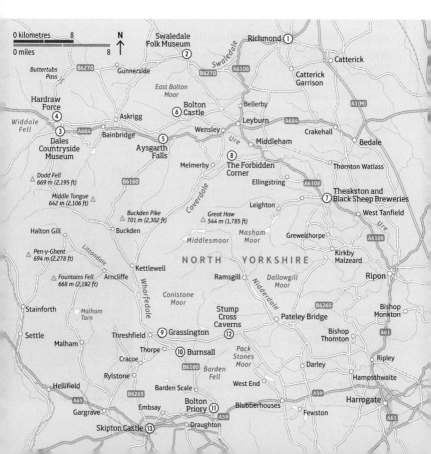

A viewing platform offering great view of the middle levels of the Aysgarth Falls

visitors with tours and tastings, a brewing museum at Theakston's and a restaurant at Black Sheep. Masham village itself has an attractive square once used for sheep fairs, surrounded by 17th- and 18th-century houses.

The Forbidden Corner

🏠 Tupgill Park Estate, near Leyburn ⏰ Apr–Oct: noon–dusk Mon–Sat; Nov & Dec: 10am–dusk Sun 🌐 theforbiddencorner. co.uk

Inspired and superbly quirky, this walled garden is dotted with Victorian-style follies, statues, underground tunnels, water fountains, grottoes and a labyrinth. With no map, it's a case of finding your own way around the oddball maze, a fun playground for kids. Visit by pre-booked ticket only.

⑤ Aysgarth Falls

🏠 Aysgarth 🚌 Aysgarth Falls National Park Centre; 01969 662910

An old packhorse bridge gives a clear view of the point at which the previously placid River Ure suddenly begins to plunge in foaming torrents over wide limestone shelves. The sight is even more spectacular after heavy rainfall. Turner painted the impressive lower falls in 1817.

There is ample parking, a café and local advice on walking routes at the National Park visitor centre, a short walk from the Falls.

> Bolton Castle's most notorious period was from 1568 to 1569 when Mary, Queen of Scots was held prisoner here by Elizabeth I.

⑥ Bolton Castle

🏠 Castle Bolton, nr Leyburn ⏰ Apr–Oct: 10am–5pm daily 🌐 boltoncastle.co.uk

Situated in the village of Castle Bolton, this spectacular medieval fortress was built in 1379 by the 1st Lord Scrope, Chancellor of England. Its most notorious period was from 1568 to 1569 when Mary, Queen of Scots was held prisoner here by Elizabeth I.

⑦ Theakston and Black Sheep Breweries

🏠 Masham 🌐 theakstons.co. uk; blacksheepbrewery.com

Pretty Masham is the home of Theakston's brewery, creator of the potent Old Peculier ale. The Theakston family has been brewing here since 1827, and in 1992 a young member, Paul, set up another brewery in the village, Black Sheep. Both breweries welcome

WHARFEDALE

This dale is characterized by gritstone moorland and quiet market towns nestled along meandering sections of river. Many consider Grassington a good point for exploring Wharfedale, but the pretty villages of Burnsall, overlooked by a 506-m (1,661-ft) fell, and Buckden, near Buckden Pike (701 m/2,302 ft), also make excellent bases.

Nearby are the Three Peaks of Whernside (736 m/2,416 ft), Ingleborough (724 m/2,376 ft) and Pen-y-Ghent (694 m/2,278 ft). They are known for their tough terrain, but this does not deter keen walkers from attempting to climb them all in one day.

Did You Know?

The Pen-Y-Ghent Café runs a "Three Peaks of Yorkshire Club" challenge to climb all three in 12 hours.

↑ The cobbled streets of Grassington, lined with traditional cottages and houses

⑨ Grassington

🏠 15 km (9 miles) N of Skipton
🚩 Grassington National Park Centre, Hebden Rd; 01756 751690

With its pretty stone houses and cobbled main square, Grassington is a small, picture-postcard Georgian market town. Don't miss the **Grassington Folk Museum**, which has displays illustrating the domestic and working history of the area, including farming and lead mining.

Grassington Folk Museum
🏠 The Square 🕐 Apr-Oct: 2–4:30pm daily 🌐 grassington folkmuseum.co.uk

⑩ Burnsall

🏠 5 km (3 miles) SE of Grassington

The village of Burnsall on the RIver Wharfe hosts Britain's oldest fell race every August. In St Wilfrid's churchyard are the original village stocks, gravestones from Viking times and a headstone carved in memory of the Dawson family by Eric Gill (1882–1940).

> 💬 INSIDER TIP
> **Scenic Railway**
>
> Take a wonderful day trip through this wild and beautiful countryside on the 116-km- (72-mile-) long Settle to Carlisle railway, and marvel at the feats of Victorian engineering, including bridges, viaducts and tunnels, along the route (www.settle-carlisle.co.uk).

↑ Burnsall's handsome five-arched bridge across the River Wharfe

Did You Know?

Skipton was voted Best Place to Live in the UK by *The Sunday Times* in 2018.

Bolton Priory

🏠 Bolton Abbey, Skipton
🕐 Times vary, check website ⓦ boltonabbey.com

One of the most beautiful parts of Wharfedale is around the village of Bolton Abbey, set in an estate owned by the Duke of Devonshire. While preserving its astounding beauty, its managers have incorporated over 46 km (30 miles) of footpaths, many suitable for wheelchairs and young families. The ruins of Bolton Priory, established by Augustinian canons in 1154 on the site of a Saxon manor, include a church, chapter house, cloister and prior's lodging. These all demonstrate the wealth accumulated by the canons through the sale of wool from their flocks of sheep. The priory nave is still used as a parish church.

Another attraction of the estate is the "Strid", a point where the River Wharfe surges through a gorge, gradually gouging holes out of the rocks.

Stump Cross Caverns

🏠 Greenhow Hill, Pateley Bridge 🕐 Mid-Feb-mid-Jan: 9am-6pm Mon-Fri & Sun, 9am-7pm Sat ⓦ stumpcrosscaverns.co.uk

These caves were formed over a period of half a million years: trickles of underground water in time formed intertwining passages of all shapes and sizes. Sealed off in the last Ice Age, the caves were only discovered in the 1850s, when lead miners sank a mine shaft into the caverns.

Skipton Castle

🏠 Skipton 🕐 10am-5pm daily (from 11am Sun) ⓦ skiptoncastle.co.uk

The market town of Skipton is still one of the largest auctioning and stockraising centres in the north. It takes its name from the Anglo-Saxon *Sceap on* (sheep town),

and its bucolic (but fiercely competitive) Sheep Day is held each year in July.

Skipton's 11th-century castle was almost entirely rebuilt by Robert de Clifford in the 14th century. Beautiful Conduit Court was added by Henry, Lord Clifford, in the reign of Henry VIII. The central yew tree was planted by Lady Anne Clifford in 1659 to mark restoration work to the castle after Civil War damage.

↑ Weird and wonderful limestone formations in Stump Cross Caverns

A LONG WALK
MALHAM

Distance 11 km (7 miles) **Walking time** 4 hours
Terrain Malham Cove is steep but the Tarn area is flatter

The Malham area, shaped by glacial erosion 10,000 years ago, has one of Great Britain's most dramatic limestone landscapes. The walk from Malham village can take over 4 hours if you pause to enjoy the viewpoints and take a detour to Gordale Scar. Those who are short of time tend to go only as far as Malham Cove. This vast natural amphitheatre, formed by a huge geological tear, is like a giant boot-heel mark in the landscape. Above lie the deep crevices of Malham Lings, where rare flora such as hart's-tongue flourish. Other plants grow in the lime-rich Malham Tarn.

Locator Map
For more detail see p372

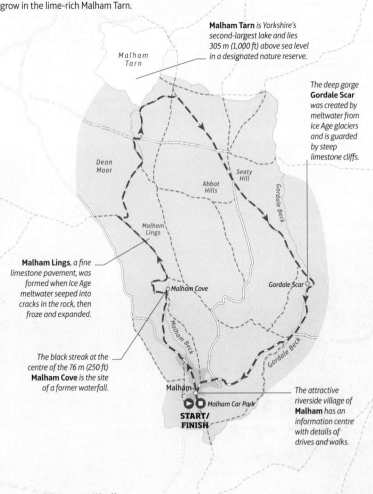

Malham Tarn *is Yorkshire's second-largest lake and lies 305 m (1,000 ft) above sea level in a designated nature reserve.*

Malham Tarn

The deep gorge **Gordale Scar** *was created by meltwater from Ice Age glaciers and is guarded by steep limestone cliffs.*

Dean Moor

Seaty Hill

Abbot Hills

Gordale Beck

Malham Lings

Malham Lings, *a fine limestone pavement, was formed when Ice Age meltwater seeped into cracks in the rock, then froze and expanded.*

Malham Cove

Gordale Scar

The black streak at the centre of the 76 m (250 ft) **Malham Cove** *is the site of a former waterfall.*

Malham Beck

Gordale Beck

Malham

Malham Car Park
START/FINISH

The attractive riverside village of **Malham** *has an information centre with details of drives and walks.*

| 0 metres | 800 |
| 0 yards | 800 |

N ↑

389

4

FOUNTAINS ABBEY

Studley Royal Estate, Ripon 10am-5pm daily (Oct-Mar: to dusk if earlier) 24 & 25 Dec nationaltrust.org.uk

Nestling in the wooded valley of the River Skell are the extensive sandstone ruins of Fountains Abbey and the outstanding water garden of Studley Royal. Built using stones taken from the Skell valley, Fountains Abbey was founded by Benedictine monks in 1132 and joined the Cistercian order three years later. By the mid-12th century it had become the wealthiest abbey in Britain.

The iconic abbey fell into ruin during the Dissolution of the Monasteries. In 1720, John Aislabie, the MP for Ripon and Chancellor of the Exchequer, developed the land and forest of the abbey ruins. He began work, continued by his son William, on the famous water garden, statuary and Classical temples in the grounds. Studley Royal and the Abbey became a World Heritage Site in 1986. The abbey buildings were designed to reflect the Cistercians' desire for simplicity and austerity. The abbey frequently dispensed charity to the poor and the sick, as well as travellers.

Within the grounds, the Fountains Hall was built by Sir Stephen Proctor around 1604, with stones from the abbey ruins. Its design is attributed to architect Robert Smythson. The building included a great hall with a minstrels' gallery and an entrance flanked by Classical columns. Also at the site is the sumptuous Victorian Gothic St Mary's Church, built by architect William Burges in 1871–8. Inside, the choirstalls are decorated with multi-coloured carved parrots. Nearby, the domed Temple of Fame features columns that look like sandstone but are constructed of hollow wood.

The Temple of Piety, a picturesque garden house that was originally dedicated to Hercules

PICTURE PERFECT
Surprise View

Also known as Anne Boleyn's Seat, this Gothic alcove was built in the late 18th century, to replace a headless statue of Henry VIII's second wife that once stood here. From this spot, visitors can take particularly fine photos of the abbey and the River Skell.

Interior of the Chapel of Nine Altars, which stands at the east end of the church

THE DISSOLUTION OF THE MONASTERIES (1536-40)

By the early 16th century, the monasteries owned one-sixth of all English land, and their annual income was four times that of the Crown. Henry VIII ordered the closure of all religious houses in 1536, acquiring their wealth in the process. This provoked an uprising of Catholic northerners led by Robert Aske, but the rebellion failed and Aske and others were executed for conspiracy. The Dissolution was continued by Thomas Cromwell, the king's chief minister, who became known as "the hammer of the monks".

Visitors exploring the grounds around Fountains Abbey, fronted by a glassy lake

↑ Traditional farmhouse amid stone-walled fields in the North York Moors

5

NORTH YORK MOORS NATIONAL PARK

⌂ North Yorkshire ⌑ Danby ⊟ Pickering (Easter–Oct)
ℹ Sutton Bank; Moors Centre, Danby; www.northyork moors.org.uk

The glorious Cleveland Way walking trail sums up the appeal of this beautiful area, crossing wild heather moorland and lush, farm-studded valleys to travel down Yorkshire's spectacular east coast, where quaint fishing villages nestle beneath plunging cliffs.

①
Whitby

⌂ 72 km (45 miles) NE of York ℹ Langbourne Rd; www.discoverwhitby.com

Once a whaling port, Whitby still has a working fishing fleet but today is more famous for its magnificent ruined abbey, its jet jewellery, and its role in Bram Stoker's *Dracula*, adding an intriguing overlay of Gothic horror to this picturesque harbour town. In the Victorian era, the red-roofed cottages at the foot of the east cliff were filled with workshops crafting the distinctive black gem into jewellery and ornaments. Today, the shops that have replaced them sell antique and modern pieces.

Whitby is divided into two by the estuary of the River Esk. The Old Town, with its pretty cobbled streets and pastel-hued houses, huddles round the harbour. Above it is St Mary's Parish Church, with a wood interior reputedly fitted by ships' carpenters.

Towering on the cliffs are the ruins of the 13th-century Whitby Abbey, still used as a landmark by mariners, just as they were when Stoker landed his vampiric Count here. From the atmospheric ruins you get a fine view over the harbour, strewn with colourful nets.

On the opposite side of the harbour is an imposing bronze clifftop statue of the explorer Captain James Cook (1728–79), who was apprenticed as a teenager to a Whitby shipping firm. The house where he lived is now the **Captain Cook Memorial Museum**.

The **Whitby Museum and Pannett Art Gallery** has a collection of 19th- and 20th-century paintings and objects illustrating local history, such

> **INSIDER TIP**
> **Whitby Goth Weekends**
>
> Whitby's Dracula connection now attracts more than 8,000 self-identifying Goths to festivals every year in April and October *(www.whitby gothweekend.co.uk)*.

as jet jewellery and Captain Cook artifacts, as well as a costume gallery.

Captain Cook Memorial Museum

 Grape Lane
Feb-Mar: 11am-3pm daily; Apr-Jan: 9:45am-5pm daily
cookmuseumwhitby.co.uk

Whitby Museum and Pannett Art Gallery

Pannett Park
9:30am-4:30pm Tue-Sun
whitbymuseum.org.uk

---

② Robin Hood's Bay

8 km (5 miles) S of Whitby
Whitby Whitby

Legend has it that Robin Hood (*p340*) kept boats here in case he needed to make a quick getaway. The village has a history as a smugglers' haven, and many houses contain ingenious hiding places for contraband. The cobbled main street is so steep that visitors must leave their vehicles in the car park at the top.

Below, narrow streets full of colour-washed stone cottages collect around a quaint quay. There is a beach with rock pools, popular with children and with jet- and fossil-hunters. At low tide, the pleasant walk south to Boggle Hole takes 15 minutes, but you need to keep an eye on the tides.

---

③ Mount Grace Priory

On A19 NE of Northallerton
Northallerton then bus
Apr-Oct: 10am-6pm daily; Nov-Mar: 10am-4pm Sat & Sun english-heritage.org.uk

In use from 1398 until 1539, this is the best-preserved Carthusian or charterhouse monastery in England. The monks took a vow of silence and lived in solitary cells, each with its own garden and an angled hatch so that he would not even see the person serving his food. The monks only met at matins, vespers and feast-day services. Attempts at escape by those who could not endure the rigour of the rules were punished by imprisonment. The ruins of the priory include the former prison, gatehouse and outer court, barns and cells. The 14th-century church, the best-preserved section of the site, was only rarely used by the community. A cell has been reconstructed to give an impression of monastic life.

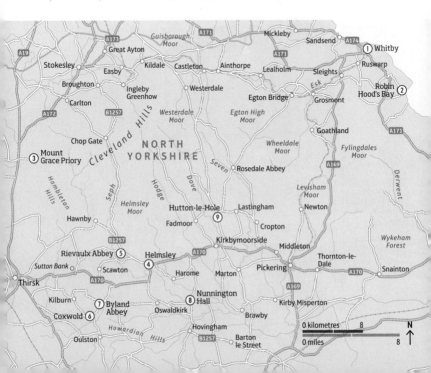

④ Helmsley

📍 40 km (25 miles) N of York 🚌 ℹ️ Town Hall, Market Place; www.visithelmsley.co.uk

This pretty market town is noted for its 12th-century castle, now an imposing ruin. The walled garden beneath the castle ruins was built in 1759 and has a lovely herbaceous border.

Other attractions include the town's church, with its 19th-century murals, and the Helmsley Brewing Co., which produces fine craft beers.

⑤ Rievaulx Abbey

📍 5 km (3 miles) W of Helmsley 🚂 Thirsk or Scarborough, then bus or taxi 🕐 Mar–Oct: 10am–6pm daily; Nov–Feb: 10am–4pm Sat & Sun 🌐 englishheritage.org.uk

Rievaulx is perhaps the finest abbey in the area, due to both its

dramatic setting in the steep wooded valley of the River Rye and its extensive remains. It is surrounded by steep banks that form natural barriers against the outside world. Monks of the Cistercian order from Clairvaux in France founded this, their first major monastery in Britain, in 1132. The main buildings were finished before 1200. The interior of the chapel, kitchens and infirmary gives an idea of monastic life.

⑥ Coxwold

📍 13 km (8 miles) SW of Helmsley ℹ️ 49 Market Place, Thirsk; www.coxwoldvillage.co.uk

Situated just within the bounds of the National Park, this charming village nestles at the foot of the Howardian Hills. Its pretty houses are built from local stone, and the 15th-century church has some fine Georgian box pews and an impressive octagonal tower. But Coxwold is best known as the home of

GREAT VIEW Sutton Bank

There's a stunning view across the Vale of York to the Pennines from this dramatic escarpment, 8 km (5 miles) west of Rievaulx. It's a steep climb, but a great visitor centre and café await at the top.

novelist and parson Laurence Sterne (1713–68), whose works include *Tristram Shandy* and *A Sentimental Journey*.

Sterne moved here in 1760 as the church curate. He rented a rambling house that he named **Shandy Hall** after a Yorkshire expression meaning eccentric. Originally built as a timber-framed, open-halled house in the 15th century, it was modernized in the 17th century and Sterne later added a façade. His grave lies beside the porch at Coxwold's church.

Shandy Hall

⊘⊘🏠 🕐 House: May–Sep: Wed & Sun for guided tours only; Gardens: May–Sep: 11am–4:30pm Sun–Fri 🌐 laurencesternetrust.org.uk

Byland Abbey

⌖ 2.5 km (1.5 miles) NE of Coxwold 🚂 Thirsk 🚌 From York or Helmsley ⏰ Apr-Aug: 10am-5pm daily; Sep-Oct: 10am-4pm Tue-Sun; Oct-Mar: 10am-3pm Sat & Sun 🌐 english-heritage.org.uk

This Cistercian monastery was founded in 1177 by monks from Furness Abbey in Cumbria. It featured what was then the largest Cistercian church in Britain, 100 m (328 ft) long and 41 m (135 ft) wide across the transepts. The layout of the monastery, including cloisters and the west front of the church, is still visible, as is the green and yellow glazed tile floor. Fine workmanship is shown in carved stone capitals, kept in the small museum.

In 1322 the Battle of Byland was fought nearby, and King Edward II narrowly escaped capture when the invading Scottish army learned that he was dining with the abbot. In his hurry to escape, the king had to leave many treasures behind, which were looted by the invading soldiers.

↑ The ruins of Rievaulx Abbey, once one of the wealthiest in England

NORTH YORKSHIRE MOORS RAILWAY

In the 19th century the arrival of the railway across the York moors to the east coast provided valuable trade transport and also brought welcome holidaymakers to Whitby. The railway link between Whitby and Pickering via Grosmont eventually closed in the 1960s, but thanks to volunteer locals it was reopened as a heritage line and is now one of Britain's most popular steam railways. The 38-km (24-mile) journey is delightful, as are the stations along the line, each restored to represent a different era in railway history - pre-World War I and 1950s, for example. The celebrity among them is Goathland, which became Hogsmeade station in the first Harry Potter film.

Nunnington Hall

⌖ Nunnington 🚂 Malton, then bus or taxi ⏰ Feb-Oct: 10:30am-5pm Tue-Sun; Nov-mid-Dec: 10:30am-4pm Sat & Sun 🌐 national trust.org.uk

Set in alluring surroundings, this manor house has a mix of architectural styles, including features from the Elizabethan and Stuart periods. A notable feature is the use of the broken pediment (the upper arch is left unjoined). It was a family home until 1952, when it was given to the National Trust. The panelling in the Oak Hall is striking, extending over the screen to the Great Staircase. Nunnington's collection of 22 miniature furnished period rooms is popular with visitors.

A mid-16th-century tenant, Dr Robert Huickes, physician to Henry VIII, is best known for advising Elizabeth I that she should not, at the age of 32, consider having any children.

Hutton-le-Hole

⌖ 15 km (9.5 miles) NE of Helmsley 🚂 Pickering then bus (seasonal service) ℹ Ryedale Folk Museum

This picturesque village is characterized by a spacious green, grazed by roaming sheep and surrounded by houses, an inn and shops. Its cottages, some with date panels, are made from limestone with red pantiled roofs. In the village centre is the excellent **Ryedale Folk Museum**, which records the lifestyle of an agricultural community from the Iron Age to the 1950s using ancient artifacts and reconstructed buildings. Visitors can step inside an Iron Age roundhouse, a Tudor manor house, a Victorian cottage and a 19th-century photography studio.

Ryedale Folk Museum

♿ ⏰ Mid-Feb-Nov: 10am-4pm daily 🌐 ryedalefolk museum.co.uk

EXPERIENCE MORE

6

Harrogate

North Yorkshire
The Royal Baths,
Crescent Rd; www.
visitharrogate.co.uk

Between 1880 and World War I,
Harrogate was the north's
leading spa town, with nearly
90 medicinal springs. The spa
waters may not currently be in
use, but you can still go for a
Turkish bath in the century-old
Harrogate Turkish Baths, a
visual feast of tiled Victoriana.

At the **Royal Pump Room
Museum**, you can still sample
the famously iron-rich waters.

Harrogate is also known for
the ornamental **RHS Garden
Harlow Carr**, owned by the
Royal Horticultural Society,
and for its spring and autumn
Flower Shows.

Harrogate Turkish Baths

The Royal Baths,
Crescent Rd Times vary,
check website turkish
bathsharrogate.co.uk

Royal Pump Room Museum

Crown Pl 10am-
4pm Mon-Sat, noon-4pm Sun
harrogate.gov.uk

RHS Garden Harlow Carr

Crag Lane Mar-
Oct: 9:30am-6pm daily; Nov-
Feb: 9:30am-4pm daily
rhs.org.uk

7

Ripley

North Yorkshire From
Harrogate or Ripon
harrogate.gov.uk

Since the 1320s, when the first
generation of the Ingilby family
lived in an early incarnation of
the castle, this village has been
largely made up of castle
employees. In the 1820s, Sir
William Amcotts Ingilby was
so entranced by a village in
France that he created a
similar one here. Present-day
Ripley has a cobbled market
square and quaint cottages.
Ripley Castle was where
Oliver Cromwell (p49) stayed
after the Battle of Marston
Moor. The grounds contain
two lakes and a deer park, as
well as more formal gardens.

Ripley Castle

Ripley Apr-
Oct: 9:30am-5pm daily; Nov-
Mar: 10am-4pm daily
ripleycastle.co.uk

→
Sunset panorama of
Knaresborough, with the
River Nidd in the foreground

8

Ripon

North Yorkshire From
Harrogate Town Hall,
Marketplace; www.
discoverripon.org

Ripon, a charming small city, is
best known for the Cathedral
of St Peter and St Wilfrid, built
above a 7th-century Saxon
crypt, which is less than 3 m
(10 ft) high and just over
2 m (7 ft) wide. It is held to
be the oldest complete crypt
in England. The cathedral is
known for its collection of
misericords which include
pagan and Old Testament
subjects. The architectural
historian Sir Nikolaus Pevsner
(1902–83) considered the
cathedral's West Front the
finest in England.

Newby Hall, just outside
Ripon, has been in the hands
of the current family since
1748. The central part of the
present house was built in the
late 17th century, in the style
of Sir Christopher Wren. You
will find 10 ha (25 acres) of
gardens, each section of which
is planted to come into flower
during a specific season.

Newby Hall

Near Ripon
Apr-Sep: 11am-5pm Tue-
Sun newbyhall.com

↑ A room with typcial Moorish design
at the Harrogate Turkish Baths

Did You Know?

Prophecies of Mother Shipton's that came true include the Great Fire of London and the World Wars.

9

Knaresborough

 North Yorkshire
From Harrogate 9 Castle Courtyard, Market Place; 01423 866886

Perched precipitously above the River Nidd is one of England's oldest towns, mentioned in the Domesday Book of 1086. Its historic streets are now lined with fine 18th-century houses. Nearby is **Mother Shipton's Cave**, reputedly England's oldest tourist attraction. It was first opened in 1630 as the birthplace of Ursula Sontheil (c 1488–1561), a famous local prophetess.

Mother Shipton's Cave

Prophecy House, High Bridge Mar: 10am–5:30pm Sat & Sun; Apr–Oct: 10am–4pm daily
mothershipton.co.uk

10

Scarborough

North Yorkshire
Stephen Joseph Theatre, Westborough; www.discoveryorkshire coast.com

A spa town since the 1600s, Scarborough has two beaches; the South Bay, with its amusement arcades nearby, contrasts with the quieter North Bay. Anne Brontë (p405) is buried in St Mary's Church. Bronze and Iron Age relics found on the site of the **castle** are at the **Rotunda Museum** (1828–9). Works by local artist Atkinson Grimshaw (1836–93) hang in **Scarborough Art Gallery**.

Scarborough Castle

Castle Rd
10am–6pm daily (Mar: to 4pm Wed–Sun; Nov–Feb: to 4pm Sat & Sun) english-heritage.org.uk

Rotunda Museum

Vernon Rd
10am–5pm Tue–Sun
scarboroughmuseums trust.com

Scarborough Art Gallery

The Crescent
10am–5pm Tue–Sun
scarboroughmuseums trust.com

EAT

The Sportsman's Arms

Dine on local game at this converted farmhouse on the edge of the moors.

Pateley Bridge, nr Harrogate sports mans-arms.co.uk

£££

Drum and Monkey

Seafood specialist with classic fare like Scottish salmon.

5 Montpellier Gardens, Harrogate Sun drumandmonkey. co.uk

£££

General Tarleton Inn

This 18th-century coaching inn serves a menu based on the day's best ingredients.

Harrogate Rd, Ferrensby, nr Knaresborough generaltarleton.co.uk

£££

STAY

Beverley Arms
Beautiful rooms are complemented by a lounge bar and a modern restaurant.

◨ 25 North Bar Within, Beverley ⓦ beverley arms.co.uk

£ £ £

The Old Lodge
This grand eighteenth-century Tudor lodge makes an ideal base for exploring the Moors.

◨ Old Maltongate, Malton ⓦ theoldlodge malton.co.uk

£ £ £

Tickton Grange
Wooden sleigh beds and Japanese-crafted tables are some of the creative features here.

◨ Tickton, Beverley ⓦ ticktongrange.co.uk

£ £ £

---

⑪

Burton Agnes

◨ On A614, near Driffield, East Yorkshire ⓡ Driffield then bus ◷ Apr–Oct: 11am–5pm daily
ⓦ burtonagnes.com

A red-brick Elizabethan mansion, Burton Agnes has changed little since the 1600s. The entrance hall has a fine alabaster chimney piece, and the massive oak staircase is an impressive example of woodcarving from the era.

---

⑫

Bempton Cliffs and Flamborough Head

◨ East Yorkshire ⓡ Bempton ⓦ Bridlington ⓘ Bempton Cliffs Visitor Centre; www.rspb.org.uk

Bempton, which consists of 8 km (5 miles) of steep chalk cliffs between Speeton and

Flamborough Head, is the largest breeding seabird colony in England and is famous for its puffins. The ledges and fissures provide ideal nest-sites for more than 100,000 pairs of birds. May, June and July are the best bird-watching months.

The spectacular cliffs are best seen from the north side of the Flamborough Head peninsula.

---

⑬

Eden Camp

◨ Malton, North Yorkshire ⓡ Malton then taxi ◷ 10am–5pm daily ◷ 24 Dec–12 Jan ⓦ edencamp.co.uk

This award-winning museum explores military and social history during the World Wars. Italian and German prisoners of war were kept at Eden

Flamborough Head's dramatic coastal landscape; a pair of puffins, among the residents of Bempton Cliffs *(inset)* ↓

Camp between 1939 and 1948. Today, some original huts built by Italian prisoners in 1942 are used as part of the museum, with period tableaux and a soundtrack.

 14

Beverley

 East Yorkshire
East Riding Treasure House, Champney Rd; www.visithullandeast yorkshire.com

The origins of Beverley date back to the 8th century, when Old Beverley served as a retreat for John, later Bishop of York, who was canonized for his healing powers. Over the centuries Beverley grew as a medieval sanctuary town.

The skyline is dominated by the twin towers of **Beverley Minster**, the resting place of St John of Beverley. The decorated nave is the earliest surviving part of the building, dating back to the early 1300s. It is famous for its 16th-century choirstalls and 68 misericords.

St Mary's Church has a 13th-century chancel and houses Britain's largest number of medieval stone carvings of musical instruments. The

↑ The ornate choirstalls and magnificent organ at Beverley Minster

brightly painted 16th-century Minstrel Pillar is particularly notable. On the richly sculpted doorway of St Michael's Chapel is the grinning pilgrim rabbit said to have inspired Lewis Carroll's White Rabbit in *Alice's Adventures in Wonderland*.

Beverley Minster

 Minster Yard
9am–4pm Mon–Sat, noon–5pm Sun beverleyminster.org.uk

---

15 (EH)

Wharram Percy

North Yorkshire
Malton then taxi
During daylight hours
english-heritage.org.uk

Discovered in 1948, this medieval village site flourished between the 12th and 14th centuries, when the Percy family lived here. However, the village suffered during the Black Death (1348–9), and with the price of wool rising, local landowners evicted families to use the land for sheep farming. By 1500, the village was deserted. Between 1948 and 2012, excavations unearthed evidence of a 30-household community, with two manors and the remains of a medieval church.

16

Burton Constable

Nr Hull, East Yorkshire
Hull then taxi Apr–Oct: noon–5pm Tue–Sun
burtonconstable.com

The Constable family has lived at Burton Constable Hall since work began on it in Elizabethan times in 1570. The house was altered in the 18th century by Thomas Lightholer, Thomas Atkinson and James Wyatt. Today Burton Constable has 30 rooms with Georgian and Victorian interiors. A fine collection of Chippendale furniture and family portraits dating from the 16th century are on display. The family still lives in the south wing.

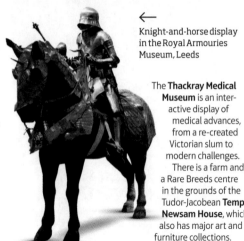

Knight-and-horse display in the Royal Armouries Museum, Leeds

The **Thackray Medical Museum** is an interactive display of medical advances, from a re-created Victorian slum to modern challenges. There is a farm and a Rare Breeds centre in the grounds of the Tudor-Jacobean **Temple Newsam House**, which also has major art and furniture collections.

17
Leeds

🅐Leeds 🚆🚌 ℹ️Headrow; www.visitleeds.co.uk

The third largest of Britain's provincial cities, Leeds was at its most prosperous during the Victorian period. An impressive legacy from this era is a series of ornate, covered shopping arcades, among them the County Arcade, decorated with faience and marble. Today, Leeds also boasts a thriving cultural scene. Opera productions at **The Grand Theatre** are of superb quality. The **Leeds Art Gallery** exhibits British 20th-century art, Victorian paintings and late 19th-century French art, including works by Signac, Courbet and Sisley.

In a 19th-century woollen mill, the **Leeds Industrial Museum** uses original equipment, recorded sounds and models in 19th-century workers' clothes to trace the history of the ready-to-wear industry in Leeds. The **Leeds City Museum** charts the city's history with ethnographical and archaeological exhibits.

In a striking development by the River Aire, the **Royal Armouries Museum** is home to a vast array of weaponry from around the world.

The Grand Theatre
🌐 🅐46 New Briggate
🌐leedsgrandtheatre.com

Leeds Art Gallery
🌐🕐 🅐The Headrow
🕐10am–5pm Tue–Sat, noon–4pm Sun 🚫Public hols
🌐leedsartgallery.co.uk

Leeds Industrial Museum
🌐🕐 🅐Canal Rd, Armley
☎0113 378 3173 🕐10am–5pm Tue–Sat, 1–5pm Sun

Leeds City Museum
🌐🕐 🅐Millennium Sq
☎0113 378 5001 🕐10am–5pm Tue–Sun & public hols

Royal Armouries Museum
🌐🕐 🅐Armouries Drive
🕐10am–5pm daily
🌐royalarmouries.org

Thackray Medical Museum
🌐🕐 🅐Beckett St
🕐Times vary, check website
🌐thackraymedicalmuseum.co.uk

Temple Newsam House
🌐🌐🕐 🅐Off A63 ☎0113 336 7461 🕐10am–5pm Tue–Sun 🚫Jan, 25 & 26 Dec

→

Hull's Queen Victoria Square, dominated by the grand Maritime Museum

18
Harewood House

🅐Nr Leeds 🚆Leeds then bus 🕐Apr–Oct: 11am–4pm daily 🌐harewood.org

Designed by John Carr in 1759, the Palladian Harewood House has an unrivalled collection of 18th-century furniture made by Yorkshire-born Thomas Chippendale (1711–79), plus paintings by Italian and English artists. The grounds by Capability Brown (p24) include the Harewood Bird Garden.

Kingston upon Hull

East Yorkshire
Paragon Interchange;
www.visithullandeast
yorkshire.com

Hull experienced the wrath of German bombers in World War II and later suffered decades of industrial decline. However, its 2017 designation as European City of Culture and new investment have significantly turned the city's fortunes around.

Start exploring in the Old Town, with its cobbled streets, old warehouses and 17th-century merchants' houses such as **Wilberforce House**, which examines the trans-atlantic slave trade that William Wilberforce campaigned to abolish. Also here are the **Streetlife** transport museum and the **Hull and East Riding**

Did You Know?

The boiled sweet was invented in Hull in the 19th century.

Museum, whose fascinating local history displays include a reconstructed mammoth. Down at the River Hull, the moored *Arctic Corsair* trawler tells the history of Hull's deep-sea fishing industry.

In the city centre, the **Maritime Museum** exhibits an ornate whale-bone bench and an engaging display of rope knots. Nearby, a 1927 grand Neo-Classical building houses the **Ferens Art Gallery**, whose collection offers a mix of Old Masters, such as Frans Hals and Canaletto; modern artists including David Hockey and Lucian Freud; and contemporary artists such as Helen Chadwick and Gillian Wearing.

Wilberforce House, Streetlife, Hull and East Riding Museum
Museums Quarter, between High St & the River Hull 10am–5pm Mon-Sat, 11am–4:30pm Sun hcandl.co.uk

Maritime Museum
Queen Victoria Sq 10am–4:30pm Mon-Sat, 11am–4pm Sun hcandl.co.uk

Ferens Art Gallery
Queen Victoria Sq 10am–5pm Mon-Sat (to 7:30pm Thu), 11am–4:30pm Sun hcandl.co.uk/ferens

EAT

Thieving Harry's
A converted warehouse bistro serving burgers and sandwiches.
73 Humber St, Hull
thievingharrys.co.uk
£££

Hitchcocks
The first person to book each night at this innovative restaurant gets to pick that evening's national cuisine. Advance booking essential.
1 Bishop Lane, Hull
Mon & Sun
hitchcocksrestaurant.co.uk
£££

Humber Fish Co
A smart bistro with nautical decor and locally sourced food.
Humber St, Hull Mon & Tue
humberfishco.co.uk
£££

Holderness and Spurn Head

🚗 East Yorkshire
🚆 Hull (Paragon St) then bus ℹ️ 11-17 Newbegin, Hornsea; 01964 536404

Holderness's flat landscape is the result of erosion higher up the coast. Tiny bits of rock washed down by the sea gradually accumulated to form a sandbank that, by 1669, was large enough to be colonized. The Spurn Peninsula is a 6-km (35-mile) spit of land whose flora, fauna and birdlife are protected by the Yorkshire Wildlife Trust.

Bradford

🚗 Bradford ✈️🚆🚌 ℹ️ City Hall, Centenary Square; www.visitbradford.com

In the 16th century, Bradford was a thriving market town, and the opening of its canal in 1774 boosted trade. By 1850, it was the world's capital for worsted (fabric made from

Bradford Town Hall and Centenary Square at night; mill machinery at the Bradford Industrial Museum *(inset)*

closely twisted wool). Many of the city's well-preserved civic and industrial buildings date from this period, such as Market Street's Wool Exchange. The **National Science and**

BRADFORD'S ASIAN COMMUNITY

Immigrants from the Indian subcontinent came to Bradford in the 1950s to work in the mills. With the decline of the textile industry, many began small businesses, especially in the food sector. As Indian cuisine became more popular, these restaurants thrived, and today there are over 200 in the city serving the spiced dishes of the Indian subcontinent.

Media Museum explores the history of image and sound. Interactive television galleries let visitors operate cameras "on set" and read the news; fans of gaming can play on classic arcade machines and consoles. The museum also has three cinemas, including an IMAX screen, and holds two film festivals each year.

Mill machinery is on display at the **Bradford Industrial Museum**, housed in an original spinning mill. Saltaire, a Victorian industrial village, is on the outskirts of the city. Created by Sir Titus Salt for his Salts Mill workers, it was completed in 1873. **Salts Mill** now contains a fascinating exhibition that explores Saltaire's history, while the **1853 Gallery** has the world's

largest collection of works by David Hockney, who was born in Bradford.

National Science and Media Museum

ⓉⓈ 🅰Pictureville 🕐10am-6pm daily 🅦nationalmedia museum.org.uk

Bradford Industrial Museum

Ⓢ 🅰Moorside Mills, Moorside Rd 🕐10am-4pm Tue-Fri, 11am-4pm Sat & Sun 🅦bradfordmuseums.org

Salts Mill and 1853 Gallery

ⓉⓈⓈ 🅰Salts Mill, Victoria Rd 🕐10am-5:30pm Mon-Fri, 10am-6pm Sat & Sun 🅦saltsmill.org.uk

---

㉒

Halifax

🅰Calderdale 🚉🚌 ℹ️Blackledge; www. visitcalderdale.com

Halifax's history has been influenced by textiles since the Middle Ages. Until the mid-15th century cloth production was modest but vital enough to contribute towards the creation of the 13th-century Gibbet Law, which stated that anyone caught stealing cloth could be executed. There is a replica of the gibbet, a forerunner of the guillotine, at the bottom of Gibbet Street. Many of Halifax's 18th- and 19th-century buildings owe their existence to wealthy cloth traders. Sir Charles Barry (1795–1860), architect of the Houses of Parliament, was commissioned by the Crossley family to design the Town Hall. They also paid for the landscaping of the People's Park by the creator of the Crystal Palace, Sir Joseph Paxton (1801–65). Thomas Bradley's 18th-century Piece Hall was where wool merchants once sold their cloth, trading in one of the 315 "Merchants' Rooms". It has a beautifully restored Italianate courtyard where Halifax's popular market takes place.

Eureka! is the hands-on National Children's Museum, with exhibits such as the Giant Mouth Machine.

Eureka!

ⓈⓈ 🅰Discovery Rd 🕐School hols: 10am-5pm daily; term time: 10am-4pm Tue-Fri, 10am-5pm Sat & Sun 🅦eureka.org.uk

㉓

Hebden Bridge

🅰Calderdale 🚉 ℹ️Butler's Wharf; www.visitcalder dale.com

Surrounded by steep hills peppered with 19th-century mills and houses, Hebden Bridge is a trendy market town with an arts community and a strong LBGT+ presence. Against this creative and welcoming backdrop, many independent galleries, second-hand and vintage shops, and organic and vegan eateries have flourished. The town's busy events calendar includes the Hebden Bridge Arts Festival (hebdenbridge artsfestival.co.uk) held for a week at the end of June.

Walking trails head out of town in all directions, including up to nearby Heptonstall, where the poet Sylvia Plath (1932–63) is buried.

↑ Restaurants lining a street in fun and quirky Hebden Bridge

24

Hepworth Wakefield

🏛 Gallery Walk, Wakefield
🕙 10am–5pm Tue–Sun
🌐 hepworthwakefield.org

Occupying a series of stark concrete blocks by the River Calder in Wakefield, this innovative sculpture gallery is named after local artist Barbara Hepworth. Several of her pieces are on display, as well as small-scale working models and her original workbench and tools. The gallery also hosts temporary exhibitions showcasing other 20th-century British artists.

EAT

The Hawthorn

This smart gastropub in an old clockmaker's shop serves beautifully presented and locally sourced food. Expect excellent grilled meats, quail's eggs and foraged ingredients on the weekly menu.

🏛 103–109 Main St, Haworth 🚫 Mon & Tue
🌐 thehawthorn haworth.co.uk

£££

Kommune

Surrounding a central craft-beer bar, this hip, high-quality food court offers a carefully selected group of acclaimed kitchens. From stone-oven pizzas and Indian street food to rotisserie chicken and gourmet burgers, you'll be spoiled for choice.

🏛 Angel St, Sheffield
🚫 Mon 🌐 kommune.
co.uk

£££

25

National Coal Mining Museum

🚉 Wakefield 🚌 Wakefield then bus 🕙 10am–5pm daily; booking advised
🌐 ncm.org.uk

Housed in the old Caphouse Colliery, this museum offers the chance to go into a real mine shaft. An underground tour takes you 137 m (450 ft) down, equipped with a hat and a miner's lamp; warm clothing is advised.

26

Sheffield

🚉 Sheffield 🚗🚌 📍 26 High St, Rotherham;
www.welcometosheffield.co.uk

There was a time when you could find Sheffield steel cutlery on dining tables all around the British Empire. Today, only a kernel of the old industry remains, but urban renewal has made Sheffield well worth a visit.

The city centre is focused on the **Winter Garden**, a 21st-century take on a Victorian conservatory. The wood supports are designed to weather naturally among the humidity of 1,000 plants.

Nearby, the **Millennium Gallery** has a Metalwork Collection that explores the history of cutlery, while its John Ruskin Collection honours the Victorian artist, writer and philosopher.

Outside the centre, **Kelham Island Museum** includes many curious and still-functioning machines and artifacts, from house-sized steam engines to giant bombs.

Winter Garden

🏛 Surrey St 🕙 8am–8pm daily (to 6pm Sun)
🌐 sheffield.gov.uk

Millennium Gallery

♿ 🏛 Arundel Gate 🕙 10am–5pm Mon–Sat, 11am–4pm Sun 🌐 museums-sheffield.org.uk

Kelham Island Museum

🏛 Alma St 🕙 10am–4pm Mon–Thu, 11am–4:45pm Sun 🌐 simt.co.uk

27

Magna

🚉 Rotherham 🚌 Rotherham Central or Sheffield then bus 🕙 10am–5pm daily
🌐 visitmagna.co.uk

A former steel works has been converted into a huge science adventure centre, with an

↑ Sheffield's Winter Garden, ressembling the ribs of a giant whale wrapped in glass

↑ *Sitting* by
Sophie Ryder
at Yorkshire
Sculpture Park

emphasis on interactive exhibits, noise and spectacle designed to appeal to 4- to 15-year-olds. In the Air, Fire, Water and Earth Pavilions visitors can get close to a tornado, operate real diggers or discover what it's like to detonate a rock face. A show features robots that evolve and learn as they hunt each other down. There are also two outdoor areas – Sci-tek, a playground with slides and trampolines, and Aqua-tek (summer only), a water play area.

28

Yorkshire Sculpture Park

🏛 Wakefield 🚉 Wakefield then bus ⏰ 10am–5pm daily 🔒 24 & 25 Dec 🌐 ysp.org.uk

This is one of Europe's leading open-air galleries: 200 ha (500 acres) of 18th-century parkland dotted with a changing display of the work of Henry Moore, Anthony Caro, Barbara Hepworth, Ai Weiwei, Sophie Ryder, Andy Goldsworthy and others. The indoor spaces include the ambitious visitor centre, which leads on to the stunning Underground Gallery exhibition space.

29

Haworth

🏛 Bradford 🚉 Keighley
ℹ Main St; www.haworth-village.org.uk

The setting of Haworth, in bleak Pennine moorland dotted with farmsteads, has changed little since it was home to the Brontë family.

From 1820 to 1861, the Reverend Patrick Brontë, his novelist daughters Charlotte, Emily and Anne, and son Branwell, lived in what is now the **Brontë Parsonage Museum**. Built in 1778–9, the house remains decorated as it was during the 1850s, with letters, manuscripts, furniture and personal objects on display.

The nostalgic Victorian Keighley and Worth Valley Railway runs from Keighley to Oxenhope and stops at Ingrow West, Damems, Oakworth and Haworth.

Brontë Parsonage Museum

♿ 🚻 🏛 Church St ⏰ 10am–5pm daily (summer: to 5:30pm) 🔒 24–27 Dec 🌐 bronte.org.uk

---

THE BRONTË SISTERS

During a harsh, motherless childhood, Charlotte, Emily and Anne found solace in writing poems and stories. As adults, they had to work as governesses, but still published a poetry collection in 1846. The following year Charlotte's *Jane Eyre* became a bestseller, arousing interest in Emily's *Wuthering Heights* and Anne's *Agnes Grey*. After her siblings' deaths in 1848–9, Charlotte published her last novel, *Villette*, in 1852. She married in 1854, but died shortly afterwards.

THE NORTHEAST

The empty, peaceful hills, rich wildlife and panoramic vistas of the Northumberland National Park belie the northeast's turbulent past. Warring Scots and English, skirmishing tribes, cattle drovers and whisky smugglers have all left traces on ancient routes through the Cheviot Hills. Slicing through the southern edge of the national park is the famous reminder of the Romans' 400-year occupation of Britain – Hadrian's Wall, the northern boundary of their empire.

Conflict between the Scots and English continued for 1,000 years after the Romans departed, and even after the 1603 union between the two crowns, which left the border much further north. A chain of massive crenellated medieval castles punctuates the coastline, while other forts that once defended the northern flank of England along the River Tweed lie mostly in ruins. Seventh-century Northumbria was the cradle of Christianity under St Aidan, until its development was stymied by Viking violence from 793 onwards, as the Scandinavian invaders raided the monasteries.

The influence of the Industrial Revolution, around the mouths of the rivers Tyne, Wear and Tees, made Newcastle upon Tyne the north's main centre for coal mining and shipbuilding.

North Sea

FARNE
ISLANDS
8

9 BAMBURGH
○ Seahouses

○ Embleton

ALNWICK
12 CASTLE
A1 ○ Alnmouth
10 WARKWORTH CASTLE
○ Newton-on-
the-Moor   ○ Amble
Longhorsley ○ Widdrington
orpeth **A697**
A1068 ○ Newbiggin-by-
the-Sea
:annington ○ Ashington
A1 ○ Blyth
○ Cramlington
A189
Newcastle
✈ **International**
Airport ○ Whitley Bay
Gosforth **A19** ○ Tynemouth
A69 ⚓ ○ South Shields
2 NEWCASTLE UPON TYNE
Gateshead ○
TYNE AND WEAR
○ Sunderland
16 BEAMISH OPEN AIR MUSEUM
○ Stanley ○ Chester-le-Street
Lanchester ○ ○ Houghton-le-Spring
A691 **A690**
DURHAM **1**
A1(M) ○ Peterlee
○ Crook ○ Wheatley Hill
Spennymoor ○ **A19**
Bishop ○ ○ Sedgefield ○ Hartlepool
Auckland
A688 **A68** ○ Newton
Aycliffe ○ Billingham ○ Redcar
Tees Stockton- Saltburn-by-
on-Tees the-Sea
○ Darlington ○ Middlesbrough ○ Loftus
A66
○ Yarm REDCAR AND
Scotch ○ Stokesley CLEVELAND **A171**
Corner ○ Whitby
○ Richmond Grosmont ○ Sleights ○ ○ Robin Hood's Bay
A1
V
YORKSHIRE AND THE **A171**
HUMBER REGION
p370

→ *Amsterdam*

0 kilometres   20
0 miles   20

N ↑

❶
DURHAM

🏛 County Durham 🚉 Durham ℹ Market Place; www.thisis durham.com

A beautiful medieval city, Durham has a magnificent Romanesque cathedral and a castle standing next to it, which has been the home of Durham University since the early 19th century. Together these historic buildings form a UNESCO World Heritage Site.

The city of Durham was built on Island Hill or "Dunholm" in 995. This rocky peninsula, which defies the course of the River Wear's route to the sea, was chosen as the last resting place for the remains of St Cuthbert. The relics of the Venerable Bede were brought to the site 27 years later. Durham Cathedral, built from 1093 to 1274, stands on the final resting place of St Cuthbert and is known for its striking geometric patterning. Durham Castle served as the Episcopal Palace until 1832, when Bishop William van Mildert gave it up and surrendered part of his income to found Britain's third university. It is now open to the public for daily guided tours. The 23-hectare (57-acre) peninsula has many footpaths, views and buildings.

Did You Know?

Durham Cathedral and Castle was one of the world's first World Heritage Sites.

CATHEDRAL ARCHITECTURE

The vast dimensions of the columns, piers and vaults, and the giant lozenge and chevron, trellis and dogtooth patterns carved into the stone columns, are the main innovative features of Durham Cathedral. It is believed that 11th- and 12th-century architects such as Bishop Ranulph Flambard tried to unify all parts of the structure. This can be seen in the south aisle of the nave below.

Old Fulling Mill, a largely 18th-century building, houses a museum of archaeology.

Monastic Kitchen

Prebend's footbridge, which dates from 1777

Church of St Mary the Less

College Green

College Gatehouse

The impressive Norman structures of Durham Castle and Cathedral ↑

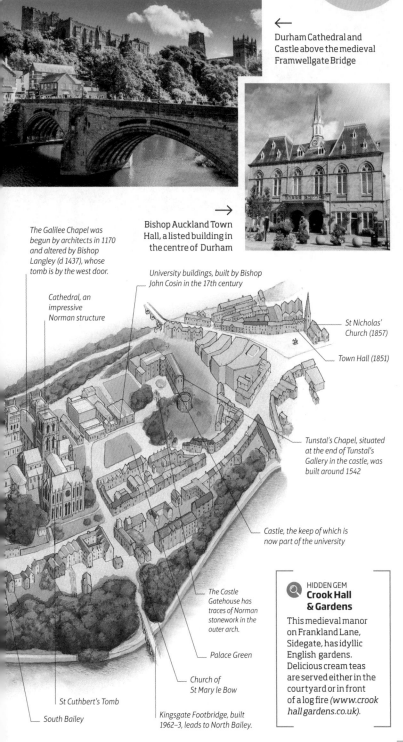

← Durham Cathedral and Castle above the medieval Framwellgate Bridge

→ Bishop Auckland Town Hall, a listed building in the centre of Durham

The Galilee Chapel was begun by architects in 1170 and altered by Bishop Langley (d 1437), whose tomb is by the west door.

Cathedral, an impressive Norman structure

University buildings, built by Bishop John Cosin in the 17th century

St Nicholas' Church (1857)

Town Hall (1851)

Tunstal's Chapel, situated at the end of Tunstal's Gallery in the castle, was built around 1542

Castle, the keep of which is now part of the university

The Castle Gatehouse has traces of Norman stonework in the outer arch.

Palace Green

St Cuthbert's Tomb

South Bailey

Church of St Mary le Bow

Kingsgate Footbridge, built 1962–3, leads to North Bailey.

HIDDEN GEM
Crook Hall & Gardens

This medieval manor on Frankland Lane, Sidegate, has idyllic English gardens. Delicious cream teas are served either in the courtyard or in front of a log fire *(www.crook hallgardens.co.uk)*.

2

NEWCASTLE UPON TYNE

🏛 Tyne and Wear 🚇🚍🚊 ℹ 26-30 Central Arcade; www.newcastlegateshead.com

Newcastle, and the city of Gateshead that faces it across the River Tyne, both have an outstanding industrial history. Today, the industrial era has largely passed; however the home of the "Geordies", as the locals are known, has emerged with a reputation for lively nightlife, excellent shops and a thriving arts scene.

①

The Castle Keep

🏛 St Nicholas St, Newcastle 🕐 10am-5pm daily 🌐 newcastlecastle.co.uk

The original Norman "new castle" here, founded by William the Conqueror's son, was built of wood, then rebuilt in stone in the 12th century. Only the thickset, crenellated keep remains, with its royal apartments, spiral staircases and battlements, from which there are great views. Visitors can explore all four floors of the building, and audio-visuals help tell its story. Nearby is the cathedral of St Nicholas, one of Britain's tiniest, with an ornate "lantern tower" – half tower, half spire – one of only four in Britain.

> ### Did You Know?
>
> Mosley Street in Newcastle was the first street in the world to be lit by electric lighting, in 1879.

②

Discovery Museum

🏛 Blandford Square, Newcastle 🕐 10am-4pm Mon-Fri, 11am-4pm Sat & Sun 🌐 discoverymuseum.org.uk

It's a proud testament to Newcastle's industrial history that its civic museum is crammed with renowned engineering creations. In the 19th century, this city was the world's foremost shipyard. Here, the scene is set straight-away with the eye-catching HMS *Turbinia* in the main hall. Tyne-built in 1894, it was once the fastest ship in the world and the first to be powered by steam. Other engineering marvels are explained with hands-on exhibits and include Joseph Swan's first light bulb and a number of Stephenson's steam engines.

---

③

Life Science Centre

🏛 Times Sq, Newcastle 🕐 10am-6pm Mon-Sat, 11am-6pm Sun 🌐 life.org.uk

The Life Science Centre, a big multicoloured complex that

↑ The 1928 Tyne Bridge, the most iconic of the seven that cross the river

④
Tyne Bridge

Linking Newcastle upon Tyne and Gateshead, the Tyne Bridge is perhaps the most iconic of the seven bridges crossing the River Tyne. Opened in 1928 to a design by Mott, Hay and Anderson, it was the world's longest-span bridge at the time.

---

⑤
Great North Museum

🏛 **Barras Bridge** 🕐 **10am-5pm Mon-Fri, 10am-4pm Sat, 11am-4pm Sun** 🌐 **greatnorthmuseum.org.uk**

From the life-sized T-Rex skeleton and hall of taxidermy to the Egyptian mummies and Japanese samurai armour, the Great North Museum mixes archaeology with natural history . Perhaps the most rewarding section is on regional Roman remains. Here an excellent display on Hadrian's Wall *(p414)* provides a good introduction to that great regional landmark.

sweeps around Newcastle's Times Square, repackages modern scientific research for children, with a science theatre, a motion ride that simulates experiences, a planetarium and a host of audio-visual gizmos. The result is an odd combination of hard science and a fairground, but kids love it.

 HIDDEN GEM
Seven Stories

Located on Lime Street, the National Centre for Children's Books has original artwork and manuscripts of kids' books from the 1930s on, including Roald Dahl's *Charlie and the Chocolate Factory*. With an interactive approach, it offers plenty of activities and events that breathe life into stories and characters.

---

⑥
BALTIC Centre for Contemporary Art

🏛 **S Shore Rd, Gateshead** 🕐 **10am-6pm daily** 🌐 **balticmill.com**

This contemporary art centre in a former grain warehouse is one of the biggest in Europe. The rooftop restaurant offers stunning views.

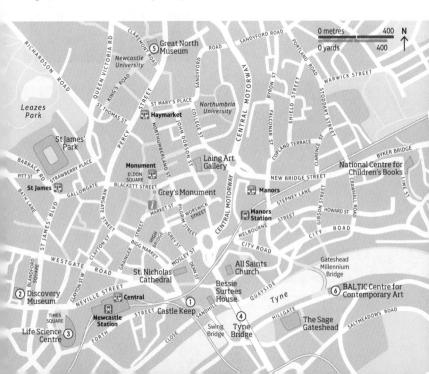

HADRIAN'S WALL

🛈 Hexham: Beaumont St; Corbidge: Hill St; www.adrianswall-country.co.uk

On the orders of Emperor Hadrian, this enormous 117-km (73-mile) wall was built across northern England to mark and defend the northern limits of the British province and the northwest border of the Roman Empire. Today you can explore the awe-inspiring sections that remain, as well as the forts and towns along this UNESCO World Heritage Site.

The most important and substantial of Roman remains in Britain, the wall runs from the mouth of the Tyne at Wallsend in the east to Bowness-on-Solway Firth in the west. It was completed in AD 122, taking about six years to build. Troops were stationed at milecastles along the wall, and large turrets, later forts, were built at 8-km (5-mile) intervals. The wall was abandoned in 383 as the Roman Empire crumbled. The best-preserved parts lie between Chesters Fort, a little north of Hexham, and Haltwhistle, about 25 km (16 miles) to the west. This area includes the Housesteads Fort and the famous site of Vindolanda, which is still being excavated.

As it moves from coast to coast, the wall offers sweeping vistas of some of England's most dramatic scenery. One of the more rugged sections is at Cawfields, 3 km (2 miles) north of Haltwhistle, which offers marvelous panoramic views of the surrounding countryside.

EXPLORING THE WALL

The best way to explore Hadrian's Wall is to walk or cycle the length of it. Running from Wallsend to Bowness-on-Solway is a 135-km (84-mile) national trail. You can walk the route in about seven days, with scenic stops along the way (www.nationaltrail.co.uk/hadrians-wall-path).

If you prefer to cycle, the 280-km (174-mile) Hadrian's Cycleway broadly follows the route of the wall, starting at Ravenglass in Cumbria and ending in South Shields in Tyne and Wear (www.sustrans.org.uk/hadrians-cycleway).

Hadrian's Wall, undulating across the rolling hills of Northumberland ↑

TOP 4 UNMISSABLE SIGHTS

Roman Vindolanda Fort and Museum
Several Roman forts have been discovered at this site. The museum also has a collection of Roman writing tablets.

Roman Army Museum
West of Vindolanda, this museum explores the life of Roman soldiers on the wall.

Housesteads Roman Fort and Museum
The best-preserved site on the wall, the remains include a Roman hospital and granaries.

Chesters Fort
Chesters Fort was a bridgehead over the North Tyne. Remains of the bathhouse are still visible.

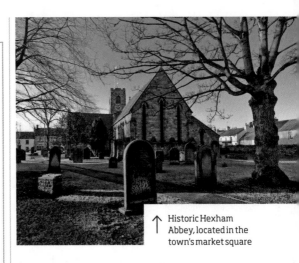

↑ Historic Hexham Abbey, located in the town's market square

EXPERIENCE MORE

❹ Hexham

🏠 Northumberland
🚌 ℹ Beaumont St; www.visitnorthumberland.com

The busy market town of Hexham was established in the 7th century, growing up around the church and monastery built by St Wilfrid, but the Vikings sacked and looted it in 876. In 1114, Augustinians began work on a priory and abbey on the original church site to create **Hexham Abbey**, which still towers over the market square. The Saxon crypt, built partly with stones from the former Roman fort at Corbridge, is all that remains of St Wilfrid's church. In the chancel is the Frith Stool, a Saxon throne made of sandstone and worn smooth over the centuries.

The 15th-century Moot Hall was once a council chamber and the **Old Gaol** (jail), built in the 1330s, contains a museum of border history.

Hexham Abbey
⊘ ⊕ 🏠 Market Place
🕐 9am–5pm daily
🌐 hexham-abbey.org.uk

Hexham Old Gaol
⊘ ⊕ 🏠 Hallgate 🕐 11am–4pm daily 🌐 museumsnorthumberland.org.uk

❺ Corbridge

🏠 Northumberland 🚌
ℹ Hill St; 01434 632815

This quiet town conceals some interesting historic buildings made with stones from the nearby Roman garrison town of Corstopitum. These include the Saxon tower of St Andrew's Church and the 14th-century tower house that protected the local clergy. Excavations of Corstopitum, now open as **Corbridge Roman Town–Hadrian's Wall**, have exposed earlier forts, a granary, temples and an aqueduct.

Since 2011, the town has hosted the annual Corbridge Festival, a family music event which is usually held in June.

Corbridge Roman Town–Hadrian's Wall
⊘ ⊗ ⊕ ⊕ 🕐 Apr–Oct: 10am–6pm daily; Nov–Mar: 10am–4pm Sat & Sun 🌐 english-heritage.org.uk

EXPERIENCE MORE

Berwick-upon-Tweed

🏠 Northumberland
🚆 ℹ️ Walkergate; www.
visitnorthumberland.com

Between the 12th and 15th
centuries Berwick-upon-
Tweed changed hands 14
times in the wars between
the Scots and English. Its
position, at the mouth of
the river which divides the
two nations, made the town
strategically vital.

The English finally gained
permanent control in 1482
and maintained Berwick as a
fortified garrison. Ramparts
dating from 1555, 2.5 km
(1.5 miles) long and 7 m (23 ft)
thick, offer superb views over
the River Tweed. Within the
18th-century **Berwick
Barracks**, the King's Own
Scottish Borderers Museum
has displays on the history of
this regiment, established
in 1689 to protect
Edinburgh. Also at
the barracks are

an art gallery and the By
Beat of Drum exhibition,
charting the history of British
infantrymen from the Civil
War to World War I.

Berwick Barracks

♿ 🅿️ 🅱️ 🏠 The Barracks
🕙 10am–6pm daily
🌐 english-heritage.org.uk

Holy Island of Lindisfarne

🏠 Northumberland
🚆 Berwick-upon-Tweed
then bus ℹ️ Walkergate,
Berwick-upon-Tweed;
www.lindisfarne.org.uk

Twice daily the long, narrow
neck of land separating
Lindisfarne, or Holy Island,
from the mainland sinks
under the North Sea tide
for 5 hours. At low tide,
visitors stream over the
causeway to the island
made famous by St Aidan,
St Cuthbert and

> **Between the 12th
> and 15th centuries
> Berwick-upon-Tweed
> changed hands
> 14 times in the
> wars between the
> Scots and English.**

the Lindisfarne Gospels.
Nothing remains of the Celtic
monks' monastery, which
was finally abandoned in
875 after successive Viking
attacks; however, the
magnificent arches of the
11th-century Lindisfarne
Priory are still standing.

After 1540, stones from
the priory were used to build
Lindisfarne Castle, which
was restored and made into
a private home by architect
Sir Edwin Lutyens in 1903. It
includes a walled garden by
horticulturalist Gertrude Jekyll.
Note that access times depend
on the tide, so check online first.

Lindisfarne Castle

♿ Ⓝ🏠 Holy Island 🕙 Mar–
Oct: times vary, see website;
Gardens: dawn–dusk daily all
year round 🌐 nationaltrust.
org.uk

Lindisfarne Castle, built
in the mid-16th century
on a craggy peak ↑

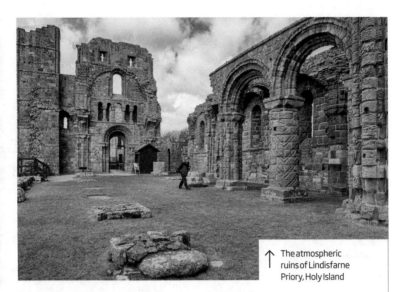

↑ The atmospheric ruins of Lindisfarne Priory, Holy Island

CELTIC CHRISTIANITY

The Irish monk St Aidan arrived in Northumbria in 635 from the island of Iona, off western Scotland, to evangelize the north of England. He founded the monastery on the island of Lindisfarne, and it became one of the most important centres for Christianity in England. This and other monastic communities thrived in Northumbria, becoming rich in scholarship, although the monks lived simply. It also emerged as a place of pilgrimage after miracles were reported at the shrine of St Cuthbert, Lindisfarne's most famous bishop. But the monks' pacifism made them defenceless against 9th-century Viking raids.

THE LINDISFARNE GOSPELS

Held in the British Library, this book of richly illustrated portrayals of Gospel stories is one of the masterpieces of the "Northumbrian Renaissance", which left a permanent mark on Christian art and history writing. The work was carried out by monks at Lindisfarne under the direction of Bishop Eadfrith, around 700. Monks managed to save the book and took it with them when they fled from Lindisfarne in 875 after suffering Viking raids.

ST AIDAN (600-651)

Aidan, an Irish monk, founded a monastery at Lindisfarne and became Bishop of Northumbria in 635. After Viking raids destroyed St Aidan's Monastery, Benedictines built the Lindisfarne Priory on its site in the 11th century. A 1960 sculpture of St Aidan stands beside the Lindisfarne Priory ruins.

← Statue of St Aidan by Kathleen Parbury

ST CUTHBERT (635-87)

The highly revered monk and miracle worker St Cuthbert lived as a hermit on Inner Farne (where a chapel was built in his memory) and later became Bishop of Lindisfarne.

8

Farne Islands

Northumberland
🚤From Seahouses (Apr-Oct) 🛈Seafield Rd, Seahouses; 01670 625593

There are between 15 and 28 Farne Islands off the coast from Bamburgh, some of them periodically covered by the sea. Nature wardens and lighthouse keepers share them with grey seals, puffins, terns and many other species of seabirds. Boat tours depart from Seahouses harbour and can land on Staple and Inner Farne, site of St Cuthbert's 14th-century chapel, or on Longstone, where Grace Darling's lighthouse is located.

Did You Know?

The Farne Islands are home to thousands of grey seals; hundreds of pups are born here every autumn.

9

Bamburgh

Northumberland
Berwick 🛈Seafield Rd, Seahouses; 01670 625593

Due to Northumbria's history of hostility against the Scots, there are more strongholds and castles here than in any other part of England. Most were built from the 11th to the 15th centuries by local warlords, including Bamburgh's red sandstone **castle**. Its coastal position had been fortified since prehistoric times, but the first major stronghold was built in 550 by a Saxon chieftain, Ida the Flamebearer.

In its heyday between 1095 and 1464, Bamburgh was the royal castle that was used by the Northumbrian kings for coronations. By the end of the Middle Ages it had fallen into obscurity; then in 1894 it was bought by Newcastle arms tycoon Lord Armstrong, who restored it. Works of art are exhibited in the cavernous Great Hall, and there are suits of armour and medieval artifacts in the basement.

Bamburgh's other main draw is the tiny **Grace Darling Museum**, which celebrates the bravery of the 23-year-old, who, in 1838, rowed through tempestuous seas with her father, the keeper of the Longstone lighthouse, to rescue nine people from the wrecked *Forfarshire* steamboat.

Bamburgh Castle

Bamburgh
11am-4:30pm daily (Nov-early Feb: Sat & Sun only)
bamburghcastle.com

Grace Darling Museum

Radcliffe Rd 01688 214910 Apr-Sep: 10am-5pm daily; Oct-Mar: 10am-4pm Tue-Sun

---

10

Warkworth Castle

Warkworth, nr Amble
518 from Newcastle
Jan & Nov-mid-Feb: 10am-4pm Sat & Sun; Mar-Oct: 10am-5pm daily
english-heritage.org.uk

Warkworth Castle sits on a green hill overlooking the

← Visitors navigating the rocky terrain of the Farne Islands, among nesting seabirds

artificial lake and has facilities for sailing, windsurfing, canoeing, water-skiing and fishing. In summer, the cruiser *Osprey* departs from Leaplish on trips around the lake. The Kielder Water Exhibition, at the Visitor Centre, covers the history of the valley from the Ice Age to the present day.

Since it enjoys extremely low levels of light pollution and some of the darkest skies in Europe, the area is a great spot for stargazing enthusiasts, with the Kielder Observatory running events and lectures.

River Coquet. It was one of the Percy family homes. Shakespeare's *Henry IV* features the castle in the scenes between the Earl of Northumberland and his son, Harry Hotspur. Much of the present-day castle dates back to the 14th century. The unusual turreted, cross-shaped keep is a central feature of the castle.

⓫

Kielder Water & Forest Park

🅰 **Northumberland**
🛈 **Tower Knowe Visitor Centre, Kielder; www.visit kielder.com**

One of the top attractions in Northumberland, Kielder Water lies close to the Scottish border, surrounded by spectacular scenery. With a perimeter of 44 km (27 miles), it is Britain's largest

⓬

Alnwick Castle

🅰 **Alnwick, Northumberland**
🚉🚌 **Alnmouth** ⏱ **Apr–Oct: 10am–5:30pm daily**
🌐 **alnwickcastle.com**

Dominating the pretty market town of Alnwick on the River Aln, this castle doubled as Hogwarts in the first two Harry Potter movies. It is the main seat of the Duke of Northumberland, whose family, the Percys, have lived here since 1309. This border stronghold has survived many battles but now sits peacefully in landscaped

grounds designed by Capability Brown. The stern medieval exterior belies the treasure house within, furnished in palatial Renaissance style with a collection of Meissen china and paintings by Titian, Van Dyck and Canaletto. The Postern Tower contains early British and Roman relics. The Regimental Museum of Royal Northumberland Fusiliers is in the Abbot's Tower. Other attractions are the Percy state coach and the dungeon.

→ Early morning frost at Alnwick Castle, its silhouette reflected in the River Aln

 13

Barnard Castle

⌂ County Durham
🚉 Darlington
🛈 3 Horsemarket;
www.thisisdurham.com

Barnard Castle, known in the area as "Barney", is a little town full of character, with old shopfronts and a cobbled marketplace overlooked by the ruins of the Norman castle from which it takes its name. The original Barnard Castle was built around 1125–40 by Bernard Balliol, ancestor of the founder of Balliol College, Oxford. Later, the market town grew up around the fortification.

Today, Barnard Castle is known for the extraordinary French-style château to the east of the town, surrounded by acres of formal gardens. Started in 1860 by the local aristocrat John Bowes and his French wife Josephine, an artist and actress, it was never a private residence

↑ The grandiose Bowes Museum in Barnard Castle; looking at the museum's art collection *(inset)*

and always intended as a museum and public monument. The château finally opened in 1892, by which time the couple were both dead. Nevertheless, the **Bowes Museum** stands as a monument to their wealth and extravagance.

The museum houses a strong collection of Spanish art, which includes El Greco's *The Tears of St Peter*, dating from the 1580s, and Goya's *Don Juan Meléndez Váldez*, painted in 1797. Clocks, porcelain, furniture, musical instruments, toys and tapestries are among its other treasures.

Bowes Museum
   ⌂ Barnard Castle ⏲ 10am–5pm daily 🌐 thebowesmuseum.org.uk

14 🎿 🏂 🍷 🖥 🛍

Cheviot Hills

⌂ Northumberland
🚉 Berwick-upon-Tweed
🛈 Padgepool Place, Wooler;
www.northumberland
nationalpark.org.uk

These bare, beautiful moors, smoothed into rounded humps by Ice Age glaciers, form a natural border with Scotland. The final stage of the Pennine Way crosses

> 🔍 HIDDEN GEM
> **Craster**
>
> A small fishing village east of the Cheviot Hills, Craster is famous for its kippers. You can enjoy superb seafood at The Jolly Fisherman. The ruins of Dunstanburgh Castle are just a short walk away from here.

> Today, Barnard Castle is known for the extraordinary French-style château to the east of the town, surrounded by acres of formal gardens.

the Cheviots, and outdoor enthusiasts can explore a near-wilderness unmatched anywhere else in England. This remote extremity of Northumberland nevertheless has a long and vivid history. Roman legions, warring Scots and English border raiders, cattle drovers and whisky smugglers have all left traces along the ancient routes and tracks they carved out here.

↑ Vibrantly coloured rhododendron creeper in bloom in the gardens at Cragside

15

Middleton-in-Teesdale

⌂ Co Durham 🚉 Darlington
ℹ Bowlees; 01833 622145

Many of the stone cottages in this old lead-mining town on the River Tees were built by the paternalistic, Quaker-run London Lead Company, which influenced every aspect of its employees' lives. Today, Middleton stands as a monument to the 18th-century idea of the "company town".

💬 INSIDER TIP
The Sun Inn

Pop in for a pint at Beamish's cosy pub, a genuine 1913 time-warp moved from its original site in Bishop Auckland and rebuilt at Beamish brick for brick. It serves a range of ales from local breweries.

16

Beamish Open Air Museum

⌂ Beamish, Co Durham
🚉🚌 Newcastle then bus
🕐 10am–5pm daily (Nov–Mar: Town and Colliery Village only, to 4pm)
🌐 beamish.org.uk

This giant open-air museum, spread over 120 hectares (300 acres) of County Durham, recreates an authentic picture of family, working and community life in the north-east in the 19th and early 20th centuries. It includes an Edwardian town and pit village with miners' houses and shops, a working Victorian farm and a Georgian steam railway. A tramway serves the different parts of the museum, which carefully avoids romanticizing the past.

17   NT

Cragside

⌂ Rothbury 🕐 Mar–Oct: 11am–5pm daily; Gardens: Mar–Oct: 10am–6pm daily; Nov–Feb: 11am–4pm Fri–Sun 🌐 nationaltrust.org. uk/cragside

Largely completed by 1880, the Victorian country home of Lord Armstrong caused a stir for its mix of old and new. Architect Richard Norman Shaw designed Cragside as a vast Tudor edifice. Meanwhile, the inventive engineering that had made Armstrong a leading industrialist resulted in hot-and-cold running water, a telephone, an alarm system and electric lighting – Cragside was the world's first house with hydroelectric power. Some of this industrial archaeology is on view in the gardens, a wild and beautiful attraction in themselves, with lakes, moors, rock gardens and a sculpture trail, along with rhododendron blooms in spring.

← A McLaren steam traction engine on display at the Beamish Open Air Museum

↑ Mountain bikers cycling over the stunning, heather-covered moorland in Blanchland

A DRIVING TOUR
NORTH PENNINES

Length 80 km (50 miles) **Stopping-off points** Several pubs in Stanhope serve bar meals, and the Durham Dales Centre provides teas all year round. Horsley Hall Hotel at Eastgate serves meals all day

Starting to the south of Hadrian's Wall, this tour explores the South Tyne Valley and Upper Weardale. It crosses one of England's wildest and most remote tracts of moorland, then heads north again. The high ground is mainly blanketed with heather, dotted with sheep or crisscrossed with dry-stone walls, a feature of this region. Harriers and other birds of prey hover above, and streams tumble into valleys of tightly huddled villages. Celts, Romans and other settlers have left imprints on the North Pennines, now denoted an Area of Outstanding Natural Beauty.

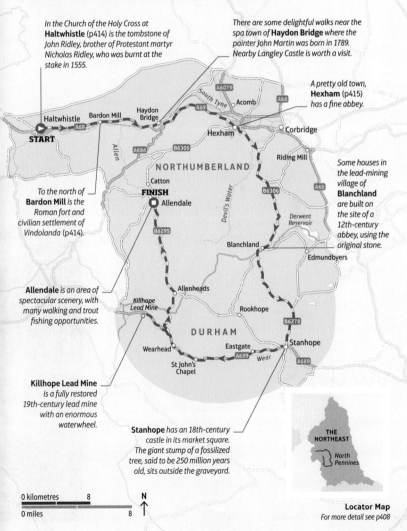

In the Church of the Holy Cross at **Haltwhistle** (p414) is the tombstone of John Ridley, brother of Protestant martyr Nicholas Ridley, who was burnt at the stake in 1555.

There are some delightful walks near the spa town of **Haydon Bridge** where the painter John Martin was born in 1789. Nearby Langley Castle is worth a visit.

A pretty old town, **Hexham** (p415) has a fine abbey.

To the north of **Bardon Mill** is the Roman fort and civilian settlement of Vindolanda (p414).

Some houses in the lead-mining village of **Blanchland** are built on the site of a 12th-century abbey, using the original stone.

Allendale is an area of spectacular scenery, with many walking and trout fishing opportunities.

Killhope Lead Mine is a fully restored 19th-century lead mine with an enormous waterwheel.

Stanhope has an 18th-century castle in its market square. The giant stump of a fossilized tree, said to be 250 million years old, sits outside the graveyard.

0 kilometres 8
0 miles 8

N

Locator Map
For more detail see p408

THE NORTHEAST

North Pennines

WALES

Sheep grazing in the Black Mountains, Brecon Beacons National Park

EXPLORE
WALES

This section divides Wales into two colour-coded sightseeing areas, as shown on this map. Find out more about each area on the following pages.

Holyhead

Anglesey

Bangor

Caernarfon

Caernarfon Bay

Snowdonia National Park

Porthmadog

Dolgellau

Cardigan Bay

Machynlleth

Aberystwyth

Cambrian

Aberaeron

Cardigan

Fishguard

St Davids

Pembrokeshire Coast National Park

Llandeilo

Carmarthen

Milford Haven

Pembroke

Tenby

Carmarthen Bay

Neath

Swansea

Swansea Bay

Bristol

0 kilometres · 30

0 miles · 30

N ↑

GREAT BRITAIN

Liverpool

Colwyn Bay
Conwy
Queensferry
Chester
Betws-y-Coed
Ruthin
Wrexham

NORTH WALES
p434

Llangollen
Bala

Welshpool

Shrewsbury

Newtown

Mountains

Wolverhampton

Birmingham

Rhayader

Stratford-upon-Avon

Llandrindod
Wells

**SOUTH AND
MID-WALES**
p452

Worcester

Hay-on-Wye

Hereford

ENGLAND

Llandovery

Brecon

*Brecon Beacons
National Park*

Cheltenham

Abergavenny
Monmouth

Gloucester

Merthyr
Tydfil

Pontypool

Cirencester

Caerphilly
Newport

Bridgend

Swindon

Cardiff

Bristol

Barry

Channel

Bath

GETTING TO KNOW
WALES

Celtic legends swirl across the Welsh landscape, an epic panorama of stirring mountains, imperious sea cliffs, mighty castles, ruined abbeys and deep-green valleys. Take your time to soak it all up and you'll soon discover why so many fall under its spell.

NORTH WALES

PAGE 434

A magnet for hikers and climbers, the jagged peaks of the Snowdonia Massif dominate the north, forming part of a national park that embraces thickly wooded valleys, tumbling waterfalls and cool glacial lakes much loved by wild swimmers. A ring of formidable coastal castles, including Beaumaris, Caenarfon and Harlech, surrounds Snowdonia, while there's more wild, untamed beauty on the remote, sand-fringed Llyn Peninsula, a stronghold of the Welsh language. To the east, nestling on the banks of the River Dee, Llangollen makes an ideal base for boat trips across the spectacular Pontcysyllte Aqueduct.

Best for
Castles, mountains and gorgeous beaches

Home to
Conwy, Portmeirion, Snowdonia National Park, Beaumaris

Experience
Puffing through the stunning Vale of Ffestiniog on the narrow-gauge Ffestiniog steam railway

PAGE 452

SOUTH AND MID-WALES

Cardiff, Wales's exciting capital, has reinvented itself since the 1980s, not least in the spectacular regeneration of the Bay. To the north, the densely populated Valleys – speckled with riveting reminders of coal-mining days – give way to the sheep-dotted uplands of the Brecon Beacons and the sylvan Wye Valley, home to Hay, Britain's premier book town. From the sweeping sandy expanses of the Gower, west of Swansea, to the jaw-dropping cliffs of Pembrokeshire, it's the coastline that elevates this beautiful region to a realm of its own.

Best for
Spectacular coastline and verdant valleys

Home to
Pembrokeshire Coast National Park, Brecon Beacons, Cardiff

Experience
Blustery walks along the Pembrokeshire Coast Path

7 DAYS

in Wales

Day 1

Start in vibrant Cardiff (p464) and spend the morning exploring the city centre on foot. Take a guided tour of the modernist Principality Stadium and check out the art and natural history collections in the National Museum, Break for lunch at Cafe Citta (4 Church St), a friendly pizzeria, and then stroll the grounds of Cardiff Castle. In the afternoon, take an Aquabus ferry shuttle down from the castle to the imaginatively redeveloped Cardiff Bay. Have dinner at Ffresh in the Millennium Centre before enjoying a show. Arrange car hire for the rest of your tour of Wales and stay overnight at Jolyons Boutique Hotel (5 Bute Crescent).

Day 2

Drive to the pretty little seaside resort of Tenby (p456). Amble along the medieval walls and stroll the narrow lanes and alleys. If the weather permits, bathe on the beach before having lunch at the cosy Plantagenet House (1 Quay Hill). In the afternoon, drive west to Britain's smallest city, St Davids (p458), and visit the

splendid medieval cathedral and Bishop's Palace. For dinner, aim for the award-winning Cwtch (p459) before hunkering down at Y Glenydd (51 Nun St), a traditional, friendly small hotel.

Day 3

In the morning, head to tiny New Quay (p471) from where there are boat trips into Cardigan Bay to spot dolphins. Back in New Quay, follow the trail of sites that inspired Dylan Thomas's Under Milk Wood. Continue northeast along the coast stopping for lunch at The Hive (Cadwgan Place) in Aberaeron (p471). In the afternoon continue up the coast to the ancient seaside market town of Abersystwyth (p473). Dine on the harbourfront at Pysgoty (S Marine Terrace), before staying overnight at classy guesthouse Gwesty Cymru (19 Marine Terrace).

Day 4

Explore the unyielding walls and stone battlements of Harlech Castle (p444) in the small town of Harlech before carrying

1 The Millennium Centre, Cardiff.

2 Picturesque Beddgelert village.

3 Boats in Tenby Bay.

4 Hikers on the approach to Penyfan, the highest mountain in South Wales, in the Brecon Beacons.

5 Second hand bookshop in Hay-on-Wye.

on to Portmeirion *(p440)*, a highly unusual private Italianate village that was the brainchild of an eccentric architect. Have lunch here and then head off towards the mighty peaks of Snowdonia – take the vintage steam trains of the Ffestiniog Railway *(p441)* to see the mountains at their best. End the day by doubling back to the hotel in Portmeirion.

Day 5

Visit Beddgelert *(p444)*, where a huddle of stone cottages cuddle up to the ancient bridge. Proceed through the mountains to Conwy *(p438)*, whose mighty castle glowers over the coast. Spend an hour exploring the fortifications and then pop over to the leafy delights of Bodnant Garden, where you can have lunch in the tea room. In the afternoon, continue inland to Llangollen *(p451)*, a handsome town beside the River Dee. Stroll around the immaculate gardens of Plas Newydd before settling down to a tasty dinner at the riverside Corn Mill *(Dee Ln)*; rest your limbs at the refined The Glasgwm B&B in a Victorian townhouse on Abbey Road.

Day 6

Begin the day by taking a boat ride on the Llangollen Canal. Then drive south to Hay-on-Wye *(p462)*, a picturesque little town famous for its annual book festival and multitude of second-hand bookshops. Browse away all afternoon or venture into the stunning scenery of the Brecon Beacons *(p460)*, where the hike up Pen Y Fan is a popular albeit strenuous excursion. Return to Hay-on-Wye for dinner at St John's Place *(3 Lion St)* and stay the night at the Old Black Lion *(26 Lion Street)*.

Day 7

Continue south to Abergavenny *(p475)*, a pretty market town, where you can stretch your legs before proceeding east to Monmouth *(p473)* for a pub lunch at the riverside Gate House *(125 Monnow St)*. Just a little south of here are the beautiful ruins of Tintern Abbey *(p474)*, which inspired both painter J M W Turner and poet William Wordsworth and where you can eat and sleep at the riverside Rose & Crown Hotel on Main Road.

A BRIEF
HISTORY

Wales's history has been shaped by many factors, from invasion to industrialization. It was a separate Celtic entity when Offa's Dyke was built as the border with England in 770. Centuries of cross-border raids followed before England and Wales were formally united by the Act of Union in 1536.

Wales was settled by waves of migrants in prehistoric times, and by the Iron Age, Celtic farmers had established hillforts. The Romans started pushing into Wales in 48 AD, but the collapse of Roman authority in the fourth century led to the splintering of Wales into a number of small kingdoms, which resisted the subsequent incursions of the Saxons. The Saxon king Offa built the defensive Offa's Dyke along the unconquered territory (*p469*), and beyond this earthwork the people called their land *Cymru*, while the Saxons called the land "Wales". The Norman invasion of 1066 did not reach Wales, but the border

1 A map of Wales and England in 1579.

2 King Henry VIII of England, descended from Welsh Tudors.

3 Young Welsh coal miners in the early 1900s.

4 A sandy Pembrokeshire beach, popular with tourists today.

Timeline of events

78 AD

The Romans finish conquering most of Wales and remain dominant until the fourth century AD.

1277

Edward I of England starts campaign to conquer Wales.

1283–1289

Conwy Castle is built by Edward I, one of a ring of fortresses.

1415

Owain Glyndŵr, the last of the native Welsh heroes, dies.

territory ("the Marches") was given by William the Conqueror to several powerful barons. These Marcher Lords controlled most of the lowlands. In the 13th century, the king of England, Edward I, embarked on a military campaign to conquer all of Wales. He introduced English law and proclaimed his son Prince of Wales. In 1400, Welsh resentment against the Marcher Lords grew into rebellions; led by Owain Glyndŵr, a descendant of the Welsh princes, these ultimately failed. King Henry VIII passed two acts of union cementing English control of Wales in 1536 and 1543.

From the late 18th century, Wales industrialized at breakneck speed. Coal mining shafts were sunk up and down the Welsh Valleys and by 1913 Barry and Cardiff had become the largest coal-exporting ports in the world. Living and working conditions were poor for industrial and agricultural workers. After World War II the coal industry went into decline; the last pit closed in 2008. The Welsh were cheered by a 1997 referendum, which resulted in a degree of self-government and the establishment of the Welsh National Assembly. A growth in tourism, thanks to initiatives such as the Wales Coast Path, has also reinvigorated this proud nation.

↑ Statue of Owain Glyndŵr, who instigated the Welsh revolt in the 1400s

1536
Act of Union is passed making Wales a part of the Kingdom of England.

1790s
Local iron ore and coal deposits launch Welsh industrialization.

1940–44
During World War II Swansea and Cardiff are battered by German bombers.

1997
Welsh devolution referendum leads to formation of National Assembly of Wales in 1999.

NORTH WALES

The Kingdom of Gwynedd emerged from the ashes of the Roman Empire in the 5th century, with Anglesey as its capital and Welsh the dominant tongue. This hegemony lasted until the Saxon incursions in the 11th century, though to this day the region remains a stronghold of the Welsh language. During the 13th century North Wales was the scene of ferocious battles between the Welsh princes and Anglo-Norman monarchs who were determined to establish English rule. A string of formidable castles was built – Beaumaris, Caernarfon and Harlech among them – otherwise known as Edward I's Iron Ring. Representing what was arguably Europe's most ambitious medieval project, these massive fortresses are as much a testament to Welsh resistance as to the wealth and strength of the invaders.

Aided by the arrival of the railway in the late 19th century, the Victorians popularised the sandy northern coastline with seaside resorts such as Llandudno. Industry, meanwhile, was largely confined to the slate quarries in the area around Snowdonia, where today, the remnants of the stark grey quarries provide a striking contrast to the natural beauty of the surrounding mountains.

Irish Sea

← *Dublin*

← *Dublin*

Cemaes
Amlwch
Carmel Head
Holyhead Bay
Llanerchymedd
Moelfre
Holy Island
Holyhead
Benllech
LLANDUDNO **7**
Trearrdur Bay
ANGLESEY
Llanfairfechan
CONWY **1**
Rhoscolyn
Gwalchmai
Llangefni
BEAUMARIS
4
A55
Llanfairpwll.
6 **BANGOR**
Rhosneigr
Bethesda
Conwy
A470
Aberffraw
Newborough
Carnedd Llywelyn
1,064 m (3,491 ft)
Llanrwst
CAERNARFON **5**
Llanberis
A5
Caernarfon Bay
Snowdon
1,085 m (3,560 ft)
Capel Curig
Betws-y-Coed
3
Penygroes
SNOWDONIA
NATIONAL
PARK
Dolwyddelan
Beddgelert
Blaenau
Ffestiniog
GWYNEDD
A487
Ffestiniog
Llanaelhaearn
Porthmadog
Maentwrog
Nefyn
Trawsfynydd
LLŶN
PENINSULA
Criccieth
2
PORTMEIRION
Tremadog Bay
9
Pwllheli
Harlech
Plas-yn-Rhiw
Llanbedrog
Abersoch
Aberdaron
Y Llethr
754 m (2,474 ft)
Braich-y-Pwll
Trwyn Cilan
Llanbedr
Bardsey Island
Llanaber
Dolgellau
Brithdi
Barmouth
Cadair Idris
892 m (2,926 ft)
Llwyngwril
A487
Cardigan Bay
Corris
Abergynolwyn
Machynlleth
Tywyn
Aberdyfi
Dyfi
Talybont
A487
Aberystwyth
Ponterwyd
A44
Cambrian
Llanilar
Llanon
Pontrhydfendigaid
Aberaeron
New Quay
A482
Tregaron

NORTH WALES

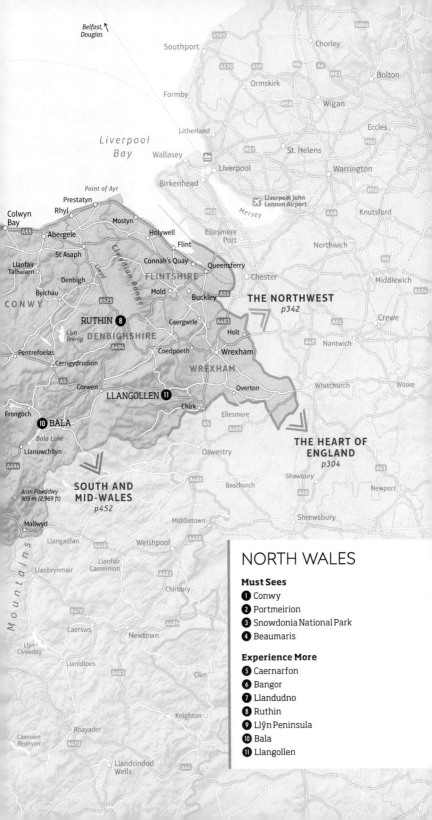

Belfast, Douglas

Southport

Chorley

Bolton

A666

A570   A59   M6   A6

Ormskirk   M61

Formby

M58   Wigan   Eccles

Litherland   M62

Liverpool Bay

Wallasey   St. Helens   Warrington

Liverpool   M57

Birkenhead   Liverpool John Lennon Airport   Knutsford

Point of Ayr

Mersey   A49

Colwyn Bay   Prestatyn   Rhyl   Ellesmere Port   Northwich   M6

Abergele   Mostyn   Holywell   Chester   Middlewich

A55   St Asaph   Flint   A534

Llanfair Talhaiarn   Connah's Quay   **FLINTSHIRE**   Crewe

Denbigh   Queensferry   **THE NORTHWEST** *p342*   A51

Bylchau   Mold   A55   A49   Nantwich

CONWY   A525   Buckley

Llyn Brenig   Caergwrle   A483   Holt

RUTHIN **8**   **DENBIGHSHIRE**   Whitchurch   Woore

Pentrefoelas   A494   Coedpoeth   Wrexham

Cerrigydrudion   A5   **WREXHAM**   Overton

Corwen   **LLANGOLLEN** **11**   Ellesmere

Frongoch   Chirk

10 **BALA**   A5   A495   **THE HEART OF ENGLAND** *p304*

Bala Lake   Oswestry   A41

Llanuwchllyn   Newport

A494   **SOUTH AND MID-WALES** *p452*   A49

Aran Fawddwy 905 m (2,969 ft)   Shawbury   A49

Mallwyd   Baschurch

Llangadfan   Welshpool   A458   Shrewsbury

Mountains   Llanbrynmair   A458   Middletown

Llanfair Caereinion   A483   Chirbury

Caersws   A489   Newtown

Llyn Clywedog   A470

Llanidloes   A483   Clun

Llyn Clywedog   Knighton

Rhayader   A470

Claerwen Reservoir   Llandrindod Wells   A44

NORTH WALES

Must Sees

1 Conwy
2 Portmeirion
3 Snowdonia National Park
4 Beaumaris

Experience More

5 Caernarfon
6 Bangor
7 Llandudno
8 Ruthin
9 Llŷn Peninsula
10 Bala
11 Llangollen

CONWY

🏠 Conwy 🚃 ℹ️ Castle Buildings, Rose Hill St;
www.conwy.com

As one of the best-preserved medieval fortified towns in Britain, Conwy has a concentration of architectural riches unparalleled in Wales. The brooding castle, built by Edward I, dominates, while the walls form an almost unbroken shield around the old town.

① 🏰
Conwy Castle

📍 Rose Hill St 📞 01492 592358 🕐 Mar–Oct: 9:30am–5pm daily (Jul–Aug: to 6pm)

Perched dramatically on a narrow outcrop guarding the town, Conwy Castle is one of the finest examples of late 13th-century military architecture in Europe. It was the most expensive of the several castles built in Wales by Edward I. Its location on the outcrop meant that it didn't need the concentric fortifications seen in the other castles built by Edward I at the time. It has two huge gateways, eight enormous towers and impressively well-preserved medieval royal apartments. A walk along the battlements provides superb views of the castle's interior and the landscape of Snowdonia.

②
The Town Walls

Conwy's impressive town walls were built at the same time as the castle, as Edward I sought to impose his control over the people of Wales. Today they still enclose a large part of the modern town, and anyone born within them is known as a *Jac y dô* (Jackdaw) after the birds that live in the walls. Among the finest in Europe, the well-preserved medieval walls include 21 towers and three sets of gateways.

Did You Know?

King Richard II hid from his rival Henry Bolingbroke (later Henry IV) in Conwy Castle in 1399.

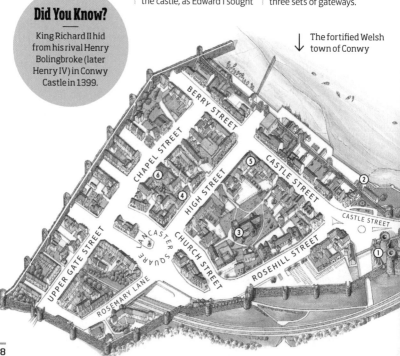

↓ The fortified Welsh town of Conwy

↑ The town of Conwy, encircled by its fine medieval walls

③
St Mary and All Saints Church

 Rose Hill St 🕑 Mar-Oct: 10am-4pm Mon-Fri, 11am-3pm Sat; services only Sun 🌐 caruconwy.com/st-marys-conwy

This parish church was originally a Cistercian abbey built between 1172 and 1186, though Edward I later moved the abbey to Maenan. Llywelyn the Great, Wales's greatest medieval leader, founded the abbey and was buried here, though his coffin was later moved to Llanrwst. The tomb of Robert Wynn, who built Plas Mawr, still stands here.

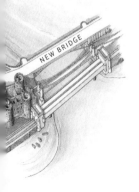

NEW BRIDGE

④
Plas Mawr

 High St 📞 01492 580167 🕑 Apr-Sep 9:30am-5pm daily; Oct: 9:30am-4pm daily

Built between 1576 and 1585 by local landowner Robert Wynn, Plas Mawr is a grand Elizabethan town house. It is impressive enough today but must have seemed palatial at the time, totally dominating the narrow cobbled streets. Wynn liked to entertain lavishly, and the house was built as an impressive backdrop to his dinners and parties. The hall plasterwork has been repainted in its original bright colours, and touch-screen displays bring the history of the house vividly to life.

⑤
Aberconwy House

 Castle St 🕑 10am-5pm daily 🌐 nationaltrust.org.uk

This 14th-century merchant's house is the only one within the town walls to have survived from that period. It has been restored as a museum, with rooms depicting various periods of its history. The gift shop is located in the room where the owner would have sold stone in the 1300s.

⑥
Royal Cambrian Academy

 Crown Lane 🕑 11am-5pm Tue-Sat; extended hours for exhibitions 🌐 rcaconwy.org

The first of its kind in Wales, this unusual art academy was founded in 1882 by mostly English artists who had settled in the town. Today it is a charitable institution representing the work of over 100 Welsh artists, including painters, printmakers, sculptors and architects.

🔍 HIDDEN GEM
Smallest House

This fisherman's cottage on the quayside is said to be the smallest house in Britain. For a small fee you can view the 19th-century interior *(www.thesmallesthouse.co.uk).*

Brightly painted
buildings surrounding
Portmeirion's piazza ↑

PORTMEIRION

Gwynedd ⬛ Minffordd ⏱ 9:30am–7:30pm daily
ⓦ portmeirion.wales

This bizarre Italianate village on a private peninsula
at the top of Cardigan Bay was created by Welsh
architect Sir Clough Williams-Ellis between 1925
and 1975. He fulfilled a childhood dream by building
a village "to my own fancy on my own chosen site".
It is now owned by a charitable trust.

About 50 colourful buildings surround a central
piazza, ranging in style from Italian to Oriental
to Gothic. Sir Clough Williams-Ellis took pieces
of demolished buildings and incorporated
them into his own designs to create a fanciful
bricolage of structures. Visitors can stay at the
luxurious hotel or in one of the charming
village cottages. Portmeirion has been an
atmospheric location for many films and
television programmes, including the popular
1960s television series *The Prisoner*.

Did You Know?

The whimsical mix of
styles in Portmeirion is
thought to have influ-
enced Postmodern
architecture.

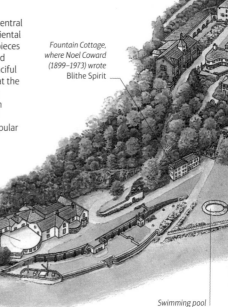

*Fountain Cottage,
where Noel Coward
(1899–1973) wrote
Blithe Spirit*

*The Portmeirion Hotel
overlooks the bay
and has a dining
room designed by
Sir Terence Conran.*

*The Amis Reunis is a
stone replica of a boat
that sank in the bay.*

→
Portmeirion, laid out
amid the greenery of a
private peninsula

Swimming pool

SCENIC RAILWAYS

Two scenic railways run from Porthmadog, the town nearest to Portmeirion. The Ffestiniog Narrow-Gauge Railway takes a picturesque 22-km (14-mile) route from Porthmadog Harbour to the mountains and the slate town of Blaenau Ffestiniog *(p443).* Designed to carry slate from the quarries to the quay, the railway closed in 1946 but was reconstructed by volunteers and reopened in sections between 1955 and 1982. The Welsh Highland Railway runs for 40 km (25 miles) from Porthamdog Harbour to Caernarfon *(p448),* past the foot of Mount Snowdon *(p442).* Both railways operate from late March to early November *(www.festrailco.uk).*

The village's huge copper statue of Hercules

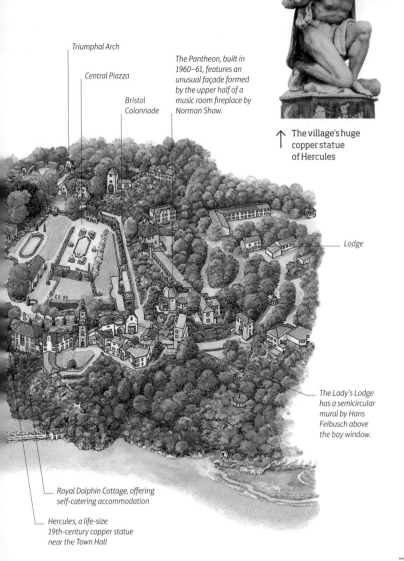

Triumphal Arch

Central Piazza

Bristol Colonnade

The Pantheon, built in 1960–61, features an unusual façade formed by the upper half of a music room fireplace by Norman Shaw.

Lodge

The Lady's Lodge has a semicircular mural by Hans Feibusch above the bay window.

Royal Dolphin Cottage, offering self-catering accommodation

Hercules, a life-size 19th-century copper statue near the Town Hall

Misty mountain trail leading to the peaks in craggy Snowdonia ↑

3

SNOWDONIA NATIONAL PARK

 Betws y Coed; www.visitsnowdonia.info

Wales's first national park, established in 1951, extends dramatically from the Snowdon massif – encompassing Wales's highest mountain – into a vastly varied landscape of high lakes, moors, river gorges and stunning coastline. While the nine mountain ranges cover more than half the park, it is full of towns and villages and much of it is used for sheep and cattle-raising.

①

Betws-y-Coed

Conwy 🚉 🚌Royal Oak Stables; www.betws-y-coed.co.uk

This village near the peaks has been a hill-walking centre since the 19th century. To the west are the Swallow Falls, where the River Llugwy flows through a wooded glen. Nearby in Capel Curig, the bizarre Ty Hyll ("Ugly House") is a tŷ unnos ("one-night house"); traditionally, houses erected between dusk and dawn on common land were entitled to freehold rights. Today it operates as a cosy tearooom (Mar–Oct only).

> ### Did You Know?
>
> The Snowdon Mountain Railway is the only rack and pinion railway in the UK.

②

Snowdon

Snowdon, at 1,085 m (3,560 ft) the highest peak in Wales, is deservedly a magnet for hikers, although the summit can also be reached by taking the 1-hour journey on the narrow-gauge Snowdon Mountain Railway from Llanberis, which opened in 1896. Trains wait at the Summit Visitor Centre and café for 30 minutes to allow a short stroll to the very top.

The easiest route on foot is the 8-km (5-mile) Llanberis Track, starting in Llanberis. From Llanberis Pass, the Miners' Track (once used by copper miners) and the Pyg Track are alternative paths. Walkers should beware of sudden weather changes and dress accordingly.

③

Llanberis

🏛 **Gwynedd** ℹ **Electric Mountain**

Llanberis was a major 19th-century slate town. Its attractions include the 13th-century shell of **Dolbadarn Castle** and, above Llyn Peris, the **Electric Mountain**, with tours of Europe's biggest hydro-electric storage station. The **National Slate Museum** has displays on Wales's 19th-century slate roofing industry.

Dolbadarn Castle

🏛 Off A4086 near Llanberis 🕙 10am–4pm daily 🌐 cadw.gov.wales

Electric Mountain

♿ ⏰ 🏛 Llanberis 🕙 Sep–May: 10am–4:30pm daily; Jun–Aug: 9:30am–5:30pm daily 🌐 electricmountain.co.uk

National Slate Museum

🏛 Llanberis 🕙 10am–5pm Sun–Fri (winter: to 4pm) 🌐 museumwales.ac.uk

---

④

Blaenau Ffestiniog

🏛 **Gwynedd** 🚉
ℹ **Betws-y-Coed**

Blaenau Ffestiniog, once the slate capital of North Wales,

sits among mountains riddled with quarries. The narrow-gauge Ffestiniog Railway *(p441)* carried the slate away to Porthmadog and beyond.

Slate Mountain, overlooking Blaenau, opened to visitors in the early 1970s, marking a new role for the declining industrial town. On the Deep Mine tour, visitors descend on Britain's steepest passenger railway to the underground chambers, while sound effects recreate the atmosphere of a working quarry. The dangers included landfalls and

floods, as well as the more gradual threat of slate dust breathed into the lungs. The Quarry tour, meanwhile, takes visitors on a 4x4 adventure through this remarkable landscape and into numerous huge craters.

There are slate-splitting demonstrations on the surface, a quarryman's cottage and a recreation of a Victorian village to illustrate the cramped and basic living conditions endured by workers between the 1880s and 1945.

Slate Mountain

♿ ⏰ 🍴 🛍 🏛 Off A470 🕙 9am–5pm daily (book guided tours in advance) 🌐 slatemountain.co.uk

←

Dolbadarn Castle, once the guardian of the Llanberis Pass

⑤ Beddgelert

🅰 Gwynedd 🅸 Canolfan-Hebog; www.beddgelert tourism.com

This village has a spectacular location, on the confluence of the Glaslyn and Colwyn rivers between two mountain passes: the beautiful Nant Gwynant Pass, which leads to Snowdonia's highest reaches, and the Aberglaslyn Pass, a narrow wooded gorge that acts as a gateway to the sea.

The name refers to an old Welsh legend, linked to the locality in the 19th century by Dafydd Pritchard, a local hotelier, to boost trade. It tells of the noble hound Gelert, who fought and killed a wolf to protect the infant son of Llywelyn the Great, at the expense of his own life. Pritchard created Gelert's Grave by the River Glaslyn, a short walk south of the village.

A particularly fine walk in the area leads south to the Aberglaslyn Pass and along a section of the Welsh Highland Railway (www.festrail.co.uk).

Northeast, the **Sygun Copper Mine** offers self-guided tours of caverns re-creating the life of Victorian miners.

Sygun Copper Mine

 🅰 On A498 🅾 Mid-Feb–mid-Nov: 9:30am–5pm daily (winter: 10am–4pm) 🆆 syguncopper mine.co.uk

⑥

Harlech Castle

🅰 Castle Square, Harlech 🅰 🅾 Mar–Oct: 9:30am–5pm daily (Jul–Aug: to 6pm); Nov–Feb: 10am–4pm Mon–Sat, 11am–4pm Sun 🆆 cadw.gov.wales

The small town of Harlech with its fine beaches is dominated by Harlech Castle, an impressive medieval fortress built by Edward I between 1283 and 1289 in a spectacular setting. The castle sits on a precipitous crag, with superb views of Tremadog Bay and the Llŷn Peninsula to the west and of Snowdonia to the north. Access to the towering gatehouse is via a suspended pedestrian bridge.

> ### ACTIVITIES IN SNOWDONIA NATIONAL PARK
>
> Hiking and cycling are not the only adventurous pursuits on offer here. Rock climbing is also popular, especially on the craggy sides of the Llanberis Pass. Go Below (www. go-below.co.uk) takes visitors beneath the surface of Snowdonia, visiting underground lakes and even zip-lining through caverns. A more unusual option is Surf Snowdonia, based at Rowen south of Conwy, with one of the biggest artificial wave machines in the world.

Did You Know?

Just to the east of Harlech Castle is Fordd Pen Llech, officially the steepest street in the world.

↑ Harlech Castle, with the mountains of Snowdonia in the background

⑦

Dolgellau

🅰 Gwynedd 🆆 dolgellau. wales

The dark local stone gives a stern look to this market town, where the Welsh language and customs are still very strong. It lies in the long shadow of the 892-m (2,927-ft) mountain of Cadair Idris where, according to legend, anyone who spends a night on its summit will wake up a poet or a madman – or not at all. The town was until 1999 one of the few centres for mining Welsh gold, used for the wedding rings of the British Royal family.

Dolgellau is a good base for walking, whether gentle strolls through beautiful leafy countryside or strenuous hikes across mountainous terrain. The lovely Cregennen lakes are set high in the hills above the wooded Mawddach Estuary to the northwest; north are the harsh, bleak Rhinog moors, one of Wales's last true wildernesses.

Cadair (or Cader) Idris is in fact a range of peaks, the highest being Aran Fawddwy, at 905 m (2,969 ft). There are several paths to the top, all popular with hikers for their varying degrees of difficulty. The visitor centre at the start of the Minffordd path offers maps, advice and a café.

⑧

Aberdyfi

🅰 Gwynedd 🆁
📱 Wharf Gardens; www.aberdyfi.org

Perched at the mouth of the Dyfi Estuary, this little harbour resort and sailing centre makes the most of its splendid but rather confined location, its houses occupying every yard of a narrow strip of land between mountain and sea. In the 19th century, slate was exported from here, and some 100 ships were built in the port.

The little Talylynn Railway (www.talyllyn.co.uk) runs not far from here. Its pint-sized steam engines pull their cosy carriages along a scenic 11-km (7-mile) track between Tywyn, on the coast, and Nant Gwernol. The Rev W Awdry, creator of Thomas the Tank Engine, enshrined the Talyllyn trains in his Railway Series book *Four Little Engines*.

DRINK

The Grapes

A 17th-century Grade II-listed coaching inn with a selection of local ales that changes weekly.

🅰 Maentwrog, Blaenau Ffestiniog 🆆 grapes hotelsnowdonia.co.uk

---

Pen-y-Gwryd

The public bar at this hotel built in 1810 has always been popular with mountaineers training in the area, including Edmund Hillary and Tenzing Norgay prior to their Everest expedition.
🅰 Nant Gwynant, Gwynedd
🆆 pyg.co.uk

Riverside Hotel Pennal

The wide range of local beers at this traditional village pub changes regularly.

🅰 Pennal, Machynlleth
🆆 riversidehotel-pennal.co.uk

↑ Climbing the mighty Cadair Idris, the *cadair* or "chair" of Idris the Giant, legendary king of Meirionnydd

4

BEAUMARIS

⌂ Isle of Anglesey 🕐 Beaumaris Castle: Mar-Oct: 9:30am-5pm daily (Jul & Aug: to 6pm); Nov-Feb: 11am-4pm daily
🌐 visitanglesey.co.uk

The most picturesque town in Anglesey, Beaumaris has sweeping mountain views, Georgian and Victorian architecture and a range of independent galleries and restaurants. The star attraction, however, is Beaumaris Castle, the most technically perfect in Great Britain.

Edward I's last, and possibly greatest, castle, Beaumaris was built between 1295 and c 1330 to command this important crossing to the mainland of Wales. The perfectly symmetrical design was intended to combine impregnable defence with comfort. Invaders would face many obstacles before reaching the inner ward. This unfinished masterpiece is today a World Heritage Site and visitors can explore its wall walks and internal passages. Among the town's other attractions are the 1614 Courthouse on Castle Street and the restored Gaol on Steeple Lane, which preserves its punishment room and a treadmill for prisoners.

STAY

The Bull
Built in 1617, this inn's celebrated literary patrons have included Dr Samuel Johnson (1709–84) and Victorian novelist Charles Dickens (*p174*). Today it offers accommodation in comfortable antique rooms and in the elegant, more modern adjacent town house. It also has an excellent restaurant serving British seasonal dishes.

⌂ 18 Castle St
🌐 bullsheadinn.co.uk

ⓔⓔⓔ

← Colourful shops and pubs lining Church Street

Mighty Beaumaris Castle against a backdrop of Snowdonia's rolling peaks ↑

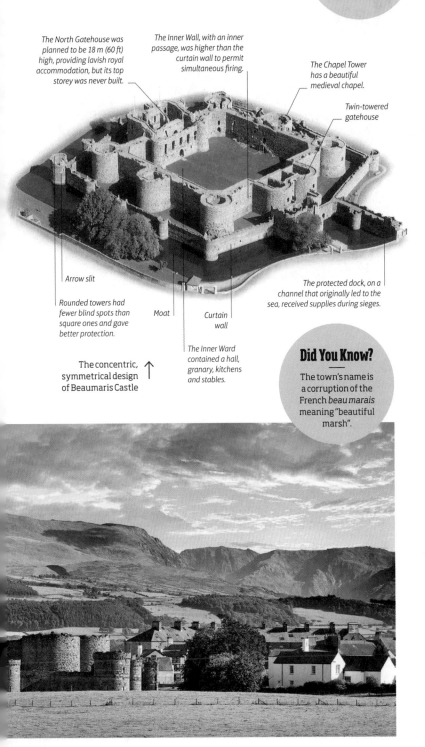

The North Gatehouse was planned to be 18 m (60 ft) high, providing lavish royal accommodation, but its top storey was never built.

The Inner Wall, with an inner passage, was higher than the curtain wall to permit simultaneous firing.

The Chapel Tower has a beautiful medieval chapel.

Twin-towered gatehouse

Arrow slit

Rounded towers had fewer blind spots than square ones and gave better protection.

Moat

Curtain wall

The protected dock, on a channel that originally led to the sea, received supplies during sieges.

The Inner Ward contained a hall, granary, kitchens and stables.

The concentric, symmetrical design of Beaumaris Castle ↑

Did You Know?

The town's name is a corruption of the French *beau marais* meaning "beautiful marsh".

↑ The imposing towers of Caernarfon Castle, overlooking the boat-dotted harbour

EXPERIENCE MORE

⑤

Caernarfon

 Gwynedd 🚌 ℹ️ Castle Ditch; www.visit snowdonia.info

The gigantic **Caernarfon Castle**, with its polygonal towers, looms over this busy town and its harbour at the mouth of the Seiont River. Both town and castle were created after Edward I's defeat of the last native Welsh prince, Llywelyn ap Gruffydd, in 1283. The town walls merge with modern streets that spread beyond the medieval centre to a market square.

In the 19th century the castle ruins were restored by the architect Anthony Salvin. Today the castle contains the Royal Welsh Fusiliers Museum and exhibitions tracing the history of the Princes of Wales and exploring the importance of the castle in Welsh history.

Situated on the hill above the town are the ruins of Segontium, a Roman fort built in about AD 78.

Caernarfon Castle

🐾🕐🖐 🏰 Y Maes 🕐 Mar-Oct: 9:30am–5pm daily (Jul-Aug: to 6pm); Nov–Feb: 10am–4pm daily (from 11am Sun) 🌐 cadw.gov.wales

---

⑥

Bangor

 Gwynedd 🚉🚌 🌐 visit snowdonia.info/bangor

Founded in the 6th century, when a monastery was established here, Bangor is the oldest city in Wales. It is also one of the smallest, and has a very young population: more than half of its residents

Did You Know?

Caernarfon was the birthplace of the first Prince of Wales, Edward I's son, in 1284.

are students at Bangor University. Cultural attractions include the 19th-century Neo-Norman **Penrhyn Castle**, a museum and an arts centre.

Penrhyn Castle

🐾🕐🖐🌀🕐 🏰 Bangor 🕐 Mar-Oct: 11am–5pm daily; Nov–Feb: 11am–4pm Sat & Sun 🌐 nationaltrust.org

---

⑦

Llandudno

 Conwy 🚉🚌 ℹ️ Library Building, Mostyn St; www. visitllandudno.org.uk

The Victorian seaside town of Llandudno has the longest seaside pier in Wales at more than 700 m (2,295 ft). Alice Lidell (the real Alice in Wonderland) holidayed here and the town is proud of its assocation with the author Lewis Carroll. Sculptures relating to *Alice's Adventures in Wonderland* are dotted all over town, including a Mad Hatter on the promenade.

The exhibits at the **Llandudno Museum** explore the history of Llandudno from Roman times onwards.

Llandudno was built between its two headlands, Great Orme and Little Orme. The former, a designated nature reserve, has a ski slope and the longest toboggan run in Britain. In the Bronze Age copper was mined here; the **Great Orme Copper Mines** and their excavations are open to the public. Local history and wildlife are described in an information centre on the summit. There are two easy ways to reach the top: on the Great Orme Tramway, one of only three cable-hauled street tramways in the world (the others are in San Francisco and Lisbon), or by the Llandudno Cable Car. Both run from April to October.

Llandudno Museum

◈ ⊙ 🏛 **⌂** 17 Gloddaeth St
🕒 Times vary, check website
🌐 llandudnomuseum.co.uk

Great Orme Copper Mines

◈ ⊙ 🏛 **⌂** Great Orme
🕒 Mid-Mar–Oct: 9:30am–4:30pm daily 🌐 greatorme mines.info

8
Ruthin

⌂ Denbighshire 🚉
🌐 ruthin.com

This prosperous market town has fine half-timbered medieval buildings, including those now occupied by NatWest and Barclays banks in St Peter's Square. St Peter's Church, on the edge of the square, was founded in 1310 and has a Tudor oak ceiling in the north aisle. Next to the Castle Hotel is the Myddleton Grill restaurant, whose unusual, Dutch-style dormer windows are known locally as the "eyes of Ruthin".

Great Orme Tramway, climbing the hills above the seafront, Llandudno

STAY

Plas Bodegroes
An intimate hideaway, this Georgian mansion has ten beautifully decorated rooms and a superb restaurant.

Nefyn Rd, Pwheli, Llŷn Peninsula bodegroes.co.uk

££££

Porth Tocyn
A charming family-friendly country house hotel with an outdoor pool and tennis courts.

Bwlchtocyn, Abersoch, Llŷn Peninsula Nov-mid-Mar porthtocynhotel.co.uk

££££

Glasgwm
This welcoming B&B is in a handsome Victorian town house.

Abbey Rd, Llangollen glasgwm-llangollen.co.uk

££££

Llŷn Peninsula

Gwynedd Pwllheli Aberdaron to Bardsey Island visitsnowdonia.info

This 38-km (24-mile) finger of land pointing southwest from Snowdonia into the Irish Sea is known for its untamed beauty.

On the south side of the peninsula is the 13th-century **Criccieth Castle**, built by Llewelyn the Great.

The windy headland of Braich-y-Pwll at the western tip of the peninsula, near the former fishing village of Aberdaron, looks out towards Bardsey Island, the "Isle of 20,000 Saints". This became a place of pilgrimage in the 6th century, when a monastery was founded here. Some of the saints are said to be buried in the churchyard of the ruined 13th-century St Mary's Abbey. Ferries take visitors to the island to see its scenery and colonies of grey seals.

East of Aberdaron is the 7-km (4-mile) bay of Porth Neigwl, known in English as Hell's Mouth, the scene of many shipwrecks due to the bay's treacherous currents. Hidden in sheltered grounds above Porth Neigwl bay, 1.5 km (1 mile) northeast of

Aberdaron, is **Plas-yn-Rhiw**, a small medieval manor house with Tudor and Georgian additions and lovely gardens.

The former quarrying village and "ghost town" of Llithfaen, tucked away below the sheer cliffs of the mountainous north coast, is now a centre for Welsh language studies.

Criccieth Castle
Castle St Apr-Oct: 10am-5pm daily; Nov-Mar: 10am-4pm Mon-Sat, 11am-4pm Sun cadw.gov.wales

Plas-yn-Rhiw
Off B4413 Apr-Oct: noon-5pm daily; Nov-Mar: 11am-3:30pm Sat & Sun (garden only) nationaltrust.org.uk

Bala

Gwynedd From Wrexham visitbala.org

Bala Lake, Wales's largest natural lake, lies between the Aran and Arenig mountains at the fringes of Snowdonia

↑ Wild flowers on Braich-y-Pwll, a wind-lashed promontory on the Llŷn Peninsula

↑ The remains of Castell Dinas Brân, a 13th-century hilltop castle in Llangollen

Did You Know?

The Irish "Ladies of Llangollen" eloped to Wales dressed as men in 1778, scandalizing Georgian society.

National Park. It is popular for watersports, and the **National Whitewater Centre** organizes exhilarating excursions along the River Tryweryn.

The little grey-stone town of Bala is a Welsh-speaking community, its houses strung out along a single street at the eastern end of the lake. Thomas Charles (1755–1814), a Methodist Church leader, once lived here.

The narrow-gauge Bala Lake Railway follows the lakeshore from Llanuwchllyn, 6 km (4 miles) southwest.

National Whitewater Centre

⌂ Frongoch ☉ Mar–Oct: 11am–2pm Mon–Fri, 8:30am–4:30pm Sat & Sun ⓦ national whitewatercentre.co.uk

---

⓫ Llangollen

⌂ Denbighshire ⊕
ⓘ Y Capel, Castle St; www.llangollen.org.uk

Best known for its annual Eisteddfod (festival), this pretty town sits on the River Dee. In the 1700s, two Irishwomen, Sarah Ponsonby and Lady Eleanor Butler, the "Ladies of Llangollen", set up house together in the half-timbered **Plas Newydd**. Their unconventional dress and literary enthusiasms attracted such celebrities as the Duke of Wellington and William Wordsworth (p358). The ruins of a 13th-century castle, Castell Dinas Brân, occupy the summit of a hill overlooking the house.

Boats on the Llangollen Canal depart from Wharf Hill in summer and cross the Pontcysyllte Aqueduct, built by Scottish engineer Thomas Telford and now a UNESCO World Heritage Site.

Plas Newydd

 ⌂ Hill St ☉ Apr–Sep: 11am–4:30pm daily ⓦ nationaltrust.org.uk

---

TOP 5 WELSH BEACHES

Abersoch
One of the best beaches on the Llŷn Peninsula, with lots of water-sports on offer.

Barmouth
This huge and scenic sandy beach, squeezed between mountains and sea, is very popular with surfers.

Trearrdur Bay
Wide and sandy, the beach at Trearrdur Bay attracts surfers and scuba-divers.

Rhoscolyn
The perfect family beach, with gently sloping sand and plenty of rock pools for children to explore.

Rhossili Bay
This 5-km (3-mile) stretch of sand has offshore islands to wade to at low tide.

SOUTH AND MID-WALES

South Wales's coastal strip has been settled for many centuries, as evidenced by prehistoric finds in the Vale of Glamorgan and Pembrokeshire. The Romans established a major base at Caerleon, where there are outstanding remains of an amphitheatre and baths; Caerleon also lays claim to being the site of Camelot, King Arthur's fabled court. Later, the Normans built castles all the way from Chepstow to Pembroke.

In the 18th and 19th centuries, coalmines and ironworks opened in the valleys of South Wales, attracting immigrants from all over Europe. Close communities developed to serve the growing coal trade, and Cardiff, which only became Wales' capital city in 1955, was transformed from a sleepy coastal town into the world's busiest coal-exporting port. The demise of the coal industry in the 1970s and 1980s devastated many Valley communities, and whilst the spoil heaps are now verdant hills and the old pits exciting new heritage sites, unemployment remains a major issue. Cardiff, on the other hand, has reinvented itself as a thoroughly modern European metropolis.

SOUTH AND MID-WALES

The Green Bridge of Wales near Stack Rocks, Pembrokeshire Coast Path ↑

PEMBROKESHIRE COAST NATIONAL PARK

w pembrokeshirecoast.wales

Running along a supremely scenic stretch of coastline in Britain, the Pembrokeshire Coast National Park has one of the most diverse landscapes of any national park, encompassing beaches, estuaries, cliffs, woodland, marshland, heathland, hills and valleys. Its 629 sq km (243 sq miles) are home to wildlife ranging from puffins and skylarks to seals and crabs, with sharks and dolphins offshore.

① Saundersfoot

🚊🚌 Tenby **w** visitsaundersfootbay.com

Beaches, a harbour, numerous watersports and great food are among Saundersfoot's attractions. Less than 6 km (4 miles) north is Folly Farm, a fun place for kids with a petting farm, vintage fairground and theme park.

② Tenby

🚊🚌 **w** visittenby.co.uk

The busiest holiday resort on the Pembrokeshire coast, Tenby has beautiful sandy beaches that are among the cleanest and best in Europe. Little remains of the Norman castle though the impressive 11th-century town walls have survived. Tenby's streets are lined with fishing-village pastel-coloured houses

Regular boat trips take visitors to the two offshore islands, Caldey Island and St Catherine's Island.

Over the years Tenby has attracted artists, and the work of visiting and local artists can be seen at the **Tenby Museum and Art Gallery.**

Tenby Museum and Art Gallery

♿ 🏛 **o** Castle Hill, Tenby
🕐 10am–5pm daily
w tenbymuseum.org.uk

WALKING THE PEMBROKESHIRE COAST PATH

The Pembrokeshire Coast Path runs the entire length of the Welsh coast, a total of 300 km (185 miles). Opened in 1970, it is the best way to experience the Pembrokeshire coastline and national park. Most of the path runs along clifftops, providing spectacular views. Even if you don't think you can tackle the entire route, you should at least try one or two stretches of it. This is best done in summer when there are bus services to help you get back to where you started, or to move on to another section.

③ Pembroke Castle

 ⌂ Main St ⏰ 10am–5pm daily 🌐 pembroke castle.co.uk

Home of the earls of Pembroke for 300 years and birthplace of Henry VII, the first Tudor king, this mighty castle was begun in 1093, but most of the present buildings date to the 13th century. Lively displays narrate its history.

④ Porthgain

⌂ Fishguard Harbour 🌐 stdavidsinfo.org.uk/porthgain

Porthgain village's harbour was used to export slate from nearby quarries in the 19th century, but today it is very picturesque. Along the coast to the south is the Blue Lagoon, a former slate quarry that has been flooded to create a popular spot for swimming and watersports.

⑤ Fishguard

 ℹ Town Hall Market Square; 01437 776636

The main town in north Pembrokeshire is a lively mix of fishing village and tourist spot. It hosts the annual Fishguard Folk Festival, held at the end of May. To the west is Strumble Head, one of the best places in Britain for seeing dolphins and porpoises.

⑥ Newport

ℹ John Frost Square; newport-pembs.co.uk

A popular holiday resort, Newport was founded in the 12th century. A castle was built by the Normans, which is now in ruins, and a later castle was added in the 19th century, which is today a private home. Newport's streets are lined with pretty cottages and the town makes a good base for walkers .

⑦ St Bride's Bay

One of the least developed parts of Wales, St Brides Bay features rugged cliffs, sandy beaches and islands with abundant wildlife, along with a cluster of fishing villages and small resorts. Boats depart for the islands of Skomer, Skokholm and Grassholm from Martin's Haven. The villages of Little Haven and Broad Haven are where most of the facilities are for this area, while the northern end of the bay includes Newgale with its large beach, and Solva, a popular village for walkers.

EAT

Sloop Inn
A traditional 1743 inn close to the harbour, with hearty food and occasional live music.

⌂ Porthgain
🌐 sloop.co.uk

£ £ £

The Salt Cellar
Superb dishes champion local produce at this restaurant with a pretty terrace.

⌂ Esplanade, Tenby
🌐 thesaltcellar tenby.co.uk

£ £ £

Coast
Enjoy wonderful sea views while dining on fish and seafood.

⌂ Coppet Hall Beach, Saundersfoot
🌐 coastsaundersfoot.co.uk

£ £ £

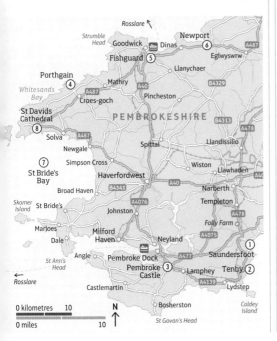

⑧ 🖊 🛍

ST DAVIDS CATHEDRAL

🏛 Cathedral Close, St Davids 🚉 Haverfordwest,
then bus ⏰ 9am–5pm Mon–Sat, noon–5pm Sun
🌐 stdavidscathedral.org.uk

The final resting place of St David, Wales's patron saint,
St Davids is officially Britain's smallest city and the site
of a splendid cathedral, which has attracted pilgrims
and visitors for thousands of years, and the Bishops's
Palace with lavish private apartments, now in ruins.

St David founded a monastic settlement in this remote
corner of southwest Wales in about AD 550, which became an
important Christian shrine. The present cathedral, built in the
12th century, and the Bishop's Palace, added a century later,
are set in a grassy hollow below St Davids city. The date of St
David's death, 1 March, is commemorated throughout Wales.

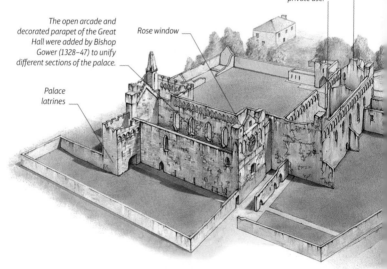

The Private Chapel was a late 14th-century addition, built, like the rest of the palace, over a series of vaults.

The Bishop's Hall, smaller than the Great Hall, may have been reserved for private use.

The open arcade and decorated parapet of the Great Hall were added by Bishop Gower (1328–47) to unify different sections of the palace.

Rose window

Palace latrines

GREAT HALL

This reconstruction shows
the hall of the Bishop's
Palace with a wooden
screen before the lead
was stripped from the roof.
Bishop Barlow, St Davids'
first Protestant bishop
(1536–48), is thought to
have been responsible for
the lead's removal.

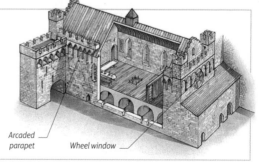

Arcaded parapet

Wheel window

↑ Remains of the Bishop's Palace, built between 1280 and 1350

EAT

Cwtch
An informal restaurant serving local dishes in a cosy, stone-walled 19th-century house.

🏠 22 High St
Ⓦ cwtchrestaurant.co.uk

£ £ £

In the nave's west end, eight stained-glass panels, produced in the 1950s, radiate from a central window depicting the dove of peace.

The roof of the nave is lowered and hidden by an early 16th-century oak ceiling. A beautiful 14th-century rood screen divides the nave from the choir.

The medieval tower's lantern ceiling was decorated with episcopal insignia when restored in the 1870s.

Bishop Vaughan's Chapel has a fine fan-vaulted early Tudor roof.

Sixteenth-century choirstalls have some interesting misericords..

St David's shrine – a statue of the saint is placed near the shrine. Thought to symbolize the Holy Spirit, a dove is said to have landed on David's shoulder as he spoke to a gathering of bishops.

St Mary's College Chapel

St Davids Cathedral, an important site of pilgrimage *(above)*; reconstruction of the Bishop's Palace *(left)* ↑

← Nave of St Davids Cathedral with rounded arches

2

BRECON BEACONS

🏠 **Powys** 🚉 **Abergavenny** 🛈 **National Park Visitor Centre, near Libanus; www.breconbeacons.org**

Stretching west from the Wales–England border almost to Swansea, this national park's dramatic and varied scenery includes four mountain ranges (one being the Brecon Beacons themselves), swathes of high open grassland, wooded gorges, waterfalls and caves.

① Llyn y Fan Fach

🚉🚌 **Llangadog**

The "Lake of the Little Hill" stands at 510 m (1,660 ft) and is surrounded by the even higher peaks of the Black Mountain range. Llyn y Fan Fach is embued with myth and legend, being one of many lakes around Britain from which a beautiful woman is said to have emerged. She enchanted a local boy and her father allowed them to marry provided he would never hit her three times. Inevitably this happened, and the woman returned to the lake, leaving her husband broken-hearted.

②  Carreg Cennen Castle

🏠 **Trapp, Llandeilo**
🚉🚌 **Ffairfach** ⏱ **Apr–Oct: 9:30am–6pm daily; Nov–Mar: 9:30am–4.30pm daily**
🌐 **carregcennencastle.com**

One of the most dramatically located castles in Wales, "The Castle on the Rock above the Cennen" stands on cliffs hundreds of feet above the River Cennen, visible for miles around. Dating from the 13th century, it was destroyed in 1462 during the Wars of the Roses and has been largely in ruins ever since.

It's a steep path up from the car park to the castle, but the reward is unrivalled views over the surrounding country-side. For anyone staying behind there are lovely tea-rooms, a craftshop and a working farm-yard to explore. The entry charge is for the castle only.

③ Hay Bluff

🚉 **Abergavenny** 🚌 **Little Ffordd-fawr**

Hay Bluff is 8 km (5 miles) south of Hay-on-Wye *(p462)* and its summit is only about 600 m (2,000 ft) from the English border. Rising to 677 m (2,221 ft) in height, it marks the northern edge of the Black Mountains. There are several paths to the top, all fairly easy walking, but check the local weather conditions

> **Llyn y Fan Fach is embued with myth and legend, being one of many lakes around Britain from which a beautiful woman is said to have emerged.**

Priory inspired JMW Turner to paint it in 1794. Its roots go back to about 1100 when it was established as an Augustinian priory. A church was soon added and more buildings followed in the 14th century, by which time the priory was one of the most important in Wales. After the Dissolution of the Monasteries the buildings fell into ruin, and today they can be seen within the grounds of the luxury Llanthony Priory Hotel.

Sunrise over the ruins of Carreg Cennen Castle, perched on a rocky crag

before setting off. If you climb up from the west then come down the eastward flank, you'll be in England before you get to the bottom of the hill.

④
Llanthony Priory

🏠 Llanthony 🚌
🚌 Abergavenny
🌐 llanthonypriory
hotel.co.uk

Surrounded by picturesque hills and woodland, Llanthony

⑤
Monmouthshire and Brecon Canal

🌐 canalrivertrust.org.uk

The Monmouthshire and Brecon Canal snakes its slow way through the Brecon Beacons National Park along the Usk Valley. Today this remnant of two longer former waterways runs for 56 km (35 miles) from Brecon to the Pontymoile basin. The ideal way to experience it is, naturally, on a narrowboat, although you can also walk or cycle the towpath. Whichever way you go, you'll come across former industrial buildings, reflecting the canal's history, and abundant wildlife.

Must See

SHOP

Penderyn Distillery
Grab a chance to taste and buy Welsh whiskies aged in bourbon barrels and Madeira casks on a tour of Wales's first modern whisky distillery, nestled in the southern foothills of the Brecon Beacons.

🏠 Penderyn, 11 km (7 miles) W of Merthyr Tydfil 🌐 penderyn. wales

⑥
Pen y Fan

🏠 Merthyr Tydfil
🚌 Pont ar Daf

At 886 m (2,900 ft) Pen y Fan is the highest mountain in south Wales and also one of the most popular with hikers. There are several paths to the top; the Beacons Way long-distance footpath runs straight across it. There are truly breathtaking views when the weather is clear, to the Bristol Channel in one direction and Shropshire in the other.

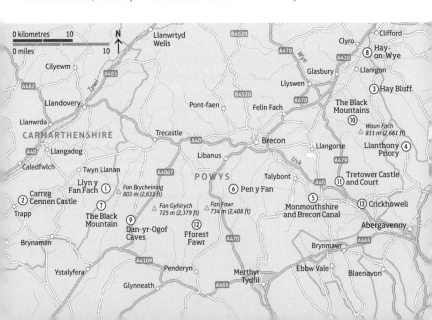

⑦

The Black Mountain

🚗 Llangadog ⛰ Dan-yr-Ogof Caves 🌐 brecon
beacons.org

The Black Mountain is a mountain range at the western end of the Brecon Beacons National Park, as opposed to The Black Mountains at the eastern end. The highest peak is Fan Brycheiniog, rising dramatically to 803 m (2,633 ft) above Llyn y Fan Fach (p460); it's a challenging hike to the top. This end of the national park is more remote, receiving fewer visitors.

The western end of the Brecon Beacons was one of the last parts of Wales where the once-endangered red kite managed to survive until a concerted effort saw this magnificent bird of prey re-established across Wales and southern England.

---

⑧

Hay-on-Wye

📍 Powys 🛈 Oxford Rd;
www.hay-on-wye.co.uk

Book-lovers from all over the world come to this small border town in the Black Mountains, just to the north of Hay Bluff (p460). Its numerous second-hand bookshops stock millions of titles, and in early summer the town hosts the prestigious Hay Festival of

> **INSIDER TIP**
> **Think Outside the Book**
>
> HowTheLightGetsIn, the world's largest philosophy and music festival, takes place alongside Hay's literary extravaganza in May or June. Past speakers have included Noam Chomsky, James Lovelock and Brian Eno.

↑ Underground lakes and cascades dramatically illuminated in the Dan-yr-Ogof Caves

Literature and the Arts. Hay-on-Wye's love affair with books began when a bookshop was opened in the 1960s by Richard Booth, who claims the (fictitious) title of King of Independent Hay. He lived in Hay Castle, a 17th-century mansion in the grounds of the original 13th-century castle. Acquired in 2011 by a charitable trust in a sad state of disrepair, it is hoped it will reopen in 2020 after a major renovation. Hay's oldest inn, the half-timbered 16th-century Three Tuns on Bridge Street, is said to have hosted some colourful visitors, including Marianne Faithfull and the Great Train Robbers.

---

⑨

Dan-yr-Ogof Caves

📍 Abercraf 🚌🚗 Brecon,
🕐 Apr-Oct: 10am-3pm daily
(to 3.30pm during Welsh school holidays) 🌐 show
caves.co.uk

The network of caves at Dan-yr-Ogof is thought to be the largest in Britain, and only part of it is open to the public. A further section is open to experienced cavers, and there is still more to be explored: at present the main cave extends for 17 km (11 miles), and some cavers believe this

> ## Did You Know?
> ―――
> Former US president Bill Clinton has called the Hay Festival "the Woodstock of the Mind".

is only about 10 percent of the full network. The caves were discovered in 1912 by three brothers who managed to cross four subterranean lakes before they could go no further. The complex also has other attractions, including a museum and a prehistoric theme park with dinosaurs.

---

⑩

The Black Mountains

📍 Abergavenny
🚌 Pengenffordd
🌐 breconbeacons.org

Standing at the eastern end of the Brecon Beacons National Park, the Black Mountains extend further east into England's Herefordshire. The range has several peaks over 610 m (2,000 ft); the highest is Waun Fach at 811 m (2,661 ft). The mountains are criss-crossed with hiking and ridge trails, providing some of the best views in the national park. Several long-distance footpaths also pass through them, including the Offa's Dyke National Trail, The Marches Way and The Beacons Way.

⑪ Tretower Castle and Court

🏰 Tretower, Crickhowel
🚉 Abergavenny 🚌 Gilfaes Turn ⏰ Apr–Oct: 10am–5pm daily; Nov–Mar: 10am–4pm Thu–Sat 🌐 cadw.gov.wales

Tretower Castle has had a chequered history in the 900 years since it was built. It began life in the early 12th century, and 200 years later the separate group of buildings forming the fortified manor house known as Tretower Court were added. In the 15th century the properties were given to the Vaughan family, remaining in their hands until sold in 1783. They then became a working farm and the buildings were neglected until a 21st-century restoration has seen them opened to the public. Several re-created rooms show what life was like in 1470, when the wealthy Vaughan family entertained lavishly.

⑫ Fforest Fawr

🕳 Dan-yr-Ogof Caves
🚉 Taffs Well 🌐 brecon beacons.org

This expanse of woodland is so beautiful that it is often used as a film and TV location. Several high peaks rise up out of the forests and fields of this former royal hunting estate – the highest is Fan Fawr (Big Peak) at 734 m (2,408 ft). There are trails for hiking and cycling, and a sculpture trail too.

The most prominent man-made feature in the area is Castell Coch (p467), the "Red Castle" whose 14th-century ruins were magnificently transformed in the 19th century by the 3rd Marquess of Bute.

⑬ Crickhowell

🏰 Powys
🚉🚌 Abergavenny
🌐 visitcrickhowell.co.uk

Standing on the River Usk, Crickhowell makes a good base for exploring the Brecon Beacons National Park. There are

Must See

THE GREEN MAN FESTIVAL

This music and arts festival takes place every August in Glanusk Park, on the edge of Crickhowell. First held in 2003, it regularly attracts 20,000 people who flock to see musicians and other artists from all over the world across 19 stages. Stars over the years have included Yo La Tengo, Ryan Adams, Richard Thompson, Fleet Foxes, Van Morrison and Mumford & Sons (www.greenman.net).

---

plentiful outdoor activities within easy reach of the town, including fishing and rock-climbing as well as hiking and biking. Other attractions include the ruins of the 12th-century Crickhowell Castle, a 14th-century church and a 17th-century bridge across the River Usk, which is unusual in having 12 arches on one side but 13 on the other. Crickhowell is also home to the annual Green Man Festival.

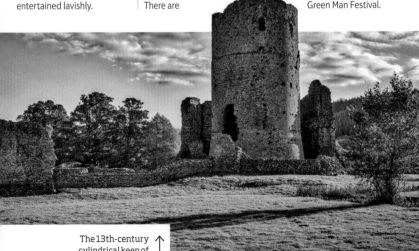

The 13th-century cylindrical keep of Tretower Castle

3

CARDIFF

⌂ Glamorgan ✈ Rhoose ▣ Central Sq 🚌 Wood St
ℹ Cardiff Castle; www.visitcardiff.com

In 1913 this was the world's busiest coal-exporting port, thanks to its rail links with the South Wales mines. Its wealth paid for grandiose architecture, while the dock area became a raucous boom town. But by the time Cardiff became Wales's capital in 1955, demand for coal was falling and the docks were in decline. The city has since been transformed by urban renewal programmes.

The Hayes, a classy shopping and dining street ↑

①

Principality Stadium

⌂ Westgate St
🌐 principalitystadium.wales

The national stadium of Wales, home of the Welsh national rugby union team, opened in 1999 to host the Rugby World Cup. It is open for guided tours – book online.

②

Wales Millennium Centre

⌂ Bute Pl, Cardiff Bay
🕙 9am–7pm daily
🌐 wmc.org.uk

Opened in 2004, this leading cultural centre stages a range of arts performances including ballet, opera, contemporary dance and musicals. It is home to leading cultural bodies such as the Welsh National Opera, National Dance Company Wales and BBC National Orchestra Wales. You can book a behind-the-scenes tour.

③

Pierhead

⌂ Cardiff Bay
🕙 10:30am–4:30pm daily 🌐 pierhead.org

This 1897 French-Gothic Renaissance building is one of Cardiff's most familiar landmarks. Formerly the headquarters of the Bute Dock Company, it now houses an illuminating exhibition on the history of the docks.

> **Did You Know?**
>
> Prior to 1955, Wales had no official capital. Cardiff is Europe's smallest capital city.

④

Craft in the Bay

⌂ The Flourish, Lloyd George Ave, Cardiff Bay
🕙 10:30am–5:30pm daily
🌐 makersguildinwales.co.uk

The Makers' Guild in Wales organizes exhibitions and demonstrations, such as weaving and pottery, at this extensive crafts gallery.

⑤

National Museum Cardiff

⌂ Cathays Park 🕙 10am–5pm Tue–Sun, public hols
🌐 museum.wales

Opened in 1927, this museum occupies an impressive building with a colonnaded

↑ A line of poetry in English and Welsh by poet Gwyneth Lewis on the Wales Millennium Centre

portico and domed roof. Its collections mainly centre on natural history and art. The art collection is among the finest in Europe, with paintings, drawings, sculpture, silver and ceramics from 1500 to the present, with works by Renoir, Monet and van Gogh.

Portland stone is set among parks and avenues around Alexandra Gardens. The City Hall (1905), one of its first buildings, is dominated by its 60-m (200-ft) dome and clock tower. The first-floor

Marble Hall is furnished with Siena marble columns and statues of Welsh heroes, among them St David, Wales's patron saint (p458). The Civic Centre also houses parts of Cardiff University.

⑥ Ⓜ
City Hall and Civic Centre

Ⓐ Cathay's Park Ⓒ Mon–Fri Ⓒ Public hols

Cardiff's Civic Centre of Neo-Classical buildings in white

SHOP

Cardiff Market

This Victorian glass-roofed market is packed with stalls selling a variety of goods from fresh fish and Welsh cakes to souvenirs.

Ⓐ Between St Mary & Trinity sts Ⓒ 8:30am–5:30pm Mon–Sat

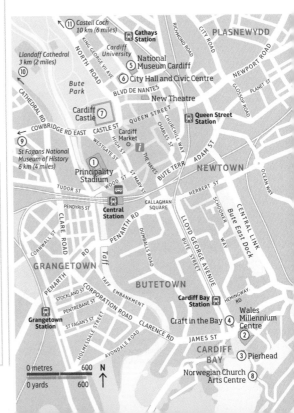

Cardiff Castle

🏛 Castle St ◷ 9am–5pm daily (Mar–Oct: to 6pm)
🌐 cardiffcastle.com

Cardiff Castle began life as a Roman fort, whose remains are separated from later work by a band of red stone. A keep was built within the Roman ruins in the 12th century. Over the following 700 years, the castle passed into the hands of several powerful families and eventually to John Stuart, son of the Earl of Bute, in 1776. His great-grandson, the 3rd Marquess of Bute, employed the "eccentric genius" architect William Burges, who created an ornate mansion between 1869 and 1881, rich in medieval images and romantic detail.

Did You Know?

Roald Dahl was born in Cardiff to Norwegian parents and was baptized in the Norwegian church.

⑧ 🖥

Norwegian Church Arts Centre

🏛 Harbour Dr, Cardiff Bay ◷ 10:30am–5pm daily 🌐 norwegian churchcardiff.com

The wooden Norwegian Church was first erected in 1868 for Norwegian sailors bringing wooden props for use in the coal pits of the South Wales valleys. The building was dismantled and rebuilt as part of dockland redevelopment in the early 1990s. Now an arts centre, it hosts changing exhibitions and arts and crafts stalls.

⑨ 🏛 🍽

St Fagans National Museum of History

🏛 St Fagans ◷ 10am–5pm daily 🌐 museum.wales

Established during the 1940s at St Fagans, on the western edge of the city, the open-air St Fagans National History Museum was one of the first of its kind. Buildings from all over Wales, including workers' terraced cottages,

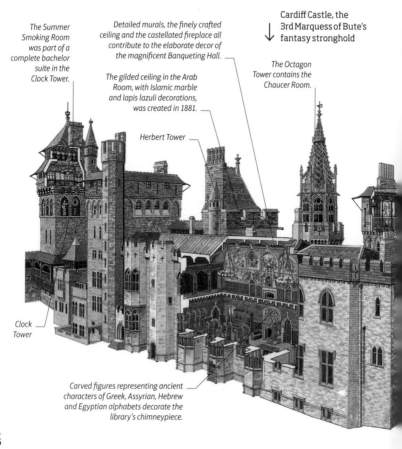

The Summer Smoking Room was part of a complete bachelor suite in the Clock Tower.

Detailed murals, the finely crafted ceiling and the castellated fireplace all contribute to the elaborate decor of the magnificent Banqueting Hall.

Cardiff Castle, the 3rd Marquess of Bute's fantasy stronghold

The gilded ceiling in the Arab Room, with Islamic marble and lapis lazuli decorations, was created in 1881.

The Octagon Tower contains the Chaucer Room.

Herbert Tower

Clock Tower

Carved figures representing ancient characters of Greek, Assyrian, Hebrew and Egyptian alphabets decorate the library's chimneypiece.

farmhouses, a tollhouse, a row of shops, a chapel and an old schoolhouse have been carefully reconstructed within the 40-ha (100-acre) parklands, along with a re-created Celtic village. Visitors can also explore a Tudor mansion that boasts its own beautiful gardens in the grounds. You can explore

Castell Coch (the "red castle" in Welsh) with its High Victorian interiors *(inset)* ↑

the story of Wales, its rich heritage and culture, through interactive exhibits in the galleries.

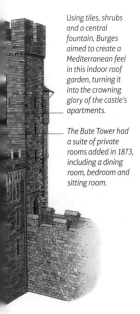

Using tiles, shrubs and a central fountain, Burges aimed to create a Mediterranean feel in this indoor roof garden, turning it into the crowning glory of the castle's apartments.

The Bute Tower had a suite of private rooms added in 1873, including a dining room, bedroom and sitting room.

⑩
Llandaff Cathedral

🏛 Cathedral Close, Llandaff 🕐 9am until after the last service of the day daily (from 7am Sun)
🌐 llandaffcathedral.org.uk

Lying in a deep, grassy hollow beside the River Taf at Llandaff, 3 km (2 miles) northwest of Cardiff city centre, this medieval cathedral occupies the site of a 6th-century monastic community. After being restored following severe bomb damage during World War II, it was eventually reopened in 1957 with the addition of Sir Jacob Epstein's huge, stark statue, *Christus*, which is mounted on a concrete arch.

⑪
Castell Coch

🏰 10 km (6 miles) NW of Cardiff, off the A470 at Tongwynlais 📞 029 2081 0101 🕐 Mar–Oct: 9:30am–5pm daily (Jul–Aug: to 6pm); Nov–Feb: 10am–4pm Mon–Sat, 11am–4pm Sun

Castell Coch is typical of the "mock castles" commissioned by the industrial barons of the Victorian era. It was built in Neo-Gothic style in the 1870s for the 3rd Marquess of Bute, over the ruins of a 13th-century castle. The design, by William Burges, aimed to reproduce a medieval Welsh chieftain's stronghold. There are ornate chambers, winding stone staircases and dark dungeons to explore, including the impressive remains of the original 13th-century castle.

EXPERIENCE MORE

4

Powis Castle

🏰 Welshpool, Powys
🚉 Welshpool then bus
🕐 House: 11am–5pm daily
(Oct–Feb: to 4pm); Gardens:
10am–6pm daily (Oct–Feb:
to 4pm) 🌐 nationaltrust.
org.uk

Powis Castle began life in the
13th century as a fortress,
built by the princes of Powys
to control the border with
England. However, this red-
stone building has served as a
country mansion for centuries.

The Dining Room,
decorated with fine 17th-
century panelling and family
portraits, was originally

designed as the castle's Great
Hall. The Great Staircase,
added in the late 17th century
and elaborately decorated
with carved fruit and flowers,
leads to the main apartments:
an early 19th-century library,
the panelled Oak Drawing
Room and the Elizabethan
Long Gallery, where plasterwork on the fireplace and
ceiling date from the 1590s.
In the Blue Drawing Room
there are three 18th-century
Brussels tapestries.

The gardens at Powis were
created between 1688 and
1722 and feature a series of
elegant Italianate terraces
adorned with statues, niches,
balustrades, hanging gardens
and sinuous mounded yew
trees. They are the only
formal gardens of this period
in Britain that have retained
their original layout.

Powis Castle seen
from the gardens;
an Antonio Verrio
painting by the Great
↓ Staircase *(inset)*

> **During the last week
> of August residents
> in Llandrindod Wells
> don period costume
> at the restored 19th-
> century Pump room
> in Temple Gardens.**

5

Llandrindod Wells

🏰 Powys 🚉 ℹ️ Town Hall,
Temple St; 01597 822600

This spa town became Wales's
premier inland resort in the
19th century and is a perfect
example of a Victorian town,
with canopied streets, wrought
ironwork, gabled villas, a
boating lake and ornamental
parklands, such as the well-
tended Rock Park Gardens.

Today Llandrindod makes
every effort to preserve its
Victorian character. During the
Victorian Festival in the last
full week of August people
don period costume at the
19th-century Pump Room in
Temple Gardens and there are

EAT

The Temple Bar

This casual bar and bistro with red-brick walls and stained-glass windows also displays contemporary art.

◫ Fiveways, Temple St, Llandrindod Wells
ⓦ thetemple bar.co.uk

£ £ £

The Horse and Jockey Inn

A 14th-century coaching inn with open fires and a great choice of locally sourced food.

◫ Wylcwm Place, Knighton
ⓦ thehorseandjockey inn.co.uk

£ £ £

↑ Bunting across the High Street in Knighton, with the clock tower at the top

free music concerts. Cars are banned from the town centre.

The **Radnorshire Museum** traces the town's past as one of a string of 19th-century spas, which included Builth, Llangammarch and Llanwrtyd. The National Cycle Museum charts the history of the bicycle, from an 1818 Hobby Horse to the present day.

Radnorshire Museum

 ◫ Temple St ☏ 01597 824513 ◷ 10am–4pm Tue–Fri, 10am–1pm Sat (Apr–Sep: 11am–4pm Sat)

---

❻ Cardigan

◫ Ceredigion ◪ Fishguard Harbour then bus
ⓦ visitcardigan.com

This small town grew up around **Cardigan Castle**. Built by the River Teifi in the 12th century, the castle eventually fell into disrepair until it was bought by the council in 2003 and renovated. It now houses exhibitions on local history and the Eisteddfod (p449).

Upstream from the town centre are the Teifi Marshes and the **Welsh Wildlife Centre**, providing nature trails, bird observation hides, a willow maze and adventure playground. Eight kilometres (5 miles) north of the town, Mwnt Beach is an attractive family beach and a good place for dolphin-watching.

Cardigan Castle

◈ ◈ ⏱ 🏠 ◫ Green Stt
◷ 10am–4pm daily
ⓦ cardigancastle.com

Welsh Wildlife Centre

◈ 🏠 ◫ Cilgerran ◷ 10am–4pm daily (summer: to 5pm)
ⓦ welshwildlife.org

---

❼ Knighton

◫ Powys ◪ 🛈 Offa's Dyke Centre, West St; www.visitknighton.co.uk

Knighton's Welsh name, Tref y Clawdd ("The Town on the Dyke"), reflects its status as the only original settlement on Offa's Dyke.

Knighton is set on a steep hill, sloping upwards from St Edward's Church (1877) with its medieval tower, to the summit, where a castle once stood. The main street leads via the market square, which has a 19th-century clock tower, along The Narrows, a Tudor street with little shops. The Old House on Broad Street is a medieval "cruck" house (curved timbers form a frame to support the roof), with a hole in the ceiling instead of a chimney.

OFFA'S DYKE

In the 8th century, King Offa of Mercia (central and southern England) constructed a ditch and bank to mark out his territory, and to enable the enforcement of a Saxon law: "Neither shall a Welshman cross into English land without the appointed man from the other side, who should meet him at the bank." Some of the best-preserved sections of the 6-m- (20-ft-) high earthwork lie in the hills around Knighton. The Offa's Dyke Footpath runs for 285 km (177 miles) along the border between England and Wales.

8

Llanwrtyd Wells

⌂ Powys
🚌🚆 To Llanwrtyd
🌐 llanwrtyd.com

With a population of less than 1,000, Llanwrtyd Wells claims to be the smallest town in Wales. It is also possibly the wackiest, with a number of unusual events. It all began with the invention of the World Bogsnorkelling Championship, which expanded to become the Bogsnorkelling Triathlon. This was followed by an annual Man-versus-Horse marathon and the World Alternative Games, which feature such events as wife-carrying and gravy wrestling. There's also a Saturnalia Beer Festival and Chariot Race Championship.

9

Machynlleth

⌂ Powys 🚆 ℹ Welshpool; www.midwalesmy way.com

Half-timbered buildings and Georgian façades appear among the grey-stone houses in Machynlleth. It was here

that Owain Glyndŵr, Wales's last native leader, held a parliament in 1404. The restored Parliament House now contains the **Owain Glyndŵr Centre**.

The ornate Clock Tower, on Maengwyn Street, was erected in 1874 by the Marquess of Londonderry; nearby, MOMA Machynlleth is a gallery showing modern Welsh art. In an old slate quarry 4 km (2 miles) to the north, a "village of the future" is run by the **Centre for Alternative Technology**.

Owain Glyndŵr Centre

🕐 ⌂ Maengwyn St
🕐 Easter-Dec: 11am-3pm daily 🌐 canolfanglyndwr.org

Centre for Alternative Technology

♿🅿🚻☕ ⌂ On A487
🕐 10am-5pm daily
🚫 24 Dec-1 Jan 🌐 cat.org.uk

10

Elan Valley

⌂ Powys 🚆 Llandrindod
ℹ Rhayader; www. elanvalley.org.uk

A string of spectacular reservoirs, the first of Wales's

artificial lakes, has made this one of the country's most famous valleys. Caban Coch, Garreg Ddu, Pen-y-Garreg and Craig Goch were created between 1892 and 1903 to supply water to Birmingham, 117 km (73 miles) away. They form a chain of lakes about 14 km (9 miles) long, holding 50 billion litres (13 billion gallons) of water. Victorian engineers selected these high moorlands on the Cambrian Mountains for their high annual rainfall. The choice created bitter controversy and resentment: more than 100 people had to move from

→
Enjoying the sunshine on one of the sandy beaches in New Quay

---

ROYAL WELSH SHOW

Established in 1904, the Royal Welsh Show (www.rwas.wales/ royal-welsh-show) takes place annually in Llanelwedd, about 80 km (50 miles) south of Machynlleth. The show features country-side sports and pursuits like sheep shearing, sheepdog trials, falconry and horse riding, plus livestock competitions, a tug-of-war and pole-climbing, along with arts and crafts displays, live music and a food hall.

The Craig Goch dam, built in the late 19th century in the Elan Valley

the valley that was flooded in order to create Caban Coch.

Finished in dressed stone, the dams here have an air of grandeur which is lacking in the huge Claerwen reservoir, a stark addition built during the early 1950s to double the lakes' capacity. Contained by a 355-m (1,165-ft) dam, it lies 6 km (4 miles) along the B4518, which runs through Elan Valley and offers magnificent views.

The remote moorlands and woodlands surrounding the lakes are an important habitat for wildlife; the red kite can often be seen here. The Elan Valley Visitors' Centre, beside the Caban Coch dam, describes the construction of the lakes, as well as the valley's own natural history. Elan Village, set beside the centre, is an unusual example of a model workers' village, built during the 1900s to house the waterworks staff. Outside the centre is a statue inspired by the poem *Prometheus Unbound* by Percy Bysshe Shelley, who stayed in the valley at the mansion of Nantgwyllt in 1810 with his wife, Harriet. The house now lies underneath the waters of Caban Coch, along with the rest of the old village.

 11

Aberaeron

🏛 Ceredigion
🚉 Aberystwyth then bus
ℹ Pen Cei; www.discover ceredigion.co.uk

Aberaeron's harbour, lined with Georgian houses, became a trading port and shipbuilding centre in the early 19th century. The town's orderly streets were laid out in pre-railway days, when the ports along Cardigan Bay enjoyed considerable wealth. The last boat was built here in 1994 and the harbour is now full of holiday sailors. The harbour can be crossed via a wooden footbridge.

The town is filled with delis, fishmongers and butchers selling local produce. On the quayside, the Hive honey ice-cream parlour serves world-renowned ice creams to a loyal clientele. The quayside is also the location for the Cardigan Bay Seafood Festival in July.

 12

New Quay

🏛 Ceredigion
🚉 Carmarthen then bus
ⓦ discoverceredigion.co.uk

A mix of small holiday resort and traditional fishing town, New Quay has several sandy beaches within easy reach. It's also a good place to see dolphins, since there is a resident pod in this part of Cardigan Bay.

Dylan Thomas visited frequently and even lived here for several months. New Quay is therefore one of several places claiming to be the inspiration for the poet's fictional town of Llareggub in *Under Milk Wood*.

 13

Mumbles and the Gower Peninsula

 Swansea
🌐 enjoygower.com

Swansea Bay leads to the Mumbles, a gateway to the 30-km- (19-mile-) long Gower Peninsula, Britain's first Area of Outstanding Natural Beauty. A string of sheltered bays leads to Oxwich and Port-Eynon beaches, popular with watersports enthusiasts. The vast beach at Rhossili leads to north Gower and a coast-line of low-lying burrows, salt marshlands and cockle beds.

The **National Botanic Garden of Wales** has a Great Glasshouse that contains a Mediterranean ecosystem.

National Botanic Garden of Wales

⊗🕐🅟🅗 🅐Middleton Hall, Llanarthne 🕐10am-6pm daily (Oct-Mar: to 4pm) 🌐botanicgarden.wales

---

 14

Swansea

🅐Swansea 🚄🚌🚢
🌐 visitswanseabay.com

Swansea, Wales's second city, is set along a wide, curving bay. A statue of copper magnate John Henry Vivian (1779–1855) overlooks the marina. The Vivians, a leading local family, founded the **Glynn Vivian Art Gallery**, which has Swansea pottery and porcelain. Archaeology and Welsh history feature at the **Swansea Museum**, the oldest museum in Wales.

The life and work of local poet Dylan Thomas (1914–53) is celebrated in the **Dylan Thomas Centre**. A permanent exhibition includes original drafts of his poems, letters and memorabilia. Thomas spent his childhood in the Uplands suburb. His birth-place, at 5 Cwmdonkin Drive, has been restored to how it would have been in 1914.

The **National Waterfront Museum** tells the story of industry and innovation in Wales over the past 300 years.

Glynn Vivian Art Gallery

◎🅟 🅐Alexandra Rd
🕐10am-5pm Tue-Sun
🌐swansea.gov.uk

Swansea Museum

🅟 🅐Victoria Rd 🕐10am-4:30pm Tue-Sun & public hols
🌐swanseamuseum.co.uk

Dylan Thomas Centre

🅐Somerset Pl 🕐10am-4:30pm Tue-Sun
🌐dylanthomas.com

National Waterfront Museum

◎ 🅐Oystermouth Rd
🕐10am-5pm daily
🌐museum.wales

EAT

Grape & Olive
On the top floor of the Meridian Tower, this restaurant serving creative cuisine offers fantastic views of Swansea Bay.

🅐Meridian Quay, Maritime Quarter, Swansea
📞01792 462617

£€£

←
Three Cliffs Bay, on the Gower Peninsula, an Area of Outstanding Natural Beauty

15

Blaenavon

⌂ Torfaen 🛈 World Heritage Centre, Church Rd; www.visitblaenavon.co.uk

Coal is no longer produced at Blaenavon's Big Pit, but the **Big Pit National Coal Museum** provides a vivid reminder of this tough industry. Visitors can see the blacksmith's forge, the

workshops and the engine house, as well as a replica of an underground gallery, where mining methods are explained. Then, kitted out with helmets and lamps, they descend by cage 90 m (300 ft) down the mineshaft, with ex-miners leading a tour of the underground workings.

Across the valley from Big Pit stand the 18th-century smelting furnaces and workers' cottages that were once part of the **Blaenavon Ironworks**, now a museum.

Big Pit National Coal Museum

🜲🜲🜲 ⌂ Blaenavon
🕐 9:30am–5pm daily
Ⓦ museum.wales

Blaenavon Ironworks

🜲🜲🜲🜲 ⌂ North St
🕐 Nov–Oct: 10am–4pm Thu–Sat; Apr–Nov: 10am–5pm daily Ⓦ cadw.gov.wales

---

16

Monmouth

⌂ Monmouthshire 🚌
🛈 Shire Hall; www.visit monmouthshire.com

This market town at the confluence of the Wye and Monnow rivers has many historical associations. The 11th-century castle, behind Agincourt Square, is in ruins but the **Regimental Museum**, beside it, remains open to the public. The castle was the birthplace of Henry V in 1387. Statues of Henry V (on the façade of Shire Hall) and Charles Stewart Rolls, founder of Roll-Royce cars, stand in the square.

Lord Horatio Nelson visited Monmouth in 1802. An excellent

←
Statue of the poet Dylan Thomas in Swansea's Maritime Quarter

Did You Know?
——
Wales is the only country in the world with a coastal path that covers the entire country.

collection of Nelson memorabilia is displayed at the **Nelson Museum**.

Monnow Bridge, on the town's western approach, is thought to be the only extant fortified bridge gate in Britain.

Regimental Museum

🜲 ⌂ The Castle 🕐 Apr–Oct: 2–5pm daily Ⓦ monmouth castlemuseum.org.uk

Nelson Museum

🜲 ⌂ Priory St 📞 01600 710 630 🕐 11am–4pm Thu–Tue

17

Aberystwyth

⌂ Ceredigion 🚌🚌
🛈 Terrace Rd; www. discoverceredigion.co.uk

This seaside university town claims to be the cultural capital of Mid-Wales. There have been no great changes along the promenade, with its gabled hotels, since the 19th century. Constitution Hill, a steep outcrop at the northern end, can be scaled in summer on the electric Cliff Railway, built in 1896. The ruined Aberystwyth Castle (1277) is south of the promenade. In the town centre, the **Ceredigion Museum** traces the history of the town.

The National Library of Wales, next to the university, has a valuable collection of ancient Welsh manuscripts.

Ceredigion Museum

🜲🜲 ⌂ Terrace Rd
🕐 10am–5pm Mon–Sat
📅 25 Dec–1 Jan Ⓦ ceredigion museum.wales

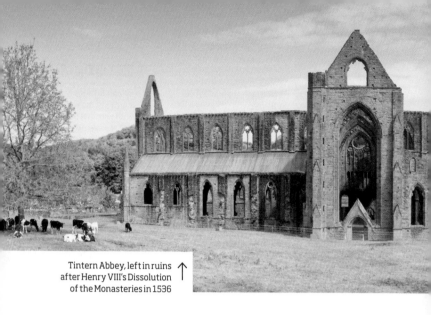

Tintern Abbey, left in ruins after Henry VIII's Dissolution of the Monasteries in 1536

Tintern Abbey

🏠 Monmouthshire
🚌 Chepstow then bus
🕐 Mar-Oct: 9:30am-5pm daily (Jul-Aug: to 6pm); Nov-Feb: 10am-4pm Mon-Sat
🌐 cadw.gov.wales

Since the 18th century, people have been enchanted by Tintern's setting in the steep and wooded Wye Valley and by its abbey's majestic ruins. Wordsworth's sonnet "Lines composed a few miles above Tintern Abbey" embodied his romantic view of the landscape:

once again
Do I behold these steep and
lofty cliffs,
That on a wild, secluded
scene impress
Thoughts of more deep seclusion

The abbey was founded in 1131 by Cistercian monks, who cultivated the surrounding lands (now forest), and it developed into an influential religious centre. By the 14th century this was the richest abbey in Wales, but along with other monasteries it was dissolved in 1536.

Caerleon

🏠 Newport ℹ️ John Frost Sq, Newport; www.newport.gov.uk

Together with York (*p374*) and Chester (*p354*), Caerleon was one of only three fortress settlements in Britain built for the Romans' elite legionary troops. From AD 74 Caerleon (*Isca* to the Romans, after the River Usk, which flows beside the town) was home to the 2nd Augustan Legion, which had been sent to Wales to crush the native Silures tribe. Covering an area of 20 ha (50 acres), Caerleon is one of the largest and most important Roman military sites in Europe. The Romans built not just a fortress for their crack 5,500-strong infantry division but a complete town to service their needs.

Outside the settlement, the amphitheatre's large stone foundations have survived in an excellent state of preservation. More impressive still is the fortress baths complex. The baths were designed to bring every home comfort to an army posted to barbaric Britain. The Roman troops could take a dip in the open-air swimming pool, play sports in the exercise yard or covered hall, or enjoy a series of hot and cold baths.

Nearby are the foundations of the only Roman legionary barracks on view in Europe. The many excavated artifacts, including a collection of engraved gemstones, are displayed at the **National Roman Legion Museum**.

MALE VOICE CHOIRS IN THE WELSH VALLEYS

Wales's nickname "The Land of Song" emerged in the 18th century with the rise of male voice choirs. The choirs were found in the docks, shipyards and industrial towns all over the country, but they are most closely associated with the mining communities of the valleys of South Wales. Famous names include the Treorchy Male Choir, the Bridgend Male Choir and the Pontypridd Male Voice Choir. As well as concerts, visitors can often attend rehearsals in return for a small donation.

National Roman Legion Museum

 🏠 High St 🕐 10am–5pm Mon–Sat, 2–5pm Sun
🌐 museum.wales

20

Abergavenny

🏠 Monmouthshire 🚉🚌
🌐 visitabergavenny.co.uk

Abergavenny is a historic market town that was the site of a Roman fort and a Norman castle. This was built to overlook the River Usk, on which the town stands. The ruins of the castle remain, and a hunting lodge added to it in the 19th century now houses the **Abergavenny Museum**. In recent years Abergavenny has become known as Wales's gastronomic capital, and it holds a popular food festival in September

Abergavenny Museum

🏛 🏠 Castle St 🕐 11am–4pm daily 🌐 abergavenny museum.co.uk

→

Twelfth-century wooden door of the gatehouse in Chepstow Castle

21

Chepstow Castle

🏠 1 Bridge St, Chepstow
🚉🚌 🕐 Mar–Oct: 9:30am–5pm daily (Jul & Aug: to 6pm); Nov–Feb: 10am–4pm Mon–Sat, 11am–4pm Sun
🌐 cadw.gov.wales

The oldest surviving stone castle in Britain, Chepstow Castle dates back to 1067 and stands in a dramatic position on top of cliffs overlooking the River Wye. Its Norman tower is open to visitors, along with the battlements. The most prominent feature, however, is a set of wooden doors dating from 1159–89 and said to be the oldest castle doors in Europe. They originally stood in the imposing gateway but have been placed on display inside the castle to help preserve them.

> **TOP 5 WELSH CASTLES**
>
> **Beaumaris Castle**
> This awesome 13th–14th-century castle has concentric defences guarded by 16 towers.
>
> **Caernarfon Castle**
> Majestic Caernarfon Castle, built by Edward I, is impressive for its scale.
>
> **Cardiff Castle**
> On the site of a Roman fort, this castle was given a Victorian Gothic makeover in the 1900s.
>
> **Carreg Cennen**
> The stunning ruins of this 13th-century castle on a limestone cliff dominate the skyline.
>
> **Conwy Castle**
> Built by Edward I in the 1200s, magnificent Conwy Castle is very well preserved.

A DRIVING TOUR
WILD WALES

Length 140 km (87 miles) **Stopping-off points**
There are many good teashops and restaurants in the market towns of Llandovery and Llanidloes

This tour weaves across the Cambrian Mountains' windswept moors, green hills and high, deserted plateaus. New roads have been laid to the massive Llyn Brianne Reservoir, north of Llandovery, and the old drover's road across to Tregaron has a tarmac surface. Nonetheless, the area is still essentially a "wild Wales" of hidden hamlets, isolated farmsteads, brooding highlands and traditional market towns.

Devil's Bridge *is a popular, romantic beauty spot with waterfalls, rocks, wooded glades and an ancient stone bridge – built by the Devil, according to legend.*

The ruined abbey of **Strata Florida** *was an important political, religious and educational centre during the Middle Ages.*

CEREDIGION

CARMARTHEN-SHIRE

↑ Conserved ruins of the old church Strata Florida

Twm Siôn Cati's Cave *is thought to have been the retreat of the 16th-century poet Tom John, a Welsh outlaw who subsequently achieved respectability by marrying an heiress.*

At the confluence of two rivers, the pretty town of **Llandovery** *has a ruined castle, a cobbled market square and charming Georgian façades.*

Llanidloes *was a centre of religious and social unrest in the 17th and 18th centuries. There is a rare example of a freestanding Tudor market hall. The medieval church was restored in the late 19th century.*

Wild Wales

SOUTH AND MID-WALES

Locator Map
For more detail see p454

Caersws
Trefeglwys
Llaninam
Dolfor
Llyn Clywedog
FINISH Llanidloes
Cwmbelan
Llangurig
Bwlch-y-Sarnau
Pant y dwr
Wye
Craig Goch Reservoir
Rhayader
Nantmel
Garreg Ddu Reservoir
Elan Village
Crossgates
Caban Coch Reservoir
Claerwen Reservoir
Llanwrthwl
Llandrindod Wells
POWYS
Newbridge on Wye
Llanafan Fawr
Abergwesyn
Beulah
Builth Wells
Llanwrtyd Wells
Llangammarch Wells
Tirabad
Trecastle

Elan Valley *(p470) is an area of lakes and important wildlife habitats.*

📷 PICTURE PERFECT
Wonderful Waters

The overflowing dam walls at the scenic Elan Valley make an impressive addition to any photo album. Capture the water flowing down the walls as the sun begins to set.

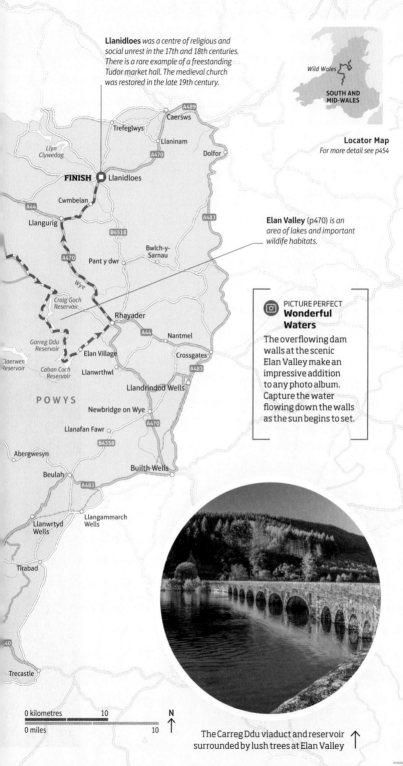

0 kilometres 10
0 miles 10

N ↑

The Carreg Ddu viaduct and reservoir surrounded by lush trees at Elan Valley ↑

SCOTLAND

Sunset over the Scottish Highlands

EXPLORE
SCOTLAND

This section divides Scotland into four
colour-coded sightseeing areas, as shown
on the map below. Find out more about
each area on the following pages.

Stornaway

Outer Hebrides

Lewis

Harris

Rudel

North Uist

Isle of Skye

Portree

South Uist

Kilbride

Inner Hebrides

Barra

Rhum

Atlantic Ocean

Coll

Tiree

Mull

GREAT BRITAIN

Colonsay

Jura

Islay

NORTHERN
IRELAND

Belfast

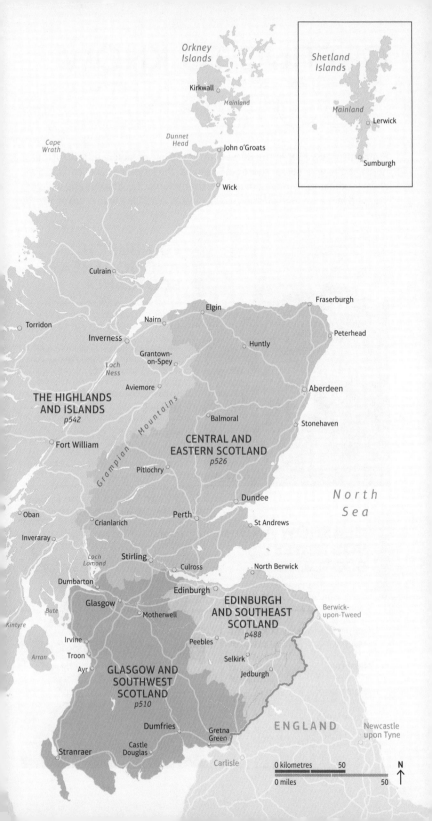

GETTING TO KNOW
SCOTLAND

From the grassy hills of the Borders up to the Isle of Skye, and still further north, to the windswept shores of Shetland, the landscapes of Scotland are always exhilarating. Added to this are the nation's cities, towns and villages, steeped in history and offering a welcome as warm as a wee dram of whisky.

PAGE 488

EDINBURGH AND SOUTHEAST SCOTLAND

Full of cultural treasures, Edinburgh is the gateway to Scotland. Beyond the Scottish capital, baronial mansions stand alongside ruins of historic abbeys and castles in the fertile farmlands and upland moors of the border country.

Best for
Sightseeing, culture and art

Home to
Edinburgh Castle, Royal Mile

Experience
Panoramic views over Edinburgh from Arthur's Seat

PAGE 510

GLASGOW AND SOUTHWEST SCOTLAND

Studded with Victorian and modern architecture, Scotland's biggest city, Glasgow, buzzes with energy. A host of historic attractions dot the rolling hills and unspoiled coastline of Southwest Scotland, including a clutch of fortresses.

Best for
Art, shopping and nightlife

Home to
Glasgow, Culzean Castle

Experience
Admiring gems of Scottish art at the Kelvingrove Art Gallery and Museum

CENTRAL AND EASTERN SCOTLAND

Encompassing wild uplands and tamer lowland landscapes, Central and Eastern Scotland is a patchwork of farmland and forest, fringed by sandy shores. Its cities have their own history, from the medieval splendour of Stirling Castle to the industrial heritage of Dundee. Stunning Loch Lomond and the Trossachs offer a range of outdoor activities, while Royal Deeside combines natural beauty with regal splendour.

Best for
Seafood feasts and royal heritage

Home to
Loch Lomond and the Trossachs National Park, Aberdeen, Stirling Castle

Experience
Teeing off at the iconic St Andrews Links

THE HIGHLANDS AND ISLANDS

For many, the Highlands and Islands epitomize Scotland. This is a vast and sparsely populated region of innumerable lochs, glens and moors dotted with majestic clan castles and ancient standing stones. Hundreds of islands lie off the coast, many of them within sight of shore or an easy ferry ride from Oban. Inverness, the Highland capital, is an excellent starting point for exploring Loch Ness and the spectacular Cairngorms, while Fort William holds the key to Ben Nevis, Britain's highest peak.

Best for
Whisky, outdoor adventures and majestic mountains

Home to
Shetland, Orkney, Outer Hebrides, Isle of Skye, Cairngorms National Park

Experience
Island-hopping on the west coast

7 DAYS
in Scotland

Day 1

Arrive in Edinburgh *(p492)* and stroll the Royal Mile, taking in St Giles' Cathedral and the intriguing Gladstone's Land. Break for a lunch of seasonal Scottish cuisine at Monteiths *(61 High St)*. In the afternoon, take a tour of the royal apartments at the Palace of Holyroodhouse before wandering around the parkland. Extend your stroll by making the 30-minute walk up to Arthur's Seat for panoramic views across the city. Dine at the Gardener's Cottage *(p493)*; sleep at The Inn on the Mile *(82 High St)*.

Day 2

Begin by visiting Edinburgh Castle *(p496)*, perched above the city on a volcanic outcrop. Allow at least an hour before strolling down to the Scottish National Gallery *(p492)* to see its outstanding British art. After lunch at the gallery's café walk 10 minutes to the National Museum of Scotland, which traces Scotland's history. Dine at The Witchery by the Castle *(p495)* and then meander back to the Inn on the Mile for the night. You will need a car for the rest of this itinerary.

Day 3

Drive northwest to Stirling *(p534)*, where the imposing castle should be your first stop. Spend the rest of the morning wandering the old town and lunch at The Birds and The Bees *(p535)*. In the afternoon head to the Battle of Bannockburn Visitor Centre, which commemorates the famous Scottish victory. Journeying on, it's a 50-minute drive to bustling Perth and Scone Palace *(p537)*, one of Scotland's most important stately homes. In Perth, enjoy dinner and a comfortable bed at the Parklands Hotel *(2 St Leonards Bank)*.

Day 4

Heading north, skirt the rugged mountains and glens of Cairngorms National Park *(p558)*. Break your journey in Aviemore for lunch at the Mountain Café *(111 Grampian Rd)* before shooting up the mountain on a funicular, the Cairngorm Mountain Railway. Drive on another 20 minutes to pretty Inverness *(p562)*, whose Museum and Art Gallery examines Highland history and culture. Afterwards, carry on to the moorland of Culloden,

① The Balmoral clock tower, Princes Street, an Edinburgh landmark.

② Cairngorms National Park forest.

③ Looking at paintings in the Scottish National Gallery, Edinburgh.

④ Interior of the Kelingrove Art Gallery and Museum in Glasgow.

⑤ Buachaille Etive Mor and River Coupal, Glencoe in the Highlands.

where the Highland Jacobite army was savaged in 1746; the visitor centre explains all. Back in Inverness, eat and sleep at the Rocpool Reserve (Culduthel Rd).

Day 5

From Inverness it's a short scenic drive to Loch Ness (p562); the Loch Ness Centre delves into the mystery of the local monster. Take a cruise around the loch or ramble (1 hour each way) to Urquhart Castle. Continue your drive through the wilderness of the Great Glen, stopping for lunch in Fort William at the Crannog Seafood Restaurant overlooking Loch Linnhe. Carry on through the stunning mountains of Glencoe (p564) until you reach Loch Lomond (p530), set amidst the glens and lochs of the Trossachs. Eat and stay at the Cameron House (www.cameronhouse.co.uk).

Day 6

In the morning head out on the scenic drive to Inveraray (p566) and explore its splendid mock-Gothic castle before

lunching at The George (1 Main St). After lunch drive a short distance over the hills to Loch Awe (p565), where the elegiac ruins of Kilchurn Castle are a 10-minute walk from the road. Continue to the Victorian seaside town of Oban (p564). Enjoy a snifter at the Oban whisky distillery before dining at Coast (104 George St); stay overnight at the Old Manse Guest House (Dalriach Rd).

Day 7

Set out on the 158-km (98-mile) drive south to Glasgow (p514). Stroll the city centre, savouring the Victorian architecture of George Square and then visit the People's Palace, a delightful museum exploring the city's past. Lunch in the museum café and then saunter along the river to the impressive Glasgow Science Centre with its interactive exhibits. From here it's a 20-minute stroll to Glasgow's top museum, the Kelingrove Art Gallery and Museum (p518). Round off the day with a seafood dinner at Gamba (225A West George St) before turning in for the night at the Grasshoppers Hotel (87 Union St).

SCHOTIA

A BRIEF
HISTORY

Scotland has been torn apart by religion and politics, coveted by a powerful neighbour, and wooed and punished for 400 years in the power struggles between England, France and Spain. The country has risen and fallen through the ages, but has always demonstrated an irrepressible spirit.

Stone Age settlers arrived in Scotland in around 7000 BC. By around 800 BC they had learned to forge iron, evolving into what Tacitus called the Picts, the "painted people". The Romans invaded Scotland in AD 82–84, but by AD 121, after several defeats at the hands of the Picts, they were forced to retreat.

In 1072 William the Conqueror led the first Norman incursion into Scotland, with little success. After Edward I's army invaded Scotland in 1286 rebels rallied behind a commoner, William Wallace, who led them in their fight for independence from the English crown. After Wallace was captured and executed, the

1 Antique map of Scotland.

2 The Battle of Bannockburn led by Robert the Bruce.

3 Factory chimneys in 19th-century Glasgow.

4 SNP leader Nicola Sturgeon.

Timeline of events

794

The first Vikings cross the North Sea to raid, trade and eventually settle in Scotland.

1314

Robert the Bruce defeats the English at the Battle of Bannockburn.

1603

Union of Crowns: James VI of Scotland also becomes James I of England.

1707

Act of Union creates United Kingdom of Great Britain.

3

2

4

rebels' support shifted to Robert the Bruce, who won a decisive victory at the Battle of Bannockburn in 1314, successfully reestablishing Scotland's status as an independent country.

The Reformation arrived during the Stuart dynasty under Mary Queen of Scots' reign, creating a long-lasting religious divide during which Catholicism was purged, albeit with revivals and impregnable strongholds in the Highlands and islands.

In 1603, King James VI (1566–1625) also became king of England, thereby uniting the two kingdoms. It was bankruptcy that finally forced Scotland into formal union with England in 1707, resulting in dissolution of the Scottish Parliament

The 19th century brought industrial revolution to Scotland and Glasgow became a great manufacturing city, but industry suffered after World War II. In the 21st century the Scottish National Party (SNP) has dominated politics, but their battle for independence was lost by a thin margin in the 2014 referendum. In the 2016 Brexit referendum, Scots voted to stay in the EU. England's vote to leave, however, means Scotland, as part of the UK, must follow against its will, which in turn has reignited calls for a second vote on independence.

THE JACOBITES

The first Jacobites were mainly Catholic Highlanders who supported James VII of Scotland (James II of England), who was deposed in 1688. Their desire to restore the Catholic throne led to uprisings in 1715 and 1745. Their failure led to the demise of the clan system and the suppression of Highland culture for more than a century.

1746
Battle of Culloden; the Jacobite army is destroyed.

1890
Opening of the iconic Forth Railway Bridge.

1999
Scottish Parliament is reinstated after 292 years.

2016
62 percent of Scots vote for Britain to remain in the EU referendum.

EDINBURGH AND SOUTHEAST SCOTLAND

Though human habitation of Southeast Scotland stretches back to 8,500 BC, the best records start with Roman accounts of Celtic tribes when they first established outposts here around 140 AD. The Romans never got a firm grip on the territory and Celtic hill-forts continued to rule the land from prominent spots such as the rock where Edinburgh's castle still stands.

Despite competition from other tribes, mainly Angles and Vikings, the Scots, who emerged as the main Celtic tribe in the 11th century, won out. Around 1130, due to its good natural defences and commanding location, the city of Edinburgh was established and quickly played a key role, becoming the national capital within 200 years. Yet Southeast Scotland remained easily approachable from the south and would for centuries be repeatedly attacked by English armies, who often ravaged the land, leaving abbeys, such as Melrose, in ruins. Over time, and with the 1707 Union between Scotland and England, life became considerably more stable.

Edinburgh began to flourish. The 18th-century Scottish Enlightenment produced world-leading contributions to almost every academic field in the city. Edinburgh's importance increased through the 20th century with the creation of a huge annual arts festival and a Scottish parliament.

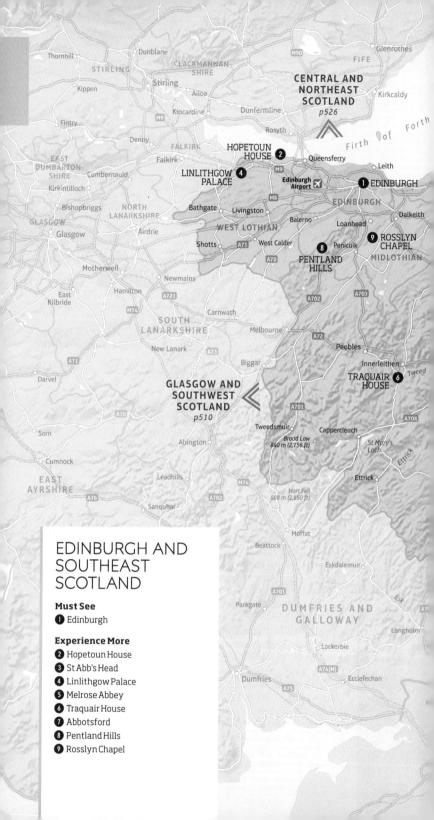

CENTRAL AND
NORTHEAST
SCOTLAND
p526

HOPETOUN
HOUSE ❷

LINLITHGOW ❹
PALACE

❶ EDINBURGH

❾ ROSSLYN
CHAPEL

❽ PENTLAND
HILLS

GLASGOW AND
SOUTHWEST
SCOTLAND
p510

TRAQUAIR ❻
HOUSE

EDINBURGH AND
SOUTHEAST
SCOTLAND

Must See
❶ Edinburgh

Experience More
❷ Hopetoun House
❸ St Abb's Head
❹ Linlithgow Palace
❺ Melrose Abbey
❻ Traquair House
❼ Abbotsford
❽ Pentland Hills
❾ Rosslyn Chapel

❶
EDINBURGH

🚉 Lothian ✈ 13 km (8 miles) from city centre 🚉 North Bridge (Waverley Station) 🚌 Elder St 🛈 3 Princes St; www.edinburgh.org

Edinburgh is one of Europe's most handsome capitals. Famous for the arts, every year it hosts Britain's largest multimedia extravaganza, the Edinburgh Festival.

The skyline at dusk, with Edinburgh Castle in the background ↑

①
Scottish National Gallery

🚉 The Mound ⏰ 10am–5pm Fri–Wed, 10am–7pm Thu 🌐 nationalgalleries.org

One of Britain's finest art galleries, the Scottish National Gallery is worth visiting for its 15th- to 19th-century British and European paintings alone. Highlights among the Scottish works include portraits by Allan Ramsay and Henry Raeburn, such as the latter's *Reverend Robert Walker Skating on Duddingston Loch* (c 1800). The Early German collection includes Gerard David's almost comic-strip treatment of the *Three Legends of Saint Nicholas* (c 1500). Works by Raphael, Titian and Tintoretto accompany southern European paintings such as Velázquez's *An Old Woman Cooking Eggs* (1620) and there's an entire room devoted to *The Seven Sacraments* (c 1640) by Nicholas Poussin.

The Weston Link is an underground complex that connects the gallery with the Royal Scottish Academy. It contains a lecture theatre/cinema, shop, restaurant, café, and an education room.

②
Georgian House

🚉 7 Charlotte Sq ⏰ Mar & Nov: 11am–3:15pm daily; Apr–Oct: 10am–4:15pm daily; Dec: 11am–3:30pm Thu–Sun 🌐 nts.org.uk

Charlotte Square is a superb example of Georgian architecture, its north side

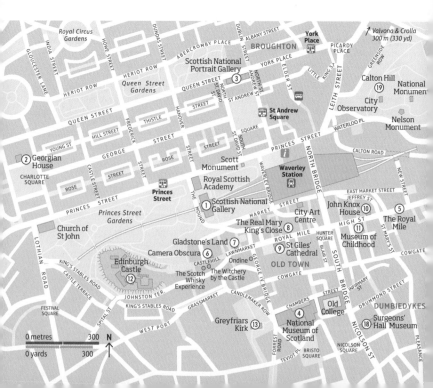

EAT

Valvona & Crolla

The godfather of Italian delicatessens, this is the place to pick up the makings of a gourmet picnic. Its café offers great pasta dishes.

 Elm Row
🌐 valvonacrolla.co.uk

£££

Gardener's Cottage

The seven-course taster menu at this cosy restaurant features fresh produce grown in the cottage's own organic garden.

📍 Royal Terrace Gdns, London Rd 🌐 the gardenerscottage.co.uk

£££

a 1790s masterwork by the architect Robert Adam. The Georgian House at No 7 has been completely restored, providing a window on to the elegance of wealthy New Town life. In stark contrast, "below stairs" is the household staff's quarters, demonstrating how Edinburgh's working class lived and worked.

③

Scottish National Portrait Gallery

📍 1 Queen St ⏰ 10am–5pm daily 🌐 nationalgalleries.org

A unique visual history of Scotland is told here through the portraits of those who created it, from Robert the Bruce (p486) to Queen Anne. Portraits of other famous Scots include Robert Burns (p525) by Alexander Nasmyth. Memorabilia includes Mary, Queen of Scots' jewellery and a silver travelling canteen left by Bonnie Prince Charlie (p487). There is also an emphasis on photography, such as the display of Alexander Hutchinson's moving record of the lost community of St Kilda.

> 💬 **INSIDER TIP**
> **Gallery Bus**
>
> The daily Gallery Bus circuit takes in the Scottish National Gallery, the National Portrait Gallery (drop-off only here) and the Scottish National Gallery of Modern Art (p501), all for a reasonable £1 donation.

④

National Museum of Scotland

📍 Chambers St ⏰ 10am–5pm daily 🚫 25 Dec 🌐 nms.ac.uk

This purpose-built museum houses the Scottish collections of the National Museums of Scotland. Exhibitions tell the story of Scotland, the land and its people, from its geological beginnings right up to the exciting events of today. Key exhibits include the famous medieval Lewis Chessmen, the Pictish Chains, known as Scotland's earliest crown jewels, and the *Ellesmere* railway locomotive. A huge *Tyrannosaurus rex* skeleton guards the entrance to the natural world galleries, and the 1930s Schmidt telescope is the centrepiece of the Earth and Space gallery. There is also a special exhibition gallery that houses temporary displays.

 (5)

The Royal Mile

 Castlehill to Canongate

This historic stretch of four ancient streets (from Castlehill to Canongate) formed the main thoroughfare of medieval Edinburgh, linking the ancient castle to the Palace of Holyroodhouse. Confined by the city wall, the "Old Town" grew upwards, with some tenements rising 20 storeys above the dark, cobbled wynds and closes below.

 (6)

Camera Obscura

 Castlehill Times vary, check website camera-obscura.co.uk

The lower floors of this building date from the early 17th century. In 1852, Maria Short added the upper floor and the Camera Obscura – a large pinhole camera that captures life in the city centre as it happens. A marvel at the

time, this feat of Victorian craftsmanship still astonishes modern visitors, and it remains one of Edinburgh's most popular attractions.

---

(7)

Gladstone's Land

 477B Lawnmarket
 10am–5pm Mon, 10am–1pm Tue–Sun nts.org.uk

This restored 17th-century merchant's house, a tall, narrow type of building known as a "land", provides a window on life in a typical Old Town house before overcrowding drove the rich inhabitants to the Georgian New Town.

66

alleys and closes lead off the Royal Mile, some to hidden courtyards.

(8)

The Real Mary King's Close

 2 Warriston's Close
 10am–9pm daily the realmarykingsclose.com

Until the 18th century most residents of Edinburgh lived along and below the Royal Mile and the Cowgate. Behind and beneath the grand houses was a warren of gloomy, narrow alleys, or "closes", leading to the cellars and basements where the lower classes lived and worked. They lacked any proper water supply, daylight or ventilation, and under these conditions, cholera, typhus and smallpox were common. Mary King's Close, under the City Chambers, is one of the most famous of these areas – its inhabitants were all killed by the plague in around 1645. In 2003 many of these closes were opened up for the first time, and in this immersive experience, costumed guides lead visitors in a walking tour of the Old Town's gruesome past.

←

Looking up Castlehill towards Edinburgh Castle at the top of the Royal Mile

of the Most Ancient and Most Noble Order of the Thistle. A royal pew is reserved for Queen Elizabeth II during her visits to Edinburgh.

John Knox House and The Scottish Storytelling Centre

⌂ 43-45 High St ⏰ 10am-6pm Mon-Sat (Jul-Aug: also noon-6pm Sun) 🌐 tracscotland.org

This beautiful medieval building with its crow-step gables, overhanging upper storeys and many surviving decorative details , was home to the great patriarch of the Scottish Reformation (*p487*), John Knox, one of the most important figures in 16th-century Scotland. Displays tell the story of Knox's life in the context of the political and religious upheavals of his time.

The building also incorporates the Scottish Storytelling Centre, a modern annex hosting local and visiting storytellers and other exponents of the spoken word, performing in English, Scots dialect and Gaelic.

St Giles' Cathedral

⌂ Royal Mile ⏰ Times vary, check website 🌐 stgilescathedral.org.uk

Properly known as the High Kirk (church) of Edinburgh, St Giles' is popularly known as a cathedral. Its Gothic exterior has a 15th-century tower; inside, the beautiful Thistle Chapel, with its rib-vaulted ceiling and carved heraldic canopies, honours the knights

↑ Statue of Scottish philosopher David Hume (1711-76) opposite St Giles' Cathedral

EAT

The Witchery by the Castle
A showcase for Scotland's finest produce. Ask for a seat in the Secret Garden.

⌂ 352 Castlehill
🌐 thewitchery.com

£££

Ondine
Sleek and sophisticated seafood dishes, plus an oyster happy hour.

⌂ 2 George IV Bridge
🌐 ondinerestaurant.co.uk

£££

DRINK

The Scotch Whisky Experience
Sample malts ancient and modern, then dine in the restaurant.

⌂ 354 Castlehill
🌐 scotchwhiskyexperience.co.uk

Museum of Childhood

⌂ 42 High St ⏰ 10am-5pm daily 🌐 edinburghmuseums.org.uk

This lovely museum is not merely a toy collection but a magical insight into childhood, with all its joys and trials. Founded in 1955, it was the first museum in the world to be devoted to the history and theme of childhood. The collection includes medicines, school books, clothing and uniforms, old-fashioned toys and a growing collection of computer games, action figures and game consoles.

⑫

EDINBURGH CASTLE

⌂ Castlehill ⏰ 9:30am–6pm daily (Oct–Mar: to 5pm); last admission: 45 mins before closing 🌐 edinburghcastle.scot

Dominating the city's skyline since the 12th century, Edinburgh Castle is a national icon and is, deservedly, Scotland's most popular visitor attraction.

Standing upon the basalt core of an extinct volcano, Edinburgh Castle is an assemblage of buildings dating from the 12th to the 20th century, reflecting its changing role as fortress, royal palace, military garrison and state prison. Though there is evidence of Bronze Age occupation, the original fortress was built by the 6th-century Northumbrian king Edwin, from whom the city takes its name. The castle was a favourite royal residence until the Union of the Crowns in 1603, when James VI of Scotland became James I of England and Ireland, after which the king resided in England. After the Union of Parliaments in 1707, the Scottish regalia were walled up in the Palace for over a century. The Palace is now the zealous possessor of the so-called Stone of Destiny, a relic of ancient Scottish kings which was seized by the English and not returned to Scotland until 1996.

> 💬 INSIDER TIP
> ### Festival Fireworks
>
> Every night during the Edinburgh Festival, the Castle hosts a fireworks display to mark the end of the Military Tattoo (p499). Climb to the top of Calton Hill (p500) to watch this pyrotechnic spectacle for free.

THE ONE O'CLOCK GUN

Resounding across the city at 1pm every day, Edinburgh's One O'Clock Gun has been startling visitors since 1861. It was originally intended to help ships moored in the Firth of Forth to synchronize their chronometers to Greenwich Mean Time, essential for accurate navigation, but it has now become a time-honoured tradition. The first guns were muzzle-loading cannons, but since 2001 a more modern 105mm artillery piece has served.

Complete with Flemish-style crow-stepped gables, the Governor's House was constructed in 1742 and now serves as the Officers' Mess.

Military Prison

The ancient fortress, built on a volcanic crag known as Castle Rock ↑

During the 18th and 19th centuries, the castle's prison vaults were used to hold French prisoners of war.

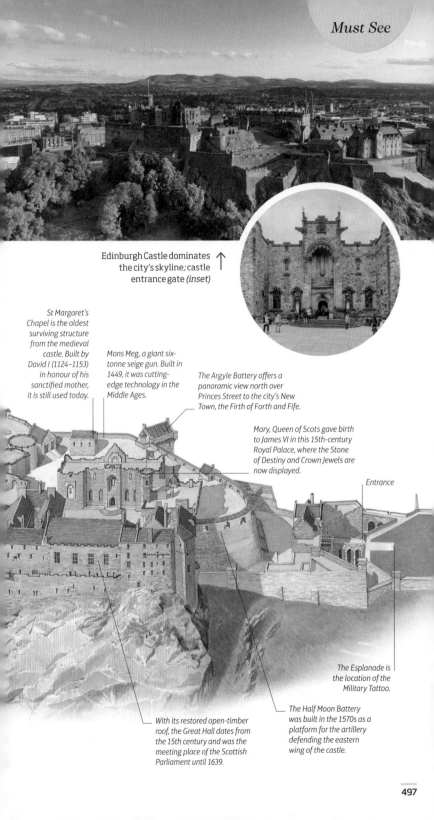

Edinburgh Castle dominates the city's skyline; castle entrance gate *(inset)*

St Margaret's Chapel is the oldest surviving structure from the medieval castle. Built by David I (1124–1153) in honour of his sanctified mother, it is still used today.

Mons Meg, a giant six-tonne seige gun. Built in 1449, it was cutting-edge technology in the Middle Ages.

The Argyle Battery offers a panoramic view north over Princes Street to the city's New Town, the Firth of Forth and Fife.

Mary, Queen of Scots gave birth to James VI in this 15th-century Royal Palace, where the Stone of Destiny and Crown Jewels are now displayed.

Entrance

The Esplanade is the location of the Military Tattoo.

With its restored open-timber roof, the Great Hall dates from the 15th century and was the meeting place of the Scottish Parliament until 1639.

The Half Moon Battery was built in the 1570s as a platform for the artillery defending the eastern wing of the castle.

Greyfriars Kirk

🅰 Greyfriars Pl ⏰ Times vary, check website 🌐 greyfriarskirk.com

Greyfriars Kirk occupies a key role in the history of Scotland, as this is where the National Covenant was signed in 1638, marking the Protestant stand against the imposition of an episcopal church by King Charles I. Greyfriars was at that time a relatively new structure, completed in 1620 on the site of a Franciscan friary. Its kirkyard was used as a mass grave for executed Covenanters. The kirk served as a prison for Covenanter forces captured after the 1679 Battle of Bothwell Brig.

Greyfriars is best known for its association with a little dog called Bobby, who, so the story goes, kept a vigil by his master's grave from 1858 until his own death in 1872. Bobby's well-loved statue stands outside Greyfriars Kirk.

Did You Know?

Some ancient traces of habitation in Holyrood Park date back as far as 10,000 years.

Holyrood Park and Arthur's Seat

🅰 Main access via Holyrood Park Rd, Holyrood Rd and Meadowbank Terr

Holyrood Park, adjacent to the Palace of Holyroodhouse, covers 2.6 sq km (1 sq mile) of varying terrain, topped by a rugged 250-m (820-ft) hill. Known as Arthur's Seat, the hill is actually a volcano that has been extinct for 350 million years. The area was a royal hunting ground from at least the time of King David I, who died in 1153, and a royal park since the 16th century.

The name Holyrood, which means "holy cross", comes from an episode in the life of David I when, in 1128, he was knocked down from his horse by a stag while out hunting. Legend has it that a cross appeared miraculously in his hands to ward off the animal and, in thanksgiving, the king founded Holyrood Abbey. The name Arthur's Seat is probably a corruption of Archer's Seat, a more prosaic explanation for the name than any link with the legendary King Arthur.

The park contains three small lochs: St Margaret's, near the Palace, is the most romantic, with its resident swans and position under the ruins of St Anthony's Chapel. Dunsapie Loch is the highest, sitting 112 m (367 ft) above sea level under Arthur's Seat. On the south side of the park, pretty Duddingston Loch is home to swans, geese and wildfowl.

The Salisbury Crags are among the park's most striking features. Their dramatic profile, along with that of Arthur's Seat, can be seen from many miles away. The Crags form a parabola of dramatic red cliffs that sweep round and up a steep supporting hillside from the Palace of Holyroodhouse. A rough track, called the Radical Road, follows their base.

Palace of Holyroodhouse

🅰 East end of the Royal Mile ⏰ 9:30am-6pm daily (Nov-Mar: to 4:30pm) 🌐 royal collection.org.uk

Known today as Queen Elizabeth II's official Scottish

residence, the Palace of Holyroodhouse was built by James IV in the grounds of an abbey in 1498. It was later the home of James V and his wife, Mary of Guise, and remodelled in the 1670s for Charles II.

The Royal Apartments (including the Throne Room and Royal Dining Room) are used for investitures and for banquets whenever the Queen visits the palace. A chamber in the so-called James V tower is famously associated with the unhappy reign of Mary, Queen of Scots. It was probably in this room, in 1566, that Mary saw the gruesome murder of her trusted Italian secretary, David Rizzio, authorized by her jealous husband, Lord Darnley. She was six months pregnant at the time of this attack. In the early stages of the Jacobite rising of 1745 (*p487*), the last of the pretenders to the British throne, Charles Edward Stuart (Bonnie Prince Charlie), held court here, dazzling Edinburgh society with his magnificent parties.

Tours are given daily from April to October, or take an audio tour; both are included in the ticket price.

EDINBURGH INTERNATIONAL FESTIVAL

For three weeks in late summer, Edinburgh hosts this spectacular arts festival, with every available space, from theatres to street corners, packed with performers. Held since 1947, it brings together international contemporary theatre, music, dance, opera, cinema and literary events. The alternative Festival Fringe contributes a host of innovative performances. The most popular event is the Edinburgh Military Tattoo, held at the Castle - massed Scottish infantry battalions marching to pipe bands.

Dynamic Earth

🏠 Holyrood Rd ⏰ Apr-Oct: 10am-4pm daily (Jul-Aug: to 4:30pm); Nov-Mar: 10am-4pm Wed-Sun
🌐 dynamicearth.co.uk

This permanent exhibition about the planet takes visitors on a journey from the Earth's volcanic beginnings to the first appearance of life. Displays cover the world's climatic zones and dramatic natural phenomena such as tidal waves and earthquakes. State-of-the-art lighting and interactive techniques provide 90 minutes of learning and entertainment.

The building is fronted by a stone amphitheatre designed by Sir Michael Hopkins.

↑ Holyrood Park and Arthur's Seat, overlooking the city

Scottish Parliament

📍 Holyrood ⏰ 10am–5pm Mon, Fri & Sat, 9am–6:30pm Tue–Thu 🌐 parliament.scot

Following decades of Scottish calls for more political self-determination, a 1997 referendum on this issue resulted in a majority "yes" vote (p487). Designed by the late Enric Miralles, known for his work on buildings at the 1992 Barcelona Olympics, the Parliament building was opened in 2004 by Queen Elizabeth II. It's well worth taking one of the regular tours of this architecturally exciting public building.

Surgeons' Hall Museum

📍 Nicolson St ⏰ 10am–5pm daily 🌐 museum.rcsed.ac.uk

Not for the faint-hearted, but certainly appealing to the morbidly curious, this off-piste Edinburgh museum opened to the public in 1832. Originally intended as a teaching facility for medical students, the museum is home to one of the oldest and largest pathology collections in the United Kingdom. It contains an extensive collection of preserved organic tissue and bone, historic scientific instruments and an array of anatomic and medical artifacts, plus state-of-the-art interactive features.

Calton Hill

📍 City Centre East, via Waterloo Pl

Towering over Princes Street, Calton Hill has an assortment of quirky Greek-style monuments. All this makes it perfect for orientation, summer strolling and picnicking amid sweet-scented gorse. There are fine views of the Old Town and across to the Firth of Forth, spanned by the magnificent Forth railway bridge, the longest of its kind when it opened in 1890. Beyond it the white tracery of the new road bridge, the Queensferry Crossing, can be seen.

Calton Hill's most eye-catching and baffling landmark is the National Monument. This 1820s half-finished imitation-Parthenon was intended to commemorate Scotland's dead in the Napoleonic Wars, before funding ran out. Glasgow's offer to complete it with its coat of arms on the building was politely declined and, over the years, shame over the bungled project has given way to local affection. Adjacent, the 1815 **Nelson Monument** commemorates the Admiral's 1805 victory at Trafalgar, and was designed to resemble a telescope. The final main building on the hill is the old City Observatory, another copy of a Greek Temple, and used by astronomers until 1895 when smoke from the trains at nearby Waverley station forced its closure. In 2018, it reopened as **Collective**, a cutting-edge contemporary art gallery. Beside it is a much-photographed eight-columned Corinthian rotunda that's become an iconic city landmark, dedicated to the little-known philosopher Dugald Stewart (1753–1828).

Nelson Monument

📍 Calton Hill ⏰ Apr–Sep: 10am–7pm Mon–Sat, noon–5pm Sun; Oct–Mar: 10am–4pm Mon–Sat 🌐 edinburgh museums.org.uk

Collective

📍 City Observatory, 38 Calton Hill ⏰ 10am–5pm Tue–Sun 🌐 collective-edinburgh.art

↑ Educational exhibits at Surgeons' Hall Museum

↑ The Shore in Leith, an attractive and bustling dining spot

Must See

📷 PICTURE PERFECT
The Forth Rail Bridge

For that stunning upwards shot of the vast framework of the Forth Rail Bridge, walk to Hawes Pier, and stand right under its massive supports at the east end of Edinburgh Road.

BEYOND THE CENTRE

 ⑳

Scottish National Gallery of Modern Art

🏠 75 Belford Rd ⏰ 10am-5pm daily 🌐 national galleries.org

Housed in a 19th-century school, the Modern One gallery features European and American 20th-century greats, from Vuillard and Picasso to Magritte and Lichtenstein. Sculptures by Henry Moore are set in the grounds. The adjacent Modern Two gallery showcases Dada and Surrealist art.

㉑

Leith

🏠 NE of the city centre, linked by Leith Walk

Leith is a historic port town that has traded for centuries with Scandinavia, the Baltic States and the Netherlands, and has always been the main trading port for Edinburgh. Although fiercely proud of its independence, it was incorporated into the city in 1920 and now forms a charming suburb. The medieval core of narrow streets and quays includes many historic warehouses and merchants' houses. Shipbuilding and port activities have diminished, but there has been a renaissance in recent years, with warehouse buildings converted into offices, apartments and, most notably, restaurants, seafood bistros and bars. This is now one of the city's most vibrant areas, with a lively Saturday farmers' market that's a delight for foodies.

Did You Know?

The former Royal Yacht Britannia, retired after 40 years' service, can be visited at Leith's Ocean Terminal.

㉒

Royal Botanic Garden

🏠 Inverleith Row ⏰ Times vary, check website 🌐 rbge.org.uk

This magnificent garden was founded in 1670 as a Physic Garden near Holyroodhouse, and moved to its present location in 1820, to be progressively enlarged. Now a world-class botanic garden, its highlights are the Chinese Hillside, rhododendron walk and the Heath Garden, filled with Scottish native plants. The glasshouses, including two magnificent Victorian structures, make fascinating green hideaways on rainy days.

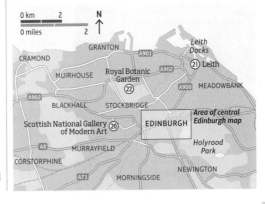

A SHORT WALK
NEW TOWN

Distance 2 km (1 mile) **Time** 20 minutes

The first phase of Edinburgh's "New Town" was built in the 18th century to relieve the congested and unsanitary conditions of the medieval Old Town. Charlotte Square, at the western end, formed the climax of this initial phase, and its new architectural concepts were to influence all subsequent phases. Of these, the most magnificent is the Moray Estate, where a linked series of very large houses forms a crescent, an oval and a 12-sided circus. The walk shown here explores this area of monumental Georgian town planning and architecture.

*The crowning glory of the Moray Estate, **Moray Place** consists of a series of immense houses and apartments, many of which are still inhabited.*

*At **Ainslie Place**, an oval pattern of townhouses forms the core of the Moray Estate, linking Randolph Crescent and Moray Place.*

Dean Bridge, *built in 1829 to the design of Thomas Telford, offers views down to the Water of Leith and upstream to the weirs and old mills of Dean Village.*

The Water of Leith *is a small river running through a gorge below Dean Bridge. There is a riverside walkway to Stockbridge.*

MORAY PLACE

AINSLIE PLACE

GREAT STUART ST

START

DEAN BRIDGE

RANDOLPH CRESCENT

QUEENSFERRY STREET

FINISH

0 metres 100
0 yards 100
N

No. 14 Charlotte Square *was the residence of judge and diarist Lord Cockburn from 1813 to 1843.*

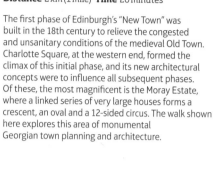

←

The Water of Leith flowing through picturesque Dean Village

The Georgian House and other grand period buildings on Charlotte Square

The Georgian House *at no 7 Charlotte Square is owned by the National Trust for Scotland and is open to the public. Repainted in its original colours and furnished with antiques, it is an insight into upperclass 18th-century Edinburgh.*

Bute House, *the official residence of the First Minister of the Scottish Parliament.*

No. 39 Castle Street *was the home of the writer Sir Walter Scott (p507).*

No 9 Charlotte Square *was the home of surgeon Joseph Lister from 1870 to 1877. He developed methods of preventing infection both during and after surgery.*

Charlotte Square *was built between 1792 and 1811 to provide a series of lavish townhouses for the most successful city merchants. Most of the buildings are now used as offices.*

Princes Street *was part of the initial building phase of the New Town. The north side is lined with shops; Princes Street Gardens to the south lie below Edinburgh Castle.*

West Register House *was originally St George's Church, designed by Robert Adam.*

MORAY PLACE

DARNAWAY ST

HERIOT ROW

WEMYSS PLACE

FOREST STREET

T COLME STREET

QUEEN STREET

CHARLOTTE SQUARE

GEORGE STREET

CASTLE STREET

CHARLOTTE SQUARE

HOPE STREET

SOUTH CHARLOTTE ST

PRINCES STREET

EXPERIENCE MORE

Hopetoun House

 West Lothian
Dalmeny Apr–Sep:
10:30am–5pm daily
hopetoun.co.uk

An extensive parkland
designed in the style of
Versailles is the setting for one
of Scotland's finest stately
homes. The original house
was completed in 1707, and
its horseshoe-shaped plan
and lavish interior represent
Neo-Classical 18th-century
architecture at its best.
A highlight of a visit here is
afternoon tea in the stables
tearoom, with the option of up-
grading to a champagne tea.

St Abb's Head

Scottish Borders
Berwick-upon-Tweed
From Edinburgh

The jagged cliffs of St Abb's
Head, rising 91 m (300 ft)
from the North Sea near the
southeastern tip of Scotland,
offer a spectacular view of
thousands of seabirds
wheeling and diving below.
During the May to June
breeding season, this 80-ha
(200-acre) nature reserve
becomes the home of more
than 50,000 birds, including
fulmars, guillemots, kittiwakes
and puffins, which throng the
headland near the fishing
village of St Abbs. The village
has one of the few unspoiled
working harbours on Britain's
east coast. A clifftop trail
begins at the **Visitors' Centre**,
where you can discover more
about the wildlife, geology
and history of the area.
Displays include identification
boards, interactive exhibits
and activities for children.
There are wonderful views
from the Visitors' Centre.

Visitors' Centre

St Abb's Head
01890 771443
Apr–Oct: 10am–5pm daily

←

Portraits lining the walls
of the elegant dining room
in Hopetoun House

The fishing village of St Abbs; Guillemots on the cliffs at St Abb's Head *(inset)*

4

Linlithgow Palace

🏠 Linlithgow, West Lothian 🚉🚌 🕐 9:30am-5:30pm daily (Oct-Mar: 10am-4pm) 🌐 historicenvironment.scot

On the edge of Linlithgow Loch stand the ruins of the former royal palace of Linlithgow, dating from the 1100s. Today's remains are mostly of the palace of James I in 1425. The scale of the building is demonstrated by the 28-m- (94-ft-) long Great Hall where monarchs would host extravagant banquets in the 15th and 16th centuries, with its huge fireplace and windows. Mary, Queen of Scots, was born here in 1542. The surrounding parkland and the loch itself provide a habitat for grebes, ducks and swans, and make this a pleasant place to visit.

Did You Know?

Linlithgow Palace's fountain flowed with wine to welcome Bonnie Prince Charlie in 1745.

5

Melrose Abbey

🏠 Abbey St, Melrose, Scottish Borders 🕐 10am-4pm daily (Apr-Sep: to 5:30pm); last adm: 30 mins before closing 🌐 historicenvironment.scot

The rose-pink ruins of this beautiful Border abbey bear testimony to the hazards of standing in the path of successive English invasions. Built by David I in 1136 for Cistercian monks from Yorkshire, and replacing a 7th-century monastery, Melrose was repeatedly ransacked by English armies, notably in 1322 and 1385. The final blow, from which none of the Border abbeys recovered, came in 1545 during Henry VIII's destructive Scottish policy known as the "Rough Wooing". This resulted from the failure of the Scots to ratify a marriage treaty between Henry VIII's son and the infant Mary Queen of Scots. What remains of the abbey are the outlines of cloisters, the kitchen and other monastic buildings, and the shell of the abbey church with its soaring east window and profusion of medieval carvings. The rich decorations on the south exterior wall include a gargoyle shaped like a pig playing the bagpipes.

An embalmed heart, found here in 1920, is probably that of Robert the Bruce *(p486)*, who had decreed that his heart be taken on a crusade to the Holy Land. It was returned to Melrose after its bearer, Sir James Douglas, was killed.

MONASTIC LIFE

The rich collection of Medieval finds at Melrose Abbey includes floor tiles, cooking pots and portable urinals. These are displayed in the late 16th-century Commendator's House, which has been restored and is now a museum.

EAT

Marmion's
Borders produce meets Middle Eastern cuisine at this friendly place.

📍5 Buccleuch St, Melrose 🕐Sun

💷💷💷

DRINK

Glenkinchie Distillery
For a whisky experience that doesn't involve a long journey into the Highlands, head to the fantastic Glenkinchie Distillery. Informative tours end with single malt tastings.

📍Pencaitland, Tranent 🕐10am-5pm daily (Nov-Feb: to 4pm) 🌐malts.com/en-row/distilleries/glenkinchie

Traquair House, which had historic links to the Catholic Stuarts ↓

7

Traquair House

📍Peebles, Scottish Borders 🚌From Peebles 🕐Apr-Jun & Sep: 11am-5pm daily; Jul & Aug: 10am-5pm daily; Oct: 11am-4pm daily; Nov: 11am-3pm Sat & Sun 🌐traquair.co.uk

Traquair has deep roots in Scottish religious and political history, stretching back over 900 years. Evolving from a fortified tower to a stout-walled 17th-century mansion (p508), the house was a Catholic Stuart stronghold for 500 years. Mary, Queen of Scots was among the many monarchs to have stayed here and her bed is covered by a counterpane she made herself. Family letters and engraved Jacobite (p487) drinking glasses are among relics recalling the period of the Highland rebellions.

After a vow made by the 5th Earl, Traquair's Bear Gates (the "Steekit Yetts"), which closed after Bonnie Prince Charlie's (p487) visit in 1745, will not reopen again until a Stuart again ascends the throne. A secret stairway leads to the Priest's Room, which attests to the problems faced by Catholic families until Catholicism was legalized in 1829. Traquair House Ale is still produced in the 18th-century brewhouse.

Abbotsford, the former home of Scottish writer Sir Walter Scott ↑

8

Abbotsford

📍Galashiels, Scottish Borders 🚌From Galashiels 🕐Mar-Nov: 10am-5pm daily (Mar & Nov: to 4pm) 🌐scottsabbotsford.co.uk

Few houses bear the stamp of their creator so intimately as Abbotsford, the home of Sir Walter Scott for the last 20 years of his life. He bought a farm here in 1811 and named it Abbotsford, after the monks of Melrose Abbey who used to cross the River Tweed nearby.

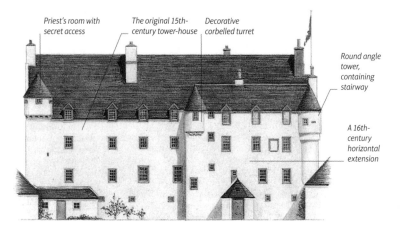

Priest's room with secret access

The original 15th-century tower-house

Decorative corbelled turret

Round angle tower, containing stairway

A 16th-century horizontal extension

Did You Know?

The Pentland Hills have served as inspiration to many Scottish poets and writers.

of Edinburgh, offer some of the best hill-walking country in the Lowlands. Leisurely walkers can saunter along the many signposted footpaths, while the more adventurous can take the chairlift at the Hillend dry ski slope to reach the higher ground leading to the 493-m (1,617-ft) hill of Allermuir. Even more ambitious is the classic scenic route along the ridge from Caerketton to West Kip.

Scott later demolished the house to make way for today's turreted building.

Scott's library contains more than 9,000 rare books and his collections of historic relics reflect his passion for the heroic past. An extensive array of arms and armour includes Rob Roy's broadsword. Stuart mementoes include a crucifix that belonged to Mary, Queen of Scots and a lock of Bonnie Prince Charlie's (p487) hair. The small study in which Scott wrote his *Waverley* novels can be visited, as can the room, overlooking the river, in which he died in 1832.

9

Pentland Hills

⌂ The Lothians
🚌 Edinburgh, then bus
ℹ Flotterstone Information Centre, off A702; 0131 529 2401

The Pentland Hills, stretching for 26 km (16 miles) southwest

---

10

Rosslyn Chapel

⌂ The Lothians 🚌🚆 Eskbank 🕐 9:30am-5pm daily (Jun-Aug: to 6pm); last adm: 30 minutes before closing 🌐 rosslynchapel.com

To the east of the A703, in the lee of the Pentland Hills, stands the exquisite and ornate 15th-century Rosslyn Chapel, which famously features in *The Da Vinci Code*, Dan Brown's bestselling novel.

The building was originally intended as a church, but after the death of its founder, William Sinclair, it was used as a burial ground for his descendants. It has remained the property of the family since 1446, and the chapel continues to be used as a place of worship to this day.

The delicately wreathed Apprentice Pillar recalls the legend of the talented apprentice carver who was killed by the master stone mason in a fit of jealous rage when he discovered his pupil's superior skill.

SIR WALTER SCOTT

Born in Edinburgh, Sir Walter Scott (1771-1832) is best remembered as a champion and literary figure of Scotland. His poems and novels created enduring images of a heroic wilderness filled with tales of the clans, while his orchestration, in 1822, of the state visit of George IV to Edinburgh was an extravaganza of Highland culture that helped re-establish tartan as the national dress of Scotland. He served as Clerk of the Court in Edinburgh's Parliament House (p500) and for 30 years was Sheriff of Selkirk in the Scottish Borders, a place he loved. He put the Trossachs (p530) firmly on the map with the publication of the *Lady of the Lake* (1810). He is buried at Dryburgh Abbey.

EVOLUTION OF THE SCOTTISH CASTLE

There are few more evocative sights in the British Isles than a Scottish castle on an island or at a lochside. These formidable retreats, often in remote settings, were essential throughout the Highlands, where incursions and strife between the many clans were common. It was King David I, who reigned from 1124–1153 in Scotland, who started building the first castles to maintain control over the lands he ruled.

TYPES OF SCOTTISH CASTLE

Those keen on visiting castles will be spoilt for choice as Scotland has more than 2,000 historic castles dotted across its landscape, most of which are open to visitors at least occasionally.

From the earliest Pictish brochs (round towers with thick stone walls) and Norman-influenced motte-and-bailey castles, the distinctively Scottish stone tower-house evolved, first appearing in the 13th century. By the mid-17th century fashion had become more important than defence, and there followed a period in which numerous huge Scottish palaces were built. The building of imitation mock fortified buildings continued into the 19th century with the mock-Baronial trend, the finest example of which is Balmoral Castle, finished in 1856 and modelled on 16th-century architecture *(p540)*.

TOP 5 SCOTTISH CASTLES

Eilean Donan
Sitting on an island in the Highlands, this is one of Scotland's most romantic castles *(p560)*.

Glamis
The legendary setting for Shakespeare's *Macbeth* resembles a fairytale château *(p536)*.

Culzean
This magnificent hilltop castle was remodelled in the late 18th century by Robert Adam *(p522)*.

Edinburgh
A world-famous icon of Scotland *(p496)*.

Duart
This 13th-century castle sits high on a crag on the Isle of Mull *(p565)*.

Evolution of Castle Designs

Motte-and-Bailey

▲ These castles first appeared in the 12th century. They stood atop two adjacent mounds enclosed by a wall, or palisade, and defensive ditches. The higher mound, or motte, was the more strongly defended as it held the keep and chief's house. The lower bailey was where the people lived. Of these castles little more than earthworks remain today. The image above shows all that remains today of Duffus Castle, Morayshire, built around 1150.
in the image above.

Early Tower-House

▲ Designed to deter local attacks rather than a major assault, the first tower-houses, such as Neidpath Castle above, appeared in the 13th century, though their design lived on for 400 years. They were built initially on a rectangular plan, with a single tower divided into three or four floors. The walls were unadorned, with few windows. Defensive structures were on top, and extra space was made by building adjoining towers. Extensions were vertical to minimize the area open to attack.

DRUMLANRIG CASTLE

Incorporating the remains of a 14th-century castle, Drumlanrig Castle *(p524)* was built in the 17th century. It has many traditional Scots aspects as well as such Renaissance features as the decorated stairway and façade, making it one of the most significant Renaissance buildings in Scotland. The castle is arranged around a courtyard.

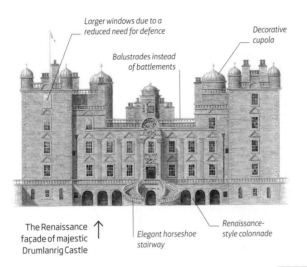

Larger windows due to a reduced need for defence

Decorative cupola

Balustrades instead of battlements

Renaissance-style colonnade

The Renaissance façade of majestic Drumlanrig Castle ↑

Elegant horseshoe stairway

Later Tower-House

▲ Though the requirements of defence were being replaced by those of comfort, the style of the early tower-house remained popular. By the 17th century, wings for accommodation were being added around the original tower, such as at Traquair House (above). The battlements and turrets were kept more for decorative than defensive reasons.

Classical Palace

▲ By the 18th century, the defensive imperative had passed and castles were built in the manner of country houses, rejecting the vertical tower-house in favour of a horizontal plan. Outside influences came from all over Europe, including Renaissance revival (Drumlanrig Castle above), Gothic revival and echoes of French châteaux.

GLASGOW AND SOUTHWEST SCOTLAND

Glasgow can trace its origins to a prehistoric fording point on the River Clyde. Romans manned outposts here to monitor their northern Pictish neighbours, but their presence was brief and the lands became part of the Kingdom of Strathclyde, which ran across the wild hills of Southwest Scotland (still sparsely populated today) and beyond today's English border.

It was religion that eventually propelled Glasgow to prominence. By the 11th century it had one of Scotland's largest bishoprics, for which it built the mighty Glasgow Cathedral in the 13th century. This helped seal Glasgow's 18th-century fortunes, when its merchants ran colonial tobacco, cotton and sugar operations in the Americas. The whole region benefited. Infrastructure grew rapidly, cotton mills such as New Lanark opened and a world-leading ship-building industry developed. This was also an era of mass immigration, including many from Ireland, who created a strong Catholic presence in Glasgow.

Military shipbuilding ensured Glasgow flourished in the early 20th century until post-war peace and global economic change caused a hard-hitting decline in heavy industries. A corner was slowly turned in the 1980s as the city diversified into financial and insurance services and refocused itself around redevelopment projects.

GLASGOW AND SOUTHWEST SCOTLAND

Must Sees

❶ Glasgow
❷ Culzean Castle and Country Park

Experience More

❸ Falkirk Wheel
❹ The Helix
❺ New Lanark
❻ Drumlanrig Castle
❼ Whithorn
❽ Threave Castle
❾ Burns Heritage Trail

CENTRAL AND NORTHEAST SCOTLAND
p526

EDINBURGH AND SOUTHEAST SCOTLAND
p488

THE NORTHWEST
p342

❹ THE HELIX
❸ Falkirk
FALKIRK WHEEL
FALKIRK

Rosyth
Queensferry
Edinburgh Airport
Edinburgh
WEST LOTHIAN
EDINBURGH
Livingston
Pentland Hills
Penicuik
Newmains
Carluke
Carnwath
Lanark
Melbourne
Peebles
❺ NEW LANARK
Biggar
Douglas
Abington
Leadhills
Hart Fell 808 m (2,650 ft)
Cappercleuch
St Mary's Loch
Ettrick
SCOTTISH BORDERS
Jedburgh
Hawick
Cheviot Hills
Moffat
Beattock
Teviothead
DRUMLANRIG CASTLE ❻
Thornhill
Eskdalemuir
Esk
Parkgate
Newcastleton
AND GALLOWAY
Nith
Lockerbie
Langholm
ENGLAND
Crocketford
Dumfries
Canonbie
New Abbey
Ecclefechan
Longtown
Dalbeattie
Annan
Gretna
Kirkbean
Carlisle
Solway Firth
Wigton
GLASGOW AND SOUTHWEST SCOTLAND
Cockermouth
Lake District
Workington

Buchanan Street, a shopping district in downtown Glasgow ↑

GLASGOW

🚇🚆 Argyle St 🚌 Buchanan St 🚊 Buchanan St; www.peoplemakeglasgow.com

Scotland's finest Victorian city reflects its era of prosperity, when ironworks, shipyards and cotton mills were fuelled by Lanarkshire coal. Today this dynamic city rivals Edinburgh in the arts and also has a superb Science Centre, plus great shopping and dining options.

①
Glasgow Cathedral

🏛 Cathedral Sq ⏰ Apr-Sep: 9:30am-5:30pm Mon-Sat, 1-5:30pm Sun; Oct-Mar: 10am-4pm Mon-Sat, 1-4pm Sun 🌐 glasgowcathedral.org.uk

One of the few churches to survive the Reformation by adapting itself to Protestant worship, Glasgow Cathedral is a rare example of an original 13th-century church. It was built on the site of a chapel founded by the city's patron saint, St Mungo, a 6th-century bishop. According to legend, Mungo placed the body of a holy man on a cart yoked to two wild bulls, telling them to take it to the place ordained by God. There St Mungo built his church.

The crypt contains the intricate tomb of St Mungo. The Blacader Aisle is reputed to have been built over an existing grave site that was blessed by St Ninian. Behind the cathedral, a likeness of John Knox (p495) overlooks the necropolis, or cemetery, containing extravagant monuments to the dead of Glasgow's wealthy.

 GREAT VIEW
Glasgow Necropolis

Glasgow Cathedral's hauntingly beautiful necropolis boasts great views over the city's rooftops. Modelled on the Père Lachaise cemetery in Paris, it's a welcome escape from the busy streets below.

St Mungo Museum of Religious Life and Art

 2 Castle St 0141 276 1625 10am–5pm Tue–Thu & Sat, 11am–5pm Fri & Sun

This museum in the cathedral precinct illustrates religious themes with superb artifacts, including a 19th-century dancing Shiva and an Islamic painting, the *Attributes of Divine Perfection* (1986) by Ahmed Moustafa. An exhibition on religion in Glasgow throws light on the life of missionary and explorer David Livingstone. Outside, you can visit Britain's only permanent Zen Buddhist garden.

Did You Know?

Glasgow's name comes from the Gaelic *glas cu*, meaning "green valley" or "dear green place".

Provand's Lordship

 3 Castle St 10am–5pm Tue–Sun glasgowlife. org.uk/museums

Built as a canon's house in 1471, this is now Glasgow's oldest surviving house. Its low ceilings and wooden furniture create a vivid impression of life in a wealthy 15th-century house-hold. Mary, Queen of Scots may have stayed here when she visited Glasgow in 1566.

Tenement House

 145 Buccleuch St 0141 333 0183 Mar-Sep: 10am–5pm daily; Nov-Feb: 11am–4pm Sat-Mon

More a time capsule than a museum, this is an almost undisturbed record of life as it was in a modest Glasgow flat on a tenement estate in the early 20th century. It was the home of Miss Agnes Toward, who lived here from 1911 until

HIDDEN GEM
Sharmanka Kinetic Theatre

Two Russians, a sculptor-mechanic and a theatre director, created this bizarre theatre on Trongate, where strange contraptions, light displays and music tell both funny and tragic tales (*www. sharmanka.com*).

1965. As Agnes never changed anything and threw very little away, the house has become a treasure-trove of social history. In the parlour, used only on formal occasions, afternoon tea is laid out on a white lace cloth. The kitchen, with its coal-fired range and box bed, is filled with the tools of a vanished era, such as a goffering-iron for ironing lace, a washboard and a stone hot-water bottle. Agnes's lavender water and medicines are arranged in the bathroom.

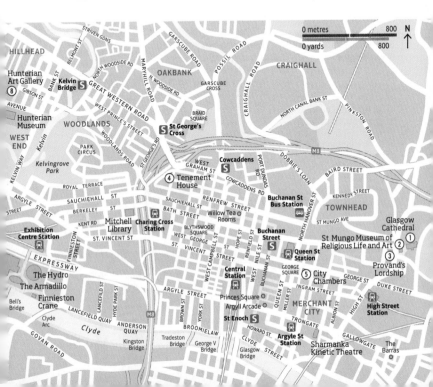

Monument to Sir Walter Scott rising above the City Chambers on George Square

project, Glasgow's glass and titanium Science Centre is located on the south bank of the River Clyde. The centre has three huge floors full of interactive puzzles, optical illusions, scientific and craft areas aimed at entertaining and educating kids. Big hits include mind control games and Madagascan hissing cockroaches. There's also an IMAX theatre that projects gigantic 3D and 2D films. The 127-m (417-ft) revolving tower, Scotland's tallest freestanding structure, provides striking views of central Glasgow and beyond.

⑦

Riverside Museum

🏠 100 Pointhouse Place 🚇 Partick 🚌 59 🕐 10am-5pm Mon-Thu & Sat, 11am-5pm Fri & Sun 🌐 glasgow life.org.uk/museums

This landmark attraction sits on the Clyde in a dramatic zinc-panelled building designed by architect Zaha Hadid. Focused on transport and its social impact on the city, the museum is crammed with Scottish-built locomotives and road vehicles of all styles and vintages, testament to Glasgow's past manufacturing supremacy. The tall ship *Glenlee*, berthed alongside, is also open to the public.

⑤

City Chambers

🏠 George St 🕐 For guided tours only, 10:30am & 2:30pm Mon-Fri

Located on the east side of George Square, the City Chambers, the headquarters of Glasgow City Council, is a magnificent civic building designed by William Young in Italian Renaissance style. The imposing building was opened in 1888 by Queen Victoria. With its elegant interior, decorated in Italian marble and mosaic – it has the largest marble staircase in western Europe – the opulence of this building makes it the most impressive of its type in Scotland.

⑥

Glasgow Science Centre

🏠 50 Pacific Quay 🕐 Apr-Oct: 10am-5pm daily; Nov-Mar: 10am-3pm Wed-Fri, 10am-5pm Sat & Sun 🌐 glasgowscience centre.org

The centrepiece of an impressive £75 million millennium

→ Iconic jagged structure of the Riverside Museum on the Clyde waterfront

Hunterian Art Gallery

🏛 82 Hillhead St 🚌 4, 4A
🕐 10am–5pm Tue–Sat,
11am–4pm Sun
🌐 gla.ac.uk/hunterian

Built to house paintings bequeathed to Glasgow University by an ex-student and physician, Dr William Hunter (1718–83), this gallery contains Scotland's largest print collection, with works by many major European artists dating from the 16th century. A collection of work by celebrated Glasgow designer Charles Rennie Mackintosh (*p520*), often cited as the father of the famous "Glasgow School", a group of painters – the "Glasgow Boys" – who found fame at the beginning of the 20th century, is supplemented by a reconstruction of his home.

The building also houses a major collection of 19th- and 20th-century Scottish art, but by far the most famous collection is that containing works by the Paris-trained American painter James McNeill Whistler (1834–1903), who influenced so many of the Glasgow School painters.

SHOP

The Barras
This most Glaswegian of markets is a glorious mix of stalls selling everything under the sun. The Glasgow Vintage and Flea Market is a regular weekend fixture.

🏛 244 Gallowgate
🌐 theglasgow
barras.com

Princes Square
This five-storey atrium beneath a Victorian glass cupola is a paradise for fans of big-name fashion, with brands such as Vivienne Westwood, Kurt Geiger and Belstaff.

🏛 48 Buchanan St
🌐 princessquare.co.uk

Argyll Arcade
Glasgow's glittering emporium of bling gleams with new and pre-loved goods, from luxury watches to diamond rings and vintage jewellery.

🏛 Argyll St
🌐 argyll-arcade.com

Did You Know?

The 2,500-tonne roof of the Riverside Museum is one of the UK's most complex structures.

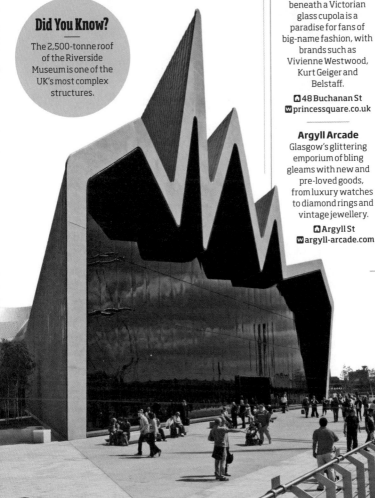

Did You Know?

In 1996 a number of works were stolen from the collection and sold on the black market.

⑨ Ⓜ ⓨ ▣ ⓐ

KELVINGROVE ART GALLERY AND MUSEUM

📍Argyle St, Kelvingrove 🚌2, 3, 11 🕙10am–5pm Mon–Thu & Sat, 11am–5pm Fri & Sun 🌐glasgowlife.org.uk/museums

Housed in a grand Spanish Baroque building in Glasgow's West End, the Kelvingrove Art Gallery and Museum is deservedly Scotland's most popular civic art collection.

Kelvingrove's 8,000-item collection includes many pieces of international significance. Included are works by 19th-century British artists such as Turner and Constable, and French Impressionist and Dutch Renaissance painters. Scottish art and design is well represented with rooms dedicated to the Scottish Colourists and the Glasgow Style.

The museum offers insight into Glasgow's evolution from its medieval beginnings to its 19th- and 20th-century economic and cultural transformation, to the 2010 Commonwealth Games, hosted by the city.

↑ Kelvingrove Art Gallery and Museum, an imposing red sandstone building

↑ Spitfire hanging dramatically from the ceiling of the West Court

Kelvingrove's collection is the world's leading portfolio of works by the dynamic "Glasgow Boys".

↑ Visitors exploring the Natural History Gallery

Must See

Gallery Highlights

The Dutch Gallery

Rembrandt's *Man in Armour* sets the tone for Kelvingrove's collection of 17th-century Dutch and Flemish masters, which is recognized as one of the UK's finest. Other paintings worth seeking out include Benjamin Gerritszoon Cuyp's *The Quack Doctor*, and the supporting cast includes Nicolaes Pieterszoon Berchem, Daniel de Blieck, and Abraham van Beyeren.

The French Gallery

Van Gogh's portrait of the red-headed, red-bearded Alexander Reid makes the Glasgow-born art dealer, a friend of the artist, look almost like Vincent's twin brother. Raoul Dufy's *The Jetties of Trouville-Deauville* is another stand-out work in a stellar portfolio of paintings by 19th- and 20th-century greats including Braque, Gauguin, Monet, Pissarro and Renoir.

The Scottish Colourists

◀ Though they are more closely associated with Edinburgh than with Glasgow, the Scottish Colourists are well represented at Kelvingrove. Cadell's elegantly poised *A Lady in Black* and Peploe's *Roses* are outstanding examples of each artist's style. Hunter's *A Summer Day, Largo* and Fergusson's *On the Beach at Tangier* are variations on the classic maritime themes that both these painters loved.

The Glasgow Boys

James Guthrie's *Old Willie; The Village Worthy*, a sympathetic portrait of an elderly man, contrasts strongly here with the colourful, almost psychedelic mysticism of *The Druids: Bringing in the Mistletoe* by George Henry and E A Hornel, illustrating the breadth of vision of this celebrated group of painters. Kelvingrove's collection is the world's leading portfolio of works by the dynamic "Glasgow Boys".

Mackintosh and the Glasgow Style

Woodwork and gesso panels, stylish furniture, beautifully detailed light fittings and other decorative elements that are hallmarks of Charles Rennie Mackintosh's distinctive style have pride of place in the reconstructed Ingram Street Tearooms, designed by Mackintosh working together with his wife, Margaret MacDonald, between 1900 and 1912. Tearooms were the first dining establishments to allow unaccompanied women, and the elegant Ladies Luncheon Room is the epitome of Edwardian elegance.

519

BEYOND THE CENTRE

People's Palace

🅰 Glasgow Green
🕐 10am–5pm Tue–Thu & Sat, 11am–5pm Fri & Sun
🌐 glasgowlife.org.uk/museums

Built in 1898 as a cultural museum for the people of Glasgow's East End, this building houses everything from temperance tracts to trade-union banners, suffragette posters to comedian Billy Connolly's banana-shaped boots, providing a social history of the city from the 12th to the 20th century. A superb conservatory contains an exotic winter garden.

Burrell Collection

🅰 200 Pollokshaws Rd
🕐 Until spring 2021
🌐 glasgowlife.org.uk/museums

Given to the city in 1944 by Sir William Burrell (1861–1958), a wealthy shipping owner, this internationally acclaimed collection is the gem in Glasgow's crown. The 9,000-piece collection features 600 medieval stained-glass panels, 150 tapestries, ancient Middle Eastern, Greek and

CHARLES RENNIE MACKINTOSH

Glasgow's most famed designer (1868-1928) entered Glasgow School of Art at the age of 16. His first commission was to design a series of tearooms in the city. He became a leading figure in the Art Nouveau movement, and his characteristic straight lines and flowing detail are the hallmark of early 20th-century style.

Roman treasures, Chinese ceramics and superb Oriental carpets and embroideries, and even celebrated works by Old Masters such as Rembrandt's *Self Portrait* (1632). Additional displays will be unveiled when the collection reopens.

House for an Art Lover

🅰 Bellahouston Park, 10 Dumbreck Rd 🕐 10am–5pm daily 🕐 Regularly for functions 🌐 houseforanartlover.co.uk

Plans for the House for an Art Lover were submitted by Charles Rennie Mackintosh and his wife Margaret MacDonald in response to a competition in a German magazine in the summer of 1900. The competition brief was to create a country retreat for someone of elegance and taste who loved the arts. As it was a theoretical exercise, the couple were unrestrained by logistics or budget and won a special prize for their efforts. The plans lay unused for over 80 years until consulting engineer Graham Roxburgh, who had been involved in the refurbishment of other Mackintosh interiors in Glasgow, decided to build the House for an Art Lover. Construction began in 1989 and was completed in 1996. The rooms on the main floor give a real insight into the

Sun shining through medieval stained glass at the Burrell Collection ↓

→

Grand exterior of Pollok House surrounded by lush parkland

vision of Mackintosh and the artistic talent of MacDonald. The Oval Room is a beautifully proportioned space in a single light colour, designed to be a tranquil retreat for ladies, while the Music Room and its centrepiece piano (enclosed within a four-poster bed), which is played to add to the atmosphere, is also bright and inspiring. The Main Hall leads into the Dining Room, which contains a long table, sideboard and relief stone fireplace. The great attention to detail demonstrated throughout the House, in the panelling, light fixtures and other elements, is enormously impressive. The exterior is also an extraordinary achieve-ment in art and design.

⑬

Scotland Street School Museum

🏠 225 Scotland St 🕐 10am-5pm Tue-Thu & Sat, 11am-5pm Fri & Sun 🌐 glasgow life.org.uk/museums

This museum, housed in a former school designed by Charles Rennie Mackintosh, contains audio-visual exhibits and reconstructed classrooms to reflect developments in education from the Victorian era to the 1960s. You can read and hear recollections of former pupils on topics such as classroom discipline, World War II, school attire and playground games.

⑭   (NTS)

Pollok House

🏠 2060 Pollokshaws Rd 🕐 10am-5pm daily 🔒 25, 26 & 31 Dec 🌐 nts.org.uk

Glasgow's finest 18th-century domestic building has one of Britain's best collections of Spanish paintings. The Neo-Classical central block of Pollok House was finished in 1750, the sobriety of its exterior contrasting with the exuberant plasterwork within.

The Maxwells have lived at Pollok since the mid-13th century, but the male line ended with Sir John Maxwell, who designed the gardens and parkland. In 1966 Anne Maxwell Macdonald gave the house to the City of Glasgow.

Hanging above the family silver, porcelain, hand-painted Chinese wallpaper and Jaco-bean glass, are William Blake's *Sir Geoffrey Chaucer and the Nine and Twenty Pilgrims* (1745) as well as William Hogarth's portrait of James Thomson, who wrote the words to *Rule Britannia*. El Greco's *Lady in a Fur Wrap* (1541) and works by Goya and Murillo adorn the library and drawing room.

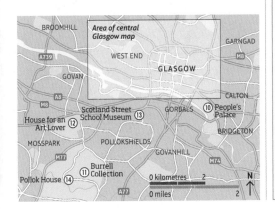

EAT & DRINK

Willow Tea Rooms
The only surviving Charles Rennie Mackintosh-designed tearoom in the city is a decorative - and delicious - delight.

🏠 217 Sauchiehall St
🌐 willowtearooms. co.uk

£ £ £

2 ⊘ ⊘ ▢ ⌂ (NTS)

CULZEAN CASTLE AND COUNTRY PARK

⌖ 6 km (4 miles) west of Maybole, Ayrshire ▦ Ayr, then bus ⏱ Castle: Apr-Oct: 10:30am-5pm (last adm 4pm); grounds: 9am-dusk daily year-round ◉ nts.org.uk

Standing on a cliff's edge in an extensive parkland estate, the late 16th-century keep of Culzean (pronounced Cullayn) is a masterpiece in a land full of magnificent castles, with a glorious estate to match.

Formerly a crumbling fortified tower-house, Culzean Castle was transformed by the great Scots architect Robert Adam into a mansion of sumptuous proportions and elegance. Work began in 1777 and lasted almost 20 years, with no expense spared in the decoration and craftsmanship of this breathtaking clifftop fortress. Culzean was fully restored and gifted to the nation in the 1970s.

The Castle Grounds

The grounds became Scotland's first public country park in 1969 and, with farming flourishing alongside ornamental gardens, they reflect both the leisure and everyday activities of life on a great country estate. Free tours depart from the Home Farm visitor centre, or you can go it alone – the views across the water to the mountains of Arran are glorious from the clifftop and shoreline trails.

ORANGES AND LEMONS

Camellia House, Culzean's elegant stone-framed orangery, was restored in 2018 and replanted with clementine, lime, lemon and orange trees. Built in around 1840, it was designed by John Patterson, a disciple of Robert Adam. Orangeries in this style, built in emulation of those created for 17th-century monarchs like Louis XIV of France, were enviable status symbols for wealthy 19th-century notables.

The clock tower was originally the family coach house and stables.

Did You Know?

During the castle's prime, the caves below were used for smuggling contraband.

Illustration of Culzean Castle perched on its magnificent clifftop setting ↑

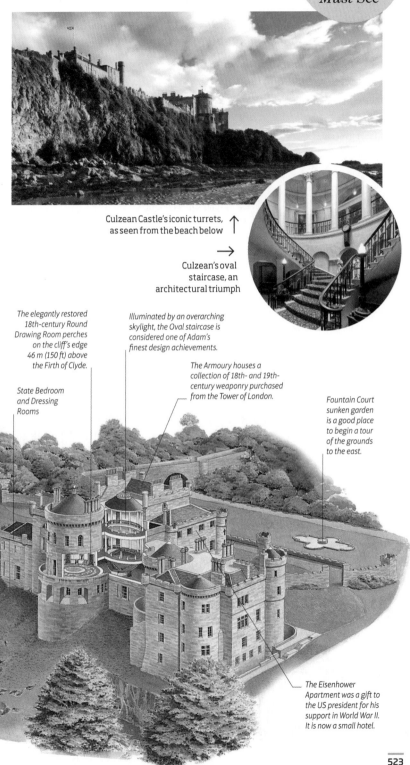

Culzean Castle's iconic turrets, as seen from the beach below ↑

→

Culzean's oval staircase, an architectural triumph

The elegantly restored 18th-century Round Drawing Room perches on the cliff's edge 46 m (150 ft) above the Firth of Clyde.

Illuminated by an overarching skylight, the Oval staircase is considered one of Adam's finest design achievements.

The Armoury houses a collection of 18th- and 19th-century weaponry purchased from the Tower of London.

Fountain Court sunken garden is a good place to begin a tour of the grounds to the east.

State Bedroom and Dressing Rooms

The Eisenhower Apartment was a gift to the US president for his support in World War II. It is now a small hotel.

EXPERIENCE MORE

3

Falkirk Wheel

⌂ Lime Rd, Tamfourhill, Falkirk ⊞ Falkirk ⏰ 10am-5:30pm daily for boat trips ⓦ scottishcanals.co.uk

This impressive boat lift, the first ever to revolve, gently swings boats between the Union and the Forth and Clyde canals. Visitors can ride the wheel on boats that leave from the visitor centre.

4

The Helix

⌂ Falkirk ⏰ 9:30am-5pm daily ⓦ thehelix.co.uk

Two glittering equine heads tower above the Forth and Clyde and Union canals. The Kelpies, 30-m- (98-ft-) tall metal sculptures created by sculptor Andy Scott, are the keynote landmark of The Helix, a large canalside park with walking and cycling trails. The visitor centre explains the history of the canals.

5

New Lanark

⌂ Clyde Valley ⊞ Lanark ⏰ 10am-5pm daily (Nov-Mar: to 4pm) ⓦ newlanark.org

Situated by the falls of the River Clyde, this village was founded in 1785 by the entrepreneur David Dale. The village became Britain's largest cotton producer by 1800. Dale and his successor, Robert Owen, proved that commercial success need not undermine the wellbeing of the workforce. Now a museum, New Lanark is a window onto working life in the early 19th century.

 HIDDEN GEM
Scotland's National Book Town

Book-mad Wigtown, in Dumfries & Galloway, is a book-lover's paradise. Home to more than 20 bookshops and literary cafés, this quaint town also hosts a literature festival every autumn.

6

Drumlanrig Castle

⌂ Thornhill, Dumfries & Galloway ⊞ Dumfries then bus ⏰ Easter-Aug: 11am-5pm daily; Grounds: Apr-Sep: 10am-5pm daily ⓦ drumlanrig.com

Built from pink sandstone between 1679 and 1691, the massive fortress-palace of Drumlanrig (p509) contains

↑ The Falkirk Wheel, a feat of engineering linking two canals

a priceless collection of art treasures, including paintings by Holbein and Rembrandt, as well as Jacobite relics such as Bonnie Prince Charlie's sash.

Whithorn

🏛 Dumfries & Galloway
🚉 Stranraer 🚌 🖥 visit dumfriesandgalloway.co.uk

The earliest site of continuous Christian worship in Scotland, Whithorn (meaning "white house") takes its name from a chapel built here in 397. Though nothing remains of this chapel, a guided tour of the archaeological dig reveals evidence of Northumbrian, Viking and Scottish settlements dating from the 5th to the 19th centuries. A visitors' centre, **The Whithorn Story**, provides information on the excavations and contains a collection of carved stones.

The Whithorn Story

🎫 🕐 🏛 The Whithorn Trust, 45-47 George St ⏰ Apr-Oct: 10:30am-5pm daily
🖥 whithorn.com

Threave Castle

🏛 Castle Douglas, Dumfries & Galloway 🚉 Dumfries ⏰ Apr-Oct: 10am-4:30pm daily (Oct: to 3:30pm)
🖥 historicenvironment.scot

This menacing tower, a 14th-century Black Douglas stronghold standing on an island in the Dee, commands the most complete medieval riverside harbour in Scotland. The feudal lord Douglas's struggles against the early Stuart kings culminated in his surrender here in 1455. Threave was later dismantled after Protestant Covenanters managed to defeat its Catholic defenders in 1640. A small boat ferries visitors to and from the castle.

↑ Sailing past Threave Castle, sitting on an island in the River Dee

9 Burns Heritage Trail

🏛 South Ayrshire, Dumfries & Galloway
🖥 visitscotland.com

Robert Burns (1759–96), Scotland's most beloved writer, left behind a remarkable body of work – from satirical poetry to tender love songs. An official Heritage Trail takes in various sights in southwest Scotland where he lived.

Among the highlights are, in Dumfries, the **Robert Burns Centre**, focusing on his years in the town, and **Burns House**, his home from 1793 to 1796.

In Alloway, the **Robert Burns Birthplace Museum** is set in beautiful rolling countryside. It comprises Burns Cottage, the poet's birthplace, with a collection of memorabilia and manuscripts.

Robert Burns Centre
🎫 🔊 🏛 Mill Rd, Dumfries
🕐 Times vary, check website
🖥 nts.org.uk

Burns House
🏛 Burns St, Dumfries
📞 (01387) 255297 ⏰ Apr-Sep: 10am-5pm Mon-Sat, 2-5pm Sun; Oct-Mar: 10am-1pm & 2-5pm Tue-Sat

Robert Burns Birthplace Museum
🎫 🔊 🏛 Alloway ⏰ 10am-5:30pm daily (cottage: 11am-5pm) 🖥 burnsmuseum.org.uk

CELEBRATING BURNS NIGHT

The birthday of Scotland's bard (25 January) is celebrated with much pomp. A Burns Supper opens with the reading of Burns's "Selkirk Grace", before the ceremonious piping in of the haggis, the event's main dish. "The Address to the Haggis", the poet's homage to the "great chieftain o' the pudding-race", and other readings follow, along with the patronising "Toast to the Lassies", traditionally met with a sarcastic riposte from a female guest. The event ends with "Auld Lang Syne".

CENTRAL AND EASTERN SCOTLAND

Lying at the gentle transition between Scotland's Lowlands and Highlands, Central and Eastern Scotland historically acted as a bridge between the two regions and cultures. This was an area once in the hands of Picts, who left beautiful geometric stone carvings before fusing their culture with that of the Gaels from the west in the 8th century. Together they became Scots and created the Kingdom of Alba, Gaelic for Scotland. Hence often dubbed the cradle of Scotland, Central Scotland is dotted with castles that organized this Kingdom. The most significant was at Stirling, which in the 13th and early 14th centuries oversaw watershed struggles. In 1314 the Battle of Bannockburn saw Robert the Bruce win the day and help secure Scottish independence from England for some 400 years.

The gentle green valleys and rising moorlands of the region, still thinly populated today, also bore witness to another era of north–south tensions when Jacobites, supporters of a rival claim to the British throne, repeatedly clashed and skirmished with the British crown in the 17th and 18th centuries. This was followed by a period of industrialization, which gripped coastal cities such as Dundee, with its jute industry, and Aberdeen, where shipbuilding and fishing thrived. The latter also began to benefit from North Sea oil wealth, which helped see it through Scotland's late 20th-century industrial downturn.

CENTRAL AND EASTERN SCOTLAND

Must Sees

1. Loch Lomond and the Trossachs National Park
2. Aberdeen
3. Stirling Castle

Experience More

4. Stirling
5. Glamis Castle
6. Doune Castle
7. Perth
8. Scone Palace
9. Dundee
10. East Neuk
11. Dunfermline
12. St Andrews
13. Falkland Palace
14. Culross
15. Balmoral Castle and Royal Deeside
16. Elgin
17. Dunkeld
18. Pitlochry
19. Killiecrankie
20. Blair Castle

Alness

Dingwall   Fortrose   Nairn

Beauly   Inverness   Ferness

Loch Ness   Carrbridge

HIGHLAND   Aviemore

Glen Mor

THE HIGHLANDS AND ISLANDS
p542

Dalwhinnie

Beinn Dearg
1,008 m (3,307 ft)

Glencoe

Garry

BLAIR CASTLE 20   Blair Atholl

Portnacroish

KILLIECRANKIE 19

PITLOCHRY

Loch Laidon

Rannoch Station   Loch Rannoch   Tummel Bridge

Carn Mairg
1,041 m (3,415 ft)   Aberfeldy

Bridge of Orchy   Kenmore

Ben Lawers
1,214 m (3,983 ft)   PERTH AND KINROSS

Benderloch   Loch Tay

Taynuilt   Killin   Ben Chonzie
931 m (3,055 ft)   Almond

Oban   Tyndrum   A85   St. Fillans   Crieff

ARGYLL AND BUTE   Crianlarich   Lochearnhead   Loch Earn   Comrie

Kilmelford   Inverarnan   Strathyre   Ben Vorlich
985 m (3,232 ft)   Auchterarder

Inveraray   Loch Katrine   STIRLING   Braco

Callander   A9

LOCH LOMOND AND THE TROSSACHS NATIONAL PARK 1   DOUNE CASTLE 6   Dunblane

Luss   Aberfoyle   STIRLING 3 4

Balmaha   Buchlyvie   STIRLING CASTLE

Loch Lomond   Balfron   M9

Balloch   Fintry

Helensburgh   A61   M80   Falkirk

CENTRAL AND EASTERN SCOTLAND

Strathblane

Dumbarton

Greenock   Clydebank   GLASGOW AND SOUTHWEST SCOTLAND
p510

Glasgow Airport   M8

Largs   Johnstone   Glasgow

Motherwell

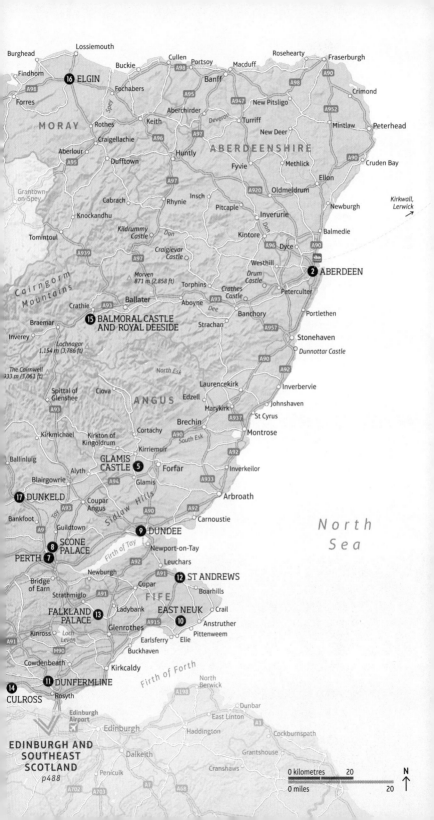

LOCH LOMOND AND THE TROSSACHS NATIONAL PARK

⬔ West Dunbartonshire, Argyll & Bute, Trossachs
🚉 Balloch; Arrochar and Tarbet 🚌 Callander; Balloch;
Balmaha 🛈 Ancaster Sq, Callander; National Park
Visitor Centre, Balmaha; www.lochlomond-trossachs.org

Combining the ruggedness of the Grampians with
the pastoral tranquillity of the Borders, this beautiful
region of craggy hills and sparkling lochs is the
meeting place of the Lowlands and Highlands.

Loch Lomond

Of Scotland's many lochs, Loch Lomond is perhaps the most
popular and best loved. Lying just 30 km (19 miles) northwest
of Glasgow, its accessibility has helped its rise to prominence.
Duncryne, a small hill some 5 km (3 miles) northeast of Balloch
on the southern shore, gives an excellent view of the loch, while
the western shore is the more developed, with villages such as
Luss and Tarbet attracting many visitors.

Walkers pass by Loch Lomond's shores on the West Highland
Way, Scotland's most popular long-distance footpath, running
from Glasgow to Fort William, and the 50-km (30-mile) Great
Trossachs Path, which runs between Callander and Inversnaid.
Boat trips operate from Balloch Pier and can be rented from
various points around the loch.

GREAT VIEW
Ben Lomond

The 12-km (7.5-mile)
hike to the summit of
Ben Lomond, 990m
(3,217 ft) above the
lochside starting point
at Rowardennan, calls
for good boots and
reasonable fitness.
The path leads through
oak and birch woods,
then up to the summit
for a breathtaking
panoramic view.

Walker overlooking Loch
↓ Katrine from the summit
of Ben A'an, Trossachs

Inversnaid Hotel Harbour and Loch Lomond *(right)* as viewed from Beinn Dubh ↑

The Trossachs

In 2002, 1,865 sq km (720 sq miles) of the Trossachs area was designated Scotland's first national park. Home to a variety of wildlife, including the golden eagle, peregrine falcon, red deer and the wildcat, the Trossachs have inspired many writers, including Sir Walter Scott *(p506)*. Loch Katrine, just north of Loch Lomond, was the setting of Sir Walter Scott's *Lady of the Lake* (1810). The Victorian steamer *Sir Walter Scott* cruises from Trossachs Pier. Callander is the most popular town from which to explore the Trossachs, while Queen Elizabeth Forest Park between Loch Lomond and Aberfoyle offers spectacular woodland walks through this vast tract of Scottish countryside.

Did You Know?

At 45 sq km (27.5 sq miles), Loch Lomond is the largest stretch of fresh water in Britain by surface area.

↑ Granite buildings of Union Street, Aberdeen's main thoroughfare

②

ABERDEEN

 Grampian ✈ 13 km (8 miles) NW of Aberdeen
🚉🚌 Union Sq 🛈 23 Union St; www.visitabdn.com

Nicknamed the "Granite City" for its distinctive, hard-edged architecture, Aberdeen is Scotland's third-largest city. After the discovery of oil beneath the North Sea in the 1970s, it became Europe's offshore oil capital and, despite some decline in recent years, its harbour still bustles with commercial shipping. At the east end of Union Street modern redevelopments surround the ornate granite walls of Marischal College. North of the centre, Old Aberdeen is a late medieval enclave of historic buildings nestled around one of the UK's oldest universites.

**① **

St Machar's Cathedral

🏠 The Chanonry
🕐 9:30am-4:30pm daily (Nov-Mar: 10am-4pm)
🌐 stmachar.com

The twin granite towers of this 15th-century cathedral, dedicated to Aberdeen's patron saint, rise above the Old Aberdeen skyline to pinpoint St Machar's Cathedral. Stained-glass windows light the interior, depicting the 6th-century saint and the cathedral's earliest bishops.

**② **

King's College

🏠 College Bounds
🕐 Daily (chapel: 10am-3:30pm Mon-Fri)

Founded in 1495, King's College was the city's first university. The visitor centre gives background on its long history. The chapel has a distinctive lantern tower, rebuilt in 1633. Douglas Strachan's stained-glass windows add a modern touch to the interior, where a 1540 pulpit is carved with heads of Stuart monarchs.

**③ **

St Andrew's Cathedral

🏠 King St 🕐 Times vary, check website
🌐 standrewscathedral aberdeen.org.uk

The Mother Church of the Episcopal Church in the United States, St Andrew's has a memorial to Samuel Seabury, the first Episcopalian bishop in the US, who was consecrated in Aberdeen in 1784. Coats of arms representing the American states and Jacobite families contrast with the gleaming white interior.

④

Maritime Museum

🏠 Shiprow 🕐 10am-5pm daily (noon-3pm Sun)
🌐 aagm.co.uk

Overlooking the harbour is Provost Ross's house, which dates back to 1593. It now houses the Maritime Museum, which traces the history of Aberdeen's seafaring tradition from medieval times to the offshore oil boom during the 1970s. The brilliant exhibitions cover numerous topics from shipbuilding and shipwrecks to rescues and oil excavation.

⑤
St Nicholas Kirk

🏛 Union St ⏰ Jun-Sep:
noon-4pm Mon-Fri;
9:30am-1pm Sun 🌐 kirk-
of-st-nicholas-org.uk

Founded in the 12th century
and rebuilt in 1752, St Nicholas
Kirk is Scotland's largest
parish church. Many ancient
relics can be seen inside,
including iron rings which
were used to secure women
accused of witchcraft in the
17th century.

⑥
Aberdeen Art Gallery

🏛 Schoolhill 🔧 For renov-
ation 🌐 aagm.co.uk

This landmark art gallery's
collection of works by British
artists including Raeburn,
Reynolds, Hogarth, Paul Nash,
Stanley Spencer and Francis
Bacon, and by Monet, Renoir,
Degas and Toulouse-Lautrec,
may once again be viewed
when a long-delayed
redevelopment is completed.

⑦
Provost Skene's House

🏛 Guestrow ⏰ Times vary,
check website 🌐 aagm.
co.uk

This 16th-century house is
one of the city's most historic
buildings. It is temporarily
closed due to the Marischal
Square redevelopment.

⑧
Marischal College

🏛 Broad St

The world's second-largest
granite building (losing out to
the Escorial in Spain for the
top spot), Marischal College
was founded in 1593 by the
5th Earl Marischal of Scotland
as a Protestant alternative
to King's College. It's austere
façade, a symbol of the
"Granite City", now houses
Aberdeenshire Council's
headquarters.

↑ Student cycling along
the cobbled lanes of
King's College campus

EAT

Musa
Contemporary art and
live music complement
the menu at this lively
bar-restaurant. Choose
from vegan, veggie
and thoroughly
carniverous options.

🏛 33 Exchange St
🌐 musaaberdeen.com

£ £ £

Moonfish
Imaginative bites
precede delightful
mains at this lovely
hideaway restaurant
off Union Street.

🏛 9 Connection Wynd
🔧 Sun & Mon 🌐 moon
fishfishcafe.co.uk

£ £ £

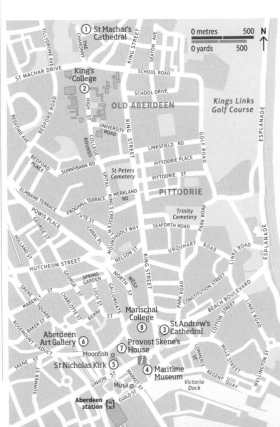

③ ⑯ 🍴 🖥 🛍

STIRLING CASTLE

🏠 Castle Esplanade, Stirling 🚃🚌 🕐 Apr–Sep: 9:30am–6pm daily; Oct–Mar: 9:30am–5pm daily 🌐 stirlingcastle.gov.uk

Rising high on a rocky crag, this magnificent castle, which dominated Scottish history for centuries, now remains one of the finest examples of Renaissance architecture in Scotland.

Overlooking the plains where some of Scotland's most decisive battles took place, Stirling Castle was one of the nation's greatest strongholds. Legend says that King Arthur wrested the original castle from the Saxons; however, the first written evidence of a castle is from 1100. The present building dates from the 15th and 16th centuries. From 1881 to 1964 it was used as a depot for recruits into the Argyll and Sutherland Highlanders.

Today you can explore the palace vaults, try your hand at some medieval crafts and rub shoulders with costumed characters as they bring the castle's fascinating history to life.

↑ Highland cattle grazing on pastures overlooked by Stirling Castle

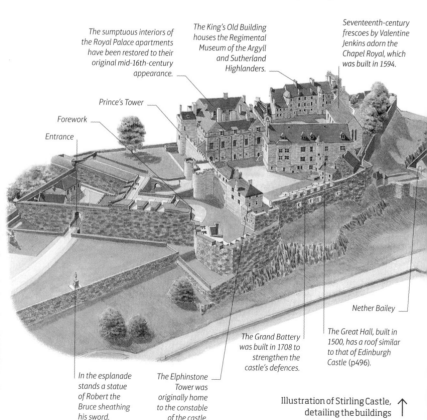

The sumptuous interiors of the Royal Palace apartments have been restored to their original mid-16th-century appearance.

The King's Old Building houses the Regimental Museum of the Argyll and Sutherland Highlanders.

Seventeenth-century frescoes by Valentine Jenkins adorn the Chapel Royal, which was built in 1594.

Prince's Tower

Forework

Entrance

Nether Bailey

The Grand Battery was built in 1708 to strengthen the castle's defences.

The Great Hall, built in 1500, has a roof similar to that of Edinburgh Castle (p496).

In the esplanade stands a statue of Robert the Bruce sheathing his sword.

The Elphinstone Tower was originally home to the constable of the castle.

Illustration of Stirling Castle, ↑ detailing the buildings within its fortified walls

STIRLING BATTLES

Standing at the highest navigable point of the Forth and holding the pass to the Highlands, Stirling occupied a key position in Scotland's many struggles for independence. Seven battlefields can be seen from Stirling Castle; the 67-m (220-ft) Wallace Monument at Abbey Craig recalls William Wallace's defeat of the English army at Stirling Bridge in 1297, foreshadowing Robert the Bruce's victory in 1314.

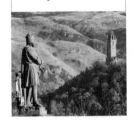

1745

The year of the last military assault on Stirling Castle, led by the Jacobite army.

EXPERIENCE MORE

4

Stirling

⌂ Stirlingshire 🚆🚌 🛈 Old Town Jail, St John St; www.destinationstirling.com

Between the Ochil Hills and the Campsie Fells, the city of Stirling grew up around its castle, historically one of Scotland's most important fortresses. Below the castle the Old Town is still protected by the original walls, built in the 16th century to keep Mary, Queen of Scots safe from Henry VIII. The medieval Church of the Holy Rude, on Castle Wynd, where the infant James VI was crowned in 1567, has one of Scotland's few surviving hammerbeam oak roofs. In front of the church, the ornate façade of Mar's Wark is all that remains of a grand palace, destroyed by the Jacobites in 1746.

Just 3 km (2 miles) south of Stirling, the **Battle of Bannockburn Experience** stands by the field where Robert the Bruce defeated the English in 1314 (*p486*), after which he dismantled the small castle that once stood there to prevent it from falling into English hands. A statue commemorates the man who became an icon of Scottish independence.

Battle of Bannockburn Experience

♿ 💬 👶 NTS ⌂ Glasgow Rd 🕐 10am–5:30pm daily (Nov–Feb: to 5pm) 🌐 battleof bannockburn.com

←
The Bruce Monument at the site of his decisive victory

↑ Medieval Glamis Castle, with its distinctive fairy-tale turrets

Glamis Castle

◎ Forfar, Angus 🚌 Dundee then bus ◯ Apr–Oct: 10am–5:30pm daily (last adm: 4:30pm) 🌐 glamis-castle.co.uk

With the pinnacled outline of a Loire chateau, Glamis Castle began as a royal hunting lodge in the 11th century but underwent extensive reconstruction in the 1600s. It was the childhood home of Queen Elizabeth the Queen Mother, and her former bedroom can be seen, with its youthful portrait by Henri de Laszlo (1878–1956).

Doune Castle

◎ Doune, Stirling 🚌 Stirling then bus ◯ 9:30am–5:30pm daily (Oct–Mar: to 4pm daily) 🌐 historicenvironment.scot

Constructed as a residence for Robert, Duke of Albany, the son of King Robert II of Scotland, in the 14th century, Doune Castle was a Stuart stronghold until it fell into ruin in the 18th century. Now fully restored, it offers a unique insight into the royal household.

The Gatehouse leads to the central courtyard, off which is the Great Hall. Complete with its reconstructed open-timber roof, minstrels' gallery and central fireplace, the Hall adjoins the Lord's Hall and Private Room. A number of private stairways and narrow passages reveal the ingenious ways the royal family tried to hide during times of danger.

Perth

◎ Perthshire 🚍🚌 ℹ 45 High St; www.perthshire.co.uk

Once the capital of medieval Scotland, Perth's rich heritage is reflected in several of its buildings. It was in the Church of St John, founded in 1126, that John Knox delivered many of his fiery sermons. The Victorianized Fair Maid's House, on North Port, was the fictional home of the heroine of Sir Walter Scott's *The Fair Maid of Perth* (1828).

In **Balhousie Castle**, the Museum of the Black Watch commemorates the first Highland regiment, while the **Perth Museum & Art Gallery** on George Street has displays on local industry and exhibitions of Scottish art.

↑ Dundee's sleek V&A Museum of Design, by architect Kengo Kuma

Balhousie Castle

⊡ RHQ Black Watch, Hay St
🕙 10am–4pm daily
🌐 theblackwatch.co.uk

Perth Museum & Art Gallery

⊡ 78 George St 🕙 10am–5pm Tue–Sat 🌐 culturepk.org.uk

Scone Palace

⊡ Scone, Perthshire
🚌 From Perth 🕙 Apr–Oct: 9:30am–4pm daily
🌐 scone-palace.co.uk

Pronounced "scoon", this 12th-century palace with an opulent interior was the historic home of the Stone of Destiny. The site has played many roles over the centuries, including as seat and crowning-place of Scottish kings. The last coronation in Scotland took place here in 1651, when King Charles II was crowned atop Moot Hill. Today the palace is a fine example of late Georgian Gothic – and a treasury of *objets d'art* such

Did You Know?

Dundee is undergoing a £1 billion transformation, centred on the new V&A museum.

---

as marble busts, ornate sculptures from mythology and elaborately crafted 18th- and 19th-century timepieces.

Scone's wooded gardens are home to red squirrels, roe deer and the rare hawfinch, as well as peacocks.

9

Dundee

⊡ Dundee City 🚆🚌
🛈 16 City Sq; www. angusanddundee.co.uk

Famed for its three Js of jam, jute mills and journalism – see the statues of publisher DC Thomson's *Beano* and *Dandy* comic-book characters near the grand venue of Caird Hall – Dundee was a hub of creative industries and science. Today, the city is undergoing major restoration and development. The **V&A Museum of Design** charts Scotland's outstanding design heritage inside a cutting-edge building by the Japanese architect Kengo Kuma.

On the River Tay is the royal research ship **Discovery**, built here in 1901 for Captain Scott's first voyage to the Antarctic. Audio-visual shows and displays describe the captain and crew's heroic journey.

EAT

The Playwright
This pioneer of fine dining in the heart of Dundee's arts quarter is perfect for a pre- or post-theatre dinner.

⊡ 11 Tay Sq, Dundee
🌐 theplaywright.co.uk

££££

The **McManus Galleries**' collection of Dundee-related art and artifacts, in a splendid Victorian building, gives an excellent insight into the city.

V&A Museum of Design

⊡ Victoria Docks
🕙 10am–5pm daily (9pm Fri)
🌐 vandadundee.org

Discovery

⊛ ⊡ Discovery Point
🕙 10am–5pm daily (from 11am Sun) 🌐 rrsdiscovery.com

McManus Galleries

⊡ Albert Sq 🕙 10am–5pm Mon–Sat, 12:30–4:30pm Sun
🌐 mcmanus.co.uk

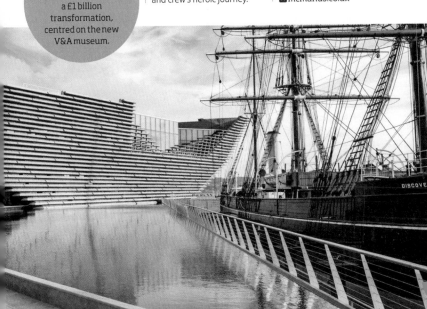

⑩ East Neuk

⌂ Fife 🚉 Leuchars
🚌 Glenrothes & Leuchars
ℹ St Andrews; www.
eastneukwide.co.uk

Pretty fishing villages pepper the shoreline of the East Neuk, from Earlsferry to Fife Ness. Pittenweem, the base for the East Neuk fishing fleet, is also known for St Fillan's Cave, retreat of the 9th-century hermit. Anstruther's **Scottish Fisheries Museum** has boats, while in Lower Largo is a statue of Alexander Selkirk, who inspired Daniel Defoe's novel *Robinson Crusoe* (1719). After disagreeing with his captain, Selkirk was left on a deserted island for four years.

Scottish Fisheries Museum

 ⌂ St Ayles, Harbour Head, Anstruther ⏰ 10am–4:30pm daily (from noon Sun) 🖥 scotfish museum.org

EAT

East Pier

This unassuming former boat shed serves home-smoked shellfish.

⌂ East Shore, St Monans ⏰ Jun–Aug: daily; May & Sep: Wed–Sun; Apr–Oct: weekends 🖥 eastpier.co.uk

Cromar's

Twice acclaimed as Scotland's finest chippie, Cromar's has been serving up quality fish suppers since 2013.

⌂ 1 Union St, St Andrews 🖥 cromars.co.uk

£££

⑪ Dunfermline

⌂ Fife 🚉🚌
🖥 visitdunfermline.com

Scotland's capital until 1603, Dunfermline is dominated by the ruins of the 12th-century abbey and palace. In the 11th century, the town was the seat of King Malcolm III, who founded a priory on the present site of the Abbey Church. With its Norman nave and 19th-century choir, the church contains the tombs of 22 Scottish kings and queens, including Robert the Bruce *(p486)*.

Dunfermline's most famous son is philanthropist Andrew Carnegie (1835–1919). As a boy, he had been forbidden entrance to the gardens of Pittencrieff Park. After making his fortune, he bought the entire estate and gave it to the people of Dunfermline. Carnegie was born in the town, though moved to Pennsylvania in his teens. There he made a vast fortune in the iron and steel industry. The **Carnegie Birthplace Museum** is still furnished as it was when he lived there.

Carnegie Birthplace Museum

⌂ Moodie St ⏰ Mid-Feb–Nov: 10am–5pm Mon–Sat; 1–4pm Sun 🖥 carnegie birthplace.com

⑫ St Andrews

⌂ Fife 🚉 Leuchars
🚌 Dundee ℹ 70 Market St; www.standrews.co.uk

Scotland's oldest university town, St Andrews is now a mecca for golfers. Its three main streets and numerous cobbled alleys, full of crooked house fronts, university buildings and medieval churches, converge on the ruins of the 12th-century cathedral, which was pillaged for stones to build the town. **St Andrew's Castle** was built for the bishops of the town in 1200. The **British Golf Museum** tells how the town's Royal and Ancient Golf Club became the ruling arbiter of the game, and to the west, the town's golf courses are open for a modest fee.

St Andrew's Castle

⌂ The Scores ⏰ 9:30am–5:30pm daily (Oct–Mar: 10am–4pm) 🖥 historicenvironment.scot

British Golf Museum

⌂ Bruce Embankment ⏰ 9:30am–5pm daily (Nov–Mar: 10am–4pm) 🖥 british golfmuseum.co.uk

←

Ruins of the cathedral in St Andrews, once the largest in Scotland

↑ Pretty Culross village, preserved by the National Trust for Scotland

Falkland Palace

🏠 Falkland, Fife 🚂🚌 From Ladybank ⏰ Mar-Oct: 11am-5pm Mon-Sat, 1-5pm Sun 🌐 nts.org.uk

This Renaissance palace was designed as a hunting lodge for the Stuart kings. Most of the work was carried out in the 1530s by James V, who hired French workmen to build the beautifully proportioned South Range. The palace fell into ruin during the years of the Commonwealth and was occupied briefly by the outlaw Rob Roy in 1715.

Culross

🏠 Fife 🚂🚌 Dunfermline 🌐 nts.org.uk

An important religious centre in the 6th century, Culross is said to have been the birthplace of St Mungo in 514. Now a beautifully preserved village, Culross prospered in the 16th century with the growth of its coal and salt industries.

During its subsequent decline Culross stood unchanged for over 150 years. The National Trust for Scotland began restoring the town in 1932.

Built in 1577, **Culross Palace** has the crow-stepped gables, decorated windows and red pantiles typical of the period. The interior retains its original early 17th-century painted ceilings. Crossing the Square, past the Oldest House, dating from 1577, head for the Town House to the west. Behind it, a cobbled street known as the Back Causeway leads to the turreted Study, built in 1610. The main room has an original Norwegian ceiling. Continuing northwards to the abbey ruins, don't miss the Dutch-gabled House with the Evil Eyes.

Culross Palace

🕑 Apr-Sep: 10am-5pm daily; Oct-Mar: 10am-4pm Fri-Mon

FIFE COASTAL PATH

This 188-km (177-mile) path *(www.fifecoastal path.co.uk)* takes in rugged cliffs, beaches and seal-spotting spots, passing through fishing villages and the historic town of St Andrews. Allow at least six days to do this route justice. With less time, visit the portion around the village of Elie, where a "chain-walk" allows you to clamber between bays and a sandy beach. Afterwards, head to the fishing village of Anstruther.

Balmoral Castle, the high point of any visit to Royal Deeside ↑

15

Balmoral Castle and Royal Deeside

🏠 Balmoral Estate, Ballater
🚌 From Aberdeen 🕐 Times vary, check website
🌐 balmoralcastle.com

Queen Victoria bought Balmoral estate for 30,000 guineas in 1852, after its owner choked to death on a fishbone. Her Prince Consort, Albert, had a hand in the design, and it reflects his Teutonic tastes. The grand ballroom is the only part of the castle open to the public, but splendid walking trails allow visitors to explore the gardens and grounds.

16

Elgin

🏠 Moray 🚌 🚆 ℹ️ 36 High St, Inverness; 01463 252401

With its cobbled marketplace and crooked lanes, the popular holiday centre of Elgin still retains much of its medieval layout. The 13th-century cathedral ruins next to King Street are all that

remain of one of Scotland's architectural triumphs, the design of its tiered windows reminiscent of the cathedral at St Andrews *(p538)*. Once known as the Lantern of the North, the cathedral was severely damaged in 1390 by the Wolf of Badenoch (the son of Robert II) in revenge for his excommunication by the Bishop of Moray. Worse damage came in 1576 when the Regent Moray ordered the stripping of its lead roofing.

Next to the cathedral are the Biblical Gardens, containing all 110 plants mentioned in the Bible, the **Elgin Museum**, which has anthropological displays, and the **Moray Motor Museum** with more than 40 vehicles exhibited.

Elgin Museum

⊚ 🏠 1 High St 🕐 Apr–Oct: 10am–5pm Mon–Fri; 11am–4pm Sat 🌐 elginmuseum.org.uk

Moray Motor Museum

⊚ 🏠 Bridge St, Bishopmill
🕐 Apr–Oct: 11am–5pm daily
🌐 moraymotormuseum.org

17

Dunkeld

🏠 Perth & Kinross
🏠 Birnam 🚌 ℹ️ The Cross; www.perthshire.co.uk

Situated by the River Tay, this ancient and charming village was all but destroyed in the 1689 Battle of Dunkeld, a Jacobite *(p487)* defeat. The Little Houses lining Cathedral Street were the first to be rebuilt and are fine examples of imaginative restoration. The ruins of the 14th-century cathedral enjoy an idyllic setting on shady lawns beside the Tay, against a backdrop of steep, wooded hills. The choir is used as the parish church and its north wall contains a Leper's Squint: a hole through

> **Blair Castle's 18th-century wing has a display containing the gloves and pipe of Bonnie Prince Charlie, who spent two days here gathering Jacobite support.**

which lepers could see the altar during mass. It was while on holiday in the Dunkeld countryside that Beatrix Potter (*p360*) found the location for her Peter Rabbit stories.

18

Pitlochry

🏠 Perth & Kinross 🚌🚏
ℹ️ 22 Atholl Rd; www.perthshire.co.uk

Surrounded by pine-forested hills, Pitlochry became famous after Queen Victoria described it as one of the finest resorts in Europe. In early summer, salmon swim up the ladder built into the Power Station Dam, on their way to spawning grounds up-river. There is a viewing chamber here to see them. Above the ladder are fine views of the Loch Faskally, an artifical reservoir. Walking trails from here lead to the pretty gorge at Killiecrankie. The tasting tours at **Edradour Distillery** give an insight into traditional whisky-making. Scotland's famous **Festival Theatre** puts on a summer season with a programme that changes daily.

Did You Know?

Pictlochry is the furthest Scottish town from the sea.

Edradour Distillery
🏠 Off A924
🕐 Apr-Oct: 10am-5pm Mon-Sat 🌐 edradour.co.uk

Festival Theatre
🏠 Port-na-Craig
🕐 10am-8pm daily
🌐 pitlochry.org.uk

---

19 (NTS)

Killiecrankie

🏠 Perth and Kinross
🚇 Pitlochry 🚌 🌐 nts.org.uk

For centuries Killiecrankie, site of a famous 1689 battle, was a staging post between lowland Scotland and the Highlands. Now a peaceful suburb of Pitlochry, it is the starting point for a walk through the scenic Pass of Killiecrankie.

20

Blair Castle

🏠 Blair Atholl, Perthshire
🚇 Blair Atholl 🕐 Apr-Oct: 9:30am-5:30pm daily
🚫 1 & 2 Jan, 25-27 Dec
🌐 blair-castle.co.uk

This rambling, turreted castle has been altered so often in its 700-year history that it provides a unique insight into the history of Highland aristocratic life. Blair Castle's 18th-century wing has a display containing the gloves and pipe of Bonnie Prince Charlie (*p487*), who spent two days here gathering Jacobite support. The Tapestry Room displays fine Huguenot silks and Mortlake tapestries. Family portraits cover 300 years and include paintings by such masters as Johann Zoffany and Sir Peter Lely. Sir Edwin Landseer's *Death of a Stag in Glen Tilt* (1850) was painted nearby.

In 1844 Queen Victoria visited the castle and conferred on its owners, the Dukes of Atholl, the distinction of being allowed to maintain a private army. The Atholl Highlanders still flourish.

↑ Blair Castle's grand ballroom, built for the Atholl Highlanders

THE HIGHLANDS AND ISLANDS

Most of the stock images of Scottishness – clans and tartans, whisky and porridge, bagpipes and heather – originate in the Highlands. But for many centuries the Gaelic-speaking, cattle-raising Highlanders had little in common with their southern neighbours. Clues to the non-Celtic ancestors of the Highlanders lie scattered across the Highlands and islands in the form of stone circles, brochs and cairns spanning over 5,000 years. By the end of the 6th century, the Gaelic-speaking Celts had arrived from Ireland, as had St Columba, who taught Christianity to the monastic community he established on the island of Iona.

For over 1,000 years, Celtic Highland society was founded on a clan system, built on family ties to create loyal groups dependent on a feudal chief. However, the clans were systematically broken up by England after 1746, following the defeat of the Jacobite attempt on the British crown led by Bonnie Prince Charlie. A more romantic vision of the Highlands began to emerge in the early 19th century, due largely to Sir Walter Scott's novels and poetry depicting the majesty and grandeur of a country previously considered poverty-stricken and barbaric. But behind the sentimentality lay harsh economic realities that drove generations of Highland farmers to seek a new life overseas.

0 kilometres 30

0 miles 30

N

Flannan Isles

Lewis

Port of Ness

North Tolsta

Barvas

Carloway

A857

Timsgarry

Stornoway

Portnaguran

Cape Wrath

Durness

Kinlochbervie

Tongue

Scourie

Altnaharra

Kylesku

A836

Drumbeg

Lochinver

Shinness

Reiff

Elphin

Lairg

A894

Strathcanaird

A837

Ullapool

A835

The Minch

Harris

Hushinish

Ardhasaig

Tarbert

Arivruaich

A859

Lemreway

Scarastavore

**OUTER
HEBRIDES**
3

*North
Uist*

Tigharry

Lochmaddy

Clachan-a-Luib

Creagorry

Benbecula

Stilligarry

*South
Uist*

Lochboisdale

Kilbride

Eriskay

Barra

*Sea of
the Hebrides*

Kilmaluag

Uig

Staffin

Kensaleyre

**ISLE OF
SKYE**
4

Portree

Bracadale

A87

Peinchorran

Glenelg

Broadford

Glenelg

Elgol

Armadale

Canna

Rum

Mallaig

Eigg

Muck

Lochailort

A830

Glenfinnan

Ardnamurchan

Ardtoe

Glenbeg

Strontian

Coll

Arinagour

Tobermory

Dervaig

Tiree

Scarinish

Staffa

MULL
18

Craignure

Iona

Fionnphort

Bunessan

Clachan

*Atlantic
Ocean*

Colonsay

Port
Askaig

JURA
23

Bowmore

ISLAY
24

Port
Ellen

Tayinloan

Muasdale

Kilchenzie

*Mull of
Kintyre*

Campbeltown

KINTYRE
25

Inverewe Garden

Gairloch

**WESTER
ROSS**
9

Kinlochewe

Shieldaig

Torridon

Balnacra

Applecross

A890

Kyle of Lochalsh

Eilean Donan Castle

Glenelg

**THE FIVE
SISTERS**
6

*Belnn Dearg
1,084 m (3,556 ft)*

*Ben Wyvis
1,045m (3,428 ft)*

Dingwall

STRATHPEFFER
7

Muir of Ord

A9

HIGHLAND

Drumnadrochit

A82

Urquhart Castle

LOCH NESS
11

Fort Augustus

A87

Invergarry

Clunes

A82

Moy

A86

Fort William

*Ben Nevis
1,345 m (4,411 ft)*

GLENCOE
16

A828

Portnacroish

Bridge of
Orchy

Benderloch

Taynuilt

Tyndrum

OBAN
17

A85

Dalmally

LOCH AWE
19

INVERARAY CASTLE
20

Strachur

AUCHINDRAIN MUSEUM
21

CRARAE GARDENS
22

Kilmartin

Lochgilphead

**ARGYLL
AND BUTE**

Dunoon

Balloch

Tighnabruaich

Tarbert

Glasgow Airport

Kennacraig

Rothesay

Barrhead

Claonaig

Pirnmill

M77

Kilchenzie

Arran

**GLASGOW AND
SOUTHWEST
SCOTLAND**
p510

THE HIGHLANDS
AND ISLANDS

Strathy
Thurso
Castletown
John O'Groats
Strathy
A897
A9
Wick
Forsinard
Achavanich
A99
Thrumster
Kinbrace
Dunbeath

Helmsdale

North Sea

Golspie · Dunrobin Castle
10 DORNOCH
Tain

BLACK ISLE
8 · Cromarty
Lossiemouth
Elgin

14 FORT GEORGE
15 CAWDOR CASTLE
12 **13** CULLODEN
INVERNESS
Tomatin
A939
Spey
Aberlour
Huntly
Carrbridge
A95
Grantown-on-Spey
Aviemore
Kingussie
Cairn Gorm
1,245 m (4,084 ft)
Ben Macdui
1,309 m (4,296 ft)
Ballater
5
CAIRNGORMS
NATIONAL PARK

CENTRAL AND
NORTHEAST
SCOTLAND
p526

Brechin
Forfar
Dunkeld
Alyth
A93
Arbroath
A9
Dundee
Crieff
Perth
Bridge of Earn
Glenrothes
Dunblane
Glenrothes
Stirling
M90
North Berwick
Denny
Dunfermline
M9
Lennoxtown
Edinburgh · Leith
Coatbridge
Penicuik
Glasgow
A703
M74
Lanark
Peebles
Galashiels
Selkirk
Sanquhar
Moffat

Shetland and Orkney

Unst
Yell
SHETLAND **1**
Brae
Walls · Tingwall Airport
Foula · Lerwick
Mainland
Fair Isle

ORKNEY **2**
Westray
Sanday
Mainland
Stromness · Kirkwall
Hoy · Kirkwall Airport
Aberdeen ↘

Thurso
John O'Groats
Wick
area of main map

0 km 50
0 miles 50
N ↑

THE HIGHLANDS AND ISLANDS

Must Sees

1 Shetland
2 Orkney
3 Outer Hebrides
4 Isle of Skye
5 Cairngorms National Park

Experience More

6 The Five Sisters
7 Strathpeffer
8 Black Isle
9 Wester Ross
10 Dornoch
11 Loch Ness
12 Inverness
13 Culloden
14 Fort George
15 Cawdor Castle
16 Glencoe
17 Oban
18 Mull
19 Loch Awe
20 Inveraray Castle
21 Auchindrain Museum
22 Crarae Gardens
23 Jura
24 Islay
25 Kintyre

↑ St Ninian's Isle, separated from Mainland by a thin isthmus of white sand

❶

SHETLAND

🏠 Shetland 🚢✈ From Aberdeen and Stromness, Orkney
ℹ Lerwick; www.shetland.org

With the North Sea to the east and the Atlantic Ocean ravishing its western shores, this windswept archipelago is where Scotland meets Scandinavia. Its rugged coastline, oceanic climate and fascinating geology will delight all who venture to this most northerly enclave.

More than 100 rugged, cliff-hemmed islands form Shetland. Severe storms are common in winter, but in summer, the sun may shine for 19 hours.

The west coast has spectacular scenery, notably the red granite cliffs and blow-holes at Esha Ness, from where you can see the wave-gnawed stacks of The Drongs and Dore Holm, a huge rock arch. The northern isles of Yell, Fetlar and Unst have regular, though weather-dependent, boat connections to Mainland. West of Mainland, Foula has dramatic sea cliffs. There are regular inter-island ferries. Most routes depart from Tingwall, on Central Mainland.

①
Lerwick

On the island of Mainland, Shetland's chief town was first established by Dutch fishermen in the 1600s and is a pretty place of grey stone buildings and narrow lanes. At the **Shetland Museum & Archive**, a fine collection of historic boats, archaeological finds and Shetland textiles trace the islands' unique and fascinating history.

Shetland Museum & Archive

🏛🖼 🏠 Hay's Dock
🕙 10am–4pm Tue–Sat
🌐 shetlandmuseumand archives.org.uk

②
Bressay and Noss

🚢 From Lerwick

Sheltering Lerwick from the winter gales is Bressay, an island with fine walks and views. The Bressay ferry departs from Lerwick every hour, weather-dependent, and boats run a regular service from Lerwick to Noss, off Bressay's east coast. **Noss National Nature Reserve** is home to thousands of breeding seabirds, including gannets and great skuas (or

↑ Adult black guillemot on Sumburgh Head, Mainland Island

SHETLAND'S BIRDLIFE

Shetland is one of the best birdwatching areas in Britain. Millions of migrant and local birds can be admired on these islands. Over 340 different species have been recorded passing through Fair Isle, one of the world's great staging posts. Inaccessible cliffs provide excellent security at vulnerable nesting times for huge colonies of gannets, guillemots, puffins, kittiwakes, fulmars and razorbills. Species found here but in very few other UK locations include great skuas and storm petrels.

bonxies), while both islands are outstandingly beautiful and abundant in bird and mammal life.

Noss National Nature Reserve

 C 01595 693345
O May–Aug: 10am–5pm Tue, Wed, Fri–Sun

---

③
Mousa Broch

A Mousa **O** Apr–Sep: daily
W mousa.co.uk

The ornate Mousa Broch, on an easterly islet reached by a summer ferry from Sandwick, is the best example of this type of ancient fortified tower in Britain. These drystone roundhouses, unique to Scotland, consist of two concentric walls, between which is a narrow passage containing a stone stairway to the top. Thought to have been constructed in around 300 BC, Mousa is the tallest of all the remaining brochs in Scotland. At 13 m (42 ft), its towering walls are clearly visible from the main road.

---

④
Jarlshof Prehistoric and Norse Settlement

A Sumburgh **B** Jarlshof
O Apr–Sep: 9:30am–5:30pm daily **W** historic environment.scot

Jarlshof, in the far south, spans over 3,000 years of occupation, from Neolithic to

Viking times. Preserved under layers of sand and grit for thousands of years, this ancient site was discovered in the 1890s. Explore ancient Bronze Age dwellings, Iron Age wheelhouses and Viking longhouses and outbuildings, and evidence of the island's Norse occupation, all set against the dramatic backdrop of the beautiful West Voe of Sumburgh.

⑤
Hermaness National Nature Reserve

A Muckle Flugga Shorestation **B** Unst
B From Lerwick to Haroldswick **O** Daily (Visitor Centre: Apr–Sep only) **W** nnr.scot

Of all Shetland's islands, Unst has the most varied scenery and the richest flora and fauna, plus an excellent visitor centre at the Hermaness National Nature Reserve, home to thousands of seabirds, including gannets, puffins and kittiwakes. Beyond the lighthouse of Muckle Flugga is Out Stack, Britain's most northerly point.

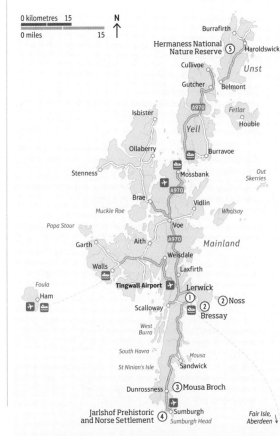

②

ORKNEY

🛫 Kirkwall ⛴ From Scrabster or Gill's Bay (Caithness),
Aberdeen, Lerwick (Shetland), and John O'Groats (May–Sep only)
🛈 Kirkwall; www.visitorkney.com

Beyond the Pentland Firth, less than 10 km (6 miles) off the Scottish mainland,
the Orkney archipelago consists of some 70 islands and rocky skerries boasting
the densest concentration of archaeological sites in Britain. Today, only about 16
of these islands are permanently inhabited. Orkney's way of life is predominantly
agricultural – it's said that, whereas the Shetlanders are fishermen with crofts,
the Orcadians are farmers with boats.

The Mainland is the archipelago's main island,
home to Orkney's two largest towns, Kirkwall
and Stromness. Almost 5,000 years ago, rings
of colossal stone walls enclosed a complex of
temples at Ness of Brodgar, the most recently
rediscovered of Orkney's Neolithic relics. In
1999, sites including the chambered tomb at
Maeshowe and the Standing Stones of
Stenness and the Ring of Brodgar were
granted UNESCO World Heritage status, and
archaeologists continue to unearth exciting
finds that tell of a sophisticated ancient
culture that flourished here long ago.

Hoy, Orkney's second-largest island, takes
its name from the Norse word for "high island",
which refers to its spectacular cliff-lined
terrain. Hoy is very different from the rest of
the archipelago, and its northern hills make
excellent walking and bird-watching country.

Orkney's outlying islands are sparsely
populated and mostly the preserve of seals
and seabirds. Rousay is known as the "Egypt of
the North" for its many archaeological sites,
and Egilsay was the scene of St Magnus's grisly
murder in 1115. The 12th-century round-
towered church dedicated to his memory is a
rare example of Irish-Viking design. Sanday is
the largest of the Northern Isles, its fertile
farmland fringed by sandy beaches, while
North Ronaldsay, the northernmost of the
Orkney Islands, is noted for its hardy,
seaweed-eating sheep and rare migrant birds.

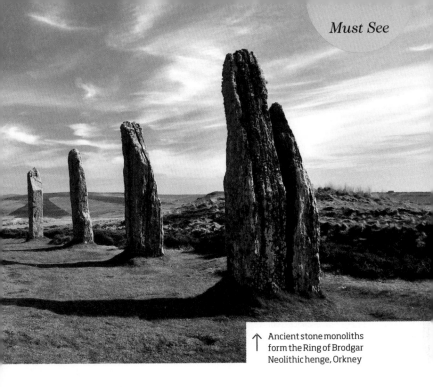

↑ Ancient stone monoliths form the Ring of Brodgar Neolithic henge, Orkney

① Kirkwall

Orkney's capital is lined with period houses. Opposite **St Magnus Cathedral**, an 870-year-old masterpiece of red and yellow stone, lie the ruins of the **Bishop's Palace**, dating from the 16th century. The **Orkney Museum** tells the history of the islands, while the **Highland Park Distillery** dispenses a fine dram at the end of its guided tours.

St Magnus Cathedral

⊗ ⊗ 🏠 Broad St ⏰ Mon-Fri
🌐 stmagnus.org

Bishop's Palace

⊗ 🏠 Watergate ⏰ Apr-Sep: 9:30am–5:30pm daily
🌐 historicenvironment.scot

Orkney Museum

🏠 Broad St ⏰ 10:30am–5pm Mon-Sat 🌐 orkney.gov.uk

Highland Park Distillery

⊗ ⊗ ⊕ 🏠 Holme Rd
⏰ Times vary, check website
🌐 highlandparkwhisky.com

North Ronaldsay
Hollandstoun
Papa Westray
The North Sound
Pierwall
Westray
Sanday
Westray Firth
Braeswick
Wasbister
Whitehall
Rousay
Eday
Brinyan
Egilsay
Redland
Wyre
Stronsay Firth
Stronsay
Marwick Head ④
Twatt
Mainland
Gairsay
Rothiesholm
Skara Brae
Ring of Brodgar
③
Balfour
Shapinsay
Auskerry
Finstown
Sandgarth
Heart of Neolithic Orkney World Heritage Sites
Standing Stones of Stenness
① Kirkwall
Stromness ②
Houton
Kirkwall Airport
St Mary's
⑤ Italian Chapel
Copinsay
Gritley
→ Aberdeen, Lerwick
⑦ Old Man of Hoy
Scapa Flow
Scapa Flow Visitor Centre ⑧
Cava
Flotta
Burray
Hoy
Lyness
St Margaret's Hope
Melsetter
South Ronaldsay
Burwick
⑥ Tomb of the Eagles
Pentland Firth
Stroma
0 kilometres 15
0 miles 15
N ↑
John O'Groats

Orcadian town of Stromness with the hills of Hoy in the background

② Stromness

Many of the waterfront buildings in Stromness date from the 18th and 19th centuries. Among them, the **Pier Arts Centre** contains a fine collection of 20th-century works. **The Stromness Museum** traces Orkney's history as a trading port.

Pier Arts Centre

 28-36 Victoria St
10:30am–5pm Tue–Sat
pierartscentre.com

Stromness Museum

52 Alfred St 10am–5pm daily (to 7pm Wed) orkneycommunities.co.uk

> **INSIDER TIP**
> **Day Trips to Remote Islands**
>
> There are flights from Kirkwall to a dozen outlying islands several times a week, and ferries run daily. Inter-island transport is very much dependent on weather conditions.

③ Heart of Neolithic Orkney World Heritage Sites

Various locations on Central & West Mainland
Times vary, see website
historicenvironment.scot

Almost 5,000 years ago, rings of colossal stone walls more than 100 m (330 ft) long enclosed the complex of temples at Ness of Brodgar, the most recently discovered of Orkney's Neolithic relics. Said to date from around 2750 BC, Maeshowe is a chambered tomb aligned with the winter solstice. Vikings plundered it around 1150, leaving a fascinating legacy of runic graffiti on the walls. Nearby are the huge Standing Stones of Stenness and the Ring of Brodgar, a megalithic henge of 36 stones. The Neolithic village of Skara Brae was discovered when a storm stripped dunes from the site in 1850 to reveal relics of everyday Stone Age life. In 1999 these ancient sites were granted UNESCO World Heritage status.

④ Marwick Head

The cliffs of Marwick Head, overlooking Birsay Bay, are one of several RSPB reserves on West Mainland, home to thousands of nesting seabirds in early summer. A memorial commemorates Lord Kitchener and the crew of HMS *Hampshire*, which was sunk off this headland by a German mine in 1916.

⑤ Italian Chapel

Lambholm, Hoy
Daily (Mass: 1st Sun of month)

East of Kirkwall, the road runs through quiet agricultural land over a series of causeways linking the southernmost islands to Mainland. The Churchill Barriers were built by Italian prisoners of war in the 1940s to protect the British fleet stationed in Scapa Flow. In their spare time, these POWs constructed the Italian Chapel, containing beautiful frescoes.

Tomb of the Eagles

 South Ronaldsay Mar: 10am–noon daily; Apr–Sep: 9:30am–5:30pm daily; Oct: 9:30am–12:30pm daily
 tombofheeagles.co.uk

On South Ronaldsay, the 5,000-year-old Tomb of the Eagles, or Isbister Chambered Cairn, contains some 340 burial sites, along with stone tools and the talons of many sea eagles. The mile-long walk from the visitor centre to the tomb through a Bronze Age excavation site teems with birdlife and wild flowers.

 ⑦

Old Man of Hoy

The Old Man of Hoy, a 137-m (450-ft) vertical stack off the western coast, is the island's best-known landmark, a popular challenge to keen rock climbers. Near Rackwick, the 5,000-year-old Dwarfie Stane is a unique chambered cairn cut from a single block of stone.

---

 ⑧

Scapa Flow Visitor Centre

 Lyness, Hoy For renovation until 2021
 orkney.gov.uk

On the eastern side of Hoy, the Scapa Flow Visitor Centre contains a fascinating exhibition on this deep-water naval haven.

STAY

Merkister Hotel
Only 15 minutes from Stromness and close to the Neolithic Orkney World Heritage Sites, this family-run hotel offers cosy rooms, and exquisite home cooking set against fabulous sunset views.

 Harray
 merkister.com

 £££

The Creel
Multi-award-winning seafront B&B and restaurant in a timeless stone village. Quaint rooms and imaginative cooking – try the wolf-fish broth.

 St Margaret's Hope
 thecreel.co.uk

£££

Temporarily rehoused in Hoy Hotel while the main museum undergoes renovation, the exhibition recounts the events of 16 June 1919, when the captured German fleet was scuttled on the orders of its commanding officer to prevent handover: 74 ships were sunk. Many have been salvaged; others provide one of the world's great wreck-diving sites. Tours from Houton Pier, using a remote-controlled vehicle with an underwater camera, give a glimpse of this sub-aquatic graveyard. Guided tours of the former Royal Naval Base depart at 11am every Tuesday and Thursday from the Ferry Waiting Room.

 ←

Orkney's iconic sea stack, the Old Man of Hoy is a popular rock climbing spot

Cliffs and sea stacks near Mangersta, on the west coast of Lewis ↑

③

OUTER HEBRIDES

⌂ Western Isles, Outer Hebrides ✈ Stornoway, Benbecula, Barra ⛴ From Uig (Skye), Oban, Mallaig, Kyle of Lochalsh & Ullapool 🛈 26 Cromwell St, Stornoway, Lewis; www.visitouterhebrides.co.uk

Western Scotland ends with this remote chain of islands, made of some of the oldest rock on Earth. Barren landscapes are divided by countless waterways, while the western, windward coasts are edged by white sandy beaches.

Hundreds of windswept and beautiful islands lie scattered off Scotland's northwest coast. Some are tiny, rocky skerries inhabited only by seabirds, while others are home to bustling farming and fishing communities. White sandy bays fringe these rugged coasts, bordered by sweet-smelling natural wildflower meadows known as *machair* that pepper the land with splashes of yellow, white, blue and pink.

In the low-lying hinterlands, vast peat bogs provide many homes with fuel, and the rich tang of peat smoke is the signature scent of the isles. These are some of the longest-inhabited parts of Scotland, with ancient standing stones attesting to over 6,000 years of human settlement, though abandoned dwellings and monuments attest to the difficulties in commercializing traditional local skills. Home to Scotland's largest Gaelic-speaking community, many islanders use the ancient Celtic tongue as their first language.

↑ Sheep in wildflower meadows on rugged and remote Harris

St Kilda
80 km (50 miles)

① Lewis and Harris

Forming the largest landmass of the Western Isles, Lewis and Harris are a single island, though Gaelic dialects differ between the two areas. The administrative centre of Stornoway is a bustling harbour town with colourful house fronts. The **Museum nan Eilean** offers a fascinating insight into the culture, language and traditions of the people of the Outer Hebrides. From here, the ancient Standing Stones of Callanis are only 26 km (16 miles) to the west. Just off the road on the way to Callanish are the cone-shaped ruins of Carloway Broch, a Pictish tower over 2,000 years old. The more recent past can be explored at **The Blackhouse** in Arnol – a showcase of rural crofting life as it was until 50 years ago.

South of the rolling peat moors of Lewis, a range of mountains marks the border with Harris, which is entered via the head of Loch Seaforth. The mountains of Harris are a paradise for hill walkers, offering views of the distant islands of St Kilda 80 km (50 miles) to the west.

The ferry port of Tarbert stands on a slim isthmus separating North and South Harris. The tourist office provides addresses for local weavers of the tough Harris Tweed. Some weavers still use indigenous plants to create the dyes. From Leverburgh a ferry sails to North Uist, linked by a causeway to Berneray.

Museum nan Eilean
🅰️🅱️🅲️ 🅳 Lews Castle grounds, Stornoway
Ⓦ lews-castle.co.uk

The Blackhouse
🅰️🅱️ 🅳 Arnol 📞 01851 710 395 🕐 Apr–Sep: Mon–Sat; Oct–Mar: Mon, Tue & Thu–Sat
Ⓦ historicenvironment.scot

White sandy bays fringe these rugged coasts, bordered by sweet-smelling natural wildflower meadows known as *machair*.

EAT

Crown Inn
This cosy inn doubles as a lively bar-restaurant that hosts occasional live performances by local musicians.

⌂ Castle St,
Stornoway, Lewis
☎ 01851 703734

£ £ £

Langass Lodge
Locally caught seafood and produce from their own garden feature on the menu at this small restaurant with rooms and great ocean views.

⌂ Locheport, North Uist
🖥 langasslodge.co.uk

£ £ £

②
The Uists and Benbecula

After the dramatic scenery of Harris, the lower-lying, largely waterlogged southern isles may seem an anticlimax, though they nurture secrets well worth discovering. Long, white, sandy beaches fringe the Atlantic coast, edged with one of Scotland's natural treasures: the lime-rich soil known as *machair*. During the summer months, the soil is covered with wildflowers, the unique fragrance of which can be detected far out to sea.

From Lochmaddy, North Uist's main village, the A867 crosses 5 km (3 miles) of causeway to Benbecula, the isle from which the brave Flora MacDonald smuggled Bonnie Prince Charlie to Skye (*p556*). Benbecula is a flat island covered by a mosaic of small lochs. Like its neighbours, it is known for good trout fishing. Here, and to the north, the Protestant religion holds sway, while Catholicism prevails in the southern islands. Benbecula's chief source of employment is the Army Rocket Range, which has its headquarters in the main village of Bailivanich. Another causeway leads to South Uist, which has golden beaches that are renowned as a National Scenic Area.

③
Eriskay

One of the smallest and most enchanting of the Western Isles, Eriskay epitomizes their peace and beauty. The island is best known for the wrecking of the SS *Politician* in 1941, which inspired the book and film *Whisky Galore*. A bottle from its cargo and other relics can be seen in Eriskay's only bar. It was at the beautiful beach of Coilleag A'Phrionnsa (Prince's beach) that Bonnie Prince Charlie first set foot on Scotland at the start of his 1745 campaign. As a result, a

The quaint village of ↑
Gearrannan Blackhouse,
Carloway, Lewis

→ Village bay and abandoned settlement of the Island of Hirta, St Kilda

rare convolvulus flower that grows here has become associated with him.

 Barra

The dramatic way to arrive on the pretty island of Barra is by plane – the airstrip is a beach and the timetable depends on the tide. The island has a central core of hills and circular road, with beaches on the western coast.

The view over Castlebay from the Madonna and Child statue on top of Heaval hill is particularly fine. The romantic **Kisimul Castle**, set on a tiny island, is the 15th seat of the Clan MacNeil. It is currently being restored. Other attractions are the **Barra Heritage Centre** and a golf course.

Kisimul Castle
⊛ 📞 01871 810313
Ⓦ historicenvironment.scot

Barra Heritage Centre
📞 01871 810413
Ⓞ May–Sep: Mon–Sat
Ⓦ barraheritage.com

 St Kilda

These "Islands on the Edge of the World" were the most isolated habitation in Scotland until the ageing population requested to be evacuated in 1930. The largest gannetry in the world (40,000 pairs) is now found here. There are three islands and three sea stacks of awesome beauty, each with sheer, soaring cliffs rising as high as 425 m (1,400 ft). Such is the islands' isolation that separate subspecies of mouse and wren have evolved here.

Tours are run by **Westernedge Charters** and **Island Cruising**. Volunteers can occasionally pay to join summer work parties on the islands, organised by the National Trust for Scotland, owners of the **St Kilda World Heritage Site**.

Westernedge Charters
⊛ ⊛ 🏠 Berneray, North Uist
Ⓞ May–Sep Ⓦ westernedge. co.uk

Island Cruising
⊛ ⊛ 🏠 1 Erista, Uig, Lewis
Ⓞ May–Sep Ⓦ islandcruising. com

St Kilda World Heritage Site
Ⓝ Ⓦ kilda.org.uk

CROFTING

Crofts are small parcels of agricultural land. They originated in the early 1800s when landlords decided to lease out poor-quality land on the coast in an effort to clear the people from more fertile areas. Crofters became dependent on wages from either fishing or collecting kelp, which was used to make commercial alkali. When these sources of income diminished, they endured extreme hardship through famine, high rents and lack of security. In 1886 an Act was passed to allow crofting families the right to inherit (but not own) the land. Today there are 17,000 registered crofts, almost all in the Highlands and islands. Most crofters raise sheep, but recent trends include tree planting and providing habitats for rare birds.

↑ Lone walker exploring other-worldly rock formations at The Storr

4

ISLE OF SKYE

🏠 Inner Hebrides 🚉 Kyle of Lochalsh 🚌 Portree
🚢 From Mallaig or Glenelg 🌐 isleofskye.com

The largest of the Inner Hebrides, Skye boasts some of Britain's most dramatic scenery. From rugged volcanic plateaus to ice-sculpted peaks, the island is divided by numerous sea lochs. Limestone grasslands dominate in the south, where hills are scattered with ruined crofts abandoned during the Clearances (p487).

①

Portree

🛈 Bayfield House, Portree; 01478 612992

With its harbour lined with colourful houses, Portree (meaning "port of the king") is Skye's mini-metropolis. It received its name after a visit made by James V in 1540 in a bid to bring peace to local warring clans. With beautiful views of the surrounding mountains, and its fair share of cosy pubs, restaurants and B&Bs, Portree is an excellent base from which to explore this rugged island.

②

Dunvegan Castle

🏠 Dunvegan 🕐 Apr–mid-Oct: 10am–5:30pm daily
🌐 dunvegancastle.com

For over eight centuries, Dunvegan Castle has been the seat of the chiefs of the Clan MacLeod. The castle's architecture is a unique mix of building styles due to numerous structural additions and renovations that took place from the 13th to mid-19th centuries. Seal-spotting adventures, a favourite with kids, and fishing trips on the loch depart from the castle.

③

The Storr

Erosion of a basalt plateau on the Trotternish ridge has resulted in the Storr's other-worldy rock formations. The Old Man of Storr, a monolith rising to 49 m (160 ft), is the highest of these curious structures. Hike the 3.8-km (2.6-mile) Storr Ascent, accessed from the main road from Portree to Staffin, and head to the north side for spectacular views of these rocky pinnacles. North of the Storr, Quiraing's terrain of

↑ Boats moored in the still waters of Portree harbour at sunset

spikes and towers is a fantastic area to explore on foot and is easily acessed off the Uig to Staffin road.

Talisker Distillery

🏠 Carbost 📞 01478 614 308
🕐 Times vary, check website 🌐 malts.com

Overlooking the Cuillins from the banks of Loch Harport at Carbost, this is the oldest working distillery on the island, famed for its sweet, full-bodied Highland malts which are often described as "the lava of the Cuillins".

The Skye Museum of Island Life

🏠 Kilmuir, Portree
🕐 Apr-Sep: 9:30am-5pm Mon-Sat 🌐 skyemuseum.co.uk

This award-winning museum takes visitors back in time to an old Highland village, comprising a community of well-preserved thatched cottages and crofts, where they can discover what island life was like 100 years ago.

EAT

Three Chimneys
A sublime cottage restaurant with an international reputation in a remote setting. Its excellent cuisine has been rewarded with a Michelin star.

🏠 Colbost, Dunvegan
🌐 threechimneys.co.uk

£££

Cuillin Mountains

Britain's finest mountain range is within walking distance of Sligachan, and in summer a boat sails from Elgol to the desolate inner sanctuary of Loch Coruisk. As he fled across the surrounding moorland, Bonnie Prince Charlie is said to have claimed: "even the Devil shall not follow me here!"

A particular highlight of the area, at the foot of Skye's Black Cuillins on the River Brittle, are the Fairy Pools. Here, white water cascades into deep stone cauldrons filled with clear pale turquoise water. The pools are also a favourite with wild swimmers daring enough to plunge into their chilly waters. Allow around an hour to follow the riverside trail that leads to the most spectacular upper pools, with breathtaking views of the Cuillins along the way.

Armadale Castle Gardens and Museum of the Isles

🏠 Armadale, Sleat 🕐 Apr-Oct: 9:30am-5:30pm daily; Mar & Nov: 10am-3pm Mon-Fri 🌐 armadalecastle.com

Once the seat of Clan Donald, who reigned over the area as Lords of the Isles, this ruined castle and its grounds make for a fascinating day out. The gardens date back to the 1790s and are home to many remarkable specimens of trees and rare plants. Beyond the gardens there are numerous woodland trails.

At the award-winning Museum of the Isles, visitors can discover the story of Scotland's most powerful clan, while its six galleries cover the 1,500 years of history and culture of the Kingdom of the Isles. An additional gallery hosts visiting exhibitions.

CAIRNGORMS NATIONAL PARK

🏠 The Highlands 🚊🚌 Aviemore 🛈 7 The Parade, Grampian Rd, Aviemore; www.visitcairngorms.com

There is no better place in Scotland to get away from it all than this rolling, near-Arctic massif of moors and lochs dotted with impressive mountain peaks. A range of activities are offered year-round.

This vast wilderness, home to reindeer, red deer, golden eagles and mountain hare, is within easy reach of all Scotland's major cities. The Cairngorm plateau is dominated by Ben Macdhui, which is Britain's second-highest mountain at 1,309 m (4,296 ft) and can be ascended from both Speyside and Deeside. It is said to be haunted by a resident spectre, the Old Grey Man. However, the brooding peak of Lochnagar, with its magnificent northern corrie, is perhaps the most coveted munro of the lot. It was immortalised in verse by Lord Byron, who lauded its wild crags and the "steep frowning glories of dark Lochnagar".

Activities for all Seasons

Aviemore, commonly considered the gateway to the Cairngorms, is a purpose-built resort town with a wide choice of places to stay, eat and be entertained throughout the year. In winter, this is Scotland's snow sports paradise, with good snow cover for skiing as late as April or even May. Chairlifts and tows provide access to almost 30 ski runs on the flanks of 1,245-m (4,084-ft) Cairn Gorm during the ski season. Visitors can also head up the mountain on Scotland's only funicular railway, which operates all year. In summer, the **Rothiemurchus Centre** offers outdoor activities including river kayaking,

Did You Know?

The Cairngorms is home to Scotland's two highest villages: Tomintoul and Dalwhinnie.

→
A mountain biker riding across bleakly beautiful moorland in the Cairngorms

white-water rafting, quad biking, off-road safaris and pony trekking on the Rothiemurchus Estate near Aviemore. Treetop-level zip wires and swings add to the excitement for families. On rainy days, the **Highland Folk Museum**, where actors in authentic period costume bring history to life on a working croft, is well worth a visit.

Rothiemurchus Centre
⊗⊗⊜⊕ 🄰Rothiemurchus, by Aviemore, Inverness-shire 🄾Times vary, check website 🅆rothiemurchus.net

Highland Folk Museum
🄰Newtonmore 🄾Apr–Aug: 10:30am–5:30pm; Sep & Oct: 11am–4:30pm 🅆highlandfolk.com

> The brooding peak of Lochnagar, with its magnificent northern corrie, is perhaps the most coveted munro of the lot.

Wildlife Encounters

Driving through the **Highland Wildlife Park** visitors can see bison alongside bears, wolves and wild boar, all of which were once common in the wilds of the Highlands. Britain's only herd of wild reindeer roam free at the **Cairngorm Reindeer Centre**, where they were introduced in 1952.

Highland Wildlife Park
⊗ 🄰Kincraig, Kingussie 🄾Times vary, check website 🅆highlandwildlifepark.org.uk

Cairngorm Reindeer Centre
⊗⊗ 🄰Glenmore, Aviemore 🄾Times vary 🅆cairngormreindeer.co.uk

Reindeer ploughing through deep snow in the Cairngorms National Park

TOP 4 **WALKS IN THE CAIRNGORMS**

Loch Brandy
An easy half-day walk from Clova village to a mirror-calm loch.

Glen Doll
A two- to three-hour stroll on a well-surfaced path from Glen Doll to Corrie Fee, a dramatic natural amphitheatre.

Lairig Ghru
This age-old mountain trail runs from Speyway side to Deeside and climbs to 835 m (2,740 ft). A tough but rewarding full-day hike with amazing views.

Jock's Road
This iconic long-distance trail traverses three Munro summits. Allow a full day to complete the walk.

EXPERIENCE MORE

6
The Five Sisters

⌂ Skye & Lochalsh
🚆 Kyle of Lochalsh
🚌 Glenshiel ℹ️ Bayfield
Road, Portree, Isle of Skye;
www.visitscotland.com

The awesome summits of the
Five Sisters of Kintail rear into
view at the northern end of
Loch Cluanie as the A87 enters
Glen Shiel. Further west, the
road passes **Eilean Donan
Castle**, connected by a bridge.
A Jacobite (*p487*) stronghold,
it was destroyed in 1719 and
restored in the 19th century. It
now contains Jacobite relics.

Eilean Donan Castle
♿ ⌂ Off A87, nr Dornie
🕐 Feb-Dec: 10am-4pm
daily (Apr-Oct: to 6pm)
🌐 eileandonancastle.com

Did You Know?

The most northerly
point of mainland
Great Britain is
Dunnet Head, not
John o' Groats.

7
Strathpeffer

⌂ Ross & Cromarty
🚆 Dingwall, Inverness
🚌 Inverness ℹ️ Dingwall
Museum, High St; 01349
865366

Standing 8 km (5 miles) from
the Falls of Rogie, this popular
town flourished as a spa
resort in Victorian times. The
grand hotels and gracious
layout of Strathpeffer recall
the days when royalty from all
over Europe used to flock to
the mineral-laden springs,
believed to have curative
powers. Today, one of the
biggest attractions is the local
pipe band and dancers who
perform in the square every
Saturday (May–Sep: 8.30pm).

8
Black Isle

⌂ Ross & Cromarty
🚆🚌 Inverness
🌐 black-isle.info

The broad peninsula of the
Black Isle is largely farmland
and fishing villages. The town
of Cromarty was an important
18th-century port and many

MORAY FIRTH

Renowned for its
wildlife-spotting
opportunities, most
notably from popular
spot Chanonry Point,
the Moray Firth is
home to a wealth of
marine life. Harbour
seals, porpoises, white-
beaked and bottlenose
dolphins and several
species of whale all
come here to feed.
Learn more about the
Moray Firth's resident
and visiting sealife
at the WDC Scottish
Dolphin Centre at Spey
Bay. Dolphin-spotting
tours are available.

of its merchant houses still
stand. The museum in the
Cromarty Courthouse runs
tours of the town. The **Hugh
Miller Museum** recalls the life
of theologian and geologist
Hugh Miller (1802–56).
Fortrose has a ruined 14th-
century cathedral, while a
stone on Chanonry Point commemorates the Brahan Seer,
burnt alive by the Countess of
Seaforth after he foresaw her
husband's infidelity. For local

↑ Inverewe Garden in Wester Ross, benefiting from the mild influence of the Gulf Stream

archaeology, visit Rosemarkie's **Groam House Museum**.

Cromarty Courthouse

⊘ △ Church St, Cromarty ⊙ Apr-mid-Oct: noon-4pm daily �W cromarty-courthouse.org.uk

Hugh Miller Museum

⊘ ⊚ ⊚ △ Church St, Cromarty ⊙ Mid-Mar-Sep: 1-5pm daily �W nts.org.uk

Groam House Museum

⊘ △ High St, Rosemarkie ⊙ Apr-Oct: 11am-4:30pm Mon-Fri, 2-4:30pm Sat & Sun �W groamhouse.org.uk

← Eilean Donan Castle, amid the stunning scenery of Glen Shiel

Wester Ross

△ Ross & Cromarty ⊞ Achnasheen, Strathcarron ⓘ Ullapool; www.visitscotland.com

Amid the great wilderness of Wester Ross, the Torridon Estate includes some of the oldest mountains on Earth, and is home to red deer, wild cats and wild goats. Peregrine falcons and golden eagles nest in the towering sandstone mass of Liathach, above the village of Torridon with its breathtaking views over the Applecross peninsula to Skye. The **Torridon Countryside Centre** provides guided walks in season and information on the region's natural history.

Along the coast, exotic gardens thrive in the warming currents of the Gulf Stream, the most impressive of which is **Inverewe Garden**, created in 1862 by Osgood Mackenzie (1842–1922). Visit in May and June for azaleas and rhododendrons; July and August for herbaceous borders.

Torridon Countryside Centre

⊘ ⊚ △ Torridon ⊙ Apr-Sep: 10am-5pm Sun-Fri �W nts.org.uk

Inverewe Garden

⊘ ⊚ △ Off A832, near Poolewe ⊙ Times vary, check website �W nts.org.uk

---

10

Dornoch

△ Sutherland ⊞ Golspie, Tain ⓘ History Links Museum, The Meadows; www.visitscotland.com

With its first-class golf course and extensive sandy beaches, Dornoch is a popular holiday resort that retains its peaceful atmosphere. A stone at the beach end of River Street marks the place where Janet Horne, the last woman to be tried in Scotland for witch-craft, was executed in 1722.

Nineteen kilometres (12 miles) northeast of Dornoch is the stately Victorianized pile of **Dunrobin Castle**, in a great park with formal gardens overlooking the sea. Many of its rooms are open to visitors. A steam-powered fire engine is among the miscellany of objects on display.

Dunrobin Castle

⊘ △ Near Golspie ⊙ Apr, May, Sep & Oct: 10:30am-4:30pm daily; Jun-Aug: 10am-5pm daily; Falconry displays: Apr-Sep: 11:30am & 2pm �W dunrobincastle.co.uk

---

STAY

Alladale Wilderness Reserve

Accommodation is offered in a luxurious Victorian lodge, a rustic bunkhouse or self-catering cottages.

△ Sutherland IV24 3BS, near Dornoch �W alladale.com

ⓔⓔⓔ

The ruins of Urquhart Castle, overlooking the still waters of Loch Ness ↑

 11

Loch Ness

 Inverness Inverness
36 High St, Inverness;
www.visitscotland.com

At 39 kilometres (24 miles) long, 1.5 km (1 mile) at its widest and up to 305 m (1,000 ft) deep, Loch Ness fills the northern half of the Great Glen fault from Fort William to Inverness. It is joined to lochs Oich and Lochy by the 35-km (22-mile) Caledonian Canal, designed by Thomas Telford. On the western shore, the A82 passes the ruins of the 16th-century **Urquhart Castle**, which was blown up by government supporters in 1692 to prevent it falling into Jacobite hands.

A short distance west, the **Loch Ness Centre and Exhibition** explores the loch's environment and the legend of its most famous resident, Nessie.

THE LOCH NESS MONSTER

First sighted by St Columba in the 6th century, the legendary creature "Nessie" has attracted increasing attention since ambiguous photographs were taken in the 1930s. Though serious investigation is often undermined by hoaxers, sonar techniques continue to yield enigmatic results: plesiosaurs, giant eels and too much whisky are the most popular explanations. Nessie appears to have a lesser-known close relative in the waters of Loch Morar (p568).

Urquhart Castle

Nr Drumnadrochit
9:30am-6pm daily (Jun-Aug: 8pm; Oct-Mar: 4:30pm)
historicenvironment.scot

Loch Ness Centre and Exhibition

Drumnadrochit
10am-3:30pm daily
(Easter-Oct: 9:30am-5pm)
lochness.com

───────────

12

Inverness

Highland 36 High St; www.visitscotland.com

As the Highland capital, Inverness makes an ideal base from which to explore the area. The town centre is dominated by the Victorian castle, now used as law courts. The **Inverness Museum and Art Gallery** provides a good introduction to the history of the Highlands with exhibits

including a lock of Bonnie Prince Charlie's (p487) hair and a collection of Inverness silver.

The **Scottish Kiltmaker Visitor Centre** explores the history and tradition of Scottish kilts, while those in search of tartans and knitwear should visit **Ben Wyvis Kilts**.

Inverness Museum and Art Gallery

Castle Wynd 10am-5pm Tue-Sat (Nov-Mar: Tue-Thu, pm only) inverness.highland.museum

Scottish Kiltmaker Visitor Centre

Huntly St 9am-5:30pm daily highlandhouseoffraser.com

Ben Wyvis Kilts

Highland Rail House, Station Square
9am-5pm Mon-Sat
benwyviskilts.co.uk

───────────

 13

Culloden

Inverness Inverness

A desolate stretch of moorland, Culloden looks much as it must have done on 16 April 1746, the date of the last battle fought on British soil (p487). Here the Jacobites, under Bonnie Prince Charlie's leadership, were conclusively

> **A desolate stretch of moorland, Culloden looks much as it must have done on 16 April 1746, the date of the last battle fought on British soil.**

defeated by Hanoverian troops led by the Duke of Cumberland. The battle is explained in the **NTS Visitor Centre**.

A short distance east are the Neolithic burial sites of Clava Cairns.

NTS Visitor Centre
 🅝 On B9006 east of Inverness ⬭ Mar-Oct: 9am-6pm daily (Jun-Aug: to 7pm); Nov-Feb: 10am-4pm daily 🆆 nts.org.uk

---

⑭
Fort George

🅐 Inverness 🚇🚌 Inverness, Nairn ⬭ Apr-Sep: 9:30am-5:30pm daily; Oct-Mar: 10am-4pm daily 🆆 historic environment.scot

One of the finest examples of European military architecture, Fort George stands on a windswept promontory jutting into the Moray Firth.

Completed in 1769, the fort was built after the Jacobite risings to discourage further rebellion in the Highlands. It houses the Regimental Museum of the Highlanders, and some of its barracks rooms reconstruct the conditions of the common soldiers stationed here more than 200 years ago. The Grand Magazine contains a superb collection of arms and military equipment. The battlements also make an excellent place from which to spot dolphins in the Moray Firth.

---

⑮
Cawdor Castle

🅐 On B9090 (off A96) 🚉 Nairn, then bus 🚌 From Inverness ⬭ Mid-Apr-Sep: 10am-5:30pm daily 🆆 cawdorcastle.com

Cawdor Castle is one of the most romantic stately homes in the Highlands. Though the castle is famed for its links to Shakespeare's Macbeth, it is not historically proven that he, or King Duncan, came here.

An ancient holly tree preserved in the vaults is said to be the one under which, in 1372, Thane William's donkey, laden with gold, stopped for a rest during its master's search for a place to build a fortress. According to legend, this was how the site for the castle was chosen. The house, which is still the home of the Thanes of Cawdor, contains a number of rare tapestries and portraits by the 18th-century painters Joshua Reynolds (1723–92) and George Romney (1734–1802). Furniture in the Pink Bedroom and Woodcock Room includes work by Chippendale and Sheraton.

TOP 5 SPEYSIDE DISTILLERIES

Speyside is home to half of Scotland's whisky distilleries. A signposted trail takes in numerous distilleries and a cooperage.

Cardhu
🆆 malts.com
Founded in 1811, Cardhu is the first distillery to be pioneered by a woman.

Macallan
🆆 themacallan.com
The state-of-the-art Macallan Visitor Experience is the perfect place to sample the "Rolls-Royce of single malts".

Glenlivet
🆆 theglenlivet.com
Enjoy multisensory tours and tastings in a remote setting.

Glenfiddich
🆆 glenfiddich.com
Traditional craftsmanship and innovation come together at this family-run distillery.

Speyside Cooperage
🆆 speysidecooperage.co.uk
Here visitors can learn about the making of the wooden casks that are used to store and age the whisky.

↑ Paintings, vases and period furniture in an elegant room in Cawdor Castle

EAT

Café Fish
Super-fresh seafood
straight off the boat
and a surprising wine
list are on offer here.
There's a quayside
terrace in summer.

📍The Pier, Tobermory,
Mull 🌐thecafefish.com

Argyll Hotel
Crofters and local
fishermen keep this
cosy restaurant well-
stocked with lamb,
game, beef and seafood.

📍Isle of Iona, Argyll
🌐argyllhotel
iona.co.uk

16
Glencoe

📍Highland 🚉Fort William
🚌Glencoe 🚶15 High St,
Fort William; 0139 7701801

Glencoe is renowned for
its awe-inspiring scenery
and savage history. The
precipitous cliffs of Buachaille
Etive Mor and the knife-edged
ridge of Aonach Eagach (both
over 900 m; 3,000 ft) present
a formidable challenge even

MASSACRE OF GLENCOE
On 13 February 1692, the Glencoe
MacDonalds chief was five days
late with an oath of submission to
William III, providing an excuse to root
out a nest of Jacobite supporters. For ten
days 130 soldiers, under Robert Campbell,
were hospitably entertained by the
MacDonalds before, in a terrible breach
of trust, the soldiers turned on them
and killed them. A political scandal
ensued, but there were no official
reprimands for three years.

to experienced mountaineers.
Against a dark backdrop of
craggy peaks and the River
Coe, the Glen offers superb
hill walking in the summer.
Stout footwear, waterproofs
and attention to safety
warnings are essential. Details
of routes, ranging from an
easy half-hour walk to Signal
Rock (from which the signal
was given to commence the
massacre) to a stiff 10-km
(6-mile) haul up the Devil's
Staircase, can be had from
the **NTS Visitor Centre**.

NTS Visitor Centre
📍Glencoe 🕐9am-6pm
daily (Nov-Feb: 10am-4pm)
🚫Mar-early Apr 🌐nts.org.uk

17
Oban

📍Argyll & Bute 🚉🚌⛴
🚶North Pier; www.oban.
org.uk

Located on the Firth of Lorne,
the port of Oban is busy with
travellers on their way to Mull
and the Western Isles (p552).
   Dominating the skyline is
McCaig's Tower, an unfinished
Victorian imitation of Rome's
Colosseum. It is worth making
the 10-minute climb from the
town centre for the superb
views of the Argyll coast.
Attractions in town include
working centres for glass,
pottery and whisky; the Oban
distillery produces one of the
country's
finest

Brightly coloured
harbourfront houses
at Tobermory, Mull

malt whiskies. Regular car
ferries depart for Barra and
South Uist, Mull, Tiree and
Colonsay islands.
   Dunstaffnage Castle,
5 km (3 miles) north of Oban,
was the 13th-century stronghold of the MacDougalls. It
has atmospheric ruins.

Dunstaffnage Castle
📍Dunbeg, off A85
🕐Apr-Sep: 9:30am-5:30pm
daily; Oct-Mar: 10am-4pm
Sat-Wed 🌐historic
environment.scot

18
Mull

📍Argyll ⛴From
Oban, Lochaline
and Kilchoan; from
Fionnphort, on Mull,
to Iona 🚶Craignure;
01680 812377

The largest of the Inner
Hebridean islands, Mull
features rough moorlands,
the rocky peak of Ben More
and a splendid beach at
Calgary. Most roads follow
the coastline, affording
wonderful sea views.
On a promontory to the east
of Craignure lies the 13th-
century **Duart Castle**, home of
the chief of Clan Maclean. You

can visit the Banqueting Hall, State Rooms and the dungeons.

At the northern end of Mull is the picturesque town of Tobermory, with its brightly coloured buildings. Built as a fishing village in 1788, it is now a popular port for yachts. The harbourside **Mull Aquarium** is Europe's first catch-and-release aquarium.

On the small island of Iona, a restored abbey stands on the site where Irish missionary St Columba began his crusade in 563 and made Iona the home of Christianity in Europe. In the graveyard of the abbey, 48 Scottish kings are said to be buried and four historic high crosses can be seen, two of them along the medieval Street of the Dead.

If you are lucky with the weather, head to **Fingal's Cave** on the Isle of Staffa. The cave is surrounded by "organ pipes" of basalt, the inspiration for Mendelssohn's *Hebrides Overture* (1833). Boat trips run there from Ulva and Fionnphort and to the seven **Treshnish Isles**. These uninhabited isles are a sanctuary for thousands of seabirds, including puffins, razorbills, kittiwakes and skuas. Lunga is the main stop for tour boats.

Duart Castle

⊛⊛ 🏛 🅐 Off A849, near Craignure 🕐 Apr: 11am–4pm Sun–Thu; May–Oct: 10:30am–5pm daily 🆆 duartcastle.com

Mull Aquarium

🅐 Taigh Solais, Tobermory 🕐 Easter–Oct: 9:30am–5pm daily 🆆 mullaquarium.co.uk

Fingal's Cave and Treshnish Isles

⊛ 🅐 Staffa, west of Mull 🚢 Easter–Oct 🕐 Timetable varies, check website 🆆 staffatours.com

---

⑲
Loch Awe

🅐 Argyll & Bute 🚊🚌 Dalmally 🅘 Wollen Mill, Front St, Inveraray; www.loch-awe.com

One of the largest of Scotland's freshwater lochs and its longest, Loch Awe fills a 40-km (25-mile) glen in the southwestern Highlands. A short drive east from the village of Lochawe leads to the lochside remains of Kilchurn Castle, abandoned after being struck by lightning in the 18th century. Dwarfing the castle is the huge bulk of Ben Cruachan, whose summit

PICTURE PERFECT
Tobermory Harbour

For that iconic snap of Tobermory's colourful waterfront, head to the aquarium end of Main Street. A lookout point here offers an excellent shot of the harbour, twinkling with the reflections of brightly coloured buildings.

can be reached by the narrow Pass of Brander, in which Robert the Bruce *(p487)* fought the Clan MacDougal in 1308. From the A85, a tunnel leads to the cavernous Cruachan Power Station. Near the village of Taynuilt, the preserved Lorn Furnace at Bonawe is a reminder of the iron-smelting industry that caused the destruction of much of the area's woodland in the 18th and 19th centuries.

Marked prehistoric cairns are found off the A816 between Kilmartin and Dunadd. The latter boasts a 6th-century hillfort from which the Stone of Destiny, an ancient symbol of Scotland's monarchy that is now housed in Edinburgh Castle, originated.

↑ Romantic Inveraray Castle, with its 19th-century conical towers

20

Inveraray Castle

⌂ Inveraray, Argyll & Bute
🚂 Dalmally 🚌 From Glasgow ⏰ Apr–Oct: 10am–5:45pm daily
🌐 inveraray-castle.com

This mock Gothic palace, the family home of Clan Campbell, was built in 1745 on the ruins of a 15th-century castle. The conical towers were added after a fire in 1877. The castle houses a huge collection of Oriental and European porcelain, Regency furniture and portraits by Ramsay, Gainsborough and Raeburn.

EAT

Loch Fyne Oyster Bar
Oysters are key at this converted loch-side stone barn, but let the day's catch rule by choosing the seafood sampler platter.

⌂ Clachan Farm, Cairndow, nr Inveraray
🌐 lochfyne.com

£££

21

Auchindrain Museum

⌂ Inveraray, Argyll & Bute
🚌 Inveraray then bus
⏰ Apr–Oct: 10am–5pm daily (last adm: 4pm); Nov–Apr: 10am–4pm Mon–Fri
🌐 auchindrain.org.uk

This open-air museum illuminates the working life of the kind of farming community that was typical of the Highlands until the late 19th century. Many of the buildings combine living space, kitchen and cattle shed under one roof.

22

Crarae Gardens

⌂ Crarae, Argyll & Bute
🚂 Inveraray then bus
⏰ 9:30am–dusk daily; Visitor Centre: Apr–Oct: 9:30am–5pm daily (Sep & Oct: Thu–Mon) 🌐 nts.org.uk

These beguiling gardens were created in the 1920s by Lady Grace Campbell. She was the aunt of explorer Reginald Farrer, whose specimens from Tibet were the beginnings of a collection of exotic plants. Nourished by the warmth of the Gulf Stream and high rainfall, the gardens are best seen in spring and early summer.

23

Jura

⌂ Argyll & Bute
⛴ From Kennacraig to Islay, then Islay to Jura
🛈 The Square, Bowmore, Islay; 01496 305165

Barren, mountainous and overrun by red deer, the Isle of Jura has only one road, which connects the single village of Craighouse to the Islay ferry. Though walking is restricted during deer-hunting season (Aug–Oct), the island offers superb hill walking, especially on the slopes of the three main peaks, known as the Paps of Jura. The tallest of these is Beinn An Oir at 784 m (2571 ft). Beyond the island's northern tip are the notorious whirlpools of Corryvreckan. A legend tells of Prince Breackan who, to win the hand of a princess, tried to keep his boat anchored in the whirlpool for three days, held by ropes made of hemp, wool and maidens' hair. The prince drowned when a single rope, containing the hair of a girl who had been untrue, finally broke.

24

Islay

⌂ Argyll & Bute ⛴ From Kennacraig 🛈 The Square, Bowmore; 01496 305165

Islay (pronounced "Eye-luh") is the home of respected Highland single malt whiskies Lagavulin and Laphroaig. Most of the island's distilleries produce heavily peated malts with a distinctive tang of the

Did You Know?

George Orwell wrote *1984* in a remote farmhouse on Jura.

STAY

Ballygrant Inn

This family-run inn set in pretty gardens offers comfortable rooms and a good restaurant serving Scottish fare.

 Ballygrant, Isle of Islay
 ballygrant-inn.com

£ £ £

sea. The Georgian village of Bowmore has the island's oldest distillery and a circular church designed to minimize the Devil's possible lurking places. The **Museum of Islay Life** in Port Charlotte contains fascinating information on social and natural history. Just 11 km (7 miles) east of Port Ellen, the Kildalton Cross, adorned with Old Testament scenes, is one of the most impressive 8th-century Celtic crosses in Britain. Islay's beaches support a variety of birdlife, some of which can be observed at the RSPB reserve at Gruinart.

Museum of Islay Life

🅰 Port Charlotte ⏲ Apr & Oct: 10:30am–4:30pm Mon–Fri; May–Sep: 10:30am–4:30pm Mon–Sat, 1–4:30pm Sun 🅦 islaymuseum.org

---

㉕
Kintyre

🅰 Argyll & Bute
🚆 Oban 🚌 Campbeltown
ℹ Riverside Filling Station, Lochgilphead; 01546 603858

The long, narrow peninsula of Kintyre has superb views across to the islands of Gigha, Islay and Jura. The 14-km (9-mile) Crinan Canal is a delightful inland waterway, its 15 locks bustling with pleasure craft in the summer. The town of Tarbert (meaning "isthmus" in Gaelic) takes its name from the neck on which it stands, which is narrow enough to drag a boat across between Loch Fyne and West Loch Tarbert. This feat was first achieved by the Viking King Magnus Barfud who, in 1198, was granted by treaty as much land as he could sail around.

Travelling south past Campbeltown, the B842 ends at the headland known as the Mull of Kintyre. Westward lies the Isle of Rathlin, where Robert the Bruce (p487) learned patience in his struggles against the English by watching a spider weaving a web in a cave.

Copper stills used to make single-malt whisky at Laphroaig Distillery (inset), on Islay ↓

A DRIVING TOUR
ROAD TO THE ISLES

THE HIGHLANDS AND ISLANDS

→ Road to the Isles

Locator Map
For more detail see p544

Distance 72 km (45 miles) **Stopping-off points**
Glenfinnan NTS Visitors' Centre (01397 722250) explains
the Jacobite risings and serves refreshments; the Old Library
Lodge in Arisaig offers excellent Scottish cuisine

This scenic route goes past vast mountain corridors,
breathtaking beaches of white sand and tiny villages to
the idyllic town of Mallaig, one of the ferry ports for the
isles of Skye, Rum, Eigg, Muck and Canna. In addition to
stunning scenery, the area is steeped in Jacobite history.

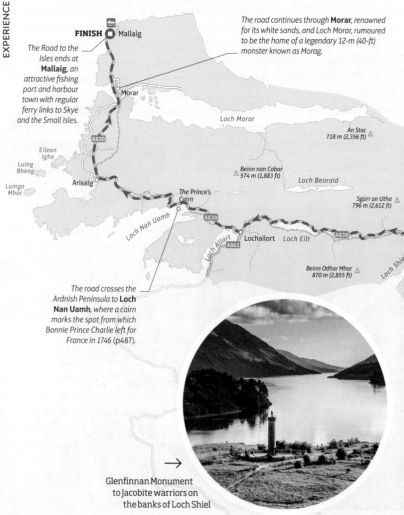

FINISH ◻ Mallaig

*The Road to the Isles ends at **Mallaig**, an attractive fishing port and harbour town with regular ferry links to Skye and the Small Isles.*

*The road continues through **Morar**, renowned for its white sands, and Loch Morar, rumoured to be the home of a legendary 12-m (40-ft) monster known as Morag.*

Morar

Loch Morar

An Stac
718 m (2,356 ft) △

Eilean Ighe

Luing Bheag

Luinga Mhòr

A830

Arisaig

Beinn nan Cabar
574 m (1,883 ft) △

Loch Beoraid

Sgùrr an Utha △
796 m (2,612 ft)

The Prince's Cairn

Loch Nan Uamh

A830

Loch Allort

A861

Lochailort   Loch Eilt

A830

Loch Shiel

Beinn Odhar Mhor △
870 m (2,855 ft)

*The road crosses the Ardnish Peninsula to **Loch Nan Uamh**, where a cairn marks the spot from which Bonnie Prince Charlie left for France in 1746 (p487).*

→ Glenfinnan Monument to Jacobite warriors on the banks of Loch Shiel

↑ Walking a dog on the beautiful white sands of Morar

0 kilometres 5
0 miles 5

N ↑

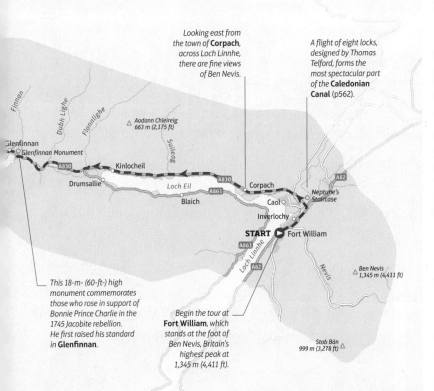

*Looking east from the town of **Corpach**, across Loch Linnhe, there are fine views of Ben Nevis.*

*A flight of eight locks, designed by Thomas Telford, forms the most spectacular part of the **Caledonian Canal** (p562).*

△ Aodann Chleireig 663 m (2,175 ft)

Glenfinnan
○ Glenfinnan Monument
A830
Kinlocheil
Drumsallie
Loch Eil
A830
A861
Corpach
Blaich
Caol ○
Neptune's Staircase
Inverlochy
START ▶ Fort William
A861
Loch Linnhe
A82

△ Ben Nevis 1,345 m (4,411 ft)

Nevis

Stob Bàn 999 m (3,278 ft) △

*This 18-m- (60-ft-) high monument commemorates those who rose in support of Bonnie Prince Charlie in the 1745 Jacobite rebellion. He first raised his standard in **Glenfinnan**.*

*Begin the tour at **Fort William**, which stands at the foot of Ben Nevis, Britain's highest peak at 1,345 m (4,411 ft).*

NEED TO KNOW

Steam train on the Glenfinnan Viaduct, Scotland

BEFORE
YOU GO

Forward planning is essential to any successful trip. Be prepared for all eventualities by considering the following points before you travel.

AT A GLANCE

CURRENCY
Pound Sterling
(GBP)

AVERAGE DAILY SPEND

SAVE	SPEND	SPLURGE
£60	£125	£200+

BOTTLED WATER	COFFEE	PINT OF BEER	DINNER FOR TWO
£1.00	£2.50	£4.50	£60

CLIMATE

The longest days occur May–Aug, while Oct–Feb sees the shortest daylight hours.

Temperatures average 15°C (59°F) in summer, and drop below 0 °C (32 °F) in winter.

October and November see the most rainfall, but heavy showers occur all year round.

ELECTRICITY SUPPLY

Power sockets are type G, fitting three-pronged plugs. Standard voltage is 230 volts.

Passports and Visas

For a stay of up to three months for the purpose of tourism EU nationals and citizens of the US, Canada, Australia and New Zealand do not need a visa to enter the country. However, this may change once the UK has left the EU. Consult your nearest British embassy or check the **UK Government** website for up-to-date information specific to your home country.
UK Government
W gov.uk

Travel Safety Advice

Visitors can get up-to-date travel safety information from the UK Foreign and Commonwealth Office, the US State Department, and the Department of Foreign Affairs and Trade in Australia.
Austrailia
W smartraveller.gov.au
UK
W gov.uk/foreign-travel-advice
US
W travel.state.gov

Customs Information

An individual is permitted to carry the following within the EU for personal use:
Tobacco 800 cigarettes, 400 cigarillos, 200 cigars or 1 kg of smoking tobacco.
Alcohol 10 litres of alcoholic beverages above 22% strength, 20 litres below 22% strength, 90 litres of wine (60 litres of which can be sparkling wine) and 110 litres of beer.
Cash If you plan to enter or leave the EU with €10,000 or more in cash (or the equivalent in other currencies) you must declare it to the customs authorities.
These regulations may be subject to change. Check restrictions before travelling.

Insurance

It is wise to take out an insurance policy covering theft, loss of belongings, medical problems, cancellation and delays. Check the **NHS** website for the latest details regarding accessing emergency national health services if you're visiting from abroad.

NHS
 nhs.uk

Vaccinations

No inoculations are needed for the UK.

Money

Major credit, debit and prepaid currency cards are accepted in most shops and restaurants. However, it is always worth carrying some cash, as some smaller businesses, markets and local public transport may operate a cash-only policy. Cash machines can be found at banks and on main streets in major towns. Though technically having the same value, Scottish bank notes are not always accepted outside Scotland, so it is best to exchange them before leaving.

Booking Accommodation

Britain offers a variety of accommodation, from luxury five-star hotels to family-run B&Bs, and budget hostels. Lodgings can fill up and prices become inflated during the summer, so it is worth booking well in advance. The lists of accommodation maintained by local tourist boards can be useful but the big international booking engines have the best nationwide coverage. The dominant accommodation search engines are **Booking.com**, **Expedia.co.uk** and **Tripadvisor.co.uk**, which is useful for the depth of user reviews. To browse curated lists of the best accommodation try **The Hotel Guru**.

Booking.com
w booking.com
Expedia
w Expedia.co.uk
The Hotel Guru
w thehotelguru.com
Tripadvisor
w Tripadvisor.co.uk

Travellers with Specific Needs

Most modern buildings and infrastructure have been designed with wheelchairs in mind while many trains and buses in Britain have been adapted. The best dedicated guide for wheelchair users is *Holidays in the British Isles* published by **Disability Rights UK**. Accessibility information for public transport is available from regional public transport websites. Many major museums and galleries offer audio tours and induction loops for those with impaired sight and hearing. **Action on Hearing Loss** and the **Royal National Institute for the Blind** offer information and advice.

Action on Hearing Loss
w actionhearingloss.org.uk
Disability Rights UK
w disabilityrightsuk.org
Royal National Institute for the Blind
w rnib.org.uk

Language

Britain is a multicultural country in which you will hear many languages spoken. Accents in English vary tremendously between regions and can at times be stronger and more challenging in certain areas.

Closures

Mondays Some museums and tourist attractions are closed for the day.
Sundays and public holidays Many shops open late and close early, and some close for the day.

PUBLIC HOLIDAYS	
1 Jan	New Year's Day
2 Jan (Scotland Only)	Bank Holiday
10 Apr (2020) 2 Apr (2021)	Good Friday
13 Apr (2020) 5 Apr (2021)	Easter Monday
8 May (2020)	May Day
25 May (2020) 31 May (2021)	Spring Bank Holiday
31 Aug (2020) 30 Aug (2021)	Summer Bank Holiday
25 Dec	Christmas Day
26 Dec	Boxing Day

GETTING AROUND

Whether you are visiting for a short city break or rural country retreat, discover how best to reach your destination and travel like a pro.

AT A GLANCE

PUBLIC TRANSPORT COSTS

LONDON

£13.10

All-day zones 1–4
Tube ticket

EDINBURGH

£4.00

All day bus ticket

BRITRAIL PASS

£146.00

3 days
unlimited train travel

SPEED LIMIT

MOTORWAY

70 mph
(112 kmph)

DUAL CARRIAGEWAYS

70 mph
(112 kmph)

SINGLE CARRIAGEWAYS

60 mph
(96 kmph)

URBAN AREAS

30 mph
(48 kmph)

Arriving by Air

London Heathrow is among the world's busiest airports and handles about a third of all UK air traffic. Three other London airports: Luton, Gatwick and Stanstead account for another third. Manchester is by far the busiest airport outside London, with Edinburgh a distant second. Another 15 or so regional airports handle the vast majority of the remaining international air traffic, with the major ones being Birmingham, Glasgow, Bristol and Newcastle.

Train Travel

International Train Travel

St Pancras International is the London terminus for Eurostar, the high-speed train linking the UK with the Continent. You can buy tickets and passes for multiple international journeys via **Eurail** or **Interrail**, however you may still need to pay an additional reservation fee for certain trains. Always check that your pass is valid on the service on which you wish to travel before boarding. **Eurostar** runs a regular service from Paris, Brussels and Amsterdam to London via the Channel Tunnel. **Eurotunnel** operates a drive-on-drive-off train service between Calais and Folkestone, in the south of England.

Eurail
w eurail.com
Eurostar
w eurostar.com
Eurotunnel
w eurotunnel.com
Interrail
w interrail.eu

Domestic Train Travel

The UK's railway system is complicated and can be confusing. Lines are run by a number of different private companies, but are coordinated by **National Rail**, which operates a joint information and ticket-buying service.

London has eight main railway termini serving different parts of Britain (Charing Cross, Euston, King's Cross, London Bridge, St Pancras, Paddington, Waterloo and Victoria). If you are

GETTING TO AND FROM THE AIRPORT TABLE

Airport	Distance to City	Taxi fare	Public Transport	Journey time
London-Heathrow	28 km (17 miles)	£50	Bus/Train / Underground	15–50mins
London-Gatwick	50 km (31 miles)	£60	Bus/Train	30–90mins
Manchester	15 km (9 miles)	£33	Bus/Train	25mins
London-Stansted	62 km (39 miles)	£75	Bus/Train	50–90mins
London-Luton	56 km (35 miles)	£70	Bus/Train	40–80mins
Edinburgh	13 km (8 miles)	£30	Bus/Train	30mins

RAIL JOURNEY PLANNER

This map is a handy reference for travel to major cities in Great Britain. Most lines radiate from London.

London to Birmingham	1 hr 30 mins
London to Bristol	2 hrs
London to Edinburgh	5 hrs
London to Glasgow	4 hrs 30 mins
London to Inverness	8 hrs
London to Manchester	2 hrs
London to Newcastle	3 hrs
London to Oxford	1 hr
London to Penzance	5 hrs
London to Thurso	13 hrs
London to York	2 hrs

Thurso

Inverness

Glasgow Edinburgh

Newcastle

York

Manchester

Birmingham

Oxford

Bristol London

Penzance

planning to travel outside of the capital, always try to book rail tickets several weeks in advance to secure a seat and a discount fare. The earlier you book the cheaper the ticket is likely to be. You can also save if you travel off peak.

The **Caledonian Sleeper** operates overnight services via the West Coast Mainline from London Euston to Glasgow, Edinburgh, Aberdeen, Inverness and Fort William. The Interrail Great Britain Pass offers a good deal on travel in the whole of the UK for 3, 4, 6 or 8 days within a one-month period.

Caledonian Sleeper
w sleeper.scot

National Rail
w nationalrail.co.uk

Long-Distance Bus Travel

In Britain long-distance buses are often referred to as "coaches" and the biggest operator is **National Express**. **Eurolines** is its European arm, offering a variety of coach routes to London from European cities. Fares start from around £20, and vary depending on distance. In Scotland the key operators between major towns are **Megabus** and **Citylink**. In all cases, it is advisable to book as far in advance as you can for the best prices.

Citylink
🌐 citylink.co.uk
Eurolines
🌐 eurolines.eu
National Express
🌐 nationalexpress.com
Megabus
🌐 uk.megabus.com

Public Transport

Public transport in the UK is a combination of private sector and city-operated services.

Most cities have only bus systems, though a few, such as Edinburgh, have tram lines. Underground subway trains and light suburban railway networks, the backbone of London's public transport system, are also rare elsewhere in the country.

Most types of public transport offer a choice of a single ticket and an unlimited day-ticket. In some cases your train ticket to a destination can be upgraded to include local public transport, which is particularly useful in London. Most public transport in London is coordinated by Transport for London (**TFL**). In Scotland **Traveline Scotland** provides ticket and timetable information for all services.

TFL
🌐 tfl.go.uk
Traveline Scotland
🌐 travelinescotland.com

Taxis

Britain has two sorts of taxis. Some, such as London's iconic black cabs, can be hailed on the street and can be identified by a yellow "Taxi" sign on the roof that's illuminated when the cab is available. The other sorts of taxi are private-hire minicabs. These are generally lightly modified regular cars and are only bookable online or by phone. All taxis are metered, with fares locally set, but usually starting at around £2.50. The following services can be booked online:

Dial-a-Cab
🌐 dialacab.co.uk
Gett Taxis
🌐 get.com/uk

Driving

For many foreign travellers, driving in Britain is a challenge simply because you drive on the left. The measurement of distances in miles can add to the confusion as can narrow roads, the many roundabouts, congestion and scarce parking in most cities. But in rural areas driving can be a pleasure and the key way to get around.

Driving to Britain

For those driving to Britain, the simplest way is to use the Eurotunnel shuttles between Calais in France and Folkestone, both of which have direct motorway access. From Folkestone it is possible to drive to London in about two hours, to Edinburgh in around eight hours. There are also a number of ferries between the UK and continental Europe (p577).

To take your own foreign-registered car into and around Britain, you will need to carry the vehicle's registration and insurance documents, a full and valid driving licence, and valid passport or national ID at all times. EU driving licences issued by any of the EU member states are valid (though this situation may change following the UK's departure from the EU). If visiting from outside the EU, or if your licence is not in English, you may need to apply for an International Driving Permit (IDP). Check with your local automobile association or consult the UK Driver and Vehicle Licensing Agency (**DVLA**) for the latest regulations.

DVLA
🌐 dvlaregistrations.direct.gov.uk

Driving in Britain

Though often busy, Britain's roads are generally good, with motorways or dual carriageway highways connecting all major towns and cities. In rural areas sealed roads connect almost all communities, though in remote areas of Scotland these may be a single carriageway, shared with oncoming traffic and using designated passing places. Convoys of slow-moving caravans can slow up traffic in peak summer holiday season and at weekends everywhere.

Driving in cities is not recommended; traffic is heavy and parking scarce and in London there is the added cost of the **Congestion Charge** – an £11.50 daily charge for driving in central London between 7am and 6pm Monday to Friday.

In the event of breakdown, contact the **AA** for roadside assistance. This should be free if you are a member of a partner organisation in your home country.

AA
🌐 theaa.com
Congestion Charge
🌐 tfl.gov.uk/modes/driving/congestion-charge

Rules of the Road

Drive on the left. Seat belts must be worn at all times by the driver and all passengers. Children up to 135 cm (4 ft) tall or of the age of 12 or under must travel with the correct child restraint for their weight and size. Mobile telephones may not be used while driving except with a "handsfree" system. Third-party motor insurance is required by law.

Overtake on the outside or right-hand lane. When approaching a roundabout, give priority to traffic approaching from the right, unless indicated otherwise.

It is illegal to drive in bus lanes during restricted hours, as posted on roadside signs. The drink-drive limit (p578) is strictly enforced and very low. Avoid drinking alcohol completely if you plan to drive.

Car Rental

To rent a car you must be 21 years of age or over and have held a valid driver's licence for at least a year. You will also need a credit card for the rental deposit. Rental cars with automatic transmission are rare, and must be booked in advance. Returning a car to a different location will incur surcharges.

Boats and Ferries

Passenger ferries have plied the English Channel for generations. Companies currently include **P&O Ferries, DFDS Seaways, Condor Ferries** and **Brittany Ferries**, which link Britain with French ports such as Calais, Dunkirk St-Malo, Dieppe Roscoff and Cherbourg. Several other countries also operate car ferries to either Hull or Newcastle in Britain, including Zeebrugge in Belgium and the Hook of Holland, Amsterdam and Rotterdam in The Netherlands. Ferries run between Bilbao in Spain and Portsmouth. **Direct Ferries** has a good website where you can book most of the above services.

Most of Scotland's many islands can only be reached by boat, with ferries connecting the largest. The majority of services are run by **Caledonian MacBrayne** (Calmac), who offer both regular tickets as well as passes valid for 8 days, 15 days or one month.

Brittany Ferries
W brittany-ferries.co.uk
Caledonian MacBrayne
W calmac.co.uk
Condor Ferries
W condorferries.co.uk
Direct Ferries
W directferries.co.uk
DFDS Seaways
W dfdsseaways.co.uk
P&O Ferries
W poferries.com

Cycling

Generally, Britain's cities are not especially cycle-friendly. Traffic is often heavy and roads are narrow. Cycle lanes and the occasional cycle-path are not unusual but only a small number of cities are particularly attractive for cycling. Among the best are Cambridge and York, where it is easy to rent a bike. Several other cities have also embraced bike sharing schemes run by **Nextbike** and modelled on the **Santander Cycles** system in London. All these involve using credit cards at one of several self-service road-side docking stations scattered around a city.

Rural areas, particularly in Scotland, are much better for longer-distance cycling though there are usually more hills to contend with. Many key routes form part of the UK's National Cycle Network and are mapped by **Sustrans**. **Wilderness Scotland** offers guided cycling tours in areas that include the Cairngorms, the Hebrides and the Great Glen, with a support van to carry your luggage. Scotland is also ideal for mountain biking. **Forestry and Land Scotland** maintains over a dozen dedicated and colour-coded route networks.

Forestry and Land Scotland
W forestryandland.gov.scot
Nextbike
W nextbike.co.uk
Sustrans
W sustrans.org.uk
Santander Cycles
W tfl.gov.uk/modes/cycling/santander-cycles
Wilderness Scotland
W wildernessscotland.com

CANAL CRUISING

The finest way to explore Britain's waterways under your own steam is by renting a boat. Two destinations stand out: Norfolk's Broads (p204) and Scotland's far wilder Caledonian Canal (p562). The following authorities give information and advice on cruising the waterways:

Canal and River Trust
Extensive information and suggestions of various "cruising rings" - trips that follow waterway loops around England.
W canalrivertrust.org.uk

Waterways Holidays
Rental of canal boats, motorboats and sailboats in many locations in Britain.
W waterwaysholidays.com.

Caley Cruisers
Choose from ten different styles of hire boats on the Caledonian Canal.
W caleycruisers.com

PRACTICAL
INFORMATION

A little local know-how goes a long way in Great Britain. Here you will find all the essential advice and information you will need during your stay.

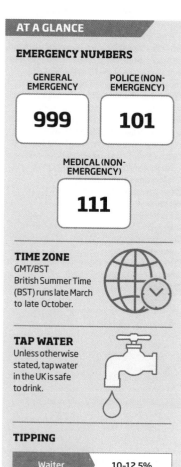

AT A GLANCE

EMERGENCY NUMBERS

GENERAL EMERGENCY	POLICE (NON-EMERGENCY)
999	**101**

MEDICAL (NON-EMERGENCY)

111

TIME ZONE
GMT/BST
British Summer Time (BST) runs late March to late October.

TAP WATER
Unless otherwise stated, tap water in the UK is safe to drink.

TIPPING

Waiter	10-12.5%
Hotel Porter	£1 per bag
Housekeeping	£1 per day
Concierge	£1-2
Taxi Driver	Round up to the nearest pound

Personal Security

Pickpockets sometimes work crowded tourist areas. Use common sense and be alert to your surroundings. If you have anything stolen, report the crime to the nearest police station as soon as possible. Get a copy of the crime report to claim on your insurance.

Contact your embassy in the event of a serious crime or accident or if you have your passport stolen.

Health

For minor ailments go to a pharmacy or chemist. These are plentiful throughout towns and cities. Chains such as Boots and Superdrug have branches in almost every shopping area.

If you have an accident or a medical problem requiring non-urgent medical attention, look for details of your nearest non-emergency medical service on the **NHS** website. Alternatively, call the NHS 24 helpline number at any hour on 111, or go to your nearest Accident and Emergency (A&E) department.

You may need a doctor's prescription to obtain certain pharmaceuticals; the pharmacist can inform you of the closest doctor's surgery or medical centre where you can be seen by a GP (General Practitioner).

When the UK leaves the European Union EU citizens may no longer be able to receive emergency medical treatment in the UK free of charge. They, like visitors from outside the EU may have to pay upfront for medical treatment and reclaim on insurance at a later date.
NHS
ⓦ nhs.uk

Smoking, Alcohol and Drugs

Smoking and "vaping" are banned in all public spaces such as bus, train stations and airports and in enclosed areas of bars, cafés, restaurants and hotels. However, many bars and restaurants have outdoor areas where smoking is permitted.

Alcohol may not be sold to or bought for anyone under 18. The legal limit for drivers is

80 mg of alcohol per 100 ml of blood, which is roughly equivalent to one small glass of wine or a pint of regular strength lager. In Scotland the limit is 50mg. If you plan to drive it is safest to avoid drinking altogether.

Possession of all recreational drugs, including psychoactive substances formerly known as "legal highs" and now classified as illegal, is a criminal offence.

ID

Visitors to the UK are not required to carry ID, but passports are required as ID at airports, even when taking internal flights within the UK. Anyone who looks under 18 may be asked for photo ID to prove their age when buying alcohol.

Visiting Places of Worship

Show respect by dressing modestly, especially when entering churches and religious buildings. Do not talk loudly or use cameras, phones or other devices without first asking permission.

Mobile Phones and Wi-Fi

Free Wi-Fi hotspots are widely available in cities. Cafés and restaurants will give you their Wi-Fi password if you make a purchase. Many buses and trains offer free Wi-Fi, as will most hotels.

Visitors should check roaming charges with their domestic provider. Consider picking up a local pay-as-you-go SIM card from a newsagent or supermarket if roaming charges are high .

Do not rely on mobile phones or other devices for navigation or emergency communications in remote areas such as rural Scotland where reception can be intermittent.

Post

Main post offices are found in the centres of major towns and cities. In suburbs and villages, post office counters are often embedded in supermarkets and newsagents or even a village shop. Hours are generally 9am–5:30pm Monday to Friday and until 12:30pm on Saturday. You can also buy 1st class, 2nd class and international airmail stamps in shops and supermarkets (in books of 12). Distinctive red post boxes are located on main streets throughout the country.

Taxes and Refunds

VAT (Value Added Tax) is charged at 20% on most products and almost always included in the marked price of anything you buy. Stores offering tax-free shopping display a distinctive sign and (for non-EU residents) will provide you with a VAT 407 form to validate in order to get a refund when you leave the country.

Discount Cards

Most attractions in Britain offer concessionary rates for children, seniors and students. If you're among the last group, it is best to secure the **ISIC** (International Student Identity Card). Some city tourist offices also offer visitor passes and discount cards (such as the **London City Pass**). These are usually worth purchasing if you're in a city for more than a couple of days.

If you intend on visiting several English castles, historic homes and ornamental gardens, an annual **National Trust** membership may be worthwhile. In Scotland, consider the **Historic Environment Scotland** Explorer Pass, which provides access to over 70 attractions over a 3-or 7-day period.

Historic Environment Scotland
W historicenvironment.scot
ISIC
W isic.org
London City Pass
W londonpass.com
National Trust
W nationaltrust.org.uk

WEBSITES AND APPS

MoneySavingExpert.com
Unbiased UK consumer website with a good travel section and active forums.

Visit England visitengland.com
Detailed tourist information, including help with accommodation.

Visit Scotland visitscotland.com
Scotland's excellent official tourist board website with a glut of up-to-date listings and activity search engines.

Visit Wales visitwales.com
The official Welsh tourist board.

INDEX

Page numbers in **bold** refer to main entries

ACKNOWLEDGMENTS

The publisher would like to thank the following for their kind permission to reproduce their photographs.

Key: a-above; b-below/bottom; c-centre; f-far; l-left; r-right; t-top

123RF.com: colindamckie 156t; Pavel Dudek 151t, 304–5, 339tr; flik47 107clb; Anton Ivanov 377tl; Serhii Kamshylin 46t.

4Corners: Massimo Borchi 430tl; Pietro Canali 282–3t; Justin Cliffe 8cl; Justin Foulkes 10clb, 424–5; Susanne Kremer 495bl, 518–19t; Nicolò Miana 4; Peter Packer 19tr; Arcangelo Piai 13cr; Maurizio Rellini 12clb, 13t, 156br; Alessandro Saffo 58, 64-5; Richard Taylor 494–5t; Sebastian Wasek 483bl, 542–3.

Alamy Stock Photo: AC Images 417br; age fotostock / Historical Views 316ca; AGF Srl / Lorenzo De Simone 484cra; AJB 540t; Antiqua Print Gallery 486t; Arcaid Images / Richard Bryant 141tl, / Peter Durant 347cra; Archive Room 432bl; Arco Images GmbH / T. Schäffer 450bl, 536t; Art Collection 2 48tl; Art Directors & TRIP / Helene Rogers 323br; Arterra Picture Library / Clement Philippe 564bc; Artokoloro Quint Lox Limited / liszt collection 315crb; Ashley Cooper pics 418–19t; Andy Aughey 2-3; Sergio Azenha 18–19t; Bailey-Cooper Photography 40t, 369tr; Adrian Baker 270tr; Andrew Barker 390–91b; Bob Barnes 229tr; Peter Barritt 97cr, 170bl; Guy Bell 136t; Herb Bendicks 431tr; Best 308–9b; Nigel Blacker 79b; blickwinkel / McPHOTO / O. Protze 22–3b; Kristian Bond 476clb; Louise Bottomley 148, 160–61; John Bracegirdle 235bl, 508clb, 538br; Rick Buettner 258bl; Janet Burdon 395cra; Richard Burdon 16crb; John Burnikell 381tc; Adam Burton 285crb, 286–7t; CBCK-Christine 173tr; Denis Chapman 263tl; Philip Chapman 459bc; Chronicle 47tr, 72bc, 73bl, 487tr; classic / Roger Cracknell 01 125tr; Classic Image 117cr, 525br; Clearview 415tr; Thornton Cohen 504bl; Donna Collett 440t; Danielle Connor 61cb, 134; Guy Corbishley 11br; Cotswolds Photo Library 231cr; Derek Croucher 485tr; CW Images / Chris Warren 387tr, 459tr; D.G.Farquhar 508crb; Ian G Dagnall 33b, 92ca, 94tl, 155tl, 166–7t, 174bl, 197bl, 200t, 203t, 225tr, 244tl, 275tl, 291bl, 294–5b, 312bl, 319cra, 322b, 325bl, 340–41t, 349tr, 353tr, 366tr, 386tl, 394–5b, 400tl, 420t, 403br, 470–71b, 485cla, 532t, 541b, 563bl; Jon Davison 176–7b; dbphots 272b; Design Pics Inc / Axiom / Ian Cumming 213b; DGB 569t; DGDImages 401; dianajarvisphotography.co.uk 218; Digital Image Library 561tl; Helen Dixon 303br; Joe Doylem 43br; dpa picture alliance archive 73br; Mark Dunn 201cr; Dylan Garcia Photography 155tr; Rod Edwards 216br; Dave Ellison 443bl; Epicscotland Ltd 41tr; escapetheofficejob 108b; EThamPhoto 68–9; Greg Balfour Evans 40bl, 187tl, 323tl; Robert Evans 215tr; Eye Ubiquitous / Mockford & Bonetti 519bl; eye35 128t, 139clb, 139bc, 464bl; eye35.pix 142–3b, 154–5ca, 206–207b, 207tl, 208–9t, 231tr, 254t, 315t, 448t; Malcolm Fairman 106–7b; Mark Ferguson 550t; David Fernie 412–13t; Andrew Findlay 364–5b; John Foreman 209bl; Fotomaton 141br; FotoPulp 469tr; Stephen French 175t; funkyfood London - Paul Williams 243b, 446–7b; Clare Gainey 149cb, 220–21; Tim Gainey 228b; Trish Gant 28–9b; Les Gibbon 388b; Jeff Gilbert 281cra; GL Archive 294tr, 487bl; 520tr; Dimitar Glavinov 274–5b; Manfred Gottschalk 285ca; John Graham 139cb; Tim Graham 176tl; Granger Historical Picture Archive / NYC 71cla, 315bl, 382cl; Dennis Hardley 19cla; Brian Harris 32bl; Michael Heath 110–11b; Paul Heaton 379cr; hemis.fr / Rieger Bertrand 567b; Heritage Image Partnership Ltd / Ashmolean Museum of Art and Archaeology 46clb, / Historic England 118crb, / Historica Graphica Collection 174cr, / London Metropolitan Archives (City of London) 73bc, / ©

Museum of London 71tc, / Werner Forman Archive / Dorset Nat. Hist. & Arch. Soc. 46bc; Stuart Hickling 339br; Nick Higham 402cra; Sue Holness 185b; David Martyn Hughes 319crb; Rachel Husband 430tr; Anthony (known as Tony) Hyde 247tl; Ian Dagnall Commercial Collection 41crb, 203cra, 239cra, 348b, 464–5t; Ianni Dimitrov Pictures 74–5b; imageBROKER / Helmut Meyer zur Capellen 92bc, / Gisela Rentsch 505cra, / Martin Siepmann 284cla; incamerastock / ICP 47br, 159tr, 267tl; INTERFOTO / Personalities 71tl; Jason Smalley Photography / Tony Morris 396bl; Jeff Morgan 14 433crb; Joana Kruse 359tr; Jeffrey Isaac Greenberg 3 63tl; John Davidson Photos 450–51b; John Peter Photography 182b, 516–17b, 535br, 539t; Shaun Johnson 379cra; Jon Arnold Images Ltd 217br; David Keith Jones 316bl; Bjanka Kadic 92clb; Susie Kearley 231cra, 365tr, / Sculpture of Alan Turing at Bletchley Park by Stephen Kettle, represented by Turner Fine Arts 37cl, / The Keasbury-Gordon Photograph Archive Ltd 433cla; Alan King 269bc; Alan King engraving 119bc; Joana Kruse 359tr; Elitsa Lambova 105tl; Lebrecht Music & Arts 486bl, / Lebrecht Authors 117crb; Thomas Lee 520b; Lenscap 35cl; Barry Lewis 34–5b; Ian Linton 509clb; Howard Litherland 43tr; Aled Llywelyn 21cl; London Picture Library 60; 100–101; Look / Franz Marc Frei 267tr; Loop Images Ltd / Bill Allsopp 210br, / Mark Bauer 189, / Tony Latham 131b, / John Norman / courtesy of the Bronte Society 405bc, / Roy Shakespeare 131cr; De Luan 72br, 314bl; David Lyons 324–5t, 383cr, 507bc; M.Sobreira 171cra; Luke MacGregor 36–7b; Mark Sunderland Photography 21b, 377br; J Marshall - Tribaleye Images 190bl; Sue Martin 374bl; Iain Masterton 506–507t, 535cl, 536–7b; mauritius images GmbH / ClickAlps 568br, / Steve Vidler 39cl, 68clb; Angus McComiskey 564–5t; David McCulloch 38–9t; Meibion 291tr; Elizabeth Melvin 327tr; MH Country 317t; Mikel Bilbao Gorostiaga-Travels 62tr; Vanessa Miles 44cr; Barry Morgan 382–3t; John Morrison 400–401b; Rosaline Napier 502bl; The National Trust Photolibrary / Christopher Gallagher 468cl, / Dennis Gilbert 263cra, / Arnhel de Serra 319tr; Natrow Images 184tl; Steve Nicholls 213cl; Dru Norris 284–5b; Alan Novelli 336bl, 449b; Michael Olivers 462tr; James Osmond 286bl; parkerphotography 180–81b; Derek Payne 191tr; Roy Perring 300tr; The Photolibrary Wales / Martin Barlow 43cr; Photopat / One Two Three Swing! by SUPERFLEX, an installation in the Turbine Hall, Tate Modern © DACS 2019 120–21b; Pictorial Press Ltd 292bl; David Pimborough 156cl; PjrTravel 117cra; Prisma by Dukas Presseagentur GmbH / TPX 43cl, 105tr, 225cra; Radharc Images 358cra; Alex Ramsay 301br; Lana Rastro 164br; Simon Reddy 296tr; Ed Rhodes 350bc; Paul Richardson 399tr; John Richmond 300bl; Paul Riddle-VIEW 257cla; Robert Kerr 533tr; robertharding / John Alexander 232–3t, Rob Cousins 256t, / Miles Ertman 386–7b, / Michael Nolan 292tl, 292–3b, / Eleanor Scriven 319tr, / Billy Stock 467t, 467cr, 470tr, / Ann & Steve Toon 559cl, / Adam Woolfitt 71br; David Robertson 530–31b; Marcin Rogozinski 260bl; Maurice Savage 179tl; Michael Sayles 366bl; Scottish Viewpoint 554–5b; Phil Seale 18cla; 539br; Alex Segre 16clb, 20–21t, 62–3ca, 82tr; SFL Travel 231crb; SJH Photography 503tr; Keith Skingle 313cr; Stephen Smith 368tc; Stewart Smith 358bc; Jon Sparks 368–9b, 558–9b; Steve Speller 63tr, 298–9t; Nigel Spooner 28tl; Kumar Sriskandan 23cl, 107tr, 168br, 236bl, 314cl; Robert Stainforth 84b; Slawek Staszczuk 183tr; Stephen Saks Photography 473bl; Steven Gillis hd9 imaging 352bl; Billy Stock 261tl, 287crb, 472–3t; StockFood GmbH / Inga Wandinger 468b; Petr Svarc 20bl; SWNS 16bl; Homer Sykes 109br; T.M.O.Buildings 204–5t, 410bl; T.M.O.Travel 411tl; Steve Taylor ARPS 249br; Marc Tielemans 432t; travelbild 168–9t, 226t, 341bl; travelibUK 72clb; travellinglight 116clb, 158cra, 258t,

MIX
Paper from responsible sources
FSC™ C018179
www.fsc.org

Penguin Random House

Main Contributers Edward Aves, Matt Norman, Christian Williams, Darren Longley, Mike Gerrard, Philip Lee, Michael Leapman, Josie Barnard, Christopher Caitling, Juliet Clough, Lindsay Hunt, Polly Phillmore, Martin Symington, Roger Thomas

Senior Editor Alison McGill
Senior Designer Bess Daly
Project Editor Rada Radojicic
Project Art Editor Ben Hinks
Designers Vinita Venugopal, Ankita Sharma, Hansa Babra, Chhaya Sajwan, Nehal Verma, Simran Lakhiani
Factcheckers Darren Longley, Matt Norman, Christian Williams
Editors Sands Publishing Solutions, Louise Abbott, Rachel Thompson, Lucy Sara-Kelly, Zoë Rutland
Proofreader Debra Wolter
Indexer Hilary Bird
Senior Picture Researcher Ellen Root
Picture Research Harriet Whitaker, Sumita Khatwani, Rituraj Singh, Manpreet Kaur, Vagisha Pushp
Illustrators Richard Draper, Jared Gilby (Kevin Jones Assocs), Paul Guest, Roger Hutchins, Chriss Orr & Assocs, Maltings Partnership, Ann Winterbotham, John Woodstock, Christian Hook, Gilly Newman, Paul Weston
Senior Cartographic Editor Casper Morris
Cartography Ashutosh Ranjan Bharti, Simonetta Giori, Suresh Kumar, Animesh Pathak
Jacket Designers Maxine Pedliham, Ben Hinks
Jacket Picture Research Susie Watters
Senior DTP Designer Jason Little
DTP Rohit Rojal
Producer Rebecca Parton
Managing Editor Rachel Fox
Art Director Maxine Pedliham
Publishing Director Georgina Dee

First edition 1995

Published in Great Britain by Dorling Kindersley Limited, 80 Strand, London, WC2R 0RL

Published in the United States by DK Publishing, 1450 Broadway, Suite 801, New York, NY 10018

Copyright © 1995, 2020 Dorling Kindersley Limited
A Penguin Random House Company
19 20 21 22 10 9 8 7 6 5 4 3 2 1

A CIP catalog record for this book is available from the British Library.

A catalog record for this book is available from the Library of Congress.

ISSN: 1542 1554
ISBN: 978 0 2414 0829 2

Printed and bound in China.

www.dk.com